Teaching English in Middle and Secondary Schools

Fourth Edition

W9-CHH-976

RHODA J. MAXWELL
University of Wisconsin–Eau Claire

MARY JORDAN MEISER
University of Wisconsin–Eau Claire

PEARSON

Merrill
Prentice Hall

Upper Saddle River, New Jersey
Columbus, Ohio

Library of Congress Cataloging-in-Publication Data

Maxwell, Rhoda J.
    Teaching English in middle and secondary schools / Rhoda J. Maxwell,
    Mary Jordan Meiser—4th ed.
        p. cm.
    Includes bibliographical references and index.
    ISBN 0–13–114007–8
    1. English language—Study and teaching (Secondary)—United States.
    2. Language arts (Secondary)—United States. I. Meiser, Mary Jordan. II. Title.

    LB1631.M393 2005
    428'.0071' 273—dc22

                                                            2004003654

Vice President and Executive Publisher: Jeffery W. Johnston
Senior Editor: Linda Ashe Montgomery
Associate Editor: Ben M. Stephen
Editorial Assistant: Laura Weaver
Production Editor: Mary M. Irvin
Production Coordination: Emily Hatteberg, Carlisle Publishers Services
Design Coordinator: Diane C. Lorenzo
Cover Designer: Jason Moore
Production Manager: Susan Hannahs
Director of Marketing: Ann Castel Davis
Marketing Manager: Darcy Betts Prybella
Marketing Coordinator: Tyra Poole

This book was set in Galliard by Carlisle Communications, Ltd., and was printed and bound by
R. R. Donnelley & Sons Company. The cover was printed by Coral Graphic Services, Inc.

Pearson Prentice Hall™ is a trademark of Pearson Education, Inc.
Pearson® is a registered trademark of Pearson plc
Prentice Hall® is a registered trademark of Pearson Education, Inc.
Merrill® is a registered trademark of Pearson Education, Inc.

Pearson Education Ltd.   Pearson Education Australia Pty. Limited
Pearson Education Singapore Pte. Ltd.   Pearson Education North Asia Ltd.
Pearson Education Canada, Ltd.   Pearson Educación de Mexico, S.A. de C.V.
Pearson Education—Japan   Pearson Education Malaysia Pte. Ltd.

10 9 8 7 6 5 4 3
ISBN: 0–13–114007–8

Preface

Teaching is a complex task, and no one text can answer all of the questions facing secondary teachers, especially novice teachers, in today's challenging classrooms. For this reason, we are quick to point out that this text is not a panacea. At the same time, we believe that this fourth edition does offer a comprehensive and realistic view of teaching the English language arts in middle and secondary schools. In providing thoughtful and practical approaches to both curriculum and instruction, this text does address, we believe to a large degree, the questions and concerns of those just entering the profession.

In this fourth edition, we have made significant changes through new chapters and new segments in every chapter. But once again, we reaffirm the value of an integrated approach to teaching the English language arts. Although we divide the language arts into separate chapters (e.g., oral language, writing, literature), we do so only to explore each area in some depth. Further, we bring the strands back together in every chapter, underscoring that we teach best when we recognize the potential for both oral and written language in every lesson or unit that we develop and implement. We also reaffirm a *constructivist* approach, where students use the language arts to make meaning—not to be handed meaning. The question that underlies every chapter is not "What can I teach?" but rather, "How can my students best learn?" Reflective practice is, then, at the core of this edition.

The most effective teachers are usually the most reflective among us; they are not afraid to question materials, instructional methods, or themselves in the daily process of working with young learners. To encourage thoughtful reflection, we ask our readers to interact with the ideas presented, whether it be to affirm, to question, or to challenge. For this same reason, we include problem solving and application as a major part of this new edition, incorporating segments that we have named **Reflection** and **Exploration** into every chapter. We have also added more student units for analysis and decision making about content and instructional methods, and we have balanced the number of middle and senior high school units. Through these, we hope that the newest members of our profession will gain useful experience, as well as the most practical of habits, thoughtful reflection and confident problem solving, as they work through this text.

 ## THE FOURTH EDITION: ORGANIZATIONAL CHANGES AND EMPHASES

In this new edition we have added new chapters, and to ensure a logical flow, we have changed the order of chapters. However, with few exceptions, the organization of this text is completely flexible, allowing instructors to follow their own course structure and wishes. For teachers with a single, two-, or three-credit English methods course, we believe this fourth edition will be ideal, comprehensive but not overwhelming. Further, its tone throughout welcomes student readers and celebrates their intelligence and dedication to their goal of teaching the English language arts.

In Chapter 1, *Becoming a Teacher,* we ask our readers to explore their motivation and goals: Why do they want to be English language arts teachers? At the same time, we describe personal and professional traits that will serve them well as teachers of adolescents. In the third edition, we used this chapter to close our discussion; here, we open with it. Why? Because we realized that this chapter, with its friendly and supportive tone, welcomes readers to the profession but also asks them to think about themselves in rather specific ways. In chapters that follow, we then ask them to extend and expand those reflections, another new feature of this edition.

We also realized that we might close this text in another very personal and pragmatic way: We take our readers through student teaching experiences. Chapter 14, *Your Starting Role: Student Teacher,* is rich with the voices of our former student teachers, who kept weekly e-mail logs, specifically to share their experiences with others. Through them, we have recreated the world of student teaching for those about to enter it. In this chapter, we don't just present our students' voices; we ask our readers to respond, to figure out the situation presented, to suggest solutions to typical problems, and to take on the role of a student teacher in the safety of their methods class. We have not made up scenarios, nor have we altered what our students told us. Consequently, we believe that this new chapter is unique among contemporary methods texts.

Another major change involved dissolving the third edition's Chapters 1, 3, and 4 into a new chapter, Chapter 3, *Understanding Curriculum, Instruction, and Planning.* Although some methods texts address these core language arts areas, we again believe that we have approached them rather uniquely in this new edition. Here, our former students' work is the foundation for understanding and applying knowledge, for making decisions about content and method. In Chapter 2, *The Students We Teach,* we added a section implementing students' activities based on theories of learning. Chapter 2's essential information about middle and high school students now folds into Chapter 3's decisions about materials, pacing, teaching strategies, and activities. The richness, once more, of student work and student voices invites not only analysis but also realistic decision making about lessons and units for senior high school.

Chapter 4, *Understanding Language, Teaching About Language,* has been updated and moved to position it as a foundation for the language arts to follow. For mainstream teachers, it offers a strong response to questions of working with second-language learners. Students who do not take a separate course in first and second language acquisition, or teaching writing to ESL students, will find in this chapter both background knowledge and teaching strategies. Chapter 5, *Oral Language: The Neglected Language Arts,* has two new features. The first addresses "the" speech, as it is often known in senior high English classes. Using a speech unit from an area high school, and a series of reflections and explorations, we ask our readers to evaluate in some cases, try out some teaching ideas in others. The second new feature is a tenth-grade playwriting and informal drama unit that uses Japanese folktales and art as its base. Here, readers will once again have the chance to apply knowledge from previous chapters, as well as that of oral language for adolescent learners.

Chapters 6 through 9 concentrate on writing, with Chapter 9, *Writing Research Papers*, a new addition. Additions to Chapter 6, *Teaching Composition*, are examples of students' demonstrating the writing process in classrooms. One example includes a teacher's comments as a model. More examples of revising strategies and response and editing guides are included. English education students have more opportunities to respond to writing classroom samples. A chart of writing levels relating to purposes of writing provides a guide for writing student assignments. Chapter 7, *Understanding Grammar*, is now placed within the composition sequence. We believe that the knowledge and issues in this chapter are essential to teaching composition, and thus should be within the sequence of those chapters. Chapter 8, *Writing for Learning*, as the title implies, focuses readers on another requirement of composition instruction, one often ignored in methods texts. Chapter 8 is expanded to include a published article so English education students have the opportunity to apply study skills that they in turn will teach. How to teach persuasion and classification are added with student papers provided. Chapter 9, *Writing Research Papers*, a new and critical addition to the text, focuses attention on appropriate methods of research and research writing—an area that has typically been the bane of both senior high teachers and students alike. Purposes of writing research papers help students through a process for teaching research. Internet sites are provided as well as handouts to guide their future students in using Internet sources. A complete student research paper is included. In the composition chapters, we use authentic student work, along with reflection and exploration, as a way to involve our readers in a careful analysis of teaching writing in secondary schools.

Additions to our literature chapters include new student units, useful Web sites for teachers, new considerations of literature, especially multicultural selections, and again a great many reflection and exploration segments. Chapter 10, *Selecting Literature*, continues its emphasis on the literature of American minorities and women without neglecting other areas such as classic, young adult, and world literature. Updated references on censorship are added. In Chapter 11, *Teaching Literature*, students learn more specifically how to design and implement literature lessons and units. Additional teacher assignments and activities are provided, including one on *Hamlet*. A student writing represents the classroom assignment. Through evaluating authentic student units, they have the opportunity once again to apply knowledge gathered through earlier chapters.

Issues of and strategies for assessment are addressed in Chapter 12, *Evaluating English Language Arts*, and are applicable to both oral and written language. Several examples of scoring guides are provided. A literature assignment is evaluated using writing levels. In Chapter 13, *Developing Units*, students learn more specifically how to design and implement instructional units, an invaluable preparation for student teaching and beyond. Teaching activities for *To Kill a Mockingbird* are greatly expanded. New units on *The Scarlett Letter* and Historic Homes are included. Internet searches are added throughout the units. Although students may study unit design in general education classes, we have found that they need such experience in English methods courses, supported by language arts specialists, models, and discussions that go to the core of the discipline itself.

The Fourth Edition: New and Unique Features

For this new edition, we have updated and revised each chapter. Here are the most significant changes:

- **Comprehensive**, addressing not only the major strands of the language arts but additional areas critical to effective teaching today.

    New chapters:

Chapter	3	Understanding Curriculum, Instruction, and Planning
Chapter	9	Writing Research Papers
Chapter	14	Your Starting Role: Student Teacher

- **Purposeful**, asking students to look through the lens of the teachers whom they aspire to be.

    New student units for *analysis and realistic problem solving:*

Chapter	3	In Constant Search of Perfection: Benjamin Franklin
Chapter	3	*All Quiet on the Western Front* and WWI Literature
Chapter	5	*Kwaidan:* A Lesson in Playwriting and Classroom Drama Integrating Japanese Legends and Art
Chapter	5	"The" Speech: A Guide for Tenth Grade
Chapter	9	The Research Paper: Full-length Student Paper
Chapter	13	*The Scarlet Letter*
Chapter	13	Historical Homes

    New student unit segments or texts for *analysis and response:*

Chapter	3	*To Kill a Mockingbird*
Chapter	6	Additional Student Papers and Examples
Chapter	6	Writing Image Poetry
Chapter	8	Student Papers
Chapter	11	*The House on Mango Street*
Chapter	13	*To Kill a Mockingbird*

- **Interactive**, involving students in their own learning.

    Chapter 1, Becoming a Teacher: Questions of personal motivation, traits, and goals central to being a teacher; student voices, secondary and college, throughout.

    Chapter 14, Your Starting Role: Student Teacher: Analysis and realistic problem solving based on authentic semester-long student teaching experiences.

    Every chapter: Two new features which relate to the information or situation just presented:

Reflection: What do you think about _____? What might you do if _____? How would you handle _____? What has been your experience with _____? Your observations about _____? How does _____ influence your ideas about _____?

Exploration: Evaluate _____, Revise _____, Design _____, Develop _____, Apply _____.

We have worked hard to make this text truly a new edition, and we believe it will resonate with the students for whom it was written, tomorrow's teachers, and their instructors, whose task we hope we have lightened somewhat.

 ## ACKNOWLEDGMENTS

Again, we thank our own students for having provided us with opportunities to learn with them—and from them. Without them, this text would be less rich, less authentic, and, more important, less fun. From middle school to senior high school to graduate school, these students remain in our memory, and here, in our text.

For this fourth edition, we wish to note in particular the contributions of Laura Apfelbeck, Sara Argabright, Mark Heike, and Becky Olien, whose sustained and insightful conversations in the past year have enriched this text. Also, we want to thank Emily Hatteberg and Carlisle Communications for their helpful advice and careful attention to detail.

Finally, we would like to thank the following reviewers for their careful reading and helpful comments: Carolyn S. Moran, Tennessee State University; John H. Bushman, University of Kansas; David Gill, University of North Carolina, Wilmington; F. Todd Goodson, Kansas State University; and Peggy Albers, Georgia State University.

Educator Learning Center: An Invaluable Online Resource

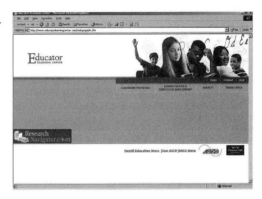

Merrill Education and the Association for Supervision and Curriculum Development (ASCD) invite you to take advantage of a new online resource, one that provides access to the top research and proven strategies associated with ASCD and Merrill—the Educator Learning Center. At **www. EducatorLearningCenter.com** you will find resources that will enhance your students' understanding of course topics and of current educational issues, in addition to being invaluable for further research.

HOW THE EDUCATOR LEARNING CENTER WILL HELP YOUR STUDENTS BECOME BETTER TEACHERS

With the combined resources of Merrill Education and ASCD, you and your students will find a wealth of tools and materials to better prepare them for the classroom.

Research
- More than 600 articles from the ASCD journal *Educational Leadership* discuss everyday issues faced by practicing teachers.
- A direct link on the site to Research Navigator™ gives students access to many of the leading education journals, as well as extensive content detailing the research process.
- Excerpts from Merrill Education texts give your students insights on important topics of instructional methods, diverse populations, assessment, classroom management, technology, and refining classroom practice.

Classroom Practice
- Hundreds of lesson plans and teaching strategies are categorized by content area and age range.
- Case studies and classroom video footage provide virtual field experience for student reflection.
- Computer simulations and other electronic tools keep your students abreast of today's classrooms and current technologies.

LOOK INTO THE VALUE OF EDUCATOR LEARNING CENTER YOURSELF

A four-month subscription to Educator Learning Center is $25 but is **FREE** when used in conjunction with this text. To obtain free passcodes for your students, simply contact your local Merrill/ Prentice Hall sales representative, and your representative will give you a special ISBN to give your bookstore when ordering your textbooks. To preview the value of this website to you and your students, please go to **www.EducatorLearningCenter.com** and click on "Demo."

Brief Contents

Contents

CHAPTER 3
Understanding Curriculum, Instruction, and Planning   30

CHAPTER 4
Understanding Language, Teaching about Language   72

CHAPTER 5
Oral Language: The Neglected Language Arts   *119*

CHAPTER 6
Teaching Composition   *181*

CHAPTER 7
Understanding Grammar   241

CHAPTER 10
Selecting Literature   *313*

CHAPTER 11
Teaching Literature   *348*

CHAPTER 12
Evaluating English Language Arts   *393*

CHAPTER 13
Developing Units   *424*

CHAPTER 14
Your Starting Role: Student Teacher   *468*

NOTE: Every effort has been made to provide accurate and current Internet information in this book. However, the Internet and information posted on it are constantly changing, and it is inevitable that some of the Internet addresses listed in this textbook will change.

Becoming a Teacher

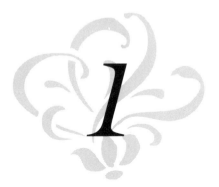

Because teaching is a vocation, no one set of guidelines will be helpful
to everyone. Our performances in one classroom will be as unique as we are;
we not only teach a subject, but we also teach who we are.

Debra C. Guyton (60)

As you read through this chapter, you'll be asked many questions about becoming and being a teacher. Thus, we'd like you to keep a response journal—a dialogue with yourself that will extend to your classmates and instructor. Self-reflection is at the core of effective teaching, of being and becoming the kind of teacher you wish to be. Like learning itself, teaching is a journey of discovery. We ask you to begin that journey now, using your journal as a reflecting pool along that path.

 ## WHY ARE YOU HERE?

Choosing a profession is one of the most profound acts of our lives, a commitment to our future. It's important, then, to know just why you chose teaching. It's not an easy career: Students live in an uneasy and complex world; funding and resources go in cycles of "feast or famine" and parental and community expectations, demands, and criticism are very public. Preparing, teaching, and evaluating go well beyond a 40-hour week, and at times, dealing with so many students can be stressful. However, working with students can also be rewarding, and teachers have a tangible opportunity to make a difference in some students' lives. We suspect you're here because you want to make that difference. Nonetheless, it's important to explore the question.

We asked some of our methods students why they wanted to teach English language arts, and Aimee Peterson's first response surprised her: "The idea of answering the question of what attracted me to teaching and more specifically teaching English *scared* me." She went on to explain that there were many answers she could give and that having to pinpoint her motivation was scary. We noted that delving into self and motivation can be unsettling, but it's also a positive act. Another student, Mike Le Bouton, had no hesitation at all: "I have never doubted that I would teach—I was raised by teachers." Complimenting his parents in his remarks, Mike explored growing up with what seemed a normal and effortless gravitation to teaching English.

Several students noted that they too had role models, though not so close at hand. Jason Hedrington told us: "The catalyst of [my] decision was a high school English teacher that opened my eyes into myself and showed me the wonderful world of English." For Mary Beth Koehler, it was a college teacher who asked the critical questions. As Mary Beth explained it, she started off as a broadcast journalism major with no interest in teaching English. In her junior year, however, she ended up in an 8 A.M. creative writing class because it was the only class open. Because she was running around "chasing ambulances and writing up stories" for the campus station, her work in creative writing was perpetually late. Finally the teacher called her in and got her to blurt out her unhappiness with her major and her desire to be like the creative writing teacher in front of her. The professor convinced Mary Beth that not knowing the difference between a noun and a verb—Mary Beth's reason for not considering teaching English—could be dealt with. She could learn all about nouns and verbs through tutoring in the peer composition lab. As Mary Beth noted, "That's what I did. My life has been pretty great, exciting, and fulfilling ever since." And we hope those adjectives remain active throughout her career—and yours.

A TEACHER? WHY?

In your journal, explore your reasons for wanting to teach English language arts. Like Mike, have you always known that teaching was meant for you? Or like Mary Beth, did someone jolt you into recognizing it? If you come up with several reasons, consider which is most important to you and why. There's a difference between explaining what drew you to teaching and what you want to accomplish as a teacher. Here, concentrate on what drew you to teaching English.

 ## AS A TEACHER, I WANT TO . . .

As you thought about why you were drawn to teaching, you no doubt also thought about what you wish to accomplish as a teacher. The first thing that comes to mind is probably a broad goal: I want to make a difference in kids' lives; I want kids to love literature and reading; or I want kids to learn the power of language. And that's an important start. But just as we have to take broad curricular goals and turn them into specific student outcomes, we need to go a step further here. For example, if you want to make a difference in kids' lives, how will you do that? You'll need to think about curricular materials and instructional methods that will help you achieve your goal. How does "making a difference" translate into cognitive or affective effects? Or into new or improved skills?

AS A TEACHER, I WILL . . .

In your journal, list at least three things you wish to do or accomplish as an English teacher. If you know you want to teach middle school or high school, you might want to consider the age level as you frame your response. First think about your broad goals as an English language arts teacher and then turn the goals into more specific student outcomes. It's okay if things seem a little fuzzy at first. We just want you to get a sense of your personal stake in your profession.

Schoolhouse Memories

Many of our methods students came to the teaching profession because of their teachers—men and women whose knowledge, care, and dedication inspired them. But they also were keen observers of unhappy teachers. Brian Quade believed that "many of them feel trapped. A couple that I had, I am sure were trapped in a job they did not enjoy. I think one of my English teachers was a teacher because he wanted to coach; unfortunately, by the time I got to high school, I don't think he liked coaching either. I think he simply didn't like teenagers—which makes secondary education a rather uncomfortable place to be." As Brian speculated on reasons that teaching doesn't work out for some people, he concluded:

Some teachers get swamped by the apathy of their students, the apathy of the administration, the apathy of the community, or an interesting combination of the above. Some get hired by districts that do not have the resources they had hoped for and simply fall into the rut of using the same materials that have always been available. Others just do not know what is available. Some have become disillusioned by the students or the system. In other cases, teachers are forced into teaching situations that they are unprepared for or do not want and find themselves with few options—other than using the curriculum established before they got there. It can be difficult to change an established curriculum when you don't know what to choose from, have no passion for the material, or simply don't know how.

Brian brings up an important point, one that we have made throughout this book: Curriculum and instruction are inextricably bound together. Moreover, teachers must have some freedom, or their creativity and motivation fade.

The most memorable teachers, however, were those who "lit a fire" in our students. Kendra Jones wrote of her senior English teacher: "He changed my life, the way I thought, the way I looked at the whole world." Jason Hedrington had similar memories: "He really opened my eyes in general. He made me see that I could really be anything that I wanted to be. 'When the dream dies, you die,' he often told me." Jason went on to note that this teacher "made us feel important, and he showed that he really cared about each and every one of us." The words *care* and *respect* came up often when our methods students reflected on their secondary teachers. Kris Westphal echoed Jason: "What it comes down to is his [teacher's] respect for his students. That was what made everything else fall into place." Later, we will share with you the remarks from current high schoolers from Green Bay, Wisconsin—remarkably similar to these college students' views. In fact, when we ask almost any generation of students to reflect on memorable teachers, the positive and negative attributes remain constant. What does this tell us?

I REMEMBER YOU

In your journal once more, reflect on your most memorable teacher from middle school or high school. Don't hesitate to use *memorable* as a negative if that is your strongest memory. We can learn from both positive and negative role models. Try to be specific about words or actions that led you to choose this person.

IF YOU HAD A TEACHING "FAIRY GODMOTHER"

If there were such a thing as a "perfect" English language arts teacher, what qualities do you think this person would possess? Make a list. Then rearrange the list into characteristics that are related to one's personality (aspects that would not be easy to change) and characteristics that one acquires through experience or development (aspects that can be added to or erased). Then rank them in importance.

We asked middle and high schoolers to tell us what characteristics they believe are important. In fact, we asked them what they would say if they could talk to a college class where students are studying to become English teachers. Here are their responses, from South Middle School in Eau Claire, Wisconsin, and due east hundreds of miles in Bay Port High School, Green Bay, Wisconsin:

respects kids	makes kids feel wanted	adjusts to the
knows material	and smart	student's level
listens	creative	can control class
thinks kids' opinions are	flexible	energetic
worthwhile	fair/evenhanded	openminded
knows when kids need help	knows kids' interests	sense of humor
keeps things interesting	shares	gives choices

Now try to rank their responses. What do you think these students considered the most important characteristics of good teachers? Before we tell you, let's listen to some of the voices from Bay Port High School:

Senior Summer Delvoye said, "It is important that a teacher acts like a human being." Think about that for a moment. What does she mean by "act like a human being"? When wouldn't a teacher "act like a human being"—at least from the perspective of a high school senior?

Tara Beth Boerner, a junior, cautions: "Be yourself—don't put up a fake front because you're a teacher." What's a "fake front"? And what does it have to do with being a teacher? What is Tara talking about here? And why would Jason Hundt, a senior, say something so similar: "Be yourself. Don't try to put on a false front for the students because they may end up taking advantage of you later." What do you think may have happened to cause these students to talk about "fake" and "false" behavior?

Another senior, Dave Vander Leest, had a different perspective: "Try not to be a popular teacher. Some teachers don't give homework and try to be everyone's friend instead of teaching like they are supposed to." What negative effects would a popular teacher have on students?

Junior Tami Gialdini believed, "English teachers should be first of all comfortable with themselves." Do you know people who aren't "comfortable with themselves"? How do you know? What would make you uncomfortable with yourself as a teacher? Why has Tami hit on something critical to the teaching environment?

Sue Johnson, also a junior, advised, "If you love what you do, then show it." How do we show a love of teaching English language arts? Is there a danger here? Consider what another junior, Jill Witthuhn, says: "Many teachers are stuck on their pedistle [sic] of superiority." How could you meet Sue's criterion without climbing up Jill's "pedistle"?

Brooke Johnson echoes Jill with rather strong words: "We're not stupid; we can pick up on negativity, and it stays with us a long time. As does anything that is said or done in class." What would you consider "negativity" in an English class? Have you ever experienced it? Since no teacher would begin his or her career with negativity, how do you think it develops?

The characteristic "stupid" came up again when Stacy Lewis talked about a memorable teacher who "always listened to both sides and never once made anyone feel as if they were totally wrong or stupid." What kind of words or actions convey to students that their opinions do count? Knowing that teens are often hypersensitive to criticism, real or perceived, how would you deal with responses that are off the mark?

"Command respect, but don't *demand* it" was the advice of Paul Sheedy. What does Paul mean? How does a new teacher command respect? Did you have any high school teachers you didn't respect? If yes, what caused you to lose it? Could that teacher have gained it back? Why or why not? What caused you to develop respect for a teacher?

Alisa Frederici's best advice to someone who wants to become a good English teacher is to remember "that teenagers try to be tricky and malicious, but it's only a flagrant attempt for attention." What would you consider "tricky" or "malicious" behavior? One of our methods students, Aimee Peterson, told us about a high school class in which she and her classmates walked across the desktops and made the teacher cry. Is this malicious behavior? Or is it simply a "looney tunes" kid response to a teacher with no discipline in place? Alisa's point, that teenagers want attention, is a good one. Despite their bravado, many of them don't receive all that much of it, at least in constructive ways. What can English teachers do other than say things like "pay attention now"? How do construction of the curriculum and care in instructional methods translate into "attention"?

How Students Rate the Teachers

Let's look at how both middle schoolers and senior high students ranked teacher qualities:

Middle School	*Senior High School*
listens	listens
gives choices	fair
values our opinions	values our opinions
fair	gives choices

Also mentioned often were humor, sharing, understanding the level of students and adjusting to it, and knowing student interests.

How did your ranking compare with that of the students? If there were significant differences, why do you think that was so?

If you had a fairy godmother who could grant your "I want to be this kind of teacher" wish, what would you tell her? As you consider the wish list, you need to be realistic about who you are and what kind of teacher you would like to be in the classroom. As a couple of the high school students pointed out, being yourself is critical. What are your strengths? What are potential problem areas when you picture yourself in the classroom? Having some "butterflies" is normal, but you want to anticipate areas where better planning and specific classroom procedures will help you start out well. If, for example, you tend to procrastinate, or if you aren't particularly well organized, you know that about yourself. You no doubt also realize that you can't procrastinate or be disorganized when more than 100 students depend on you to frame and facilitate their work. That's why it's important that you reflect on potential problem areas as well as on your strengths. We know the strengths are there, recognized by others as good "teacher traits"—or you wouldn't be this far along in becoming a teacher.

The Best of Me

List what you consider your best personality traits—and don't be modest! Then from this list, choose three that you believe will help you as a teacher. Next to each trait, indicate how it will play a role in your classroom.

 ## No Fairy Godmother Needed

Although there are studies and tests of personality traits linked to the teaching profession, we don't need such measures to tell us the basic qualities of effective teachers. What's more, people with remarkably different personalities are considered good teachers by both their students and professional peers. We suspect part of the reason lies in the different personalities and learning styles found among us all. We need and benefit from different kinds of teachers throughout our academic career. But an underlying thread links most successful teachers; they share certain qualities.

Realism

As we have already noted, successful teachers know something about students, both from what research tells them and from what students themselves say. Successful teachers also know things about themselves. For example, our upbringing, culture, and social class do influence us. Many English teachers come from middle-class backgrounds that may conflict with those of some students. Further, we aren't facing a classroom full of prospective English teachers for whom English is easy and pleasurable. Being knowledgeable and realistic about ourselves and our students is an important base for teaching.

Openness

Being honest with both ourselves and our students is an important characteristic. If we don't know something, we should say so. We can tell the students that we will find out, or better yet, we can find out together. We can also share some experiences with students, not divulging sensitive or highly personal incidents, but certainly recounting experiences that meant something to us. We also need to do what we expect students to do: read, write, and share ideas. A certain hypocrisy is involved when English teachers require students to read and to write, but fail to do so themselves.

Positive Expectations

We need to see students as individuals, not as the fifth-hour class or the slow group. Developing or strengthening the attitude that every student has a right to learn is an essential part of teaching. Believing that every student brings to the classroom knowledge that enriches others in the learning community is equally essential. Similarly, effective teachers believe that their students *can* learn. These attitudes foster both individual growth and class cohesiveness. Students who know their ideas are taken seriously and their efforts valued are far more likely to participate in the learning process.

Responsiveness

Our attitude is always the baseline of what happens. The time we spend initially getting to know students and allowing them to know one another and us is time well spent. Similarly, being honest, genuine, and responsive sets the tone for productive work. We are not advocating being "the friend" and throwing discipline and structure aside. Students need us to take charge, orchestrate, and lead; neither we nor they can function in an environment that lacks structure, planning, and leadership. At the same time, we can do this in ways that incorporate students rather than dominate them. Being a good listener is another important form of responsiveness; in fact, it is listed as number one among our student respondents. Listening, not just hearing, *will* make a difference.

Flexibility

Planning well is part of teaching well. However, plans are carried out among individuals who hear, respond, and think in unique ways. Every classroom experience is full of surprises, and while teachers need carefully thought-out plans, they also need to be ready to change those plans on a moment's notice. We cannot remove the equivocal nature of teaching, nor would we want to when we consider that our focus is teaching people, not subject matter.

Sense of Humor

Laughter is important to our well-being. Our classrooms should be places of shared laughter, the light-hearted and playful moments that tell us we are connected and connecting with one another. However, what might pass for humor among peers—biting humor, sarcasm, and mockery—could quickly disconnect us and dissolve any sense of community. Keeping these harsher elements outside the classroom and operating instead from a gentle humor within helps build a classroom climate in which students feel safe to be themselves.

Evenhandedness

Few things bother teenagers more than the sense that a teacher is "unfair." And when we think about it, we realize that we adults react pretty strongly to real or perceived unfair treatment, too. No one likes it. For this reason, teachers need classroom procedures that are evenhanded and fair to all students. Students need to know these procedures on day one and to see consistent application throughout the school year. Favoritism is quickly noted and resented, as is changing rules in midstream. Even teachers who are thought to be "tough" receive high marks from their students if they are also considered "fair."

Intellectual Curiosity

Effective teachers like to map the territory, to try out new paths, discover new places, and venture into "foreign" lands. In brief, they have a strong desire to be perpetual learners. Intellectual curiosity is a critical trait. Without it, teachers depend on the same materials and methods, and as one high school student pointed out, they bore themselves and us. Moreover, with these approaches, student thinking will never be engaged, pushed, or fostered—the very core of teaching and learning. The best teachers we know continue to be students 20 years into their careers by reading professional journals, participating at conferences, and attending graduate courses in summer or night school.

Drawing Conclusions

In 1986, Richard Lloyd-Jones, then president of the National Council of Teachers of English, outlined qualifications for future teachers of English language arts. He listed many of those we have just discussed and, like us, believed insatiable curiosity and a strong will to discover and try out new ideas were critical (3). It is not enough, however, just to try out new ideas; we must reflect on them. The habit of reflection, of thoughtful analysis of what we do and observe in our classrooms, is a critical part of teaching well. Mitch Cox, a high school teacher, describes the connections among planning, teaching, and reflection:

> Planning is the prewriting stage where attention must be given to the connections among the teacher/writer, students/audience, and the needs and goals of the two. It is also recursive, involving revision not only after an initial delivery of a lesson but also during the act of teaching itself. In fact, planning for the present always requires looking back to the previous year and being ready to adjust ideas to past experience. (33)

Looking back requires a written response to teaching activities: how one feels about the day, what could have gone better, and what went right, too. Given this, teachers' most valuable tool in assessing their teaching is a reflective journal. With a journal, patterns of problems and successes are easier to see and to understand. Too often, students are blamed for the failure of plans or activities that didn't work. When we transfer blame for poor results to students, we close the door to considering how and what we ourselves might change to achieve better results. To be effective teachers, we must continue to be learners as well.

Part of your learning in English language arts rests in the chapters that follow, but much of it rests in you. Because you have reached this point in your quest to become an English language arts teacher, we know you have already demonstrated knowledge in two fields: English and education. However, now we are going to ask you to pull that knowledge together, extend it, and apply it through sustained reflection on and exploration of each strand of English language arts—from the perspective of the teacher you are preparing to be, the teacher you know you can be. As that teacher, you really must be first and always a learner. Thus, the journey continues, with pen in hand.

REFERENCES

Cox, Mitch. "Bards and Beatles: Connecting Spontaneity to Structure and Lesson Plans." *English Journal* (Mar. 1991): 33–41.

Guyton, Debra C. "Good Teaching: Passionate Performances." *English Journal* (Feb. 1995): 59–60.

Lloyd-Jones, Richard. "What English Teachers Need to Know—and to Be." News Release. Urbana, IL: National Council of Teachers of English, 1986, n.p.

The Students We Teach

Perhaps most important, interdisciplinary, inquiry-centered learning often includes something that has been ignored in a great many recent reform reports: the joy of learning. By "joy" I do not mean the "fun of easy gratification and quick laughs," but the genuine joy of mastery, the pleasure of gaining control. The same intellectual joy can be found in the mastery of language and learning.

Stephen Tchudi (30)

 ## THE JOY OF LEARNING

Stephen Tchudi's observation that most recent educational reform reports ignore the "joy of learning" reflects a national loss. In the past decade, U.S. citizens appear to be less resilient, less optimistic, and less intellectually curious. It is no surprise then, that students in U.S. schools fail to grasp what Tchudi, a prominent English educator, believes is the heart of teaching—the intellectual joy of learning. Given the complexity of educating young people, the multiple roles and expectations placed on schools and teachers, and the difficult lives of many students, it is understandable that joy in learning is infrequent in many schools. Sara Lawrence Lightfoot, professor of education at Harvard University, believes that "When you're worried about discipline, or preoccupied with completing a prescribed curriculum in a particular amount of time, you lose the sense of joy and possibility—the sense of play" (157). Like Tchudi, Lightfoot is concerned about the nature of learning and of teaching.

Many new teachers go into the classroom with unrealistic expectations. They go into teaching because they love the subject and like young people, but that is often not enough to create in their students the sense of joy they are looking for.

The following scenario describes a situation first-year and student teachers often find themselves in: The second week of August, Chris was excited to receive a job offer to teach tenth grade English at a suburban school of approximately 1,500 students. Although he realized he would not have much time to prepare for his new teaching assignment, he felt fairly confident because his student teaching had been a positive experience. He had worked with a supportive teacher in a small high school of 400 students teaching juniors and seniors American and British literature. For the first weeks of school, Chris prepared lessons using literature selections that he had particularly liked from his college literature class and ones he taught during student teaching. He spent hours designing discussion questions and related information he thought would interest students, but Chris became increasingly frustrated and discouraged because most of his students did not seem interested, would not pay attention, and did not become involved in the discussion. He thought about the pleasure he had experienced when he was a high school student and studied similar literature, and asked himself, "What was wrong with these students? Why weren't they interested?"

Chris has realized that his classrooms are not full of the kind of students he and most of his college friends were in their high school years. For Chris, the joy of teaching and learning does not seem to be present in his classes. Rather than blame students for his frustration, however, Chris needs to look at the reality of his students' lives and remind himself of the nature of adolescents and their worlds.

 ## ADOLESCENT TRAITS

Students of middle school age differ developmentally and socially from high school students. Although the language arts involve basic processes that are similar across age levels (for example, a 12-year-old and an 18-year-old both use a similar writing process), maturation differences are critical in performance and product. An eighth grader and a junior may complete the same writing assignment, but the results will be vastly different. We cannot expect the same level of knowledge, skill, or performance from a middle school student that we might from one in high school. Nor could we expect the same attention and concentration levels. Young adolescents are quite different from their high school counterparts; therefore, creating activities for middle level students is not only a matter of making lessons less sophisticated.

Early adolescence is generally considered to occur between the ages of 10 and 14. Because this period is a time of profound developmental changes, students at this age require different educational experiences that acknowledge the significant physical, cognitive, and social changes they are undergoing as they mature. These changes, of course, continue into senior high school, and maturation varies with individual students.

To help students cope with these changes, educators developed the middle school concept, the recognition that young adolescents require an environment that matches their attributes more closely than junior high schools do. Junior high schools are patterned after high schools, with separate classes throughout the day and little or no integration of classes or teaching staff. Although middle schools do vary, they are all based on the philosophy that students at early adolescence need a wealth of experiences so they can develop in a wide variety of ways. Integrated activities, small-group work, and a hands-on approach to learning are all ways of accommodating their diverse needs and acknowledging that they are not quite as grown up or independent as high schoolers. The National Association of Secondary School Principals (NASSP) published a statement in 1983, and although dated, the observations hold true today. Middle school students are described as "in the middle," noting that, "We know that at no other period in the life cycle does such variance exist in the rate of individual development" (n.p.). These differences are apparent in students' intellectual, emotional, social, and physical development. According to NASSP, these changes may lead middle schoolers to be

middle schooler traits

- Impulsive in actions and impatient with restrictions
- Preoccupied with popularity and self-conscious about appearance
- Deeply influenced by mass media and responsive to advertising
- Plagued by mood swings and subject to forgetfulness and boredom
- Assertive in independence and moved by competitive situations
- Charged with energy, confused by self-doubt, and fearful of failure
- Embarrassed by social situations and veneered with wisecracks

Considering these characteristics, middle schools organize their curriculum and activities to emphasize emotional and social needs and to develop a positive self-esteem during these critical years. Instead of individual classes with little or no interaction with other students, middle school students need group work to help them develop social skills, choices of activities to help them explore their many interests, and units of study that help them take responsibility for their own learning.

We asked our English education students to reflect on their memories of middle school. Their journal entries reinforce educators' perceptions of what life is like for these young people.

At ages 12 and 13, fitting in with my peers was most important to me. I started to wear makeup and I remember spending hours on my hair and never being satisfied with it. I started to go shopping a lot, any opportunity I had, in order to use my saved money to buy cool clothes. What I remember most about this age was being very self-conscious and always worried about my appearance and what others thought of me. (Brenda Meyer)

I was unpopular because I was smart and a bookworm. I made a pact with myself that I would work to become popular. My favorite movie was Grease and I wanted to turn out like Olivia Newton-John (heaven forbid). I worked hard at not paying attention in class and not reading anymore and acting stupid so that everyone would think I was not smart anymore. I became the class clown. (Mary Beth Koehler)

Mary Mercer Krogness, an eighth-grade teacher, observes that body and soul, from eighth-grade boys and girls, young adults are emerging. These mysterious young people vacillate between behaving like toddlers who are going through the terrible twos and acting like young adults who scrutinize their parents' and teachers' behaviors and debate what's equitable and inequitable with these authority figures (47).

Not surprisingly, early adolescents may feel misunderstood and misjudged by their parents and teachers. Further, many believe adults do not listen to them or consider their ideas seriously. These young people may face an unfair bias. Store clerks, for example, often ask them to leave, people frown at them, and many adults expect that they will be noisy and rude. Even though they appear to be "little kids," they are not. They know things, have experiences to draw on, and deserve credit for having worthwhile ideas. It is critical that teachers not trivialize their words and ideas, but try to understand that adolescent emotions run high and are even volatile in some students.

Working with young adolescents can be difficult for teachers, but also extremely rewarding. Middle school students may challenge authority, but they rely on their teachers for guidance and support. They expect and need structure, despite words to the contrary. Even though there are individual differences, they have in common an overwhelming sense of fairness. They also expect people to be fair with them, and react strongly when they believe they have been treated unfairly. To work well with these students, teachers need to explain their reasons for and expectations of behavior and social interactions. They must be willing to listen to students and to provide a supportive environment and opportunities for choice within structure.

Linda Rief, a teacher, loves to work with young teenagers, but warns that teaching at this level requires patience and humor (90). She adds that it is important to support teenagers in their search for self-discovery and self-making: "We must laugh with them, respect them, and help them find out what's good about their lives" (91). Although high school students need this same support, they differ some because of their increased maturity.

HIGH SCHOOL STUDENTS

Socially, students in late adolescence have the same need for peer interaction as do younger middle schoolers. Although high schoolers may be able to sit still longer, they still require a classroom in which they interact with classmates. They want desperately to belong to a group and sort themselves out based on mutual interests and characteristics. To develop a sense of belonging as a protection against the world, students often label themselves (as jocks, druggies, preppies, brains, or shop rats, for example) and hang out with like-minded peers.

Physical growth in this age group varies greatly depending on their rate of maturing. It can be fairly rapid and uneven. Teenagers develop a growing self-consciousness about their bodies, which may take different forms—from flaunting to camouflaging. Psychological changes continue, but not all students go through crises, nor do all feel alienated or rebellious. For some, growing up is very difficult, for others less traumatic. Some of our English education students recall how they felt in high school:

> *At 15 and 16, music became the center of my life. I still thought about sex, too. I began getting serious about the piano and I began to play the guitar. My close friends and I spent Friday and Saturday evenings listening to or playing music; we had no social life, nor did we desire one. (Jason Hedrington)*

> *When I was 15 and 16, all I could think about was driving a car and going to school dances with the "right" boy. Athletics was very important to me and so was school. Friends and peer pressure were my only worry. As a 17-year-old, I was very concerned about my boyfriend and how moving to college would affect our relationship. I was scared to death of losing him. I was so in love. (Aimee Peterson)*

> *As I went through high school, I always struggled with the acceptance thing. I never stopped yearning for friends and significant relationships. By the time I graduated, I had begun to find some. (Brian Quade)*

 *Reflection*

Think back to your middle and high school days. When was it difficult to keep your attention on school subjects? What interfered with your concentration and attention?

———————————

DEVELOPMENTAL STAGES

Our understanding of the intellectual changes that adolescents undergo has been dominated by a Piagetian view of developmental stages: adolescents moving from concrete observable experience to abstract, speculative thought. However, this view is theoretical and not necessarily a reality. The stages of development are not discrete or predictable. Some students, even as juniors and seniors in high school, struggle with abstract thinking. In late adolescence, generally students are more able to entertain diverse points of view, a widening from the self-centered stance of childhood and early adolescence. Moreover, cognitive awareness is heightened during the high school years.

However, society expects high school students to act like adults, forgetting that these young people have not had time to reach full maturity. They must, however, make critical decisions that will affect them for the rest of their lives. To make these decisions wisely and bridge the difficult transition to adulthood, they need teachers who listen and respond to them in sensitive and caring ways.

∽ *Reflection* ∽

Thinking back to Chris, the first-year teacher described earlier in this chapter, how might he change his approach to teaching that takes into account traits of high school students? What could he do to involve his students more in the learning process and thus generate more interest?

 ## LIFE IN THE CLASSROOM

No matter how orderly the school or good the control, tension exists between students and teachers—just as it exists in any situation where interaction is an hourly activity. The students are in same-age groups, reinforcing both the best and worst of young adolescents. Teachers work with over 100 students each day, and all teachers, no matter how experienced and talented, will experience bad days and encounter students who confound, puzzle, and trouble them.

Some students consistently please others, and just as consistently challenge and frustrate us. No matter how good our efforts, we will lose some along the way, some dramatically and tragically to death or prison; others will simply fade into oblivion as soon as the law permits them to leave school. Apathy and alienation are real and take varying forms.

Some students do absolutely nothing and bother no one. They do not open books or bring writing materials to class. No amount of teacher effort can encourage them to participate. Other students can be physically threatening and verbally abusive, despite the fact that a teacher has done nothing to provoke such a response. You will experience these students in both inner-city schools and in rural or suburban areas. Why? Because in many schools and classrooms, students have not been part of the teaching and learning process: teachers have centered instruction around themselves rather than on their students. Further, until recently, school curricula have focused on college-bound students. The tightly controlled classroom and curriculum appear to some students to be artificial, irrelevant, and exceedingly boring. Sitting in rows while one or two students recite what the teacher already knows or filling in worksheets or end-of-chapter questions sends at-risk students into their own world, into the role of the outsider.

∽ *Reflection* ∽

What activities could you use to determine students' interest in a unit of study you are planning? No matter how carefully you choose the material and plan the activities, you must generate student interest and enthusiasm.

STUDENTS AT RISK

Although all adolescents can feel like outsiders at times, most grow out of it. Those who do not are labeled "at risk" by the school system. Lloyd Tindall, in a study of at-risk students, identified the following factors that contribute to those at risk:

- Family trauma, such as divorce and abuse
- Low parental expectations and apathy
- Alcohol and drug abuse
- Poverty
- Minority status
- Lack of basic academic skills (6)

Student characteristics that may contribute to increased risk range from a desire to be left alone to being combative if students believe teachers or administrators are controlling them. At-risk students typically do not often participate in whole-class activities and do little, if any, homework. They will not have books or class-related materials with them when they do show up, and their attendance rate is poor. Many at-risk students are underachievers and are relegated to remedial or learning disabled classes because of it, even though they have ability.

Tracking such students into homogeneous classes creates assumptions about their learning abilities. Lower-track students are often taught through the use of skill sheets, creating a boring and superficial curriculum. Pamela Adams, a high school teacher, describes two problems with this type of instruction. One is the assumption that if students can't read well, they can't think well either. The other problem is that these students do not have the opportunity to practice critical thinking or learn the type of knowledge valued in our society (424). Rather than dummy-down the curriculum, Adams suggests changing teaching methods to increase student interest and engagement. For instance, she makes a convincing case that *Romeo and Juliet* is an appropriate literature selection for classes with lower-ability students if it is taught with students' interests and knowledge in mind. These students have relevant experiences—for example, interfering parents and faulty decision-making—that help them to relate to what happens to Romeo and Juliet. Teachers need to allow students to share their experiences and to listen to others, thus increasing their knowledge.

VARYING SOURCES OF ALIENATION

"Typical" at-risk students are not the only students who experience alienation in our schools. Racial and ethnic background, gender, and disabilities also contribute to some students' sense of alienation. Being a minority student, even if one has been born and raised in the United States, can cause some students to feel alienated. Immigrant students may face even more prejudice, especially if economic times are hard and communities believe that immigrants are taking away jobs. Because different cultures have specific ways of "knowing and doing," schools serve best those who have been practicing "those ways" since childhood; in other words, mainstream American kids. Because they may be outside of the mainstream culture, minority students sometimes find little in the curriculum that is familiar and consequently give up.

Only recently has gender been recognized as a source of alienation in the schools. In long-term studies of gender differences in school settings, Harvard psychologist Carol Gilligan and her associates found that female students often lose confidence as they move through middle school, becoming less sure of their intellectual abilities. As a result, they may participate less and not challenge male students or teachers. Teachers, too, have recognized that they may unwittingly favor male students by calling on them more often and allowing them to take center stage. However, teachers tend to help females more than males by supplying answers and hints. Female teachers are also more likely to tell males to figure something out on their own. The result can be that males learn to find answers independently, whereas females look to authority figures for answers. These are not deliberate actions, but they nonetheless create gender inequity. Mary Jett-Simpson and Susan Masland, university educators, remind us that "with gender inequity a prevalent part of our society, teachers have a special role to play in being able to help their students identify where it exists in the classroom and school environment" (107). Too, they need to closely examine their own behavior so they do not unwittingly continue the status quo.

Students with learning disabilities, such as dyslexia or other perceptual or neurological problems, may have a hard time with reading and writing, the heart of language arts classrooms. These students may have serious problems, but they are capable of learning and can often participate fully in a "regular" classroom. As James and Kathleen Strickland point out, labeling such students allows schools to provide a less stimulating, less challenging curriculum, and worse, to expect a lot less of them. Further, once a label is attached, it sticks, and all other reasons for educational failure may be ignored. For this reason, it is vital that, for every activity and unit, teachers provide materials with varying levels of difficulty so that everyone in the classroom can find appropriate material.

Other students may be alienated because they have sought their identity through gangs, drugs, or sex. Teens with babies have become a national problem, one that some schools try to address through better sex education, counseling, and day care so that young mothers can complete high school.

Gifted adolescents may also suffer alienation, appearing bizarre or challenging to teachers, and simply "weird" to classmates. Their interests and talents may leave them bored with classroom materials and routines. Often teachers long for a class of gifted students. The reality of such classes, however, is often surprising. Some gifted students are considered "gifted" because they have been teacher-pleasers, not because they have exceptional academic talent. Others may have an inflated sense of their own worth and, thus, are critical of teachers and peers. Gifted students may also expect high grades and rewards for everything they do. And many students are under intense pressure from family and themselves to perform. For these students, performance can be nothing less than excellent, leading some educators to refer to a "cult of excellence" surrounding gifted students. Robert Johnson, a Colorado high school teacher, notes that gifted students "have been taught by teachers and culture that by creating anything less than perfection at the first attempt, they have shown themselves to be ordinary—the worst adjective of all" (37). He also observes that his students believe "excellence has come to mean never trying anything scary in case [their] grades should suffer" (38). Their GPA is the magic number on which they and others pin further education, scholarships, and entrance to prestigious post-secondary institutions. Accordingly, competition with peers may be far stronger than cooperation.

Gifted students need to be challenged but not isolated from classroom activities. To do so is to focus solely on content or academic matters and ignore the social aspects of learning. In the past, gifted students were too often pulled out of the classroom to engage in activities unrelated to what their classmates were doing, or teachers would send gifted students to the library, not knowing how else to keep them busy. Probably even more than other students, gifted students need to learn how to get along with and respect others. Teachers can help build these skills by giving material and activities that are related to the regular students' classroom work to gifted students when they finish their class assignments. This is not busy work, but work that is closely related to what the other students are working on. For example, when reading *Hamlet*, a gifted student who finished early did research about dreams and reported his findings back to his classmates.

 ## THE FORGOTTEN "ORDINARY" STUDENTS

Because schools have so many levels of tracked and labeled kids, it is easy to ignore the vast middle, the "average" kids. For the most part, they do not cause any trouble; they do their homework, participate in class, and get along with teachers and peers. Therefore, it is even more important that we remember they need individual attention, praise, and reinforcement. Within that "average" group are students at both ends of the academic spectrum—some talented, some struggling. And ordinary kids can get into extraordinary trouble. A case in point: At a small suburban Midwest high school, students labeled as "basically good kids" vandalized their high school with eggs, paint, oil, and lawn-killing chemicals. They also flung a deer carcass onto a teacher's car. The superintendent had this to say: "It's unfortunate that this happened because many of these kids have not been discipline problems. That's what makes this more difficult. Some of these kids have been fairly good students" (*Leader Telegram*, 10A). At least 15 students were suspended and banished from graduation, and several were issued tickets for property damage and disorderly conduct.

Mary Mercer Krogness reminds us:

> Good students get attention for being good. Not-so-good students get attention for their misdeeds. And the rest of the students, the large group in the middle and lower middle, may get little attention at all. These are the young people who neither wow their teachers with brilliance nor inundate them with problems; they just come in every day and settle down to work. In the average classroom, these quiet students—especially those who have learning problems and don't meet school requirements,

such as achieving certain levels of proficiency on standardized tests or passing proficiency tests—can easily get lost. Because they usually don't make noise, they don't get
acknowledgment or support, and without these they can lose momentum and interest. Next thing you know, they have quietly fallen through the cracks. (281)

But among the "average" are also the apathetic and mediocre, the unspecial and
unmotivated.

The *English Journal* devoted its symposium section to "Being Unspecial." In the
introduction to this section, editor Ben Nelms states: "I have always wondered when
parents of so-called average students would realize how their children were being neglected and initiate lawsuits for equity" (44).

Nelms' remark was prompted by Sharon Thomas's symposium article in which
Thomas concludes that "the number of needlessly mediocre students could be considerably lessened if average students were given the same attention we have provided special education" (46). Thomas, a high school English teacher in Washington state,
makes a strong case for eliminating the educational waste that occurs when reluctant or
unmotivated learners are left alone, pointing out that the kids themselves don't mind:

> In fact, they like it that way because it means they don't have to work very hard. These
> students have learned that no real consequences spring from lack of effort in high
> school. (45)

These students, says Thomas, "prompt leaders in business and industry to complain
about education in the United States" as they continue their "slipshod ways in the
work world" (45). Most secondary teachers would agree that kids understand early on
that if they don't want to go to college, they'll not be held accountable for demand-
ing academic performance and, thus, the self-fulfilling prophecy.

 ## TEACHING ALL STUDENTS

Teachers are responsible for teaching, to the best of their ability, every student in their
classrooms. Through inclusion, more students with special needs (such as emotional
disturbances, mental and physical disabilities, and limited language proficiency) are in
a regular classroom, at least for part of a class period. Resource teachers may be present in the class and meet with regular classroom teachers outside of class to help them
work with special needs students. Teachers have many resources to help them with
special needs students and need to ask for the help that is available. It is not a poor reflection on teachers to ask for help; rather it shows a concern and knowledge about
helping their students. Parents, retired teachers, literacy volunteers, and others available outside the school can help with small groups, thus allowing a teacher to address
individual needs. Within the school the gifted coordinator, librarian, Chapter One
teachers, and counselors can help with reading groups. Inclusion has many benefits for
all students because they learn to work and socialize with others of varying capabilities. Such knowledge helps to dispel fears about differences among us, a major source
of prejudice.

HELPING STUDENTS TO LEARN

Many factors in the classroom affect how children learn: class size, environment, motivation, teacher encouragement, appropriate lessons that interest students and are matched to their abilities, and group work. Throughout this book, we have included ways of taking these factors into account in lesson plans and selection of student material. Two particular areas of research have contributed to our understanding of creating classrooms that optimize students' learning: learning styles and multiple intelligences.

Whether we are ordinary, gifted, or disabled, we all have a learning style that is a "biologically and developmentally imposed set of personal characteristics that make the same teaching method effective for some and ineffective for others" (Dunn, Beaudry, and Klavas 50). One's learning style is the way he or she concentrates on, processes, internalizes, and remembers new and difficult information and skills. Learning styles affect how we respond to an environment, how we remember information, and how we learn. Styles can vary with age, achievement level, culture, and gender (Shaughnessy 141). Learning style is a "multidimensional construct; many variables have an impact on each other and produce unique patterns" (Dunn reported in Shaughnessy 142). Some students learn best by listening, others by reading, note-taking, seeing, manipulating, or some combination (Dunn, Beaudry, and Klavas 50). Students who cannot sit still, for example, might be responding to a strong learning style that requires movement or interaction.

A wealth of research has accumulated on various learning styles, methods for determining individual styles, and the effects of optimal styles for individuals (Dunn, Beaudry, and Klavas 51). Research studies show that in environments where instruction is compatible with one's learning style, students learn more and retain that learning longer (51–52). "Most people can learn anything when they know how to capitalize on their learning style" (reported in Shaughnessy 143). Learning styles can be determined by "The Learning Style Inventory." Different grade-level forms are used to analyze specific conditions under which students prefer to work (Shaughnessy 142). However, if a teacher is unable to give the inventory or does not want to, it is important to be aware that every class has a mixture of styles that may or may not be the same as the teacher's.

Since we tend to use the style that works best for us, we should identify our own style by taking a reliable identification instrument. By learning about diverse learning styles, teachers become more understanding of other's learning style as well as their own (Stevenson and Dunn 484). Then they can deliberately use other methods when presenting material and creating learning environments. For example, if a teacher learns best by listening, then presentations might follow that style by explaining verbally in addition to written material. To effectively reach more students, teachers need to present information through discussion, written material, visual approaches, and opportunities to discuss in small groups. It is vital that teachers vary their methods and presentations to give students options and alternatives that accommodate more students more of the time.

Howard Gardner, a professor at Harvard University, has developed a theory of multiple intelligences, a theory that calls into question traditional ideas about learning. Intelligence is multidimensional and occurs at multiple levels: mind, body, and brain (Lazear 8). We all have multiple ways of processing understanding or ways of knowing the world. People have separate and equally valid types of intelligence (Viadero 24). Gardner refers to these multiple levels as multiple intelligences and has identified seven areas or ways of knowing:

1. verbal/linguistic
2. logical/math
3. visual/spatial
4. body/kinesthetic
5. musical/rhythmic
6. interpersonal
7. intrapersonal

We possess at least these seven intelligences and have the capacity to strengthen each one, but to do so takes intention and practice.

American schools focus on linguistic and logical–mathematical intelligence. Gardner explains that we need to place equal value on individuals whose strengths lie in other intelligences. People differ in their ways of knowing and in their ability to combine their intelligences (Armstrong 1). Gardner explains, "When teachers provide different ways for students to learn, that is various approaches and opportunities, students are more able to expand the intelligences they use" (17). The different ways of teaching speak to disparate learning styles and cultural backgrounds. Gardner suggests five different ways of connecting with the multiple intelligences to help students learn a concept:

1. narrational: explaining about a concept
2. logical–quantitative: using deductive reasoning
3. foundational: philosophical background
4. esthetic: including related music and art
5. experiential approach: hands-on experiences

how to connect to students w/ multiple intelligences

Teachers can apply these approaches to diverse situations (Gardner 245–246).

Students have different kinds of minds and "therefore learn, remember, perform, and understand in different ways" (Gardner 11). We don't have to teach or learn using all of the intelligences; however, to help students learn, teachers must both teach and assess in several ways. Armstrong suggests that teachers do not have to teach in all seven ways, but see what the possibilities are and then decide what might be the most effective learning tools (Armstrong 3).

Teacher Laura Apfelbeck designed student-learning projects for *Romeo and Juliet* using the Multiple Intelligences Approach.

ᕙ LESSON PLAN FOR *ROMEO AND JULIET* LEARNING PROJECTS

After discussing Howard Gardner's Multiple Intelligences Approach to learning, group students according to their favored intelligence. Groups of three or four usually work well. Once groups have looked at the examples of learning projects below, they may have their own ideas about how to use their learning strengths to demonstrate their understanding of *Romeo and Juliet*. In addition to reading, watching a dramatized version of the play is helpful to students.

1. *Verbal/linguistic*— these learners will be interested in the language and in oral discussions. They may want to explore the archaic words creating Shakespearean equivalents to contemporary slang expressions or rewriting a scene in modern English. Oral interpretation such as a reader's theater approach to presenting a scene might appeal to this group.

2. *Logical/mathematic*— these learners will probably be interested in the meter of the verse, the structure of the Globe Theater, or the choreography of the staged version. Some might be interested in creating a web page featuring the play or one of the characters. Others may enjoy a close look at the timing of the events. What happens each day? Is the timing logical? Those with a more biological slant may enjoy studying Friar Laurence's plants.

3. *Visual/spatial*— these students will most likely learn well by watching a performance of the play and may enjoy comparing two versions of the performance, sketching costumes for characters or drawing stage sets for scenes. Some may also enjoy creating models of the Globe, making a diorama of a specific scene, or sketching a character, such as Mab or Juliet, based on the textual description.

4. *Body/kinesthetic*— these students will appreciate and learn from acting out scenes from the play, creating choreography, especially for intense scenes such as sword fights or street scenes with multiple actors, developing gestures and characteristic movements for central characters in specific scenes.

5. *Musical/rhythmic*— these learners will be interested in the cadence of the oral language and may enjoy listening to a tape recording of key scenes by professional actors. Also, musical/rhythmic learners may like analyzing the theme music chosen by professionals to accompany various versions of the play or choosing their own score for a scene or two. Others might like finding a theme song for each key character or creating a song in rap, blues, country, or pop style.

6. *Interpersonal*— these students will enjoy learning through discussion or reflection on character motivations and interactions, talking to others about their interpretations, perhaps surveying class members to learn their reactions to specific characters and their opinions of those characters.

7. *Intrapersonal*— these learners will probably like discussions that connect the play to themselves such as "What expectations do you have for someone you love?" or "What would you have done if your parents disapproved of your

girlfriend/boyfriend?" or a journal in which the student choose a scene and imagines himself/herself in the same situation as the character and writes what he/she would do under the same circumstances.

By letting students choose how they react and explain their understanding of a novel allows them to take advantage of their strongest intelligence.

EXPLORATION

Teaching to Student Intelligences

Choose a novel appropriate for student interest and, following Apfelbeck's example, develop ways students could respond in a final project demonstrating their understanding of the work. Not all literature will present opportunities for all of the intelligences. Select any novel suitable for either middle school or high school.

REALITIES OF STUDENTS' LIVES

Most educators are painfully aware of the conditions that many of our students experience. Gene Tucker explains that while we can't change the harsh realities, we can create viable environments in schools.

Violence of all kinds is a fact of life in many homes and neighborhoods. An increasing percentage of our youth live in unstable homes, most with single mothers earning marginal incomes or on welfare. Transience rates are exceptionally high, with some schools experiencing turnover approaching 100% in any given year. Large numbers of children come to school with limited primary language development and very poor social skills. In many instances, alienation and despair about the prospects for a better future generate attitudes that denigrate traditional values (1). Tucker explains that rather than being overwhelmed by the enormity of the problem, teachers can make a difference in children's lives. "Teachers who have effectively adapted to today's students while maintaining high standards and expectations for all" create classrooms "where pupils are actively engaged with challenging content and positive learning outcomes are evident" (2). This may sound too idealistic, but teachers who know the content of their field, apply diverse strategies, and create a learning community do have success.

Our classrooms must reflect an awareness of the nature of our students' lives and the content we teach. Teachers and students need to interact if they are to create the most effective learning and teaching conditions. How teachers structure their classrooms is critically important and dependent on many factors—from resources to personalities, personal knowledge to school policy. Although many factors influence teachers' decisions about how and what to teach, one of the major ones must be the nature of the students. Age, gender, race, ethnicity, socioeconomic status, and language proficiency all contribute to individual differences. Students' lives and experiences greatly influence their ability to learn in both positive and negative ways.

Consequently, we cannot ignore the conditions of students' lives. We must be aware of deaths, separations, or serious illness in students' families. We must not ignore the student whose girlfriend just dropped him, the student who failed an important exam, the student who works nights or who gets up at 4 A.M. to do farm work, or one who has major responsibility for younger siblings. In every class, some students are struggling with difficulty, responsibility, uncertainty, or pain. Given this reality, teachers must be both understanding and flexible. A head on the desk or turned toward a window does not necessarily indicate disrespect or lack of interest, but could be evidence of a larger, more compelling concern.

Increasingly, students' lives have become more troubled, reflecting a society with a widening gap between the "haves" and "have nots," a society of uncertain values, questionable ethics, and periodic violence. We need, then, to be aware of a student whose parent or sibling is in jail, whose brother has been injured or killed in a gang fight, whose alcoholic parent is abusive, whose household is overcrowded, whose home revolves in a cycle of poverty. For such students, just getting to school is a major accomplishment. Keeping this perspective is not easy, but it is important that our students' experiences influence our teaching and expectations. We cannot, for example, expect students who have neither the physical space nor emotional support to complete homework assignments.

We cannot continue to teach students as if they had no life outside of the classroom. In reality, their lives can be frightening, exhausting, and overwhelming. Candy Carter, a high school teacher, argues, "students often come to school with so much unfinished business from home that it takes a real master to bring art and life together" (27). She adds that few students today, regardless of socioeconomic class, have not "been confronted with opportunities to use drugs or drink to excess" (26). Thus, our idealism as teachers may be sorely tried by circumstances beyond our control.

Teachers cannot always solve students' problems, but we can make our classrooms places where they can find temporary refuge and provide them with understanding, empathy, and patience. Through responding to literature, writing in journals, listening, and talking with peers, students may find answers to their questions and make sense of their lives.

We can say one thing with certainty. Every teacher will have a wide range of students—from the bookworm to the defiant, from students who absorb everything placed in front of them to those whose silence says, "I dare you to teach me." Their varying attitudes reflect our world at large, one that Alvin Toffler described in *Future Shock* as "the shattering stress and disorientation that we induce in individuals by subjecting them to too much change in too short time" (2). Our world is a complex kaleidoscope of changing values and attitudes. In addition to personal problems in families and relationships, students grapple with societal problems. If students in past decades lived in fear of nuclear annihilation, ours live in an equally frightening world of terrorism and a sense of shrinking opportunities.

HOW TEACHERS CAN HELP

Over thirty years ago Dwight Burton and his colleagues asked students what they needed. They responded that "they needed some hope, some feeling that mankind will not merely survive but that it deserves to survive" (17). Sobering words, words as likely to arise from the students of the 21st century.

What do these realities mean for our classrooms? Mainly that we provide personal integrity, a modeling if you will, and opportunities for students to explore their beliefs and values. Through literature, classroom drama, and writing, students can safely explore themselves and their world, find people to admire, and see beyond the limits of their present situation. Students also need a classroom environment that encourages and respects the range of human emotions. In his important study of American schools, John Goodlad tells us:

> Data . . . suggest to me a picture of rather well-intentioned teachers going about their business somewhat detached from and not quite connecting with the "other lives" of their students. What their students see as primary concerns in their daily lives, teachers view as dissonance in conducting school and classroom business. (80)

Goodlad goes on to note that "classes at all levels tend not to be marked with exuberance, joy, laughter, abrasiveness, praise, but by emotional neutrality" (112) and "whether we looked at how teachers related to students or how students related to teachers, the overwhelming impression was one of affective neutrality—a relationship neither abrasive nor joyous" (111). Knowing how deeply felt the emotions of adolescents are, the affective desert presented here astounds us. What is more, we can think of no worse environment for students or ourselves. To prevent it, we need to seriously examine students' needs and interests as we choose materials and plan lessons. And even though, as teachers, we are the ones who structure learning, we have to remember that we do not own it.

No matter how well we teach, learning ultimately belongs to the student. Janet Emig explains this idea in a talk entitled "Exploring Theories of Learning for Teaching Writing": "Learning doesn't always follow teaching, but leads a marvelously independent life of its own." As English language arts teachers, we can structure, facilitate, and nurture learning, but we can neither impose nor control it. "Marvelously independent," we believe, captures the essence of learning, for it suggests our students follow diverse, individual paths of learning, measuring time and demonstrating growth uniquely, and finally coming to know in their own ways. This view of diversity reminds us that we ourselves have learned in different ways, in different times, and in different places. Our own learning has not been limited to the classroom; therefore, we must value and draw on our students' experiences as we plan for teaching. Moreover, we cannot separate teaching and learning; as teachers we learn, and our students, in many respects, become our teachers.

When we plan lessons for the myriad of student types we have in our classrooms, we need to keep in mind the following points:

1. Always provide multiple ways to learn
2. Generate interest in the lesson by connecting to students' lives and to the world outside the classroom
3. Encourage student responsibility
4. Connect the lessons to other areas they have studied
5. Encourage self-confidence by helping students achieve success

In the first chapter of this book, "Becoming a Teacher," we use the voices of real high school students to describe the importance of seeing our students as teachers. Some veteran English teachers share their thoughts as well. One of them, Eileen Simmons, tells us to trust our students and ourselves to explore our subject areas together:

> No teacher's guide taught me the connection between Shakespeare's play *The Tempest* and Ray Bradbury's *Fahrenheit 451*. But a high school sophomore saw that Prospero and Beatty were both into "mind control." A junior English literature student spotted the similarity between King Arthur's court and modern society: Gang members are controlled by a code as rigid as that of any medieval knight. (73)

Simmons is right. Students are wonderful teachers, smart and insightful, if only we share with them the journey of learning and emphasize the importance of their responses. And they are much more fun than a teacher's guide.

As teachers plan lessons, they must keep students' needs in the forefront. Joy Hoffmann, who teaches at a residential treatment facility for children with emotional disturbances or behavior disorders, has students with special needs. Her materials and resources are extremely limited, a fact that has her "constantly fighting the budget and scrounging around for the stuff from which learning experiences are made." Some of her students are extremely bright and would benefit from higher-order thinking strategies.

Hoffmann developed an instructional unit based on heroic values because her students have few positive role models and even fewer heroes; they need people to look up to and emulate. She further explains that her students have "value systems that are antisocial, dangerous, and/or fragmented, but they seldom know how to develop more workable practices and beliefs." Although what follows is an abbreviated version of the unit Hoffmann developed, we can explore what she planned in light of her specialized student group.

INSTRUCTIONAL UNIT

HEROIC VALUES

Joy chose the following materials listed in chronological order to use in a six-week unit on heroic values: newspaper or other nonfiction articles about people who students would consider heroic, speeches by John F. Kennedy and Martin Luther King, Jr., one or two short stories or poems, *Beowulf*, *Hamlet*, and *Beloved* by Toni Morrison.

Activity: Begin the unit by playing rap tapes and other popular songs. Ask students why these songs are popular, easy to remember, and fun to sing. What do these songs have in common? The students practice writing their own lyrics after discussion of rhythm, diction, and structure in class. Or they may develop their own unusual style.

The unit also develops the idea of audience, word choice, style, and imagery. The students do some oral reading of *Beowulf* with emphasis on rhythm and discuss diction and style. For the final assignment, students create a narrative that would be attractive to an audience with little education or literary background.

Reflection

1. How has Joy considered the variety of learning styles of her students?
2. Discuss how appropriate you think her literature selections are for her students.
3. Where has Joy focused on student interests? In what other ways might she use student interest as the basis for activities?
4. What are Joy's objectives? Based on this unit, what do you think is her philosophy of teaching and learning?
5. What activities from Joy's unit could you use in an academically heterogeneous classroom?

EXPLORATION

1. Many new teachers get caught up in subject matter content without considering who that content is for. Think back to your own high school experience. How would you characterize the students? What might account for these characteristics? In particular, try to recall groups of students who were labeled as troublemakers. If you had these students in your classroom today, what activities would you use to reach them?
2. Talk with as many experienced teachers as possible to learn their views on the variety of students they teach. How do they adjust content to fit the students' needs? Observe classrooms, concentrating on the students' behavior, not the teacher. Keep a log of your observations. How do you know if assumptions you make about the students are right?
3. Design an opening day activity that will help you be a more successful teacher throughout the year. Share the activity with peers and discuss which activities would be the most helpful. What goals are the most beneficial for all students?
4. Survey college students who are non-English majors to learn their views of the characteristics of "good" English teachers and classes. Then survey the students in an English education class. What are the similarities and differences? Discuss the implications for future teachers.

5. What are some ways you could get to know your students better at the beginning of the school year? What are the most important things to tell them? Usually the first day of class is spent handing out a list of rules, textbooks, course expectations, and what a teacher will not accept or allow. Reflect on your own first-day experiences and those of classes you have observed. What might you do? Why?

RELATED WEB SITES

http://www.thomasarmstrong.com/multiple_intelligences.htm
http://www.nassp.org (high school)
http://www.nmsa.org (middle school)
http://www.ed.gov/databases/ERIC (education articles on many subjects)

REFERENCES

Adams, Pamela E. "Teaching *Romeo and Juliet* in the Nontracked English Classroom." *Journal of Reading* 38.6 (Mar. 1995): 424–31.

Armstrong, Thomas. *Multiple Intelligences* 13 July 2003 <http://www.thomasarmstrong.com/multiple_intelligences.htm>.

Burton, Dwight, et al. *Teaching English Today.* Boston: Houghton Mifflin, 1975.

Carter, Candy. "Are Teenagers Different?" *What Is English?* Ed. Peter Elbow. New York: Modern Language Association; Urbana: National Council of Teachers of English, 1990.

Dunn, Rita, Jeffrey S. Beaudry, and Angela Klavas. "Survey of Research on Learning Styles." *Educational Leadership* (Mar. 1989): 50–58.

Emig, Janet. "Exploring Theories of Learning for Teaching Writing." Conference on Teaching Composition to Undergraduates. Clearwater Beach, FL. 5 Jan. 1992.

Gardner, Howard. *The Unschooled Mind.* Basic Books/HarperCollins, 1991.

Gilligan, Carol, Nona Lyons, and Randy Hanmer, eds. *Making Connections: The Relational Worlds of Adolescent Girls at Emma Willard School.* Cambridge: Harvard UP, 1990.

Goodlad, John. *A Place Called School.* New York: McGraw-Hill, 1984.

Hoffmann, Joy. "Heroic Values." Unpublished manuscript, 1996 Eau Claire: University of Wisconsin.

Jett-Simpson, Mary, and Susan Masland. "Girls Are Not Dodo Birds! Reading Against the Grain: Gender Bias in Children's Books." *Language Arts* (Feb. 1993): 104–08.

Johnson, Robert. "Challenging the Cult of Excellence." *English Journal* (Oct. 1992): 37–40.

Krogness, Mary Mercer. *Just Teach Me, Mrs. K.: Talking, Reading, and Writing With Resistant Adolescent Learners.* Portsmouth: Heinemann, 1995.

Lazear, David G. *Teaching for Multiple Intelligences.* Bloomington: Phi Delta Kappa Educational Foundation, 1992.

Lightfoot, Sara. Interview. *Conversations With Bill Moyers.* Public Affairs TV. WNET/NIV and UTTW/Chicago, 1988.

National Association of Secondary School Principals. *On the Threshold of Adolescence.* Reston: Author, 1983.

Nelms, Ben F. "Being Unspecial. Introduction to Symposium." *English Journal* (Oct. 1992): 44.

Rief, Linda. *Seeking Diversity.* Portsmouth: Heinemann, 1992.

Shaughnessy, Michael F. "An Interview with Rita Dunn about Learning Styles." *The Clearing House* (Jan/Feb. 1998): 71.

Simmons, Eileen. "A Quarter of a Century and Not Finished Yet." *English Journal* (Feb. 1995): 73.

Stevenson, Joseph, and Rita Dunn. *College Student Journal* 35.4 (2001): 483–91.

Strickland, Kathleen, and James Strickland. *Uncovering the Curriculum*. Portsmouth: Boynton/Cook, 1993.

Tchudi, Stephen. "Invisible Thinking and the Hypertext." *English Journal* (Jan. 1988): 22–30.

Thomas, Sharon. "The Forgotten Half." *English Journal* (Oct. 1992): 45–46.

Tindall, Lloyd W. "Retaining At-Risk Students: The Role of Career and Vocational Education." Washington: U.S. Department of Education, ERIC 303–683 Report.

Toffler, Alvin. *Future Shock*. New York: Random House, 1970.

Tucker, Gene. "Teaching Today's Students." *UCLA Graduate School of Education Quarterly* (Fall 1993): 1–2.

"Vandals Barred From Graduation." *Leader-Telegram* 28 May 1995: 10A.

Viadero, Debra. "Staying Power." *Education Week* 22.39 (4 June 2003): 24–28.

Understanding Curriculum, Instruction, and Planning  3

Good teaching consists of the making and adjusting of day-to-day plans and depends
upon a delicate balance between rational order and intuitive spontaneity.

Editorial Staff, *English Journal*

 ## A PHILOSOPHY SHAPING WHAT WE DO AND WHEN WE DO IT

At times we have heard our English education majors say that they don't want to
write one more philosophy statement for courses in the School of Education. At
times we have also heard experienced English language arts teachers say that they
don't really have a philosophy of teaching. To our students, we say: "You need to develop, indeed trust in, a philosophy, one resting on reputable research and best practice." To those veterans, we say: "Yes, you do. You illustrate it every day in every
class." How we view our students, structure our classrooms, and choose instructional
methods or materials affects the learning of every student entrusted to us. A teacher
who believes that English is a subject to be taught, mastered, and tested will structure learning very differently than one who believes English is a process through
which students seek to understand themselves and others. A teacher who believes
English is a collection of basic skills or a body of knowledge to be transmitted creates
a different learning environment than one who believes students acquire basic skills
through sustained, authentic experience in oral and written language. Similarly, a
teacher who tells students about literature, rather than asking them to respond to it,
demonstrates one philosophy; a teacher who believes students must connect with literature through their own experiences before they move on to abstract and universal
considerations, has quite another.

Reflection

If you have been asked to write a philosophy statement, what did you include? From being a student for more than 14 years, what do you already know about teaching philosophies—about what a teacher believes, and thus acts upon, in his or her classroom?

ANCHORING OUR PHILOSOPHY: WHAT WE KNOW ABOUT THE ENGLISH LANGUAGE ARTS

Several decades of research and classroom practice have provided us with good information upon which to build a useful and effective philosophy of teaching. That is, as we plan our lessons and units, we know what generally works well and why.

- The language arts are interactive processes, each influencing and strengthening the others, as we construct meaning. This means students need to use the language arts actively and consistently to make sense of themselves and their world. It means their teachers have a philosophy where students construct, rather than are given, meaning.

- Because the language arts influence and strengthen one another, students need lessons where their teachers have consciously balanced listening, speaking, reading, and writing activities. In developing units and lessons, teachers may emphasize one area, but their students should be actively engaged in all the language arts. Students soon tire of a curriculum that puts them through two weeks of giving speech, followed by three weeks of writing essays or four weeks of reading literature. Further, the real world does not use oral and written language in such artificial, isolated constructs—and students know this.

- Whether we listen, speak, read, or write, we are engaged in communication—with purpose, audience, and context to guide our choices of language and style. If teachers want their students "to stay the course," this language principle must permeate curricular and instructional design. Student motivation comes from purpose, from students who have something to say and want to say it.

- When we use language, we are engaged in an ongoing cognitive process. Because the language arts have traditionally been viewed as a subject to be taught, we have sometimes forgotten that they are first and foremost active processes. Teachers who plan and implement lessons from this point of view know that students need time and experience to achieve competency or proficiency in each of the language arts. Moreover, these teachers' lessons acknowledge that language processes occur holistically; that is, we don't master one skill and then move to another. When we speak, listen, read, or write, we use various skills all at the same time, reaching competency or proficiency in different skills at different times. In this classroom, the choice of materials and methods is altered by the knowledge of cognitive processing and complexity, as is the view of errors as normal, necessary even, to student growth.

- When we listen, speak, read, or write, we are limited by maturation—physically, cognitively, and linguistically. Some tasks are too difficult for us at the time at which they are introduced; some are too easy. Within a single classroom, students may be similar in age yet vary in maturation, and thus in their ability to complete certain assignments. They may also vary considerably across the language arts, performing well in one area but not another. Similarly, student performance may vary from task to task, even within one language arts area—something that confounds and frustrates teachers who forget that teenage development is ongoing and changing. Without this knowledge, and appropriate action to follow, assessment may be resting on absolutes and expectations that push students away or convince them that they cannot learn.

All of these points are part of a philosophy of teaching and learning: knowledge about how students learn most effectively. These guide our choice of materials, activities, and assessment. They also suggest how classroom climate will evolve and how learning will be nurtured. Mostly, they help us focus more on learners and less on ourselves.

A philosophy of teaching, then, is not a dry, unmotivated essay written to satisfy requirements of a college class; it is the heart of what we do in the classroom. From reputable research and best practice nationwide, we know that a philosophy based on such knowledge evolves into a set of beliefs that guides our planning:

- Students are active participants within a community of learners.
- Teachers facilitate learning rather than "hand it out."
- Students construct meaning through sustained, meaningful experience.
- The language arts are learned through purposeful communication, not exercises.
- Teachers respect and plan for individual differences and the unique needs of some students.
- The classroom environment, emotionally safe, fosters and supports intellectual risk-taking.
- Students work cooperatively as well as independently.

However, holding a sound philosophy for teaching English language arts, and acting upon it, are not the same. We need to know how to translate that philosophy into everyday lessons and units—and that's just ahead as we explore both the "what" and the "how" of the English language arts for secondary level students.

EXPLORATION

In Full View: A Philosophy of Teaching

As homework, list your most memorable secondary teachers. Choose one. With a pseudonym for this person, list specific teaching characteristics (e.g., style, materials, assignments) that you now understand illustrated his or her philosophy of teaching. In class, with a partner or small group, compare your findings. What stands out and why?

DEVELOPING CLASSROOM CURRICULUM

Sometimes, teachers think in terms of "What can I teach?" rather than "How can my students best learn?" The English language arts curriculum should arise out of the latter perspective. We can best help our students learn by providing them with experiences that will help them grow both intellectually and imaginatively, individually and socially, cognitively and emotionally. Curriculum and instruction, then, should acknowledge and prepare for the inevitable changes that our students will undergo as they mature. Knowing, for example, that the capabilities and needs of a 13-year-old differ from those of a 15-year-old is useless information unless we act on it. Intervening in the lives of our students demands that we do act on the best knowledge our profession has to offer. Once teachers focus on the learner, other questions follow about students' ability levels, learning styles, and interests.

From Goals to Outcomes

The English language arts curriculum consists of a common set of goals, outcomes, and topics for each of the language arts at each grade level. For example, a general goal for high school literature, such as these from Wisconsin's Model Academic Standards, might state: "Students will read, interpret, and critically analyze literature." A specific goal for eleventh grade would then state: "Students will draw on a broad base of knowledge about universal themes of literature such as love and duty, heroism, or illusion and reality, and explain how these themes are developed in a particular piece of literature." The eleventh-grade curriculum might also specify pieces of literature that all students will read to focus on this goal. At the same time, eleventh-grade teachers would choose other pieces that both complement the mandated literature and provide for greater reading diversity. From goals, we extract learner outcomes: What students are expected to know or accomplish as a result of our instruction. Returning to our eleventh-grade literature goal, we can state learner outcomes more specifically. For example: "Students will differentiate between illusion and reality in *The Great Gatsby*." "Students will define heroism through the character of Atticus in *To Kill A Mockingbird*." How students achieve these outcomes, the methods and materials through which they learn, is up to us, classroom teachers. The means through which students demonstrate achievement is also up to us—fair and appropriate assessment. Thus, as we develop outcomes, we must also develop the daily activities through which students will achieve them and the assessment measures through which we know that they did.

Textbooks, Trade Books, and Software

In some districts, English language arts textbooks *are* the curriculum, representing the scope and sequence for specific grade levels. The terms *scope* and *sequence,* as the names suggest, refer to the range or amount of curricular content and its order of presentation. In brief, *scope* tells teachers what to cover and *sequence* tells them the order of instruction. Moreover, textbooks lay out not only "what," but also, through their questions and activities, they lay out instructional methods—the "how." Some are far better than others at the "how." When textbooks are congruent with how students learn, allow for diversity, and challenge the learner, this textbook curriculum may be a good one. The goals and outcomes inherent in the texts would closely align with those of the district and its teachers, as well as with state and national standards. The oral and written activities would be appropriate and stimulating. However, teachers don't often get to choose their textbooks, largely because textbooks represent a major financial investment for a district and are not replaced all that often, especially in fields less subject to factual change. Although we can argue that recent English language arts texts do represent important changes in the field, especially in more diverse literary selections, teachers are still unlikely to have new textbooks more than once in a decade.

Nonetheless, teachers make important curricular choices. First, teachers determine which segments of a textbook will be used, and in which order, and second, they choose from or create an array of supplementary materials. Fortunately, we have a plethora of good trade books, usually well within a year's budget, that provide the kind of diversity we want and complement selections in the basic literature textbook. We can also become good scavengers, supplementing textbooks with acquisitions from the school library, the public library, used book stores, and book sales. School librarians are a wonderful resource, not only in providing a constant flow of information about new works of fiction and nonfiction but also in assisting us as we develop units. When I was teaching junior high school in a rural district, the school librarian helped me to pull 20 or more adolescent novels off the shelves to stash in my classroom for several weeks. Similarly, a children's librarian at the nearest public library, once drawn into my unit's theme and goals, prepared stacks of adolescent fiction and nonfiction for my classroom—all taken out on my library card for several weeks. With the help of these professionals, I was able to meet diverse student needs and interests, ranging from learning disabled to intellectually gifted in one eighth-grade class.

The public library is also a good source of audio and video tapes, often matching or complementing literary selections in the textbook. With the abundance of video stores, we have yet another low-cost alternative for special films. Used book stores offer us plenty of fiction and nonfiction at bargain prices, meeting a classroom need for alternative reading selections. Meeting the diverse needs of students is challenging, but maintaining a classroom supply of paperbacks and periodicals is not only economical but practical. Even students who appear to dislike everything about school in general and reading in particular appear to like the *Guinness Book of Records,* books with trivia from sports, cars, music or any aspect of popular culture, and word games or puzzles. It is not "selling out" to provide trade books or materials that appear nonacademic or too heavily representative of popular culture. Through them, we help many students discover the pleasure of literacy or make the transition to more complex, challenging reading.

Although textbooks for composition and grammar are plentiful, they are not really needed. Student drafts can and should provide the core of composition and grammar instruction. A good composition textbook can, of course, be a useful reference text, but handbooks—if students are taught how to use them and required to use them for editing their own drafts—will work perfectly well. In most cases, composition will not be handled as a textbook unit; thus, there is no need for a textbook devoted solely to writing as units of study. Novice teachers will probably find composition and grammar textbooks a useful reference for themselves; they can borrow ideas and teaching strategies from them as warranted or desired. But as noted earlier, funding for textbooks is usually very limited, and teachers are wise to spend it in ways that meet the diversity of learners through interesting reading materials or student-friendly handbooks, rather than through costly textbooks.

What about computer software? It is readily available for language arts, but just as we make judgments about any text or material through examining it, we need to try out the software. The options range from CDs that give students a chat with an author, for example, to an interactive game with a toucan gulping fruit when the right subject-verb agreement is chosen. These can be intriguing, and, in some cases, respond well to the diversity of interests and needs in our classrooms. But again, we should check out software ourselves to learn if it's right for our students and the outcomes we have set for them. To locate appropriate software or pare down options, read reviews in professional English journals and ask around. Other English teachers may have experience with specific software, or know someone who does. The web site for The National Council of Teachers of English is a good resource for finding them.

EXPLORATION

Making the Most of Pop Culture

One of our student teachers was surprised to find a corner in her middle school classroom that was devoted solely to pop culture items (e.g., paperbacks, magazines, games, puzzles). As the weeks unfolded, Martina was grateful for that corner. With partners, make a list of specific items that could add to students' language development, critical thinking or reading skills—or just plain interest them. Then review your list, sorting items as appropriate for middle school, senior high, or both. Put a star next to items that kicked in some biases, where you believed an item was quite "unworthy" of classroom space or time. Share your findings in large group.

Cliffs Notes for Teachers: Guides and Web Sites

Although the very term *Cliffs Notes* conjures up visions of students slugging their way through classic novels, there are times when teachers might use similar guides to good advantage. When planning a unit, the first glance at unfamiliar texts could be through a good synopsis or a teacher's guide of some sort. The teacher edition of secondary literature anthologies usually carries both synopses and teaching suggestions, some of which may be very helpful, especially for special needs students. Other suggestions may be superficial, unimaginative, or wrong-headed in terms of effective classroom practice, but just scanning them is in itself a useful activity. As we learn from both good and poor suggestions, ideas pop into our heads, and we see potential.

The same can be said for web sites devoted to teaching English language arts or related areas in other disciplines. There is a wealth of good web material available; on almost any topic, author, or theme, you will find some useful ideas. However, checking the source of the web site is always a good idea: You need to know if the site has been posted by reliable educators or a reputable agency. For example, in the Ben Franklin unit that closes this chapter, student Sarah Nyberg used eight web sites, originating from government sources to public television, from school districts to national teacher organizations. When we tried some Ben Franklin sites ourselves, we were met with literally hundreds of responses. Sorting them out had a lot to do with recognizing the reputation and reliability of their origins. We knew we could trust the web site for public television, for example, which featured a teacher's guide to their recent three-part series on Ben Franklin, along with eight lesson plans. We didn't go into the lesson plans themselves, but from the synopses on their web site, it was clear that useful and creative information could be found there. Additionally, the web site granted permission for teachers to videotape the series for classroom use. So part of your planning task, and your time allocation for planning, should include that of "surfing" relevant and reputable web sites.

We are not, however, advocating that you take specific lesson plans or teaching ideas and use them exactly as presented to you, but rather, that you simply consider materials and activities matching your developing unit plan. When you find some that you believe would work well with your students, adapt them to your teaching style, your classroom. Using someone else's lessons verbatim rarely works. Preparing to be an English language arts teacher means deciding what to teach and how to teach it. What's more, one of the most satisfying and pleasurable parts of teaching is the development of interesting and worthwhile units. We shouldn't let anyone take that responsibility and pleasure away, but we should be open to good ideas from other educators.

Some Curricular Issues

Tracking, sometimes referred to as ability grouping, is a curricular issue that has a powerful effect on students. The points of view about this effect are polarized, despite several decades of research suggesting the effect is largely negative, especially on students who are already marginalized. Noted English language arts educator Nancy Atwell believes that tracking allows us to blame students for our failure to teach them well—all those low-tracked adolescents of whom we ask and expect less and less (40). And this is the crux of the academic effect: low expectations, coupled with work that is largely rote and unimaginative. We wish to emphasize, however, that educators who oppose tracking are not suggesting that students of like ability should never be grouped— only that creating a permanent group labeled "slow" is a poor response to a serious problem.

If tracking appears a poor option for students already struggling or alienated in some way, the other extreme is equally problematic, what we will call the "feel good" curriculum. To base all instruction on whether students will feel good about themselves while learning is dangerous; it becomes a purely affective curriculum, leaving students without the content knowledge, skills, and experience critical to their academic development. Intuition and common sense tell us that kids need self-esteem to succeed in school and in life. Consequently, we must remember that we are teaching kids—not just where to put a comma. At the same time, we must act on the knowledge that self-esteem comes from authentic learning and achievement, both of which are the by-products of an interesting and developmentally appropriate curriculum, a curriculum that involves kids in their own learning. Educator Alfie Kohn argues that we can facilitate such learning through the "three C's of motivation: collaboration, choice, and content," all of which are integral to our earliest planning (281). Kohn states, "Students do not come to believe they are important, valued, and capable just because they are told this is so"; instead, they "acquire a sense of significance from doing significant things, from being active participants in their own education" (282). This, we believe, is the real "feel good" curriculum, one intimately linked to good curricular content. Without such content, just what are those "significant things"?

Student needs and interests can become another curricular issue, one arising when teachers believe that "they alone know best." Well-educated teachers do know "best" about most things—but not everything. Some things they need to find out directly from their students, whose needs and interests change rapidly in the course of an academic year. So, finding out what kids are interested in, building choice within lessons and units, and ditching elitist views about what is "proper" in English are all part of curricular planning. For example, that Batman comic dumped as trash—even though its characterization and theme may echo those of classic literature—may be a missed chance with a whole group of students, ages 12 through 17.

When we think about classes where we tuned out, and ask why, several reasons come to mind. But before we discuss them, we would like you to reflect on your experience with "tuned out" secondary classes.

⟡ *Reflection* ⟡

In your journal, make a list of times you recall feeling disconnected, frustrated, angry even, because a high school class just didn't work for you—not for a day or two, but for a significant period of time. What factors might have contributed to this situation? Be as specific as possible—and as honest. Don't discount your young, adolescent self at that point in time.

If you were consistently bored, the materials and instructional approaches probably weren't connecting with your needs and interests. If you were lost, the materials and instructional approaches weren't connecting with your level of understanding or background knowledge. If you felt as though you were in a perpetual cycle of "been there, done that," you probably were—no diversity or challenge, thus no purpose, no motivation. Into a curriculum, then, teachers put not only concepts, skills, and topics, but also attitudes about what and how students best learn. Failure to connect academic experience with adolescent experience may result in students who disconnect altogether or who do the work, but superficially or resentfully.

 ## DEVELOPING CLASSROOM TEACHING PLANS

Effective teachers plan well, laying out units and daily lessons designed to provide their students with a coherent course of study. Despite this, they face days when the reality of teaching, dealing with students with diverse and complex needs, defies even the best planning. Teaching is more complex, more unpredictable than we like to admit, or as Joseph McDonald, a 17-year teaching veteran, puts it: "Teaching is a messy, uncertain business" (54). McDonald voices what many veteran teachers know: that experience allows them to cope with uncertainty—not eliminate it. He depicts what he calls a "wild triangle of relations—among them teacher, students, and the subject—whose dimensions continually shift," at the core of teaching. Consequently, he believes, teachers rarely have "clean evidence" of what is happening both to themselves and their students. He notes the following:

> Technique, however proved by research and practice, however skillful the application— is always hostage to so much else: the appearance of spring in the air or a bee in the room, the complicated chemistry of a roomful of humans constructing meaning together, the extent to which the conditions of their lives outside the room that day weigh on any of them that day. (54)

Like McDonald, we believe that "beginning teachers are astounded by these complexities and may try to pretend them away" (54). However, there is no magic answer to the complexity, other than to expect it.

Peter Smagorinsky adds to this view: "All too often methods texts suggest that teaching isn't so difficult if only you know the proper techniques" (qtd. in Johannessen and McCann ix). Smagorinsky goes on to note that he is not diminishing the importance of theory or technique, but rather, he is emphasizing judgment: Teachers have to know how and when to use particular techniques and how to deal with the complex daily situations every teacher faces (cited in Johannessen and McCann ix).

No matter how well we plan, we cannot eliminate all the variables in how and when people learn. If we need a rule of thumb for dealing with the inevitable clash between reality and our planning, it would be "go with the reality." Even with 18-year-olds, the sight of a wasp swooping around the lights causes a lesson to cease. But the loss of five minutes is hardly cause for alarm. Neither is a lesson that bombs, for whatever reason. No matter how experienced we become, we will always be confronted with situations that are neither planned nor desired. The saving grace of these situations is experience. The more we have, the more confidence we gain. Consequently, we are far less likely to be totally surprised or devastated by events or people that sweep in and destroy our carefully designed plans.

Variables within Our Grasp

Although good planning is an essential part of success, it is by no means the only part. You can plan well and still have an unsuccessful class. And it isn't necessarily your fault. Many variables interact simultaneously in a classroom, and you cannot always control all of them. Because a class rarely goes awry for a single reason, understanding the major variables affecting the outcome of a class is important—especially when these variables are within our grasp.

Classroom Variables

- *Content.* The subject matter of your lesson or unit. Is it familiar or new material? Does it generally appeal to students, or is it part of the curriculum students typically view as "dumb, too hard, boring"? How much content is being presented at one time? Have students had any choice in the content?
- *Method.* The way content is delivered to students. Via lecture, seatwork, or discussion? In large or small group work? Individuals or pairs? In oral or written activities? Led by teacher or students?
- *Time.* The amount of time estimated for the lesson or unit. Three weeks for a novel? Two days for revision? One week for classroom drama?
- *Situation.* Time of day or year. Does the class meet the first hour on Monday or the last hour on Friday? Is the class split, with lunch falling between two parts? Are special events coming up—athletic tournaments, homecoming week, holiday break, prom day, deer hunting season, school musical?
- *Students.* The class mix. Are there 20, 25, or 30 students? Are they of average grade-level ability? Are any students gifted? Do some students have limited English proficiency? Do students come from varying racial or ethnic backgrounds? Are they all sophomores or college-bound seniors? Do any students have learning disabilities?
- *Teacher.* The background and experience he or she brings to the classroom. What is the level of academic preparation? What experience has he or she had with varying racial or ethnic groups? With special needs students? How many years of teaching experience? In rural, urban, or suburban areas? What is his or her dominant teaching style? What kind of personality does he or she have? What is the confidence level?

EXPLORATION

Playing the Variables Game

To understand how variables interact and affect outcomes, Leila Christenbury, an English language arts methods teacher, suggests playing a card game with them (50–52). We'd like you to try it. But before you do, take a look at what one of our student groups came up with.

Content:	Selected poems of Robert Frost *Huckleberry Finn* *The Tempest* *Rime of the Ancient Mariner* Hawthorne short story
Method:	Read aloud in class Complete a short-answer worksheet Write journal response Read material for homework and have small group discussion Teacher lectures
Time:	One class period One week Eight class periods Three weeks Two class periods
Situation:	Early fall, homecoming week, Friday First period Monday Winter, last class period, Friday Spring musical underway Class period split by lunch break
Students:	Class of 31, high ability seniors. 10 African American, 3 Hispanic Class of 23, reluctant juniors, mostly boys, mixed ability Class of 18, average but 2 with learning disabilities, seniors Class of 25, mixed ability, 1 ESL, sophomores Class of 27, sophomores, 3 gifted
Teacher:	Every card had "you"—in other words, the teacher in each situation was a new teacher with the personal background and traits of the person who had drawn the card.

Drawing one set of cards, Ryan ended up with this scenario:

Very outgoing, fairly confident new teacher with a class of 23 juniors, mostly boys of mixed ability levels, somewhat reluctant learners. The class meets on Friday; it's Homecoming week. The teacher has Rime of the Ancient Mariner *on planner, allowing only that one day— for a lecture.*

Ryan quickly decided that this set of variables was a scenario for disaster. And right he was. It is doubtful his class would pay much attention, let alone come away with any significant learning. What could he do?

With your group, figure out a few alternatives to the variables that Ryan could control, but assume that the *Rime of the Ancient Mariner* is on the required list for his district. He can't just dump it.

Playing the Variables Game

Here are Christenbury's directions:

In small groups, prepare index cards representing each variable listed in the exploration. Each group member writes a card for each of the variables. Then, the cards for each category (e.g., content, method) are shuffled together, making six small decks of cards. Each person then draws a card from each of the six decks, ending up with six cards, each representing a category. At this point, each player silently studies the six cards, perhaps for 5 minutes, and makes a few notes about the mix received, as though this were representative of his or her class. Then, group members present their class mix, noting what the possible results might be: Problems? Adjustments? Scrap the lesson? Each group member leads the discussion for his or her set of cards, but everyone contributes ideas on what works—or not—and why. This is a problem-solving activity.

There's no question that the variables game sometimes results in extreme or bizarre combinations unlikely to occur in a real classroom. Nonetheless, the game forces us to think about options and changes that are within our control. As Christenbury warns: "Deciding that an instructional pattern just 'doesn't work' is rarely the case. You must try to get an eye for the variables; while the class may not have 'worked,' there may be more reasons or different reasons [why it didn't] than what you might automatically assume" (52). This is good advice, especially for new teachers who are only beginning to develop "that eye" and a hefty file of options for both materials and teaching strategies.

Sorting, Organizing, Preparing to Plan

The phrase "preparing to plan" may sound a bit strange. However, for an English language arts teacher it is an essential step: We really do face organizational challenges unknown to colleagues in mathematics or science, for example. We are awash in paper, each sheet representing a potential poem, a strategy for discussion groups, a web site for a novel; we are swimming in lesson plans, units plans, and ideas for chaotic days. For this reason, we urge our methods students to create a filing system immediately: colored folders or plain folders with colored labels, and a number of crates to hold them. An alternative system using three-ring binders with colored dividers and tabs would work well, too. Methods students accumulate material from three major resources: English content classes; English methods classes; education classes. Here, we will concentrate just on methods classes and how a crate and some folders not only save time and frustration, but provide the options, the variables, well within your control.

EXAMPLE:
Choose a color and stick with it.

Yellow folders:	Oral language
Green folders:	Literature/novel, short story, nonfiction
Orange folders:	Literature/poetry
Red folders:	Literature/drama
Blue folders:	Composition

If an article or a piece of literature fits into two categories (e.g., usable as writing prompt and also as discussion prompt), then photocopy it and place it in each appropriate file. When you use it in a specific lesson, make a third copy that stays with material for that lesson. It's worth the dime. You could subdivide your filing system once more, depending upon how you like to organize. Under composition, for example, you could have divisions for writing projects, writing prompts, writing activities, grammar, sentence structure, and so forth. And again, you might have double copies of some. If you develop writing projects for a specific literature unit, you would have a copy in both the composition file and the appropriate literature file.

As you develop units, you will also be developing a new file—perhaps quite thick—with everything specific to and needed for the unit. This file would contain: the state standards it meets, your goals, student outcomes, reading materials, supplementary materials (e.g., films, music, readings), student handouts, models/examples, transparencies, assessment—whatever is needed to teach this unit. Over time, you will add to this file: from your own notes when teaching the unit (e.g., reflections on what worked and what didn't, ideas for "next time"); from reading English journals, professional teacher texts, or teacher's web sites; from conferences, or from talking with teachers informally. This file would be labeled with the specific unit name, which may be a literary title, a thematic one, or topical (e.g., *The Great Gatsby*, the American Dream, families), depending on just where you are in the process and how you have envisioned or fashioned the unit.

EXPLORATION

Finding and Selecting Unit Resources

Finding resources is one of the most challenging, but also the most creative and stimulating things we do as teachers. And as just noted, keeping good files of what we have collected is imperative; otherwise, we must reinvent and search again, wasting time and energy.

Steve Wisner, a student in Literature for Teachers, decided to develop a unit centered on World War I. His final resource list for this twelfth-grade unit included the following:

Novel	*All Quiet on the Western Front* Erich Maria Remarque
	Short Story "Big, Two-Hearted River" Ernest Hemingway
Poetry	"To Lucasta, Going to the Wars" Richard Lovelace
	"Dreamers" Siegfried Sassoon
	"Channel Firing" Thomas Hardy
	"Anthem for Doomed Youth" Wilfred Owen
Video	*Gallipoli*
	All Quiet on the Western Front
	Newsreel footage of trench warfare
Music	"Waltzing Matilda" The Pogues
Visual Texts	World War I propaganda posters
	Map of Europe circa 1914
	References Variety of WWI historical texts for in-class library

a. With your group, figure out what file folders or binder divisions/tabs Steve might have made as he collected and sorted through potential materials for this unit. How many different ways might he have organized his resources? Keep in mind that each of us has preferred ways of organizing materials, but make a case for a way that you believe would benefit future development of his unit.

Two of Steve's goals affected his choices: (1) that students understand the effects of WWI on individuals and Western culture; (2) that students understand how war shaped literature and art, both during the war and after. Similarly, Steve's desired student outcomes were central to choices: that students will understand how historical events and literature are related; that they will understand propaganda; that they will understand the experiences of men at war. In the case of WWI, Steve also wanted his students to see how these experiences in WWI led to the "lost generation" that followed, which was the next unit he was planning. As he sifted through resources, then, Steve knew what he was after: pieces that fit his goals and student outcomes. As he read Wilfred Owen's poetry, for example, he chose only one piece of many; he could have used Rupert Brooke's WWI poetry but didn't. He chose certain propaganda posters for his major unit project, and rejected others that didn't meet his goals and outcomes or that would have required technology too complex for his students. All of these activities were a prelude to laying out his teaching plan, the daily lessons, and thus all a part of what we are calling "preparing to plan."

b. Now, consider what Steve might collect if he were to enlarge his scope, from WWI to a more general "war and peace" topic, but still for twelfth grade students. Keep in mind key concepts around which to select resources: attitudes toward war, reasons for going to war, learning from war, changes in people and society because of war, visions of peace both before and after war. As a group, choose one major goal and one student outcome derived from that goal. Then, search for material that fits them. Divide up the major categories Steve used (e.g., novel, short story) and check out the following resources:

- Senior high school textbooks for pieces that fit the topic. Do not use college-level textbooks, as the reading level and format may be too advanced.
- Educational publishers' catalogues, where topical or thematic texts (paperbacks) are often grouped; some carry video titles as well.
- Video titles from a local store or public library
- Music and art
- Indices from the *English Journal*
- Internet resources for teachers

Keep in mind that you have the American Civil War, WWII, Korea, Vietnam, Persian Gulf, Afghanistan, and Iraq as potential sources of material. Some of these conflicts, of course, offer far more potential than others in both fiction and nonfiction, a diversity of genres, music and art—and high interest.

Standards and Students

Another part of planning involves state standards. Most teachers work from two directions to meet standards in English language arts: the standards guiding the choice of material and activities, or the material and activities, already chosen, meeting various performance standards. Steve worked from the latter plan. He chose his material, worked out the activities and projects, and then noted that his unit worked toward meeting the following Wisconsin Academic Standards.

Students will:

- Use effective reading strategies to achieve their purpose in reading.
- Read, interpret, and critically analyze literature.
- Read and discuss literary and nonliterary texts in order to understand human experience.
- Read to acquire information.
- Create or produce writing to communicate with different audiences for a variety of purposes.
- Plan, revise, edit, and publish clear and effective writing.

- Understand the function of various forms, structures, and punctuation marks of standard American English and use them appropriately in written communication.

Notice that this list of content standards looks very much like teachers' goals for a lesson or unit. From there, Steve would specify student outcomes—what he wanted his students to know or to be able to do better as a result of his unit. For example, under the Wisconsin content standard for the critical analysis of literature is the more specific performance standard: "Investigate and report on ways in which a writer has influenced or been influenced by historical, social, and cultural issues or events" (4). Steve's entire unit speaks to this standard, but within it, he has activities that require his students to show that they understand author Erich Maria Remarque.

Steve was very clear about whom he was teaching:

"I have designed this unit for an enriched twelfth grade class. This is reflected in the volume of reading, variety of texts, and intellectual demands I place on students."

In addressing student diversity specifically, he says:

"Because I have designed this unit for an enriched English class, the needs of severely learning disabled students and the disengaged reluctant reader have not been taken into account. That having been said, the unit does allow for the inclusion of students with a variety of academic strengths and weaknesses. The daily reading requirements are such that most students could finish their reading under one and one-half hours. If a student has a learning disability limited to reading, such as dyslexia, All Quiet on the Western Front *is available as a book on tape, which I would provide. Other reading is done in class and aloud. The variety of assignments in this unit allow for gifted and talented students to remain engaged, plus I would make any adjustment necessary to allow motivated students to participate. Students are at the center of this unit, and in fact, it depends on their diversity to be an effective unit."*

Steve was planning his unit for a specific group of students; consequently, he chose texts and developed assignments with their characteristics in mind. If he were planning for a more typical group of mixed ability students, he would have made very different decisions. Similarly, had he been planning for students with a history of resistance or learning difficulties, he would have geared up to meet their needs and interests. One thing Steve would not have done is consider any group as "dumb" or "unteachable." Instead, he would have marshaled his thoughts and resources around the students, who are the real heart of the curriculum and the focus of planning.

Same Novel, Different Students

While Steve was planning *All Quiet on the Western Front* for a group of enriched twelfth graders, Alison, a student teacher at a large area high school, was actually using this text with a group of mixed ability juniors, early in the fall semester. Here is a sample of Alison's planning calendars, keeping both her and her students on track.

Using a unit calendar, Alison worked out a daily schedule for the students:

All Quiet on the Western Front

16 Computer lab Finish peer biographies	**17** Begin war unit Explore thematic elements of war through poetry **HW:** Come up with 3 things you associate with either WWI or Germany	**18** Journal activity Pre-reading activity on WWI Discuss the historical background of WWI	**19** Introduction to the novel and writer Begin reading Chapt. 1 **HW:** Finish reading Chpt. 1 Note character descriptions	**20** Mini-lesson on characterization Character group activity **HW:** Start reading Chpt. 2
23 Mini-lesson on aphorisms Create own aphorism Explain sticky note discussion **HW:** Finish chpt. 2	**24** Have Chpt. 2 read Quiz on Chpts. 1 & 2 Sticky note discussion on chpt. 2	**25** SILENT READING DAY **HW:** Finish Chpt. 3	**26** Have Chpt. 3 read Receive handout for final project Discuss final project Imagine activity	**27** Watch *All Quite on the Western Front* **HW:** Read Chpt. 4
30 Journal activity Mini-lesson on imagery Group activity on imagery **HW:** Start Chpt. 5	**1** Quiz on Chpts. 3 & 4 Mini-lesson on symbolism Symbolism activity **HW:** Read Chpt. 5	**2** Have Chpt. 5 read Comradeship activity Conference about final project	**3** SILENT READING DAY **HW:** Read Chpt. 6	**4** Have Chpt. 6 read Quiz on Chpts. 5 & 6 Trench warfare activity **HW:** Start reading Chpt. 7
7 Propaganda activity Computer lab **HW:** Have Chpt. 7 read	**8** Finish propaganda activity **HW:** Read Chpt. 8	**9** Quiz on Chpts. 7 & 8 Watch *All Quiet on the Western Front* **HW:** Read Chpt. 9	**10** NWEA	**11** NWEA
14 Mini-lesson on point of view Activity on point of view **HW:** Read Chpt. 9	**15** Have Chpt. 9 read Read "Dulce et Decorum Est" Work on Final Project Conferences	**16** SILENT READING DAY	**17** Have Chpt. 10 read Quiz on Chpts. 9 & 10 Similarities & differences between war discussion	**18** Hero activity Discussion of recurring themes in the novel **HW:** Read Chpt. 11
21 Have Chpt. 11 read Read Chpt. 12 aloud in class Journal activity	**22** Finish watching *All Quiet on the Western Front*	**23** Presentations of final project	**24** Review for the unit exam	**25** Unit exam

Notice how Alison varies the instructional methods: mini-lessons to introduce or strengthen literary elements, small-group activities and discussion, large-group discussion, independent reading days, film, and lecture on needed background (e.g., WWI, trench warfare). She also plans diverse measurements: quiz, exam, project. Additionally, Alison had to plan around a major break, the Northwest Education Association's annual conference, a time when students will be anticipating the break and perhaps be a bit sluggish following it. The large calendar was not cast in stone, as she did add activities and homework, and she did make some changes in sequence as she went through the unit.

Here is her detailed plan for the week of September 30–October 4.

September 30–October 4

Monday, September 30	Mini-lesson on imagery Group activity with sensory images from *AQWF* Discussion of Chpt. 4 HW: Find an illustration (an article, picture, news clipping) of war or violence that shows how prominent these images are in society.
Tuesday, October 1	Share images of violence and war. Journal activity Discussion of life on the home front during WWI Quiz on Chpts. 3 & 4 HW: Read Chpt. 5 and do sticky note worksheet
Wednesday, October 2	Mini-lesson on theme and comradeship in *AQWF*. Sticky note discussion
Thursday, October 3	SILENT READING DAY HW: Read Chpt. 6
Friday, October 4	Mini-lesson on symbolism Group Activity with symbolism Quiz on Chpts. 5 & 6

Now look at her daily lesson plan for one day, September 30.

∽   LESSON PLAN ON IMAGERY IN *ALL QUIET ON THE WESTERN FRONT*

Student Outcomes:
- Students will understand the effect of sensory images in *AQWF*.
- Students will work effectively in small group.
- Students will explain, and justify their response through reference to the text, what they believe is the most horrifying part of Chapter 4.

Wisconsin Academic Standards:
- Use effective reading strategies to achieve their purposes in reading.
- Read, interpret, and critically analyze literature.
- Read and discuss literary and nonliterary texts in order to understand human experience; listen to, discuss, and comprehend oral communication.

Materials:
All Quiet on the Western Front
Transparency with imagery examples

Procedure:
Conduct a mini-lesson on imagery (examples from *AQWF*)
Explain small-group activity (on handout): to find examples of sensory imagery in Chapter 4.
Small groups share one example of found imagery.
Large-group discussion of horrific aspects of Chapter 4.

Journal write: Paul seems so hardened by the war. Do you think we are hardened by images of war and violence?

Homework: Find an illustration (article, photo, newspaper clipping, magazine) of war or violence that shows how prominent these images are in our society today. Be prepared to present your illustration to your classmates.

Evaluation: Informal "look" at small-group discussion and oral presentation of image.

Although Alison had originally planned to work with symbolism on the following day, she switched that lesson to a later date. Why? Because she realized that her homework assignment required more time for student presentation and discussion—not a repeat day of mini-lesson followed by group work. She also made a decision to work with theme before working with symbolism, which is the more abstract concept. There isn't always congruence among the planners for the entire unit, the week, or the day. Teachers have to be flexible, taking enough time when and where students need it, and making changes to accommodate their diversity. Although "conferences about final project" is on the unit planner, it is not on the weekly one. Alison's homework assignment for that day is very specific, however:

> Write a paragraph in which you tell me the option you have chosen for your final project; discuss what you have already done and what you intend to do. You will turn in the paragraph tomorrow during silent reading time. At that time, I will meet with you to discuss your project.

With only 20 students in her class, Alison could talk with each during the class period. If she'd had a larger class, she would have had to plan differently.

Alison's students had received a handout outlining their final project options about one week into the unit. A week later, she asks them for a commitment to one and tells them the due date, at the completion of the unit, three weeks away. In her planning for the unit, Alison had decided on the options well in advance of students receiving them.

All Quiet on the Western Front

FINAL PROJECT

For your final project, choose one of the options listed below. Your written project is due October 23, and you will present a brief (1–2 minutes) summary of your work at that time. The project is worth 50 points.

1. *Conduct an interview with someone who has either been directly involved in a war or who has had his or her life affected by a war. The interview should be written in script or dialogue form without the use of quotation marks.*

   For example: Jon: What do you remember most vividly about being in Vietnam? Mr. Smith: Seeing men die right in front of me. Feeling helpless.

   The interview should include an introduction: Whom you interviewed, the relationship, if any, to you, the war that he or she was involved in. Include a very brief background on the war itself. And finally, reflect on what you learned through this interview.

2. *Take a character from AQWF and place him in the current conflict in Afghanistan or Iraq. What might this character witness? Would he encounter the same situations? Feel the same emotions as Paul, for example, 70 years ago on the Western Front? Be sure to address some of the themes we have discussed in class. Do the same themes apply to a war that is taking place nearly a century later? This is a creative writing task.*

3. *Make a collection of war poetry or songs. Separate the poems or songs by the wars (e.g., WWI, WWII, Vietnam) with which they are associated. At the end of your collection, provide a reflection on the various themes*

found in the poems or lyrics—and how these relate to themes found in AQWF. What affected you the most as you worked with these poems or lyrics? Why?

4. *Write an editorial that either supports or opposes the war effort in AQWF. To support your opinion, this editorial must include textual evidence from AQWF and/or other literature that we have read.*

5. *Devise your own oral or written project for AQWF. Sketch out what you wish to do, and we will discuss it.*

In addition to planning the final project, Alison had to plan smaller tasks. Journal writes, for example.

What If . . .

What if war had been declared, and while thousands of men and women are defending America, on ships, on bases abroad, in a war zone, you remain at home, on the Home Front. Would you feel as though you are contributing to the war effort? How? Would you feel as though we need to sacrifice some individual rights for the good of the country as a whole? Do you think you could be upbeat when writing to someone close to you, now far away and in harm's way?

Choose one of the journal prompts and reflect on your situation.

In order to lessen America's dependence on foreign oil, the government decides to ration the amount of gasoline each person may use in a week.

In order to provide better security for all traveling Americans, the government decides to issue I.D. cards to be used on planes, trains, or buses. Without a government-issued card, people will be restricted in interstate travel.

Someone in your family or close to you is on the front line. What would you write to this person about life at home? Would you note what has changed since—or because of—the war? Why or why not? Would you write of feelings of loss or feelings of pride? Why?

Exploration

Review Alison's project options. Even if you have not read this novel, you should be able to judge whether or not the list meets basic unit criteria: provides for diversity of ability and interests; appropriate for age level; appropriate for application of knowledge. Then, review the sample of journal writes. In your opinion, is her basic premise, in the introduction to the prompts, a good one? What might you change and why? Or do you believe that Alison got it right: that she chose questions that will resonate with teens who have been through 9/11 and continued terrorism threats at home? Explain.

Reading through these portions of Alison's unit, you should have gleaned some ideas about planning a unit. Before we go into principles of good planning, we would like you to spend a little more time with Steve's unit on *All Quiet on the Western Front* starting with his rationale for creating this particular unit. In Alison's case, remember, she was required to use *All Quiet on the Western Front* in English 11. Steve, by contrast, chose to use it. Here, in his own words, is why.

THOUGHTS ON CREATING THIS UNIT

The idea to do a unit on WWI literature came to me as I was trying to remember my favorite books as a high school student. The list contained the usual suspects: Catcher in the Rye, Lord of the Flies, *and* Huck Finn. *But when I searched for the book that stood out as the one that affected me the most, it was* All Quiet on the Western Front. *This book does more work than almost any text I have read. It is a lesson in history and culture. It is a compelling story of a young man's fight to retain his humanity, despite the horrors around him. It is a harrowing portrait of the brutality of trench warfare. And, perhaps most important, it is so beautifully written. Why, I then wondered, did I never read this novel in school.*

So that was the genesis of this unit. As I began looking at other WWI literature, I found thematic similarities in almost every text. As a body of literature, there is an overwhelming current of hopelessness and despair running throughout. I then realized that Western culture has never inflicted so ghastly a wound on itself as it did between 1914 and 1918. The effects of that war have never really left the culture. This is why I designed this unit to show how terrible the war was for those involved in it.

Steve's rationale should be linked to his goals as a teacher. And three of his goals *are* directly tied to his rationale. As a result of this unit, he wants his students to: understand the effect of WWI on individuals and Western culture; understand how WWI shaped literature and art during the war and after; identify themes in literature and make thematic connections among a variety of texts. With his goals in mind, Steve moved to the next part of his planning:

I read as much WWI literature as I could in an attempt to choose pieces that illuminated ideas in my primary texts (AQWF and Gallipoli); I have chosen texts in a variety of forms, including visual art and music. I have tried to make each day's activity meet at least one, and often several, state standards, and I have made every effort to make the usefulness of activities readily apparent to students. Finally, I made a conscious effort not to branch out, to deal with life on the home front, minority soldiers, or any of the other hundreds of possible tangents relating to the war. I wanted a narrow focus, with AQWF firmly in the center. I have heard WWI described as 'Europe's suicide attempt,' and I designed this unit to reflect that.

Although this may sound a bit grim, Steve was preparing the unit for advanced seniors who had studied world history and who had lived through 9/11—and thus understood something of what man can to do man.

Like Alison, Steve laid out an abbreviated set of lesson plans for himself. This is far more difficult than it sounds. First, as noted in his rationale, he had to read an enormous amount of fiction and nonfiction, pore over lists of videos—and view some—and find music with lyrics appropriate to his unit's goals. Next, he had to select those pieces that fit his unit's goals. Then he had to determine the sequence and the pacing. Although the central novel provides a sequence, the pacing—the amount of reading or activities per day—is a difficult decision. Similarly, he had to match the poetry, for example, to the novel—ensuring that the themes were reinforced. But did he want students to read a piece of poetry and then read the novel—or vice versa? More decisions involved the methods of instruction, activities, student tasks, and evaluation. Steve knew that once teaching this unit, he might have to make some changes (as we saw with Alison's unit in progress); nonetheless, his first responsibility lay in planning well, start to finish, before he ever handed out texts and assignments.

Let's look at a few days of Steve's two week unit, first in his abbreviated sequence notes, very similar to what teachers put in their "on my desk" planners, and then in the more detailed daily lesson plan for the same day.

LESSON PLAN ON WWI LITERATURE

Day 1   Desktop Planner

In-Class Reading: "To Lucasta, Going to the Wars"

Directed Journal Entry: Compare/contrast text of poem to personal knowledge of warfare

Video Newsreel: Clips of trench warfare

Lecture: Short history of WWI, focus on effect of this "scientific" warfare on individual soldier and idea that war could be glorious

Day 1

Student Outcomes

- Think, write, speak of cultural and personal beliefs about warfare and the individual's role in warfare
- Have a basic understanding of the history of WWI, sufficient to understand novel

Advance Preparation

- Copies of "To Lucasta, Going to the Wars"
- Newsreel clips of trench warfare and cue
- VCR and monitor
- Map of Europe circa 1914
- Notes for history lecture
- Create class library of WWI reference materials and other WWI fiction

Development
- Read aloud "To Lucasta, Going to the Wars" by Richard Lovelace
- Journal write: Make connections to the poem and what it says about the role of the individual and warfare (e.g., Do citizens have a duty to fight if asked? Can warfare be an adventure? Is war a place to prove you are courageous?)
- Short discussion on journal write. Explain that views of Lovelace were fairly universal until 1914; some continue today
- Show newsreel clips of trench warfare
- Short lecture on history of WWI, emphasis on how this war differed (e.g., trench warfare, machine guns, flame throwers, gas, barbed wire); effect of this "scientific" warfare on the individual soldier and Western culture
- Discussion/Questions

Closure
- Explain why we are going to read *AQWF*, difficult but important subject matter. Reading will begin tomorrow

⌛ *Reflection* ⌛

Although Steve's unit overall is thoroughly grounded in small group and collaborative tasks, he chose to lecture on the first day. What was his rationale for doing so? Why do you think he held off passing out the novel or assigning reading for the next day?

_____

Day 6   Desktop Planner

Discussion/Response: Student questions on pp. 137–185 of *AQWF*

Art Work: Examples of wartime propaganda posters

Collaborative Art/Writing Assignment: Use Photoshop software, scanners, and color printer; design "reality posters" by scanning and altering propaganda posters viewed in class

Work Due: Poetry assignment from Day 4

Day 6

Student Outcomes
- Relate their reading of Chapters 1–7 of *AQWF* to actual historical events
- Understand propaganda as tool for changing or reinforcing public perception
- Understand ways in which truth is manipulated in propaganda materials

- Use techniques of mimetic criticism to evaluate and offer new readings of propaganda
- Use computers, scanners, and Photoshop software to alter and create visual images

Advance Preparation
- Varied examples of WWI propaganda posters (book size for scanning)
- Arrange use of two computers, scanners, and a color printer in classroom
- Arrange for computer assistance (school staff and student "experts")
- Ensure Photoshop software has been installed on computers
- Ensure scanners and printer are online and functioning

Development
- Student questions and comments on pages 137–185 of *AQWF*. Brief discussion.
- Break class into five groups and distribute copies of propaganda posters
- Hand out "Reality Poster" assignment
- Student work time (analysis of posters, choice of poster, writing time)
- Assign rotation order for use of computers
- Groups not on computers continue with analysis, writing

Closure
- Remind students to save all unfinished computer work to disks
- Remind that there will be ample class time over the next two days for each group to complete assignment and do quality work
- Assign pages 187–231 of *AQWF*

Before we ask you to reflect on Steve's choices and order, you need to read the Reality Poster assignment that his students would receive.

WWI Literature: Reality Posters

Propaganda posters were an interesting element of WWI. The governments of the countries involved seemed to sense that people need to be convinced that the war was necessary. All of the major countries involved in the war produced propaganda posters; however, none of the countries felt that an accurate description of their foe or conditions at the "front" would be very compelling. As such, they need to turn the enemy into an abstraction and their own soldiers into heroic, willing combatants. Each side, through propaganda, made the other out to be monsters.

Your assignment is to use these posters to set the record straight. Using a computer scanner and Photoshop software, your group will scan a chosen poster and alter the text to reflect reality instead of propaganda.

Look through the examples of propaganda posters and choose one that you would like to alter. Your alteration will be limited to changing the text. This process will work best if you choose a poster that has its text written on a single background color rather than on an image. The reason for this is simple: You will destroy some of the background when you remove the text, and it is easier to repair the damage to a single color background than to a complex image.

Instructions for scanning, removing existing text, repairing the background, and inserting your "corrected" texts are printed on each computer. Computer experts are on hand to help, and do not hesitate to ask for help. Once you have competed your changes, print your "Reality Poster" on the color printer. When the entire class has finished, we will discuss the posters and your reasons for the changes you made. Good luck! Dazzle me!!

Your group will be evaluated on the following criteria:

_____   *1–10 Alteration based on reality as found in required reading and viewing*

_____   *1–10 Original and thought-provoking*

_____   *1–5   Group followed instructions and used technology effectively*

Total points possible = 25

ᦙᧉ *Reflection* ᦙᧉ

Steve's student outcomes center on an understanding of propaganda. Although he has limited the focus to only one type of war propaganda, has he provided students with enough background on elements of propaganda? Or, is he relying on their reading skills and experience in WWI literature, and past class discussions of war as reality, to carry them through the poster assignment? What's your view on his plan and assignment? Why do you think Steve planned to control both the group membership and rotation order for computer use?

Planning Well: Principles and Practice

As you saw with Steve's unit, he was very clear about his reasons for "why this unit, why this literature." Rationale is a starting point for planning, whether it be a single day's lesson or a three week unit. Then, you move to specific questions that will guide you in hands-on planning.

- What do I want my students to learn?
- What resources do I have? What will I need?
- What will I need to modify instruction for special needs students (e.g., learning disabled, gifted, second language learners)?
- How will I get from "wanting them to learn" to "learning it"?
- About how much time will I need to accomplish this?
- What skills or knowledge do my students already have? What will they need?
- How will I know if my students have met the outcomes I set for them?

Experienced teachers will tell you that planning a lesson or a unit is an immense amount of work, yet it is also among the most enjoyable tasks that teachers do. You bring your special "stamp" to this process—a highly creative process. Underneath this process, however, regardless of content, lie specific principles of planning.

As you plan, you should choose texts, activities, and materials that:

- build on students' life experiences and interests
- build on students' prior knowledge
- engage students in meaningful talk and tasks
- engage students in critical thinking and problem-solving
- provide for decision-making, both individually and with others

As you plan, you should develop activities and assignments that:

- use a variety of texts and materials
- include a variety of instructional strategies
- include as many of the language arts as feasible
- possess an appropriate, logical sequence
- have a clear structure, linked to goals and outcomes
- are open to modification, based on student needs
- lead to fair and appropriate assessment

Because sequence is essential and often challenging for novice teachers, let's look at what Susan J. Tchudi and Stephen N. Tchudi suggest. They first state that "this [preparation] is the hard part—and the fun part" (32). They then make an important point:

> Every teacher has his or her own way of preparing for a course or unit. Some like to have a day-to-day plan that they know they will have to adjust as they go along. Some

like to have more structured activities at the beginning of the unit and leave more time at the end for student projects and student-initiated work. Some like to build in time throughout the unit for issues and questions that come up during reading, writing, and discussion. (32–33)

Nonetheless, Tchudi and Tchudi note that their general practice involves starting with a fairly specific set of plans and activities and then opening things up later, as they see how students respond, what students may need, or what students are interested in. Here is what Tchudi and Tchudi suggest for movement within the unit:

- from whole-class to individualized activities
- from teacher-initiated to student-developed projects
- from core or common to individualized readings
- from basic or introductory tasks to more difficult ones
- from where we perceive the students to be, to where we think they can or probably should go
- from where the students see themselves to where they want to be (33)

The last two points are arguably the most difficult, especially for novice teachers. We sometimes hear our methods students both worry and complain that they don't have any students yet; therefore, how can they develop appropriate lessons or units in methods classes? We agree that it is more difficult without knowledge of the students, but nonetheless, new teachers have to start somewhere; moreover, there will always be those first classes, students whom they will not know in September. Knowing principles of curriculum and instruction, therefore, is foundation knowledge—one that will be used without specific knowledge of students at first, but one that will also be used with students who are well known.

Choosing resources, activities, and tasks are the first part of the planning process. Deciding where and how to use them, as well as what you need to teach, is the second part: thinking about implementation.

As the teacher, you must:

- know where you need to model learning strategies, to introduce or review
- know where you need concrete examples, on paper or transparency
- allow enough time for processing, for absorption of new material or tasks
- allow enough time for in-class work (e.g., writing)
- allow enough time for group work and instruct students in group behavior
- set aside time to talk with students about your rationale, goals, and outcomes
- set aside time to ask the students what they need to accomplish them

Reflection

Search your memory for a specific class that either adhered to or violated any of these principles of planning. What stands out? Why?

Good Advice for Implementation

Diana Mitchell and Leila Christenbury believe that "despite the varied circumstances of your students, classes, and needs, whatever you implement in your classroom needs to have the three characteristics of *simplicity, relevance,* and *workability*" *(Both Art and Craft)*. Let's explore what they mean by those terms.

First, simplicity: keeping a single, major focus. Mitchell and Christenbury point out that "teaching ideas that rely on multiple, complex components—most of which necessarily would be interconnected—can fall apart due to their own elaborate nature. Both teachers and students can become hopelessly confused if a teaching activity has too many parts, too many concepts, too many grading rubrics, too many components" (5–6).

Second, relevance: the idea that the student activity is directly tied to text or concept, that it's part of the instructional point you are making. Third, workability: this means that the activity has a real chance of being successful in your school, with your students. School circumstances may involve things like computer access, a good media staff, or access to a good public or university library for resources. Student workability lies in their skills: what they bring to the task and what they will need to be successful (6–7).

EXPLORATION

Evaluating Steve's Unit

Although you have not seen Steve's entire unit, you have enough material to evaluate if or how he meets these three characteristics. Check first for simplicity: Does Steve have a single focus, a major thrust for this unit and for each lesson that you have read? Does anything seem overly complicated? Then, does his Reality Poster activity have relevance? Is it tied to the literature the students are reading and to a concept that he wants them to grasp? Finally, is his Reality Poster activity workable? Is he knowledgeable about the technology (hardware and software) needed? Does he need access to the school's computer lab, or has he thought through how to ensure that his students have the access they need at the point they need it? Has he overestimated the students' computer literacy skills? Or has he made plans to ensure that all students can do the assignment? Is his plan for group work also part of "workability"?

Gifted but Resistant

Steve was planning for high ability seniors, a class where students were already self-selected or grouped. However, we want to point out what Larry R. Johannessen and Thomas M. McCann call the "myth of honors"—the notion that teaching these students is easy, that all the kids are smart and sophisticated, with few behavior problems. In a hypothetical but realistic teaching scenario, Johannessen and McCann note that efforts to produce critical thinking or problem-solving may end with disappointing re-sults. These high ability students may read, take notes, do the work assigned, but not think critically. Their response to questions may be short and literal, or not answer the question at all. Further, they may not work as well as expected in groups; in fact, they may appear to be just like "regular" kids—talking about the weekend or letting one student do all the work. They may also challenge your tests or grading and call you "unfair" (81–84). We don't tell you this to discourage you—only to emphasize that even students grouped as "gifted" are subject to loafing, disinterest, or defiance.

EXPLORATION

Smart But Resistant: Rethinking Steve's Unit

Based on what you have seen of Steve's planning, what do you believe reinforces or in some way underscores this class's talent? What do you think Steve might do with his plans and materials if confronted with the bright but non-thinking students described by Johannessen and McCann? Be Specific.

There has been a great deal of attention and print devoted to "special needs" students, and with good reason. Whether they are "special" in terms of ability (learning disabled or gifted) or language (limited English proficiency), the odds of them dropping out of school is high. The odds of them tuning out is even higher. Most people don't think of gifted and talented students as "special needs," but they are, and the astounding rate of one in five are dropouts. Sometimes teachers make the fatal error of acting as though gifted students will do fine on their own, that they don't need any attention or adjustments in curriculum or instruction. Gifted students may be quirky or chal-lenging, not the picture of the bright, highly motivated and self-initiating learner a teacher expects when assigned an enriched class. Sometimes, they decide to fail, as a measure of control over their lives or because they are afraid to compete at a higher level. Sometimes they hold back for fear of being called names or isolated by those less capable, especially within their immediate peer group or friends. Whatever the case, we owe them attention. Not by singling them out as "brainy" or turning them into class tutors, but by providing them with interesting, challenging texts and materials and with provocative assignments, rather than just more work, more of what everyone else is doing.

Resistant, Reluctant, but Not Unteachable

Rena B. Lewis and Donald H. Doorlag remind us that students with behavior disor-ders are a heterogeneous group; they exhibit a wide range of classroom behaviors, from disobedient and aggressive to very shy (66). We also have to remember that many of these kids have low self-esteem, patterns of negative treatment and response, and little confidence that they can be successful academically—despite the fact that many of them are very bright. Figuring out the best way to manage a class with some resistant or reluctant learners will take time, patience, and experimentation with materials and methods. It will take good, thoughtful planning and flexibility in implementation. When we consider classroom environment, materials, and instructional methods for these students, we strongly advocate for a community of learners, which incidentally is the core of any classroom, but here is essential. As you plan, keep the following practical suggestions in mind:

- Establish a classroom community, beginning with the first class. Don't worry about how much time it takes or that you aren't on page 36 at the end of the week.
- Survey student interests immediately. Act on that knowledge as you select texts and materials.
- Use young adult literature that speaks to adolescent experience; let students choose texts that interest them; structure diverse ways of response.
- Find out areas of student expertise. Build your activities to use them.
- Plan many large-group activities, chosen to build relationships and class cohesion.
- Read to the class, choosing material that offers discussion on important ideas or feelings.
- Do as much in-class work as possible, modeling strategies and expected level of response; provide samples of student work.
- Let students choose from a variety of activities within a skill area.
- Model processes that students will need to succeed in an activity or task.
- Vary activities, sometimes within a single class period.
- Plan for pairs and small-group work.
- Plan for clear, immediate feedback.

Special Needs Students: A Different View

Another group that raises curricular questions is students with special needs. Lewis and Doorlag state: "It is likely that at least 75% of the special education population has mild learning needs that can be met, at least in part, in the regular classroom" (66). However, they explain the perplexing situation facing the mainstream teacher:

> Teachers often use the word *puzzling* to describe students with learning disabilities. These students are average, even bright, learners who encounter difficulties in specific school subjects. Because they seem capable and learn some things quickly and easily, their failure to learn in other areas is perplexing. Students with learning disabilities have adequate intelligence. Their learning problem is not due to hearing or vision impairment, physical or health disorders, or emotional disturbance. The reason for poor school performance is much more subtle and elusive: they have difficulty processing information. (66)

To many mainstream teachers, this is a startling revelation. And one to consider care-fully in planning. There are, of course, other realities under the general heading of "learning disabilities," among them issues of attention deficit disorder, hyperactivity, and emotional distress—challenging for teachers, frustrating for students. Keep in mind that special needs students may have a long history of being told to sit still, stay in their seats, don't talk, and finish a worksheet. They may have been isolated from classmates, if not physically, then emotionally. Further, because these students often share two cur-ricular worlds, special education and mainstream English language arts, the curricular models may be very different. Consequently, you need to know the curriculum and the instructional methods of special education teachers in your school. You need to work with these teachers in whatever manner possible, consistently and positively.

In your classroom, development of a community of learners is the first priority for special needs students; simply stated, they need to feel like part of the group, to *be* part of one group. Specific instructional procedures to assist special needs students are not significantly different from those effective for all students:

- Use a weekly assignment sheet on which students can check off work.
- Give special needs students the same assignment as "regular" students, but quietly and privately accommodate their special needs with smaller chunks of work at one time and more time to complete the work.
- Break information into sequential parts and review frequently.
- Design handouts with simple, clear discourse and use graphics when feasible.
- Use concrete examples and explicit models.
- Use an overhead projector to illustrate or explicate more complex tasks or knowledge.
- Provide a series of tasks at different levels, letting students start at their own pace before setting a time limit for completion.
- Involve students in some planning.
- Use pairs and small groups.
  (Adapted from Mercer and Mercer 38; 42; 83–85; 163; 199–200)

In addition to planning for curriculum and instruction, teachers with special needs stu-dents need to know how to use praise appropriately, reward improvement, and pro-vide sustained feedback. Adolescents know when they have problems, so it is not surprising that those with learning problems may become aggressive, frustrated, or withdrawn. At the same time, they know when adults are patronizing or insincere. Thus, teachers need to find the right supportive balance. When a special needs student requires a different or modified assignment, he or she should receive it privately. Grouping students with similar needs together and working with different groups is one means of handling the situation. And, suggest Lewis and Doorlag, if the rest of the class asks what's going on, be matter of fact and tell them that everyone may get more, fewer, or different materials throughout the year (83).

We wish to emphasize that the term *special needs* covers a diverse group: from stu-dents with learning disabilities to those with emotional or physical disabilities, from students who are learning English as a second language to those who are talented or gifted in their native language. However, as we have already pointed out, the curricular and instructional strategies appropriate for special needs students are those also appropriate for all students. Of course, you will do some tweaking, but the basic foundation of an authentic community of learners doing meaningful things holds for all kids. This basic foundation also includes high, though reasonable, standards that may be met through alternative ways. Students with learning disabilities fear appearing stupid; thus, what they need to know and experience are different ways of being smart. Could there be a better class than English language arts to do just that? We don't think so.

INSTRUCTIONAL UNIT

In this chapter, you have analyzed parts of Steve Wisner's unit, examining what he planned and why he made certain choices. Now, we'd like you to explore a complete unit, developed by Sarah Nyberg for one of her English methods courses. Keep in mind that Sarah's unit was originally written with a narrative that provided a great deal of information about her materials and methods. To provide you with this evaluative opportunity, we have removed her commentary. We have also made some changes to her unit, again to provide you with more analysis and decision-making about planning a unit.

First, read through the unit to gain an overview of its content. Next, read the questions and directives at the end of the unit, carefully noting what you will need to accomplish in your next reading of the unit. After you complete your individual analysis, share your views in small group. Try to reach a consensus on what you believe would strengthen the Ben Franklin unit (e.g., additions, deletions, changes in sequence). Prepare to present your ideas, along with your rationale, to your classmates.

IN CONSTANT SEARCH OF PERFECTION: BENJAMIN FRANKLIN
Teacher Materials and Resources

Eight web sites on Franklin, Teaching Ideas
Franklin, Benjamin. *Autobiography*
Franklin, Benjamin. *Poor Richard's Almanac*
Fritz, Jean. *What's the Big Idea, Ben Franklin?*
Lawson, Robert. *Ben and Me.*
Randolph, Ryan P. *Benjamin Franklin: Inventor, Writer, and Patriot*

Day 1
Student Outcomes

- Students will understand Ben Franklin's virtues (concepts and vocabulary) and "translate" them into 21st century terms.
- Students will define traits of a "perfect" person and a "good" life in today's society.

Materials

Journals
Ben Franklin packet: Timeline and virtues segment from *Autobiography*
Virtues log

Procedure

Student Activity. Journal write: Think of someone whom you believe leads a good life. What makes his or her life "good"? Are there certain ways a person can act, or should act, in order to have a good life? What are they?

Teacher Activity. Introduction to Ben Franklin, link to American history class. Large-group question and answer to discover background knowledge on Franklin and his era in American history. Introduction to week's unit. Read excerpt (virtues) from Franklin's *Autobiography;* students follow on their copies.

Whole-Class Discussion. Do Franklin's virtues (i.e., temperance, silence, order, resolution, frugality, industry, sincerity, justice, moderation, humility, cleanliness, tranquillity, chastity, and humility) seem relevant today? Do you think his pursuit of perfection was realistic? Do you know of areas of life or professions where people do just that, seek perfection? How do we, in general, respond to people we perceive as "perfectionists"? Does our culture reward certain kinds of perfectionists and not others? As teenagers, what's your view of perfectionists? Is Franklin using this term as we would understand it or use it in the 21st century?

Student Activity. In self-selected groups of five, develop a list of Franklin's virtues that you believe are ignored today. Next to each virtue, make a note of why you believe it to be generally ignored. Choose a recorder/spokesperson to report your ideas to the class.

Whole-Class Discussion. Students share their ideas on Franklin's virtues. Discussion is led by each group's spokesperson.

Student Activity. In their groups, students develop a list of five virtues for the 21st century (i.e., qualities or traits needed to be a "good" or "perfect" person). Each virtue must have a title, along with a definition or description/example. The group will choose a new recorder and spokesperson for this activity.

Whole-Class Activity. As students report their list of virtues, teacher will write the list on the board or a transparency, erase doubles, and ask for clarification as needed. From this list of virtues, students will choose a common list of virtues for their personal virtues log.

Teacher Activity. Assign and explain the virtues log, which will be kept for a full week. Students will enter a brief explanation next to each virtue *not* obeyed that day.

Example:

MY VIRTUES LOG			
	Moderation	Resolution	Industry
Monday	ate bag of Oreos		blew off math assignment
Tuesday	bought new jeans at full price		

Assessment

Journal entry

Creation of group virtues list with definitions

Day 2

Student Outcomes

- Students will view Ben Franklin as an inventor, not just as an author or politician.
- Through effective use of the Internet, students will successfully research American inventors/inventions.

Materials

Journals

What's the Big Idea, Ben Franklin?

Handout with relevant web sites and nonfiction titles

Handout "American Inventions"

Note cards

Media center reservation

Procedure

Student Activity. Journal write: What, in your opinion, is the best or worst invention we have today? Why?

Teacher Activity. Read pages 17–28 from *What's the Big Idea, Ben Franklin?* Go over assignment, explain expectations, clarify as needed.

AMERICAN INVENTIONS: MORE THAN WE EVER KNEW

Ben Franklin was always seeking out new and better ways of doing things. Because of his constant search for perfection, he was responsible for many inventions that we benefit from today (e.g., bifocals, swimming flippers, lightning rod, odometer, wood stove). We have many American inventions that we use unthinkingly every day, and your task is to become an expert on one such invention. You will present your knowledge of this invention to the class. Your research notes should provide the following information: Name of inventor and invention; date and place of invention; circumstance of invention (experimentation, accident); reason for invention; invention's impact on our lives. Web sites and texts to help you identify, choose, and gather information on an invention are provided on the attached sheet.

Use note cards to record information. You will present your information from a single note card; plan on 3–4 minutes for your "report."
(Adapted from "History Dig: American Inventions")

Student Activity. Research in media center

Assessment

Journal
Use of time in media center

Day 3

Student Outcomes

- Through jig-sawing [instructional strategy where students contribute individual research/information to form a whole picture, like working a jigsaw puzzle], students will gain overview of plethora of American inventions.
- Students will enhance listening skills (attentive, eye contact with speaker).
- Students will enhance presenting skills (volume, pace, eye contact, gestures).

Procedure

Student Activity. Journal write: If I could invent anything, it would be _____ . I would invent this because _____ .

Student Activity. Present research on invention to class. Some students will present on the following day.

Student Activity. In groups of five, brainstorm ideas for "In Ben's Footsteps . . ." assignment.

In Ben's Footsteps . . .

Many of Franklin's inventions arose from his ability to recognize a need or problem in daily living. He then problem-solved and came up with a solution. Sometimes, he based his solution or invention on the work or ideas of other people; other times, he came up with an original idea or invention.

Either way, people benefited from his desire to help others and improve life in the 18th century.

Your task is to identify a problem or something needed in our school or community, and then come up with a solution that would benefit the general good. You need to include the following in your written, informal report: A statement of the problem or need; the people who would most benefit from a solution; a description of the solution—which may be an invention or a policy.

Your text should be no less than one page and no more than three pages. Feel free to draw or use print images to support your solution; you may use such images as part of the text or as an appendix to it. Be sure to document any print or media resources used in your report.

Your report must be ready for peer review in one week. The final draft is due two days following peer review. You will have class time to work together, but you must also plan for work outside of class.
(Adapted from Twin Cities Public Television)

Assessment

Journal entry
Presentations

Day 4

Student Outcomes

- Students will enhance listening skills.
- Students will enhance speaking skills.
- Students will work effectively in small groups.

Procedure

Student Activity. Complete invention presentations.

Student Activity. Continue group work on solution/invention.

Teacher Activity. Circulate, assist groups as needed.

Assessment

Presentations
Group work

Day 5

Student Outcomes

- Students will understand the role or purpose of proverbs.
- Students will increase their understanding of Franklin as a "picture of perfection."
- Students will relate *Poor Richard's Almanac* to their own lives.

Materials

Journals
Overhead of proverbs from *Poor Richard's Almanac*
Handout of proverbs from *Almanac*

Procedure

Student Activity. Journal write: Make a list of proverbs that you have heard as you were growing up. For example: "A penny saved is a penny earned." "Good fences make good neighbors." "The early bird gets the worm."

Whole-Class Activity. Share list of proverbs generated in journal write. What is the point—or benefit of—such sayings? Do they have a purpose? Are proverbs culturally based? Are they limited by historical period of origin?

Teacher Activity. Introduce *Poor Richard's Almanac.*

Relation of proverbs to Franklin's list of virtues. Explore meaning, tone, and rules that appear to govern the form of a proverb.

Student Activity. Students break into self-selected pairs to translate some of Franklin's 18th century proverbs into proverbs for 21st century teens. Teacher then puts two pairs together, who discuss their translations. As a group of four, students choose one of their modern proverbs to share with the class. The person with the birthday closest to today's date is the recorder. Proverb translations will be handed in.

Whole-Class Activity. Following discussion, students will vote on the proverb most appropriate and/or needed by their teenage peers.

Assessment

Proverb assignment

Day 6

Student Outcomes

- Students will work effectively in small groups.
- Students will show progress on their "In Ben's Footsteps" task.

Procedure

Student Activity. Groups work on their solution/invention task.

Teacher Activity. Circulate, assist students as needed, evaluate progress.

Assessment

Group progress

Day 7

Materials

Virtues log

Procedure

Student Activity. Journal write: After keeping my virtues log for a week, I have discovered _____ (e.g., Which, for you, are most commonly ignored—and why?). Are there different virtues for different age groups? For different cultures? Why or why not?

Whole-Class Activity. Discuss journal write, reflections on keeping virtues log, comparisons of virtues then and now.

Assessment

Virtues log

Day 8

Student Outcomes

- Students will produce a rough draft of their "In Ben's Footsteps . . ." report.
- Students will work effectively in their groups.

Materials

Model of report draft.

Procedure

Teacher Activity. Show students a model draft. Discuss acceptable formats for this informal report. Remind students of purpose and audience. With students, develop evaluation criteria for final product.

Student Activity. Work on draft: completeness of information, organization of information, background and interest of audience. Draft for peer review must be ready in two days.

Day 9

Student Outcomes

- Students will recognize poorly written sentences and revise for clarity and correctness in their drafts.

Procedure

Teacher Activity. Mini-lesson on sentence structure, use of punctuation to achieve clarity and voice.

Student Activity. Draft revision.

Day 10

Materials

Handout Peer Review Guides

Student Outcomes

• Students will respond thoughtfully, with helpful criticism, following peer review guide as directed.

Procedure

Student Activity. Peer review of drafts. Final edited draft is due in two days. The solution/invention will be posted on the "Search for Perfection" bulletin board, and as appropriate, sent to school or community leaders for their consideration of your ideas.

Assessment

Peer review guides when turned in with final draft.

Coming up next:

Continuing with "A Search for Perfection"—the life and works of Phillis Wheatley.

QUESTIONS FOR THE BEN FRANKLIN UNIT: ANALYSIS AND DECISION-MAKING

1. In this chapter, you have seen how Steve and Alison use brief planners, in one case similar to what teachers put in their daily lesson plan books, and in the other, as a topic and assignment reminder given to students on the first day of a unit. Develop two such planners for the Ben Franklin unit: one for the teacher and the other for students. For the student planner, use boxes, as Alison did, to delineate each day's topic and/or work.

2. We have discussed principles of good planning as noted by educators Alfie Kohn, Diana Mitchell, and Leila Christenbury. Examine this unit for Kohn's three C's of motivation (collaboration, choice, content) and for Mitchell and Christenbury's three standards (simplicity, relevance, and workability). If the unit does not meet these, what might you do to achieve them? Where and how would you make these changes?

3. Appropriate sequencing of materials and activities is essential in planning a lesson or unit; without it, students will flounder. Evaluate the sequencing in *Ben Franklin,* making note of any changes that you believe might benefit the tenth graders. Also consider the time frame. Will students have enough time to complete assignments, both in and outside of class?

4. In a typical tenth-grade class, you would have a diverse mix of student abilities, backgrounds, interests, and achievement levels. Review the materials and activities in this unit against this mix. If you believe that this mix is not being addressed, suggest specific ways to do so (e.g., teacher

modeling, examples of written products, more time allocated, etc.) at the spot where you would make any changes.

5. Reluctant learners are a reality. Is Ben Franklin, usually a required American literature author, a compelling character study for these students? Why or why not? What, if anything, would you do differently to motivate or engage them?

6. Assessment is part of initial planning—not an afterthought. Look at the general assessment plans found in each lesson. What do you believe should be evaluated formally? Informally? Provide a rationale for your response.

7. Teachers need to consider state standards as they plan. Here are the Wisconsin's Model Academic Standards most relevant to this unit. How does the Ben Franklin unit respond to them? Be specific.

Reading/Literature

Students will

Use effective reading strategies.

Read, interpret, and critically analyze literature.

Read to acquire information.

Writing

Students will

Create or produce writing to communicate with different audiences for different purposes.

Plan, revise, edit, and publish clear and effective writing.

Oral Language

Students will

Prepare and deliver formal oral presentations appropriate to specific purpose and audience.

Participate effectively in discussion.

Media and Technology

Students will

Use computers to acquire, organize, analyze, and communicate information.

Research and Inquiry

Students will

Conduct research, organize, and use an appropriate format to present their findings.

Consult your state's standards for English language arts. Do you believe that you will have difficulty meeting state standards, or do you see them as "common sense"—what you would be doing regardless? Can you think of any barriers to implementing state standards successfully?

REFERENCES

Atwell, Nancie. *In the Middle: Reading, Writing, and Learning with Adolescents.* Portsmouth: Boynton/Cook, 1987.

Christenbury, Leila. *Making the Journey: Being and Becoming a Teacher of English Language Arts.* Portsmouth, NH: Boynton/Cook, 1994.

"History Dig: American Inventions." April 2003. http://www.tccsa.net/webquest/colejohnsons/

Johannessen, Larry R., and Thomas M. McCann. *In Case You Teach English: An Interactive Casebook for Prospective and Practicing Teachers.* Upper Saddle River: Merrill/Prentice Hall, 2002.

Kohn, Alfie. "The Truth about Self-Esteem." *Phi Delta Kappan Magazine* (Dec. 1994): 272–82.

Lewis, Rena B., and Donald H. Doorlag. *Teaching Special Students in the Mainstream.* 4th ed. Upper Saddle River: Merrill/Prentice Hall, 1995.

McDonald, Joseph A. "A Messy Business." *Teacher Magazine* (Nov.–Dec. 1991): 54–55.

Mercer, Cecil D., and Ann R. Mercer. *Teaching Students with Learning Problems.* 5th ed. Upper Saddle River: Merrill/Prentice Hall, 1998.

Mitchell, Diana, and Leila Christenbury. *Both Art and Craft: Teaching Ideas That Spark Learning.* Urbana: National Council of Teachers of English, 2002.

Nyberg, Sarah. "A Constant Search of Perfection: A Unit on Benjamin Franklin." Unit prepared for English 404, Literature for Teachers. University of Wisconsin-Eau Claire. Spring 2003.

Smagorinsky, Peter. "Forward." In *In Case You Teach English: An Interactive Casebook for Prospective and Practicing Teachers.* Ed. Larry R. Johannessen and Thomas M. McCann, Upper Saddle River: Merrill/Prentice Hall, 2002.

Tchudi, Susan J., and Stephen N. Tchudi. *The English Language Arts Handbook: Classroom Strategies for Teachers.* 2nd ed. Portsmouth: Boynton/Cook, 1999.

Teacher's Guide. *Ben Franklin: An Extraordinary life, an Electric mind.* <http://www.pbs.org/benfranklin/teachers guide.html>. 2002 Twin Cities Public Television. Accessed 13 Oct, 2003.

Wisconsin's Model Academic Standards for English Language Arts. Madison: Wisconsin Department of Public Instruction, 1998.

Wisner, Stephen. "World War I Literature: The War to End All Wars." Unit prepared for English 404, Literature for Teachers. University of Wisconsin-Eau Claire, Spring 2001.

Understanding Language, Teaching about Language

Language is not only the principal medium that human beings use to communicate with each other but also the bond that links people together and binds them to their culture. To understand our humanity, therefore, we must understand the language that makes us human.

Clark et al. (1)

 ## THE IMPORTANCE OF LANGUAGE STUDY

Although most teacher education programs include the study of language, we don't always grasp the significance of language principles on the first exposure. Nor do we necessarily make the cognitive leap from principle to practice—that is, to teaching adolescents—when we are not yet involved in designing and implementing lessons in listening, speaking, reading, and writing. Similarly, our understanding of language diversity may remain academic until we must consider diversity in our own classroom. For this reason, we address basic language principles before we discuss language activities for middle and secondary level students. We will look first at those things common to all languages, and what native speakers intuitively know about their language. We will then explore the acquisition of our native language, and how the acquisition process differs when we acquire a second language. Because

English language arts teachers are key to the acquisition and development of written language, we also look at this process for both native and non-native speakers of English. Finally, we explore linguistic diversity in America and in our schools, the richness of American dialects. With this base, we then consider classroom activities that foster language awareness and development in adolescent learners.

 ## LANGUAGE CHARACTERISTICS

Wherever you find human beings, you find language. It binds us into communities of shared meanings, where our thoughts reach across time and space and connect us to those who have been and those who will be. In some cultures, oral language is the sole means of communication; in others, both oral and written language form the base of communication. No language is any less complex than any other. It is a mistake to believe that the language of an Amazon tribe, for example, is "primitive" simply because the culture is less technological than our own. Every language is equally complex and complete as a system of communication. That is, no language or dialect is inherently superior or more satisfactory as a means of communication, a fact that has implications for teaching students with dialects or limited English proficiency.

Commonalities among Languages

All languages share certain characteristics. One of the most obvious is the arbitrary relationship between the sounds and the meanings of spoken language or, in the case of languages for the deaf, between the signs and the meanings. There is no connection between an object and what a language group has chosen to call it. Nonetheless, we tend to believe that our language alone has the "right" names for things in the world, just as millions of other people all over the globe are equally certain their language got it "right." However, no language group is right or wrong in their choices—merely different.

What makes a language different from others is the discrete set and combinations of chosen sounds. As we listen to French or Arabic or Chinese, we are instantly aware of this phenomenon. Similarly, all languages have distinct rules for forming words and sentences. When we learned our native language, mainly between birth and age five, we learned these language patterns. No one taught us; we simply absorbed them from the language around us. Native speakers, then, come to school with considerable intuitive knowledge. We can use this knowledge when we work with students. The intuition of how English words group together, for example, is already present; students don't need text exercises to understand the concept. Many textbooks, however, fail to draw on a native speaker's knowledge, and approach students as though they were learning English as a non-native speaker.

EXPLORATION

Sound and Sense

Our native intuition guides us in deriving meaning from the combination and positioning of English sounds—even if they are nonsense. With this linguistic intuition, we also have a cultural context in which to unravel combinations of sound and word groups and extract meaning. For example, e.e. cummings's "hist whist" would make little sense to a non-native speaker lacking both linguistic and American mainstream knowledge—in this case, Halloween. Similarly, Jack Prelutsky's rhymes in *Ride a Purple Pelican* would be far less fun without an American geographical background. What would we know of "Cincinnati Patti" or "Timble Tamble Turkey who lived in Santa Fe"? Or what might happen "Late one night in Kalamazoo"? The linguistic fun lies in the combination of sounds, and the cultural fun in both sound and place names. As native speakers, we untangle and appreciate both.

With a partner, find examples of poetry or prose that illustrate these principles. Then in small group, discuss your findings, choose two of your best examples—and have some fun in large group!

All normal children are capable of learning any language to which they are exposed. Nationality or race has nothing to do with the acquisition of language per se: It is the sustained language environment (e.g., family, peers, community) that provides the child with a native language. Children all over the world acquire their native languages in remarkably similar ways. Without instruction, they grasp the rules of the language—the basic sounds, how sounds are arranged to form words, and how words are arranged to form sentences. In the process, children also learn social behavior, that is, how to use their language appropriately in their cultural community. Because this knowledge does not always transfer easily to classroom culture, we have to help students adjust to school language and to ways of knowing and doing within the mainstream school culture.

COMPETENCE VERSUS PERFORMANCE

There is a difference between *competence*—what every native speaker carries as a linguistic system—and *performance*—how we use that knowledge in actual behavior. All normal children are competent in their native language, but every child differs in performance. Unfortunately, judgments of performance are linked to deviation from what is termed "standard American English." This is a social issue rather than a linguistic one. There is no such thing as linguistic superiority; every grammar is equally complex and equally capable of expressing whatever thoughts the speaker intends.

The rules of our grammar may differ from someone else's, but neither set of rules is better—only different. Thus, grammar as we discuss it here includes everything speakers know about their native language: the sound system, the system of meanings, the rules of word order and sentence formation, and a dictionary of words. The amazing thing is that we know this complex system unconsciously and intuitively and that we learned most of it by the time we started school.

 ## WHAT NATIVE SPEAKERS KNOW

Recognition of Grammatical Sentences

As native speakers of a language, we know which strings of words form acceptable arrangements and which do not, and other speakers of the language agree with us; native speakers know the grammar of their language. "Grammar" in this instance refers to what we know intuitively about our language: specifically, its structure.

> Alex hit the red ball into the street.
> It was a red ball that Alex hit into the street.
> *That was it red ball hit into the street Alex.
> *It was street that red ball hit Alex into the.

These are extreme examples of either grammatical or ungrammatical sentences. However, there is an in-between area where native speakers still recognize English sentences that deviate from their normal expectations. Authors and poets know that native speakers will not only understand these "derivations" but also appreciate them. As native speakers, our ability to judge sentences for both sense and nonsense comes from our knowledge of the possibilities of meaning. When we work with students who have syntax problems, it is important to remember that this native ability does not come from studying formal grammar, diagramming sentences, or labeling parts of speech. Rather, we need to tap students' intuition about how English words characteristically form meaningful groups. Asking questions about what goes together and why is a more effective approach.

Recognizing Relationships within Sentences

One of the key principles in language is that of the relationships among parts. We know that acceptable sentences are not randomly ordered groups of words. The conversation between Alice, the March Hare, and the Mad Hatter makes the point:

> "Then you should say what you mean," the March Hare went on.
> "I do," Alice hastily replied; "at least—at least I mean what I say—that's the same thing, you know."
> "Not the same thing a bit," said the Hatter. "Why, you might just as well say that 'I see what I eat' is the same thing as 'I eat what I see'!" (Lewis Carroll)

In English, word order does make a difference in meaning:

The angry teacher scolded the naughty boy.
The naughty boy scolded the angry teacher.
The angry boy scolded the naughty teacher.
Scolded the angry teacher the boy naughty.

Who does what to whom is altered considerably by the arrangement of words. Thus, word order is an important clue for native speakers. Conversely, it represents a body of knowledge to be acquired by the non-native speaker.

In a basic English sentence, we can also determine where to break word groups into units. Look, for example, at this sentence:

The thoughtful teacher was chewing on her pen.

We would probably make a major break between *teacher* and *was* and between *chewing* and *on*. No native speaker would see *the thoughtful* as a major unit. It is also unlikely that anyone would note *teacher was chewing* without also noting what was being chewed. The intuitive sense of "incomplete" would take over. If we take a longer, more complex sentence, we would still be able to break it into units of meaning.

EXPLORATION

Units of Meaning

Break the following sentences into their units of meaning:

- The old man raised his voice when he saw the mayor coming onto the platform.
- Driving like a madwoman Lulu hit the neighbor's mailbox last night around midnight.
- The desperate student sat at his computer staring blankly at the screen hoping for inspiration.

How many units did you find? How many of them could be written as separate sentences if you add other elements to them? How do commas help us to process chunks of information? Where would you add commands?

Native speakers have unconscious knowledge of how words cluster together and function as units. Again, we need to consider this linguistic reality when we ask students to revise sentences. With our help, they can use that knowledge to construct and manipulate sentences: What goes together? Why? Can we move the word group to another spot in the sentence? Should we? Why or why not? Why do we need commas to help us understand word groups within a sentence? Teachers can and should approach sentence work inductively, drawing out students' native language ability.

Recognizing Relationships among Sentences

As native speakers, we are able to move beyond the parts of a single sentence. We also recognize relationships among sentences, something that allows us to construct meaningful discourse, both oral and written.

EXPLORATION

Recognizing Relationships

What is the difference between the two tales of Alice's mother and the cat?

    a. Alice's mother fed the cat at midnight.

       The female parent of Alice provided food for the feline at the bewitching hour.

    b. Alice's mother fed the cat at midnight.

         Alice's mother dislikes the cat.

         The cat knows Alice's mother dislikes him.

         The cat refused to eat.

         Alice's mother didn't care.

What difference does it make that we have this native ability? How can teachers use this ability when teaching young writers?

Recognizing Ambiguities

Another language ability of native speakers is knowing how to resolve ambiguity.

EXPLORATION

Resolving Ambiguity

What do each of the following sentences mean? How do you know? Or can't you know?

- The shooting of the hunters was terrible.
- They are eating apples.
- Visiting relatives can be boring.

How would you help students approach and resolve ambiguity in their own writing? Does studying literature play a role in this skill?

In each of these sentences, the reader could come to two different conclusions about meaning. As native speakers of English, we know the possibilities. That does not mean that every student will recognize all of them; the ability to recognize and deal with ambiguity varies with individuals.

Creating Novel Sentences

Perhaps the most remarkable ability of native speakers is the ability to create and understand sentences never before uttered. If we keep track of our utterances for a few hours, we will no doubt be astonished at the number of novel sentences. Aside from some stock sentences or phrases (e.g., see you around, how are you doing, nice to see you), we are constantly creating and listening to new sentences. The human mind creates rather than stores. This ability has led some linguists, notably Noam Chomsky, to believe that we come "wired" for language, which is now one of the leading theories of language acquisition. English language arts teachers need to know something of the acquisition process because it affects how we approach writing instruction.

 ## ACQUIRING OUR NATIVE LANGUAGE

Although you have probably studied language acquisition in other areas of your pre-service program, it bears repeating here. Knowledge of the acquisition process can help teachers understand the importance of providing an appropriate classroom environment and using authentic oral and written language activities. And it is essential knowledge for developing and fostering writing processes among novices.

Despite considerable research, we do not have complete knowledge of the language acquisition process; nonetheless, we do know some of the things that children do in acquiring a native language. Understanding this knowledge is critical to teachers in the English language arts, for it allows us to intervene successfully in the learning process. This knowledge can provide us with answers when we are frustrated by what appears to be a lack of progress. It can also help us tap into students' intuitive knowledge of language. The following are some of the most basic principles of acquisition:

- Children do not learn a language by storing words and sentences in a giant mental dictionary. Although the number of words in a language is finite, the number of sentences that children can construct is infinite.
- Children learn to put sentences together, the vast majority of which they have never heard before, without direct instruction.
- Children understand sentences they have never heard before, again without instruction.
- To utter or understand sentences never spoken or heard before, children must learn "rules" that allow them to use their native language creatively.
- No one teaches children the "rules." Parents or caregivers are no more aware of the various rules than the children are. Children internalize these rules, the grammar of their native language, through language experience.

It appears, then, that normal children acquire their native language rather effortlessly, at least with regard to the complex rules of grammar. They must, however, also learn how to use this language appropriately, adapting to various audiences and situations. How children manage this complex undertaking continues to be a central research question in linguistics and psychology.

 ## ACQUIRING ENGLISH AS A SECOND LANGUAGE

If acquiring our native language is mostly effortless, we must consider learning a second language, at least as an adolescent, as somewhat more difficult, despite some similarities in language processing (e.g., acquiring aspects of sounds, words, and syntax in a specific order). Stephen Krashen's model of second language acquisition explains why. The difference lies in the distinction between language learning and language acquisition. We *acquire* language through immersion in it; in a school setting, we *learn* language through study of its parts and its rules. This distinction suggests why native speakers become frustrated when confronted with "rules" in their own language; they know the "rules," although unconsciously. In both first and second language acquisition, says Krashen, we must have comprehensible input; that is, we must be able to understand enough language to construct meaning. With second language learners, however, not only is there an issue of time and sufficient comprehensible language from which to learn, but also one of risk-taking. Making language mistakes is normal and necessary, but also more embarrassing as an adolescent or adult. Krashen thus hypothesizes that second language learners, conscious of error, use a "monitor" when using their new language. And in so doing, they slow down the process and miss the normal trial and error that fosters real language acquisition (cited in Weaver 48–52). In our classrooms, then, adolescents may be struggling with processes that remain somewhat hidden to us, and not just linguistic ones.

Issues of cultural identity, of family, affect the acquisition process, especially for students who have already reached adolescence. They may find themselves in a psychological limbo in a school setting. The native language has been the linguistic system associated with basic concepts. If students are forced to drop it altogether, the loss affects both conceptual development and identity. In extreme cases, students can end up with neither the native language nor English as a useful tool. The language limbo extends beyond the classroom; students who lose their native language lose important family ties as well. Listen to the following voices of high school Hmong students, refugees from Laos in Southeast Asia. Youa, at age 15, reveals a very personal and poignant side of language loss:

Even though I love my mother very much, I hardly talk with her. We do not sit down and discuss things like most American girls do with their mother. I do not talk to her much because my vocabulary in Hmong is very limited and she has no English vocabulary.

She goes on to explain other family communication difficulties:

Once when we went to the cities [Minneapolis/St. Paul] for a visit, a relative of ours thought I was deaf because I did not answer him.

And as 16-year-old Ye tells us, the loss of native language becomes a source of tension within the family:

As a result of lack of communication, many of the Hmong generation have lost their language and their culture. The lack of communication and culture causes a big deal of anger between the parents and the young generation. (Meiser Teaching 1–2)

Bilingualism, then, is critically important in maintaining family relationships, tradition, and culture. For Southeast Asian students like Youa and Ye, there was no bilingual program available. Having to make a choice between English and their native Hmong, they chose English, a pragmatic decision—but one with a high price in terms of family and culture. As David E. Freeman and Yvonne S. Freeman explain:

> Some students are unable to move successfully between worlds because they never fully enter the mainstream school community. They are marginalized by the instruction they receive and the attitudes they encounter. Eventually, many of them drop out or are pushed out of school. Unfortunately, these students are often not able to succeed in school or return to their home community. They may be in a state of cultural ambivalence, not accepted at school or at home. When this happens, increasing numbers of students turn to alternate communities, such as gangs. Rather than experiencing the best of both worlds, they cannot participate fully in either one.
>
> Other students succeed in school, but in the process become alienated from their home community. These are students who enter school as monolingual Spanish or Korean speakers and leave school as monolingual English speakers. They are unable to communicate with family and friends in the home community. These students may reject their heritage language and culture to become part of the mainstream. Rather than experiencing the best of both worlds, they simply trade one world for another. (*Between Worlds* 3)

Unfortunately, bilingual education is, and will no doubt continue to be, controversial; it is an issue of politics, economics, and emotions. People have strong feelings about English and *only* English being spoken in America; further, many believe that students become fluent in English only by being taught in English, despite reputable research that tells us otherwise. Although appearing to be counterintuitive, programs that provide limited English students with significant content instruction in their native language result in more English acquisition than do programs in which all instruction is in English. The students' native language helps them develop expressive skills and conceptual understanding that then build a strong conceptual base for the acquisition of English.

 ## LEARNING ACADEMIC ENGLISH

The difficulty experienced by the limited-English student in the mainstream classroom stems from the differences between conversational and academic English. When nonnative speakers become reasonably fluent in English, we can easily forget the level of difficulty they must confront in academic language, both spoken and written. Research reminds us that immigrant students may reach proficiency in basic oral communication in two to three years; however, the level of proficiency needed in school requires five to seven years (Chamot and O'Malley 109). The language of school is both unique and complex, although as teachers we don't often consider this fact. The higher the curricular level, the more abstract we become, moving even farther away from experiential and contextual learning. For the second language student, this situation can be a formula for failure.

At greatest risk are students arriving in U.S. schools at age 12 or older. The heavy cognitive demands and level of academic language used in secondary schools make it very difficult to catch up. Consequently, students need content area instruction in their native language rather than only intensive English language instruction (Chamot and O'Malley 110). Moreover, secondary students can't afford to lose two to three years of academic instruction while mastering English if they expect to go on to post-secondary institutions (Collier 520). English language arts teachers can help by including materials and concepts from various content areas in their classrooms.

We must remember, however, that students may or may not have developed academic language skills in their native language, thus affecting whether they must learn to transfer these skills to English or learn them for the first time. Teachers need to make English comprehensible, fully contextual, and rich in nonverbal cues. The higher the grade level, the more decontextualized the language and instruction. Language no longer refers to the concrete, the here and now, but to ideas and events far removed from the student. Immigrant students also lack a historical and cultural context for these ideas and events, which compounds the level of difficulty.

A student's progress through the stages of language acquisition is both personal and uneven. The amount of time each learner spends in each stage and the consistency of performance depend on several variables. One is the individual development of the student, another is willingness to learn the second language, and yet another is the quality of instructional planning and language environment in the classroom. Self-esteem, the ability to take risks, and good learning strategies are critical to the process. Age may also be a factor (Raimes "Working"). However, assumptions that young children are faster and more efficient in acquiring a second language have been disputed by research (Collier 510). At the same time, research has not provided information of an optimal age. What is not disputed is that age cannot be separated from other key variables in language acquisition, such as cognitive development and proficiency in native language.

Concerning students' acquisition of a second language, Ann Raimes ("Working") notes some agreement among researchers on the following points:

- Acquisition is complex, gradual, nonlinear, and dynamic.
- Acquisition of certain structures follows a definite order.
- Students acquire competency gradually; some learners remain stuck at one stage of competency.
- Learners develop an interlanguage midway between the native language and the target language, a system that approximates the target language but is neither the native nor the target language.

- Learners transfer cognitive strategies, which may be positive or negative for learning in the second language.
- Learners rely on native language when the target language is not adequate for their communicative needs.
- Fewer errors can be attributed to the native language, to interference, than previously thought.

Because of the nature of language processes themselves, some obvious parallels exist between native and second-language acquisition. As with native language, a sustained and comprehensible second-language environment fosters students' progress in both listening comprehension and oral production. And in both native and second-language learning, grammatical and pronunciation errors are normal, indicating important developments in learning. Purposeful language—that is, authentic communication—is also central to both native and second-language learning.

Despite some striking similarities, profound differences also exist between native and second-language learning. One of these is time. Students learning a second-language cannot return to infancy and enjoy a similar time frame for growth and the unconditional tolerance for error it provided. A necessary variable for the second-language learner is the provision for as much comprehensible language (i.e., that they can understand) as possible in whatever time is available. A great deal of talking, reading, and writing is basic to acquisition; looking at language, analyzing it, and writing things down all assist the non-native speaker in the secondary classroom.

Unfortunately, many ESL students are hurried into literacy, attempting to gain reading and writing skills while their oral language base is still being formed. Although development of oral and written skills may occur simultaneously, time may be a significant problem for the secondary student. Like other young adults, second-language students are faced with many demands, complete with variables that affect the rate and level of competency or proficiency. Another problem with acquiring literacy is the effect of the native language because rhetorical patterns are culturally based. For example, in Japanese texts, writers do not provide full explication, relying more on nuance, hints, and other devices; the reader is responsible for "filling in the gaps." In most English texts, the writer is responsible for clarity, for delineating everything for the readers. The concept of the topic sentence, for example, is very American. How students link sentences is also culturally based. In Arabic, the written language is linked to the Koran, resulting in rhythmic coordination and balance. Arabic students writing in English thus rely heavily on *and* and *so* rather than on subordination. An ESL student, then, must learn an entirely new rhetorical system (Raimes "Working").

With our native language, we also acquire, gradually and naturally, its social uses and applications. Because expectations of speakers and writers vary from culture to culture, students cannot simply transfer this knowledge to English. Similarly, academic expectations vary considerably from culture to culture. Some students may be from a culture that venerates the written word and thus may have great difficulty with the expectation that students challenge it. Others may be from a culture where rote learning is the accepted method of instruction; self-discovery would be very alien to them. Cultural differences also affect motivation for learning the second language. If students have negative feelings about U.S. culture, they may resist its language. In any case, students acquiring a second language are finding and processing a new identity, an American one (Raimes "Working"). Mainstream teachers should not underestimate the emotional and social complexity of this undertaking.

 ## WRITTEN LANGUAGE ACQUISITION: IMPLICATIONS FOR TEACHING

Native Speakers of English, American Dialects

Drawing on our knowledge of oral language acquisition, we already know what works well for written language acquisition:

- a language-rich environment, both oral and written
- authentic purpose, a reason to communicate
- active participation
- sustained practice
- positive reinforcement
- tolerance for error
- a concentration on meaning and fluency prior to correctness
- awareness of variable rates of development and competency

Teachers who maintain a perspective of "this takes time" are far less likely to become frustrated with the forward and backward movement of students learning to write. Similarly, teachers who use folders or portfolios will see individual growth more quickly than those who don't—allowing them to say with honesty and confidence, "You can do it." As with oral language acquisition, those words do wonders.

Although speakers of other American dialects such as black English or Appalachian are native speakers of English, we wish to acknowledge some differences. Teaching writing to students with different dialects can be a challenge, mainly because it is difficult to use conscious strategies to change a largely unconscious process. This difficulty also explains why the direct teaching of grammar may fail, no matter which dialect students speak. It is only with sustained contact with meaningful, full discourse text—written and spoken—that students gain fluency with standard written English. Mina Shaughnessy's powerful study of writing, *Errors and Expectations,* adds another view—and a warning. Teachers should not be misled by errors in writing. The problem has less to do with dialect than it does with lack of exposure to written English. The problem is one of making sense on paper, in an academic setting; the problem is not the home dialect per se (5). Because fundamental language processes work the same for all students, there is no reason to believe that the process of learning to write is different for nonstandard dialect students. We are not suggesting that instruction is identical or that we don't need to make some adaptations for nonstandard dialect speakers, but on the whole, we teach writing—not writing to various subgroups within our classrooms.

Teachers with knowledge of the dialect can anticipate errors in usage and syntax, and be prepared with a positive procedure for reinforcing the standard forms. Developing brief, but targeted, mini-lessons in usage and syntax and providing this type of instruction systematically is one method to address the expected patterns of "error." Allowing ample time for writing in class, where conferencing on both content and skills can take place, is another necessary element in the process. Similarly, allowing time for reading adds to the visual sense of standard forms. Many students acquire their sense of English prose from reading, from seeing in print the standard forms, the standard rhetorical patterns, and the like. While we often recognize the need to work with usage and syntax, we may overlook the need to work with rhetorical patterns. Standard American English is linear, very "get to the point quickly," and we use topic sentences to do so. This is not the pattern in other cultures, where such directness would be considered not only inelegant but unskilled.

Again, knowing the home dialect's pattern is important in guiding the student into standard dialect patterns. In that all secondary students need work with rhetorical patterns, these lessons can be directed to an entire class. However, ensuring that students with different dialects read a great deal should be a priority. Secondary students have enough cognitive and linguistic maturity to discuss their patterns of usage and syntax, and some straight talk about dialects will open discussion to language itself. The lessons are natural: What is a dialect? What features do our dialects share? What features of pronunciation, usage, and syntax are different? Which vocabulary words are different? How does vocabulary reflect our culture? How does rhythm differ? These lessons can be taught by the students. We need only lead them into critical listening and thinking, to keen observation of themselves and others as users of language, and then, into discussion. Such discussions provide both awareness of language and respect for the diverse cultures represented.

Non-Native Speakers of English

Often, mainstream teachers believe that they have no knowledge of how to work with students for whom English is a second language (ESL). However, teachers who understand the underlying concepts of native language acquisition and its relevance for teaching composition to native speakers do have a good base for working with ESL writers. Similarly, teachers who approach writing instruction holistically, emphasizing process skills before turning to product evaluation, are already using beneficial strategies. Teachers who have integrated the language arts—weaving reading, writing, speaking, and listening into all instructional activities—also have a sound basis for working with these students. Nonetheless, it is important that mainstream teachers treat ESL writers neither exactly the same as nor completely differently than native speakers (Chan 85).

One of the most critical aspects of working with ESL writers is the teacher's awareness that these students should write, regardless of how limited their English vocabulary is. Based on her research and extensive experience with ESL writers, Ann Raimes believes "the acquisition of adequate vocabulary does not necessarily have to precede writing. If ESL students are given enough time, shown ways to explore topics, and given enough feedback, they will discover and uncover the English words they need as they write" ("What Unskilled" 248). Raimes goes on to note that ESL writers need more of everything: talking, listening, reading, writing; instruction and practice in generating, organizing, and revising ideas; attention to rhetorical options; and an emphasis on editing for linguistic form and style (250). Reading—lots of it—is another essential component of learning to write. Because ESL writers do not have native intuitiveness to guide them in revision, they need to read a great deal of well-written English prose (Chan 84). Providing a wealth of reading resources, along with sustained time for reading, helps students see how the language functions.

Understanding ESL Students' Errors

Traditionally, teachers focused almost entirely on anticipated interference from a student's native language. Although teachers must, of course, be aware of the major differences between English and the student's native language, recent studies have demonstrated that second-language learners often make errors that have less to do with interference from their native language and more to do with their developing competency in English. Another major consideration is the uniqueness of each student. The type of errors that occur in one student's work may be very different from those of another student sharing the same native language. Errors generally fall into patterns, which makes it easier for teachers to analyze the source and devise instruction. Errors also provide evidence of systematic decision-making, providing a key to the student's language development and understanding of English.

ESL students make errors for some of the same reasons that native speakers do. One is simply performance—making a mistake despite underlying competency. Another is lack of exposure to the correct form or lack of correction, often in an oral pattern that the student simply transfers to paper. However, ESL writers also make mistakes due to transfer from the native language or applying an idiosyncratic set of rules in an effort to approximate English.

Recognizing and Working with "Smart Errors"

For mainstream teachers working with ESL writers, a useful perspective is one of "smart errors." Many written language errors provide evidence that the ESL student is gaining insight into how English works because the errors are logical. For example, a student may have learned the plural rule and has overextended its use to an irregular plural (e.g., "Childrens are playing."). Applying the rule, however wrong in this case, is evidence of growth. Similarly, a student who writes "It made me cried" or "It was very complicated for me to learned" is making connections about English verbs and tense, despite the obvious problem with infinitives. Further, when we consider the sophistication of the syntax used, we realize just how much progress the ESL writer has made. Seeing the logic in ESL errors is important, not just to guide the student's development but also to save both teacher and student from unnecessary frustration.

Examples from high school Hmong students, whose native language is from the Indochinese family, provide striking evidence of "smart errors" (Meiser adapted from *Teaching*):

> Our parents complain that our generations are losing our own language and culture.
> I have been losing my Hmong's big vocabularies.

This student has an amazing control of English syntax. She also understands plurals well enough, lacking instead specific word knowledge; in the context she has used them, *vocabulary* and *generation* remain singular.

The same student might use the word *everythings* in a sentence. Although grammatically singular, *everything* is psychologically plural, and again, the student writer has applied the plural rule logically. Most ESL students demonstrate inconsistency with plurals—omitting when needed and adding when not needed. An additional confounding element for ESL writers lies in the English system of using *-s* to indicate plural on a noun and singular on a verb. And in some instances, the error may relate to semantic constraints on the word itself, such as the word *vocabulary*. Learning these constraints takes a great deal of time. For this reason, sustained reading experience is critical. The more often ESL students see how English words function in full discourse, the better. Similarly, sustained oral interaction with native speakers promotes an "ear" for the correct forms. Sustained writing experience—not drills on plurals, but full discourse—is the appropriate response.

Should you point out the errors? Yes, but only if you are going to discuss them with the student. Annotating papers does little to foster the kind of internal grammatical knowledge ESL writers need to acquire. Individual conferences or small-group minilessons on a specific problem will help. As with native speaker writing instruction, you should use examples from the students' text and limit your instruction to one or two concepts at the very most. If you provide students with samples of similar, correct text, they can often draw conclusions about the appropriate forms. One advantage of working with secondary students lies in their higher level of cognitive development. They do understand language as an object to be worked with.

Pronouns often cause trouble. The choice of subject or object forms, for example, can be confusing, as can demonstratives:

> Those delicious food . . .

If you talked with this student about "those delicious food," you would probably learn the logic of her construction. The word *food* covers both a single apple and a table filled with 15 desserts. Before determining whether to teach pronoun forms once more, check the consistency of the error. If you do decide that a review of forms is warranted, don't present them all at once. Also, group them (i.e., work with subjects only). And keep in mind that when you work with demonstrative pronouns, such as *this, that, these,* and *those,* you are also working with agreement. The student has to understand the concepts of singular and plural before agreement makes any sense. One pronoun error, the bane of every English teacher, has little or nothing to do with logic or ESL:

> . . . because me and Blia have to go to the store.

This error is common among native speakers, probably because of students' oral language patterns. Unfortunately, ESL speakers make the same kind of transfer.

One of the characters in *Alice in Wonderland* notes that English verbs have a temper. ESL students would no doubt agree. For many, the system of verbs and tenses is the most challenging and frustrating part of the learning process.

> Many people get marry.
> I haven't master . . .

Using the base form of the verb is a reasonable thing to do because the meaning is clear even if the form is incorrect.

> We can laugh, giggling, teasing, and all kinds of things.
> We were arguing for a while and then she sort of accept . . .
> We came back to my house for a drink and get relax.

The inconsistency in verb forms in these sentences can be viewed positively because, again, they show normal development.

Note how Hmong student Youa changes her use of verb forms from draft to draft in the following example:

> Draft 1: Some of the kids that was born in this country could speak Hmong anymore.
> Draft 2: Many Hmong kids that were born in this country could speak Hmong anymore.
> Draft 3: Many Hmong kids that born in this country can not speak Hmong very well.

ESL writers, just like novice writers in their native language, are limited in their ability to focus on multiple problem areas. As Youa corrects the verb form in the subordinate clause in Draft 2, she ignores the main clause. When she turns her attention to the main clause, she reverts to an incorrect verb form in the subordinate clause. This is not cause for despair, only an indication of normal cognition at work. And Youa needs to know that. Similarly, Blia needs support for her sophisticated expression:

> As long as life goes well, my dream could always be accomplish any time. Whenever I feel I could handle my life, that's when it will be accomplish.

As teachers, our attention quickly focuses on the incorrect verb form. What is far more significant, however, is this student's sophisticated intent. Blia is using a combination of tenses to convey abstract ideas. We can best help her by focusing first on her intended meaning and working with tense as appropriate to that meaning before turning to the incorrect verb form. Because most high school students use increasingly complex structures, mere notations in the margins don't work well. Talking with Blia would be far more effective.

When we work with errors of tense, we must necessarily work with full discourse. Notice how our understanding changes when we look beyond a single sentence:

> My family and I usually stayed home for we have not learned to survived the jungle of America. We spend most of our time sitting in the living room.

Without additional information, we cannot know the time sequences Xiong intended or which tense is appropriate. It's always tempting to focus immediately, and usually solely, on the obvious errors, but we need to keep a different perspective. Xiong is writing fairly complex sentences, showing remarkable progress with English. His intended meaning should be the first priority.

Subject–verb agreement is another problematic area for ESL students, but one in which we often see "smart errors":

Children thinks . . .
. . . they feels . . .

This student is no doubt thinking of *-s* as the plural marker, and therefore, making a logical use of it. However, some errors result from sheer sentence complexity and are typical of native speakers as well:

The kinds of hardship encounter varies greatly with different people.

Instead of giving students a rule or assigning work in the grammar text, give them examples of interrupted subject–verb agreement and ask them to draw conclusions about the appropriate form. You'll be teaching them to be critical readers and conscious observers of how English functions.

Subordination is a late-developing skill. These sentences, with no identification of ESL writers, would easily serve as examples of many high school students' writing:

The reason why I do not talk to her is because my vocabulary is limited.
Not having many friends also leads me to not wanting to join any school activities.

Other sentence errors occur because spoken English is a powerful influence, and in speech we are often redundant:

. . . so Ka and I, we invited them to our picnic.
The part where E. T. was about to die, it made me cried.

And, similar to other novice writers, ESL students make punctuation errors that are logical, often related to oral language:

Once when we went to the cities for a visit; a relative of ours thought I was deaf because I did not answer him. So when he asked our neighbor about me; she told him that I spoke mostly English and very little Hmong.

Youa doesn't need a drill on semicolons and commas—only an explanation based on her own text and continued encouragement to use both marks. A few conventions aside, punctuation must be learned as part of syntax. ESL students need to learn the punctuation marks when they are constructing sentences that need them. When students need the marks to make clear *their* intended meaning, motivation remains high.

Your view of error will be a powerful factor in how you approach and work with ESL writers. Substantial and credible research in language and learning processes tells us that errors are a normal part of language learning. Students who understand that their errors most often show increasing competency in English, "smart errors," are more likely to take risks in learning a second language (Meiser adapted from *Teaching* 26–32).

Errors and Grades

If teachers follow a "smart errors" approach, along with a writing folder for each student, we believe they will establish a basis for fair and useful evaluation. Nonetheless, the question of grades looms large, especially when school districts insist on a single letter grade at the end of a quarter or semester. A useful solution with secondary students involves the ESL students themselves: Ask them to formulate goals for their writing. With your help, these students can set realistic and useful "exit" goals. Further, ESL writers often insist on knowing how they are progressing, what grade their drafts would receive. Thus, they expect to see errors marked, and most want their errors marked. Following strategies discussed earlier, mainstream teachers need not fear to do so.

Monitoring Classroom Language

Teachers should monitor their classroom language for clarity, pacing, and word choice; they should use natural rhythms and pronunciation, normal tone, and gestures. Although we may slow down a bit, we shouldn't do so to the point where English is unnatural, a form that students may not be able to relate to outside of class. We should use complete sentences and be continually aware of the importance of giving examples and paraphrasing. As we present information, we should provide as much context as possible, such as concrete objects, pictures, manipulatives, and demonstrations. Similarly, the chalkboard or overhead projector can serve as visual background, providing key words or other graphic representations.

When we give instructions, we should remember that "one of the hardest listening tasks for ESL learners is to understand and remember a string of instructions" (Freeman and Freeman *Teaching* 21). Although we have suggested earlier that teachers don't repeat instructions for native speakers, as it may make them lazy listeners, non-native speakers need repetition. Thus, using a variety of formats, teachers with ESL students will repeat instructions.

In the oral language chapter, we discuss the art of asking questions and directing large-group discussion. Here, we will add only that "language use differences can be especially confusing in the realm of teacher questioning," where "wait time" for responses is, if possible, even more critical for students with limited English proficiency (Peregoy and Boyle 12). Moreover, students may be more or less comfortable with different instructional formats, dependent both on cultural contexts and personal preference. In some cultures, for example, the teacher is the authority and the source of all learning; consequently, cooperative learning groups are virtually unknown—and may be questioned by both student and parent (Peregoy and Boyle 13).

Teachers need to be aware of the density and specialized vocabulary of classroom texts, texts that assume native language competency. At the same time, we should beware of workbooks that deprive students of the rich context of real books. ESL learners should use trade books that support their language development. Vocabulary lists do not promote acquisition, simply because there is no context and the words are thus easily forgotten. Contextualized vocabulary, both oral and written, relates to meaning and is therefore more easily retained. The emphasis must be on meaning first. Because reading aloud has a significant effect on both literacy acquisition and language development, we should provide many opportunities for this activity.

Grouping Students

Students with limited English proficiency (LEP) need to be with native speakers. Being in a language-rich environment with real interaction and students their own age is critical to language development. The teacher should organize lessons so that small groups of LEP and native speakers work together on meaningful tasks. If a task involves particularly difficult information, the teacher may want to keep LEP students together and provide them with extra help. For the most part, however, groups should be a mix of LEP and native speakers. For writing activities in particular, the LEP student can see how peers handle the various problems inherent in the composing process. For work with LEP students, teachers need to provide specific questions to guide revision and editing; however, these may not differ significantly from those provided for native speakers.

Using Peer Partners

Assigning a native speaker peer partner to the LEP student provides many benefits: a stable relationship between two students; the opportunity for interpersonal conversation "kid-style"; and the effective use of native speaker knowledge to help the LEP student gain academic language, knowledge, and skills. In writing activities, a peer partner is key to the oral rehearsal inherent in prewriting, as well as in response during the drafting and revising processes. With peer tutors, LEP students would be less likely to develop self-segregating behaviors that limit their linguistic and social development (Holdzkom et al. 3). At the same time, native speakers would learn far more about language and about another culture. Because peer groups and peer response are integral features of the integrated English language arts curriculum, such pairing is both natural and desirable. As noted in Chapter 5, "Oral Language: The Neglected Language Arts," however, we need to teach students how to work together, and not just expect that they know how.

Ensuring Effective Learning

A second language, like the native one, develops gradually and not linearly. That is, "language is not learned as a jigsaw of tiny bits of mastered skills, each fitting into a pattern, but rather as an entire picture, that is at first blurred, only gradually coming into focus" (Riggs and Allen xi). The classroom implication is clear: Teachers should not waste students' time with worksheets, word lists, or pronunciation drills. Students need to be actively engaged in real activities, have a context for language, and hear and participate in conversations. Because teachers worry, justifiably, about student error and its correction, a better technique would be the inclusion of double-entry notebooks for "drill." Here, LEP students would record their errors, enter a corrected version, and an explanation of what went wrong or why they made the language choice resulting in the error.

Providing Experience with Written Language

Literacy is part of the LEP students' language development. "Writing, speaking, listening and reading all nourish one another; we don't wait for mastery of one before encouraging development of the other three" (Riggs and Allen xiii). Given this, teachers should encourage reading and writing and not wait until the LEP student is a fluent speaker of English. Teachers must choose comprehensible reading materials and, as noted earlier, stay away from workbooks that fragment language. Teachers must also provide age- and skill-appropriate models of rhetorical patterns (e.g., narration, exposition). Writing should be authentic, that is, not for purposes of answering text questions or evaluation. Dialogue journals provide an important place for student writing and teacher comment—not on form, only on content. Asking students to reflect on their own writing processes in a journal is good way to find out just how the student perceives his or her progress. Frequent oral conferences with LEP students will also help alleviate some of the anxiety that accompanies writing in a new language. An essential tool for the LEP student is a dictionary, native language/English if possible. If a dictionary with the native language isn't available, then one specialized for the nonnative speaker should be part of classroom resources for writing.

Reflection

The 2000 U.S. Census reported that "nearly one in five Americans speaks a language other than English at home . . . some 47 million Americans 5 and older." The Bureau also noted that the "percentage of people 5 and older in 2000 that spoke English less than 'very well' was 8 percent, up from 6 percent in 1990 and 5 percent in 1980." Nearly half of the 47 million non-English speakers' native language was Spanish, but the number of Russian speakers has tripled since the last census. Perhaps the most startling statistic was that of isolation: The Bureau found that "11.9 million people lived in linguistically isolated homes, meaning nobody in the home 14 or older knew English 'very well.' That [number] was up 54 percent from 1990." (*St. Paul Pioneer Press* 10-9-03 2A). Clearly, mainstream English language arts teachers at all curricular levels should expect a linguistically diverse classroom, and increasingly, students with limited English proficiency. If you have not studied a foreign language nor spent sustained time outside of the United States, how will you gain insight into the linguistic, cognitive, and social challenges of students struggling to fit into an American classroom, an American society? Do you think teachers should be required to learn a few basics of Spanish, for example, if they have Hispanic students? Why or why not?

LANGUAGE VARIATION: AMERICAN DIALECTS

Each language has variations in sounds, words, and more rarely, in grammar. In the United States, regional, social, and ethnic differences provide our language with a rich diversity known as American dialects. Despite differences in pronunciation, vocabulary, or grammar, we can understand a speaker from any dialect region. Everyone in America speaks a dialect, although usually only one dialect rises to a position of prestige and is named "the standard." This position has nothing to do with that dialect being superior, but rather, with its speakers having achieved social prestige and power. Value judgments about dialects are common; consequently, some people hold a deficit view, portraying some American dialects as incomplete, illogical, or impoverished—in short, a substandard version of some "ideal" English. Marilyn Wilson, a university English teacher, argues that:

> Negative attitudes toward other dialects are rarely developed on the basis of the dialect differences themselves; rather they are formed because of attitudes toward the *speakers* of those dialects. A suspicion of difference arises mostly from viewing other ethnic or social groups as less deserving, less educated, less intelligent, less acceptable— and those attitudes get transferred to the languages these groups of people speak. Language becomes the scapegoat for racist and classist stereotypes and biases. (34)

These are strong words, but they are supported by several decades of research in the schools, by classroom experience that cautions us again and again: for second dialect or language students to succeed, they must have teachers who not only believe they can but also capitalize on the language strengths inherent in these students' home languages. The goal is linguistic flexibility, variations that help students live comfortably in their homes and neighborhoods, their schools and communities.

⌘ *Reflection* ⌘

What is your response to Marilyn Wilson's assertion that we form responses to dialect variation not on the basis of the language itself but rather on our attitudes toward the speakers?

———————————————————

Language variation allows us to adjust to social situations. With some people we speak informally; with others, formally. We use certain vocabulary with one group but not with another. We know what is appropriate to the situation and the audience. These language adjustments are learned as part of our native language, and they explain one of the most difficult aspects of learning a second language or dialect as an adult. We can learn the sounds, words, and sentences, but that is only half the knowledge. We also have to learn the appropriate contexts for them. In the classroom, we have to be continually aware of both the social and cultural implications of language as we work with students from cultures different from our own. We also need to acknowledge the time involved in learning not only form but also function, especially in academic settings. Years of sustained practice are needed for students to learn new ways of using language. Expecting too much too quickly only sets a stage for frustration and, ultimately, high potential for failure.

Understanding Linguistic Diversity in Our Schools

Diversity is the foremost characteristic of oral language in America. Everyone in America speaks with a dialect that marks each of us as belonging to a certain race, gender, social class, and geographic region. With the exception of speech related to age or profession, most people retain their original dialect throughout their lives. Only when speakers change their status or role do they find it necessary to acquire a second dialect; many speakers, therefore, have little need to learn a new American dialect. There is, however, a dialect marked as "standard American English," which is the form taught in schools. This dialect is useful because it facilitates communication in many situations. However, we must be aware of our attitudes toward it.

Because teachers tend to value the role of the standard forms of English, we may easily fall into linguistic chauvinism: We assume that our dialect, standard American, is the most appropriate way of speaking. Further, we may assume, as Jean Berko-Gleason points out, that "differing dialects are . . . degenerate, illogical, or 'simpler' versions of our own" (334–35). Nothing could be more damaging in the classroom than the assumption that students with nonstandard dialects are less than competent—linguistically or cognitively. Standard American English may be the dialect of status, but it is not intrinsically better or any more complete as a means of communication than any other English dialect. Further, actual differences between standard dialect and its variants are few. Thus, linguistic variance should be regarded as part of the rich linguistic life of America and as the foundation for teaching and learning the standard dialect (Meiser "Note" 6).

All students bring to school a wide range of backgrounds that is reflected in their language. Marcia Farr and Harvey Daniels point out that although "all students have a highly developed linguistic competency, a set of underlying rules that enables them to use their language, they do not share exactly the *same* set of rules" (13). This is true even within a dialect. For example, in African American English, there is considerable variation in its speakers' use of the dialect. This variation may be related to gender, age, social class, or context of the situation. Speakers of standard American English demonstrate the same variations, but they are not usually perceived as linguistically undeveloped or inadequate. Educators have consistently valued "standard dialect" more highly than American dialects such as black, Appalachian, and Puerto Rican (Farr and Daniels 24). The low prestige attached to these dialects is a serious matter because dialect differences do act as social class barriers (Schwartz 49). Gary Young, a high school teacher, delineates just how serious this can be:

> In the American mind, rural dialects, especially rural Southern dialects, are equated with ignorance, stupidity, and lack of sophistication. When Hollywood wants us to perceive a character as an ignorant bumpkin, he is given a rural accent and nonstandard usage. If we are to see him as a racist, too, he is given a rural Southern accent. (21)

A native Texan, Young is brutally honest about his own situation, that he was academically aware that no dialect is superior to another, but he had never applied that principle. "In my mind, Southern English, East Texas English, wasn't just different, it was inferior, and part of a good education was getting rid of it" (21). Young goes on to tell how he worked with his students, not to eradicate their native dialect, but to be more receptive to Standard English:

> People who speak other dialects aren't stupid and probably aren't ignorant; they're just unconvinced. And we're not going to convince them with shame and browbeating. They have to understand why it's in their best interest to learn Standard English and when it's appropriate to use it. No matter what their native dialect, regional or ethnic, we need to give them a new source of pride, not strip them of the pride they already have. (21)

Some educators cannot understand why students entering school with nonstandard dialects leave school 12 years later with the same nonstandard dialect. These educators forget a basic principle of language: Our ways of using and understanding language are deeply ingrained through years of social interaction; they are not easily changed through direct teaching (Farr and Daniels 24). Thus, failure to learn a second dialect may be the result of cultural differences within society and the mainstream classroom. Shirley Brice Heath's *Ways with Words*, a study of home and school cultures, illustrates the phenomenon. Children, she found, are socialized into ways of using language, both oral and written, and are thus bound up in the patterns of their own culture. When they enter school, they generally enter the mainstream culture. It is no wonder, then, that complex differences between two ways of using language may cause difficulty.

Dialect, Identity, and Linguistic Competence

Research has demonstrated that a nonstandard dialect is not a barrier to learning. Thus, we need to look beyond dialect differences when students don't do well in our classrooms. Students who feel deficient and devalued because of their language will most certainly fail, thus continuing a cycle of illiteracy and poverty. We also know that attitude is a critical factor in a student's acquisition of a second dialect or language; thus, teachers often become the critical link between the student and competency in the standard American English dialect. Moreover, teachers whose classrooms focus on linguistic and cultural diversity enrich all students, not just those who are acquiring a new dialect. The issue is sensitive, however, because before students can understand and appreciate language variation, they first must feel comfortable speaking in class. They must also learn that their home dialect, a valued vehicle for thinking and communicating, is nonetheless not always appropriate for all audiences or in all situations.

African American English

African American English, also known as black English, is perhaps the most widely discussed dialect of English; it may also be the most misunderstood. Too often, people believe that it is simply sloppy talk. Pronunciations such as *jus* for *just* cause some teachers to label black Americans as careless or lazy, despite the fact that white speakers of southern variants demonstrate similar pronunciations. There isn't one correct way of speaking, only variations that are appropriate to the audience and situation. Attempts to erase black dialect differences by correcting "errors" are ineffective, as well as insulting. Our goal should be to increase communicative competence—the student's ability to use language effectively in a variety of settings for many purposes and diverse audiences.

Our job, then, is not to change a student's language but to expand the potential. Accepting black dialect, recognizing it as different, not defective, is the first step in the process. We also need to recognize that the label itself, "black English," is misleading. It equates ethnic identification with a genetic characteristic, being black. Many African Americans never speak this dialect, whereas people of other ethnic groups do. Moreover, certain standard dialects share some of the features of black English. To establish respect for the culture it represents and as a base for teaching, teachers with black dialect speakers in their classes should learn something of its most basic features and rules.

The dialect has the same number of sounds as standard dialect but a different pattern of distribution; the real distinction is in rhythm, inflection, and tone. Anyone who has listened to the public speech of Martin Luther King Jr. or Jesse Jackson, who keep the cadence of black dialect even when using standard dialect and vocabulary, has no doubt been struck by these elements.

As with any dialect, notable variations in pronunciation (e.g., substitutions and deletions of certain sounds) are standardized and predictable. Teachers familiar with black dialect are thus able to recognize the difference between an error and a mere substitution of sounds, a return to the home dialect, when speaking or reading aloud. For example, a student who reads *with* as *wif* is not making an error; in black dialect the final /th/ is pronounced /f/. Similarly, a student who reads *sore* as *saw* and *star* as *stah* is following a regular rule of black dialect that deletes both the middle and final /r/. Most final consonants or consonant clusters are also deleted. A student who asks about her *tes* grade demonstrates a regular feature of her home dialect—not an error.

After an initial period of adjustment, most people readily understand the pronunciation differences. Some southern dialects have similar characteristics, and few people have real difficulty understanding a speaker from Georgia or Mississippi—if they want to. As Geneva Smitherman, a noted African American scholar, reminds us: "Southern Black speech sounds pretty much the same as Southern White speech . . . when you talk about pronunciation, there is no national standard, even among white speakers" ("It Bees" 522).

Grammar is the most rigid part of our language system and is the least likely to change over time. Therefore, differences in grammar are fewer than those in pronunciation, but at the same time, they carry a greater stigma. Most people, regardless of dialect, find grammar differences irritating and unacceptable. Teachers are no exception. Despite their knowledge of the integrity of every dialect, many English language arts teachers respond negatively not only to black dialect but to any variance in grammar. Teachers who work with speakers of black dialect must not only overcome such a response but also learn the distinctive features of the grammar.

It is most often the attitude of school personnel toward the dialect, rather than the dialect itself, that contributes to poor scholastic performance. No one assumes a speaker of a Boston dialect who says *idear* cannot learn to write *idea*. Yet, many African American students are victims of an assumption that says their dialect is a barrier to learning.

Native American Languages

There is no such thing as an "Indian culture" or an "Indian language." In fact, the word "Indian" itself is a misnomer, coming from Columbus' mistaken belief that he had reached the East Indies. It is the "most commonly used name for the Indigenous people of North America" . . . [however] The best way to refer to Indigenous people is by their tribal names," according to Cornel Pewewardy, a university professor, a Comanche-Kiowa (71). The approximately 300 different tribal groups in the United States each have, to some degree, their own distinct cultures, languages, and traditions (Knop 24). It is not surprising, then, that more than 200 Native American languages are in use today, and among them, many dialects. However, the degree to which Native American students speak a native language or a dialect of English varies considerably. Moreover, Pewewardy suggests that the "type of English spoken by many Indian children today has been influenced by the geographical regions in which they reside and exposure to predominately English speakers" (74). Consequently, students who live in Texas, for example, may reflect that regional dialect rather than one associated with their tribal heritage. Lee Little Soldier also cautions that the language of Native American students who live on reservations or in rural areas will differ from those who live in urban areas. In either case, it is essential to determine the home language of the students, along with the degree to which they use or are comfortable with school language. Little Soldier explains:

> Is English the first or a second language for them? Do they communicate in what some researchers are beginning to recognize and label as a "reservation brogue"? Teachers should not simply assume that all their Native American pupils are "ready" for English to be the medium of communication in school. Nor is it appropriate to assume that these students know their native languages. (651)

Although many Native American students appear not to have a distinct dialect when they enter mainstream schools, they nonetheless come from a cultural background that may use language in very different ways. As Lynn K. Wilder et al. remind us:

> Culture is more than race or ethnicity. It comprises one's beliefs, values, expectations, customs, and perceptions. Culture is a pervasive influence on behavior . . . similarly, schools are characterized by particular cultures, including sets of beliefs, values, customs and behaviors. (120)

As noted earlier, there is no single "Indian" culture, and "there can be as much variation within a culture as between cultures" (Little Soldier 653). Further, teachers cannot assume that each student believes in or follows the values of his or her tribal culture. Nonetheless, most educators point to a core of Native American values and learning styles that influence how these students will or will not mesh with mainstream classrooms.

Pewewardy points out that communication between a white teacher and a Native American student can be challenging. For example, expressing an opinion, which may be viewed as challenging authority, may not be part of many students' cultural background (70). Conversational exchanges may also be played out with a degree of misunderstanding, as teacher and [Indian] students "assign different social meanings to the same utterance or gesture" (70). Patterns and organization of classroom talk, it should be remembered, best fit white, middle-class students; talk may thus neither fit with nor build on the interpersonal skills held by Native American students. Further, ways of "knowing" and "doing" may offer another significant difference in the way these students respond to classroom activities and lessons.

Susan Philips's study of the Warm Springs Indian Reservation, *The Invisible Culture,* illustrates how Indian children's verbal and nonverbal communication patterns may conflict with those in the mainstream school. Philips argues that this conflict results in less interaction and less student participation in the normal sequences and structure of classroom talk. This in turn leads to more instances in which Native American students suffer the consequences. Philips also points out that even well-intentioned teachers may find minority students' efforts to communicate incomprehensible. Unfortunately, because many American classrooms are built around the teacher as authority, the students, rather than the school system or environment, end up being defined as those responsible for breakdowns in communication (128). We believe that the model of "teacher as authority" has indeed lessened, at least in best practice, since Philips's study. Nonetheless, to most students, the teacher is still "authority." Building a classroom community of learners, including the teacher as learner, helps "teacher authority" translate into a more student-centered model of communicative exchange. Further, talking with students about language, about cultural differences in communication, will go a long way in promoting understanding and tolerance in a multicultural classroom.

Teachers must also remember that most of the curriculum and materials of the mainstream school are designed for the middle-class white culture (Pewewardy 74). The traditional literacy backgrounds, honed since early childhood with most white students, may be completely lacking or limited. Thus, teachers cannot assume what has worked in the past will work with minority students, nor that Indian students have prior content or cultural knowledge assumed at that grade level. Indian students whose families have surrounded them with books and encouraged reading will come to English language arts with a better background, a better fit, than those who have not. Obviously, this will hold true for all minorities and white students alike, but white students have the advantage in being part of mainstream ways of knowing and doing from the start.

Another important classroom consideration lies in work with peers. Scott Sparks notes that "Cooperative strategies tend to work very well with Native American students," but warns that they will "do better in cooperative rather than competitive learning environments" (262). While most teachers will say that is true for all students, they may not fully recognize the competitive reality of mainstream classrooms, where most things *are* competitively based. Pewewardy concurs that cooperative strategies and small-group strategies are best, but adds that an Indian student may be most comfortable when the group itself has identified desirable behaviors and goals, and then, working for the benefit of the group, has formulated the rules to accomplish them (76). This model fits well with cultural values, as well as with mainstream best practice at all curricular levels.

Sparks provides one more characteristic of some Native American learners that may have a direct bearing on the classroom: their concept of time. "Native American students frequently have a different concept of space and time and more often than not see life as an unhurried event" (262). Mainstream schools run on time constraints, and teachers often respond to time, their classroom demeanor and pace thus perhaps a bit more frenetic than many Indian students are used to or understand. Little Soldier believes that "To learn to work within the larger American society, Native American students do need to come to grips with time, but the manner in which they do depends on their teacher" (652). In other words, mainstream teachers should discuss time: its use in classroom and school settings; its restrictions with assignments, short and long term; and its periodic frustrations for teacher and student alike. Moreover, teachers should take a view that all students, not just Native Americans, need both reasonable working time and reasonable time limits—and plan accordingly.

Hispanic English

Also known as Latino dialect, Hispanic English is spoken by students whose native language is Spanish. Although Spanish is the native language of students of Mexican, Cuban, Puerto Rican, and Central American descent, each of these cultures has its own ways of "knowing and doing"—and its own way of using language. Thus "one cannot speak of a homogeneous Latino dialect" (Fromkin and Rodman, 6th ed., 418). In fact, "the identification 'Latino' means something very different in Latin American than it does in the United States. In Latin America, one's identity is foremost national: one is Salvadoran, Guatemalan, or Mexican. Each national identity embodies a distinct history, geography, and culture . . . the term 'Latino' is too broad to be truly significant," states Susan Katz in her study of Latino secondary students (608). Katz further notes that "Latino ethnic identity in the U.S. is not just shaped by members of the ethnic group itself" but by external factors, often resulting in stereotypes, all labeled "Latino" or "Hispanic" (609). In her study, Katz found negative images repeating themselves in the writing of Latino students, who saw themselves represented as "stupid, gang members, thieves, and prostitutes . . . perceptions which the students believed others had of them, undoubtedly very painful perceptions to accept" (610). Needless to say, mainstream teachers must address a fuller view of cultural identity than simply native language or dialect.

Among Latino students, the degree of proficiency in both Spanish and English varies greatly, from passive to full competency; *bilingual*, then, can be a relative term—one that teachers must determine and address for classroom instruction. Julia Lara and Gitanjali Pande note:

> Most Latino students are not limited English proficient; however, the overwhelming majority of limited English proficient students are Latinos (75%). There are significant numbers of these students who come to school at the middle or high school level . . . [who] need second language development support. . . . Unfortunately because native language instruction is not generally provided at the secondary school level, Latino students who are LEP face a difficult challenge in meeting content class expectations

and learning English. This is a particularly daunting task for those students with limited schooling in their home language. (5)

Secondary teachers, then, also must determine literacy levels, student by student, especially for those whose parents are migrant workers or have recently immigrated to the United States.

Hispanic English is found mostly among bilingual speakers. In areas of the United States that border Mexico, the Spanish influence reinforces and maintains the dialect, as does the social cohesion of its speakers. In other areas of the United States, social cohesion alone provides a stable community of speakers. As with all dialects, there are systematic differences in pronunciation, stress, and syntax (Fromkin and Rodman, 4th ed., 270). Hispanic English, nonetheless, is comprehensible to speakers of other American dialects. Ricardo Garcia tells us that "while speaking his *colo*, or dialect, the Chicano thinks little of borrowing or mixing Spanish and English, whether it be sound, vocabulary, or grammar" (540). This process, called code-switching, is a universal phenomenon that reflects two languages, in this case Spanish and English, working simultaneously. It also results in the misperception that people who code-switch speak "broken" English, sometimes called Tex-Mex or Spanglish (Fromkin and Rodman, 6th ed., 418). However, code-switching follows a set of rules. For example, a phrase inserted into a sentence always keeps the syntactic rules of that language. Consider these original English and Spanish sentences:

> English: My mom fixes green tamales. (Adj N)
> Spanish: Mi mama hace tamales verdes. (N Adj)

A bilingual speaker, code-switching, might say:

> My mom fixes tamales verdes.

or

> Mi mama hace green tamales.

However, this speaker would not say:

> *My mom fixes verdes tamales.

or

> *Mi mama hace tamales green. (Fromkin and Rodman, 418)

In a classroom with bilingual Spanish–English speakers, teachers who are aware of the "rules" for code-switching recognize that their students know two languages. Moreover, mainstream English teachers who learn some basics of Spanish sentence structure will demonstrate respect for students' home language and judge more accurately their students' continuing growth in English.

As just noted, there is no one form of Hispanic or Latino English. Nor is there one form of perhaps the most widely spoken Hispanic dialect: Chicano English. Nonetheless, it is recognized as a distinct dialect of American English, "one that is acquired as a first language by many children and which is the native language of hundreds of thousands, if not millions of Americans" (Fromkin and Rodman, 6th ed., 419). Like African

American English, Chicano English is not a "wrong" version of standard American English—nor is it simply American English with a Spanish accent. It is, rather, a systematic variation in sound and syntax. For example, Chicano speakers may substitute Spanish vowels for English ones or not voice some consonants. They may also simplify some English consonant clusters (e.g., *start* becomes */star/*) or delete past-tense (e.g., *poked* becomes */pok/*) and third person singular agreement (e.g., *he loves her* becomes *he love her*).

Stress and intonation also differ, with stress placed on a different syllable in an English word. In syntax, double negatives are a regular rule of Chicano English (e.g., *I no want nothing*), as is using the comparative *more* to mean *more often* (e.g., *I use English more*) (Fromkin and Rodman, 6th ed., 420).

Roseann Duenas Gonzales offers additional information for mainstream teachers. Chicano English is:

> . . . distinguished by characteristics such as incorrect or incomplete verb formations (no *ed*, no *s*, no *ed* on past participle), inappropriate prepositions (such as *in* for *on*), and inappropriately used vocabulary and syntactic patterns that differ from those acceptable in edited American English. (21)

She adds that the lexicon of this dialect is limited both in breadth and precision. Consequently, these students need to understand the difference between oral and written English, and to acquire an extended and enriched vocabulary (21). Many teachers would respond, at least in this instance, that the needs of Hispanic students differ little from those of mainstream American students.

Because Hispanic English derives from Spanish, these students may be placed in programs or classes for non-native speakers. However, appropriate placement or instruction is complicated. According to Gonzales, "Understanding Mexican American students demands familiarity with their complex, yet simply perceived, linguistic situation" (20). She explains that too often people assume that all Chicanos are bilingual, whereas "their linguistic situation reflects a complex spectrum of bilingualism" (21). In reality, students may be Spanish dominant with limited oral and written English skills or English dominant with limited Spanish language ability or somewhere along a language continuum in either or both languages. Too often we miss the reality of linguistic variability with non-native speakers, thus complicating issues of competence and performance.

 ## ACHIEVEMENT AMONG MINORITY STUDENTS

Citing information from the Diversity Project, which he directed at the University of California-Berkeley, Harvard educator Pedro Noguera argues that differences in achievement, the gap between white students and those of color, usually originate outside of school:

> They originate in inequities in homes, in socioeconomic status, and that sort of thing. We know that schools exacerbate those disparities, and they exacerbate them because

we consistently give less to students who need more and more to students who have more. We'll take the kids who are in remedial classes and [have them work with] the weakest teachers and the most boring materials. So we set kids up for failure. (1)

We wouldn't disagree; however, we would define "weakest teachers" a bit differently. In our experience, the newest, least experienced teachers may be those placed in the most challenging, most diverse classrooms. Thus, "weak" may be inexperience, not a lack of academic knowledge. Such classes may represent an overwhelming situation, especially when students represent diverse cultures, languages, and educational profiles. "Boring materials," we believe, are those that focus on drill, on anything but purposeful reading and writing, and fail to include multicultural materials or activities.

Noguera also believes that student motivation arises from teachers:

Kids will tell you that when they encounter a good teacher who can inspire them about the subject matter, they become motivated. So I would suggest that, rather than focusing on the kids and saying they are lazy and unmotivated, the real challenge is to figure out how teachers can create conditions where more kids become motivated. What are we doing in our classrooms to tap into what I believe is an intrinsic desire to learn in all kids? I think that is the challenge of education. (2)

We don't believe any teacher starts out by characterizing students as "lazy" or "unmotivated." What can happen is a series of disappointments (e.g., lessons or units don't work well, students don't appear to make progress) that may leave a sense of failure all around. But it shouldn't. We will always have a second chance to adjust, and our students will have a second chance to learn. Noguera is right that motivation is linked to classroom conditions, and to the "fire" that we bring to our subject matter. And he is right that most students want to learn. Thus, his question of "what are we doing?" is an apt one—and we can address it. That's what this textbook is all about.

Angela Elder Quinn, in her article on marginalized Latino migrant students, directs mainstream teachers who want to nurture that intrinsic learning desire to evaluate their classrooms: Do they recognize the interests, needs, and cultures of every student?

Every aspect of the curriculum should contain elements of all the students' native cultures. The incorporation of these elements should be a substantial, regular occurrence. Using literature that reflects various cultures, asking students to share stories and poems that they have heard in their homes, and exploring the history as well as the immigration process of the cultures are all excellent ways to introduce students to others' ways of life. (48)

As we have discussed earlier and consistently, such an environment will encourage not only motivation, but also the oral and written language environment needed for academic success. Similarly, mainstream teachers should acquire some basic knowledge of the dialect or home languages of their students. It is not just a matter of respect, but also one of pragmatism. The more fully we understand and implement elements of native cultures, the more fully our students will participate in the lessons we set for them, and the more easily we will find our classrooms developing into a real community of learners.

Reflection

From your own cultural perspective, what may be most challenging for you as a teacher in a multicultural classroom, perhaps one with several home dialects or languages?

ACTIVITIES FOR LANGUAGE AWARENESS AND DEVELOPMENT

Whether they are 12 or 17, adolescents are inherently interested in language. Jokes, board games, the magic decoder ring in the cereal box, music lyrics, love notes, cheers, jeers, and even taunts are examples of their everyday experience with language. However, language is often transparent to them, something they see "right through," use constantly, but rarely think about. Our job, then, is to make language more opaque. Developing units that focus primarily on language is one way to do it; another, and arguably, better way is to find the potential for language study in all of our units. With an integrated language arts curriculum, that potential is virtually unlimited. The activities that follow represent major language concepts, as well as language standards recently enacted at both national and state levels.

Origins and Relationships

One of the most basic principles of language is its arbitrariness. People all over the world use different sets of sounds and symbols to represent the same object or phenomenon. Although the impulse to label our world is universal, the result is specific to our cultures. Most Americans, for example, have no need to define and label eight varieties of rice. But some people do need such definition within their culture. We can introduce students to the principle of language as both universal and culturally specific through activities in naming.

Naming People

Naming is a basic human impulse and a lesson easily introduced through an old friend of many American students, Dr. Seuss. The correlation between naming and physical description is easily seen in such characters as the Star-Bellied Sneetch and the bug named Von Fleck. Illustrations from various Seuss books allow students to make other connections very quickly. Once provided with a representative list of American surnames, students can work deductively to discover other basic characteristics of naming: derivation from physical characteristics, occupation, place of dwelling, character traits, from parent (e.g., *-son, mac*). With the vast influx of names from diverse cultures, students have a rich field of inquiry. Once students have discovered the ways in which we name, they might enjoy researching their own names. Although given names are fairly easy to research, surnames require teacher assistance. For this project, bringing public library books into the classroom is a good idea. Depending upon race and ethnicity, some students may have to rely on family information rather than texts for their research. For senior high school students, name research offers an easy introduction to formal research methods and requirements. It also offers an excellent way to combine library and people sources, because most students will talk with parents and relatives in the process of gathering data.

Naming Places

Investigating place names is another worthwhile activity. Students can use any level (e.g., city, street) or geographic site (e.g., river, mountain) to explore how and why these places received their names and if there is any relationship between the name and the site. Many states have a rich cultural heritage in place names, so students of Hispanic or Native American cultures may become important informants. City malls also offer an interesting view of naming places, which in some cases is linked more to Madison Avenue advertising rather than to regional logic. The mall also offers first-hand research into the naming of businesses and restaurants. A telephone book, of course, could also be a resource for such investigation. Library resources are available for searching for place names, many of them appropriate for middle level as well as for senior high students.

Naming and Culture

A lesson on the arbitrariness of naming "things" within a culture naturally emerges. Projects that present language as both a universal and culturally derived phenomenon help students see that what is needed and thus named in one culture may be superfluous in another. Students can discover this principle through a bit of field research in a subculture. One way is to group students by activities in which they participate, such as music and sports. Together they would develop a list of vocabulary words they need to participate in this group. A group of skiers, for example, would differentiate snow into *corn snow*, *powder snow*, and so forth, something of no interest or importance to people who merely shovel it or never see it. People outside of music would have no use for the term *pianissimo* or *allegro*. Students who are whiz kids with computer programming could easily exclude everyone else with a specialized vocabulary. Using the subculture of "teen," both middle level and senior high students could devise a vocabulary relatively unknown to most adults. This vocabulary could be used in a multitude of oral or written tasks demonstrating the principle of language and cultural relativity.

Students from diverse cultures could draw on their native languages to develop informative oral presentations, informal classroom drama, or miniature written dictionaries for their classmates. Considering naming and culture from another perspective, students could demonstrate how things in mainstream culture have very different connotations if one is African American, Native American, Asian American, or Hispanic.

Sounds, Rhythms, Rhymes

Students need to understand that although human beings are physically capable of making many sounds, we choose and use a finite set for English. Again, this is a basic language concept that many students are surprised to learn. Unless they are bilingual or have studied foreign languages, they tend to assume that all people, regardless of their native language, hear and represent sounds in pretty much the same way. Literature, of course, has wonderful examples of the onomatopoeic features of English, as well as its rhythms and rhymes. Using children's literature as a way to illustrate these capacities works well—and it is not beyond the sophistication levels of senior high students. Even college freshmen light up when they hear the familiar sounds of Dr. Seuss, Maurice Sendak, Shel Silverstein, Jack Prelutsky, and many more.

If Words Imitated Meaning

Just as onomatopoeic words try to sound like what they mean, some words try to look like what they mean—when forced to by people who like to play with language. For example, one of our eighth graders wrote a poem in the form of her favorite dessert, while her classmate developed her poem using the shape of a chess board, one of his passions. If students work with form and meaning in these enjoyable ways, they will come up with remarkable examples of relationships. Sometimes teachers think that such "experimentation" is a waste of time, perhaps because it appears to be frivolous. But students actually learn a great deal about words and meanings as they create their own poetic forms. These language tasks also provide freedom for students with varied ability. Right or wrong is not an issue; only individual perception and personal interest matter.

More than Just Fun

Relationships among language, thought, and culture are important concepts in their own right. But they should have a place in the English language arts curriculum for another reason: They lay the foundation for later considerations of dialect and latent prejudice. Discussion of the complexity and integrity of all languages, of their usefulness as communication systems, and of the tendency to make value judgments about those different from our own must have a place in the classroom.

Discovering Relationships

Relationships among various languages is another area of study well within the reach of middle and senior level students. With foreign language dictionaries, students can examine words across language families. Teachers can designate a corner of the room for gathering and recording data and provide a supply of foreign language dictionaries—not just Germanic and Romance languages but also Asian and Middle Eastern. If the class has students from various language groups, these students can be resources as well. Students should look up words that are certain to be part of every language group (e.g., family members, numbers, and geographical terms). They can record their findings on a large chart and later analyze the information to draw conclusions about language families.

Word Searching

We most often take words for granted; they're simply there. Students can begin to develop awareness of words by first hypothesizing about the origins of common idioms and both literal and figurative expressions. Once they have made some educated guesses, they can search for origins. The library will have resources for this inquiry. Students can also trace the origin of various American English words; most are surprised at the extent of global borrowing in our language. Students could work in small groups or pairs to search particular categories, such as food or holidays.

Searching for Meaning

Words can be real chameleons, changing right in front of our eyes. We need to understand the context before we can use and respond to words appropriately. We also need to understand the difference between literal and figurative language. A humorous way to remind students of this reality lies in the *Amelia Bedelia* books, tales of the loveable maid who takes directions and idioms literally. Another way for students to discover shades of meaning in our language is through advertisements. The word *body*, for example, has various meanings, depending on whether shampoo or diets are being sold. Middle level students can gather and analyze the data themselves; they can then formulate language principles from their own conclusions. Similarly, older students can examine the language of politics and discover just how many ways words can be turned around, blurred, and generally misused. The National Council of Teachers of English (NCTE) Doublespeak Awards are good sources of such language in action. Older students should also study euphemisms, which can be approached from two directions: words that soften realities (e.g., *passed on* or *putting the cat to sleep* for *death*); or words that cover up, deceive, and hide harsh truths (e.g., *final solution* for *killing Jews* in World War II; *soft targets* or *collateral damage* for *killing human beings* in the 1991 Gulf War and again in the 2003 Iraq conflict). Cultural values also come into play. NCTE's 1991 Doublespeak Award, for example, went to the U.S. Department of Defense for its use of language during the Persian Gulf War. Because Saudi Arabia has significantly different views of women's roles, our female military personnel became "males with female features." Studying these aspects of language with civics, social problems, or history is an excellent way to help students see how meaning permeates and directs our lives.

Word Magic

As Lawana Trout points out:

> For primitive people, words were alive before all else. Words were here before the sun, the earth, the dawn, and even man. Words had special power. If you lived in a tribal society, words could make things happen for you. You could sing songs to cure the sick, to scare enemies, to fight danger and fear, or to make someone love you. (46)

Today, people may be more sophisticated, but the power of words nonetheless affects them. Unfortunately, students often fail to see how language influences and shapes how we think about ourselves and others. For this reason, they may not understand our concerns about sexist language in their essays, why it makes any difference whether we use *he* or *she*. We can address the power of language through a discussion of labels. Senior high students can quite easily come up with lists of labels applied to males and females throughout their school years; with some nudging, they might classify labels by reference to animals and plants (e.g., old hen, bat, fox, pansy, peach). Although we have to caution them about language that is too offensive for class, that in itself is a lesson in language as a social phenomenon. Also, we must make clear our point: We are influenced by labels. Referring to women as *girls* or *chicks* or *broads* demeans them, just as references to black males as *boy* is demeaning. Younger students could work with "sticks and stones may break my bones but words will never hurt me," a modern incantation. Most students could supply personal examples to disprove the old taunt; however, it might be more challenging to work through appropriate literature, where characters rather than students are the focus of discussion. Young adult fiction offers powerful material for exploring the effect of language in everyday life. The important thing is to get students to recognize just how language does influence us.

The Symbolic Nature of Language

A good way to introduce students to the symbolic nature of language is through logos. Students can easily collect logos by examining the yellow pages of phone books. Once they have a good sample, they can analyze the logos to determine what the symbol represents. Younger students might like to design a personal logo, a symbolic representation of themselves.

Ancient writing systems are another good way to introduce symbols. American Indian pictographs and Egyptian hieroglyphics are two interesting places to start. After students have read and discussed pictographs, they might read a creation story and draw pictographs in the margins. Or they might create both the story and the pictographs. Students would need a good sense of myth and how ancient peoples wanted to explain the universe and its creatures before doing this task.

Egyptian hieroglyphics are no doubt familiar to students from their cultural geography classes or movies. However, they may not have studied them from the viewpoint of a symbolic language system. With limited examples, they could figure out passages, as well as create some.

Less familiar are Aztec symbols. Children's literature provides wonderful access to symbols and their connections with culture. Deborah Nourse Lattimore's *The Flame of Peace* contains authentic illustrations, vibrantly presented. Students can examine the endpapers, where Lattimore has provided an additional key to the illustrations, and then explore the symbols in the text itself. The mythic tale echoes those of many cultures, so students might pursue comparisons of cultures and symbols.

Viking *runes* are yet another example of an early writing system. Our writing system represents sounds we make, but runes are symbols both for things and ideas. The Vikings came to believe in the magic of the runes. An *X,* for example, offered protection against a poisoned cup; an arrow pointing upward would ensure victory in battle; a figure somewhat like our letter *p* was a safeguard against giants (Born 2, 9). The runes, left on thousands of stones, are part of Norse mythology, as well as an authentic writing system. Students could link history and mythology and try writing with runes. With all writing activity, students should have a clear purpose in mind, associating purpose with their mythical audience and setting. The fact that ancient peoples developed various writing systems should make clear to students the power of words and the basic human need to communicate across time and distance.

Using Young Adult Literature to Teach Language Concepts

The Importance of Names

As noted earlier, names carry significance. It is not surprising, therefore, that young adult literature often addresses them in connection with characters' personal identities. Susan Ohanian provides some examples:

> *"Galadriel Hopkins. What a beautiful name! From Tolkien, of course."*
> *"No," muttered Gilly. "Hollywood Gardens."*
>
> (*The Great Gilly Hopkins* Katherine Paterson)

Discussion could center on the use of nicknames (Gilly for Galadriel), the advantages and disadvantages of being given a very unusual name (or even one that is considered old-fashioned), and connections between attitudes about names and how we act (65).

Another discussion could focus on public and private names (73). In *Julie of the Wolves*, the main character has two names, one English and one Eskimo; because she was bound to her family with her Eskimo name, Miyax, she decides that it alone will be the name used with her father.

Students may have private names, not only with special family members but also with best friends. Talking about the ways in which a name may bind us to another person or group of persons—sometimes in negative ways—is another facet of naming.

Ohanian also provides examples of literature that address the Americanization of foreign names, as well as teens dealing with their non-American names (71):

> My name is Stepan Bakaian, or Step for short. I've been called Bak also, which isn't as cool, but it's better than Steven, which is my 'American' name. (*Asking the River* David Kherdian)

Sandra Cisneros's adolescent narrator in *The House on Mango Street* also comments on her name, Esperanza, meaning "hope" in Spanish:

> At school they say my name funny as though the syllables were made out of tin and hurt the roof of your mouth.

Esperanza explores other aspects of her name, including her desire to baptize herself with a name is the "real" her. This declaration would be a good starting point for discussion on naming in general, and the feelings we attach to our names, regardless of culture.

With America continuing to welcome many immigrant groups, the issues of names and cultural identity are important, especially because young adults may tease or taunt those who are different in any way. And it is not just foreign names that elicit this language behavior. In a novel by Zilpha Keatly Snyder, a character notes that *Okie* is applied to more than just people from Oklahoma. Another character affirms: "You're shorely right 'bout that . . . When Californians say Okie they mean dumb and dirty and lazy and most everthin' else bad they can think of" *(Cat Running)*.

Ohanian has many examples of naming, taken from both young adult literature and that for younger readers. Students need not read an entire text to benefit from such examples, and if classroom literature does not lend itself to the concept of naming and its effects, preparing brief examples for such a discussion is a worthwhile teacher activity.

Noticing Language

Young adult literature is a powerful vehicle for getting students to notice and discuss language. In *Using Young Adult Literature in the English Classroom,* John H. Bushman and Kay Parks Bushman provide teachers with a wealth of resources. They note, for example, how author Chris Crutcher is bound to catch kids' attention through his vivid descriptions: "In *Chinese Handcuffs,* Crutcher uses the language most effectively. He describes Mrs. Crummet's cat as a 'three legged alley Tom with a face like a dried-up creek bed and the temperament of a freeway sniper.' "(qtd. in Bushman and Bushman 103). Crutcher also describes Mrs. Crummet herself: "Mrs. Crummet starts to speak, her skinny finger aimed at Preston like a poison dart gun" (10).

Chris Lynch, another favorite author of young readers, provides powerful and suggestive descriptions. Here Lynch sets the physical and emotional scene of a locker room he introduces as "big and chilling":

> The white-tiled floor and walls, under harsh florescent lights, maybe made it seem larger and colder than it was. But the real thing of it, probably, was the nobodyness of it. (*Iceman* 112)

Because Lynch's characters often revolve in a world of male sports, his novels provide a good base for discussion of language as key to our ability to read and describe our everyday world.

Similarly, S. E. Hinton's use of Robert Frost's poetry focuses attention on the role of poetic language in everyday life, when Johnny states: "Too bad it couldn't stay like that all the time," and Ponyboy responds, "Nothing gold can stay," and then recites the familiar Frost poem of the same title. (*The Outsiders* 77)

This use of language, because it points out the relevancy of poetry and symbol, can be a powerful message to adolescents who may believe poetry is "not for them."

In another example, Bushman and Bushman discuss Katherine Paterson's *The Great Gilly Hopkins:*

[This novel] provides students with an interesting use of language. Questions about Trotter often surface due to the language that she uses. Most realize that, although Trotter speaks less-than-perfect English, she is a truly admirable human being. A study of Trotter's language patterns could be productive. For example, such a study should determine whether Trotter's English actually enhances her powerful use of language and her image. In addition, students should explore the effects of Mr. Randolph's old-fashioned, flowery, highly literate style of speaking. What effect does this language style have on the reader's image of Randolph? (105)

In a section called "Word Wonder," Ohanian uses examples to do just that—focus adolescent attention on specific words (74–78).

> . . . promise is a meaningless word. . . . Sometimes I think the word is just useless. You can't promise anything that matters, and if it doesn't matter, why use such an important word. (*Noonday Friends* Mary Stolz)

Such a discussion focuses on meaning and can lead students into thinking about the expectations they set up by their use of specific words.

> *"An enemy? What's that?"*
> *"That's hard to explain," I said again.*
> *"An enemy is someone who wants to beat you up." I said that because I couldn't think of a better explanation.*
> (*Dinosaur with an Attitude* Hanna Johansen)

Some words are hard to define, which doesn't stop us from using them relentlessly. Students could have a fruitful discussion on this language phenomenon, noting not just words that are difficult to define but also words that carry many, and perhaps confusing, connotations. Students might also keep a record of their own lexicon, build their own dictionary or thesaurus, and then work with classmates on "the" definitive class text—for kids, by kids.

A Matter of Style

Just as young adult literature provides teens with opportunities to see the descriptive power of language, it similarly allows them to discuss language as a stylistic device important to authors: Is the language used by a character appropriate for his or her age, educational level, and social background? How does a character's language reveal his or her identity to a certain degree? How does dialogue enhance our understanding of that character? (Bushman and Bushman, *Using* 31–32). Teens would be quick to notice characters not "acting their age," perhaps being too adult for the situation at hand. Extending to language, a discussion focused on "kids don't talk that way" could lead to increased appreciation of language's role in readers' acceptance or rejection of a character. S. E. Hinton was a teenager herself when she wrote *The Outsiders,* a text that has remained a favorite for at least two generations of students. Paul Zindel's *The Pigman* has similar staying power. These novels might be a good place to start an investigation of language as integral to appropriate characterization.

Arthea J. S. Reed, in discussing young adult novels as a way of modernizing *Romeo and Juliet*, points to Cormier's *The Chocolate War* as a good bridge to understanding Shakespeare's use of language in character development. She suggests comparing the language of the villain, Archie, with that of the hero, Jerry: How does language convey their personalities, identify their social class, and help readers predict outcomes? From their experience with this contemporary model, students might more easily approach the more challenging language of *Romeo and Juliet* (103–104).

Another discussion might focus on language, character, and context, especially in novels where profanity is used. Bushman and Bushman argue that in the context of particular situations, along with a specific character developed by the author, *not* to use profanity would be ridiculous. They note Cormier's novels and Meyer's Vietnam War novel, *Fallen Angels*, as examples of profanity appropriate to events and characters (*Using* 31).

American Dialects

Young adult literature can help students both understand and appreciate our country's linguistic diversity. In addition to three major geographical dialects (Northern, Southern, Midland), we have many social dialects. The most prominent of these are, arguably, African American English and Southern. Nonetheless, other social dialects are also important (e.g., Appalachian English, Alaskan English, Hawaiian nonstandard English, New York nonstandard English, and Spanish-influenced). To interest students in dialect, teachers could use *To Kill a Mockingbird*, where attitudes about language are revealed in the dialogue between Jem and Calpurnia, a black dialect speaker (Bushman and Bushman, *Using* 107).

Bushman and Bushman point out that young adult literature can be used to showcase the standard features of black dialect, like omitting the *be* form of the verb. Good pieces for such study include Tate's *Secret of Gumbo Grove*, Meyer's *Scorpions*, Childress's *Rainbow Jordan*, Irwin's *I Be Somebody*, and Taylor's *Let the Circle Be Unbroken*. In Reaver's *Mote*, black dialect itself is discussed by two characters. Interestingly, in some novels with black characters, like Hamilton's *M. C. Higgins, The Great*, no black dialect is used. This "omission" could lead to interesting speculation about why some authors choose not to use it (*Using* 109–10).

A Window on History

American English has been influenced by many languages, both those brought by settlers and those already here, the rich languages of Native Americans. Speare's novels, whose settings take us back to colonial America, introduce young readers to words commonly used earlier in our history but not in use now. Borland's *When the Legends Die* uses words borrowed both from Native Americans and Spanish. George's novel *Julie of the Wolves*, a favorite among young readers, provides a fascinating look at language, culture, and identity. In accepting or rejecting English, Julie reinforces cultural links embedded in one's native language. An added language feature lies in the wolves, who have their own "language" but nonetheless communicate with Julie (Bushman and Bushman, *Using* 114–15).

A medieval English setting for *Catherine, Called Birdy* by Cushman, introduces students to vocabulary and an occasional phrasing that might pave the way for later enjoyment of Chaucer. Additionally, Birdy plays with language for its shock value and comments on her experimentation with it. The characterization of Birdy rests heavily on her language and offers another chance to explore the role of language in developing our knowledge of characters and predicting their fates.

Language as Manipulation

Young adult fiction provides many examples of the manipulative aspects of language and, when paired with classic novels, serves as a bridge to more sophisticated language devices. Bushman and Bushman suggest pairing *1984* and *The Chocolate War* to investigate both motivations for and the effects of abusive language ("Dealing" 221). Additionally, *The Chocolate War* is a rich resource for exploring the language devices characters uses to get others to act and think in a certain way. Blume's *Tiger Eyes* and Sleator's *Singularity* are other books suggested by Bushman and Bushman (*Using* 113–14).

Being a Book Sleuth

Young adult literature, as well as children's literature, are arguably the richest resources available for focusing on language. Texts are interesting, accessible, and versatile—but you need to search, read, and catalogue your findings. Because language concepts in children's and adolescent literature lay the foundation for later, more complex literary understanding and appreciation, the preparation is well worth both time and effort—and an oasis of sheer enjoyment.

INSTRUCTIONAL UNIT

A study in language, culture, and identity: *Julie of the Wolves,* Jean Craighead George's young adult novel, is a wonderful resource for learning about language and its relationship to culture and personal identity. As a popular piece of survival literature, the novel also easily pairs with other young adult novels also rich in cultural identity (e.g., *Island of the Blue Dolphins, Dogsong, The Cay*). The importance of such literature is noted in national and state standards for secondary language arts classrooms:

Students will develop understanding of and respect for diversity in language patterns and dialects associated with culture, ethnic groups, geographical regions, and social roles. (NCTE 1996)

As you explore the blueprint for a language study unit centered on *Julie of the Wolves*, consider how it addresses or could address not only this specific standard for language, but also language concepts more broadly. Also consider the unit's potential for the other language arts standards and classroom diversity:

- integrated language arts (listening, speaking, reading, writing)
- potential for integration with other content areas
- inquiry skills
- critical thinking skills
- variety of writing forms
- variety of oral language forms
- special needs students (e.g., learning disabilities, limited English)
- student ability and interests

LANGUAGE, CULTURE, AND IDENTITY: JULIE OF THE WOLVES

Summary of Novel

Julie/Miyax finds her home life in an Alaskan village intolerable, and dreams of a new life in California. Hoping to reach her California pen pal, she runs away. But without compass or provisions, she soon loses her way in the Alaskan wilderness. With memories of her father's training and the help of Arctic wolves, Miyax survives. In the process, she is forced to rethink her identity and the traditional values of her Eskimo heritage: intelligence, fearlessness, and love.

Teacher Goals

To illustrate relationships among language, culture, and personal identity.

To provide students with fictional teen role models demonstrating resourcefulness, courage, and intelligence.

To develop or reinforce the following skills:

- critical reading
- discussion
- storytelling
- improvisation
- critical thinking
- inquiry
- decision-making
- writing as a tool for thinking and discussion

Introduction of Unit

Teacher Activity. Read (or play cassette) the first 36 pages of the novel to the class, Part I, Amaroq the Wolf.

Assign peer partners for reading/dialogue logs. Introduce the required class project and the optional projects.

Required Class Project. Create a culture: Students will form groups of five and develop the following for their culture: a name, a language, an oral history/folklore and legend, a calendar, feasts/rituals, and a totem.

Individual Choice Projects. Students may choose one of the following ideas or develop their own:

- a field study involving observation of animal behavior and communication
- a field study of language within a specific group of people or a place
- an investigation of nonfiction topics related to Julie's Arctic world (choice of topic and presentation mode)
- selection and reading of a book representative of a specific culture or ethnic background other than their own (choice of presentation mode)

Teacher Activities for Unit

Although teachers should not dilute the pleasure of reading this novel through excessive exercises, they must nonetheless help students develop higher-level thinking skills. Thus, many possibilities are presented with this unit. Choosing the most appropriate, the most appealing, and the most needed are all part of a teacher's skill.

Introduce "think pads"; have students make their own response booklets for this novel. Illustrate the split page "What I Read/What I Think About It" approach. Model some entries. Introduce "quick writes"; have students write for 2 minutes, then share their remarks with a partner. Students circle what's alike in their entries and talk about what is different.

Use photographs to introduce vocabulary or concepts specific to setting. Place heavily illustrated nonfiction texts of Alaskan geography, wildlife, and native peoples in resource center.

Provide reading structures for critical analysis:

Characterization Chart

Based on what	Julie is . . .	Example/Page
Julie herself says		
Julie thinks		
Other characters say		
The narrator says		

Running Lists

List examples	(and page numbers) where:
Julie faces a new challenge.	
Julie learns something new:	
about herself	
about her environment	
about the wolves	
Jean Craighead George had to know specific, researched information:	
about wolves	
about Eskimo culture	
about the arctic environment	

Provide "Thinking" Structures for Personal Exploration

a. Miyax identifies the leader of the wolves through human characteristics she learned as a child from old Eskimo hunters on Nunviak Island: intelligence, fearlessness, and love. What do you believe are characteristics of a good leader? Why? How did you come to believe in these characteristics? Through someone you know personally? Through observing? Through reading or viewing on television?

b. Miyax recalls the words of her father as she evaluates what to do. He believed fear is a warning to "change your ways," that if you feel fear, you are doing something wrong. Have you ever observed or experienced a situation where fear was linked to something you knew or sensed was wrong? Explain what happened.

c. Imagine Miyax is a classmate whom you know quite well. One day, you learn that she is facing a serious problem. First describe the situation; then, explain what you think Miyax's actions would be and why.

d. Other than the wolves, Miyax is alone in the tundra. How might her story be different if she had a teenage friend with her? Do friends always prove to be dependable or helpful in tough situations? What have you observed or experienced?

Cause/Effect Chart

Single cause with multiple effects
[e.g., Julie becomes Miyax]

Single effect with multiple causes
[e.g., Julie is able to survive in the tundra]

Thematic Web

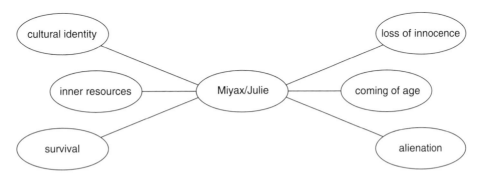

Create Mini-lessons on Language

Effects of Figurative Language. The novel has abundant similes and metaphors. Provide a few examples (e.g., wolf's eyes as jewels, fur as metal, voice as violin or flute); then, invite students to explore how their mental "image-making" is affected throughout the novel. Ask them to keep a running list of figurative language, starring those that they found especially appealing or striking.

Understanding Language as Ritual. Miyax's songs, to draw strength from the natural world, provide accessible examples of language used as ritual. Illustrate through examples from the novel (e.g., Kapugen's song of the Bird Feast, song to Amaroq the wolf), asking students to "translate" the songs into Miyax's needs or desires. Then, ask students to note where ritualistic language is used in our everyday world and why it has been an essential part of every culture throughout our long history.

Understanding Language as Cultural Identity. Because language, culture, and identity are wrapped around and within each other, Miyax faces unexpected issues. Provide examples for discussion (e.g., when she could express sadness only in Eskimo), asking students to explore how our native language or dialect: (1) affects our ability to express ourselves clearly, fully, or easily; (2) links us to our culture—family, community, nation.

Create Mini-lessons and/or Model Writing Forms
Expressive writing: journal, diary, learning log
Narrative writing: storytelling, personal narrative
Expository writing: news writing, researched pieces
Alternative forms for reporting research findings:
    Elements of folklore/legend

EXPLORATION

JULIE OF THE WOLVES UNIT

1. Review the teacher's goals for this unit. Then list some appropriate student outcomes for the unit.
2. Which activities are particularly effective for students with special needs? Which activities would require teacher or peer assistance for students with limited ability? Which activities would challenge gifted and talented students?
3. Suggest written and oral activities that would capture student interests and address diverse learning styles.
4. How would you assess student learning in this unit? How would you know that students are meeting state and national standards? Is *assessment* the same as *meeting standards?*

REFERENCES

Berko-Gleason, Jean, ed. *The Development of Language.* 2nd ed. Upper Saddle River: Merrill/Prentice Hall, 1989: 334–35.

Born, Thomas. *Understanding Language I: The Magic of Words.* Columbus: American Education Publications, 1969.

Bushman, John H., and Kay Parks Bushman. *Using Young Adult Literature in the English Classroom.* Upper Saddle River: Merrill/Prentice Hall, 1993.

———. "Dealing with the Abuse of Power in *1984* and *The Chocolate War.*" *Adolescent Literature as a Complement to the Classics.* Vol. 1. Ed. Joan F. Kaywell. Norwood: Christopher-Gordon, 1993.

Cazden, Courtney B. *Child Language and Education.* New York: Holt, 1981.

"Census Report." *St. Paul Pioneer Press* 9 Sept. 2003: 2A.

Chamot, Anna Uhl, and J. Michael O'Malley. "The Cognitive Academic Learning Approach." Ed. Pat Riggs and Virginia G. Allen. *When They All Don't Speak English: Integrating the ESL Student into the Regular Classroom.* Urbana: NCTE, 1989: 108–25.

Chan, Michele M. "What We Already Know About Teaching ESL Writers." *English Journal* (Oct. 1988): 84–85.

Cisneros, Sandra. *The House on Mango Street.* New York: Vintage, 1983.

Clark, Virginia, et al., eds. *Language: Introductory Readings.* 5th ed. New York: St. Martin's, 1994.

Collier, Virginia P. "How Long? A Synthesis of Research on Academic Achievement in Second Language." *TESOL Quarterly* 23 (1989): 509–31.

Farr, Marcia, and Harvey Daniels. *Language Diversity and Writing Instruction*. Urbana: NCTE, 1986.

Freeman, David E., and Yvonne S. Freeman. *Between Worlds: Access to Second Language Acquisition*. Portsmouth, NH: Heinemann, 1994.

Freeman, Yvonne S., and David E. Freeman. *Whole Language for Second Language Learners*. Portsmouth, NH: Heinemann, 1992.

_____ . *Teaching Reading in the Multilingual Classrooms*. Portsmouth, NH: Heinemann, 2000.

Fromkin, Victoria, and Robert Rodman. *Introduction to Language*. 4th ed. New York: Harcourt, 1993.

_____ . *Introduction to Language*. 6th ed. New York: Harcourt, 1998.

Garcia, Ricardo I. "Linguistic Interference and the Chicano." Ed. Virginia P. Clark, et al. *Language: Introductory Readings*. New York: St. Martin's, 1981: 539–45.

George, Jean Craighead. *Julie of the Wolves*. HarperCollins, 1972.

Gonzales, Roseann Duenas. "Teaching Mexican American Students to Write: Capitalizing on the Culture." *English Journal* (Nov. 1982): 20–24.

Heath, Shirley Brice. *Ways with Words*. Cambridge: Cambridge UP, 1983.

Hinton, S. E. *The Outsiders*. New York: Penguin, 1967.

Holdzkom, David, et al. "What Teachers Can Do With Non-English Speaking Children in the Classroom." *Research Within Reach: Oral and Written Communication*. Washington, DC: National Institute of Education, n.d.

Knop, Constance K. *Limited English Proficiency Students in Wisconsin: Cultural Background and Educational Needs*. Part III. Madison: Department of Public Instruction, 1982.

Lara, Julia, and Gitanjali Pande. "Latino Students and Secondary School Education." *Gaining Ground Newsletter*. May/June 2001. CCSSO Resource Center on Educational Equity. Washington, D.C.

Lattimore, Deborah Nourse. *The Flame of Peace*. New York: Harper, 1987.

Little Soldier, Lee. "Is There an 'Indian' in Your Classroom? Working Successfully with Urban Native American Students." *Phi Delta Kappan* April 1997: 650–52.

Meiser, Mary Jordan. "A Note on Diversity." *Classroom Activities in Speaking and Listening*. Madison: Wisconsin Department of Public Instruction, 1991: 6.

_____ . *Teaching Writing: A Guide for Teachers of Hmong and Other ESL Students*. Wisconsin Council of Teachers of English, 1992.

NCTE and IRA. *Standards for the English Language Arts*. Urbana: NCTE, 1996.

Noguera, Pedro. "Challenging Minority Underachievment: A Conversation with Dimon Professor Pedro Noguera." *Harvard Graduate School of Education News*. January 2002. Accessed 10-2/02. <http://www.gse.harvard.edu/news/features/noguera123202.html.>

Ohanian, Susan. *145 Wonderful Writing Prompts from Favorite Literature*. New York: Scholastic, 1998.

Parrish, Peggy. *Amelia Bedelia*. New York: Harper, 1963.

_____ . *Thank You, Amelia Bedelia*. New York: Harper, 1964.

Pewewardy, Cornel. "Fluff and Feathers: Treatment of American Indians in the Literature and the Classroom." *Equity & Excellence in Education* 31.1 (April 1998).

Peregoy, Suzanne F., and Owen F. Boyle. *Reading, Writing, and Learning in English as a Second Language: A Resource for K–12 Teachers*. 3rd ed. New York: Longman, 2001.

Philips, Susan Urmstorm. *The Invisible Culture*. New York: Longman, 1983.

Quinn, Angela Elder. "Moving Marginalized Students inside the Lines: Cultural Differences in the Classroom." *English Journal* (March 2001): 44–50.

Raimes, Ann. "What Unskilled ESL Writers Do As They Write: A Classroom Study of Composing." *TESOL Quarterly* (June 1985): 229–58.

_____ . Lecture. "Working with International Students and Immigrants." CCCC Winter Workshop on Teaching Composition to Undergraduates. Sheraton Sand Key Resort, Clearwater Beach. 6 Jan. 1992.

Reed, Arthea J. S. "Using Young Adult Literature to Modernize the Teaching of *Romeo and Juliet*."

Adolescent Literature as a Complement to the Classics. Ed. Joan F. Kaywell. Vol. 1. Upper Saddle River: Merrill/Prentice Hall, 1993.

Riggs, Pat, and Virginia G. Allen. *When They All Don't Speak English: Integrating the ESL Student into the Regular Classroom*. Urbana: NCTE, 1989.

Schwartz, Judith, ed. *Teaching the Linguistically Diverse*. New York: State English Council, 1980.

Shaughnessy, Mina. *Errors and Expectations*. New York: Oxford UP, 1979.

Smitherman, Geneva. "It Bees Dat Way Sometimes: Sounds and Structures of Present-Day Black English." Ed. Virginia Clark, et al. *Language: Introductory Readings*. New York: St. Martin's, 1981: 521–38.

Sparks, Scott. "Classroom and Cultural Accomodations for Native American Students." *Intervention in School and Clinic* 35.5 (May 2000).

Trout, Lawana. *Myth: Student Log*. New York: Scholastic, 1975.

Weaver, Constance. *Teaching Grammar in Context*. Portsmouth: Boynton/Cook, 1996.

_____ . (ed). *Lessons to Share: On Teaching Grammar in Context*. Portsmouth, NH: Boynton/Cook, 1998.

Wilder, Lynn K., Aaron P. Jackson, and Timothy B. Smith. "Secondary Transition of Multicultural Learners: Lessons from the Navajo Native American Experience." *Preventing School Failure* 45.3 (Spring 2001).

Wilson, Marilyn. "The Changing Discourse of Language Study." *English Journal* (March 2001): 31–36.

Young, Gary, "Shame on Whom?" *English Journal* (March 2001): 20–22.

Oral Language: The Neglected Language Arts 5

Schools are language saturated institutions. They are places where books are thumbed, summarized, and "revised"; notes are dictated, made, kept, and learned; essays are prepared; examination questions are composed and the attendant judgments made. Teachers explain, lecture, question, exhort, reprimand. Pupils listen, reply, make observations, call out, mutter, whisper and make jokes. Small knots gather over books, lathes, easels, or do nothing in classrooms, laboratories, workshops, craft rooms, corridors and toilets to chatter, discuss, argue, plan, plot, and teach one another.

Douglas Barnes

 ## BASIC PRINCIPLES

As Barnes reminds us, oral language is the most pervasive environment of our schools. We seldom perceive of it in this way, and tend to forget that oral language is an important instructional area in the English language arts. At the secondary level, responsibility for oral language has most often been relegated to the speech course or fragmented into isolated units. John Fortier, a former high school English and speech teacher, reflects on a possible reason for this:

> A number of factors have combined to prevent oral language instruction from achieving the gains that writing instruction has. We sometimes perceive speaking, unlike writing, as a competence which develops independently without instruction. After all, students come to school talking, but few are able to write. (2)

An additional factor may lie in the traditional preparation of secondary English teachers, where written language has been the focus for methods courses. As one of our English education majors put it, "I know it was sort of a shock to some of the methods students to think about teaching speaking and listening skills, because they didn't

119

really consider that 'English.' " Quite often, secondary English textbooks reinforce the notion of the primacy of written expression, which generally appears in two varieties: literature and composition/grammar. Fortunately, a renewed emphasis on an integrated and balanced English language arts program has also brought more resources for teaching oral language. Similarly, national and state standards for oral language instruction and performance have focused attention on these critical language arts.

Before looking specifically at listening and speaking, we need to focus on some oral language principles. Fortier summarizes these:

1. Not all students share the same level of competency in oral language; in fact, some students enter school impoverished by a lack of verbal interaction in the home. The implication for teachers is clear: Students do need to talk in school, not "idle chatter, but focused discussion" (3).

2. Similar to other language skills, the acquisition of oral language skills is developmental. We should not expect all students to progress at the same rate or demonstrate the same ability, regardless of similar chronological age.

3. Students need varied and purposeful experience in oral communication, just as they do with written communication. This means a shift from familiar audiences and contexts to more distant ones, as well as opportunities to share feelings, entertain, give information, and persuade. Each of these purposes has its own problem relative to audience and setting; therefore, students would learn to solve diverse communication problems. Our responsibility is to create these contexts, everything from role playing to group activities, from conferencing to public speaking before an entire class.

4. We should not break speaking into subskills, nor should we isolate speaking from the other language arts. Oral language activities integrated with reading and writing, a planned part of every unit and daily classroom interaction, enhance student competency.

5. Since speaking is not totally oral, students need to learn about body language, eye contact, gesture, and so forth. Being aware of how listeners are responding is a critical skill. Similarly, students need to be sensitive to how culturally bound these areas are. For example, in mainstream American culture, eye contact is expected to be direct, indicating honesty and self-confidence. In other cultures, such directness would be ill-mannered. (3–5)

TEACHER TALK, STUDENT TALK

The most obvious characteristic of classroom talk is that there is so much of it.

A. D. Furlong and V. J. Edwards (10)

A. D. Furlong and V. J. Edwards, although referring to British secondary classrooms, characterize our classrooms as well: "The theme is simply 'everybody listen.' For much of the time in classrooms, there is a *single* verbal encounter in which whatever is being said demands the attention of all" (11).

All of us recognize the truth in this, although the use of peer response groups and cooperative learning groups has brought about more varied voices in genuine dialogue. However, the perception still exists in many schools that a quiet classroom is a good classroom, that the appropriate role of the teacher is to speak and of the student to listen. This tradition may be linked to more than just respect for authority and for the teacher as the source of knowledge. Unfortunately, as Furlong and Edwards point out, teachers are judged by their ability "to keep [the class's] collective attention on the matter at hand" (12); that is, discipline is very much a part of classroom talk. Increased student interaction brings with it the threat of loss of control; therefore, some teachers prefer to control most of the talk. Furlong and Edwards put it this way: "Teachers usually tell pupils when to talk, what to talk about, when to stop talking, and how well they talked" (14). Or as Michael Stubbs, another British researcher, noted, "There is a sense in which, in our culture, teaching *is* talking" (12). Research supports this view. In a famous study of classrooms, Flanders learned that in the traditional "chalk and talk" classrooms, teachers talk about 70 percent of the time (cited in Stubbs 12).

A contemporary classroom must improve this ratio. In a classroom preparing students for a viable future, students would be involved in far more talk, both structured by the teacher and more informally. The teacher's role shifts from "dispenser of information" to "facilitator of learning." The curriculum also shifts from teacher-centered to student-centered, as the teacher plans activities in which work is no longer a solo, silent affair. Students interact with one another in pairs or small groups to share or pool information, provide feedback, and develop material together. A truly integrated language arts curriculum—one where listening, speaking, reading, and writing are part of nearly every lesson—demands student interaction. Although teachers structure such interaction by determining tasks and stipulating whether students should work in pairs or small groups, for example, teachers thereafter function as consultants. Most teachers "drift" around the room, spot-checking the work under way, relinquishing their traditional role as sole provider and controller of information.

Does this suggest that teachers should never lecture or lead discussions? Of course not! In fact, it is critical that we do so, modeling processes and questions that students need to internalize. The issue is one of ratio and balance between teacher talk and student talk. A related concern is classroom arrangements that facilitate more student interaction. The straight, orderly rows of desks seldom encourage interaction and genuine exchange. The flexibility to move into circles, pairs, or small groups is an important consideration of classroom space. Similarly, having a corner where students can curl up with a book or have access to a quiet space for quiet work is equally important.

Reflection

Think about talk, your high school, and you. What were the contexts in which "meaningful" talk took place? Why do you recall these and not others?

TALK AND CULTURAL DIFFERENCES

Differences between students' home language and the school language can be a critical factor in student achievement. As Courtney Cazden, professor emerita at Harvard, reminds us: "Ways of talking that seem so natural to one group are experienced as culturally strange to another" (67). School language is, in some ways, strange to all students. However, it is especially strange to students outside the mainstream culture. We need to be aware of this reality, observe our students, and find ways to facilitate their adaptation to this new culture, the mainstream classroom. Lisa Delpit, a researcher in language and literacy, notes: "All students deserve the right both to develop the linguistic skills they bring to the classroom and to add others to their repertoire" (264). Linguistic skills include not only syntax and grammar but also discourse style and language use. How we ask questions, give directions, listen, and interpret are culturally bound. As teachers, we must plan accordingly for an increasingly diverse classroom and ensure that no student is marginalized in the world of classroom discourse.

 ## TALK AND GENDER EQUITY

Research into classroom discourse and gender differences suggests that male students are the more frequent respondents—as well as the object of more frequent teacher response, both positive and negative. While we can cite examples to the contrary, we nonetheless must acknowledge a dominant pattern in mainstream classrooms and be aware of our own pattern of calling on and responding to our students. For a novice teacher, this may be a challenge because there are so many aspects of classroom management to analyze and confront. But failure to recognize the domination of either gender will have a negative effect overall, both for individuals and for the learning community in our classrooms.

Researchers have also found that teachers may fail to recognize or stop female students' tendency to make self-deprecating comments. For fear of appearing too tough on them, some teachers end up patronizing them, rather than forcefully rebutting such negative self-commentary. All students need to hear teachers attribute academic success to effort and ability, not to docile behavior, as has been the case with some females. At the same time, we should not overreact to male students' verbal one-upmanship or horseplay, which most often commands teacher attention. There are ways to quietly indicate "that's enough" without singling out either gender for punishment. We tend to teach as we have been taught; therefore, we need to be more conscious of how we acknowledge and respond to our male and female students, or risk continuing patterns of gender inequity that research has recently uncovered.

⟲ *Reflection* ⟲

Do you recall times in your secondary classrooms where race, ethnicity, or gender played a significant role in who talked and who listened? Where peers were included or excluded in small- or large-group discussion? Make a list of examples. Then compare verbal exchanges outside of the classroom (e.g., halls, lunch areas, school-sponsored events). What changed? Why?

LISTENING: NOT THE SAME AS HEARING

> *Listening is both the most used and the least understood of all communication arts.*
> Wisconsin Department of Public Instruction (1986, 67)

Considering the percentage of school time in which students are expected to be quiet and listen, we might assume they develop into good listeners. However, this is far from true. To begin with, there are many misconceptions about listening, the first being that listening cannot be taught. Listening can and should be taught, not through talking about listening skills but rather by engaging students in authentic communication. A second misconception is that listening and hearing are the same thing. Given the continual bombardment of "noise" in modern life, we can hardly blame students for tuning out. Nevertheless, as teachers we are responsible for teaching students the difference.

Another misconception is to confuse the statements "you're not listening" with "you don't agree with me; therefore, you're not listening." Parents and teachers often chastise students for not listening when what they mean is the students have rejected what they heard. The implication for the classroom is serious, for it concerns the integrity of speaking and listening as a shared experience. Sometimes we also fail to differentiate among the varying purposes of listening. There is, however, considerable difference between listening critically and listening aesthetically, for example.

Major Curricular Goals and Classroom Barriers

With awareness of general curricular goals in listening, we can structure lessons to include them. On the most basic level, students should be able to recognize the speaker's purpose, as well as their own in listening—whether to gain information, to analyze, or to appreciate aesthetically. Students must also be aware of the verbal and nonverbal cues that help them understand a verbal text. Their own role in providing feedback in both of these forms is similarly critical. The skill of giving *effective* feedback is learned.

Teachers must also be aware of barriers to effective listening. Unfamiliarity with the vocabulary, syntax, or content may be one cause; dialect and native language differences may be another, but *any* student may face barriers. A much more difficult situation occurs when students simply tune out when lessons involve complex content. Some students choose to not listen to ideas or explanations that demand their full attention. At other times, they may tune out a one-to-one exchange between a classmate and the teacher—and wait for the teacher to give the "real and true" answer. If classroom discourse is consistently recitation rather than discussion, students' "why bother?" attitudes may be justified. Others may stop listening when they don't agree; usually, they will be framing their rebuttal or preparing some sort of response before the speaker has completed his or her message. Adolescents can be sensitive to situations in which their words are ignored, so some straight talk about being fair might help.

Structuring classroom activities to encourage or compel students to listen is an important part of teaching listening skills. Although high-interest lessons capture students' attention, we must still consciously incorporate activities that develop good listening skills. Teaching purposeful listening involves two major activities: (1) listening to follow spoken directions and (2) listening to recognize the organization of spoken discourse. The latter is particularly important because students comprehend much better when they recognize the plan. For example, students who recognize cause and effect or comparison and contrast as the organizing principle will grasp the content far more efficiently. We enhance this ability by giving the students a plan for what they will hear: an overview and an explanation of new or difficult words or concepts in advance.

Listening to oral directions is, of course, a basic part of most classes. However, teachers tend to repeat directions too frequently, and students quickly learn they don't have to listen the first time. Without making an issue out of it, we can help students by not being so generous with repetition. For students who comprehend more slowly, we do need to make adjustments; however, this can usually be done individually as needed.

Listening as Process: Student Outcomes

Ideally, listening is part of student activities that involve the other language arts. The following listening skills are among the most important in curricular planning.

- Accurately remember significant details and simple sequences of words and ideas.
- Follow oral directions accurately.
- Accurately paraphrase an oral message.
- Follow a sequence in plot development, character development, and a speaker's argument.
- Understand both literal and connotative meanings.
- Understand meaning derived from a spoken context.
- Listen for significant details.
- Listen for main ideas.
- Distinguish between old and new material.

- Distinguish between relevant and irrelevant material.
- Predict outcomes.
- Draw conclusions.
- Identify and summarize main ideas.
- Relate the speaker's ideas and information to their own life. (Devine 5)

Students also need to develop critical listening skills. These skills are perhaps most associated with argument and persuasion; therefore, some curriculum guides list these skills as part of a unit dealing with media. However, students need sustained experience. Sara Lundsteen, professor of education at North Texas State University, notes the most important skills for students. Again notice that this list provides student outcomes.

- Using criteria, distinguish "fact from fancy."
- Judge the validity and adequacy of main ideas, arguments, and hypotheses.
- Distinguish well-supported statements from opinion and judgment.
- Evaluate the use of fallacies (e.g., self-contradiction, false analogy, failure to present all choices).
- Recognize emotional appeals and loaded words.
- Detect and evaluate speaker bias.
- Evaluate qualifications or credentials of the speaker.
- Recognize basic propaganda devices. (60–61)

These skills are, of course, linked to critical thinking. Thus, in devising ways in which students practice listening, teachers are also devising ways to promote higher-order thinking skills. As you plan lessons and units, then, you need to review these outcomes and ensure that students have structured ways in which to practice them.

 ## LISTENING: AN ESSENTIAL FOR GROUP WORK

Teachers offer mixed reviews on group work, along with many myths, but research findings on group work and cooperative learning are generally positive. Virginia O'Keefe, a communications education instructor, provides some reasons:

> Group work produces more actively engaged, task-oriented behavior than when students work alone on "seatwork." The struggling student profits from an interactive situation where he or she receives feedback from peers. And, students at all achievement levels benefit from the opportunity to "rehearse" new concepts as they talk through problems.
>
> Social cooperation increases as students learn more about each other. They reveal their achievements . . . [and] also admit their vulnerabilities—dropping out of football, failing typing, not winning a debate tournament, and losing parents through

death or divorce. That kind of information may not seem relevant to language arts, but those same human experiences are ultimately the stuff of any literary text. (91)

We know from our experience with composition classes that what O'Keefe says is true: Students help one another, find a comfortable niche despite (or because of) mixed abilities, and share both academic and personal ups and downs. As a result, their writing is far richer, as is the class overall, because student cohesion results from sustained group work. A critical factor in this achievement is listening.

As O'Keefe puts it: "Improving our relations with others really begins with listening" (91). As we have already pointed out, we listen for different purposes. But regardless of our purpose, we can improve listening through nonverbal behavior, which is critical to the success of working groups. O'Keefe lists the attributes of good listening behavior:

- maintaining natural eye contact
- nodding head in agreement
- leaning forward
- adopting a pleasant facial expression
- facing the speaker(s)
- keeping arms open (not folded)
- taking position at the same elevation as the speaker (91)

She goes on to note that "if these nonverbal behaviors are choreographed for effect without sincerity, they will have the opposite effect" (91). Kids are especially good at ferreting out nonverbal behavior that doesn't mesh with the speaker or the message, but we also need to "school" them to the importance of nonverbal behavior. Otherwise, they may send unintentional negative messages and impair group relationships.

Whether it is small- or large-group work, students should face one another, preferably in a circle where eye contact is easily gained. And they should learn to give verbal signals, such as a simple nod of the head or a smile, to show they are attending to the speaker. If appropriate, taking notes is another way to signal interest in the speaker's ideas, as is avoiding some listening distractions.

We agree with O'Keefe that "active listening requires conscious effort"—and that the skills and behaviors are indeed teachable (92). But we must see listening both as part of ongoing classroom discourse and a curricular focus.

To improve students' group work, we can provide tangible instructional strategies for listening well:

1. *Be prepared:* Have pens, paper, and materials at hand and have assignments read in advance. For example, if students are dividing up some research, they need to arrive at the group with a sense of the parameters of that research and be ready to discuss their interests and potential tasks. If they are working through a literary text, they need to read it before class.
2. *Set goals:* Plan how group information will be used when students are working on their own. Students need to set a purpose for their listening. If

they know that they will have to depend on what they take away from their group, their motivation will likely increase.

3. *Use time well:* Human beings think three or four times faster than they speak, so we process messages quickly—faster than a speaker sends the words. What happens in the gap? Mostly distracting thoughts! Students need to recognize this phenomenon and have some strategies to use the gap productively (e.g., take notes, write out questions, reorder information, or find patterns in what is being said).

4. *Minimize distractions:* Students react quickly to all kinds of distractions, whether it is a wasp or a word laden with emotional impact. Teaching them the power of "high blood pressure" words is part of teaching them to be listeners. They need to recognize and control their emotional responses; if they don't, the intellect is turned off. Then they get an argument rather than a discussion. Similarly, kids need to know that developing counter-arguments at the same time they are still receiving the message is counterproductive. Remind them how they feel when their parents or teachers appear not to listen or are too ready with a response.

5. *Avoid evaluation:* Although there is a place for evaluative listening and response, such as when someone makes a claim without sufficient support, evaluative listening should be the last part of a process, not the first. That is, students should not say things like "that's dumb" or "it'll never work" in the group. Again, remind them how they feel when their ideas are greeted with such responses.

6. *Use feedback:* Verbal or nonverbal feedback is how a speaker knows group members listened and got the message. Nonverbal feedback, such as smiles, nodding of the head, or laughter, is effective in signaling "understood." Verbal feedback may be a simple "okay" or it may be a question, paraphrase, or request for clarification. Even negative responses, such as "no" or "maybe," provide evidence of listening. (O'Keefe 92–94)

Preparing students to listen, then, is part of the process. Just placing them into groups and telling them to get to work usually results in little work—and leads many teachers to abandon group work altogether. There is, however, more to this process than providing information on how to listen. Understanding how groups should be formed, structured, and conducted is also critical to success.

⁓ *Reflection* ⁓

In our methods courses, we have heard students complain about group work in other classes. It is with some trepidation, then, that many approach our first major task: form a group and develop a unit collaboratively. How would you characterize your group experiences, especially where a major (and graded) project is involved? Note why your group was or was not successful. What did you learn about yourself in the process of being a group member (e.g., liked to lead, didn't quite trust partners, liked hearing so many ideas)?

MAKING GROUP WORK EFFECTIVE

Forming Groups

Group work is essentially oral work, and as such, it is vital experience for young people. Whether they pursue some type of post-secondary education or go right into the workforce, they need to know how to work with others. This ability to work cooperatively and effectively depends largely on both oral language and social skills. Some students will be more comfortable than others in group work, depending on personality and learning style, but all students need regular group experience.

A question most teachers face when planning group work is how to construct the groups: Should students choose their own group members? Should the teacher assign them? Should groups be of mixed ability or homogeneous? Should groups be balanced by gender, race, or other considerations? Research findings on these questions are mixed when high-ability students are considered, but the research findings concerning lower-ability students are consistent. Heterogeneous groups benefit less-able students. Explanations from peers improve their understanding, and the more skilled question/answer processes of higher-ability students provide good models and cues. Additionally, research supports group work as especially good for students from cultural backgrounds where shared discussion and work are the norm.

Gender can affect how groups work, so teachers need to consider what research and classroom experience have revealed: boys tend to talk whereas girls tend to listen, question, and support. Some girls, as noted earlier in this chapter, tend to be verbally subservient and thus may take non-speaking roles in group work; others may be subjected to verbal harassment and shut down completely. That is not to suggest that such harassment doesn't happen to boys. With either gender, such linguistic behavior is unacceptable. What can we do about it? We can talk about gender differences in linguistic behavior, making students aware that there is such a thing. We could also form same-sex groups for some projects. However, building a classroom community, a safe place, from the first day of the semester will go a long way in avoiding gender communication issues.

Groups can be formed in rather spontaneous ways, depending on the type of classroom activity that is planned. If a small group is needed for buzz sessions, brainstorming, or similar all-class projects, then counting off will work fine. If students need to devise or respond to questions, or to plan some activity or response, working in twos might be best, especially if you want to ensure full participation. Some teachers let students choose their partners; later, the teacher will assign two pairs as a foursome. This method is a comfortable way of introducing students to small-group work and active participation.

Another method of grouping is a natural for class projects with multiple topics of interest or inquiry. Students select and list their choice of topics; they also list three classmates with whom they would like to work. They are then told that they will receive either one topic from their list or one person of their choice—and perhaps more. Because students participate in the selection process, they usually respond well to the work to follow.

For whole-class activities such as brainstorming or single-class projects, students can count off into groups. For responding and devising questions or planning, dyads often work well and offer some assurance that students fully participate. From dyads, forming larger groups is easy: Two pairs become a group of four. If the number of pairs is uneven, one group could have more students, but three to five students per group is preferable.

Teaching Students to be Group Members

Working with small groups in a classroom does not come naturally to most students. Even adults usually work in groups only when they share similar interests and goals, and then it takes time for people to become comfortable with others in the group. In a classroom setting, students may experience similar discomfort and must learn and apply behaviors that foster cooperation. Without some training and a firm structure for their group work, they will flounder—mainly because groups must be self-directed, a skill that requires planning and monitoring.

Experienced teachers suggest using preliminary activities that will bring out the individual interests and talents of each group member or engage them in shared creative responses—in brief, activities for sheer fun. For example, in small groups, students write the last names of every teacher they can remember. They then pool their lists and arrange the names into a rhythmic pattern, later "chanting" the list for the entire class. One enterprising group we know delighted classmates by aligning their teacher list with "Twinkle, Twinkle Little Star" and singing it for us. Another activity that works well is similar to an old elementary ritual, Show and Tell. Each group member brings an object that has significance for him or her and explains why to the group. We've seen everything from a tattered teddy emerging from a backpack to a locket belonging to a cherished grandmother, a dog-eared photo and a dog collar without its owner, a pair of well-worn athletic shoes and a pair of equally worn ballet slippers. One student even brought a bottle of insulin and explained to her classmates that she was dependent on it. In every case, the groups learned something important about each of its members. Many resources exist for group activities—the key is to use them.

If providing students with preliminary activities is a key ingredient to group success, equally so are clear, specific objectives and directions for group work. These include everything from establishing time limits to expecting a product from the group. Depending on the complexity of the project and the length of the class period, groups might work anywhere between 15 and 30 minutes. Whatever the time period, teachers need to establish it and stick to it; otherwise, staying on task may become a game of avoidance and delay. Some students may need specific roles within the group: a discussion leader, a recorder, a reporter, and a manager of notes and materials. Another way of looking at specific roles is to divide them into those contributing to the task product and those that maintain group interaction and dynamics. For example, the group would need at least one student who is knowledgeable about the topic or task and another who has good people skills and can reconcile differences or bring humor to the group. Another group member might have fine analytic or synthesizing skills, and yet another might be a detail person, someone capable of taking good notes. In the beginning of the semester, assigning roles is probably wise. Later, as students become accustomed to group work, they can set more of the roles and rules themselves. Moreover, they will know the strengths of their group and, assuming rapport, use those strengths to get the task done. All of this depends, however, on the task being worthwhile. If students see no reason for it, no group will work well.

Before any group work begins, students need direct instruction on asking questions, summarizing, paraphrasing, offering constructive criticism, and providing positive feedback. They also need to learn how to deal with classmates who monopolize or dominate the group. A session in which you ask the kids to identify good speaking and listening habits can get at the problems likely to occur in any group of adolescents. If there is conflict within a group, you may need to intervene; if you see more than one group having similar problems, you need to stop group work, discuss what is happening and why, and reteach group processes as needed.

Finally, requiring a product at the end of each group work period will help keep students focused on the task. The product can be as simple as the answer to a question, a list of things to be done, a suggestion, a scratch outline, or questions to be pursued. Early in the semester, you may need to be specific about the product; later, students may come up with various products, depending on the nature of the project itself.

EXPLORATION

Analyzing Group Tasks

Example 1
As you know from Chapter 3, Steve Wisner developed a group project based in technology for his unit on World War I literature. We are repeating this group assignment here; we want you to examine it from a different perspective. As you read Steve's directions to a twelfth-grade class, make a list of the oral and social skills needed to complete this project successfully. Which skills do you think will be most critical?

REALITY POSTERS

Propaganda posters were an interesting element of World War I. The governments of the countries involved seemed to sense that people needed to be convinced that the war was necessary. All of the major countries involved in the war produced propaganda posters; however, none of the countries felt than an accurate description of their foe or the conditions at the front would be very compelling. As such, they tended to turn the enemy into an abstraction and their soldiers into heroic, willing combatants. Each side, through propaganda, made the other out to be monsters.

Your assignment is to use these posters to set the record straight. Using a computer scanner and Photoshop software, your group will scan a chosen poster and alter the text to reflect reality instead of propaganda.

Look through the books of propaganda posters and choose one to alter. Your alteration will be limited to changing the text. The process will work best if your poster has the text written over a single background color rather than an image, mainly because you will destroy some background when you remove text and repairing damage is easier with a single color.

Instructions for scanning, removing existing text, repairing background, and inserting your "corrected" text are printed on each computer. Our computer staff and peer experts are on hand to help. Once you have completed your changes, print your "Reality Poster" on the color printer. When the entire class has finished, we will discuss the posters and your reasons for the changes your group made. Good luck—and dazzle me!

Example 2

As noted earlier, group products may be small and limited, part of the on-going daily work within a unit. Here is a small poster task developed by methods students working with *To Kill a Mockingbird*. Again, note the oral and group skills needed to complete this assignment.

EXPLORING PERSONAL AND SOCIETAL ATTITUDES

In your group, use 10 minutes to individually find quotations that show characters' attitudes toward one another or society's "attitude" in general. Share your ideas with your group. Then, as a group, use your poster board to write five quotations that you believe illustrate an important attitude in this novel. We will hang the poster boards around the room, using them to chart how attitudes may or may not change throughout the novel. In the final 10 minutes of class, each group will present its poster board.

Example 3

Small-group discussion tasks may be as simple as this one, but the key element is direction; students know what to do and have the tools to do it. Here is an example from a student unit, again using *To Kill A Mockingbird*. Comment on the clarity of directions in this example. Also comment on the oral and group skills needed for this work.

In the chapters you have just read, Jem and Scout ponder how Tom Robinson could be convicted of a crime he did not commit. On page 226, however, Jem tells Scout that he has it all figured out:

There's four kinds of folks in the world. There's the ordinary kind like us and the neighbors, there's the kind like the Cunninghams out in the woods, the kind like the Ewells down at the dump, and the Negroes . . . The thing is, our kind of folks don't like the Cunninghams, the Cunninghams don't like the Ewells, and the Ewells hate and despise the colored folks.

With your discussion partners, figure out what sets each of these groups apart: Why do they have a "need" to dislike one another? Think about reasons for social oppression (e.g., social or economic class, race, education, gender). One person should act as group scribe, writing your group's ideas on a transparency for our class discussion.

Example 4

This group task, for eleventh graders, is challenging but clearly directed. What skills will the eleventh graders need or develop?

A River Runs Through It ends with one of my favorite paragraphs in the English language:

> *Eventually, all things merge into one, and a river runs through it. The river was cut by the world's great flood and runs over rocks from the basement of time. On some of the rocks are timeless raindrops. Under the rocks are the words, and some of the words are theirs. I am haunted by waters.*

As much as I [methods student Steve Wisner] love this passage, I am not entirely sure I understand exactly what it means. What are the words and who is the "they" referred to by "some of the words are theirs." And why is the author "Haunted by waters"? Take 10 minutes to write individually about what you think this passage means. Then meet up with your group and compare responses. Make a list of all the similarities among group members' individual responses. See if there are enough similarities to write a three-paragraph group interpretation. If this is not possible, write three-paragraphs summarizing the different ways in which group members interpreted the passage. Whatever the result, I will ask each group to present their results to the class.

EXPLORATION

Creating a Group Task

With a partner, develop a small-group task around this passage from *To Kill a Mockingbird*, where Atticus Finch tells his daughter Scout a way to live her life.

If you can learn a simple trick, Scout, you'll get along a lot better with all kinds of folks. You never understand a person until you consider things from his point of view . . . until you can climb into his skin and walk around in it.

Before you design the task itself, list the oral and group skills (the student outcomes) that you want students to learn or enhance through doing it. Also note the "product"—oral or written or both—that will result from the group's discussion and work together. Then, design the procedures that will get them there.

 ## SPEAKING: MORE THAN JUST TALK

Speaking is a process, not a series of episodes, units, or courses.

Wisconsin Department of Public Instruction (1986, 90)

Speaking has most often been perceived as "something the speech teacher takes care of," rather than as one of the major strands of the English language arts curriculum. Consequently, in many school districts, a curriculum for speaking translates into a single speech course. When this occurs, speaking is essentially isolated from conscious attention in the development of daily lessons and units in English classrooms. However, speaking is essential in all language arts classes, not only for its own sake but also because it influences the development of other language arts competencies.

Major Curricular Goals

As a curricular area, speaking parallels writing in important ways. Like writing, speaking must be purposeful, serving an authentic communicative need geared to audience and context.

The major goals of the speaking curriculum revolve around five communicative functions:

- expressive (express or respond to feelings and attitudes)
- ritualistic or formulaic (culturally determined, responsive to patterns of social interaction)
- imaginative (storytelling, dramatizing, speculating, theorizing)
- informative (stating, questioning, explaining)
- persuasive (convincing, arguing, justifying, rejecting)

The first goal, of course, is that students learn to speak effectively in all five functions. This does not mean that teachers should develop units around them; rather, the goal should be an integrated language arts curriculum in which all four language arts are present in daily lessons. For example, students may be reading novels as part of a unit. Although we would expect and plan for discussion, we would also consciously build in questions and activities that focus specifically on one or more of the speech functions. Asking students to speculate on plot, imagine future character development, or to justify a character's action are different speech functions. Asking students to choose a scene for dramatizing or to write and then perform a scene using characters from the novel draws once more on different language competencies. If we keep the competencies in mind when we plan unit activities, we can be reasonably sure that our speaking curriculum is balanced.

As we plan classroom activities, we also need to consider the different levels of audience—from pairs to small groups to the whole class. Students need varied experiences in developing speaking competencies and audience awareness. Some students may be comfortable in pairs but not in front of an entire class; others may feel inadequate in group work. Without consistent experience in all types of speaking situations, they might not develop a level of comfort that will serve them well as adults. Another related goal is competency and comfort among diverse racial and ethnic groups. Teachers fortunate enough to have a diverse student population find that cultural differences in speaking and listening can be easily identified and discussed. Lacking such diversity, we must find ways to increase student awareness of the cultural base of language. All languages express the five communicative functions, but how they do so is a matter of culture.

It might be argued that if students are engaging in these various functions through conversation alone, there is no need to place them in the curriculum. The problem is that student talk *is* culture-bound and, equally important, is not the talk of academic discourse. Moreover, students will not necessarily extend or evaluate talk, or ask good questions, or consider the significance of a message. They are not quick to determine the presence or lack of evidence or evaluate a line of reasoning. Nor are they necessarily aware of language strategies, such as those in argumentation and persuasion, or able to evaluate strategies for social acceptability and civic responsibility. These are critical competencies in a modern, democratic society. We also have another important role: teaching students the responsibility inherent in freedom of speech. Freedom of speech is one of the United States' most cherished values; however, it can be abused. Students need to understand the difference between the right to express an opinion and the "non-right" to verbally abuse, defame, or denigrate another human being.

All students, regardless of ability level, need classroom experience in speaking. All too often, speaking opportunities and training appear only in honors classes or advanced placement, where teachers view students as future leaders. However, "talk is as essential to thought as exercise is to health" (O'Keefe 15). From this perspective, talk must be at the center of the English language arts classroom. Unfortunately, teachers trained in English language arts generally lack training in oral language; moreover, student textbooks provide little assistance. The occasional discussion section at the end of a reading selection or chapter leaves the teacher trying to figure out how to initiate, maintain, and close a good discussion. But without planned "talk" for students, teachers tend to monopolize classroom talk—a situation that negates a student-centered classroom and integration of all the language arts into units and lessons.

IMPROVING DISCUSSION QUESTIONS

Jane Schaffer gives us a candid appraisal of her skill as a novice teacher:

> In my earlier days, I remember asking such inane questions as, "What about the river in *Huckleberry Finn?*" and then becoming irritated when students did not respond. I figured they had not done their homework or were not really trying hard enough. I look at this question now and understand several problems with it. (40)

Consider this principle for classroom discussion: Students need to care about the questions. They aren't going to care about questions that are simply a test of whether they read the assignment, nor do such questions advance their thinking or oral language skills. Too often, questions at the end of textbook selections are useless, mainly because they are mini-tests of the worst sort—they call for facts that students can locate in the text. Such questions are mindless and boring. Mainstream students are accustomed to such questions, but non-mainstream students may be baffled by why teachers want them to answer something the teachers already know. As Shirley Brice Heath's *Ways With Words* illustrates, in many cultures adults don't ask questions to which they already know the answer. We need to figure out what kinds of questions will interest and make sense to students.

Most students respond to questions that relate the material to their own lives. The idea is not to infringe on their privacy, but to link themes or ideas to the contemporary situations faced by adolescents or young adults. Joy F. Moss suggests this type of question to draw students into reflection on their own life experience:

> Do you think this [story, event] could really happen?

The trick, of course, is to be specific enough, and at the same time, non-threatening. To answer "could it really happen," students ultimately are drawing on their own experience, but are saved from personal revelations.

Students also respond well to interpretative questions for which they know there is no right or wrong answer, where they know their genuine response counts. Again Moss suggests a general prompt:

> How did you feel about this character's behavior? Why did you think this character behaved the way he or she did? Clues?
>
> What did you find that was surprising, puzzling, or disturbing about the characters or events in this story?
>
> As the story unfolded, did you change your mind about specific characters? (68–69)

An excellent way to make students better respondents to interpretive questions is to train them to write the questions themselves. Schaffer suggests requiring students to address topics they really want to discuss and to ask for three questions per student. The teacher would then choose several for discussion, dictate them to the class, and allow students time to think about their responses (40). Allowing time for reflection is another critical feature of good discussions. We often tend to avoid silence and call on the first student to respond, thus cutting off thinking time and recognizing the same students too frequently.

Another feature of good discussion is planned closure. All of us have experienced classes where discussion was suddenly cut off in midstream because the class had run out of time. Because we cannot truly re-create the discussion later, it is better to plan for closure. Stopping 5 or 10 minutes before the end of the hour and asking students to summarize, either orally or on paper, is one method. Another is asking them to describe what they learned during that discussion using specific and well-focused comments. Students could also write one question that had not been answered in the discussion (Schaffer 41). All of these activities require good listening skills. For this reason, we cannot initially expect very complete or very good responses, but responses will improve with experience and the knowledge that our request is genuine.

In addition to personal experience or interpretive questions, we need to train students to support their responses by citing references to the text. This is a critical skill, the one most lacking in American students according to National Assessment of Educational Progress reports in the past decade. In order to answer questions such as these, students would have to give specific examples from the text:

How did the author make the characters and events believable?

Do you think the author revealed his or her own attitudes? biases? opinions?

Moss believes that "the art of teaching is, in large part, the art of asking significant, well-timed questions," but she also cautions that "too many questions can turn the enjoyment of literary exploration and discovery into the drudgery of meaningless drill" (78). We have seen this happen. A teacher we knew chose wonderful young adult novels for her eighth graders, only to destroy their enjoyment through an "answer these 20 questions" approach with each novel. The students dutifully filled out the identical list of questions, novel after novel, missing the heart of the novels and any thread of active participation through significant and well-timed questions.

Reflection

Returning to Schaffer's question about *Huck Finn*, you can easily detect her reasons for calling it "inane." Just what *is* wrong with it? How would you initiate a whole-class discussion on *Huck Finn*?

CLASSROOM STRATEGIES FOR FOSTERING AUTHENTIC DISCUSSION

Too often, teachers lead discussions that are really recitations: The teacher asks a question, and a student responds; the teacher asks the next question, and another student responds. The rest of the class remains passive, most not even listening. Many textbooks, unfortunately, reinforce this teacher-centered model through the questions at the end of the reading or chapter.

As Nancy Rost Goulden points out, "Perhaps the first rule of a fully participatory classroom is that the teacher will not depend exclusively on volunteers in class discussion" (92). Setting up a pattern of full participation is the teacher's responsibility, and students will soon learn that they are expected to do more than sit quietly throughout the class period. However, as Goulden also notes, students need help in preparing their response, whether it is in a small- or large-group format. Giving students a few minutes to think about the topic, write some notes to themselves, and thus organize their ideas is a good strategy. She suggests that students use a claim–support pattern, where they "jot down a phrase or sentence that summarizes their answer and then map out the support for this central response claim" (92). Early in the year, a good strategy to involve students can be found in those little pads of sticky notes. Each student has a small sticky note, and as the teacher reads a poem or a short passage of fiction or nonfiction, students record their thoughts, deliberately kept brief, on the sticky note. With no discussion, students then put their sticky notes on the chalkboard, where they will be read silently as students rotate among them. When students return to their seats, they should be ready to discuss their ideas and those of their classmates. Since no sticky note is signed, students feel relatively free to talk about ideas.

If students have been in classrooms where either the teacher or a few assertive classmates have carried the discussion, they may be reluctant speakers initially. However, once they realize that you are going to insist on full participation, give them time and strategies to prepare for it, and truly value their response, most will become comfortable. Becoming comfortable with their own voices and ideas lays the groundwork not only for discussion but also for more formal speaking activities. Goulden argues that the total amount of time devoted to speaking doesn't have to change—only the pattern, a shift from limited to full participation (93).

Authentic and sustained opportunities for speaking arise when teachers plan them as a matter of course throughout the year. *English Journal* featured some of these teachers, and their good ideas for student discussion are easily adapted for both middle and high schoolers.

Personal Response, Small Group, Large Group

Wilbur H. Sowder Jr., a teacher at Ridgefield Park, New Jersey, found that techniques developed in his Advanced Placement (AP) English class also work well for his average seventh graders. Sowder uses reading journals (personal response to reading and discussion) as the basis for small-group response. For example, he began a discussion of Zindel's *The Pigman* with a 15-minute journal writing on "Pigmen I have known." Students shared their journal entries with their circle of four or five classmates. Then, as Sowder tells it, from across the room he heard a student read:

> My grandmother had old-timer's disease for six years, and she walked around as if she were searching for a special god. (39)

Sowder noted that the student's entire circle snapped to attention with that line. And that line was the springboard to a whole-class discussion on family relations and the death of a loved one. The progression Sowder followed—individual thinking and response, to focused group discussion, to whole-class discussion—is a good one, regardless of age group or piece of literature. In AP English, Sowder removed the final word, *death,* from T. S. Eliot's "Journey of the Magi" and asked students to complete the poem. Because Sowder uses a reader response approach, the groups are actively engaged and not worried about a "right" response. Later, he gave the class Adrienne Rich's "Living in Sin," without the final image. He found student response so intense that he scrapped plans for only 10 minutes of group discussion. Sowder believes, "A reader cannot seriously attempt to choose the final word for 'Journey of the Magi' or 'Living in Sin' without integrating the poet's ideas and images, without evoking the world of the poem" (40). Benefits of this methodology extend to the teacher. Says Sowder:

> I rely on student ideas, questions, and even misconceptions to promote group and class discussion. I'm becoming a better reader and a better teacher as I learn to see literature through students' eyes. I'd rather respond to their ideas than ask them to grapple with mine. Above all, I want them to be active. (41)

Sowder's success with everything from Hinton's *The Outsiders* to Kafka's *The Metamorphosis* rests on his determination to make students the center of his classroom:

> If I devise thought-provoking, open-ended activities, student momentum often carries discussion further than I ever did in a teacher-centered classroom. I now spend a lot of time preparing questions: unexpected questions, puzzling questions. Questions that ask students to examine their own lives and read literature with a purpose. The students have become the center of my classroom, and I wouldn't have it any other way. (42)

The Fishbowl

In another New Jersey high school, Haddonfield, other teachers are finding similar success. Terry Willis's eleventh graders have taken on *Macbeth* and through a "fishbowl" strategy, are having animated, informed discussions (Bolche 30). Classroom chairs are arranged in a "fishbowl," two circles, one inside the other. As students enter the room, Willis assigns students to one circle. The inner circle is then given about eight minutes to discuss the statement: "Men who have been on the battlefield may come home to act like criminals in time of peace." Students are told to relate this statement both to *Macbeth* and contemporary life—an idea that they have already explored in their journals. The ground rules are simple: State an idea and support it with evidence; agree with the speaker and add additional evidence; disagree with a speaker and offer evidence.

Each student in the outer circle spends the eight minutes listening to the discussion and making notes on the interaction of their "fish." Willis provides students with a worksheet to make note-taking easier and more precise:

> Throughout the discussion, students tally each time their "fish" contributes an idea, describes feelings, paraphrases, expresses support or acceptance, encourages others to contribute, summarizes, relieves tension by joking, or gives direction to the group's work. (Bolche 43)

Willis notes that students in the inner circle treat each other with courtesy. What's more, "the positive, enthusiastic acknowledgement of peers has a certain magical quality" (Bolche 43). After eight minutes, students exchange places, those in the inner circle become observers in the outer ring, and those in the outer ring become the inner ring "discussers" of a second focus statement. At the end of class, students reflect on the fishbowl as a discussion strategy. In Willis's experience, students have enthusiastically endorsed it, perhaps for the same reason that teachers employ it: "The best part of this fishbowl is a controlled free-for-all—a spontaneous explosion of ideas with nothing held back—exciting and argumentative" (Bolche 43).

Creative Controversy

Just down the hall at Haddonfield High School, Marilyn Lee Mauger's tenth graders are studying *The Crucible* through a cooperative group technique (Bolche 90). Mauger divides the class into groups of four, and within the foursome, students are paired. Each pair has to build a case, taking opposite positions on the dilemma faced by John Procter in Act IV. For homework, students use the text to build evidence for their positions; in class, the pairs integrate ideas and evidence into a coherent position. Mauger then has each pair separate and consult others who prepared the same position. Following this sharing, students return to their own partners, assimilating new ideas. The next class period, each group presents its positions. While one pair is presenting, the other pair takes notes. They then ask clarifying questions, request further evidence, and openly challenge one another: "Book pages fly, bodies lean forward, and voices are raised in earnest excitement" (qtd. in Bolche 44).

Mauger notes that following this rather intense discussion, each pair prepares "for what might be the most interesting and challenging phase of this creative controversy—perspective reversals" (qtd. in Bolche 44). As they switch positions, students have to add at least two new pieces of evidence for the argument, and present the new positions the following class period. Finally, they drop advocacy and strive to reach a consensus. For the final task, the foursome presents its decision to the class through oral presentations, written statements, and visual displays. As with most authentic discussion, students are enthusiastic about their experience with this strategy. As one of them said: "It was much more helpful to hear the views of classmates rather than just listen to the teacher" (qtd. in Bolche 44). In a student-centered classroom, such views would be the norm, not the exception.

Teach Each Other: Guided Instruction in Group Participation

Margo Sorenson, an eighth-grade teacher from Harbor Day School in Corona del Mar, California, has found "the open-discussion method energizes the classroom and stimulates me to encourage students to challenge themselves" (43). Colleagues report her method has been successful at every grade level between fifth and twelfth and with students of all ability levels. Sorenson teaches the format in one class period, beginning with questions about student–teacher discussions. Students readily relate their history with traditional class discussions: boring; never learn anything; teacher does all the talking; a couple of smart kids do all the answering. Sorenson then explains the format and expectations for a discussion unlike those just described. Students will be the center of discussion and will in fact teach one another. At the same time, she explains a bit of reader response to them, emphasizing there are no right or wrong opinions as long as opinions are supported with details from the readings.

Three rules exist for open discussion:

Courtesy

Participation grades depend on contributions, and each comment receives a check mark, regardless of its merit. Each student calls on another student, with raised hand and a finger signal to indicate if it is the first or second entry into the discussion. Students are expected to keep track of participation and ensure that those who have spoken little or not at all become participants. To encourage silent students, Sorenson teaches the class to do the following:

1. Alert the student who will be called on first by stating that student's name.
2. Give an opinion so the student to be called on has something to react to.
3. Ask about the stated opinion.

Sorenson says, "This procedure ensures that no students are caught mentally flat-footed in discussion . . . and promotes the belief that the students really are engaged in helping each other learn" (44).

Don't Look at the Teacher!

Sorenson tells her students that she will not show approval or disapproval, nor will she contribute or ask questions unless it is essential that she clarify some point. She explains that they are a community of learners, teaching one another, and that includes her—and that each year she gains insights and new approaches to literature through her eighth graders.

Tolerate Silence

Explaining that thinking takes time and silence is fine, Sorenson again places leadership within the student group:

> When the discussion on a particular question seems to have ended and no one has anything more to say, or when comments are becoming repetitive, any one of the students may ask, "Are we done? Shall we go on to another question?" Students manage their own discussion and end it when they want. (44)

However, Sorenson also helps students with "food for thought" by providing discussion cue sheets. The cue sheets serve as a reminder of thoughts and questions that might otherwise be fleeting:

- What did you like about the previous contribution?
- What new ideas did that contribution give you?
- What puzzled you in that last statement?
- What in the last statement had not occurred to you before?
- How did the person making the statement arrive at that conclusion?
- Can you elaborate, explain, or give another example? (44)

Sorenson also asks students to do some self-evaluation in their journals, using these questions to help them consider their contributions before another discussion:

- Did I contribute to the discussion?
- Did I encourage others to contribute or clarify ideas?
- What would I like to do in the next discussion?
- How can I do this?
- Who contributed the most interesting or valuable comments?
- Who was the Most Valuable Player in keeping the discussion going?
- Who encouraged me the most in discussion? (44)

As further incentive, Sorenson gives some "silly reward" to students named by peers, like a "little gummed gold star (which they promptly stick on their shirts or noses for the rest of the day) or a crazy rubber stamp on the back of their hands and in their spirals" (45). She has found the process "does wonders for motivating students to recognize each other's contributions and do well enough to be nominated next time by one of their peers" (45).

Preparation for discussion begins with journal writes, perhaps responses to some open-ended questions about the literature or developing their own questions. These form the basis of the student-led discussion. Sorenson reports that "the teacher's hardest job is often to be quiet when a 'right' answer seems so obvious and let the students be accountable for their own investigation and inquiry—to teach each other" (46). She also notes that patience pays off as students become more experienced with the format: Insights are deeper, note-taking becomes common, listening habits improve. Students also become skilled at monitoring themselves and capable of assessing when too many similar comments are made or discussion is off track.

Through this discussion method, students make significant gains in oral and analytic skills. These in turn transfer to better writing about literature. Perhaps the most significant aspect of the method lies in students' initiative and responsibility for their own learning—at the core of a student-centered classroom where students build self-esteem and confidence through sustained experience with oral language and an integrated language arts approach.

TALKING ABOUT LITERATURE

Whether using traditional or contemporary literature, teachers can structure oral language activities that provide a scaffolding for substantive and stimulating discussion. In the model activities to follow, notice that the teacher is facilitator, not "dominator." And in most cases, the teacher, having structured the activity, becomes an observer.

Small-Group Activities for *The Giver*

As a popular and powerful young-adult novel, *The Giver* provides students with rich thematic material for thinking and discussion. The following activities intertwine written and oral language skills, but, as used here, writing serves the development of good oral discussion. Through structured discussion activities, students can explore all major literary elements of the novel and relate important themes to their lives.

A. Write for five minutes on one of the following. Then discuss in small group for five minutes. Repeat the cycle.
- Everything in life is a trade-off.
- What's right with Jonas's society?
- What's wrong with Jonas's society?
- Can the "release" be considered a humane act?

B. Write a brief dialogue; then, with your partner or your group, enact it.
- An interview with author Lois Lowry.
- A discussion between you and Jonas.
- A discussion between you and Jonas's father.
- A discussion between you and The Elder/The Giver.

C. Fill in the "what if?" Then, with your group, categorize the "what if" by character, and discuss (e.g., everything that pertains to Jonas, everything that pertains to his father).
- How would you feel about _____ if _____?
- How would you react to _____ if _____?
- If you were _____, what would you do about _____?

D. Imagine that you are one of the characters in *The Giver*. As that character, write three questions [choose one of the situations below]. Be sure to use the language, tone, and so on, that are appropriate for this character.
- To the author about the way this character behaves or is treated.
- To another character about his or her attitudes or behavior.
- To the reader of this novel about his or her reaction to this character.

Pass your questions to your group partners, going to your left. Each person will answer and pass the questions on, again to the left. When the original writer has his or her questions back, discuss both the questions and the responses. Finally, each group will report to the class as a whole.

E. Select one character who intrigues you. Create a one-minute monologue to tell this character what you think or how you feel about an issue or idea that he or she raises. Then create a one-minute monologue for this character to talk back to you. What helps or hinders you from saying what you really think? What helps or hinders you from taking the viewpoint of the other character? Form groups based on your choice of character, read your monologues and discuss commonalties and differences.

F. Pick one character from *The Giver* and answer the following questions.
- Why did I choose this character?
- What information do I want to obtain about this character?
- Why do I want to know this? Why does it matter to me?
- What questions will I ask my character?

Compare your responses with those of others who have chosen the same character.

G. On your own, generate at least one question that you would like answered about this novel (e.g., Why did the Giver accept his life without question?). Bring the question to your group for discussion. Small-group work can, of course, lead to whole-class discussion. Usually, students come well-prepared for the large group since they have had the chance to try out their ideas. A mix of small- and large-group discussion about the novel will sustain readers throughout the novel, encouraging more students to understand and comment on important ideas and themes.

Large-Group Activities for *The Giver*

Making Themes Tangible
Provide students with simple art materials and ask them to paint an image of a telling moment in the novel (e.g., something they consider important, disturbing, memorable). Then take them through this process:

- Ask students to create a title for their image, writing it on a separate sheet of paper.
- Have students share the image and title orally with classmates.
- Collect the titles, and as a class, have students put them into a poetic form reflecting the novel. Each person should suggest at which point his or her title is most effectively added.
- Read the poem aloud. Negotiate changes the class believes would improve the poem in terms of impact, rhythm, and so on.
- Reflect on the process. What themes emerged? What happens to individual ideas when all titles are merged into one piece? Do new ideas about a title emerge from seeing it as part of a new and larger whole? Does the poem "work"? What happens in the process of collaboration and negotiation?

In a similar exercise involving art, collaboration, and negotiation, students create a class quilt based on themes in *The Giver*. The following process is suggested by Nancy King (26–27).

- Write: On a small piece of paper, a memory that Jonas should receive. Don't sign your name.
- Pass: Place it in the box. Shake the box to jumble all the papers. Then take one paper out (not your own).
- Share: Read aloud the memory you found on the slip of paper.
- Reflect: What kind of memories seem to be important? Is hearing all the memories different than simply writing yours in private? Why?
- Consider: Which memory is so important that you will work together to share it, your vision as a single group?
- Select: From the list on the board, choose a theme of interest to everyone, making it large enough to encompass the possibilities suggested in the novel.
- Design: A class quilt from papers cut into four inch squares. Each one will create an image that symbolizes the theme you've chosen. Upon completion of the individual pieces, you'll assemble the quilt pieces [using tape or glue, a large piece of tag board as a base].
- Reflect: How is the theme of the novel affected by the piecing into a single quilt? What is the impact of looking at the quilt? How does making the quilt affect your connection to your classmates?

Although some teachers might find working with art materials a bit cumbersome at first, the integration of physical material with collaborative decision-making and discussion is helpful. The final products are a concrete reflection of the work, the ideas taking form. This strategy has been successful for both middle school and high school teachers, especially in conjunction with works of literature.

    The Giver is a good example of the quality of young-adult literature today and its potential to explore social issues. Teachers can and should use such literature as a bridge to the more complex literature of senior high school; the patterns of discussion established through less challenging texts will serve all students well, but especially those less skilled.

 ## OTHER STRATEGIES FOR LITERARY EXPLORATION AND DISCUSSION

As a means of understanding social issues underlying a complex piece of literature, students would first brainstorm possibilities (e.g., in *Wuthering Heights* they might focus on class and race prejudice, alcoholism, women's rights, abuse, and inheritance laws). They then research those issues as they relate to today's society, with each student or group presenting research findings orally. Each student or group must compile a list of related examples or observations from the literary text, followed by a student-led whole-class discussion of the issue as it relates to the novel. This is the kind of discussion that allows everyone to speak and offer opinions, whether about the issue or the text (O'Keefe 18–19).

If small groups of students are reading a single novel, Pam B. Cole suggests using literary circle discussions to illustrate how an individual response to a piece of literature is not only possible but appropriate. After students have had a few days to immerse themselves in their reading, they meet three times a week to share their responses to the novel. Using their journals as a springboard to discussion, students share their reactions to specific words, lines, or passages. Cole notes that "a more challenging group activity is to have students perform think-alouds" (31). Her teacher directives are as follows:

> Before their groups convene, have students choose passages that depict levels of growth and psychological changes that occur in the characters. When they meet in their groups, have students read their chosen passages to the group and then speculate about the changes that are taking place within the characters. These activities, while encouraging group participation, will allow students to explore their own questions and reactions to the text. (31)

Not only does the literary circle discussion foster good listening and speaking skills, but it eliminates the idea that a single interpretation, especially that of a teacher, is the definitive one.

Literary Interviews

Literary interviews offer students experience in written and oral language. In a model suggested by Terry Johnson and Daphne Louis, students take on the role of a literary character. They are then interviewed both by a partner and later by the entire class. Although the first questions are based on story information, additional questions can relate to events not in the actual story but to events that are plausible given the plot and characters. In planning, both partners develop the questions to be asked, but they do not rehearse the responses. As Johnson and Louis note, "The keys to success are well thought-out questions and an interviewee who is able to enter into their chosen character" (134). Teachers will need to model interviewing strategies or provide some television clips for analysis and discussion.

The literary dinner party is yet another way to establish discussion with a purpose. Students choose a character from literature they have all shared and role-play at a dinner party. To do this well, students must understand their character: dress, speech, mannerisms, point of view, and so forth. Most students are enthusiastic about choosing and portraying an intriguing character, and teachers learn a great deal about each student's knowledge of the character through his or her table talk.

Telling the Story with a Tangram

As a strategy to check on comprehension of a literary text—and perk up student involvement—ancient Chinese puzzles known as tangrams can be used at any curricular level. Tangrams are squares that have been cut into seven pieces, each called a tan. In traditional Chinese storytelling, the teller places the tans so they touch each other without overlapping, forming a "picture" related to the story. The teller may use as many of the seven pieces as he or she wishes, but the tans cannot cross over one

---

Figure 5.1 Planning sheet

Book Title _____   Author _____

A. Think about the main character(s). Use the tans to create a puzzle that looks like or represents this character. Make a simple drawing of your puzzle in the box.

B. Think about an important event or important place. Use the tans to make a puzzle that looks like the event or the place.

C. Think about an important idea in the story. Use the tans to make a puzzle that represents this idea.

D. Think about the story's ending. Use the tans to make a puzzle that represents something from the ending of your book.

E. Practice telling your story.

---

another in any way. The preparation for this literary storytelling event calls on students' ability to isolate a main character, a major plot event, and so forth. Teachers need to provide both an example and a framework for an initial activity. For example, Christine Boardman Moen (15–16) suggests reading the children's book *Grandfather Tang's Story* to introduce the concept, putting each animal figure mentioned into a tan representation. She then retells the story through the tans. Next, in small groups, students receive a set of seven tans. As she reads aloud another children's story, *Where the Wild Things Are,* each group creates four puzzles to use during retelling of the story. Traditionally, the Chinese storyteller would use all seven pieces, but it is not a requirement for this class activity. A planning sheet (see Figure 5.1) helps students create their puzzle.

This activity acts both as a introductory tool for retelling the literary piece and for helping students into the role of storyteller.

 STORYTELLING

Building Class Cohesion Through Stories

Nancy King's *Storymaking and Drama* is an exciting resource for secondary teachers. Because many high school teachers believe that their students will find story activities "kid stuff," they tend to exclude these activities from the curriculum. King, however, believes that old stories are the best way to introduce new ideas: "The experience of telling connects me with the world tradition of storytelling and helps to create an environment that is special, apart from the usual classroom interaction" (26). As a way of beginning, King tells students a story, shown on the next page, that she heard from a Thai woman, who told her that she first heard it from her Laotian mother.

EXPLORATION

The Water Buffalo's Letters

A Community of Knowing

In former times, the Akha people had letters. One year, all the letters were swallowed by the water buffalo and imprinted on its skin. When the time came to make their yearly move, the people discovered the water buffalo's skin was too big and too heavy for them to move to their new location. The people were perplexed. They did not want to leave their letters, and they could not move the skin.

They went to Headman. He thought about the problems, "If we cannot move the water buffalo's skin, we must eat the water buffalo's skin. This way we keep the letters inside us forever."

And so the water buffalo's skin was cut up into the number of people in the group. Each person swallowed a piece. Thus the letters were kept within the tribe forever. (King 26)

King then takes students through this process:

1. Write: On a small piece of paper, write a small bit of information that you would like to see remembered, perhaps to be shared with people you don't know. Don't sign your name.
2. Pass: Pass your paper to another person.
3. Share: Share the bits of information.
4. Reflect on the story and the process. Consider the following: What kinds of information are important? Is hearing the bits of information different from writing it in private? If so, in what ways? (26–27)

Creating stories may appear to be an unusual activity for many students, particularly in classrooms with time constraints and academic standards to be met. However, image-making is a productive means of evoking stories and drama, all of which improve student understanding of a text (King 5).

King offers another important reason for teachers to incorporate story-making and drama into their literature and language units:

Many of us already feel a sense of isolation, a lack of real community. We live very separate lives, often at great distance from family and childhood homes. We learn to keep our thoughts and feelings to ourselves. Many teachers have told me that they wish their students would be more forthcoming in class discussion. Sharing stories and making drama are excellent ways to build community within the classroom, to create a communal space where students feel safe to express opinions not yet fully formed or clearly understood and to discover the stories of their lives and their society. (4–5)

In a student-centered classroom, "stories of their lives and their society" are a critical element in student response to literature and language, as well as the taproot of authentic writing.

Larry Swartz's *Dramathemes* offers many ideas for storytelling, and work particularly well for initial "comfort" in groups. One activity involves imbuing ordinary objects with importance and a history. As Swartz explains it, each student brings an object and works in a small group to invent a story about it, which he or she then shares with the group. Students could weave their stories from history or cultural folklore (e.g., the jewelry box belonged to Cleopatra; the stone was given to the first settlers on the Great Plains) or even a mythical alien civilization. Students should be encouraged to be very detailed in their storymaking. As an extension, Swartz recommends telling students that these objects belonged to someone important, but now deceased. Each group would build a story about the person, incorporating each of the group's objects into it. Two groups could work together. Another extension would have groups exchange their objects and repeat the exercise; then, they would tell each other the stories they invented for that set of objects (25).

Another storytelling activity recommended by Swartz involves students' working with a novel. The class would be divided into small groups, with each group responsible for conveying important information from one chapter. Each group can dramatize the story in one of the following ways:

- by becoming storytellers
- by telling the story in a role and from that character's point of view
- creating an improvisation based on a scene in that chapter
- through tableaux
- through song
- as Story Theatre (narration, dialogue, and movement)
- as Readers' Theatre (reading the text aloud)
- as an interview
- as diary or letter
- as a poem
- as a series of illustrations
- in movement only
- using sound and movement (Swartz 55)

Swartz also uses fairy tales for storytelling activities. Because fairy tales are familiar to most students, they offer a good springboard for oral work—and fun as well. Fairy tales are passed down from one generation to the next; therefore, students are asked to imagine that one of the characters was able to tape his or her story for future generations. Students could reread a tale they enjoy or try out an unfamiliar one, but in either case, they must retell the story without using the book. The students will tape-record their tales as told from the point of view of any character they choose. They are free to change or omit details from the original story, and perhaps add details of their own. The tape recordings would be shared with the whole class (77).

STORYTELLING: EVOKING A CULTURAL TRADITION

Creating a Storyteller

In developing oral language activities, our methods students discovered some wonderful ideas in the journal *SchoolArts*. With the lessening of oral tradition in American culture today, we need to provide students with experiences that reflect and draw on cultural traditions. In *A Tradition of Storytelling*, Gail M. Dickel used the storyteller figurine (a seated, open-mouthed adult figure covered with listening children) as the basis for her students' understanding both the rich oral tradition and the culture of the Native American pueblos. Texts on art of the Southwest will feature the clay storytellers, as well as shops carrying authentic art from this region, and students do need to see the storytellers as preparation for their work—first to create a storyteller and then to create the story.

Slides of the Taos Pueblo and its storyteller sculptures, for example, will open discussion to storytelling as a means of teaching people about their history, their values, and their relationship with the earth. From this discussion, students can focus on their own lives and the storytellers and stories within them. Then Dickel's students made storyteller figures out of clay, although it could be done with colored paper or other media. In creating their storyteller, students had to confront questions: Why do we tell stories? Why do families and entire nations need stories? Who is your storyteller? What is the relationship of your storyteller to you? What kind of stories does your storyteller tell? Who listens? Why? In brief, a great deal of classroom discussion and thought went into the creation. Upon completion of the storyteller figure and the story, each was photographed and placed in a class book (22–23).

Creating a Story Cloth

In introducing her students to cultural history, Candice J. Schilz used the Korhogo Story Cloth, a traditional art form from Africa's Ivory Coast. After discussion and interpretation of the story cloth, including how designs and techniques are passed down through generations, Schilz extended the discussion to early African American quilts and a comparison with African colors and symbols. She then had students explore fabric designs from various countries, including the United States, both for motifs and the communication of ideas through this story art. Schilz asked her students to discuss ideas that have been passed down in their families, and how storytelling is part of the process of passing on traditions. Finally, students created their own story cloth, using a variety of art media. Both the storyteller figure and the story cloth provide students with a rich environment for oral language activities, as well as with important links to their national, ethnic, and racial heritages. And, putting the "arts" into language arts is not only important but rewarding.

Multilingual Folktales

In classrooms where non-native speakers need sustained experience in all the language arts, projects designed to engage students in good listening and speaking activities, followed by writing, hone important skills. At the same time, tapping into folktales from students' cultural backgrounds celebrates their heritage. Pat Egenberger, a middle school teacher from Modesto, California, had her students put together books of folktales from their cultures of origin, which they then wrote in both their native language and English (King and Stoval 79–80). Optimally, Egenberger notes, students gather the tales from family or older members of the community; however, they might also use library collections written in the native language. With the help of family members, students retell the tale, not translating but in their own words. They then write the tale in both the original language and English.

In preparation for the written product, however, oral work is essential. Egenberger first did a storytelling project in which she taught everyone a folktale that was a Spanish equivalent of "The House That Jack Built." Half the class told the story in Spanish, and the other half in English, until, as Egenberger notes: "We shouted out the lines, one after another, until the whole story was told in both languages" (80). Public libraries usually have a collection of children's folktales written in two languages, which serve as models for oral and written work. For a classroom with predominately native speakers of English, teachers can pair or group native and non-native speakers and modify the project accordingly.

Creating Masks for Stories

Although written for elementary students, Bette Bosma's text on using folk literature is a rich resource for teachers of all grade levels. Bosma points out that students will "become less inhibited doing pantomime and improvisation when using masks" (56). It isn't that masks hide the student, Bosma notes, but rather that the mask facilitates the student's releasing self into the character. Students could use children's stories or turn to Native American or African folklore, in which masks play a significant role. Bosma suggests consulting *Who's in Rabbit's House?* by Verna Aardema, where Leo and Diane Dillon's illustrations "depict the story as being performed by masked players" (57). After exploring various types of folklore (e.g., myth, fable, legend, fairy tale, folktale), students could write their own and then create the masks for pantomime or oral presentation.

Telling Stories Through Puppets

Bosma believes that the "sharply drawn characters of fairy tales and animal tales make wonderful puppets. From the simplest paper-bag puppet to the most elaborate papier-mâché model, storybook characters can be easily identified by accentuating particular features" (59). For students who have had no experience with puppets, regardless of age, this might be the best way to start. Writing conversation for the puppets, adding background music, and supplying other props can all be handled by the students themselves, with very little teacher guidance. Puppets could be used for various literary pieces, everything from dramatic poetry to *The Canterbury Tales*. Older students could prepare a production for presentation to younger students, either within the school or within the community, such as in a hospital or retirement home. It is important to remember that no student is too old or too sophisticated for puppetry.

Although working with the district's art teachers would be a helpful collaboration, language arts teachers can "go it alone." Materials can be simple and still provide the basis for storytelling activities. In classrooms with diverse ethnic backgrounds, the results will be especially rich. Moreover, such work fulfills national and state standards in both oral language and language.

Oral Histories

An oral language project resting firmly in family and culture is that of oral history. Susan Katz Weinberg, in response to a classroom representing diverse cultures and languages, developed this project for her middle school students, especially for those whose native language was other than English. Interviewing family members in their native tongue underscored the importance of maintaining that language, and at the same time, provided a bridge from oral to written language. Most adolescents experience a generation gap, with its resultant breakdown in communication, at some point, but for ESL students negotiating two languages and cultures, that gap widens. Through the oral language project, students can close or narrow the gap.

Katz Weinberg selected a topic for interview based on her students' lives; potential topics include immigration or migration, a particular event or decade with significance to their parents or grandparents (e.g., Vietnam, Persian Gulf War, 1960s, civil rights). However, students could select their own topics, with one requirement: face-to-face interviewing as the source of their information. Katz Weinberg cautions that students must be taught the skills of interviewing, and she invited a guest speaker as a way to model appropriate and useful interviewing. As a class, her students prepared and categorized questions in advance of the speaker's visit. During the class interview, each student was required to ask one question and to write down all the responses; each then wrote a summary of the interview. The next day, Katz Weinberg played back the tape recording she had made of the session, and the written transcript, thus modeling the process. After the students prepared questions for their family interviews, they practiced them with a peer partner, then conducted their interviews.

Following the interviews, students transcribed them, then transformed them into narratives—which could be oral or written or both. If family members refused to be interviewed, which Katz Weinberg notes was rare, she arranged for the student to interview an adult at school or to work with a peer. Parents were notified before the start of the project that their privacy would be protected and that their children would not suffer in any way if they did not interview a family member.

Instructional Unit

Here you will explore a student's unit, this one geared to oral language activities. In addition to evaluating the unit's use of these activities, we would like you to review principles of planning and evaluate their application in Mary Beth Koehler's unit, The Trickster. Each unit, regardless of its emphasis, should reflect conscious decisions about materials and methods. To allow you to discover and evaluate Mary Beth's decisions, we have removed her statements about them. We also omitted her thoughtful and thorough reflection on the process of developing this unit for eighth graders.

As you read Mary Beth's unit, look for the following:

1. What are Mary Beth's goals? Do they reflect all three developmental areas: cognitive, affective, and social? Is one area emphasized more than the others? If yes, why do you think it is? If they are balanced, do you think it would be appropriate in this unit to stress one area more than the others?
2. What does Mary Beth want her students to understand or be able to do better as a result of this unit? What are her objectives or student outcomes?
3. What materials has she selected? What activities has she planned? What knowledge of English language arts is guiding her decisions? Do you think a narrow focus such as this one makes one's decisions more or less difficult? How does her unit reflect Mary Beth's knowledge of both concepts and kids?
4. Has Mary Beth provided for students with varying ability levels? Would students from diverse ethnic and cultural backgrounds be comfortable with this unit? Does she celebrate cultural diversity with this unit?
5. Has Mary Beth considered student interests and needs as she planned this unit? How do you know?
6. How will students be evaluated?
7. Does Mary Beth's time frame of two weeks seem about right for the activities planned? Does her sequence of activities seem appropriate for 13- and 14-year-olds?

Again, keep in mind that Mary Beth's unit was originally written as a narrative with a great deal of reflection about her goals, anticipated outcomes, methods, and materials. To provide you with this evaluative opportunity, we have removed her commentary.

Storytelling: The Trickster

In this unit, students will work with storytelling. To provide for a common structure, we will concentrate on the character of "trickster" in folk and fairy tales.

Teacher Materials and Resources:

Iktomi and the Buffalo Skull
All-Jahdu Storybook
Paper Faces
Paper Masks and Puppets for Stories, Songs, & Plays
Puppets, Methods and Materials
Plenty of Puppets
The Art of Kabuki (video)
The Family Storytelling Handbook: How to Use Stories, Anecdotes, Rhymes,
    Handkerchiefs, Paper & Other Objects to Enrich Your Family Traditions
American Indian Resource Manual for Public Libraries
Keepers of the Earth

Day 1

Teacher-Led Activity. As students come into the room, I will have dim lights and Native American flute music playing. As they file in, I will whisper and tell them to go to their seats, attempt to sit quietly, and close their eyes. When everyone is in the room, I will help them to imagine Native American life over one hundred years ago.

Discussion Questions:
    1. What did Native American people do for entertainment?
    2. How did Native American people explain natural phenomena?

Story. How the Loon Got Its Red Eyes and Tail Feathers. Demonstration of Menominee Song and Dance/Loon Story.

Student Activity. Journal Response to Loon Story/Song and Dance

Day 2

Teacher Activity. Whole-class discussion from journal writing. Introduce the two-week unit, provide handout with oral project options, and give book talk on the following trickster tale resources:

Keepers of the Earth
The Girl Who Married a Ghost
The Adventures of Nanabush: Ojibway Indian Stories
Why the Possum's Tail Is Bare and Other North American Indian Stories
Teepee Tales of the American Indians
Iktomi and the Buffalo Skull
Iktomi and the Ducks
Iktomi and the Berries

Tricky Rabbit
Favorite Folk Tales from Around the World
Folk and Fairy Tales
Time-Ago Tales of Jahdu
Time-Ago Lost, More Tales of Jahdu
The All-Jahdu Storybook
Anasi and the Talking Melon
Spiderman Anancy

Student Activity. Gain familiarity with resources; begin to select tale for oral project.

Day 3

Teacher Activity. Show and read stories from *Iktomi and the Buffalo Skull* and *The All-Jahdu Storybook.* Encourage students to interact and respond during the reading. Using overhead transparencies, show students how Iktomi's thoughts (and witty asides to audience) are shown in print.

Discussion Questions:

Iktomi—How do the story elements suggest a Native American tale?
How is humor handled?
All-Jahdu—What words give a traditional African flavor to the story?
What words give a contemporary flavor to the story?

Student Activity. Brainstorm ways students could retell tales they are interested in and maintain cultural flavor.

Student Assignment. Preparation for guest speaker, Kimberly Blaeser, Ojibway storyteller from White Earth Reservation (also a college instructor). Students will bring five questions on storytelling or the trickster for the guest speaker to answer.

Day 4

Workshop with Ms. Blaeser.

Day 5

Evolve criteria for effective storytelling. Review from workshop and excerpt from *Keepers of the Earth* where authors provide ideas for good storytelling.

Student Activity. Following review and *Keepers of the Earth* work, small cooperative working groups develop criteria.

Whole-Class Discussion. Discuss and merge criteria from the small-group lists into one list for class evaluation/oral project (list to be typed and distributed by teacher).

Conferencing/Peers and Teacher. Select and retell a tale.

Day 6

Teacher Activity. Show taped excerpts from the video *The Art of Kabuki.* Excerpts will feature use of makeup (masks), methods of walking, gesture, movement, and voice.

Teacher Mini-lesson. Relate Japanese techniques to Native American and African storytelling, emphasizing commonalties in storytelling.

Student Activity. Students will write in their journals on ideas received from tape and mini-lesson on how to adapt some to their own process of storytelling. Share ideas with classmates.

Conferencing/Peers and Teacher. Students' specific tales and plans for storytelling.

Day 7

Teacher Activity. Show students a variety of simple masks, teacher-made from old billboard signs. Give book talk on resources for mask making, asking students to apply the information to their chosen tales.

Conferencing/Peers and Teacher. Mask-making application for students' specific tales.

Day 8

Teacher Activity. Introduce puppetry as a form of storytelling. Give a book talk on resources for making and using puppets, explaining how different styles of puppetry create different tones in storytelling (e.g., simple kid-type masks are lighthearted; shadow puppets are a bit more scary). Encourage student involvement and ask them to apply different mask styles to different types of tales.

Conferencing/Workshop.

Day 9

Teacher Activity. Introduce origami in storytelling; explain and demonstrate "Something Special" from *The Family Storytelling Handbook.*

Student Activity. With an excerpt on how to perform "Something Special," work with partners. Practice origami storytelling; focus on criteria for effective storytelling.

Whole-Class Discussion. Origami practice and application for storytelling; comparisons of origami and other storytelling techniques.

Conferencing/Workshop.

Day 10

Conferencing/Workshop. Individual storytelling projects.

Day 11

Conferencing/Workshop. Projects.

Day 12

Student Activity. Performance of storytelling projects.

Teacher Activity. Evaluation based on criteria evolved at start of unit.

Day 13

Storytelling and Evaluation.

Day 14

Student Activity. Writing reflection on own experience of storytelling and observation of peers.

Questions About The Trickster Unit

Mary Beth began the "summary reflection" on her unit with this paragraph:

When I did my student teaching in middle school, my cooperating teacher gave me an assignment of creating a speech unit for the students. After spending nights after school and in the library developing lessons and techniques that I thought would help the students create the perfect speech, I walked up to another English teacher and tried to explain step by step what I thought I was going to do with the students. Then I asked what he thought. After my recitations of all the fancy-schmancy things I told him I was going to do, he looked at me and simply said, "I would think the main reason for this would be to make the students comfortable with speaking because most of them are going to be terrified." The next night, I completely overhauled my unit with that in mind, and it ended up a success. I tried to keep that in mind when I created this storytelling unit.

1. Where do you see evidence of Mary Beth's late night "middle school education" in her unit?
2. Why must you understand the trial and error of unit development if you want to be an effective teacher?
3. Why must you be able to "roll with the errors" and believe in yourself and the second chances we get as teachers?
4. If you were developing a storytelling unit for high school juniors, roughly 16- to 17-year-olds, what might you do differently? Can you think of ways in which the greater independence and self-direction of older students might influence your decisions? How might working with older students make this lesson more difficult?
5. How could Mary Beth involve other grade levels, parents, or the community in this unit? Why must you be alert to the potential for involvement beyond your classroom?

INSTRUCTIONAL UNIT

Nancy Koehler, a classmate of but no relation to Mary Beth Koehler, decided to focus her oral language unit on pourquoi stories or etiological animal tales—folktales. As Nancy explained them in her introduction:

> Pourquoi stories, according to Bosma, "explain the origin of certain characteristics. They are written to entertain and are not believed to be true by the storyteller" (57). Often there is an element of trickery in the plot. The characteristics described are not usually attributed to logical or natural causes. (1)

Nancy says she chose them because she believes "that almost all students delight in these stories, in their cleverness, and elements of surprise" (1). She also chose middle schoolers as the focus of her unit, and with a similar subject, her unit offers an interesting comparison with Mary Beth's.

Once again, we have removed the author's voice and her many insightful comments and reflections about motives, materials, and methods, although the sequence is presented as Nancy originally prepared it. Consider what goals and student outcomes Nancy had in mind as she chose the elements of this unit. Similarly, we would like you to speculate on her philosophy of teaching: What does she believe about kids and English language arts? How do you know? Review the questions that led into Mary Beth's unit before you read Nancy's unit.

STORYTELLING: POURQUOI STORIES—HOW AND WHY

Time. Fourteen class periods. Students will each receive a calendar of events and due dates for the unit. The schedule will also be posted in the classroom.

Materials
Just So Stories
Why Mosquitoes Buzz in People's Ears
Mask-making kit

Mini-lesson. Characteristics, form, and history of pourquoi stories through reading "How the Leopard Got His Spots" and other stories from Kipling's *Just So Stories.*

Student Activity. Silent reading of both traditional and modern pourquoi stories.

Mini-lesson. Readers' Theatre, criteria for evaluation

Student Activity. Small groups (chosen by teacher), choice of story for Readers' Theatre activity, rehearsal.

Student Activity. Performance and evaluation of Readers' Theatre performance by peers (form provided).

Whole-Class Activity. Brainstorm ideas for pourquoi stories (e.g., animal characteristics, possible story elements, formats, and possible use of narrator); diversity of animals/cultures (e.g., Kipling's Asian animals, Aardema's African animals).

Student Activity. Small groups, brainstorm ideas for development of an original pourquoi story.

Student Activity. Small groups, following decision of pourquoi story (animals, characteristics), begin mask making from kit materials provided (five days for completion/drying before performance).

Mini-lesson. Story mapping or storyboards; example from Kipling story; preparation for story/script writing.

Whole-Class Activity. Brainstorming, story mapping and formatting of pourquoi stories.

Student Activities.

1. Small groups, writing pourquoi story (use of storyboard or mapping, forms provided); mask-making activities continue.
2. Peer editing of story/script drafts; sharing drafts among groups; mask-making activities continue.
3. Rehearsal of scripts; students may either read parts dramatically or memorize parts for performance.
4. Performance for classmates; if possible, performance for other students or family. Self-evaluation of participation both in writing and performing.

Teacher Activity. Evaluation of each small group on their written product, group participation, and performance.

Student Activity. Self-reflective journal entries on the unit's activities.

References for Unit of Study

Aardema, V. *Why Mosquitoes Buzz in People's Ears.* New York: Dial, 1975.

Bosma, B. *Fairy Tales, Fables, Legends, and Myths: Using Folk Literature in Your Classroom.* New York: Teachers College Press, 1987.

Creative Educational Systems. *The New Playmaking: The Latest in Integration of the Arts in Education.* Chicago: Creative Education Press, 1993.

Creative Educational Systems. *Creative Mask-Making Kit.* Chicago: Creative Education Press, 1993.

Kipling, R. *Just So Stories.* New York: Doubleday, 1973.

Rief, L. *Seeking Diversity.* Portsmouth: Heinemann, 1992.

Wisconsin Department of Public Instruction. *Classroom Activities in Speaking and Listening.* Madison: Department of Public Instruction, 1991.

DISCUSSION QUESTIONS FOR STORYTELLING UNITS

1. What similarities do you find between Mary Beth's and Nancy's units? Do you think similarities arise because Mary Beth and Nancy share a philosophy of teaching and learning? Or is it simply a matter of similar interests?
2. What differences do you find between Mary Beth's and Nancy's units? What accounts for the differences?
3. Mary Beth had a strong background in theatre and drama; Nancy had one in special needs children. Are their specific interests and talents evident in their respective units? Why is it important for teachers to honor their strengths and interests as well as recognize their weaker areas?
4. How do Mary Beth and Nancy show that who they teach is as critical as what they teach? How are they meshing materials, methods, and learners in appropriate ways?
5. What additions or changes would you make in Nancy's unit? What rationale do you have for making them?
6. How could you use this unit with high school seniors? What adjustments would you make and why?
7. Some senior high school teachers believe that their students are too old or sophisticated for fairy tales and folklore. How would you respond to criticism that you are using "little kid stuff" as a basis for oral and written language activities with juniors and seniors?
8. Mary Beth and Nancy include both student and teacher evaluation as part of their units. We have not provided you with their criteria or forms because we would like you to devise some. With a partner or small group, choose one unit and develop appropriate criteria and evaluative methods. Review your understanding of Mary Beth's or Nancy's goals and intended student outcomes before evolving criteria. Be sure to keep the age level in mind, and keep things as clear, simple, and fair as possible.

SPEAKING FORMALLY: TEACHING "THE" SPEECH

Today's teens have grown up in a world of surround-sound media and glitzy technological devices. It's not surprising, then, that they may have some reservations about being the ones front and center, both writing and producing an oral event—and being judged on its merits. Therefore, before you assign formal speeches, consider smaller oral assignments, more formal than discussion but less so than "the" speech. Here are some ideas:

- *Demonstration.* The speaker, usually with props or visual aids, and using a subject he or she knows extremely well, both shows and tells "how to."
- *Story Time.* Without notes, the speaker tells a story, again something that he or she already knows very well.

- *In or On the News.* The speaker summarizes, without notes or reading, a brief piece of interest to peers, taken from print or television.
- *Roundtable.* A small group of students, in front of the class, discusses a topic of interest to them—and to their peers. They may use notes but not read. (adapted from Burke 220–222)

While being on the spot is one consideration, voice is another—and quite surprisingly, most students are not used to their own voices, especially in formal situations. Joseph O'Beirne Milner and Lucy Floyd Morcock Milner have some ideas that give those voices a place to warm up.

- *First person poems.* Collect poems that reflect different cultural, ethnic, and racial perspectives, as well as appeal to a wide range of interests and abilities. Have students choose and read one for their peers.
- *Hero worship.* From public figures, past and present, find speeches or documents that were meant to be spoken, not just read. Collect sound bites and arrange them chronologically (e.g., Lincoln, King, Angelou) and read to class.
- *Accidental power.* Using either a contemporary or past news event, be the reporter live on the scene, responding to the news of the day. (53–55)

Choral reading is another good vehicle for students to hear themselves speaking in front of their peers. Paul Fleischman's works, written for two or more voices, are easy and fun to use with all grade levels.

⟳ *Reflection* ⟳

Almost everyone, no matter how experienced or polished, gets butterflies at the thought of giving a formal speech in front of peers. With a partner or small group, brainstorm "I gave a speech" memories of your high school years. Then, take the other side of the desk and consider what secondary English teachers can do to net those butterflies.

The secondary English classroom must provide students at each curricular level with a range of speaking opportunities, some of which should be formal. The formal speech is, for most students, a difficult assignment—not because they can't put a speech together but because they are afraid they will "blow it" once in front of their peers, or that peers may tease or even ignore them. These are not baseless fears, and you have to address them. First, establish some ground rules for conduct during formal presentations (e.g., applause required, no comments during presentation unless asked for by speaker). Second, make sure each student is well-prepared before he or she ever stands in front of the class (Burke 220). This preparation starts with the student's topic. In response to weekly "sound-off" topics in ninth grade, Ann wrote this brief, unedited piece:

I'D LIKE TO TELL YOU WHAT I THINK ABOUT
Welfare being canceled

"It shouldn't have happened. I don't like Tommy Thompson [then governor] for making that decision. I have a few friends who because of him are flunking school. They have to stay home and baby sit their younger siblings. It's because their parents are single parents receiving minimum wage. They don't even have enough money for daycare. Some people can't help it if they are single parents and have only one income to pay for everyday needs. Plus, they don't have time to watch their kids since they are working extra hours. With welfare, they'd be able to get themselves back on their feet and get a better job."

Ann's issue was a heated one, with plenty of newsprint and TV talk, as well as "on the street" commentary. But how does a teacher help her focus and prepare this topic for a speech? What will help Ann understand the difference between writing to be read and writing to be heard?

To begin the process, Ann needs to address some questions, and here is where you provide her with concrete guidance:

- Why do you care about this topic?
- What is the purpose of your speech?
- Who is the audience and what do they already know about your topic?
- What will they need to know in order to understand it?
- How will you engage them right away? (e.g., story, statistics)
- What resources (e.g. visual aids, props) might you need?
- Why should your peers believe what you say? Care about what you say?
- Where will you get information to support your topic?

EXPLORATION

Playing Ann—And Her Teacher

Re-read Ann's ideas in her "sound off" piece. Using the questions just presented, personalize them for Ann's welfare topic. Should she give an informative speech or a persuasive one? Why? With a classmate, role-play.

Because formal speaking has often been ignored in the English language arts curriculum, some districts have formalized the process. One of our area high schools, for example, developed a three-week persuasive speech unit to be used in every tenth-grade class. Here is an abbreviated version of some unit basics, which includes readings on speech strategies and language, handouts on developing and writing a speech, peer help, and an evaluation rubric. As you scan excerpts from this student guide, note the similarities and differences between preparing a speech and preparing a written essay.

English 10 A Speech Guide

- What is your topic?
- What makes your speech persuasive rather than informative?
- What kind of audience do you expect to have: supportive, uncommitted, opposed?
- What kind of appeal will you use: emotional, logical, personal?
- What kind of attention-getter are you using in introduction?
    (question, quotation, tell story, startling information)
- What organizational pattern are you using?
    (climactic, topical, cause-effect, problem-solution)
- What forms of support are you using?
    (statistics, facts, examples, opinions, statistics, anecdotes)
- Will you use a visual aid?
    (poster, video, overhead, slides, video, object)
- How will this aid your speech?

Although students use only note cards while speaking, they are required to have a written outline, a written version of the speech, and peer "editing" completed prior to the speech itself.

∞ *Reflection* ∞

Below is the evaluation rubric (using a 4 point scale) for the English 10 speech. As you read through it, consider its strengths and weaknesses. Further, what does this rubric say to you, as a teacher, about your instructional role in this unit?

Rubric for Speech

1. Outline complete
        Full sentences
2. Speech content
        Introduction
                use of attention-getter
                clear, focus thesis/persuasive
        Body
                organization clear effective
                variety of support strategies
                no faulty reasoning
                used at least 3 arguments
                had adequate proof for all arguments
                cited sources
                used good transitions
                appropriate concluding strategy

3. Delivery
    spoke from note cards
    maintained eye contact with a variety of peers
    good posture
    clear, loud voice
    no nervous mannerisms
4. Time frame
    maintained 4–6 minutes

We will talk more about evaluation criteria in Chapter 13, but for now, keep in mind that when students give formal presentations, they should know the criteria before they begin working on the presentation. Although the above rubric is rather formal, you can develop criteria that speak very directly to the kids.

For example, "no nervous mannerisms" can be more colorful and specific:

"ahs, ers, mmms, uhs, ums" or "tapping fingers" or "blinking eyes"

We can use a lighter approach to an evaluative 4 point scale:

"wow!"   "lots and lots"   "some along the way"   "almost none"

Evaluation is a reality of oral work, just as it is in the other language arts strands. The trick is developing clear and fair criteria, and then, applying them consistently. An informal evaluation to presentations can be done through note cards, stating only what was most memorable or stood out most in the speech (Burke 225).

ᨠᨠᨠ *Reflection* ᨠᨠᨠ

What do you think about using speech as a unit rather than as an integral part of other lessons and units (e.g., literature, media)? Do you get a sense of "let's get it over with" or "let's focus on it"? List some advantages and disadvantages of speech as a unit.

HEADING OFF "FRONT AND CENTER" ANXIETY

When you work with students, address anxiety as a normal response. At the same time, remind them that the best way to alleviate it lies in their preparation. Knowing their audience, in this case peers, will help them anticipate and deal with resistance to their ideas, or conversely, to activate a positive response early and easily. Since you want students to talk rather than read, coach them with note cards, help them isolate key words and phrases that cue the main ideas, and suggest that they memorize the opening to their speech, thus freeing their eyes for contact with their audience. Suggest visual aids that may provide added security. Have them read aloud their entire text, editing out words or phrases that cause them to stumble. Show them how to block their speech into segments and to work on each segment separately for awhile. Give them rehearsal time in class, using a peer partner for feedback, and remind them that that old saying about "practice makes perfect" has some truth to it. Their comfort level will increase the more often they do formal speaking, even though their body may turn up their heart rate and sweat production. That too is completely normal—and kids need to know that it is (Burke 220–222).

EXPLORATION

In Tyler's Shoes

Tyler, a classmate of Ann, had something to say about the world of pro athletes in his "I'd Like to Tell You What I Think About" piece.

> *I think the athletes are paid way too much. For example, Kevin Garnett, on the [Minnesota] Timberwolves, gets $120 million dollars, just for playing basketball. I was reading the sports section in the newspaper and I saw an article on Major League Baseball. The headline was "Baseball Puts 314 millionaires to work." Over 5 NBA players earn over 100 million dollars. The NFL has many millionaires, and every day it seems I read about another football player getting a million dollar bonus, just for signing with some team. His whole contract of course is worth many millions more. Many people never see even $50,000 in their life and these athletes see millions in a year. If you want to be rich someday, all you have to do is be good at sports.*

Make a list of questions or comments that you would use with Tyler to help him turn his interest in pro sports salaries into a good speech for his tenth-grade class. You already know that Tyler is nervous about speaking up in class discussion, let alone being in front of the class. How can you use the evaluation rubric on "delivery" to ease rather than rev up his fears?

INFORMAL CLASSROOM DRAMA

Informal classroom drama is a teaching strategy that enhances various academic and social skills. Among these are the improvement of all language skills, analytic thinking, problem solving, and sustained concentration. Betty Jane Wagner points out that "improvisational drama, perhaps more obviously than other oral language activities, ties directly into both literary and nonverbal knowing" (196). John H. Bushman and Kay Parks Bushman concur: "Role playing and improvisation expand the boundaries of experience for students so that they develop a more complete understanding of themselves and of the literature they are reading. . . . Students get inside the characters and play out their emotions, making choices and decisions based on the readers' under-standing of those characters" (35). Bushman and Bushman argue that young adult novels offer a particularly rich source for drama because "moral dilemma is most often at the heart of the novel's conflict" (35). The analytic and problem-solving skills needed for successful role playing and improvisation based on young adult literature are the same skills most teens need in daily life. Through vicarious experience, teens can safely test their decisions and explore the consequences of words and actions. Students involved in classroom drama also strengthen their self-concept and their ability to work cooperatively (Wisconsin Department of Public Instruction, 1986, 108). Because stu-dents are both the "inventors and actors," the role of the teacher is one of facilitator.

Wagner suggests using informal drama in various ways: (1) as a whole-class activ-ity in which students pantomime the action as the teacher or a student reads the text aloud; (2) plan a dramatization ahead of time (not reading from script) with two groups of student volunteers to act it out, followed by class discussion comparing the two versions; or (3) dramatize a scene that was not part of a story they have just read but a scene that would fit contextually. Wagner believes that "drama in the classroom entails unremitting pressure to develop listening and conversational skill" (197–198). Moreover, students "grow in their capacity to send and receive increasingly complex and mature verbal messages effectively, independently, creatively, and symbolically" (210). What's more, most students enjoy it, which is why Wagner believes its educa-tional importance is often underestimated. Moffett and Wagner make an important point, especially for teachers unfamiliar with informal drama: "Teachers should not feel that time spent on [these activities] takes away from reading and writing or basic literacy. Drama will definitely further such goals" (91).

More specifically, drama serves these important purposes:

- Fosters expression of all kinds
- Develops concentration and focuses energy
- Habituates students to self-directed small-group work
- Fosters intuitive understanding of rhetorical style
- Channels emotions
- Makes language in school fun

Further, informal drama can play an important role for students with limited English proficiency; second language acquisition depends on an interesting and lively oral language environment, which informal drama provides (Moffett and Wagner 91–92).

Drama Activities

Johnson and Louis make an important distinction between drama and theatre: "Drama encompasses every person in the room; there is no stage and no audience. Theatre, on the other hand, involves actors and a passive audience" (162). They also suggest avoiding any type of star system or an emphasis on performance. Drama and mime can be used in connection with a story, with students acting out the events. Al-ternatively, teachers can introduce students to some of the dramatic situations that arise from the narrative before they read the story themselves. This requires breaking the story into a series of dramatic scenarios to which the students would respond. Partner and group work are appropriate here. After students have read the story, they can then dramatize actual scenes.

Readers' Theatre is a class activity in which students sit in a group and read their parts directly from a script, as though it were a radio production. Neither movement nor memorization of lines is required. But students do need to use their voices extremely well to create their characters and the action.

EXPLORATION

Preparing Students for Readers' Theatre

In preparing a unit for *To Kill A Mockingbird*, our methods students included a Readers' Theatre activity for tenth graders. They first remind students that Readers' Theatre is participatory, interpretive reading—that they will be reading, not memorizing lines—and that they need to develop gestures, movement, and especially voice to create their characters. The class will be divided into groups of four, and each group will receive a script of the testimony from Tom Robinson's trial. The groups will decide who plays each role (e.g., Atticus, Tom Robinson). As each group performs, the other groups will form the jury, the white spectators, and the black spectators.

With a partner, decide on the speaking and listening skills these tenth graders would use in this activity. From a teacher's point of view, how would you prepare the students for a successful Readers' Theatre?

Regardless of the activity, before a group performs for the class, the students need rehearsal. Here are several ways this can be done: Teacher reads alone, modeling; Teacher reads a line, students repeat it; Teacher and students read lines together; Students work in pairs, alternating lines in the script. Although the activity works well with prepared scripts, Johnson and Louis believe that students are engaged more fully if they begin with a narrative and transform it into a play themselves (166). Teachers prepare students for this activity by modeling this process:

- Take part of a story and create a play script.
- Ask the class to examine both, noting the changes.
- Then, take a second part of the story and have the class transform it.
- Finally, have students take another part of the story, work on it in pairs, and eventually exchange their work with another pair of students.

Students are expected to provide constructive criticism. After this experience, students could work with a story of their own choosing, either alone or in pairs. Johnson and Louis recommend that teachers go over criteria for story selection first to ensure that students choose a story with ample conversation and several characters (166).

EVALUATING ORAL LANGUAGE ACTIVITIES

The contemporary English language arts classroom provides many varied opportunities for evaluation. Watching students working in pairs and small groups or listening to student-led discussions, for example, leads to important observations on student participation: Who responds easily and well? Who holds back despite obvious knowledge? Who is reluctant to respond? Who is left out? If you use a seating chart of each class, you can quietly make check marks or symbols to indicate what's happening orally. To be fair, however, you need sustained and varied observation. "Kid-watching" is an important component of evaluating oral language, but there are others. Just as written pieces can be evaluated with holistic or analytic scales, oral language activities lend themselves to similar measures, and students can share in the process. Simple written criteria for evaluating peers can be part of their experience with oral presentations of all kinds, both individually and as groups. Additionally, self-reflection on oral expression, whether class discussion or performance, is important—just as it is with written expression. Chapter 13, which deals exclusively with assessment, contains some examples of oral evaluation. The discussion there will also help you to devise appropriate measures for most oral language activities.

INSTRUCTIONAL UNIT

Nicole Kind, a graduate student in English 604, Literature for Teachers, developed this tenth-grade unit to take advantage of her knowledge of, and affection for, another culture. Having lived in Japan, Nicole brought to this unit a blend of its art forms through folktales and woodblock prints. We believe such combinations are too often ignored, despite the richness they bring to students. Similarly, we believe that both writing and performing classroom drama is an area not visited in many high school classrooms. Although elementary students are involved in both, the practice seems to vanish somewhere in middle school, despite state and national standards that clearly state students at all curricular levels need to experience diverse oral language activities.

We want you to review Nicole's plan with a critical eye. As you read, take notes on the following:

1. Does Nicole fulfill her goals? List specific ways in which she plans to engage students in activities reflecting what she envisions in those goals. Note especially the verbs used in her goals statement. These are key to her inclusion of specific materials or methods.
2. Nicole has addressed diversity in one sense, using another culture as the base of her unit. However, follow *diversity* as she notes it in "Planning for Diversity." How does she address the variety of learning styles and abilities present in a typical tenth-grade class?
3. Assessment should be part of your initial unit or lesson planning; it should not be an afterthought. Is Nicole's plan varied? Fair? Does it

allow students some choice? Which evaluation tool did you like best? Why? How would you characterize her criteria for evaluation in the rubrics? She lists and delineates her major assessment tools (i.e., three projects), but what of other, somewhat informal means of evaluating students? Should Nicole consider not formally grading some activities? Why or why not?

4. Nicole's student outcomes are noted on her daily plan. Examine each day's activities against her outcomes. Will students be able to achieve her desired outcomes? How do you know?

5. As you saw with Steve Wisner's unit in Chapter 3, advance preparation in terms of materials is mandatory. Make a list of the materials Nicole *must* have ready prior to launching this unit. Then, consider what she had to sort through to arrive at her choice of both materials and methods. Make a list of what you believe to be essential to success with the Kwaidan unit.

Again, take notes as you read, and when you complete your reading of this unit, return to these questions once more. Fill the thoughts that occur at this point.

PLAYWRITING AND INFORMAL CLASSROOM DRAMA: KWAIDAN— A LESSON PLAN INTEGRATING JAPANESE LEGEND AND ART

Time. Ten class days

Teacher Goals

- To expose students to Japanese culture through a study of folktales and woodblock prints.
- To encourage students to consider cultural similarities (i.e., between America and Japan) through analysis of folktales.
- To engage students in folktales through playwriting and performance.
- To make effective use of small- and large-group discussion.
- To provide students with projects that will actively engage them in all the language arts.

Note: Nicole designed this unit to fit into a larger folktale unit.

Teacher's Plan for Diversity

- Texts: Japanese folktales, oral and written; Japanese art, visual
- Learning Styles: Visual, kinesthetic, oral, written, independent and group work
- Ability Levels: Group work, jig-sawing, children's versions of folktales available, Akira Kurosawa's films available
- Motivation: Provocative foreign content, rich artwork, physical performance, planned for calendar time typically a "low spot" in the semester

Unit Assessment
- Journals
- Group Research Project
- Ukiyoe Print Project
- Folktale Drama Project

Day 1

Student Outcomes
- Understand the purposes of legends and fairy tales.
- Become acquainted with Ukiyoe prints.
- Analyze and draw conclusions from art.

Materials

Journals
Copies of Tsukioka's *Okiku*
Fishbowl
Transparencies and books of Ukiyoe [a time period in Japanese art] prints

Procedure

Student Activity. Journal write: Think about a legend or fairy tale that you know well. What purpose does it serve? Does it simply tell a story or is there more to it?

Whole-Class Activity. Short discussion on journal write. Create class chart to show purpose (e.g., "Beauty and the Beast," Teach a Lesson, Lesson: Don't judge by outside appearance).

Teacher Activity. Introduce Ukiyoe prints.

Student Activity. Transparency of Tsukioka Yoshitoshi's *Okiku*; individually, students write their interpretation of what they see.

Whole-Class Activity. Students put interpretations in fishbowl; some slips drawn for discussion; continue discussion of visual cues and student perspectives.

Teacher Activity. Tell the legend of Okiku: a ghost story with many variations, but all of them include a description of wrongful and cruel treatment of a poor girl, a servant, who was thrown into a well. Her ghost comes out of the well every night, howling and sobbing.

Teacher Activity. Introduce the unit (a whole new cast of creatures and creepies) and the research task.

Teacher Activity. Break students into pre-determined groups for research on characters from Japanese mythology (*tengu, kappa, rokurokubi, obake, yurei*); this information is readily accessible on Internet. Remind class that the results of their research will be presented verbally and visually on Day 3.

WORD SLEUTHS RESEARCH PROJECT

Word Sleuths! I need your help. I have discovered some mystery words in my reading of Japanese legends found in the Kwaidan. *It is your job to research one of the following words:* rokurokubi, kappa, tengu, obake *or* bakemono, *and* yurei. *Use the Internet to research your word; then, create a poster of your word for presentation and display. Your poster must include a definition of your word, a verbal explanation beyond the definition (a story or example), and a visual explanation (picture or drawing). You will receive a group grade based on how successfully you meet the criteria just given. You will also be evaluated on your overall presentation, as well as on the "mechanics" of your poster. You will report your findings on Day 3. Good luck, Sleuths!*

WORD SLEUTHS RESEARCH RUBRIC

Group projects will be graded on the following:

Definition:
How well did you define your word?   _____ /3

Verbal explanation/description:
Did you give good examples? Use good description?   _____ /3

Visual explanation (picture, drawing):
Is your visual relevant? Does it fit the definition?   _____ /3

Overall presentation:
Is your poster visually pleasing? Is it easy to understand?   _____ /3

Mechanics:
Did you use correct usage, punctuation, and spelling?   _____ /3

Comments:

Day 2 Research Day/Computer Lab

Student Activity. Work on Word Sleuth Project.

Teacher Activity. Assist groups as needed.

Day 3

Student Outcomes

- Learn aspects of Japanese folklore from classmates; effective use of jig-sawing strategy [students each contribute segments of information to form a larger piece of information, like working a picture puzzle].
- Find connections between art and literature.
- Analyze and draw conclusions from artwork.
- Develop oral "reporting" skills.
- Develop note-taking skills.

Materials

Journals

Tsukioka's Tokaido Yotsuya transparency (Hokuei's *The Lantern Ghost of Oiwa*)

Story of Tokaido Yosuya

Procedure

Student Activity. Student presentations (in alphabetical order) of assigned word. Listeners take notes on information presented, to compare with American ghosts/creatures.

Whole-Class Discussion. Comparison of each culture's ghosts.

Student Activity. Transparency of Hokuei woodcut; journal write on ideas behind the print: What story does it tell you? What conclusions can you draw from the print? What do you believe to be the story behind the print?

Houkuei, Japanese active 1824–1837. Lemon and His Wife's Ghost (Lemon nyobo oiwa) from the series One Hundred Ghost Stories & Hyaku monogatari), circa 1830–1832. Color woodcut, 36.9 × 25 cm. Fine Arts Museums of San Francisco, Achenbach Foundation for Graphic Arts purchase, 1980. 1.85

Whole-Class Discussion. Share ideas on Hokuei woodcut.

Teacher Activity. Tell legend of Tokaido Yotsuya, a tale of a samurai fallen on hard times. The master-less samurai, Lemon, poisons his sickly wife, Oiwa, with a "medicinal" drink; she dies a brutal death. To justify her murder, Lemon fabricates a story that she was having an affair with his servant, whom he also murders. He is now free to wed the granddaughter of a wealthy neighbor. However, Lemon keeps seeing the face of his murdered wife, and mistakenly ends up murdering his new wife and her grandfather. Wherever Lemon goes, he faces the grisly spirits of those he has murdered. In his final flight from torment, the lantern that swings over his head has the image of his first wife, Oiwa.

Whole-Class Discussion. Why do you think this story is recorded in art?

Teacher Activity. Assign stories in groups: from *Kwaidan Mimi-Nashi-Hoichi, Rojuro-kubi, Yuki-onna, Oshidori,* and *Jikininki.*

Day 4
Student Outcomes
- Create art inspired by literature.

Materials
　　Art supplies
　　Poster board
　　Examples of other Japanese woodblock prints
　　Index cards
　　Children's books of legendary creatures
　　Final group project assignment, rubric, and prompt

Procedure

Student Activity. Students break into groups to discuss stories. Each group decides which scenes they will create in a Ukiyoe print (a drawing, not actual printmaking). Their Ukiyoes must reveal an aspect of the story through their art. Encourage students to look at children's books.

Teacher Activity. Remind of project components: the "print" and an index card explanation of the significance/relevancy of the story. Completion of this project counts as a 10 point quiz.

Teacher Activity. As students finish their projects, post prints on wall for class viewing.

Teacher Activity. Assign and explain final group project, due Day 10.

FINAL PROJECT: FOLKTALE DRAMA

Dear Distinguished Company of Players,

A great honor has been bestowed upon you! Important visitors from Japan are visiting our school, and we are having a welcoming party for them. The party needs entertainment, and the committee has selected your theatre company to write, direct, and perform a Japanese folktale for these festivities.

Your Company's Task:

Adapt your assigned folktale to a play format: 30 pts.

- *Your play must include good characterization, appropriate dialogue, stage directions, explanations of setting, and sound effects (if needed).*
- *Your script will be evaluated on adaptation, elements of originality, elements of theatre listed above, and elements of writing.*
- *Your play should be 10–15 minutes long. If the folktale is lengthy, you may do a cutting from the story. However, you must then give the audience an explanation of events leading up to and following your chosen scene.*
- *You may add your own twist to the tale (e.g., create a modern interpretation or change the setting). Have fun with this!*

Perform your play: 20 pts:

- *Your 10–15 minute performance must be rehearsed— and professional. Feel free to use costumes, properties, music, or whatever else you believe would enhance your performance. Ask me if you need help.*

We, the committee, look forward to your performance!

Sincerely,

Miss Kind, Chairwoman

FOLKTALE DRAMA RUBRIC

Script:
Dialogue   _____ /5
   Realistic speech reflecting state or personality of characters
Elements of Theatre   _____ /5
      Setting, stage directions, sound effects
      Story related clearly
Originality   _____ /5
      Fun with tale, put own "twist" or "stamp" on it
Style   _____ /5
      Language and voice
Mechanics   _____ /5
Editing   _____ /5

                                                             _____ /30

Presentation:
Evidence of rehearsal   _____ /5
Volume/articulation   _____ /5
Characterization   _____ /5
Visual/action   _____ /5

                                                             _____ /20

Total _____ /50

Comments:

Day 5
Student Outcomes
- Visually organize folktale through map.
- Convert folktale to drama form.
- Work and write cooperatively in small groups.

Materials
   Story organizer
   Paper
   Journals

Procedure
Student Activity. Journal write: Brainstorm ideas for your play. What part of the tale should you include? What can be cut out? What could be added? Do you have costume ideas? How should the main character speak? What does the setting look like?

Teacher Activity. Explain story organizer, a group project.

Folktale Organizer

Name: _____ Date: _____

Opening	Conflict
1.	2.

Rising action	Rising action
4.	3.

Climax	Resolution
5.	6.

Student Activity. Share ideas for play. Complete organizer.

Teacher Activity. Remind students that draft is due on Day 8. Performances will be given on Days 9 and 10.

Day 6
Student Outcomes
- Successfully convert folktale to drama form.
- Work and write cooperatively in small groups.

Materials
Paper
Reserve computers
Transparency of play format

Procedure

Teacher Activity. Mini-lesson on play format.

Student Activity. Group work/playwriting.

Teacher Activity. Assist groups as needed.

Day 7
Student Outcomes
- Convert folktale to drama.
- Work and write cooperatively in small groups.

Materials
Computers
Paper

Procedure

Student Activity. Work on plays.

Teacher Activity. Assist groups as needed. Remind hard copy due tomorrow.

Day 8
Student Outcomes
- Create a character through movement, dialogue, and costume.
- Produce dramatic interpretations of assigned folktale.
- Efficient use of rehearsal time.

Materials
Art supplies
Costume material
Construction paper
Newspaper

Procedure

Student Activity. Rehearsal, costume creation, properties, setting.

Teacher Activity. Assist as needed. Collect hard copies of plays.

Day 9

Student Outcomes
- Effectively embody a character from their folktale.
- Peer critique well.

Materials
    Peer critique forms
    Video camera
    Rubrics

Procedure

Teacher Activity. Review peer critique. Remind of theatre etiquette.

Student Activity. Performances of *Yuki-onna*, *Rokuro-kubi*, and *Jikininki*.

PEER CRITIQUE FOLKTALE DRAMA

Volume/Articulation
Can I hear the actors?
Can I understand what is being said?

Visual
This group used props and/or costumes such as:
The visuals added to the performance by:

Characterization
Some examples of good characterization:
My favorite character was _____ because:

Rehearsal
I could tell this play was rehearsed because:
I could tell this play was not rehearsed because:

Overall
I really liked it when:
I thought this part was confusing:

Comments:

Day 10

Student Outcomes

- Effectively embody a character from folktale.
- Critique peers well.
- Reflect honestly on experience.

Materials

Peer critique forms
Video camera
Rubrics
Journal

Procedure

Teacher Activity. Review peer critique. Remind of theatre etiquette.

Student Activity. Performances of *Mimi-Nashi-Hoichi* and *Oshidori*.

Student Activity. Journal write: Reflect on your experience working in groups, writing as a group, and performing your play. What went well? What didn't? What was most difficult? Most fun? What surprised you about the experience?

QUESTIONS FOR THE KWAIDAN UNIT

1. In her reflection on development of the Kwaidan unit, Nicole notes: "Once I began, I just kept digging and digging." For what and where do you think she was doing her digging? Does a decision to use material from a foreign culture necessarily involve more work than using material from American culture? Or is "digging" a part of every unit plan?
2. Later in her reflection, Nicole states: "It would be interesting to integrate comics and movies. It would be very easy to incorporate the manga [Japanese comics in many genres, very popular with Americans as well] into the woodblock prints." What, then, should Nicole's file for this unit include?
3. Early in the unit, Nicole introduces students to Ukiyoe prints. These are art pieces from a specific time period; she concentrates on the woodblock prints of 19th century artist Yoshitoshi. Due to copyright restrictions, we could not reproduce these images here, but we urge you to take a look at some when you are in the library. They are vivid, captivating in content and design. What is gained from teacher time and energy devoted to integrating art into secondary English units?

EXPLORATION

A World of Possibilities

Make a list of foreign cultures that you either know well or wish to know better. Now pick one that you believe would be of high interest to both you and your students, mixed ability tenth graders. Consider the potential for an integrated language arts approach (i.e., balanced use of listening, speaking, reading, and writing), but with special emphasis on oral language and drama. Also consider how much background knowledge (or time to achieve some!) you might need to successfully develop a unit based in foreign literature, art, and music. Make a few notes for yourself, just enough to discuss your ideas in small group.

REFERENCES

Barnes, Douglas. *From Communication to Curriculum.* Harmondsworth, UK: Penguin, 1976.

Bolche, Linda, et al. "Fishbowls, Creative Controversy, Talking Chips: Exploring Literature Cooperatively." *English Journal* (Oct. 1933): 43–48.

Bosma, Bette. *Fairy Tales, Fables, Legends, and Myths: Using Folk Literature in Your Classroom.* New York: Teachers College Press, 1987.

Burke, Jim. *The English Teacher's Companion.* 2nd ed. Portsmouth: Heinemann, 1999.

Bushman, John H., and Kay Parks Bushman. *Using Young Adult Literature in the English Classroom.* Upper Saddle River: Merrill/Prentice Hall, 1993.

Cazden, Courtney B. *Classroom Discourse.* Portsmouth: Heinemann, 1988.

Cole, Pam B. "Bridging *The Red Badge of Courage* With Six Related Young Adult Novels." *Adolescent Literature as a Complement to the Classics.* Ed. J. Kaywell. Vol. 2. Norwood: Christopher-Gordon, 1994. 21–39.

Delpit, Lisa D. "Language Diversity and Learning." *Perspectives on Talk and Learning.* Eds. Susan Hynds and Donald Rubin. Urbana: NCTE, 1990. 247–66.

Devine, Thomas. *Listening Skills Schoolwide: Activities and Programs.* Urbana, NCTE, 1982.

Dickel, Gail M. "A Tradition of Storytelling." *SchoolArts* (April 1996).

Egenberger, Pat. "Multilingual Folktale Book." *Classroom Publishing: A Practical Guide to Enhancing Student Literacy.* Eds. Laurie King and Dennis Stovel. Hillsboro: Blue Heron, 1992: 79–82.

Fortier, John. "What to Do Until the Doctor Comes: Speech in the English Language Arts Classroom." *Wisconsin English Journal* (January 1987): 2–6.

Furlong, V. J., and A. D. Edwards. *The Language of Teaching: Meaning in Classroom Interaction.* London: Heinemann, 1978.

Gonzales, Roseann Duenas. "Teaching Mexican American Students to Write: Capitalizing on Culture." *English Journal* (Oct. 1982): 20–24.

Goulden, Nancy Rost. "Implementing Speaking and Listening Standards: Information for English Teachers." *English Journal* (Sept. 1988): 90–96.

Heath, Shirley Brice. *Ways with Words: Language, Life, and Work in Communities and Classrooms.* Cambridge: Cambridge U. Press, 1983.

Johnson, Terry D., and Daphne R. Louis. *Literacy Through Literature.* Portsmouth: Heinemann, 1985.

Katz Weinberg, Susan. "Unforgettable Memories: Oral History in the Middle School Classroom." *Voices from the Middle.* 3.3 (Sept. 1996).

Kind, Nicole. "Kwaidan: A Lesson Plan Integrating Japanese Legend and Art." English 604. University of Wisconsin-Eau Claire, Spring 2003.

King, Nancy. *Storymaking and Drama.* Portsmouth, NH: Heinemann, 1993.

Koehler, Mary Beth. "The Trickster." English 606. University of Wisconsin-Eau Claire, 1995.

Koehler, Nancy. "Pourquoi Stories: How and Why." English 406. University of Wisconsin-Eau Claire, 1995.

Lowry, Lois. *The Giver.* New York: Bantam Doubleday Dell, 1993.

Lundsteen, Sara W. *Listening.* Urbana: NCTE, 1979.

Milner, Joseph O'Beirne, and Lucy Floyd Morcock Milner. *Bridging English.* 2d ed. Upper Saddle River: Merrill/Prentice Hall, 1999.

Moen, Christine Boardman. *Better than Book Reports.* New York: Scholastic, 1992.

Moffett, James, and Betty Jane Wagner. *Student-Centered Language Arts, K–12.* 4th ed. Portsmouth: Boynton/Cook, Heinemann, 1992.

Moss, Joy F. Literary Discussion in the Elementary School. Urbana: National Council of Teachers of English, 2002.

O'Keefe, Virginia. *Speaking to Think/Thinking to Speak: The Importance of Talk in the Learning Process.* Portsmouth: Boynton/Cook, Heinemann, 1995.

Schaffer, Jane C. "Improving Discussion Questions: Is Anyone Out There Listening?" *English Journal* (April 1989): 40–42.

Schilz, Candice C. "Korhogo Story Cloth." *SchoolArts* (April 1996).

Sorenson, Margo. "Teaching Each Other: Connecting Talking and Writing." *English Journal* (Jan. 1993): 42–47.

Sowder, Wilbur H. "Fostering Discussion in the Language-Arts Classroom." *English Journal* (Oct. 1993): 39–42.

Stubbs, Michael. *Language, Schools and Classrooms.* London: Methuen, 1972.

Swartz, Larry. *Dramathemes: A Practical Guide for Teaching Drama.* Markham, Ont.: Pembroke, 1988.

Wagner, Betty Jane. "Dramatic Improvisation in the Classroom." *Perspectives on Talk and Learning.* Eds. S. Hynds and D. Rubin. Urbana: NCTE, 1990. 195–212.

Wisconsin Department of Public Instruction. *A Guide to Curriculum Planning in the English Language Arts.* Madison, WI: Department of Public Instruction, 1986.

_____ . *A Guide to Curriculum Planning in Classroom Drama and Theatre.* Madison, WI: Department of Public Instruction, 1990.

_____ . *Classroom Activities in Speaking and Listening.* Madison, WI: Department of Public Instruction, 1991.

Teaching Composition

6

What more important service can we perform for ourselves than to write; to write, that is, not to get a grade or pass a course, but to sound the depths, to explore, to discover; to save our floundering selves.

James E. Miller Jr. (7)

 BACKGROUND OF TEACHING COMPOSITION

Writing is a complex skill, and the teaching of writing is multidimensional. We must help students discover their own knowledge and their own voices. We need to help young writers develop the techniques necessary to write their ideas coherently in a form comprehensible and appropriate for others. No one method is best for teaching writing, but the work of educators and researchers during the past 20 years has helped us understand how to improve the teaching of writing.

 RESEARCH ON WRITING

Concerns with how we teach composition are not new. From the first issue of the *English Journal* in 1912, teachers have struggled to find the most effective ways of helping students write well. Although the emphasis has changed over the years, many of the same issues that teachers of the 1920s worried about are still with us, including (1) writing in other subjects, (2) lessening the burden of grading, (3) balancing the teaching of skills with content, and (4) choosing topics of interest to students (Maxwell, "So What's New?" 2–4). In the 1930s, the emphasis was on motivating students to write and finding ways to make writing meaningful to them, while correct

181

punctuation was also a concern. Although we may think of journal writing as a fairly new idea in teaching writing, Eleanor Brown introduced it in 1934 as a way to avoid the stiffness of formal writing (Maxwell, "So What's New?" 7).

Articles during the 1940s focused on the importance of students writing about subjects that mattered to them. The 1950s reemphasized the concern with errors and ways to help students learn the basics of writing, although many of the *English Journal* authors continued to examine ways of bringing real-life experiences into student writing (Maxwell, "So What's New?" 9–11).

A growing concern in the 1960s was that, although teaching composition had been an established part of English programs since the early 1900s, there was no comprehensive understanding of how to teach writing. Educators were moving from a concern with the written product to an emphasis on the process of writing, but not until a 1966 conference at Dartmouth College in Hanover, New Hampshire, did process writing become integrated with the teaching of writing in the schools. The Dartmouth Conference emphasized personal growth in both writing and literature, and the participants advocated moving from product to process in the teaching of writing.

John Dixon, one of the participants, described the thinking, discussing, and sharing that went on at Dartmouth in *Growth Through English*. He stressed the need for students to talk about their experiences before attempting to write. "Talking it over, thinking it over, and (as confidence is gained) writing, can be natural parts of taking account of new experiences" (28). The ideas of exploratory talking before writing and talking in groups as part of the writing process were quite different ways of viewing the teaching of writing.

Traditionally, when writing instruction focused on the product, teachers told students what they did wrong, hoping they would then learn. Such an approach has the wrong emphasis. Learning is much easier when we are praised for what we do right. If we concentrate on what we do wrong when we are learning to ski, golf, or roller skate, we tend to repeat our mistakes. If we are praised for what we do correctly, we learn more easily because we concentrate on what we do right. Praise must always be honest and specific to be helpful. We all find learning easier and more pleasant when we receive praise and encouragement.

Writing instruction, before the writing process, took just the opposite approach. On Monday, teachers typically assigned a theme, explained it carefully, and asked if there were any questions. The students handed in the themes on Friday, and dedicated teachers spent the weekend going over the papers, noting every error. The model was a negative one: what not to do. As a result, students did not write well, nor did they like to write. In the traditional model, a teacher was usually the giver of information and the hunter of errors, the examiner.

Writing did not improve for the majority of students. The more red ink and negative comments, the less students paid attention to what teachers wrote on their papers. What a discouraging situation for teachers! Students looked at the grade, and without reading the comments, threw the paper away because there was no opportunity for revision. This situation was just as discouraging for students, particularly for those who had difficulty with writing. They did not know what area or skill to begin working on and the frustration kept them from writing.

⟲ *Reflection* ⟲

Describe yourself as a writer. Do you consider yourself a writer? What kinds of writing do you do and how often? What purposes does writing serve for you? What types of writing did you do in elementary and secondary schools? How might your own experience in writing influence how you will teach writing?

WRITING PROCESS

Teaching writing as a process means that writers can improve their writing at any or all stages from first thoughts about a topic to finished draft. Teachers do not treat each paper as though it had to be carefully scrutinized. The following example illustrates the frustrations a new teacher may experience:

> Joellen, a first-year teacher, planned on putting the writing process into action in her sophomore English class. She liked to write, especially poetry, and was determined to help her students succeed at writing. She assigned a variety of writing activities and included brainstorming and discussion to help students get started. Before long, Joellen felt completely swamped with the amount of grading she had to do and found she was devoting evenings and weekends to a seemingly endless pile of papers. She considered cutting back on the amount of writing she was requiring, but because of her commitment to have students experience a wealth of writing activities, she felt guilty about that. Her students began to complain that they were not getting their papers returned quickly enough, and some rebelled about turning in any more work. With each passing week, Joellen became more and more frustrated with the situation.

Joellen's experiences are not uncommon among both new and experienced teachers. Part of the problem is that she is trying to improve students' writing by looking at a finished product, when the main difficulty with the papers may have occurred much earlier when students were generating ideas for their topic. When evaluation occurs only after the paper is turned in to the teacher, the basic problems may be engulfed in a morass of red-penned punctuation errors. By contrast, teaching writing as a process is an ongoing activity in which teachers can help students whenever problems occur. With movement to a more process-oriented approach to writing, the teacher's role had to be redefined.

The writing process is described as loosely fitting into stages: prewriting or discovery, drafting, revising, and editing. However, the writing process is not made up of a series of discrete linear steps leading to a finished product; it is recursive. That is, a writer goes back and forth from one stage to another as the writing progresses. For instance, a writer first considers what to write about and how best to get started. As the draftings, or first attempts at writing, proceed, the writer may return to the discovery stage to rethink what to write or to explore other ideas and feelings. A writer will have several drafts as the writing develops. At the revision stage, the writer may return to discovery activities when it becomes clear the writing needs more than minor revising. Throughout the process, writers move in and out of stages as the writing demands. The following diagram illustrates the recursive nature of the process approach to writing:

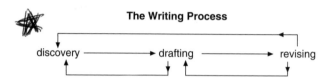

The Writing Process

discovery ⟶ drafting ⟶ revising

STAGES IN THE WRITING PROCESS

1- discovery
2- drafting
3- revising
4- editing
5- publishing

Discovery Stage

discovery
prewriting

The discovery stage is the most important step in writing something interesting, honest, and lively. Various activities help writers discover what they know and what they want to say. These activities might include creative dramatics, films, discussion, reading, and writing. Many people call this stage *prewriting,* but that term does not reflect the many writing activities that occur at this stage. Because this beginning step is discovering a topic and how to explore it, *discovery* is a more apt name for this stage.

D. Gordon Rohman coined the term *prewriting* in 1965 when he conducted a study on first-year writers at Michigan State University. He believed students needed time for thinking to develop their ideas and plans for writing. He used journal writing as the prewriting activity and found students improved their writing when given the time and method to discover what and how they would write.

In a 1971 study, Janet Emig found that prewriting was a much longer process when students wrote on self-chosen topics than when writing school assignments. This is true partly because teachers do not provide time for prewriting, but also because students cannot explore their thoughts for writing when the topic is unfamiliar or uninteresting. Allowing time for students to think and talk about writing is essential.

Without discovery activities, writers tend to develop papers that lack their own voice. The writing also lacks depth and details to make the writing interesting. The papers look more like writing done to fill a required assignment rather than writing a student cares about. Discovery activities help from the beginning, at the point students are trying to decide on a topic.

students must choose their topics

To be successful writers, students must be interested in what they are writing about. This means giving students the freedom to select their own topics. A teacher can provide a general area or a list of possible topics, for example, "Choose one of the characters in *Great Expectations* and explain how he or she changed throughout the novel" or based on the novel *The Giver,* "What if we had a Giver/Receiver in today's world? What kind of burdens would he or she have to carry around?" Within this broad idea, students need to be able to choose their specific topic. Even with choices, some students cannot think of what they want to write about. Teachers may suggest alternative topics, but other students are often a better source of help. As noted earlier, John Dixon recommends exploratory talk before writing and talking in small groups. Class discussions about possible choices and small-group discussion provide a rich source of possible topics. After students select their topic, they meet in groups and the teacher instructs them to talk about their choices—why they think they would like to write about a particular one or what they already know about it. Members of the group help anyone who is having difficulty in deciding on a topic.

After a topic is chosen, several discovery activities help students develop their thoughts. Discussing ideas and getting immediate feedback are a tremendous help. If the general topic is writing about how a character in a novel changed over the course of the story and the reasons for the change, hearing how others perceive the character's development can help someone decide what to write about. The same is true with other kinds of assignments. If students are writing persuasive letters, for example, taking part in discussions about why and to whom a particular letter needs to be written helps generate ideas. Sharing ideas about writing is the most effective way to help writers get started.

A contemporary writing classroom is a talking classroom. In traditional classrooms, students wrote in isolation. Opportunities for exchanging ideas did not exist. In the real world, however, we share our writing. When we write a line or paragraph that we believe is particularly good, our first impulse is to read it to someone. We all have turned to someone and said, "Listen to this!" Except for private journal writing (and even that sometimes), writing is meant to be shared.

At the point where we are generating ideas and drafting, we need to think of what it is we mean—in other words, the content—and save the urge to correct for later in the process, when editing and proofreading are appropriate. As Tom Romano reminds us:

> We [teachers] must strive to keep editing skills in perspective—a part of the writing process. Countless people have had their attitudes about the creative act of writing permanently darkened by a teacher who emphasized perfection in editing to the point that all other parts of the writing process did not matter. (74)

Discovery Activities

Depending on the writing task, a variety of discovery activities help students get started. All of the activities need to be modeled for the students, either by the teacher and students or a group of students. Student work from previous classes can be used to illustrate how others used the various discovery activities.

1. *Free writing.* At the top of a page students write the name of their topic or idea—such as a person they admire. Then for a specified amount of time, not more than 10 minutes, they write everything they can possibly think of connected with that subject. The term *free* means that the writer is free to put down anything that comes to mind and free from any concerns of mechanics or spelling. Often, we discover what we want to say in the very act of writing; thus, early concern about correctness may block the discovery. When time is up, students read what they wrote and then circle phrases and words that seem especially appropriate to them. At this point, if time permits, they meet in groups and share their writing with others. The

next step is to write again, elaborating on the circled phrases, although they can develop the piece any way they want. Free writing often brings thoughts to mind that more structured writing would not tap into, as shown by the following example by a ninth-grade writer:

I wish I had a show dog because I like dogs & my friends have animals to show-Skippy would like another dog-small-female-laid back Mom would object-too much work-??? Sheltie-really cute-love the long nose- I would clean up after it & it would be good responsibility for me Sheltie good size-wouldn't be that much work after house trained.

2. *Drawing.* Like free writing, drawing taps hidden thoughts and new connections. One does not have to be good at drawing for this to be a successful activity. If the assignment is to describe an incident from childhood, drawing a location or scene helps fill in vivid details and spurs the memory into recalling more details. When writing a description of my grandmother, I drew a sketch of the pantry in her house. Although I didn't include the pantry itself in the essay, the act of drawing it brought to mind several incidents I had not thought of. Unfortunately, after students leave elementary school, drawing is no longer incorporated into language arts and they lose an important way of thinking. The figure below shows a sketch drawn by a student to create a setting for her story. She probably will not refer directly to the plan but can now picture it clearly as her characters and plot develop.

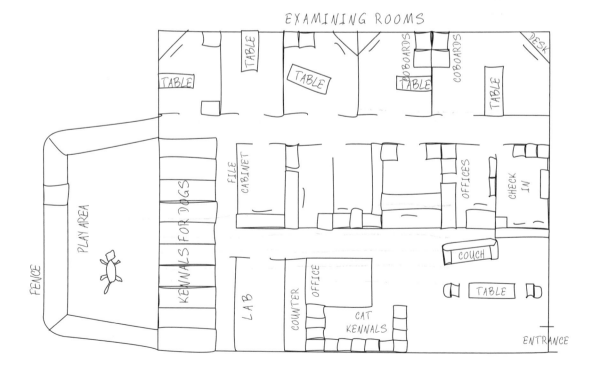

3. *Mapping*. When the writing topic is not familiar to the writers, mapping helps generate ideas and organization. Mapping is sometimes called *webbing* because the resulting diagram resembles a spider web. By either name, the intention is to generate and connect subtopics. The subject is placed in the center of the paper, and topics are added on extending lines as the writer thinks of them. If students prefer to use a computer for discovery activities, Inspiration is a helpful software program. A map on the topic of changing the school calendar might look like the one below.

4. *Outlining*. After the map is completed, students can prepare an informal outline to help structure their thoughts as they begin to write. A more formal outline with the traditional Roman numerals and capital letters can also be used. For some students, though, the structure gets in the way. People have different ways of organizing their thoughts, and teachers need to keep the differences in mind. The learning styles discussed in Chapter 2 play an important part in how students use the techniques to organize. When English teachers require a formal outline with the writing assignment, many students write the paper first, then the outline. They cannot plan the whole paper before actually beginning to compose. One writer said, "How can I do an outline when I don't know yet what I'm going to write?" However, not everyone would have that difficulty. Some writers will find particular discovery activities helpful whereas others may not. For that reason, it is best to suggest two or three activities, and let students use the ones that are most helpful to them.

5. *Creative dramatics.* This discovery technique works for many kinds of writing. The definition of creative dramatics includes impromptu acting, role playing, and skits, all requiring little preparation time. The audience is the class. The objective is not to put on a performance but to engage in an activity that promotes better writing. For example, if the assignment is to write a persuasive letter about a desired change in school policy, students role-play for each other, taking the parts of parents, school administrators, school board members, and other community members. Exchanging roles helps to clarify the issues and encourages students to see different sides of the arguments. As a result, their letters are more convincing.

Taking the role of a character in a story helps students understand the personality and motivation of a character better. The actors do not memorize lines but improvise dialogue. Empathy for and realization of a character's behavior are reflected later in the student's writing. To be successful, creative dramatics should be introduced gradually and always presented as an informal activity.

A creative dramatic activity that always produces enthusiasm is a discovery technique designed to help students write dialogue. In groups of four to six, each group receives a bag of props that the teacher has filled with an assortment of items. A bag could contain a hammer, a hair clip, and a copy of Robert Frost's poems, an apple, a feather, knife sharpener, and a pair of safety glasses. The students have about 25 minutes to think up a skit, and then each group performs the skit for the rest of the class. The one rule is that every prop must be used. During the following period, the students discuss how the dialogue carried the skit along.

This discovery activity provides practice for future writing assignments, but does not necessarily lead immediately into the writing. A teacher might provide several activities to help students discover how dialogue can be used effectively before having students write a short story.

EXPLORATION

Writer's Block

Students occasionally have difficulty in choosing a topic. How could you help a student who often has "writer's block"? Think of some assignment-specific ways as well as general ways to help students generate writing ideas.

(2) Drafting Stage

For successful writing, students must realize the importance of multiple drafts. First drafts should be messy. After the discovery stage, a writer has a great deal to say. Because the brain thinks more quickly than the hand can write, there is no time to worry about spelling or punctuation. Helping students realize that putting something down

Why do they have to be messy? What if a stud. doesn't work that way?

worth reading is far more important than putting something down right is an important lesson at this stage. The need for correctness at this early stage gets in the way of successful writing. Writers attend to correctness later in the process. There are several ways teachers can help students become fluent writers.

1. Always refer to the writing as *drafts*. Asking if someone is on a second or third draft helps establish the notion of multiple drafts. The version students turn in is called a *final draft* rather than a *final paper* because no paper is really ever "finished." That's not to discourage writers, but to acknowledge that given more time, they could have polished it even more.

2. Drafting does not have to proceed from beginning to end; in fact, papers are usually better if one does not start at the beginning. At one time or another, we all stare at a blank sheet of paper not knowing where to start. Even when using discovery techniques, writing that first line is difficult. By encouraging students not to start at the beginning, we can help students overcome that writing block. Middle school students can actually fold down the top third of the sheet of paper to concretely show they are not writing the beginning sentence. It is amazing how freeing that can be. When students complain to a teacher they "don't know what to say," the best help is for a teacher to ask them what it is they "want to say." Writers can usually articulate their thoughts, but cannot figure out how to get started. The teacher may respond, "Why not write what you just said?" Some seem to need permission to write what they want to write—to be told yes, that sounds good. Often beginnings are best written after the rest of the paper is done, particularly in expository writing.

3. When drafts are first shared in writing groups, no one but the writer actually sees the paper. Authors read their own papers aloud to the other students in the group, so that no one is embarrassed by errors or poor handwriting. The emphasis is on what is being said, and that is exactly where it should be at this stage. Multiple drafts are needed for students to improve their writing.

(handwritten margin note: interesting technique)

 ## Revising Stage

An important point here is that not all writing goes through every stage of the writing process. To get better at anything we must practice, and practice activities are usually not revised. Revision is important, but it takes time, and usually time is in short supply in our classrooms. If all writing assignments go through the entire process, we cannot teach the different kinds of assignments that provide the experiences in writing our students need.

Revision always begins with the writer. We all need help from other readers to improve our writing, but first students need to read their own work with as critical an eye as possible. Reading the piece oneself is an essential first step before getting help from others. In addition, reading the piece aloud helps the writer hear redundancies, omissions, and incorrect word choices. When the revision process is first introduced to students, filling out a memo is a useful strategy (see Figure 6.1).

Figure 6.1 Revision memo

Your name _____ Title of writing _____

step 1 → Date you read this piece aloud and made revisions _____

step 2 → Date your writing group heard your paper _____

Names of writing group members   _____ _____

_____ _____

_____ _____

step 3 → Date your partner read your piece _____

Signature of writing partner _____

Later, when they are experienced with the three steps, the memo is no longer required. Perhaps this seems more detailed than necessary, but as students are learning the process they need to be reminded of each step.

The second step involves the writing group mentioned in the memo. The groups are fairly large—five or six members—so that each writer benefits from hearing several responses. Groups can be formed in several ways. The teacher may form the groups so that a variety of ability levels is in each group, do a random selection, or select students based on their personalities, such as putting quiet students with more outgoing ones. Many teachers allow students to form their own groups. Perhaps the key to success is to use a variety of ways. Working in groups helps students to know each other; if they always work with ones they know best, they won't expand their circle of friends. On the other hand, students resent always being told with whom they can work. The groups stay together through the process for one piece of writing. With a new assignment, new groups form. Even though students may want to remain in the groups they have worked with, reforming group membership helps develop social interaction, eliminates the problem of cliques, and provides fresh perspectives for their writing.

When students meet in their writing groups, each student reads his or her piece aloud to the others. At this point, it is important for students to not read others' papers silently, but to listen carefully as the author reads. In this way, the listeners concentrate on writing as a whole: Is it interesting? Are there enough details to make the meaning clear? Does it have a flow of ideas? Are there gaps making it difficult to understand?

The others respond with suggestions for improving the writing, which takes some guidance from the teacher. The first time a teacher tries response groups in class, they may not work. One problem is that students will not stay on the task of talking about their papers, which is a natural outcome when friends meet together. A second problem is that students often are overly pleasant to each other. They tell each other how wonderful everyone's writing is, which is no help at all. Again, this is not surprising because everyone has to read his or her paper aloud, and no one wants to be too critical. To make response groups work, teachers need to provide guidance through the use of response sheets or some form of written response.

Response sheet like those from Victor's room

Figure 6.2 Response sheet

Writer's name _____

1. What is the paper about? Sum up in a sentence or two what points the author makes.
2. In what ways is the paper interesting?
3. Where could more detail or explanation be added? How would the additions help?
4. What words or phrases are especially effective?
5. What information is unnecessary?
6. What parts should be changed?
7. What other advice can you give to the writer to make this a better paper?

Your name(s)   _____

_____

Figure 6.3 Response sheet for informational or expository writing

Writer's name _____

1. What is your overall impression of the paper?
2. What is the thesis (implied or stated)?
3. In what ways is it interesting? Where should detail be added? Be sure there is enough detail for you, as a reader, to understand the idea the author wants to convey.
4. In what ways could sentences be improved?
5. Look for transitions, especially between paragraphs. Where should transitions be added?
6. What words and phrases are especially effective?
7. What words are unnecessary?
8. What words should be changed?
9. Sum up in a sentence or two what the paper is about. What points does the author make?
10. How could the author make this a better paper?

Signed _____

One way that helps students is to have them fill in response sheets, such as the one shown in Figure 6.2, after each writer reads the piece.

A second example of a response sheet intended for informational or expository writing is shown in Figure 6.3.

On the actual response sheet the students receive, spaces are left between questions to allow for written responses. Students respond to all these questions without actually looking at each other's papers, so they must listen closely when the paper is read aloud. Students often ask the writer to reread a section or repeat a sentence. Usually each student fills out a sheet so that the writer has five different responses if there are six in a group. Students may also work with a partner and fill one out together, and then both sign. We do not recommend having all of the students work on just one response sheet because it ends up being the response of only one or two. They discuss what they liked the best and ask for clarifications so that the writer and responders are all talking together about the paper. The procedure continues for each member of the group. This process takes an entire class period, and a teacher needs to make the groups small enough to make sure everyone has a turn during the same class. Students make revisions, usually as homework, before the next step in the writing process.

Students need to realize they do not have to take all the advice they receive. They should give it careful consideration, but the writers must decide if the suggestions are appropriate for their paper. They won't agree with some of the suggestions, but they need to take them seriously. Students who have trouble writing can offer suggestions that are just as valid as those who write with little difficulty. They know as well as anyone whether a paper is interesting and makes sense.

Sometimes students will say that the response group did not help them. This is partly the writer's responsibility and teachers have to help students use the writing group in the most effective way. When students know they have difficulty with a particular area, they need to ask the group for specific help. Someone might be marked down consistently for not using enough detailed description and that student needs to ask specifically for help with including details.

Editing Stage

Dan Kirby and Tom Liner support keeping skills in perspective, suggesting that we "treat proofreading as something to be done quickly and efficiently, rather than as a climatic step in the process of composing. Only when proofreading is made a mysterious and complex part of the mastery of Standard English does it become intimidating and therefore difficult for students" (235).

Editing and proofreading are necessary only when the writing is published—that is, when it has a wider and perhaps unknown audience. If students work with word processing, they bring a clean copy to the editing session. Otherwise, students do not have to copy the entire piece, but it should be revised and ready to be copied for the final draft. A paper may look messy with corrections written above a word, words crossed off, and other words inserted, but everything should be as correct as possible, including spelling and punctuation.

The editing stage is the first time students are allowed to read each other's papers. The students meet in the same group they did in the revising stage. The first procedure is the same as last time; each reads the revised paper to the others. This time, however, they do not fill out a response sheet, but rather talk about the changes, and the writer usually explains the thinking behind the changes. Often writers make more

[Handwritten margin note, top left:] But, when asking people it's like specific questions, etc. Isn't it necessary to actually see the paper? transitions, etc. to what if they can't remember them? listening + then don't give an effective response?

[Handwritten margin note, bottom left:] If the papers are long, this is going to take a lot of time

revisions than the group suggested because once they start revising they see the need for more changes. The writer may jot down notes as the others respond.

After everyone has read the papers, the members pair up and edit each other's papers. With less experienced writers, many teachers use editing guides. These vary with assignments and with the age of the students. The guides are used to focus attention on various problem areas; they are not handed in. At this point in the writing process, students may write on each other's papers. An editing guide for an expository writing assignment for juniors or seniors might look like the one in Figure 6.4.

The points on the editing sheet will change depending on the assignment. Also, students' developmental level affects the direction of editing. An editing guide for middle school students writing a descriptive personal experience paper might look like the one in Figure 6.5.

Figure 6.4   Editing guide for an expository writing assignment

1. The paper must support the thesis. Read the paper over and come back to the thesis, making sure it is appropriate.
2. Semicolons are causing problems for some. Check especially for proper use. A semicolon followed by an incomplete sentence is the most common mistake.
3. Transitions between paragraphs are another trouble spot.
4. Borrowed material needs to be introduced. Why is this source being used? Who is this person? Is the source outdated?
5. Any questions about spelling should be answered at this point. Remember that it is better to look up a word than to take a chance if you are unsure.
6. Do a final check on punctuation, subject–verb agreement, and pronoun reference.

Figure 6.5   Editing guide for descriptive personal experience writing

1. Together check every adjective and verb, making sure the editor knows what the writer means.
2. Look at the sentences. If they all begin with a subject followed by a verb, decide which ones to change.
3. Read for clichés and change to more appropriate comparisons.
4. Check for spelling. Remember to look up words you are not sure of.
5. In the last papers many students had trouble remembering to use commas. Together check each other's papers, reading sections aloud where you are not sure about comma placement.
6. Check over the paper carefully for any mechanical errors. Remember this takes patience and is a responsibility of both the writer and the editor.

Student editors, at any grade level, are more effective if they receive guidance in what to look for. Telling students to check everything is too unfocused, and they catch few mistakes that way. Also, giving them checklists is not helpful. It is easy to go down a list of yes or no questions and not really look for ways to improve the paper. Checklists are particularly useless when writers use them for their own work. The lists are meant to be reminders, but if a writer already believes the paper is in good shape, the questions are answered with a yes, with little thought. The more the editors are involved in the process, the better they will do. Sometimes teachers ask students to copy the writer's best sentence and explain why it works so well. They may also copy the sentence that most needs to be rewritten. Editing guides can focus on specific areas the class as a whole is having trouble with.

Just before the editing sessions, teachers should do a mini-lesson for the whole class on problem areas. A mini-lesson deals with one skill; for example, using semicolons. In about 10 minutes a teacher should cover the uses and show examples. Because the students are going right into editing groups, they can focus on that particular skill.

Students need to bring writing handbooks to class to use as a reference when editing. Without them, they rely solely on the teacher to answer questions of usage and punctuation. We want our students to learn how to function without us—in this case, to know how to write polished papers. Most students often underuse a handbook, and teachers can show them how to use it, much as they would a dictionary. When students ask a question during an editing session, the teacher should help the students find the answer in a handbook rather than supplying the answer. Also, when a teacher evaluates a paper, rather than only marking an incorrect usage, they note the handbook page the student can refer to. In this way, students learn a skill that helps them with future papers as well as the one they are working on.

Publishing Student Writing

In some cases, publishing is listed as the final step in the writing process. Although publishing is important for widening the audience for student writers and can be used successfully for many writing activities, students need to produce many different kinds of writing and for many different purposes to increase fluency. Public expectation is that published writing should be free of errors. The emphasis for writing, then, is always on a polished final draft. When students know their work is going public, they have more motivation to check usage, mechanics, and spelling; however, creating a polished paper worthy of publication takes a good deal of time, time away from learning different uses and modes of writing.

The time taken up in editing cuts down on the variety of writing experiences. During the year a few assignments can be considered for publication, but not many, so that fluency remains a priority.

Places that publish student work are plentiful. The National Council of Teachers of English sponsors writing contests for students in middle and senior high school. Various national publications for young people also solicit original writing. We can use students' interest in issues to encourage them to write persuasive letters to newspapers and school publications. Organizations and businesses usually respond to a student letter asking for information. Many businesses publish student work in their own publications. Clinics or medical offices might allow a student anthology in their waiting areas or nursing home residents might welcome student work or correspondence. The class may want to set up its own literary magazine and publish works by student authors. Many outlets for young writers are available.

Submission requirements for many publications are described in the yearly editions of *Writer's Market (Writer's Digest Books)* and *The Writer's Handbook (The Writer, Inc.)*. Both of these publications are excellent sources for writers and are readily found in libraries.

THE WRITING PROCESS IN ACTION

As we have discussed earlier, the writing process is recursive; writers move back and forth among the stages as they write. During drafting, writers may come to a standstill and be unable to think of what to say next. The best way to overcome this problem is to go back to discovery activities. Students could brainstorm on what they are trying to say or try mapping with the specific area they are working on or free-write all they know about the topic and move on to drafting again. At the revision stage, writers often return to drafting, rewriting sections or whole pages; here, too, they may use discovery activities again. Teachers need to remind students repeatedly of the recursive aspect of writing. The strength of the process is that writers are learning to improve their writing as they write, not after the writing is finished. Two major points are important in teaching writing using the writing process method:

1. The process is recursive. Writers move back and forth among stages as the need arises.
2. Not all writing tasks go through all of the stages—in particular, the stage of editing.

Laura Apfelbeck describes how she implemented a writing process in a seventh-grade class.

> In the first writing workshop, we study the writing process—discovery, rough drafts, revising, editing, final draft. During the writer's workshop, we produced descriptive, narrative, and persuasive pieces—most were about two pages long. For the descriptive and narrative pieces, the assignment was quite open. In class, I led mini-lessons on creating word pictures, using sensory images, writing good hooks and endings, and adding dialogue. After brainstorming topics, students could choose anything to write on except it had to be realistic (no alien abductions, etc., because they write only plot with no description, characterization, or theme). Many of the writings combine description and narration—and that's okay because it's a natural way to write. After discovery activities, drafting, and revising on their own and with peers, students hand their work in to me for a teacher edit. I write lots of comments, about the good and bad stuff on their papers. It is their choice whether to take my comments or improve in a different way. After they receive their papers back, they revise again with peers, and then can turn it in for another teacher edit or write a final draft.

In some cases, peer groups are not all that helpful and students who can't get the help they need and want become very frustrated. A teacher has the skill and insight to help a student discover what it is he or she wants to communicate when the student might not be clear of this himself or herself. In the following example, Apfelbeck writes comments and questions on a secondary student's paper. (Her comments are in brackets.) Notice how she coaches and probes the author into defining purpose and point of view, while also helping with standard writing skills.

MORE THAN JUST FISHING
By Scott Miller

Every year around late fall fishermen anxiously await the dawn of the new ice fishing season. *["Every year around" is vague as an opening image and doesn't help readers visualize. Try and think of images that bring the reader into a particular place.]* It takes a rare person to actually enjoy the sport. To most it is just sitting on a barren, enormously large chunk of frozen water staring into a tiny hole. *[Good image.]* To the ice fisherman that black seemingly endless whole is where all of your hopes lie. *[Here you show that hope is your main point. Check for shifts in viewpoint (the ice fisherman. . . you).]* To them dangling that brightly colored piece of lead into the volleyball sized whole *[Great description],* in the frozen water is more excitement and more enjoyment than anyone could imagine. *[Be specific to help the reader imagine.]* There is always that faint glimmer of hope that below the frozen surface, maybe right beneath where you are sitting there is predator stalking that tiny insignificant piece of lead. Waiting to give you the fight of your life, or maybe easily be pulled from his home into ours. *[Think about the main point of your essay. Do you want to emphasize a fight for the fish or an easy catch?]*

The thought of maybe catching the big one is not the only thing that draws the ice fisherman out of there warm and protective houses into sub zero days of winter, which to the fisherman can seem more like a cave than warm and cozy house. Believe it or not we actually head out the frozen desert every chance we can to enjoy that sub zero weather. The sun spreads whatever warmth it has fighting the cold winds offering some comfort, but mearly seeing the inviting glow of the sun during the dreary weather of winter is enough to satisfy most fishermen. The wicked and chilling winds can pierce right to the bone at times causing your body to sting and feel almost if there are millions of microscopic needles piercing the skin. Relief however lies just inches from you in your ice shanty. Inside your ice shanty is the inviting hum of your heater, warding away the toughest winds. *[Maybe connect to hope again in this paragraph, if that's the main focus. You get close (warmth of the sun, inviting hum of the heater) but maybe take the idea of hope a bit further.]*

One of the most peaceful and serene places in the entire world is on the middle of an abandoned lake in the middle of the night. *[Here you've switched from hopeful to peaceful. Maybe you want both ideas in the thesis, or maybe you want to focus on one exclusively. You'll need to either revise the thesis or refocus this body paragraph.]* When you look outside of your shanty all you see is the tiny lights on the opposite shore, like hundreds of fireflies. The only sounds you hear is the wind gently whistling and rustling the bare branches of the trees, and the humming and occasional pinging of the heater keeping the harsh winter air from chilling you.

[Notice the viewpoint shifs—earlier you focused on WE (first person plural), but here you focus on YOU (second person plural).]

Friends and family are very important attractions ice fishing. It gives my dad and I time to just sit and enjoy each other's company. *[Okay, the shanty is hopeful, peaceful, and _____. You need a word to describe this togetherness thing. And, you need to get that idea into your thesis, or refocus the paragraph and concentrate on hope—hope in terms of the relationship, perhaps.]* There are times when the fishing is the best that the lake is almost transformed into a frozen community of sportsmen. The air is filled with the sound of ice augers scraping and chipping through the rock hard foundation *[Describe the sound.]* which we all depend on to keep us from the black icy water that lies beneath us. Meaningless but enjoyable chatter fills the air as friends and family catch up and new friends are made. *[Examples?]* Charcoal and barbecue are distinctly noticed as the smell fills your nose warming you up instantly. The whine of snowmobiles is heard in the distance. Fish are far and few in between during the ice fishing months, but that really doesn't matter to most of the fishermen out there to most of them it is the things that I mentioned earlier that draw them out day after day, year after year. *[Avoid this style of announcing what you've done. It doesn't fit the rest of the essay.]*

EXPLORATION

Helping Students Improve Their Writing

The following essay has gone through peer editing; however, the student still needs help in focusing on his theme and main idea. Write comments as if you were his teacher helping him improve his writing.

MY FAVORITE PLACE: THE YMCA

By Steve Reiner

When most people think of a favorite place they think of a place where you can relax and do something you love to do. Well I am no different with the place I have chosen. I have chosen a place where I can go to do different activities such as basketball, swimming, running, and lifting weights. Also the YMCA gives me a place where I can hang out with the guys and just have a good time. My favorite place in the world to be is the YMCA.

I can do almost anything I want at the YMCA. First I would go up to the hardwood floors of the beautiful gym and get in a pick-up game with my friends. The gym is a great place for me to improve my game, make new friends, and also gain skills such as competitiveness, teamwork, and sharing. There is no better feeling in the world then hitting a clutch game winning a basket, or desperately diving after a loose ball, the gym is a special place inside of my very favorite place. Then I would hop in the bright blue water of the pool and get a good workout by swimming laps or I would just aimlessly float around the pool lost in thought about the previous day. The warm waters of the pool are a very pleasing place for me. Then I would go into the musty weight room and tone my bulging muscles. Working on each and every part is what I try to do. I just try toning my muscles that I have already. The weight room is a place of complete solitude for me. I usually work out alone thinking to myself about how I am improving my undeveloped body and what this will do for me in the long run. Finally I might end up in the whirlpool after a grueling days workout. The bubbles swirling around my aching body, soothing my muscles, and relaxing me from head to toe. I think to myself what I could do better and what I did well in the workout that I just completed. I also think of how I feel afterwards. SO refreshed and rejuvenated that I don't even think about the pain that might come on in the coming night. Those are some of the many great activities that I perform at the Y. Each helping my body while I have fun and enjoy myself also.

The YMCA is a place for me to come and relax from a hard days work. Sure I am working out but I see it as doing something I truly love to do and it is improving my health and my body. After a hard day of classes or work I come to just think about the strenous day that I had. Was it a good day or bad? What do I have to do tommorow? These are some of the mind bending questions I ask myself. For the most part I let my mind free of every thought and just play ball with the guys. I relax my achy muscles and mind in my place of silent peace. I just have a feeling when I walk in the huge building that I'm going to have a good time, each and every time. It's just a place where I can go to unwind the think.

My favorite place is also a place where I can play with friends and make new friends. I make friends by going to the YMCA and getting involved in the competitive activities. It shows people I am seriously interested and that I care about the well being of my body. Also it keeps you out of trouble. Sometimes if me and my friends have nothing to do we will go take a swim or go shoot some hoops. No matter what we do, it is a good time. We bond and connect together as guys when we play basketball. Playing basketball to me is like going on a fabulous vacation for someone else. It's a time for me to bond with friends and relax.

I have explained many reasons why the YMCA is my favorite place in the whole world. They include such things as the many activities that I can do there, the relaxation that occurs when I am in my happy place, and the time I can share with my friends. It also keeps me out of trouble and from doing something I probably shouldn't be doing. Not to mention doing something I love to do while improving my body at the same time. For all of these great factors the YMCA is my absolute favorite place and it will always be that way until the day I fall over cold and dead.

 ## CLASSROOM CLIMATE

Students will not be able to write well unless they feel comfortable in the classroom. Writing requires mutual respect and trust. To help students succeed at writing, the teacher must establish a rapport with them from the first day. The more the classroom is a place students feel at home, the more willing they are to write. A classroom should never look bare, but should be filled with colorful posters that have something on them besides punctuation rules. Part of a wall should be set aside for each class so students have a place to display their work—not the "best" work, but everyone's work.

Small-group activities also help to establish a friendly atmosphere, and arranging desks in a circle will enhance discussion. Using a variety of activities helps maintain interest and involvement. Most of all, the sense that the teacher cares about them, listens to them, and respects them as individuals ensures that students become active learners.

THE TEACHER'S ROLE

A process approach to writing redefines the teacher's role from a giver of information and the hunter of errors to the teacher as facilitator. If a teacher is a facilitator rather than an error hunter, students are given what they need most—the chance to internalize skills through guided experience. Too often, we have been neurotic about errors, focusing on them to the exclusion of everything else. Establishing a classroom model that provides students with time, strategies, and experience will go far in developing self-reliant students.

Ensuring that students write is the first step in mastering writing skills; allowing time for the writing process is the second. Teachers need to validate the importance of revising and editing by allowing in-class time for these processes. Another aspect of teacher-as-facilitator involves modeling revising and editing. Modeling is best accomplished through student drafts on overhead transparencies or duplicated copies for use with an entire class.

Teachers are part of the entire writing process, providing suggestions, helping, and listening to writers read their papers to them. But teachers also need to know when to stay out of the student's way. The writing belongs to the writer, and when teachers suggest specific ways to change the piece, they take away some of that ownership. A teacher's opinions carry far more weight than a student's. Teachers are the authority figures; they give the grades. Although we want to be supportive, we do not want to interfere with students finding their own voices.

When teachers mark rough drafts with specific suggestions and correct the punctuation, they are doing all the work for the writer. The ones who are getting practice in editing are the teachers, when it is the students who should be practicing. Teachers should guide and suggest but not mark papers with specific changes that need to be made because then the students have only to make the corrections, and not think about why they are making them. Teachers may help by asking questions and making general suggestions on rough drafts, particularly for students who ask for help or those who have trouble writing. The more a teacher takes over, the more students write to please the teacher rather than themselves, and their writing loses vitality and originality.

IMPROVING WRITING SKILLS

Along with the process of writing, there is a need to both directly teach and provide practice time for improving writing skills. Lessons usually take the form of mini-lessons because short, directed teaching on specific skills repeated often is the optimum method for student learning and remembering. Writing skills need to be linked to the act of writing; further, they need to be kept "in their place." There is no argument over the need for the skills or for students learning standard usage, syntax, and mechanics as part of their versatility with language. However, a useful perspective for both teacher and student comes from Emily Meyer and Louise Z. Smith: "Standard written English is a dialect nobody speaks" (219). Given this, it is even more important that students view writing skills as a critical part of their own written expression, not as lessons to get out of the way as quickly as possible.

Writing skills generally improve when students care about their writing. Writing skills—usage, syntax, and mechanics—are part of the process of developing a written text, of making meaning; they are part of revising and editing. When writing has an audience beyond the classroom, correct writing skills become essential. Knowing that others will read their work, students are more likely to make an effort to do their best work. The writing groups are indispensable in helping students achieve correctness. However, students also need direct teaching to improve writing skills.

Teaching improvement in sentence construction, punctuation, and word usage is best done in short segments with reinforcement over an extended period of time. Certain areas of skills need to be taught to a whole class; others are particular to only a few students and should be taught individually or in a small group.

Teachers frequently make two mistakes in teaching writing skills. First, they overteach esoteric areas that few people need to know. This overabundance of information clouds the pertinent skills students do need to know. Second, the skills are taught out of context, using examples that would rarely appear in student writing, making transfer of the information to their own writing difficult if not impossible.

Choosing what skills to teach should come out of the papers your own students write. No universal list of skills is assigned to a particular grade level. Of course, lists of writing skills that need to be reinforced have common elements across the country, but your own classroom is the source for identifying skills that need to be taught. Here, we cover writing skills that many students in secondary grades have trouble with—sentence structure, punctuation, usage, and spelling—but teachers have to adapt what they teach to their own classes.

Understanding and Improving Sentence Structure

The main concern in many teachers' minds is sentence fragments. When teachers introduce the concept of *sentence* in elementary grades, the problem of fragments is important; however, in the upper grades, other elements of sentence construction become more compelling.

As Rei Noguchi reminds us, traditional definitions of sentences are either opaque or vague, leading to even more confusion. For example:

> Defining a sentence as a sequence of words having a complete thought only shifts the problem to the equally perplexing task of defining "a complete thought." Defining a sentence as a unit with a complete subject and predicate (or, alternately noun-phrase subject and a verb phrase), necessitates defining "subject" and "predicate" (not to mention the notion of "complete"). . . . (65)

[Handwritten margin note: Idea: keep "writing records" for individuals + whole class – keep tabs of which areas are weakest/strongest while looking at papers – focus on weakest points]

In Noguchi's opinion, run-on and comma splice errors, "far from being mere instances of random error, reveal writers' efforts to organize meaning," regardless of violating written conventions for marking sentence boundaries. If this is so, then teachers need to work from what Noguchi believes is a latent but "powerful semantically based system for punctuating sentences" (73). In other words, we can profit from the knowledge that native speakers chunk sequences of words based on meaning, not on syntax. From that perspective, we can approach run-ons and comma splices with questions that allow students to understand both the error and its correction. Noguchi explains, "Yet just as complete sentences do not necessarily reflect a wholly rational and coherent mind, so fragments do not necessarily reflect a fragmented and incoherent one" (87). With increased sophistication in writing, students learn to manipulate sentences to create meaning, and this may include a fragment on occasion.

Noguchi believes that fragments are not only natural, but also useful. Our speech is peppered with fragments, mainly because the face-to-face context allows us to use them; moreover, the speed of speech and our interactions make fragments desirable. We couldn't hang onto everything in long, complete, and complex sentences. Thus, in speech, fragments are acceptable. In formal writing, however, they are not—at least, not when they are unintentional. Noguchi also points out that intentional fragments can enhance our writing, providing voice, liveliness, and a sense of spontaneity to what might otherwise be cold prose (85–87).

We need to work with the students orally, asking them to analyze the fragment: How is this information related to another sentence? Where should the fragment connect? Why? Isolate the fragment from its context and ask the students if it can stand alone as a piece of information. We need to discuss the differences between oral and written language again and again, so students understand that written language is not just speech "written down."

The main difficulty students have with sentence construction is that they use simple sentences over and over. All too often, students reduce their writing to short, simple sentences because they know that more complex sentences require punctuation and hold greater potential for making errors. Revision of sentences is a fairly complex task, especially for inexperienced writers. Mina Shaughnessy summarizes the processes:

> The ability to re-scan and re-work sentences . . . assumes several things: a memory for unheard sentences, an ability to store verbal patterns visually from left to right, as in reading, and beyond this, an ability to suspend closure . . . until, through additions, deletions, substitutions, or rearrangements, the words fit the intended meaning. (80)

This perspective also explains why textbook or worksheet exercises fail to help students gain control of sentence structure. First, students create sentences that are more complex and ambiguous than those found in exercises. Second, we make choices about sentences based on what we have already said and what we are planning to say, that most exercises fail to consider. Third, trying to untangle our own sentences to express the meaning we ourselves want is at the heart of composing.

When students have no investment in the sentences, the work is nothing more than busywork. Sentence-combining exercises, although valuable, also suffer from this third important consideration. By giving students pages of exercises with sentence errors, teachers may actually reinforce the error. Further, students have to become readers of their own text and habitual reviewers of their own sentences in their own essays.

From another perspective, reading experience is critical. Erika Lindemann points out the connection:

> Some students have troubles with sentences because they can't depend upon the eye or ear to help them identify prose rhythm. If they read poorly, have rarely been read to, infrequently converse with adults, or passively watch a great deal of television, they may have a limited repertoire of comfortable sentence options. (132)

The most obvious way to improve sentences is through guided experience, both in reading and writing. Major problems of secondary students include these:

- *Tangled, confused sentences.* Students try to say too much in one structure and thus lose focus, meaning, and emphasis.
- *A series of short, choppy sentences.* The sentences are unconnected and often redundant.
- *More than one idea.* The relationship between ideas is unclear.

As students mature and their cognitive abilities increase, their linguistic potential to express more complex ideas increases as well. For this reason, students need to know how to condense, simplify, join, and combine; they need to understand various ways to connect ideas through punctuation and connective words. Such instruction can and should be done through various means, and in all cases, with a minimum of grammatical terms. Subject, verb, modifier, and connector are probably all that is needed. Although *sentence* is often not technically correct, it serves just as well as *clause* and has been part of student vocabulary for many years. Teaching from a perspective of function, we ask these kinds of questions: How does this word or word group work in this sentence? What does it do? How does it help the reader?

Students need to understand the concept of *sentence* from a written, not oral, sense. Various activities provide some experience and insights into understanding the concept of sentences. R. Baird Schuman suggested many of these (71):

1. Give students word groups to arrange into sentences. A variation on this activity: List the words alphabetically. After they have arranged them in one sentence, ask them to change the sentence without adding words—that is, to do variations. Then ask them to rank their creations and discuss which they liked best. You can also ask students to bring in the word lists, limiting the list to 20 words.
2. Isolate typical sentences from a social studies text (or any content area textbook). Make a placard of each word or word group in the sentence and

distribute them to students. Ask students to find a word they can "attach to" (e.g., adjective searching for a noun; auxiliary searching for a verb). Once students have arranged their placards into an acceptable sentence, discuss it. Question them about the functions of the sentence parts, if the part can be moved, if so where, and so forth.

3. Give students "jabberwocky" sentences in which they can demonstrate their knowledge of how English sentences function and carry meaning. This is a good way to reinforce the notion of noun and verb markers, tense, suffixes, and word position.

These suggestions work well with native speakers but are not appropriate for non-native speakers. Students for whom English is a second language may not understand what a complete sentence is as we typically use it. The concept is not a language universal. For example, some languages omit the subject or a linking verb and rely on contextual understanding.

Sentence Combining and "Decombining"

Sentence combining helps students build fluency; however, it requires cognitive and linguistic maturity. William Strong, an early advocate of sentence combining, cautions that the ability to "tighten up" sentences is a later psycholinguistic development than expanding them; therefore, teachers need to delay this work until the upper levels of high school (18).

Sentence combining should always first be done as a whole-class activity, with the teacher modeling the process and asking questions. The value of the exercise lies in discovering the range of options in constructing the sentence. Usually it is not a matter of right or wrong, but of improved effectiveness or clarity. If some sentence parts are wrong, usually because a modifier is in the wrong place, we are able to discuss modifiers from the perspective of "what is happening here?" A helpful exercise is to give students wordy sentences and have them take out words without changing the meaning of the sentence. Working on sentence constructions can then be done in a group or pairs of students because the discussion helps students learn. Following whole-class experience, sentence combining can be an individual, paired, or small-group activity as well. Asking groups to work on a "problem" is a good way for students to learn in a risk-free environment. For this reason, sentence-combining work should not be graded.

Although students need sustained work to ensure improvement, sentence-combining exercises that are given too frequently can lead to boredom and a perception of busywork. Consequently, students must be directed to the potential for sentence combining and decombining in their own drafts. Strong reminds us that, "A basic aim of intelligent sentence combining is to make good sentences, not merely long ones. It follows that 'decombining' may be at least as important as putting sentences together" (18). With guided instruction in untangling and tightening sentences, students become more competent in writing effective and interesting sentences.

Embedding: A Special Problem

The most common problem with embedding occurs with the decision of whether that information is essential and whether to add commas. A textbook gives rules for punctuating restrictive and nonrestrictive clauses, but this concept, one that befuddles even college freshmen, seldom takes hold easily or firmly. The problem often lies in textbooks and handbooks where students are given rules rather than observation and questions about function and meaning. Students who can pick out a nonrestrictive clause in an exercise often fail to note one in their own writing, where the language is more complex. It is no wonder that there has been nearly universal confusion and noncompliance with the rule. Take these two sentences as examples:

Boys who put snakes in the teacher's desk should be expelled.

My brothers, who put snakes in the teacher's desk, should be expelled.

For many students, the distinction between these two sentences will be unclear, at least as it relates to essential information. You will need a thorough discussion with ample examples, drawn from student writing, of how meaning is affected with or without the clause. At the same time, you need to underscore the meaning of essential information—information that is needed to identify someone or something and without which the meaning of the sentence would change. Students have to understand that removing *who put snakes in the teacher's desk* not only removes identification of the boys but also changes the intended meaning of the sentence.

EXPLORATION

1. *Padding with Purpose.* In reading student drafts, you realize that your eleventh graders would improve their writing if they used more appositives and relative clauses. You know that embedding is a late-developing skill, so you have to teach it in concrete ways. Knowing that most students won't see the similarity between these structures, you develop some mini-lessons. Which structure would you teach first? How would you present the required punctuation? With a classmate, prepare a mini-lesson on these structures. Each of you might prepare just one, but work together to ensure that students have coherent bridges from one lesson to the other.

2. *The Active Appositive.* Your class has a number of students who respond best to kinesthetic methods; that is, to movement and action. You also have two students with learning disabilities who seem to do better when "action" is part of explanations. How would you help these students understand the appositive as a useful structure for their writing? Think in terms of physical objects, color, shape, and manipulation of parts. With a small group of classmates, design an activity that helps these students in particular, but that also appeals to all students in the class.

John Fortier, a veteran senior high English teacher, offers a valuable perspective on student errors: a developmental pattern. The first sentence errors are usually run-ons, probably a "response to outside suggestions or inner feelings that ideas should be combined." Fortier believes that students who are not developmentally ready for complex transformations simply run their sentences together. The next developmental error occurs when students begin to subordinate sentences, but maintain the punctuation for independent sentences. The result is a fragment. Correcting the fragment, speculates Fortier, may result in yet another error, the comma splice. We tell students to attach the fragment but separate it with a comma. If students generalize this concept, they may produce sentences separated by commas. Fortier concludes, "This predictable pattern of error suggests normal linguistic development for many students and may emerge earlier or later, depending on the individual student" (n.p.). Fortier's analysis, based on years of teaching, illustrates the importance of teachers thinking about student errors and the logic behind them. Knowing that some errors are part of normal development and that students have an individual pattern of development can be comforting both to teacher and student.

Understanding and Improving Punctuation

Punctuation should be taught as part of syntax, not as a separate skill area, because very few marks are unrelated to syntax. Some students avoid various constructions because they don't know where to place any necessary commas, thus limiting their versatility considerably. Punctuation is a response to sentence structure and should be part of sentence work. The codes, once mastered, seem easy. However, we need to understand just how long it takes for mastery. We also need to keep motivation in mind. Students should know why punctuation is useful: to signal intonation, vocal nuance, and pause, and to help readers predict grammatical structures. It's tempting to think that all punctuation errors stem from student carelessness, but that is not the case. Some punctuation errors certainly occur because students don't think marks are important or don't take the time to proofread. But among inexperienced writers, errors are seldom a lack of care. Students gain control over various aspects of writing over a long time, achieving control gradually and unevenly. This means they are juggling various skill areas when they write, and all areas will be in different stages of development and competency.

Language handbooks too often overexplain the rules of punctuation, resulting in confusion for students. Teachers need to choose the areas in which their students are having problems. For example, some might never use certain punctuation, such as semicolons. Teachers know what areas their students need help with, not from a test, but from students' writing. As they read student papers, they keep a log of errors and use the information to design appropriate lessons.

Just as a dictionary is essential, language handbooks are useful as reference books and every student needs to have one. A problem arises when handbooks are used as textbooks and not reference tools. In elementary grades, teachers design lessons to teach children how to use a dictionary, and the same technique is important for secondary students learning how to use a handbook. Handbooks are essential in revising groups and peer editing, but many students do not know how to use them. When students are working in writing groups and someone asks how to punctuate a sentence, an impromptu mini-lesson on locating a particular reference is a valuable teaching strategy. We want students to learn how to use reference tools; they do not have to, nor should they, memorize every possible use of a specific punctuation mark. Nor should the teacher be the only resource when students are capable of using reference books.

Commas

The correct usage of commas can be difficult for students to learn. Many students believe there are so many rules governing commas that there is no way they can ever keep them straight. To help with the problem, limit your teaching to students' specific problems and ignore the rest. Use as few grammatical expressions as possible. When students are confused about setting off appositives with commas, teach only that use of the comma, using many examples. Another time, teach the use of commas after introductory clauses or phrases.

Commas used with relative clauses, appositives, and participial phrases most often mark descriptive or qualifying information. For example, commas usually follow a prepositional phrase. When students see the connections and understand the function of the comma as the same function in these constructions, their grasp of them usually increases significantly. They are not learning six rules; they are learning one, by function. Some commas are simply convention, such as separating the parts of dates and places within a sentence. Most students do fine with commas separating month from year and city from state but fail to add commas to separate year or state from the rest of the sentence. This can be taught as a mini-lesson in 5 to 10 minutes.

Quotation Marks

Even young writers understand and use these marks in their own writing. Most students are plagued not by the quotation marks themselves but by punctuation setting off the speaker: which punctuation mark to use and if it goes in or outside of the quotation marks. If a teacher puts examples of quotation marks on large posters after doing a lesson on them, students can refer to the correct usage. Posting the rules is not effective, but examples of correct usage posted around the classroom are helpful.

Apostrophes

Inexperienced writers often misplace or omit this mark altogether. In black dialect, the possessive is often omitted in speech (e.g., "Tom hat on table" is understood as possessive). Thus, we have to draw attention to the physical mark and the pronunciation of *s*. Because many students, regardless of dialect, omit the apostrophe, you need to teach it. Thomas Friedmann offers a particularly helpful view of the problem, noting that most texts and all handbooks lay out every possible use of the apostrophe all at once. Students are told in quick succession that they need the mark to indicate ownership, contractions, and use of plural. Explaining all of the uses at once can cause confusion because students associate a plural with the letter *s*, possessive form, and *-es*. Friedmann notes that for students who don't notice the apostrophe at all, explanations and rules appear absurd (111). If students do understand that they need the apostrophe for ownership, we can expect that some will extend that notion to *hers'* and *his'*. This overextension of the rule shows students actively thinking about how the language works. Therefore, this is a "smart error," an error of growing competency rather than regression.

Contractions offer another opportunity for confusion. Contractions are nearly as mysterious as possessives because students may not understand the fusion of two words and the role of the apostrophe. Thus, they may omit the apostrophe altogether or place it incorrectly (e.g., *did'nt*). They assume the apostrophe has something to do with the juncture of the words rather than with an omission.

As noted earlier, texts and handbooks have a fatal flaw: teaching the exceptions rather than the rule. But when young children learn their native language, they learn to make a plural by adding *-s* or *-es* and apply that rule, no matter what. Most of the time, the child is right, but "tooths" and "foots" pop up now and then. No one seizes the moment to give the child all the exceptions to the plural rule (Friedmann 112). Students should master the rule of most frequent occurrence first; later, we can add the exceptions, as they present themselves in student writing. Textbooks that state a basic punctuation rule and then follow with a list of every exception possible are better left on the shelf.

Daily Oral Language

Two educators, Neil Vail and Joe Papenfuss, originally developed Daily Oral Language (DOL). DOL provides students with two or three sentences daily with various errors in usage and mechanics. Most teachers put the sentences on the board or a transparency and ask students to make corrections in their journals; full-class discussion of corrections and the reasons for them follows. The value of DOL is its brevity, immediate correction, and discussion. However, it should not be used as a test nor should teachers overuse it—otherwise, DOL is simply another drill, prone to mindless response. As with other skill lessons, there may be little transference to students' own writing.

Lisa, high school student, wrote the following essay:

JUDGING A PERSON

You cannot judge a book by its cover. Many do not take this cliché seriously. When a student is assigned to do a book report he will most likely look for external features such as the books length. He should actually be concerned with the content—something that is not evident at first glance. People judge individuals in the same manner they judge books. When a person is judged he is judged on his physical features instead of his personality.

On October 23, at 11:00 AM I was watching Geraldo on the television set. While I was looking at all the guest speakers on the stage I noticed a woman was wearing only half a shirt and a short miniskirt. Geraldo introduced the womans name and her profession which was modeling. She looked like a model to me and also looked like the type of woman who would sleep around. After the commercial break Geraldo introduced the topic for the day. It was on chastity. People sitting in front of him, belonged to a group who believed in chastity. The woman I described to you was one of these people. I could not believe this woman believed in chastity but you see I was judging the woman on appearance not personality. In this example, I showed that I am guilty of judging people by their cover.

EXPLORATION

Helping Students with Punctuation

Lisa has a good example in her essay about judging people, but she also has punctuation problems. How would you help her to recognize and correct the punctuation in this essay? Look for patterns among the errors.

EXPLORATION

Untangling Sentences

Each of the following student sentences needs revision. Determine where the problem or problems occur. Then decide how you would work with this student on sentence revision. The sentences were written by 18-year-olds, and you can assume they are capable of thinking about syntax and making appropriate revisions. Approach the problem from a functional perspective and use these questions to guide your analysis:

1. Where is the reader derailed and why?

2. What is the main idea?

3. What information is missing?

4. What can you do to help the reader understand the intent?

5. What options do you have to repair the sentence?

6. What punctuation is needed and why?

1. For example in football I had a coach who wanted me to gain 30 pounds on the off season and when he found out that I wasn't even going to try he had a long meeting with me about the poor attitude in sports.

2. But for more than eight days before this weekend the maintenance employees had not even touched the roads and sidewalks with any effort to clear the ice, except with a machine that has a brush type roller that brushed the snow off the ice.
3. Another point about athletics is is for all types of people.
4. As you can see owning a car can be very expensive. Especially if you are going to school.
5. A car can be a pain at school. For many different reasons. Like people borrowing it and costs to the owner.
6. An example of this is somewhat like a mutual relationship. When you do things together and have some fun.
7. The frustration would consist of not having money, no transportation and no time, I wouldn't like that.
8. The solution to the problem was that he thought what he wanted the most, if his friends didn't want to share in what he wanted, they shouldn't have to.
9. After careful consideration of these reasons my decision was made, it was not easy to do.
10. The reason I remembered this is because of the way it looked (reference to a candy bar).

 ## IMPROVING SPELLING AND VOCABULARY

Learning to spell is learning about words—their meanings, forms, and uses in communication.

Richard Hodges (15)

Spelling errors tend to be publicly offensive errors, the ones most damaging to the writer's reputation. Mina Shaughnessy believes that the public views correct spelling as the hallmark of an educated person, and that failure to meet that standard causes others to question both the quality of the writer's education and native intelligence. Despite this, notes Shaughnessy, out of all the writing skills, spelling is viewed by most teachers and students as the one most resistant to instruction and least related to intelligence: "It is the one area of writing where English teachers themselves will admit ineptness" (161–62). Hodges points out:

> Individuals make few, if any, random spelling errors. Each incorrect spelling has a cause, whether from carelessness or from insufficient or erroneous knowledge about the written language. (13)

Moreover, says Hodges, some aspects of spelling are learned best at the secondary level, when students have both greater intellectual maturity and life experience (13).

Students with spelling disabilities have most likely been told for years that they must "do something about spelling." Consequently, these students dislike writing and fear putting anything on paper, where each new word opens up more potential for making errors. However, it is critical that they write, for it is within the context of their original writing that spelling instruction must take place. Forget the textbooks and handbooks, forget the gimmicks offered by various commercial vendors, and stick to student drafts. In the first place, drafts have words that students want to use—in context and with a purpose. Students need to separate composing from editing, and composing well from spelling well.

Elizabeth Grubgeld offers some useful suggestions for helping students emerge from the fog:

1. Analyze the errors as they emerge in student drafts, "find clues to the hodgepodge of rules, visual memories, and systems of logic" by which students make spelling choices (59).
2. Once you have imposed order on the chaos of errors, provide the student with a limited number of words for proofreading, allowing the student ownership and control of the words.
3. Help the student see structures within his or her words that provide keys to words with similar structures.
4. Isolate words with similar structures and let the student work inductively to discover the patterns and principles.
5. Consider various alternatives for ways in which students can describe their own spelling rules: Write a series of conditions (questions) that help to examine the word in question; conversationally write an answer to the question, "What confuses me about this word?"
6. Forget the common practice of teaching confusing words together (e.g., *there* and *their*—put *there* with *here* and *where*).
7. Teach students the concepts of syllable, root word, and affixes, so they see words as divisible rather than as arbitrary groupings of letters.
8. Suggest that the student "read as slowly and with as much choppiness as someone who can barely read" to increase the ability to hear unstressed syllables.
9. Combine oral reading with practice in visual recognition of the grapheme-phoneme correspondence (i.e., written letters to sound).
10. Establish ways to emphasize blurred pronunciations, such as associating *major* with *majority* to prevent spelling *majer*. (48–50, 58–61)

Although this method is time consuming, Grubgeld believes that students become critical readers in the process, recognizing spelling errors as they proofread (58–61).

Many teachers have students keep their own spelling notebook. Students note what words they have trouble spelling and a quick look at their notebook will show them the correct spelling. On occasion, teachers will suggest students add words they consistently misspell in their papers. The words need to be ones commonly used and not esoteric ones that are better looked up as needed.

Vocabulary

Hodges's monograph *Improving Spelling and Vocabulary in the Secondary School* has many suggestions for increasing student awareness and proficiency with language. Using a variety of word games and puzzles helps to keep student interest high. Commercial games such as *Scrabble*, *Probe*, *Balderdash*, and *Wheel of Fortune* offer enjoyable experience with words. Several publishers offer helpful sources to teachers as they plan for vocabulary experiences for students.

Vocabulary development is critical to all aspects of the English language arts. However, don't give students lists of words to memorize or match to definitions. This approach does little or nothing to improve students' vocabulary, mainly because the words are decontextualized and the routine is rote and meaningless to the students. They may memorize a list of words and definitions but don't use them in their writing. Remember that we do not have to know the precise spelling of a word to recognize it in reading, or even to use it in writing. As with any learning, students need context and motivation, a genuine purpose. Thus, reading and writing are central in the acquisition of new words.

Middle school teacher Lisa Sassano devised a contest called "I Spy" that sparked her students' interest in vocabulary. For every class vocabulary word students found in "out-of-class" material, they would receive one point. Students could not use dictionaries, thesauruses, or encyclopedias; however, they were encouraged to use any other printed material including textbooks. The students' responses were enthusiastic and following the vocabulary contest, they had an "I Spy Figurative Language" contest. She found that students began using the words in their writing and speech (24–25).

The study of words (e.g., roots, commonalities, affixes) can be fascinating and purposeful if students apply this knowledge in their writing. Poetry is an excellent way to explore and exploit the power of vocabulary. Working with vocabulary from students' other courses is also important. Content area teachers often fail to teach their students about discipline-specific vocabulary, despite students' need to understand the web of definitions found in texts and related materials. William E. Nagy's monograph, *Teaching Vocabulary to Improve Reading Comprehension*, is an excellent resource for teachers who wish to learn how to link vocabulary study to students' prior knowledge. Nagy explains why traditional methods either fail or create problems and offers strategies for more effective instruction.

EXPLORATION

Helping Students Improve Their Writing

Alan's passion is football, not English class. He has turned in the following essay, and you schedule a conference with him. How would you approach the problems?

Wide recievers and lineman are two different kind of people. One is a alusive and quick person and the other is purely brut strength. The wide reciever has to relay on his fleet feet and his ability to get open for a wining TD. The linemen has to block his man so he doesn't get to the quarterback. He has to go threw endless pain. The obvious difference between the two are there role in the game. The wide reciever gets all the glory. He makes the spectacular catches with no time left. A wide reciever is thought as an artist in a game of violence. The linemen gets no recognition. J am happy J choose to be a wide reciever in high school.

 ## WRITING FOR A VARIETY OF PURPOSES

Teachers who believe that writing and learning are inseparable often find themselves in the same situation as Joellen, the teacher described earlier. For teachers who use the writing process and include writing throughout classroom activities, the paper load can become overwhelming. A system of writing levels developed by Rhoda Maxwell alleviates the problem. By developing levels of evaluation to fit the different levels of writing, the evaluation is simplified, thus cutting down on the time required to complete the process. The original work is based on speech theory, particularly that of Dell Hymes. Maxwell devised a levels-of-writing approach to use in the classroom (Maxwell *Writing*, xiii).

Many areas of our life are affected by the concept of different levels or standards. For example, we use different levels of eating behavior. How we eat pizza sitting on the floor with a circle of friends as we watch television is quite different from our behavior when eating at an upscale restaurant. One behavior is not better than the other; each is appropriate for the context.

Contexts determine speech levels as well. We use different levels of speech for different purposes and audiences (Maxwell *Writing*, 33–34). Martin Joos describes five levels or scales of language based on the social utility of language and stresses that all of the scales are respectable and necessary depending on purpose (Joos 4). We need different levels to assure communication in different settings (Maxwell *Writing*, 36). We use various levels of speech throughout the day depending on whom we are speaking to and what we want to communicate; in other words, audience and purpose.

Sociolinguist Dell Hymes agrees and explains that the level of speech is determined by the settings and activities surrounding the speech act (43). Within a community, listeners expect and understand a particular linguistic form. A formal speech level can be inappropriate in some settings (57). For example, we wouldn't use a very formal style when talking to friends but when giving a presentation our speech should be more formal.

Informal speaking is for sharing with a familiar audience. Characteristics of this level are unfinished sentences, slang, and jokes known only by the intimate community that has a shared knowledge (Maxwell *Writing*, 36). Donald Rubin describes such language as elliptical and choppy; he agrees that audience affects the language style (5).

A second level of speech typical in school settings is sometimes formal in style and vocabulary, although still familiar, because it reaches a wider audience than the students' intimate community. The third level, formal speech, is infrequently used and is reserved for an unfamiliar audience or one not known at all. All three levels of speech are important; we need to know not only how to use the levels but when to use them.

LEVELS OF WRITING

Levels of writing, too, depend on our audience and our purpose. When should we as writers and teachers concern ourselves with correct punctuation and spelling? What determines how formal our writing and speaking need to be? Because of their purpose, the language used in discovery activities is informal, whereas the language in a published article is naturally quite formal. But what about the writing we plan for in school and the writing we do outside of school? By differentiating among writing purposes to establish levels of writing, we provide activities for students that mirror real-life writing. If we want our students to value writing and to see the reasons for writing, then the assignments we make must include all the levels (Maxwell *Writing,* 33–49).

Level 1

We use Level 1 in casual situations; for example, when we write notes to ourselves or a list of things to do. The writing is shared only with people familiar to the writer, and in fact, probably understood only by the writer and people close to the writer. The counterpart in speech is talking to close friends where it is often unnecessary to finish a thought or sentence to be understood. The writer takes for granted the interest of the audience regardless of how casual the communication (Martin, Medway, Smith, and D'Arcy 42).

The purpose of Level 1 writing includes writing to remember, to sort out our thoughts, to organize, and to communicate (Maxwell *Writing,* 36). Many opportunities for Level 1 writing are present in school as well as one's personal life. Note-taking is a common example, whether we are taking notes to remember what we have to do today or notes from readings, lectures, or viewing films. The purpose of writing notes is to remember, and also to figure things out. When we have notes in front of us we can organize information and see connections much better than relying on thoughts only. Journals and learning logs are all Level 1 writing. The audience is the author, though on occasion, classmates might read Level 1, but the writer is always present to offer explanations.

Level 2

Level 2 is more formal and can be read and understood by most people in the writer's social circle. Audiences include people we communicate with daily—store clerks, acquaintances, teachers, and classmates. Vocabulary, grammar, and delivery must follow an understood style. Informality is acceptable as long as communication occurs (Maxwell *Writing,* 37).

Writing at Level 2 includes informal letter writing, notes to people outside the intimate circle of friends, written instructions or directions, and all situations where communication does not depend on the author being present. Writing in school that is shared with others is largely at this level. Examples include exams, homework, informal reports, and drafting. Because Level 2 is more formal than Level 1, an added degree of correctness in spelling, punctuation, and grammar is necessary. However, the writing does not have to be flawless. If a teacher expects every word to be spelled correctly, then students are apt to use words that are easy to spell rather than words that reflect nuances or connotations that make writing lively and interesting. Insisting on correct punctuation has a similar outcome. Students tend to write short simple sentences that they know how to punctuate. Level 2 is a time for exploring language and conventions and only in Level 3 writing is a higher level of correctness desired and expected.

Level 3

Level 3 is formal writing or speech and occurs in situations where the form is as important as the message, and the audience includes readers the writer may not know. All three levels are appropriate for school writing and are important for helping students improve their writing, although traditionally, Level 3 has been used almost exclusively.

The audiences are outside our immediate circle and probably include readers we do not know. The author is not present to explain what is meant; the writing by itself must state what the writer means. Résumés, job applications, business letters, and all writing intended for publication are examples of Level 3 writing. Because of the more formal requirements, Level 3 writers must go through all the stages of the writing process: discovery activities, multiple drafting and revisions, editing, and proofreading. Because of the time involved in producing Level 3 papers, they should be assigned sparingly.

Using levels of writing in the classroom cuts down on the paper load for teachers. Evaluation is clearly defined by levels; therefore, much of the writing required of students is evaluated quickly and easily. Once students understand the levels, they know the appropriate expectations. Teachers need to inform parents by sending them a letter about the writing levels so that they understand the teacher's expectations. Then they can understand the evaluations better. The purpose of evaluation is to help students improve their writing, and everyone involved needs to understand the purposes of the writing assignments. By knowing the purpose, a teacher knows what to look for when evaluating. The time involved in evaluation is greatly reduced. Planning for evaluating by levels is explained in detail in the chapter on evaluation. The characteristics of writing levels are shown in Figure 6.6.

Writing levels are inherent in any writing assignment. When teachers plan activities or units, the writing is designated at the appropriate level. One advantage to writing lesson plans this way is that a teacher can see at a glance if the balance of levels is appropriate. A second advantage is that students know the teacher's expectations before they complete an assignment. Anne Elliott, an English education student, wrote a series of writing assignments for a young adult novel, *Crazy Lady*. By designating writing levels, she conveys her expectations to her students and establishes the basis for evaluating the writing.

Figure 6.6 Levels of writing

Level 1

Style: Informal in speech, similar to talking with close friends

Audience: Writer and, in some cases, teacher and peer group

Function: Thinking through writing, organizing thoughts, generating ideas, developing fluency, helping with memory

Form: Note-taking, journal writing, responses, lists, brainstorming, mapping, first drafts

Evaluation: Content only, often not evaluated at all; mechanics, word usage, organization, spelling, and grammar are not considered

Level 2

Style: More formal in speech, similar to talking to an audience outside one's close circle of friends

Audience: Writer, classmates, teacher, parents; audience may not be known well

Function: Organizing thoughts coherently, developing ideas, explaining, informing, practical—to get work done

Form: Exams, homework, multiple drafts, reports, summaries

Evaluation: Evaluated for content and form; common writing conventions expected as appropriate for grade and ability

Level 3

Style: Formal in speech, similar to talking to people not known, like giving a formal speech

Audience: Writer, classmates, teacher, parents, audience outside the classroom, an unknown audience

Function: Learning the value of producing error-free writing, reaching a wider audience, learning to edit and proofread

Form: Letters, reports, poetry, research papers, books, final drafts

Evaluation: Content and form of equal weight; all writing skills are expected to be correct; neat handwriting or error-free typing important

INSTRUCTIONAL UNIT

A NOVEL: *CRAZY LADY*

Summary

In the novel *Crazy Lady* by Jane Leslie Conly (1993), Maxine Flooter (Crazy Lady) is the neighborhood joke, especially for a group of adolescent boys who continually tease her and her retarded son, Ronald. Vernon learns that he is closer to these outcasts than he thought. Through his relationship with Maxine and Ronald, Vernon begins to understand his own loss of his mother and to appreciate his own special gift.

Possible Themes

Family relationships, death, love, fear, growing up, and independence.

Writing Assignments

1. Before reading the book, write in your journals about one thing you wish you could do or could do better. It can be anything you have difficulty with—studying, writing, drawing, speaking, and so on. Is there something you would really love to do but your friends don't know about it? (Level 1)

2. Observe your family life for two to three days. Keep notes of your observations in your journal. Notice any family or individual routines such as who cooks at mealtime, who cleans, where people sit, and so on. Make no judgments; just report facts (Level 1).

3. Based on the notes you took, describe your family. Write a one-page response about what you observed (Level 2).

4. Answer discussion questions based on the book. (Answers are Level 2.) For example: Although Vernon doesn't have a lot of parental guidance at home, he is still taken care of. What are some ways he takes care of himself? What are some things the others outside the family do to care for him? Do you think Ronald will be better off at his aunt and uncle's house? Why or why not? Both Vernon and Maxine have experienced the loss of a loved one. Compare and contrast the coping methods each uses and explain which one you think is more effective.

5. Using some of the major themes in the novel, create a five-line poem using the following structure:

Theme

-ing, -ing

adj., adj., adj.,

-ing. -ing

theme

Experiment with as many themes as you want (Level 1).

6. Crazy Lady got her name from people in her neighborhood who did not know her. Take the time to get to know a person in school who you do not know, such as new students, faculty members, or school staff. Conduct interviews with that person. After you have gathered all of your information, write a biography of the person (Level 3). The Level 3 assignment goes through the entire writing process, incorporating Levels 1 and 2.

EXPLORATION

Experiencing Student Assignments

Reread and complete Elliott's discovery activities 1 and 2, the ones about something you wish you could do better and your observation of family life. Use the sense of family to mean people you are living with now, for example, roommates. The purpose of your doing the activity is to give you a better sense of how a student might respond to the assignment. Share your results with others in your class.

TYPES OF WRITING ASSIGNMENTS

James Britton, Tony Burgess, Nancy Martin, Alex McLeod, and Harold Rosen of the University of London Institute of Education did major research on rethinking types of writing assignments. Britton and his colleagues examined ways to classify schoolchildren's writing according to the nature of the task and the demands made on the writer (3). Out of that study some fundamental ideas about writing emerged that shape our current thinking and teaching.

Writing has been classified traditionally into the rhetorical categories, or modes, of narrative, descriptive, expository, and argument. Britton and his colleagues explained that using these four categories presents difficulty in teaching writing. The modes are "derived from an examination of the finished products of professional writers" (4). The result is a prescription for how people should write, not how they write. Britton and his colleagues argued that the categories essentially leave out the writer and ignore the process of writing. As a result, writing evaluation is concerned only with whether the writer uses the collection of rules that rhetoricians in 1828 decided were the "best sorts of things to say in various argumentative situations" (I. A. Richards qtd. in Britton et al. 4).

Through the 1950s, these traditional categories shaped writing in secondary schools. In the 1960s, educators began to distinguish between personal and objective writing, and school writing was dominated by objective writing—in other words, writing that was abstract and generalized (8).

As their study of writing progressed, Britton and his colleagues developed a description of writing based on the function of writing and the sense of audience based on research done on speech (13). They describe three categories of writing based on the intended audience and purpose: (1) expressive, (2) transactional, and (3) poetic.

The most informal type of writing occurs when writers focus on themselves. Britton and his colleagues used Dell Hymes's term *expressive* to designate language the writer is most familiar with; a writer assumes that the reader is interested in what the writer has to say. Such writing is informal and natural; the kind people like to do.

In the second category the focus shifts from the writer to a listener or a topic and is defined as *transactional*. In this type of writing, the author is trying to interpret, to shape, to represent experience (Britton 41). When writers use transactional writing, they write about events that have already happened from the "role of spectator" as they view past events. The more the writing "meets the demands of participation in the world's affairs, the nearer will it approach the transactional" (83). Transactional language gets things done in the world and is the kind of writing taught in schools, usually to the exclusion of expressive and poetic language.

When the focus is on the message or particular words, it is called *poetic*, which is defined as language in art. The purpose of writing in the poetic form is to create a verbal object, an end in itself (Britton 83). Poetry is the most obvious example of the poetic form, but the categories are not exclusive, and poetic writing can occur in any form. Britton and his colleagues explain that the words themselves are selected by the writer to form an arrangement, a pattern (90).

Like Britton and his colleagues, James Moffett also examined categories of writing. He describes the spectrum of discourse as a hierarchy of levels of abstraction: recording, reporting, generalizing, and theorizing. As in Britton's classification, the levels or kinds of discourse overlap. Shifting from one kind of discourse to another, "say, from narrative discourse to that of explicit generalization necessarily entails shifts in language and rhetoric." For example, as the audience changes for students' writings, the form and formality of the writing changes. Moffett explains that language structures such as transitions, organization, and sentence elaboration shift from one level of discourse to another depending on the purpose of the writing and for whom it is intended. Moffett makes a strong point about teaching the language structure in the context of students' writing. They experience a normal growth in sentence elaboration through their actual writing (53). The basic premise of the writing process is that writing can and should be taught as writers write, rather than after the paper is handed in to a teacher.

The personal involvement in writing affects not only the process but also the types of writing students are asked to do. Traditionally, school writing has been transactional writing, and its purpose has been to show what the student knows by repeating or rephrasing information gained through reading or listening (Maxwell *Writing*, 35). In literature, students wrote essays and exams explaining what literary critics thought. In research papers and report writing, they read library material and wrote other people's words and opinions. Students were not allowed to use the word *I* because their own voices and ideas were not considered appropriate.

In most cases, informative writing is more prevalent than personal. One characteristic consistent throughout curricula is that personal narrative becomes progressively less frequent at the higher-grade levels. Writing for "the real world" takes over composition classes: reports rather than stories, analyses rather than opinions, formal rather than informal. Other serious consequences of the emphasis on expository assignments are the reliance on sources outside the students' experiences, and the omission of *I* in this type of writing. Some teachers tell students they must never use *I* in expository writing, yet in major magazines like *The New Yorker*, first person is commonly used, as are personal experiences to make a point. When the writing must not reflect the identity of the writer, the students' importance diminishes greatly.

Journal Writing

Journal writing has a place in every subject and is indispensable in an English class. Because journals are not evaluated, students soon learn to rely on them for recording thoughts and ideas about a multitude of subjects without wondering, "Am I doing this right?" You may read students' journals and write comments in a conversational tone, but the comments should never sound negative. The only criterion you should use to evaluate journal writing is effort, which is an elusive quality. Counting pages does not help because some students write larger than others. Also, a writer may put a great deal of thought into one page, whereas another could write pages of rambling prose. Reading the journals to see if students did the work is all you have to do.

Journals in the classroom have many different purposes: recording thoughts and feelings, organizing plans, figuring things out, observing life, keeping track of projects, and recording research. The latter two are discussed in Chapter 8, "Writing for Learning." As with all assignments, classroom journals must have a purpose that reflects a learning objective. Assigning journals without a clear purpose does not benefit students and becomes "busywork."

Personal Response Journals

A frequently assigned journal is one for personal response in which students write about anything they want. Janet Burroway explains that journal writing is indispensable to developing fluency:

> There are, though, a number of tricks you can teach yourself in order to free the writing self, and the essence of these is to give yourself permission to fail. The best place for permission is a private place, and for that reason a writer's journal is an essential, likely to be the source of originality, ideas, experimentation, and growth. (3)

An example of a writer capturing a mood and feeling is evident in the following two entries from the same person:

1. *She was so happy she tried to swallow the smile and it landed in her stomach. The feeling of pride she knew was dangerous. It could grow into a self-satisfaction that might bring a loss of effort, maybe even bad luck. Watch out, she thought as she kept her lips straight ahead in parallel curves. But inside, her intestines were singing to her pancreas, and her stomach was dancing to its own flip-flop rhythm.*

2. *The voice that came out was that of an angry gander honking and hissing. It wouldn't stop but continued on for an entire hour. I was a prisoner held by a grinding noise, sound waves pressing me to my chair, held by my eardrums. The group in here murmured a polite chuckle. They must be deciphering some meaning from those sounds that are grating into my ears. He knows. He knows I'm not listening. He keeps stepping closer on the worn wood floor, throwing out words with hand motions.*

By writing responses of this nature, the student has captured the experience and may later use it in a story. Without written responses, we all tend to forget what we were thinking and feeling.

Students need to write daily. Burroway says, "It doesn't matter what you write and it doesn't matter very much how much, but it does matter that you make a steady habit of the writing" (4). Some students, though, have a difficult time thinking of anything to write, and a teacher may provide open-ended questions to help solve the problem (e.g., What I remember best from last year is . . . What I like least about school is . . .).

List-making is also a good place to start:

My 10 favorite songs, or the ones I dislike the most.

Ten things that could never happen. Choose the one you most wish would happen and explain why.

Name your three favorite people and describe them.

Name three famous people. Why are they famous?

Name three places you would like to visit and explain why.

Some high school teachers write a quotation on the board each day and students write a response to it. They have the option of writing about something else, but they all have to write. The purpose of personal response journals is to help students practice putting their thoughts into writing. They also help students become more observant about their own reactions to the world. To keep personal journals interesting to students, you may want to assign them occasionally for a short time. It is better to require them for a week or two, then after a period of time, assign them again.

Even though it takes time, reading student journals is important because they won't put effort into something we don't care about. The following suggestions make the job a little easier:

1. Read journals quickly. Responding every page or two seems to be enough. Students just want the sense that teachers are reading.
2. Stagger the dates students hand in the journals so teachers have journals from only one class at a time.
3. Have students keep a journal for a few weeks, stop for two weeks, and then start keeping them again.

Language Journals

Paying attention to language in use is one way to appreciate its playfulness and diversity. Talking about language serves the purpose, too, of learning how new words come into our vocabulary, how punctuation patterns change, how language belongs to the people who use it. A language journal might begin with an assignment to look for unusual signs, especially ones that use a play on words. Students note the signs in the language journal and share them in class. Even with a new focus each day, students continue to look for examples of all the suggestions for about a week. We take a few minutes at the beginning of each class period to share what they found. Another suggestion is to find unusual—but authentic—names, including connections between name and occupations. We had a dentist, Dr. Toothacker, and a doctor, Dr. Paine. Students come up with unbelievable examples. They have to be authentic, though. Names of businesses provide unusual examples, especially barbershops and hair salons. Advertisements are a rich source, as are newspaper headlines. Overheard conversations can provide examples of clichés. The language journal is a good starting place for discussions about language.

Writer's Journal

The purpose of this journal is to provide ideas for stories and poems. Many students are shy about writing poetry; in their journal they can practice phrases, beginnings, and endings without having to write a completed poem. The same is true of stories. Perhaps they think of a description of a house; that might be all they write. Or they can write a plot outline. If they see an interesting-looking person, they should write the description in the journal; that person might become a character in a story later. However, the connection between what one sees and, later, writes, may not always be concrete, as author Joan Didion explains. She keeps a notebook to record what she sees around her for the purpose of remembering her own sense of self at the time. Although a line or image may appear in her writing, the journal is a private recording of the world as she relates to it (136). Likewise, students can use their journals to recapture a mood, outlook, or frame of mind.

An interesting source for writing is newspaper stories. Students tape the stories in the journal, or even just the headline, and use them for ideas later on. If students have difficulty getting started in noticing the world around them, teachers might provide leads. For instance, a teacher can suggest describing someone or something students noticed on the way home from school, unusual signs, bumper stickers, newspaper headlines, scraps of conversation, one side of a telephone conversation, any use of language that catches their interest. Once students begin to notice language use, they will become more aware of real-world language. Entries in the writing journal are a rich source for sharing in the classroom.

Learning Logs

Another purpose for student journals is an ongoing log used for assignments that cover several days. These journals are referred to as *learning logs* and are used, for example, for literature assignments. Students write vocabulary words in the log, reflections on what they read each day, comments on themes, quotes they find interesting—anything related to the readings, lectures, and discussions. The learning logs are immensely helpful to students for discussions and papers based on the literature, as well as a source when studying for exams.

WRITING SHORT STORIES

Discovery activities are especially important when students write stories. Plot, characterization, setting, descriptions, and dialogue all combine to create a well-written story. The writer's journal can provide help as mentioned in preceding sections. In addition, a teacher can design many other activities such as round robin stories, developing characters, story strips, and personal narratives.

Round Robin Stories

Round robin stories are one way to get students interested in writing stories, and they work for a wide age span. These stories foster creativity and provide an enjoyable writing activity for students, which is an important result. Once a teacher uses round robin stories in class, students will probably ask to do it again. Because it takes only about 15 minutes, it is handy to use when there isn't enough time to begin something else—like the 15 minutes left in a class period after a fire drill. The class is divided into groups of four. Each student has a sheet of paper. At a signal from the teacher, each student begins a story. Sometimes teachers provide the kind of story it must be: mystery, science fiction, or adventure, for example. After a minute and a half, students stop writing. They finish a word if necessary, but not a sentence. They fold the part they've written down except for the last line so that only the last line is visible; this might be one word or a whole line. Then they pass the paper to the right. This time they have one minute to write and follow the same procedure as before. It works well if the stories go around about three times, but the process can be adjusted to the time available. Just before the last pass, students know they have to write an ending, and when they hear the word *stop,* they finish the sentence rather than just the word. Students love to read the stories to their group.

Developing Characters

Students seem to have the most trouble in this area. Plots are the easiest, so most of the time, characters appear in the story to carry the plot along and nothing more. An especially successful way to show students that characters should have personalities is an activity described by David Sudol, a high school teacher. Sudol begins by telling his class that characters have to be developed, and he discusses different levels of character development. He places an empty chair in the center of the room and announces that Stanley Realbozo is sitting in it. He explains that the students have to bring him to life. He guides the discussion that follows with these questions.

1. What does Stanley look like? Can you describe him sitting there or doing something?
2. Where does Stanley live, work, and play?
3. What does Stanley think about? What is he thinking?
4. What is Stanley's conversation like? How does he speak?

5. How does Stanley react to people, places, and things?
6. How do others characters react to Stanley? What do they think and say about him?
7. What does the author think about Stanley? (The author is the class.) (64)

When students have discussed all the questions, they put together a composite picture of Stanley. How real he is depends on the amount of detail in the class's answers. As Sudol notes, "But no matter what his level of development, he always comes alive. More than the responses to the questions, he is now an actual member of our class" (65).

At this point the students create a plot for Stanley using five questions as guides.

1. What is the situation of the story? What is happening at the beginning?
2. What is the main conflict of the story? What are the generating circumstances? What gets the action going?
3. What events in the story increase the conflict and push forward the action?
4. What is the climax or highest point of the story?
5. How are the conflicts resolved? (Sudol 63–66)

Sudol used the activity to help his students understand literature better; it can also be used as a discovery activity for short story writing. The first part—describing Stanley—is a whole-class activity; the plot questions help students individually write a story about Stanley. Teachers can adapt this and other activities to meet the particular needs of the class.

Story Strips

As mentioned earlier, most students are fairly good at writing plot, but have trouble with characters and settings. Story strips are an activity that helps them connect all three elements. Before the class activity, a teacher cuts strips of paper about 8½ inches long and 4 inches wide from three different colors. The lesson begins with a discussion of what a setting could be, using examples from stories they've read. In some literature, the setting means a great deal and, in others, it makes no difference at all. With help if necessary, students come up with a long list of what settings could include: time of day, season, location, length of time, environment, place, year, month, day. The teacher hands out strips of one color, and they each write a description of a setting.

Next, the teacher discusses how characterization can be described in several ways, such as physical appearance, personality traits, and behavior. Using the second colored strip, students write a character description.

The last strip is used for a single line of plot. At first, students tend to write too much for plot, so it is better to narrow it to one sentence. They might write, "She opened the door slowly," for example.

When students finish the three strips, they place the strips in a hat and choose one strip of each color. Their assignment is to write a story incorporating the information on the strips. Some combinations bring out loud cries of "This is impossible!" "No way will this work out!" But the stories are always interesting and creative.

Figure 6.7 Examples of story strips	
Setting:	1890s, old saloon with damaged wood floor, good drinks (cheap), regulars sitting around, smoke-filled air, few small tables besides the bar stools, a dog—black with white spots.
Character:	A quiet young adult, about 22 or 23. Heavy heart, melancholy, friendly, but shy, enjoys biking, observant, poor self-esteem.
Plot line:	They suddenly realized the rocket was without fuel.

This activity is an excellent way to teach students how to use flashbacks in story writing. Sometimes a flashback is the only way the writer can weave together dissimilar elements into a coherent story. When they say with despair, "I can't put a guy in a desert in 1834 in the same story as someone taking off in a rocket!" they might be encouraged to consider flashback as one solution (Maxwell *Notes,* 2–3). An example of the three strips that one student had to base his story on is in Figure 6.7.

Personal Narratives and Writing Stories

Personal experience and fiction writing go hand in hand. Professional writers often use their own experiences for stories, but we seldom ask students to do that. Students are not easily convinced that it is permissible to change facts when writing fiction. A student once said, "That's lying." But as Ben Logan explains in the afterword of *The Land Remembers,* writers can ignore the facts and capture the truth. When people ask Logan how factual his book is, he explains it is "feeling-level truth" (280). That's what realistic stories are, and we can help students create stories based on their own experiences.

When students begin a personal narrative, thinking about each sense one at a time can help them remember details. Logan explains, "The line between memory and invention is confused" (280). He made up some details to capture an image he knew to be true, only to discover later they were indeed accurate. If writers want to convey an idea to a reader, for example, how cold the day was, they can make up a temperature that conveys the coldness to the reader. A former student wrote a wonderful story about helping out his first-grade teacher, or so he thought, by painting leaves of the classroom plants with shellac. When Mark retells that story now, some of the facts change: the number of plants he shellacked, the grade he was in, and so forth. But what never changes is the image of a little boy trying so hard to please and failing because he did not have an adult's knowledge of the world. Mark is using "feeling-level" truth.

 ## WRITING POETRY

Before attempting poetry, students should be familiar with reading and hearing poetry. Concentrating on poetry writing is often done as a unit for a week or more, but poetry itself should be integrated throughout the year. Once poetry writing is familiar to students, it, too, can be part of many units.

To begin the unit we write a class poem based on Kenneth Koch's suggestion of the "I wish" poem in *Wishes, Lies, and Dreams*. Everyone in class completes the line that begins "I wish." It is easier to organize the lines if students write them on 3- × 5-inch cards. All the cards are laid out on a table and arranged to create a poem. If the same line or similar lines are written by more than one student, this becomes the refrain in the poem. It is important to put in everyone's line; students look for their own. Even students who are "anti-school" eagerly anticipate seeing their contribution in the completed poem. Teachers type the poem that evening, run off copies for everyone, and hand them out the next day. Staggering the activity for multiple classes makes it easier on the teacher. The poem always comes out sounding like a "real poem" and impresses everyone. This activity works with students in elementary grades through the graduate students in the writing project. English education students composed the following:

I WISH

I wish there were 40 hours in a day and weekends were 4 days long.
There's so much to do, so many places to go
And so much to experience in this life!
I wish I could travel throughout the world.
I wish that every child could have a peaceful, enjoyable childhood
Free of all abuse, hunger, and drugs.
I wish everyone could accept others as easily
As they accept themselves.
I wish I could read the minds of others
When I'm particularly confused about things they say
Or the way they act.
I wish it was Christmas time all the time
And nobody would ever stop being excited about it.
I wish for long, lazy, fun-filled days with nothing to worry about
Except for long, lazy, enjoyable evenings in which I'd share
Living and loving with forever friends.
I wish I were a preying mantis so powerful, tall and green.
I wish Coke was still sold in 16 oz. bottles.
I wish the sidewalk between my house and campus
Wasn't under two inches of water.
I wish it was spring.
I wish I was walking on a sandy beach near tranquil waters.
I wish that I could walk to the moon upon silver beams
Reflecting on the still serene waters of Lake Michigan.
I wish the skies were always clear, the weather always warm,
And the grass always green.
I wish for a beautiful multicolored sunset.
I wish for mornings like this one—cool and crisp.
To walk with my friends and enjoy the freshness of the air.
I wish the summer sun would radiate its bright yellow fingertips
Across my grandfather's sparking crystal blue eyes
Just one last time.

The "I wish" poem is a list poem, sometimes called catalog verse. Larry Fagin suggests many different subjects and types of list poems to use with student writers because they "draw on specific details of everyday experience," and use the rhythms and patterns of everyday speech (2). He suggests beginning with a theme or topic, modeling poems by using a variety of examples, and pointing out characteristics (3). Many of the list poems are collaborative efforts and help to increase students' confidence in writing poetry (8).

Writing a poem can be difficult for some people, and using a pattern to create poetry can help. Fagin suggests beginning lines with a color word (e.g., "Red is . . .") or phrases like "If I were . . . " and "I remember . . . " List poems can be organized around topics as well, such as beautiful things, emotions, definitions, and reasons.

Several explanations and examples of pattern poems are described below. All of the poetry examples used in this section are written by students.

1. *Five liners.*
   - Write the name of someone on the first line.
   - Write two adjectives describing the noun.
   - Write three words describing what they do (end in -*ing* or -*s*).
   - Write a phrase about the person.
   - Repeat the same name as on line 1 or another name for the same person.

Holden   Hester
Confused, introspective   Spirited, Censored
Wandering, wondering, running   Sins, Sews, Survives
Looking for answers   Nobel brave victim
Holden   Hester

Gail Servoss

Light   Summer
Reflect, shimmer   Hot, fun
Shining, sparkling, glowing   Swimming, playing, traveling
Taking away the dark   Free from school
Light   Summer

Becky Olien   *Jessica Olien*

2. *Diamond shape poem.* This poem form is similar to the five liners but has a twist in the middle. The first half refers to the noun on the first line; the second half refers to the noun on the last line.
   - Begin with a noun.
   - Write two adjectives describing the noun.
   - Write three participles referring to the noun on the first line.
   - Write four nouns: The first two refer to the top name, the second two to the name on the last line.
   - Write three participles referring to the noun on the last line.
   - Write two adjectives describing the noun on the last line.
   - Write the second noun on the last line.

Lady Macbeth
Greedy, ruthless
Scheming, controlling, cleaning
Blood, death-king, trouble
planning, killing, worrying
paranoid, superstitious
Macbeth

Laurie Anderson

3. *Concrete poem.* A concrete poem is one in which the words project not only an image but also the actual shape of the subject of the poem. These can become trite unless writers use descriptive words, but with creativity they are enjoyable to eyes and ears as in the two students' examples shown here:

MY CAR

a customized
window of plexiglass and
bolts. The windshield is graced
with a crack and a scratch from the
stub that was once a windshield wiper a hole in the floor to complement
the heater that works! -- constantly. and a back seat which folds down! --
permanently the ashtray is lost, the seatbelts won't click the radio is falling
out, but who needs the extra noise with the sputtering clanging   spft
rattling   banging   pft
clink   clunk   t.

Victoria Gillhouse

Jenel Korkowski

4. *Preposition poem*. The poem is seven lines long, each of which begins with a preposition. Authors write about themselves, their feelings and emotions. Giving students a list of prepositions is helpful.

> In a place of wind and sun
> As far as can be seen
> Upon the mind a vision forms
> Of grass and trees and green.
> Throughout the swing I concentrate
> About the ball so white
> Against all odds I hit the thing and sent it out of sight.

Cheryl Mortensen

> Through the azure sky the sun shines
> Upon my waking spirit.
> Before me, the day lies unexplored.
> Into the morning, I step boldly
> In spite of the chill in the air,
> Before the night covers the world
> In a velvet blanket, I shall triumph.

Lisa Willert

5. *Mood poems*. Students begin with a one-word description of the mood they are in at the time or one they felt recently. On the first line they write the mood. The next two lines begin with the word *not*, describing the mood by writing what it isn't. The fourth line is also a *not*, but is stated as a comparison. The fifth line is what the mood is, followed by three lines of description of the mood.

> I'm happy
> Not silly
> Not falling off my chair happy
> Not like the happiest I've ever been in my whole life
> But quietly satisfactorily happy.
> Happy that vacation is starting soon
> Happy that my brother is coming home
> Happy that I'm going skiing with my friends

6. *Found poems*. Poetry defies definition: Some rhyme, some do not; some are long, others short; some tell a story, or evoke a feeling, or describe a single image. The spacing of lines and arrangement of white space can create a sense of poetry. Found poems illustrate that point vividly. A found poem is "found" from any printed material: *TV Guide*, cereal boxes, student handbooks, textbooks, advertising, newspaper headlines, and so forth. Students have fun creating the layout of the words; some are silly, others more serious.

Why Brown Rice?
Brown rice is the most
nutritious
Rice of all.
It's also the least
Processed.
While most rice is
Polished
To remove the bran, brown rice is
Whole
With only the outer hull
Removed.

Kellogg's Kemmei Rice Bran

7. *Bio poem.* A bio poem usually is about oneself, but could also be about a character from literature.
   - In line 1, write the first name of the person.
   - In line 2, write four traits that describe the character.
   - Line 3 begins with the words "relative of _____ ." The student fills in the blank.
   - Line 4 begins with the words "lover of." Then the student lists three things or people loved by the character.
   - Line 5 begins with the words "who feels." Then the student describes three things the character feels.
   - Line 6 begins with "who needs," and the student writes three items.
   - Line 7 begins with the words "who fears," and the student writes three things feared.
   - Line 8 begins with the words "who gives," and the student lists three examples.
   - Line 9 begins with the words "who would like to see," and the student lists three things.
   - Line 10 begins with the words "resident of _____ ," and the student fills in the blank.
   - Line 11 lists the last name of the character.

8. *Terse verse.* The poem itself is only two or three words, but the titles can be quite long and suggest, almost like a riddle, the subject of the poem. An example by a student, Jennifer Hartzell, follows:

Daring Fungus That Adheres to Dated Vittles
Bold Mold

Experimenting and playing with words becomes the focus of poetry writing. Students, of course, can write haiku, limericks, sonnets, parodies, and so on, but the goal is always to enjoy writing poetry and increase confidence. Writing structured poems helps achieve these goals.

Linda Wall, a middle school teacher, uses the following activity to help students connect images with the five senses:

> Begin by passing out peppermint candy. The students list the five senses in columns on a sheet of paper, then write down words or experiences beside each of the five senses that come to mind as they eat the candy (provide sugarless candy for diabetics). For example, the smell of mint might remind them of their grandparents' house. Or the sight of the mint might cause them to remember candy canes or Christmas decorations. As students share their responses with the class, even more images will come to mind. (9–10)

Taking Wall's suggestion further, students could describe other food, a location, or a color. What images come to mind? A poem is created when the images are written in phrases.

Poems from phrases can also be created by having students select a color, writing the name of the color at the top of a page, and then writing every association they can think of related to that color. For example, the color green might make one think of lichen on an old stone wall, oil glistening in a water puddle, a mother's eyes, the first spring mantle of grass, moldy bread, a slow-moving stream, frogs, lime popsicle, a fading bruise. The more they write, the better. Contemplating their list, students mark the images they especially like. From this example, one might choose

> Lichen on an old stone wall
> Green of mother's eyes
> A frog by an algae-covered pool

Each phrase can become a poem:

> How much has the soft green lichen on the old castle wall seen of strife, pain, and glory.

> How much has the large solemn frog by the still green pond seen of life and death and miracles?

> How much have my mother's green eyes seen of stress, neglect, and love?

EXPLORATION

Writing Poetry

Write five poems using five different styles. Which ones are the easiest? Which are the hardest? Develop some ways of including poetry writing with literature study and thematic units.

Collaborative Writing

Students working together to create a single work has many advantages. Writing alone never provides opportunities to see how others figure out what to say and how to say it. In a group, students see what discovery techniques others use: a mapping outline, free writing, listing, and so forth. Brainstorming in a group is more productive than doing it alone. One idea leads to another; what one person says makes another think of something else. And working together in a group helps improve social interaction.

Many students loudly proclaim the disadvantages when a teacher brings up collaborative writing. Two areas cause the main difficulties: grades and workload. In collaborative writing everyone in the group receives the same grade. Students who usually receive high grades for their writing worry that their grade will drop. Some students worry that not all group members will do their share. Both are legitimate concerns, but there are ways around them, or at least ways to ease the problem.

Because cooperating with people is a skill we need throughout our life, learning to work with others is a major goal in collaborative writing, as important as writing a well-organized, interesting paper. To make collaborative writing work, teachers need to make sure the students work on both goals. By stressing the need to listen to others and respect what they say, teachers help students work through difficulties.

Receiving the same grade as others in the group bothers some students, and they have to know from the beginning there will be no other way of weighing the grade. Knowing they receive a common grade encourages students to work at cooperating with the others. When they hand in their final draft, ask them to evaluate individually how the process worked out—for instance, if they thought everyone did a fair share. Often, just having an opportunity to tell the teacher they think they did more work than others is enough satisfaction.

Helen Dale, an English education professor, sets up collaborative assignments that more evenly distribute the workload. She puts as many students in a group as there are collaborative writing assignments. If she plans three collaborative writing assignments, she puts three people in a group. Each assignment has a primary writer, so the responsibility shifts from student to student. All the group members contribute to each writing stage, but one person is responsible for collecting the others' work, doing the final polishing, and writing transitions so that everyone's writing blends together, and whatever else needs to be done. For the next group writing assignment, a different member has that responsibility. Obviously the groups have to remain the same throughout the semester or year.

Dale finds that the quality of the papers improves through collaboration. "There is peer pressure to think well and to write well. Students test ideas against each other, so you get their best and clearest thoughts" (14). When she first started assigning group papers, she thought students would write "patchwork prose," but found students "seem to integrate ideas, organization, and style" (15).

Collaborative groups provide firsthand experience in working together, an ability important in our life work. Dale believes that "Wonderful things happen when students are allowed to see other minds at work, puzzle things out, search for the right example or the right word, and arrive at a completed piece of work" (16). Although there are some negative aspects of collaborative writing, the positive outweighs the negative, and with planning teachers can make the experience worthwhile for students.

We have used a collaborative writing assignment in which students write a Level 3 paper on the advantages and disadvantages of birth order in a family. The groups were formed on the basis of their birth orders; for example, students who were the youngest in their families work in one group and produce one paper and so on. Each group was responsible for deciding on the topics and the organization of the paper. The students decided on goals for the group including work due the following day. The students wrote outside of class and then brought their work in the next day for revision and editing.

Our students responded to the experience of working on a collaborative paper:

I found that working in a group is very different from being on your own. I tend to worry about what they think of my writing and whether or not everyone agrees and is happy with the decisions. In a group you have such different styles and opinions that it can be hard to come to agreement. In our group these differences were evident but not a major problem. I think my role in the group was to help get everyone talking. It took a couple of days to learn and understand each person's style, but I am happy with the experience. There now are six more people I know better. (Shawna Sullivan)

During the first week of working together some people were a little hesitant to express their opinion or critique someone else's work but as time passed the entire group relaxed and seemed to feel more comfortable sharing their thoughts and ideas. I believe the workload was pretty evenly distributed. Aside from what I learned from the other six people in my group, I learned that it is very difficult collaborating on a paper because there are many different ways a person can approach this type of paper, and with some people in the group it made it more difficult to decide on things—not necessarily because everyone has a different opinion but because one person does not want to make decisions for six others. Overall though it has taught me how to work in a big group. (Justin Hurd)

Overall working in a group was a welcome change from writing everything individually. Our group worked well together and we accomplished a lot. The finished product turned out to be a really good paper reflecting various experiences. I think we each shared the workload evenly although Erin did more on the final draft. We each did different things at different times, which balanced out. Everyone gave input and turned in paragraphs. I learned various things about the group members and their families. I also learned group work is a lot of compromising and combining of ideas. (Dominich Walsh)

 ## COMPOSITION AND THE WORLD OF WORK

Many teachers and business people are concerned about the schools' ability to prepare students for the world of work. Teachers Mitch Cox and Christine Firpo concluded that "the majority of what we were teaching would never make a difference in their lives" (42). They realized they had to identify what their students needed to succeed in the workforce. They learned that managers were concerned with their employees' lack of ability to work on teams (42). They also identified other skills their students needed: to read technical manuals, to maintain records, to write correspondence, and to communicate orally. In addition, they needed creative and logical thinking.

Carol Pope describes five areas of proficiency that students need as they enter the labor force.

1. *Ability to communicate.* Workers must be able to use language effectively in a variety of contexts. They need to function in teams and work in a collaborative setting (38).
2. *Ability to work in a multicultural setting.* Workers need to listen, be empathetic, and be knowledgeable and open-minded of other cultures (38).
3. *Ability to adapt.* They need to learn new skills quickly and adjust to changing demographics and cultures of fellow workers. They must know how to learn (39).
4. *Ability to think critically.* Workers need to have "an inquiring responsive mind that sees relationships and considers alternatives, predicts, and analyzes" (39).
5. *Ability to use available technology.* Workers need to be familiar with computers and multimedia so that they can communicate across worlds and be able to deal with various cultures and ideas (39).

English language arts classrooms can facilitate these five proficiencies and many already do. To begin, a class structure where students move around the room, where desks are not in tidy straight rows, and where talking is going on is preparing future workers to learn adaptability, accept others, and work in diverse settings.

When you are not the focal point of learning, students learn how to plan for their own needs, where to look for information, and how to find the help they need. Response groups in writing are a good example of creating an opportunity for this to happen. You set up the situations, but students must take responsibility for the learning.

When students work collaboratively, they are learning how workers write grants and reports and plan for the future. Meeting in small groups to plan a research project teaches the necessary cooperation needed in the workforce. Developing an awareness of audience when composing is an important skill as students learn to consider how to explain information and their own views to others. The entire writing process reinforces the five proficiencies and, in particular, reinforces cooperative learning.

To help students become more self-directed learners, we can incorporate the reading/writing workshop into their class structure (Cox and Firpo 43). Within this structure, students select what they want to read and write and generate their own writing topics. The students are "encouraged to think of themselves as cooperative team workers" when they collaborate on revising and editing (43).

The more we have students work together, the more students realize they learn from each other as well as from the teacher, and the better able they are to function in the world of work.

In addition to structuring our classrooms to help students achieve the five proficiencies Pope describes, teachers can provide technical writing activities to sharpen student skills in this area. Technical writing is appearing more frequently in high school curriculums as a separate class. A teacher of such a class, Marvin Hoffman, explains the objectives for his course:

> We wanted our students to write rich, accurate, precise, objective description; to develop a sensitivity to honest, uninflated language in their own work and the work of others; and finally to demonstrate their ability to synthesize these skills by producing an action proposal on a problem or issue of their own choosing for a real audience. (59)

Hoffman used a wide range of activities to help students develop objective description. Students read a variety of literature and examples of job-related writing throughout the course. Much of the job-related writing was a negative model, and students became adept at rewriting convoluted, confusing memos into understandable English (61). Hoffman found that some of the "sharpest writing emerges from fields like nature, science, and sports" (61), and he provided many opportunities for students to read from these areas. As a final project, each student chose a problem to research and wrote about one that had a real audience. Through library research, interviews, and observations, students wrote their findings and recommendations for a specific audience (62).

If teachers stress cooperative learning through the writing process and collaborative activities, students learn the essential skills for writing in the world of work. Writing assignments that have real-world audiences and purposes help students understand the necessity of clear writing. Teaching English does not have to seem esoteric to our students.

Teaching Sources

Many sources for teaching ideas are available to us. One in particular that secondary teachers find useful is *Notes Plus,* a quarterly publication from the National Council of Teachers of English and written, for the most part, by teachers. A typical issue includes these topics: Ideas from the Classroom, Classic of the Month, A Writing Assignment of the Month, and A Literature Assignment of the Month. The following writing ideas appeared in *Notes Plus:*

1. *Customized holidays.* Begin with a discussion of holidays. Ask students why they think people create and celebrate holidays. Brainstorm about what holidays students think should be on the calendar, but aren't. Then have students design or create a special day. They write a description of the special way in which this new holiday will be celebrated, and design a logo, slogan, or whatever trimmings it takes to make the new day a complete holiday. The final step is an illustrated poster or commercial announcing the new holiday. As a continuation, ask students to think of special experiences in their own lives that should be celebrated. A children's book, *I'm in Charge of Celebrations* by Byrd Baylor, is a great starting point for this discussion. Students deepen their awareness of the value of their observational experiences (Hellman 3).

2. *The rewards of the wanted poster.* To help students focus on what they like about themselves, they design their own wanted poster. Using a form that looks roughly like the real thing, students write information about themselves: name, date of birth, a photo or caricature, physical description, caution, and reward. Students may choose which of their physical descriptions they feel comfortable sharing. Under the heading "caution" students list short phrases that describe problem areas; for example, sarcastic sense of humor, selfish, disorganized. The real focus of the activity is the reward section. Unlike the real wanted posters, this is reserved for a list of positive personal characteristics—a list that highlights how others are rewarded by knowing this person. Many students have trouble with the reward section because they minimize their good attributes. The poster is not complete until their reward section is at least as long as the caution section. This activity can be a real eye-opener for students when they discover that their good qualities outweigh their less desirable traits. (Meisner 7)

The writing ideas throughout this chapter illustrate the variety of activities you can include in frequent writing assignments. Many of the assignments are for practice and not for polished drafts. Writing at all levels should be part of ongoing activities of a classroom.

 EXPLORING AN INSTRUCTIONAL UNIT

Aimee M. Peterson, an English education student, developed a unit on family pressures for ninth- or tenth-grade students. Throughout the unit, Peterson designated levels of each writing assignment. As you read Peterson's unit, notice in particular how she creates student interest for the unit as a whole and for specific assignments by selecting a level of writing suited to the purpose of the writing. Peterson's unit is more thorough than the edited version presented here. We selected activities that highlight the use of levels and the inclusion of the writing process in planning a thematic unit.

INSTRUCTIONAL UNIT

FAMILY PRESSURES

Objectives

By teaching this unit, I believe my students will feel more comfortable about discussing family pressures that occur in their lives. It is important that they realize everyone has family pressures and to recognize that there are many types of family pressures—positive as well as negative. Also, I want them to gain knowledge about how to handle pressures. It isn't easy to deal with parents and siblings who pressure us to do what they think we should do. I want my students to enjoy the unit and, also, be able to apply what they learn to their own lives.

Introductory Activity. As students enter the classroom, I will hand each one a slip of paper that describes an incident/statement that illustrates a possible family pressure. Examples are "Your mom dislikes your new boyfriend/girlfriend," or "You spent all your allowance getting your hair colored/permed, and when you get home a parent tells you that if you don't change your hair you are not allowed to go to the school dance." Each student reads the statement on the slip aloud, and a class discussion follows led by the following questions:

1. What would you say all of these incidents/statements have in common?
2. What are some ways your family has pressured you?
3. Why did you feel pressures?
4. Think of some conflicts you've had. Why do you think parents or siblings sometimes pressure you?
5. In what ways can pressuring be for our "own good"?
6. Is there such a thing as a good pressure?

Journal Assignment. Write one page describing pressures dealing with your family that you believe are positive and one page you believe are negative (Level 1).

Writing Assignment. Using your journal entries, write a short essay comparing and contrasting positive and negative pressures (Level 2). The essays will be shared in groups and discussed the following class period.

Literature Assignment. Students choose a book to read from a selection of four, which are listed by level of difficulty:

The War with Grandpa by Robert K. Smith
Cattail Moon by Jean Thesman
Romeo and Juliet by William Shakespeare
West Side Story by Leonard Bernstein

I give a brief description of all four books. Each student chooses one book to read. They have the option to change their minds or read more than one book.

The assignments listed below are given in the first week so students have a great deal of time to think about what they want to do. The choices are as follows:

1. Find a newspaper article about a family pressure/conflict. This could be a parent pressuring a child, a child pressuring a parent, or something dealing with siblings or grandparents. Write a response to the article in your journal (Level 1). Write a story about the article. Include events that led up to the event and explain what happens after it. Use your imagination. Or you may choose to write an article of your own dealing with a family pressure.

2. Write a true story about a time when someone in your family pressured you. Explain using details so your readers can understand how you felt and why. Brainstorm, web, or free-write to get ideas for your story (Level 1). Write a rough draft and share in peer groups (Level 2).
3. Compare and contrast the main characters or characters in the novel you read with yourself or with a character from another novel. Include details about the situation of the character and why you chose to examine the particular character(s).
4. Write about an imaginary person. Give the person different problems than any character from the novel you read. Write a short story about his or her life and describe specifically the family pressures your character goes through.

Journal Assignment. Write your thoughts and opinions about the novel you are reading, including whether you are enjoying it or not and explain your reasons (Level 1).

Music Activity. The students will listen to the song "Papa Don't Preach" by Madonna. They then will write their reaction to the song and examine the family pressures that are evident (Level 1). In groups of four or five, students discuss other songs with a similar theme. Each group is responsible for selecting a song and preparing a short presentation for the whole class that explains the family pressures in the song (Level 2).

Literature Activity. Students are placed in groups so that each group represents all four novels. Group members discuss the different family pressures present in their novel. They write a short description of the differences and similarities among the books (Level 2).

Literature Activity. Next the students are placed into groups with others reading the same book. Each group creates a skit, radio show, or a TV show based on the novel. Each group writes what it plans to do (Level 2). The presentations are given to the whole class.

Discussion Activity. I will read the essay "You Don't Love Me" by Erma Bombeck to the class. This essay is about why parents don't want their children to do certain things. A class discussion follows, beginning with the following questions: What kinds of things do most people do to show their love? How does this essay relate to the positive pressures you have discussed and written about?

Poetry Activities. I will distribute the poem "the drum" by Nikki Giovanni to the class. After reading it aloud, we discuss what being an individual means. Students write their own poem inspired by "the drum" (Level 1).

Students are encouraged to bring in and share poems they think represent family pressures or decision-making.

Students write an "I wish" poem expressing how they wish things were (Level 2).

Students read the following poems and then discuss and write responses in their journals (Level 1).

"The Possessive" by Sharon Olds
"Legacy II" by Leroy V. Quintans
"Those Winter Sundays" by Robert Hayden
"Women's Program" by Marie Luise Kaschnitz
"Legacies" by Nikki Giovanni
"The Road Not Taken" by Robert Frost
"The Other House" by David Wagoner

Non-Print Media Activities. Students view the film *The Three Warriors*. Students write a response to the film (Level 1). Using their responses, students write a short essay about the pressures evident in the film (Level 2).

We will have a class discussion on TV shows that portray family pressures. Each student writes a list of shows and a short description of the pressures (Level 1).

Students watch the film *West Side Story,* and a discussion follows on pressures we may experience from peers and siblings. In journals, they write an entry from each day we watch the film, responding to the film and compiling a list of pressures that are present (Level 1). In an essay they compare this film with one of the novels they are reading (Level 2).

To conclude the unit, I plan on reading "Parents Can Be a Problem" by Shirley Schwarzrock aloud to the students. There is no assignment planned because the students will be working in writers' workshop on a Level 3 final paper from the assignment they chose at the beginning of the unit.

EXPLORATION

Examining Peterson's Unit

1. In what ways do Peterson's activities reflect her objectives? Write what you see as her purpose in including each activity. Describe how the level of writing matches the objective. Discuss where you might change a level and for what purpose.
2. Using Peterson's unit as a model, write a letter to Joellen, the teacher described at the beginning of the chapter. What are some ways she could match her goals to assignments using levels of writing?
3. How does Peterson integrate the writing process into the unit? She doesn't explicitly state all of the stages she plans to use. What discovery activities does she include? Where would additional ones be appropriate? Develop a response guide for one of her Level 3 activities.
4. Either individually or in small groups, write activities for teaching a topic, a theme, or a reading. Plan for at least five Level 1 assignments, three Level 2 assignments, and one Level 3 assignment.

RELATED WEB SITES

http://www.users.drew.edu/~sjamieso/Webresources.html
http://leo.stcloudstate.edu/catalogue.html
http://longman.awl.com/englishpages/basic-wkbk-write.htm#6
http://sites.unc.edu/teaching/newbies.html
http://www.poetrypoetry.com/Workshops/00–04ParellelPoetry.html
http://owl.english.purdue.edu/index.htm

REFERENCES

Apfelbeck, Laura. Letter to the author. 1999.

Britton, James, Tony Burgess, Nancy Martin, Alex McLeod, and Harold Rosen. *The Development of Writing Abilities (11–18)*. London: Macmillan Education Ltd., 1975.

Burroway, Janet. *Writing Fiction*. New York: HarperCollins, 1992.

Cox, Mitch, and Christine Firpo. "What Would They Be Doing If We Gave Them Worksheets?" *English Journal* (March 1993): 42–45.

Dale, Helen. "Collaboration in the Writing Process." *Wisconsin English Journal* 31.2 (1989): 11–16.

Didion, Joan. *Slouching Towards Bethlehem*. New York: Dell, 1968.

Dixon, John. *Growth Through English*. Reading: National Association for Teaching English, 1967.

Elliott, Anne. "Unit of Study for *Crazy Lady*." English 406/606. University of Wisconsin–Eau Claire. April 1995.

Emig, Janet. *The Composing Process of Twelfth Graders*. Urbana: National Council of Teachers of English, 1972.

Fagin, Larry. *The List Poem*. New York: Teachers & Writers Collaborative, 1991.

Fortier, John. Letter to the author. 15 Oct. 1991.

Friedmann, Thomas. "Teaching Error, Nurturing Confusion: Grammar Texts, Tests and Teachers in the Developmental English Class." *College English* (April 1983): 390–99.

Grubgeld, Elizabeth. "Helping the Problem Speller Without Suppressing the Writer." *English Journal* (Feb. 1986): 58–61.

Hellman, Sally. "Customized Holidays." *Notes Plus*. Urbana: NCTE, Nov. 1990: 3.

Hodges, Richard E. *Improving Spelling and Vocabulary in Secondary School*. Urbana: NCTE ERIC, 1982.

Hoffman, Marvin. "On Teaching Technical Writing: Creative Language in the Real World." *English Journal* (Feb. 1992): 58–63.

Hymes, Dell. "Models of the Interaction of Language and Social Life." *Directions in Sociolinguistics*. Eds. John J. Gumpetz and Dell Hymes. New York: Holt, Rinehart & Winston, 1972. 35–71.

Joos, Martin. *The Five Clocks*. New York: Harcourt Brace & World, 1961.

Kirby, Dan, and Tom Liner. *Inside Out: Developmental Strategies for Teaching Writing*. 2nd ed. Portsmouth: Boynton/Cook Heinemann, 1988.

Koch, Kenneth. *Wishes, Lies, and Dreams: Teaching Children to Write Poetry*. New York: Vintage, 1970.

Lindemann, Erika. *A Rhetoric for Writing Teachers*. 2nd ed. New York: Oxford UP, 1987.

Logan, Ben. *The Land Remembers*. Minocqua: Heartland Press, 1985.

Martin, Nancy, Peter Medway, Harold Smith, and Pat D'Arcy. "Why Write?" *Writing Across the Curriculum*. Eds. Nancy Martin, Peter Medway, and Harold Smith. Montclair: Boynton/Cook, 1984. 34–59.

Maxwell, Rhoda J. "So What's New?" Unpublished essay, 1982.

_____. "Story Strips." *Notes Plus*. Urbana: NCTE, April 1987.

_____. *Writing Across the Curriculum in Middle and High Schools*. Boston: Allyn & Bacon, 1996.

Meisner, Mark. "The Rewards of the Wanted Poster." *Notes Plus*. Urbana: NCTE, April 1991: 6–7.

Meyer, Emily, and Louise Z. Smith. *The Practical Tutor*. New York: Oxford UP, 1987.

Miller, James E. Jr. *Word, Self, and Reality: The Rhetoric of Imagination*. New York: Dodd, Mead & Co., 1972.

Moffett, James. *Teaching the Universe of Discourse*. Boston: Houghton Mifflin, 1983.

Nagy, William E. *Teaching Vocabulary to Improve Reading Comprehension*. Urbana: NCTE ERIC, 1988.

Noguchi, Rei. *Grammar and Teaching Writing*. Urbana: NCTE, 1991.

Peterson, Aimee M. "Family Pressures." English 406/606. University of Wisconsin–Eau Claire, May 1995.

Pope, Carol A. "Our Time Has Come: English for the Twenty-First Century." *English Journal* (March 1993): 38–41.

Rohman, D. Gordon. "Prewriting: The Stage of Discovery in the Writing Process." *College Composition and Communication* 16 (1965): 106–112.

Romano, Tom. *Grammar and Teaching Writing*. Urbana: NCTE, 1991.

Rubin, Donald L. "Introduction." *Perspectives on Talk and Learning*. Eds. Susan Hynds and Donald L. Rubin. Urbana: NCTE, 1990: 1–17.

Sassano, Lisa. "I Spy Engaged Learners." *Voices from the Middle* (May 2001): 24–25.

Schuman, R. Baird. "Seeing and Feeling Sentence Structure." *English Journal* (Jan. 1990): 71–73.

Shaughnessy, Mina. *Errors and Expectations*. New York: Oxford UP, 1977.

Strong, William. *Creative Approaches to Sentence Combining*. Urbana: NCTE ERIC, 1986.

Sudol, David. "Creating and Killing Stanley Realbozo or Teaching Characterization and Plot in English 10." *English Journal* (Oct. 1983).

Vail, Neil, and Joseph Papenfuss. *Daily Oral Language*. Evanston: McDougal Littell, 1989.

Wall, Linda. "Seeing Is Believing: A Method for Teaching Imagery in Poetry." *Notes Plus* (March 1994): 9–10.

Ziegler, Alan. *The Writing Workshop: Vol. 2*. New York: Teachers & Writers Collaborative, 1984.

Understanding Grammar 7

It appears that the teachers of English teach English so poorly largely because they teach grammar so well.

Linda Enders, high school student

Grammar is perhaps the most contested and the least understood area of the English language arts curriculum, despite being the area most taught in U.S. schools. Many people associate English classes with grammar: learning terminology and rules, diagramming sentences, filling in blanks and worksheets, and taking quizzes. Presumably, these activities enable students to speak and write acceptable English. The presumption, however, is false. Considerable research and classroom practice have shown that these activities have little effect on student competency and performance (Bamberg; Braddock et al.; Haynes; Hillocks).

Researchers continue to tell us what many classroom teachers already know: Practicing skills in textbooks or worksheets doesn't work. The skills fail to transfer when students are engaged in the messy business of composing a full essay. A student who has done 10 exercises and passed a quiz on a specific skill may make errors in that skill on the very next essay. There are several reasons for this. First, the isolated study of language skills has a limited effect on the permanent language knowledge we carry in our heads. Second, we make choices about language through the context in which we use it; a drill sheet has no context, only unrelated sentences. Third, the "dummy runs" in texts and worksheets are far less complex than the students' own language. If students don't learn to untangle their own language and judge effectiveness and correctness in an entire piece of writing, they will gain little or no proficiency. But even more damaging is the time factor: Students who are doing exercises are not writing. They are not learning about standard usage, appropriate mechanics, and correct spelling in the one context where these skills are both meaningful and mandatory: real communication. Student drafts provide ample opportunities for teaching the various language skills as they relate to communication, to what students themselves want to express.

Because grammar evokes personal, and even emotional, responses, teachers need to understand the diverse meanings applied to the term *grammar*. When teachers say they are going to do a "grammar unit," they usually mean they are going to concentrate on some aspect of standard American usage, such as conventions or sentence patterns. For example, they will block out two weeks to cover subject–verb agreement, three weeks to study comma use, or two weeks to work on sentences with a subject–verb–object pattern. Even though the notion of a grammar unit is outdated, many teachers nonetheless persist in it. An examination of school curricula and textbooks demonstrates its resistance to change, despite research and classroom practice that refute teaching these skills as isolated units.

Reflection

How did you learn formal "grammar" (i.e., parts of speech, usage)? Do you believe that knowing parts of speech had an effect on how well you read or wrote in secondary school? Why? What would you consider essential "grammar" knowledge for an English language arts teacher?

 ## What Is Grammar?

As noted earlier, controversy and confusion arise when the word *grammar* is used. People usually give three reasons why they think students must study grammar: Students can't put a sentence together; students don't know a noun from a verb; students can't speak or write without making mistakes. In exploring these reasons, we can find underlying definitions of the term *grammar*.

Students Can't Put a Sentence Together

In this context, grammar refers to the set of rules native speakers know intuitively, the rules we acquired without lessons, as we acquired our native language between birth and age 6. Grammar here is tacit, unconscious knowledge. As native speakers of English, we know how to form words and sentences, no matter how simple or complex, and we do so without making any conscious decisions about word order, word endings, and so forth. In brief, we know the grammar of our native language.

Assuming normal development (that is, no damage to the brain and capacity for language), all native speakers know the grammar of their language. They recognize non-grammatical English sentences immediately. For example, the construction

sees boy the ball red

would be rejected by every native speaker of English. Teachers and others may not like some students' sentences, which may be poorly constructed, awkward or unclear, suffer from weak vocabulary, or punctuated incorrectly. However, these weaknesses are not grammar problems, at least not to teachers who understand grammar as the system of language we learn as native speakers.

Students Don't Know a Noun from a Verb

In this context, the term *grammar* refers to the ability to talk about the language system; it is our conscious knowledge about our native language. In the United States, tradition has dictated that educated people know some basic language terms, such as *noun, verb, adjective, adverb*, and *sentence*. An understanding of these terms is not acquired naturally, the way the language itself is. We have to learn the terms through instruction—thus the heavy emphasis on them at every curricular level. In reality, few students learn all the terms. Their textbooks often define the terms poorly, probably because the concepts they represent are far more complex than people like to believe. For those who do learn the terms, the knowledge is often fleeting, largely because students quickly realize that labeling nouns and defining verbs does not have a significant effect on their lives. As one tenth grader recently remarked: "Does anyone really believe that we have to know this stuff, that someday a person will jump out from behind a tree and say, 'Tell me what a verb does'?"

Students' aversion to learning terms for terms' sake is supported by research; understanding the function of language is more effective than memorizing terms and definitions. However, some English teachers persist in their belief that sustained doses of directed study do improve language skills, especially writing. As Rei Noguchi puts it: "Like the near mythical omnipotence of cod-liver oil, the study of grammar became imbued with medicinal power it simply did not possess, particularly with respect to writing ills" (15). Under the pressure of state standards and tests, teachers have again mistakenly stressed exercises over a more functional, contextual approach to learning grammar.

Thus the labeling of parts of speech, the diagramming of sentences, and other activities designed to "name" language rather than to use it in authentic communication, continue. The same tenth grader who questioned the validity of studying terms also commented on their domination of the curriculum: "Different cover, same old stuff." A well-educated student must possess literacy skills, that is, to be able to read and write competently, but these abilities are not the result of knowing definitions for the parts of speech. Moreover, forcing such knowledge before students have a reason for knowing or the cognitive maturation to understand it is futile. We are not advocating that students never learn "grammar" terms, only that they do so within the context of reading and writing.

Students Can't Speak or Write without Making Mistakes

Here grammar refers to rules of language etiquette or verbal manners: We adhere to a standard use of language in the academic or business world. This standard has nothing to do with communication, for nonstandard forms communicate meaning as well as standard forms. For example, there is no confusion of meaning when we hear non-standard forms such as *she's taller than me* or *he can't hardly talk*, just as there is no confusion when we read *them boys did pick a fight*. What is involved is a continuum of verbal manners. Many people would not notice the error in *she's taller than me*, but few would fail to notice the deviations in *them boys did pick a fight*. "Mistakes," then, translate into a view of what does and does not constitute standard American English, the dialect used in the world of formal communication and taught in schools, the dialect of social prestige.

Because standard dialect is the dialect of schools, English language arts teachers want students to use it. Most parents, similarly, want their children to know and use it appropriately. The key, however, is flexibility and appropriateness to the communication situation. Teachers sometimes assume that all mistakes are equally serious and that all rules apply in every type of communication. This is simply not the case. Some mistakes derail readers, causing them to go back and sort out the meaning; these errors are serious because they interfere with meaning. Other errors, however, may irritate the purist but cause no confusion for the general reader. The issue of "mistake" is serious nonetheless. Teachers face a challenge in presenting students with a standard dialect and, at the same time, honoring other dialects used at home and in the community. Patrick Hartwell (105–27) offers a cogent explanation of the two grammars that get lumped together under the term *grammar:*

> School grammar. This grammar is the one of school textbooks. Although linguists cringe at fuzzy definitions (e.g., a sentence expresses a complete thought), school grammar makes no claims of scientific accuracy. School grammar presents the student with parts of speech, sentence patterns, standard usage forms, conventions of writing and spelling. Another name for school grammar is traditional grammar.
>
> Grammar-as-etiquette. When speakers or writers deviate from certain forms or conventions (those taught in school grammar), they are accused of having "bad grammar." This grammar refers to standard American English, the dialect of school and business.

The basic controversy and debate over grammar are found in school grammar and grammar-as-etiquette. Does school grammar improve grammar etiquette? Researchers have tried to determine whether instruction in traditional grammar improves student writing. That is, do grammar exercises or drills make any difference? To date, the findings suggest they do not, mainly because this approach does little to affect the internal language system.

What it does affect is the use of authentic language: students listening, speaking, reading, and writing standard English; students manipulating language, their own language. English language arts teachers who recognize and teach standard usage and sentence clarity as products of revision enter into a process that, over time, affects the internalization of language. There is no debate over the basic issue—that students can and should become more effective and flexible users of their language—only over the method by which to achieve it. Few curricular areas are as visible or as open to criticism as grammar. Given this, the issue will no doubt remain a force in the English language arts curriculum.

Grammar study as a means of improving students' language is a major reason for its place in the curriculum. Other reasons also exist, associated with everything from studying language for its own sake to preparing students for standardized tests. Teachers need to be aware of these reasons and be prepared to discuss them with colleagues, administrators, and parents.

STUDYING GRAMMAR FOR ITS OWN SAKE

Language is a uniquely human phenomenon; as such, it is worthy of study. However, studying English grammar at the expense of time for listening, speaking, reading, and writing costs most students dearly. To solve the dilemma, many high schools offer an elective course in English grammar at the junior or senior level. Such courses validate the study of language but reserve it for those students who are motivated and capable of undertaking such a study, a study that demands advanced cognitive and analytic skills. A grammar course should in no way replace English courses that offer students a well-balanced experience in the language arts.

WHY GRAMMAR UNITS PERSIST

Why does grammar continue to dominate the English language arts curriculum? Cultural mythology is one reason. People tend to believe that studying grammar is a necessary discipline, contributing to their ability to use language correctly and well. They either forget or ignore the fact that effective language skills arise out of a great many language activities and a supportive environment. People may also associate grammar study with "real" schooling, their own school days when the "3 R's curriculum" was the standard for literacy. This is, of course, a simplistic—indeed romantic—notion of schools. These schools educated fewer students in a less complicated society and dealt with fewer social ills. Even then, literacy skills came from active listening, speaking, reading, and writing; literacy came from a motivation to become literate and an environment that supported it.

A second reason for the persistence of grammar study lies in English language arts teachers' convictions about themselves. They reason that their own language skills came from studying grammar, diagramming sentences, and so forth. If we think for a moment who the English teachers were, we quickly realize the falseness of their reasoning. Today's English teachers were students for whom reading and writing were constant companions; they were students who liked playing with language. They were highly motivated and probably reinforced continually. A secondary classroom often has at least one student with an aptitude for language in the same way someone else has an aptitude for and intense interest in math. In brief, English teachers forget that they were the exceptions throughout their own schooling. Similarly, as Connie Weaver points out, teachers are well aware that their students who are good readers and writers find grammar easy; however, "this correlation encourages faulty cause–effect reasoning: students can read/write well because they know grammar; therefore, teaching grammar will make students better readers and writers" (*Teaching Grammar* 24). Only it doesn't. Just like their English teachers before them, good readers and writers have not only practiced their craft for years, they have done so out of personal pleasure.

A third and pervasive force in maintaining traditional grammar lies in texts and workbooks. Here explanations, exercises, and drills come nicely packaged and easily tested. The problem is that grammar study has not and will not solve literacy problems, nor does it enhance the skills of our best students, at least not as long as it is taught as a subject to be mastered. As Rei Noguchi points out, there is considerable difference between "teaching grammar as an academic subject and teaching grammar as a tool for writing improvement" (15). Unfortunately, some teachers are unaware of this difference; others, responding to state tests, believe that grammar is the key to high percentile scores in language arts. Thus the cycle continues. Weaver also reminds us that some school districts require that grammar be taught, and some teachers, having neither the energy nor knowledge to use grammar in less traditional ways, won't abandon it (*Teaching Grammar* 25). While this situation is understandable, given today's knowledge about learning to write, it is also indefensible in the contemporary English language arts classroom.

There are, however, aspects of grammar that are very relevant to writing, just as some grammar terms are helpful in our discussions of writing. The problem lies in not knowing the difference. Weaver notes:

> Students can learn and apply many grammatical concepts without learning to analyze and label the parts of speech and various other grammatical constructions. While this recognition does not solve all our problems in teaching grammar, it can certainly be a starting point for experimenting with other approaches to teaching those aspects of grammar that are most relevant to writing. (*Teaching Grammar* 25)

Later in this chapter, we will explore some ways in which a conscious knowledge of grammar may assist novice writers, but first, we need to understand the major components of grammar study.

WHAT TEACHERS NEED TO KNOW ABOUT GRAMMAR

Historically, the English language arts curriculum has shifted back and forth among different notions of teaching grammar. In the late 1960s, many educators turned away from traditional grammar; structural and transformational grammars became the new base of instruction. It was not uncommon in the 1970s to find junior high school texts worthy of a college English major taking a course in structural–transformational grammar. However, these new grammars worked no better than traditional grammar in producing more effective writers. With the perception of an impending literacy crisis, people determined that if the new linguistics had not worked and had perhaps added to the problem, then traditional grammar should be revisited. Thus, the emphasis on formal grammar and correctness in the 1980s reflected a more conservative view of education after the turbulent 1970s.

It is not surprising that veteran teachers are skeptical of any claims related to grammar and language improvement. However, the 1980s also brought advances in our knowledge of how people acquire, process, and improve their language abilities. Studies of students and classrooms, such as those done by Donald Graves, Lucy Calkins, and Nancie Atwell, demonstrated the difference between talking about grammar and applying grammar. The Bay Area Writing Project, under the direction of James Gray, also promoted teaching standard usage and conventions through student writing; as state after state initiated a writing project, more and more teachers became convinced of the value of teaching grammar contextually. At the same time, teacher–researchers such as William Strong and Donald Daiker applied principles of transformational grammar and developed sentence-combining to improve syntactic fluency. Most textbooks today reflect, even if briefly, the contribution of this new grammar. However, they also cling stubbornly to the old, causing dissonance for many teachers educated with a writing process approach to grammar and mechanics.

English language arts teachers should be acquainted with all descriptions of grammar: traditional, structural, and transformational. We may be called on to respond to concerns of parents, administrators, and other teachers to explain what we are doing and why, to make informed decisions on materials and methods, and to evaluate our school curriculum. But most importantly, a good grammar background also enables us to help our students make effective language choices and to determine the source of language difficulties.

 ## TRADITIONAL GRAMMAR

The English grammar that we call "traditional" was modeled on the classical languages of Greek and Latin. Roman scholars took both the terms and descriptive methods of the Greeks and applied them to Latin. Because there are some similarities between the two languages, the application was fairly successful. This is not the case when these same terms and methods are applied to English; the result is a distortion of English. For example, one of the rules of Latin grammar was never to split an infinitive, a rule still found in English handbooks today. A sentence such as "To fully appreciate this movie, you need some background in African history" would be judged flawed because the adverb *fully* is placed between parts of the infinitive *to appreciate*. Not splitting an infinitive in Latin made sense because it meant splitting a one-word verb; however, there is no reason not to split an infinitive in English. Sometimes, the rhythm of the sentence makes splitting an infinitive exactly what a writer *should* do. The traditional admonition not to do so is the result of applying Latin grammar to English. Just recently, however, English style manuals have come to the conclusion that splitting infinitives is not an error, and as just noted, often the very action to take.

From models of classical Greek and Latin, English grammar moved into medieval times and acquired yet another emphasis that persists today: to "fix" the language, to stop its degeneration, and to eliminate error. This view of grammar matched the focus and instruction of the medieval church. Again in the 18th century, the emphasis on correctness and rules was reinforced in an Age of Rationalism. Today, therefore, traditional grammar is Latin-based, rules-oriented, and prescriptive. Despite the fact that English is structured differently from Latin or Greek, the tradition of teaching the parts of speech is almost unchanged. Since Latin had more word endings than English, we ended up with more categories than we needed, along with rules that were equally inappropriate (Weaver, *Grammar for Teachers* 101).

The insistence on rules, and a belief that learning rules will teach students to write correctly, is another part of this heritage. Rules such as "It is I" rather than "It is me" exist because Latin takes the nominative form *I* in a mathematical equation: *it = I*. We are to utter, "To whom do you wish to speak?" rather than "Who do want to talk to?" because "To whom do you wish to speak?" is the base, and prepositions take the objective form *whom*, not the nominative form *who*. Following Latin dictates, definitions became singularly unhelpful and downright obtuse, as the passage from a tenth-grade textbook demonstrates.

- An adjective is a word that modifies a noun or pronoun.
- An adjective clause is a dependent clause that functions as an adjective.
- An adjective clause may be introduced by a relative pronoun or by a relative adverb.

When Nora arrived later, the old playground—empty and unkempt—shimmered in the heat of the Hawaiian afternoon. Crushed cans and paper cups littered the brown grass. The swings rocked slowly, creaking their rusty chains. The pond was dry.

Adjectives are not the only words that can modify nouns. For example, the second sentence above begins with the phrase *Crushed cans. Crushed* would appear to be an adjective, modifying *cans,* but it is not. It is a verbal—specifically a past participle—which functions in the same way that an adjective does.

It should be clear that students learn little from this type of textbook and the heritage of Latin grammar—other than a firmer conviction that this work has nothing to do with them, their language, and their world. Learning to work with adjectives and verbals is important in the world of making meaning and seeing options, but not as a study of arcane terms.

The preoccupation with defining and classifying words and labeling and diagramming sentences also left us with some strange definitions:

> A verb is a state of being.
>
> An adverb modifies another adverb.
>
> A noun is the name of a person, place, or thing.

Many of us memorized these and similar definitions, and because we liked English, we had little trouble with them, nor did we resist such tasks. However, they did little to improve our writing skills. Being bookworms and closet writers did that. Many of our classmates, however, those less thrilled about English, not only had trouble with the definitions, but also developed negative attitudes about English class in general. That seems a high price to pay for definitions that are unhelpful and unnecessary for authentic language activities.

Reflection

Which grammar terms (e.g., gerund, appositive, relative clause, participial phrase) still leave you a bit puzzled? Or anxious at the thought of finding them a required part of the curriculum you will teach? Why do you think you are a proficient reader and writer but still don't know all the formal terms?

_____

Traditional Grammar in the Classroom

Of what use is traditional grammar? For one thing, there is no reason to invent a new vocabulary for nouns, pronouns, verbs, adverbs, and adjectives. As Weaver explains it:

> Traditional grammar is important, if only because its terminology is widely known and because its appeal to meaning is often vital in determining the precise function of a grammatical unit. (*Grammar for Teachers* 105)

Pointing out, for example, that a certain verb doesn't provide the reader with a good sense of the action or that an adjective conveys just the right sense of description *within the context of the student's draft* provides a common vocabulary without drilling labels. The extreme, of course, would be terms such as *gerund,* which students really don't need to know in order to construct effective sentences.

Do students have to learn every part of speech? No. The most common categories of noun, pronoun, verb, adjective, and adverb will do. Some teachers collapse adjective and adverb into *modifier* and find that it works just fine. Rather than teach a list of prepositions, teachers can concentrate on the function of prepositional phrases—how useful they are in adding detail, for example. The same holds true for adjective and adverbial clauses, and again, the term *modifier* helps students to see function. However, native speakers can discern for themselves the function of such clauses, without drill. Students at all curricular levels benefit from sentence analysis of function: Just how does that word or word group contribute? Is it in the right (i.e., correct) place? Is it in the most effective place? Thus, questioning how the sentence works, and what could be done to improve clarity or interest, is an important classroom strategy.

EXPLORATION

Focus on Function

Respond to the questions following each sentence.

- Jeff sat at his computer, staring at the screen and wishing for a miracle.
  1. What is the function of the word group after the comma?
  2. Could we move the word group to a different position?

3. Would it work as well in a different position? Why?

4. Why do we need the comma?

- Watching the football game, the television suddenly blew up.

  1. What is the function of the introductory word group?

  2. What's wrong with its position?

  3. How many ways could we correct it?

- Annika Strum, who is a world-class athlete, won the gold.

  1. What is the function of the word group between the commas?

  2. Could we eliminate some of the words and not change the basic meaning?

- Annika Strum, a world-class athlete, won the gold.

  1. Could we move "a world-class athlete" to any other position?

  2. Do we need punctuation if we move it?

  3. Which version do you like better? Why?

As the examples in this Exploration show, use of the term *modifier* would cover the discussion. There is no need to talk about an absolute, a participial phrase, or a relative clause and its cut-down cousin the appositive, but there is need to talk about what modifiers do and how to use them correctly and effectively.

Some teachers wonder if they should use the more accurate term *clause* rather than *sentence*. Because *sentence* is the common term, the traditional descriptor, we believe it's fine for student use, especially with younger writers. However, with older students, capable of more complex syntax, *clause* will probably become a familiar term. In either case, teachers do need to understand *clause* and the difference between a grammatical sentence and a rhetorical one. Weaver provides us with workable definitions:

> Grammatically, a *sentence* consists of an independent clause plus whatever dependent clauses may be attached to it or embedded within it.
>
> *Rhetorically*, a *sentence* may be defined as whatever occurs between the initial capital letter and the final period, or between the onset of speech and the utterance's final pause. Hence a rhetorical sentence may be as short as a single word, or as long as several hundred words. (*Grammar for Teachers* 118)

Sometimes, teachers need to explain to students why their "sentence" is not a sentence. The definitions, as just given, would be unsuitable for students, but the idea of "rhetorically correct," as well as some discussion of the differences between oral and written language, would be very helpful. What is neither helpful nor appropriate, however, is dodging sentence construction issues altogether. For example, linguist Martha Kolln explains the "Because–Clause Myth" that has become rather pervasive in high school. Because a subordinate clause often looks like a complete sentence, it often results in a fragment (e.g., "Because we didn't get the review. It's an unfair test."). Kolln notes: "It appears that some teachers have discovered a sure-fire way to prevent such fragments: Ban *because* as a sentence opener" (121). This results in a poor strategy and, very likely, choppy sentences. *Fragment* is a traditional grammar term, and it works well in student discussion; however, *subordinate clause* may not work at all, nor is it needed to help repair the fragment. Teachers who know their students' developmental levels and capabilities can choose the right terms to discuss sentences in understandable ways.

As noted earlier, a great deal about traditional grammar is unhelpful, if not downright confounding to students, but English language arts teachers should view it as part of their professional background and draw on it for common-sense applications.

There are many interesting ways for students to learn basic grammar terms without formal study. Young adult literature and nonfiction from popular culture are rich resources for pausing over parts of speech—not as drill but as wonder. Teachers can read or show phrases, sentences, or passages that use nouns, verbs, adjectives, and adverbs effectively; referring to the text, they can use grammar terms without "preaching" about them. In the same way, using student drafts to point out a strong verb or a powerful adjective also introduces and reinforces traditional terms without the workbook. Other strategies for teaching about parts of speech without an emphasis on labels or drill involve activities from students' everyday lives. The activities in this Exploration are adapted from Randy Larson's enjoyable text, *Hot Fudge Monday* (163–64).

EXPLORATION

Play Ball!

With a small group, divide up the following tasks as homework. When you return to your group, discuss the tasks and decide on one "to teach" the entire class.

Turn to the sports pages of several newspapers. Look for verbs that sportswriters use to make the game come alive for their readers, many of whom would not have seen it in person or on television.

- Make two columns: verbs used to describe the action of the individuals or teams; verbs used to describe the team's performance.
- Make columns for three major sports: list verbs used to describe the action in each. Are they the same? Why or why not?
- Find a photograph of an athlete (or several in the same event) in action. Make a list of verbs that describe that action.
- Listen to a sportscaster during an athletic event or a sports anchor on the evening news. Make a list of the colorful words used to describe the event or athletes.
- Rewrite these sentences, energizing them with strong, interesting verbs:
    The basketball team entered the gym and looked at their opponents.
    Melissa took the ball down the field.
    Jason went back to the wall and caught the high fly ball.

Selling Suki

Newspapers can also be used to explore the use (and misuse) of adjectives (adapted from Larson 55).

Suppose Mindy wants to sell her beat-up car. She can't honestly use adjectives like *dependable,* so she finds other adjectives that, if not honest, are not exactly lies, either. However, her choice of descriptors belies the facts: the car is nearly 20 years old, has had five owners that she knows of, and has more than 250,000 miles on it. The rear window was hit by a rock, so it has a spider web of cracks and a hole. Another hole in the front floor is covered by carpet samples from the local Carpetland; samples are also glued to every floor surface. The current paint job is purple, with yellow racing stripes and pink doors. When it works, the AM radio is stuck on YYUK.

Here's Mindy's ad: Mature, well-traveled auto; bright, sporty exterior. Fully carpeted and air conditioned. Traditional sound system.

- Write a classified ad to get rid of the really obnoxious pet that your family insists must go—and soon.

The value of "exercises" like those Larson has devised for every major part of speech lies in their context. Students are asked to explore how the parts of speech work for us, why we need to pay attention to them, and how we can choose precise and interesting words to improve our writing. Kids use them—not just label them.

 ## STRUCTURAL GRAMMAR

Whereas traditional school grammar was largely prescriptive, telling us what we should or shouldn't do, structural grammar attempted to describe language as it exists. Thus structural linguists divided language into three levels: (1) individual sounds (phonology), (2) groups of sounds with meaning (morphology), and (3) arrangement of words, relationships among parts (syntax). They also classified words differently. For example, *gangsters* is a noun not because it is the name of a person, place, or thing but because its inflection (*-s*) marked it as a noun. This suffix belongs to nouns, marking a plural in English. *Gangster* is a noun because of another suffix that marks nouns, *-ster* (cf. *youngster*). And finally, the placement of *gangster* in English sentences marks it as a noun: The *gangsters* were put in jail. I saw the *gangsters*. Nouns lead off most English sentences; nouns often have *the* or *a* in front of them; nouns are in predictable places in English sentences.

We can see how this system works by examining what native speakers do:

1. The + kitten + s + jump + ed + play + ful + ly.
2. The + kit + tens + jum + ped + pl + ayfully.

No native speaker of English would divide the sentence as in no. 2 because the system of affixes carries meaning to a native speaker: *-s* = plural on noun; *-ed* = past tense on verb; and *-ful* + *-ly* = adverb. This knowledge is part of the internal grammar, the tacit knowledge, of a native speaker. A few irregular forms aside, we automatically add an *-s* when we want to make nouns plural, *-ed* when we want to make verbs show past tense. Structural linguists used this knowledge as the base of their description of the language.

In English, the flexibility of affixes is characteristic:

green greener greenest   earn unearned
soft softer soften   visual vision visible

These are derivational affixes—changes in the form of the word that may change its function in the sentence. For example:

She will sweeten her coffee with sugar.

Do you have a sweetener here?

I find the sweetness sickening, but I will sweetly comply and bring the sugar.

English also has inflectional affixes:

for plurals: boy boys   church churches
for tense: work worked

Unlike derivational affixes, these do not change the part of speech. A noun remains a noun, and a verb a verb. But the inflectional suffix became an important descriptor: with rare exceptions, English nouns take a plural ending in *-s* or *-es*.

These characteristics, then, became part of structural linguists' attempt to describe English as native speakers know and use it. Structural linguists also looked at sentence patterns. These are the most common in English:

| *Subject* | *Verb* | *Direct Object* | |
| The boy | hit | his neighbor. | |

| *Subject* | *Verb* | | |
| The boy | lies. | | |

| *Subject* | *Linking Verb* | *Complement* | |
| The boy | is | angry. | |

| *Subject* | *Verb* | *Indirect Object* | *Direct Object* |
| The boy | gave | his neighbor | a black eye. |

Sentence features such as noun and verb markers were also identified: *a, an,* and *the* are common noun markers; *can, should, would, will,* and *might* are common verb markers. Adjectives typically precede the noun, providing another clue. A native speaker can recognize the role of a nonsense word because of these features, the affixes, and the word order common to English sentences.

EXPLORATION

Not Really Nonsense

Before reading the explanation that follows, identify the parts of speech in the nonsense sentence below. Note how you knew a noun from a verb and so forth.

The twany wibbels ruped lifly on the jip during the zilwo nop.

A native speaker would indicate that *wibbels* is the subject, a noun. *Wibbels* is placed between the noun marker *the* and a word recognizable as a verb (*-ed* marking its tense). The *-s* on *wibbels* indicates plural form, a sign of a noun. The verb *ruped* is marked by the *-ed,* indicating past action. *Lifely* has an *-ly* to indicate how the wibbels ruped; the typical *-ly* ending of English adverbs, as well as their position near the verb, is another indicator of English structure. The phrase *on the* marks *jip* as place, another noun; *during the* marks *nop* as another noun. The words positioned between *the* and the nonsense nouns fill the role of descriptors, adjectives. Even in nonsense, a native speaker of English can identify how the parts fit together. Structural grammar helped us understand that.

Structural Grammar in the Classroom

Structural grammar is important, says Weaver, because "it lends precision to definitions and to procedures for identifying grammatical units and their functions" (105). Whereas traditional grammar defines a noun somewhat vaguely as "name of a person, place, or thing," which can get teachers into all kinds of trouble, structural grammar identifies a noun by certain endings, such as a plural or a derivational affix. Verbs, traditionally defined as words that "express an action or a state of being," are defined structurally by their endings or a distinctive verb form (Weaver, *Grammar for Teachers* 111). Trying to explain "state of being" to a 12-year-old is something most teachers never want to do; in fact, we're not even sure what it means. On the other hand, verbs can be identified by the inflectional endings we use to show tense. The verb also functions as the beginning word, or *headword* of a predicate; it's essential to meaning. Structuralists identify adjectives and adverbs similarly, both by characteristic endings and by function. Youngsters can relate to concrete endings and function more easily than to definitions, which may fail them in complex sentences.

By the time students enter middle school, they have been successful communicators, using nouns, verbs, adjectives, and adverbs at will, stringing them together in acceptable sentences. The problems occur as students enlarge their vocabulary and their capability for more sophisticated syntax and increasingly have to deal with written rather than oral language. Recognizing endings, understanding the flexibility of English words, and recognizing the function of words or word groups can help them make this transition. Students don't need to practice sentence patterns; they already know them. However, teachers usually have to bring this tacit knowledge into consciousness. Through questions that make students analyze their own words and sentences, teachers are encouraging independence and empowering students. Students soon realize how much they already know about their language: how it combines sounds, how it forms words, and how it structures sentences. And without foreign language experience, they also realize what makes English "English." Structural grammar, then, has a place in the classroom.

EXPLORATION

Mostly Hidden—but There

The following examples are taken from Thomas E. Murray (71; 172–184).

- Pronounce the following words, concentrating on the sound of /t/.

  time cat mitten butter stop

  As you listened to yourself, what did you learn about the difference between the alphabet letter "t" and the English sound /t/? Does it matter to you? Would it matter to someone who is just learning to speak and read English as a second language? (example from Murray 79)

- Place the label *loomalah* or *kratchak* on each figure below. Which seems most natural to each? Why?

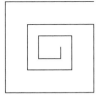

- How do you pronounce the following (and real) names:

  Ngaio   Hrbek

  What do you know about how English combines sounds?

- What is the relationship between each set of words below? What happens when we add on?

  house/houses walk/walking red/redder

  do/undo happy/happily work/workable/worker

How does this stuff of help me teach grammar

- Is the *-er* on redder the same as *-er* on worker?
- How is the grammatical relationship between house/houses different from that between happy/happily?
- Decode the following. Put each in an English sentence.

    imfligged transbaluizing blegs

- What is happening in the examples below?

    vibrations/vibes   delicatessen/deli   examination/exam

    address (accent first syllable)/address (accent second)

    Levis for any brand of blue jean

    brunch   smog

    AIDS NASA NATO

    cornflake   busybody

    Jell-O

    nitwit   wishy-washy   lovey-dovey

    buzz boom sizzle

- Arrange the following words:

    fast hit Tim ball the

    a bought Lila bean noon burrito at

How do you know how to do it correctly? How important is word order?

TRANSFORMATIONAL GRAMMAR

Other linguists saw a flaw in structural grammar's description of English: its inability to account for the creative use of language. As native speakers, we produce thousands and thousands of sentences never before uttered or written, yet understood perfectly by other members of the language community. When linguists asked how we can do this, transformational grammar took its place among the English grammars.

Transformational grammar attempts to explain the production of sentences through a number of basic (kernel) sentences that transform or expand into various patterns. Whereas the base of structural grammar was empirical, based on what native speakers actually say, the base of transformational grammar is theoretical. No one actually knows if these language structures exist or work in the way presented by linguists.

Transformational grammar assumes the existence of deep structures that lead to surface structures, or what is actually said or written. According to transformational grammar, we have two basic sentence types: kernel and transformed. A kernel sentence could be:

John is my friend.

A transformed sentence could be:

A negative: John is not my friend.
A question: Is John my friend?

A passive: The ball was hit by John.
Embedded: John, who is my friend, hit the ball.

According to linguists, we use these patterns in producing sentences, automatically and effortlessly in the case of speech. Noam Chomsky, whose work in transformational grammar was revolutionary, claims that we are born "wired" for this language activity, that we acquire a set of rules and learn how to transform sentences, all without instruction. With this ability, we are able to create endless numbers of sentences. Transformational linguists devised a set of rules, called phrase structure rules, to describe how we form and transform sentences. They represented sentences in symbol strings:

NP   +   pres + Be   +   NP
John   is   my friend
Subject noun phrase (John) + present tense of the verb Be (is) + a noun phrase
    (my friend)

The basis of the English sentence is the noun phrase and verb phrase, and without these two parts (also called a subject and predicate in many grammar books), we don't have a complete grammatical sentence.

- a noun phrase, consisting of either a noun or a pronoun.
    John/went home.   The green apple/is tart.
    They/stayed.   I/will do the work.
- a verb phrase, consisting of a main verb, which may or may not have auxiliaries, and in the case of certain verbs, a word or phrase to complete the meaning.
    John/left.
    John/is my friend.
    John/is in the living room.
    John/is happy.
    John/found a bike.
    John/seems angry.

Linguists also showed us how we continually, and unconsciously, combine sentences:

John is my best friend. He left at noon today.
John, who is my best friend, left at noon today.
John, my best friend, left at noon today.

Transformational grammar shows the patterns of English at work, how native speakers construct novel sentences out of basic patterns. For students of language, this was a useful view of the creativity of language, of what happens each time we utter an English sentence. It also gave pause to wonder about the relative ease of children acquiring their native language: Complex patterns in place and in use within a matter of years.

Transformational Grammar in the Classroom

For many English language arts teachers, transformational grammar was a revelation, a means of viewing English from a very different perspective. When viewed as product, the language appears static, and teachers are often hard pressed to explain how certain sentences got that way or how the language was working. Transformational grammar answered these questions, providing teachers with useful knowledge about patterns in English sentences. For teachers with second language learners, such knowledge was an unexpected and much-welcomed gift.

EXPLORATION

It Always Happens When . . .

Examine the following sentences. What is the pattern in each verb type? (For example, if you use a form of BE, what always happens?) Note the parts of speech that complete each sentence pattern.

- Main verb BE

    Lulu is late. Lulu is outside. Lulu is the new chairperson.
- Main verb LINKING

    Lulu seems ill. Lulu stayed in the house. Lulu appears the winner.
- Main verb TRANSITIVE

    Lulu saw Waldo. Lulu baked cookies. Lulu broke her leg.
- Main verb INTRANSITIVE

    Lulu responded. Lulu screams. Lulu smiles.
- Auxiliary "helping" verb

    Lulu is running. Lulu was talking on the phone.
- Auxiliary "helping" verb: what happens when we use a form of *have*?

    Lulu has seen that movie. Lulu had talked with him.
- Modals: what happens when we use *should, will*, etc.?

    Lulu should see that movie. Lulu must eat now.

How can you use this knowledge of how English works to good advantage with student writers? With second language students? In small group, create five sentences for discussion with your entire class. What traditional grammar terms would you plan to use? What terms would you avoid? How do you discuss sentence patterns without resorting to "transitive," for example?

With an understanding of embedded sentences, teachers found another useful classroom tool. Sentence combining (and "decombining") became the most visible and applied means of transformational grammar. Indeed, this instructional strategy remains one of the best ways to improve student awareness of syntax, rhetorical effectiveness, and the usefulness of punctuation.

EXPLORATION

- Combine the following sentences into one sentence. *Sentence combining*
    My parents found out about the party.
    They were furious.
    They kicked all our friends out of the house.
  How many options did you have? Why did you choose one over the other possibilities?
- Examine these sentences for the main idea; then, rewrite each sentence to make it clearer.
    1. Ann took finally driving lessons to which I had to drive her but things sure were different when she got her license than when I did.
    2. It is my belief that it is a matter of great importance for a student to plan a schedule for one semester in order to get prepared for all the papers and exams.
  As you clarified this text, what specific changes did you make (i.e., what was deleted or added) and why?
- Expand this sentence.
    Her hair is unusual.
  What was your first grammatical instinct when you wanted to make this sentence better through expansion? Why?

It's important to note that sentence combining or expansion does not require the use of complex terminology. Again what is critical is student awareness of the many options we have to combine or expand—and, importantly, the reasons to do so.

Making Useful Distinctions

As teachers, we need to keep the distinction between grammar and usage very clear. We have a native ability to create and comprehend sentences; this is our internal grammar. Usage, on the other hand, is linguistic etiquette, a set of socially acceptable styles of language. Problems arise when we insist on one standard usage as an absolute, the only way to say or write something. English permits many forms of language, a range of choices dependent on situation and audience. Approaching usage from this perspective allows students to maintain their many voices. Often usage is extended to mean mechanics as well—punctuation, capitalization, and so forth. Again, the notion of an absolute standard causes both student difficulty and apathy. For example, students partially learn a comma rule for *and*; then, they add a comma every time *and* pops up on their paper, incorrectly breaking apart phrases most of the time. If, instead, students learned that commas function to help us read more easily and comprehend more quickly, the world would be blessed with fewer commas and less red ink.

We also need to help students see the distinction between speaking and writing, that writing is *not* speech written down. Again, the more useful lessons about varieties of English come into play. Students do know their native language grammar orally but may be inexperienced with manipulating it on paper or even seeing it on paper. If their vocabulary is impoverished, they struggle even more. If we work from a perspective of native language competence, from what students *do* know, we can influence student performance and increase language flexibility in everyday life. Teachers who substitute grammar drills for experience in oral or written language, on the other hand, will seldom have that pleasure. Grammar is alive, something we use—not a subject to be taught.

UNDERSTANDING STUDENT ERRORS

Novice Writers

In her masterful exploration of unskilled writers, Mina Shaughnessy offers some of the most cogent explanations of student error. Shaughnessy first reminds us that "errors count, but not as much as English teachers think" (120). Teachers, she notes, are trained to evaluate students by absolute standards rather than by developmental standards. Teachers forget that their students, for the most part, *are* novice writers. Thus, serious grammatical errors may stem from a lack of experience in academic writing rather than a problem with the language itself. Shaughnessy also argues that if we view novice writers in the same way we view foreign students learning English, where errors are accepted as part of normal development—and not as evidence of their incapability of learning, their inability to be educated—then we, and the students, would be better off (90). This view does not suggest that teachers ignore errors. Allowing students to write in a fashion in which we merely "catch the meaning" is irresponsible. However, as Shaughnessy suggests, many teachers embark on an error hunt that fails to distinguish between the important errors, those that seriously impair our ability to comprehend, and the merely irritating, those that bother only the English language arts teacher.

 errors are NORMAL in learning to write

⚛ *Reflection* ⚛

What does Shaughnessy mean when she says: "Errors count but not as much as English teachers think"? Have you ever been in a situation where you felt that errors, rather than your ideas, were the major focus of your writing? Have you ever been in a situation where your errors were ignored? Looking back through your personal writing history, comment on either or both of these situations.

Expecting Too Much

Shaughnessy raises another issue in asking us to consider whether it is realistic to expect unskilled writers to learn what we set out for them in the time allocated. The acquisition of writing skills is highly individual, and for students lacking a good background in reading and writing, the process takes time. Moreover, students from homes where literacy is lacking and poverty is commonplace are disadvantaged to begin with. We cannot expect them to meet timetables based on some mythical average student or laid out by publishers unconcerned with adolescent growth and development or societal problems.

[margin note: As a teacher, I just want my stud's to progress]

[margin note: but what about standardized tests?]

Inexperienced teachers often have unrealistic expectations of student learning, which may bring frustration both to teacher and student. Textbooks can reinforce these expectations, especially if they present chapters of separate grammar skills, a linear plan that is contrary to how we actually acquire and process language. Further, cognitive and linguistic maturity limit what we do, when we do it, and with what degree of competency or proficiency. Another human reality lies in the gap between cognition and production, between the time in which we comprehend something and when we can produce it ourselves. This gap between cognition and production parallels the way we acquire oral language. We could understand far more than we could produce, a problem that time and sustained language experience solved. Thus, student failure to correct grammar errors immediately is not necessarily a reason to repeat the lesson; rather, students may just need more opportunities to apply the lessons in original writing (Shaughnessy 120).

Smart Errors: Rethinking "Remedial"

Another view of error, but one seldom discussed anywhere, is a positive one: Many errors are errors of competency, a demonstration of student progress toward more complex language. This phenomenon is perhaps recognized more often with second-language students, but it occurs in native speakers as well. In middle school, for example, students begin to use more complex syntax, thus increasing their potential for error. The errors are the result of progress, not regression; they're really "smart" errors. Kids need to know that.

Unfortunately, this view is somewhat uncommon in many secondary classrooms, especially in school systems where less able English students are routinely assigned to remedial classes. These classes are often designed on the deficit model, a model that assumes students are incapable of recognizing and self-correcting language errors.

This model also elevates the status of error; entire courses are built around stamping out various errors of syntax, usage, and mechanics, usually through rote drill and exercise formats. We are not suggesting that students in remedial English courses have no deficiencies; they do. However, these deficiencies lie in written language only and relate to inexperience in reading and writing—not to native language competency. Thus, many remedial courses fail to build on what students *do* know, continuing a cycle of discouragement and frustration for all involved.

In *Errors and Expectations,* Shaughnessy speaks of student capabilities:

> Students themselves are the best sources of information about grammar. Despite difficulties with common errors, their intuitions about English are the intuitions of the native speaker. Most of what they need to know has already been learned. What they have not learned and are not used to is looking long and carefully at sentences in order to understand the way in which they work. This involves a shift in perception which is ultimately more important than the mastery of any individual rule of grammar. (129)

In this view, remedial courses would be built around a great deal of oral and written language experience; error would take its place as a normal part of learning to write academic English. Texts and exercises focused on error would vanish; texts that proceed deductively would vanish. In their place would be wonderful reading materials, time, and an environment that allows for inductive learning.

Reflection

From your high school or college field work experience, what do you know of how remedial English classes in composition are designed and taught? Comment on what you have observed for yourself or what you have seen in textbooks for these classes.

Sources of Errors

When teachers are confronted with student errors, they must make certain assumptions about the source and then consider the implications for teaching. Three basic assumptions are common:

1. The learner doesn't know the grammatical concept.
2. The error is due to a lack of information and habit.
3. The errors are developmental.

We would be wise to limit the first assumption, that the learner doesn't know the grammatical concept, to students for whom English is a second language. For these students, a particular concept may not exist simply because their native language lacks this feature (e.g., tense, articles). To assume this situation with speakers of American dialects, however, is wrong. A student whose first dialect is African American English understands grammar and has a grammar very similar to standard dialect. Some of the surface features do differ from standard dialect, including pronunciation. Therefore, we need to know these features to avoid error judgments when students are merely "translating" the standard printed dialect into their spoken dialect. For example, in reading, a student may turn *John's hat* into the oral *John hat*, indicating she does understand the concept. In her dialect, *'s* is not needed.

There may be times when our least experienced readers and writers do not understand the grammatical concept, but these will be infrequent with native speakers of English. If students don't understand the concept, we have to break it down, analyze its parts, and then present it to them in a way that allows them to see the function. Subject–verb agreement, for example, relies on an understanding of singular and plural. We need to start there, not with agreement itself.

If a lack of grammatical concept is seldom a source of error, then what is? Some errors may stem from a lack of information or a language habit. In this view, language equals behavior, and that "bad" behavior can be fixed. This notion often leads to intense correction of oral and written language, the fate of students labeled "remedial." The first problem with this approach is its lack of judgment about which errors count most. Some teachers attack every error as though each were equally important in derailing meaning. This shotgun approach to error usually overwhelms students and contributes to further confusion, indifference and, in some cases, hostility. Moreover, the approach takes on a life of its own if worksheets and workbooks are around. Such practice doesn't transfer when students do their own writing, where they are not told what to pick out, label, or underline. Shaughnessy puts it this way:

> It may well be that traditional grammar-teaching has failed to improve writing not because the rules and concepts do not connect with the act of writing but because grammar lessons have traditionally ended up with experiences in workbooks, which by highlighting the feature being studied rob the student of practice in seeing that feature in more natural places. (155)

"In more natural places" refers to genuine discourse, people involved in communication and making meaning. Because habits of any type involve a will to change, we need to link language habits to genuine discourse. Students need a reason to edit and proofread.

ERROR ANALYSIS

Error analysis, a more developmentally based approach, asks us to discover the pattern and frequency of errors in student writing. Because it asks for an explanation of what is happening, the approach is more aligned with language acquisition than with behavior. We discover that some errors are performance errors, which students should be able to correct. An oral check quickly sorts these out because they are the types of error most associated with editing and proofreading. These errors often form the basis of mini-lessons linked to student writing; the errors mar the final product but don't interfere with meaning. A grammar-based error, one for which the student lacks the information to self-correct, is best handled one on one. In any event, error analysis assumes that one keeps a record of errors: types, where most pervasive (i.e., in which types of discourse), and frequency.

Keep student writing portfolios

Another view of error, but one seldom discussed, is that of avoidance. We can't assume that the absence of grammatical or mechanical errors means mastery. Some learners simply avoid certain words and constructions, knowing that they have had trouble with them in the past. Students, for example, who have had trouble punctuating clauses may not use them. College freshmen often admit to this "play it safe" approach to writing when confronted with questions about their "look-alike" sentences. Thus, the absence of error does not necessarily mean competency or proficiency, especially among some of our best students. They may be afraid to take risks and thus need to learn about "good errors," about growth through errors.

TAKING ON ERROR

Shaughnessy warns us about ignoring errors for fear of inhibiting students, a nonhelpful approach with students who already feel helpless (127–128). Students are well aware that they make errors and lack knowledge about academic writing. Thus, ignoring errors—either from a sense of kindness or a belief that errors are not that important—does nothing to help students. We need to convince them that they can take on errors and, most important, we need to provide them with the environment, strategies, and time to do so.

Errors: For Editing Only

Shaughnessy also reminds us that "correcting errors is an editorial rather than a composing skill and requires the writer to notice features of a sentence he would ordinarily have to ignore during composing" (128). Given this, students must learn to look at their own sentences analytically. If they do a great deal of original writing and take the writing process through editing and proofreading, they will get this experience. However, they need strategies to guide them, and such instruction must come from teachers who model and explain the strategies.

Errors cause so much trouble with novice writers because, as Shaughnessy notes, they "seem to demand more concentration than they're worth" (123). Students have been communicating successfully for years, something they have learned to do without direct instruction. Writing correctly is a learned behavior, requiring them to shift vision and to analyze a text, something they don't normally do in informal speaking.

WHAT GRAMMAR TO TEACH

Teachers understandably wonder which aspects of grammar should be part of the curriculum, and what they are responsible for teaching. As we have pointed out in this chapter, grammar does have a role in the curriculum, and it does need to be taught. It is the method, however, that separates effective lessons from busywork. Grammar must also be considered developmentally: Some aspects cannot be taught until students reach a level of cognitive and linguistic maturity to benefit from it.

Certain grammatical concepts are basic to writing: subject, verb, sentence (or clause), and phrase. Students must learn to identify sentence boundaries and methods of joining words, phrases, and sentences. To achieve a mature writing style, students will need sustained experience with both combining and untangling their sentences; thus, coordination, subordination, and parallelism should be part of the secondary curriculum. To achieve correctness, students need to understand the concept of agreement: subject and verb, noun and pronoun. And for some students, tense as it is used in standard written English must also be addressed. Although many contemporary textbooks take a more enlightened approach to teaching grammar, there is nonetheless a tendency to ignore student drafts as the most effective and authentic source of instruction. Lessons of sentence revision and editing taught through mini-lessons, small group, and individually—and based on student writing—are the heart of students learning "good grammar."

EXPLORATION

Adverbs without the Advil

You have noticed in student drafts that too few juniors are expanding their sentences; it is time to focus on modifiers. Your eleventh-grade composition and grammar textbook has the following explanation of the adverb phrase: *An adverb phrase is a prepositional phrase modifying a verb, an adjective, or another adverb.* Although you want your students to use adverb phrases correctly and well, you see nothing but trouble ahead as you scan the examples given in the textbook.

> The fire moved like dancers.
> The hat looked strange on her head.
> Leo arrived late at night.
> Ms. Jones has lived there for 10 years.

An adverb phrase may come before or after the word it modifies.

Examples:

> The reporter interviewed the attorney before the trial.
> Before the trial, the reporter interviewed the attorney.

More than one adverb phrase may modify the same word.

> On October 2, the space shuttle *Pegasus* was finally launched into space.

Exercise 1: Identifying Adverb Phrases

Each of the following sentences contains at least one adverb phrase. Identify each and the word it modifies. [Twenty sentences follow these instructions.]

At this point, you shut the book and decide to develop your own lesson on adverb phrases. One of your colleagues stops in just as you utter a large sigh, and he wants to know what the problem is. What do you tell him?

The two of you decide to develop this grammar lesson together. Your classes are composed of native speakers of English, but they also have a range of skill levels—and a number of uninterested students. Sketch out a plan. What activities will you include and why?

As you prepare to teach composition in middle or senior high school, you may face some issues of how to teach grammar—perhaps from required texts, colleagues, or parents. Always keep in mind that you *are* going to teach grammar, and it is more likely to be the method that's at issue, not the content. However, when you are clear about grammar's inclusion in your teaching plans, you will probably find that the issue goes away. Thus, a clear explanation of your methods, their proven effectiveness, and your desire to keep students engaged in writing itself should be ready to go—along with a positive attitude as you make that explanation. Good "grammar" is important, and as one of the most visible skill areas in English language arts, it holds people's attention. Understanding this is also part of your professional knowledge base in the world of teaching grammar in secondary school.

REFERENCES

Atwell, Nancie. *In the Middle: Reading, Writing, and Learning with Adolescents*. Portsmouth: Boynton/Cook Heinemann, 1987.

Bamberg, Betty. "Composition in the Secondary English Curriculum." *Research in the Teaching of English* (Oct. 1981): 257–66.

Braddock, Richard, et al. *Research in Written Composition*. Urbana: National Council of Teachers of English, 1963.

Hartwell, Patrick. "Grammar, Grammars, and the Teaching of Writing." *College English* (Feb. 1985): 105–27.

Haynes, Elizabeth. "Using Research in Preparing to Teach Writing." *English Journal* (Jan. 1978): 82–88.

Hillocks, George. *Research in Written Composition*. Urbana: National Council of Teachers of English, ERIC, 1986.

Kolln, Martha. *Rhetorical Grammar: Grammatical Choices, Rhetorical Effects*. New York: Allyn & Bacon, 1996.

Larson, Randy. *Hot Fudge Monday*. Fort Collins: Cottonwood Press, 1993.

Meiser, Mary. *Good Writing!* 2nd ed. New York: Allyn & Bacon, 1998.

Murray, Thomas E. *The Structure of English: Phonetics, Phonology, Morphology*. New York: Allyn & Bacon, 1995.

Noguchi, Rei. *Grammar and the Teaching of Writing*. Urbana: NCTE, 1991.

Peterson, Scott. "Teaching Writing and Grammar in Context." *Lessons to Share: In Teaching Grammar in Context*. Ed. Constance Weaver. Portsmouth: Boynton/Cook, 1996.

Rowe, Sue. "Using Minilessons to Promote Student Revision: Helping Students Realize Their Power Over Words." *Lessons to Share: In Teaching Grammar in Context*. Ed. Constance Weaver. Portsmouth: Boynton/Cook, 1996.

Shaughnessy, Mina. *Errors and Expectations*. New York: Oxford UP, 1977.

Weaver, Constance. *Grammar for Teachers: Perspectives and Definitions*. Urbana: NCTE, 1979.

———. *Teaching Grammar in Context*. Portsmouth: Boynton/Cook, 1996.

———. "Teaching Grammar in the Context of Writing." *Lessons to Share: In Teaching Grammar in Context*. Ed. Constance Weaver. Portsmouth: Boynton/Cook, 1996.

Writing For Learning

8

Secondary education should provide students a way
of thinking, not a set of facts.

Anne Ruggles Gere

Writing has many purposes, takes many forms, and serves many functions. We teach students how to improve their writing, but writing itself enhances learning in many ways. Through writing, learners memorize easier, retain information longer, organize thoughts effectively, learn how to persuade and inform.

We can teach our students to use this property of writing to remember and learn. If students write what they want to remember from their reading, the information is remembered much longer. The same is true when studying for exams, remembering characters in a long novel, or writing points they want to include in a story or essay.

In addition, we use writing to communicate, to organize our thoughts, and to figure things out. Thus, writing has many practical aspects, and when we teach writing to students, it is important to help them realize that writing is not an esoteric skill used only in school. We can help students understand the importance of writing to learn by helping them become self-sufficient learners through acquiring skills for learning.

We have many ways to help students learn through writing and we cannot assume students have the skills of using writing as a major technique for learning. Teaching these skills is an ongoing process because we want students to internalize the various ways they can increase their abilities to study, analyze, and understand. Also, because of the various ways that students learn we need to give them many different writing strategies and allow them to select ones that help them the most.

STUDY SKILLS USING WRITING

Too often, teachers assume that by the time students are in high school, they will have at least a rudimentary level of skill in note-taking, and to a lesser degree in summarizing and paraphrasing. However, teaching these skills often consists only of a brief explanation, followed by the expectation that students can now use the skill adequately. Secondary teachers may direct students to take notes on readings or lectures with no further instruction. The reality is that most students do not take useful notes, or summarize efficiently, or know what paraphrasing is—yet these skills are essential for competence in writing as well as for learning in general. Knowing and using effective study skills strengthens academic competence.

In a recent article, Maribeth Gettinger and Jill K. Seibert, educational psychologists, discuss the benefits of study skills. They state that when capable students have difficulties in school it may well be a lack of good study skills (350). Over the past 20 years, research has shown that when students are taught study skills, they become more efficient and independent learners (353). Practice is essential when students are learning these skills. Several skills techniques should be taught because not all students will use the same ones. Therefore, a wide array of study strategies is necessary. The most effective strategies are those that students find work the best for them (359).

For students to become independent and successful learners, they need to learn strategies that help them understand what they read, and then to retain these understandings. Educators have examined and compared various strategies to discover which are the most effective.

Alison King, a university teacher who specializes in cognitive strategy instruction, designed a study to compare students who used self-questioning, summarizing, or reviewing techniques when studying their lecture notes. Most students do only the latter when preparing for a test; however, King found that the more students interacted with the material, the more they comprehended and remembered (304). By using the more active strategies of questioning and summarizing, where students wrote in their own words, they had more success in both immediate and delayed comprehension. Passively reading their lecture notes was the least effective method. Consequently, we need to actively involve students with using study skills as an important part of effective learning.

We need to teach students how to study on their own if they are to be successful. A study by Carol Dana and Margaret Rodriquez supports the belief that students need strategies that they do outside of class for optimum learning. "Teaching study procedures that students can use on their own time can improve learning and retention of vocabulary" (84). When students read only their highlighted printed material, they do not remember what they've read and often do not understand the material. The act of taking notes requires them to read with more care and transfer what they read into their own words. Even if they do not read their notes over again, they still remember them better than if they had not taken the notes. When we write, we must think—in other words, we must become active learners.

Students need strategies to guide them and teachers to model implementing the strategies. However, teaching the skills cannot be isolated from actual use. We must realize that it takes instructional time for students to learn skills. Several mini-lessons are needed followed by repetition and practice. Students also need time to practice using the skills, not only when first introduced, but also during the learning process, so that the skills are reinforced and become an integral part of writing for learning.

While all students benefit from learning study skills, special-needs students are particularly helped by methods to enhance learning. The more senses they use in learning, the better they understand and remember. For example, when learning vocabulary words, students need to hear the word spoken by you and then they repeat the word, perhaps several times. Then you write the word in large letters and the student says the word and traces each letter with a finger, saying the letter aloud. Only when the word is familiar to the students is the meaning discussed. You begin by asking students if they know or can guess what the word means. Give several examples of the word used in a sentence, and each time ask again if they can guess the meaning. At this point, if students have not figured out the meaning, you tell them, and together you discuss when and how the word could be appropriately used. Students make up their own sentences that include the new word, first orally and then in writing. Finally, students write the word in their vocabulary notebook. It is important to revisit the words frequently to help them remember.

All students require vocabulary study, and portions of the study procedures described for special-needs students are appropriate for everyone. Hearing the words spoken, discussing the meanings, and writing the meanings in their own words enhance vocabulary study for all. However, we must remember not to confuse writing with spelling.

While writing is important to help them remember, students need to concentrate on the correct meaning, not the correct spelling. We want students to recognize the words in their reading; however, they can do that without getting every letter correct. Vocabulary and spelling have two different purposes and should not be taught as if they are one skill.

Reflection

What study skills do you use now? What did you use in middle and high school? Which ones might you plan on teaching your future students?

LEARNING LOGS

Learning logs are a form of journals, but because the purpose is specialized, the format is more structured. Journals used as learning logs facilitate learning when related to specific assignments. At the beginning of a unit, teachers find it helpful to determine their students' understandings of concepts and vocabulary. For example, a teacher who is planning a unit on addictions might ask students to write in their logs what they think *addiction* means. Learning logs provide a way to do this with no awkwardness for students. When we use a word such as *irony,* we cannot assume all students know its meaning even though no one asks for clarification. Asking students to write an explanation of the word shows us where to begin. Students know from experience that journal entries are not graded and, therefore, are more willing to risk being wrong. The information helps us plan where to begin and how much detail and what types of examples to use.

Throughout a unit, students can use the learning log to record predictions, questions, unknown words, notes from readings and lectures, and any problems they encounter as they study. Learning logs are most often used for projects and are a place for planning and recording. Some teachers may not collect them even for a quick read, but others check the logs, not to assign a letter grade, but to help students know how they are doing. A ✓ −, ✓ , ✓ + type of evaluation works well. This "grading" is helpful for middle school students who often need help with staying on task. We can check to see if students are on task and on schedule.

Another type of journal that works as a learning tool is the project journal. When students do long projects, a journal helps them remember deadlines, organize tasks, and keep track of where they are. A project journal begins with notes from the teacher's description of the assignment and the dates each part is due. At the end of the project, the journal must be handed in, too. The teacher checks to see that each part is completed. Notes from outside readings, outlines, mapping, and brainstorming are all part of the project journal. When students meet in response groups, they use the journal to jot down notes to use when revising. Keeping a project journal is a great help in staying organized, something many secondary students have trouble with.

 ## NOTE-TAKING

Note-taking is a necessary life-long skill.

Regie Routman

Learning how to take notes is important for several reasons. Of course, we need to take notes when we read material for information and when we listen to oral presentations. But notes not only help us remember, they help us to learn. As Judith Langer and Arthur Applebee, educational researchers, explain

> The more one engages in thinking about text, the more learning occurs. The more content is manipulated, the more likely students will be able to remember and understand. Any written response leads to more learning than reading without writing. (130)

Even when students' notes are sketchy, students do better on tests when they have their own notes to review. Mary Ann Rafoth found that even if students did not review their notes before a test, they did better than those who did not take notes at all.

Figure 8.1   Self-questions

What is the main idea?

How does _____ relate to _____ ?

How do I agree or disagree?

What conclusions can I draw?

Those who took notes and reviewed them did better yet; clearly, taking notes improves recall and comprehension.

Note-Taking from Oral Presentations

Beginning at about seventh grade, we increasingly rely on oral presentations as a means of giving students information, and expect them to be able to take notes. Teachers themselves took so many notes in college listening to lectures that it became second nature. But secondary students, especially at middle school level, lack the maturity and experience to take beneficial notes. Many students are poor note-takers because they have not been taught strategies (Rafoth et al. 124). At secondary level, much learning depends on students understanding and remembering information they receive orally. Even successful students often fail to remember important ideas from a teacher's lecture (Potts 3). We must teach specific strategies for note-taking if students are to be successful learners.

Alison King suggests using generic self-questions, such as those in Figure 8.1, with students to help them process the information from a lecture. She found that using generic questions as guides helped students ask higher-order questions and elaborate more in their responses (305). Both comprehension and recall improve when students use this method.

Rafoth suggests the following strategies for improving students' note-taking skills:

1. *Skeletal notes.* For complicated material, skeletal notes provide a framework. The basic outline is provided with blank spaces for students to fill in. The more space provided, the more students write. The framework helps students organize material.

2. *Note-taking clues.* Putting notes on the board and using particular words or phrases help students to know when and what to write. For example, you might say, "The reason that. . . ." Or "There were three causes. . . ." Or "An important point is. . . ."

3. *Note-taking reviews.* You should periodically collect students' notes, review them, and make suggestions for improvement. The suggestions need to be specific, not just telling them to take more notes. Do not evaluate the notes for a grade.

4. *Organization and elaboration.* Encourage students not only to read their notes but also to organize and classify the information. This helps them understand and remember. Rafoth cautions that students should not attempt to relate lecture material to previous knowledge while taking notes but should do so later.

5. *Using a split page.* Students divide a page in half vertically, using the left side for the major points and the right for supporting ideas. This helps them recognize major points and helps in their self-study when reviewing notes. (Rafoth 124–128)

When students write their own notes, even if incomplete ones, compared with notes provided by teachers, they remember and understand the material better. We need to provide many opportunities for students to practice the skills of taking notes. You begin by explaining to students that they need to listen carefully to the information they will hear during the lecture, and that they are required to write down points they believe are important. However, don't have them take notes when you are giving the information orally (Maxwell 65). Rafoth agrees that note-taking should not compete with paying attention to the lectures (124).

After the presentation by the teacher, which should be no longer than 10 minutes, students, without discussion, write down the major points. Then they share what they wrote in small groups, followed by a whole-class discussion. The teacher guides the discussion by asking why a point should be noted and how students decide what is important. You can help students understand by modeling how to abbreviate and not use complete sentences, writing just enough so that later they will remember and understand the information. Continue this practice frequently and allow time for students to compare their notes in small groups (Maxwell 65).

If there are specific names and dates students might have trouble remembering or spelling, teachers need to write that information on the board or overhead projector and students can copy them into their notes. Until students are proficient in note-taking, and that does not happen until later in high school, they need to concentrate on listening to the speaker. If they try to write what was already said, while continuing to listen, they miss information.

Taking notes helps students not only remember the material, but helps in understanding the content. They may not realize during a lecture that they have questions to ask, but when going over the material later they will likely find gaps in the information or confusing comments.

We must do our part too, and lecture at a pace conducive to note-taking with frequent pauses to accommodate students. Potts suggests the following points to consider when lecturing:

- Speak slowly.
- Segment the lectures, pausing every six or seven minutes to allow students to write notes.
- Give verbal clues to the importance of particular points.
- Make connections among the points.

Note-Taking from Films

When viewing a film or video, students should take very few notes except for pertinent words or dates. Before watching the media, you need to direct students to scenes or areas of importance, such as characters' conflicting values, or influences that shape behaviors. Immediately after the viewing, students write what they think is important to remember, and then share what they have written within a small group. Encourage them to make additions or changes based on the group discussion.

Note-Taking from Written Material

Students need instruction on how to select, organize, and synthesize information from reading, particularly in recognizing the main idea (Washington 24). Students have trouble knowing what to write down and often resort to copying verbatim. Many students highlight passages from their reading that they want to remember, but the problem with highlighting is that it requires little decision-making and uses a minimum of skills. Writing notes, on the other hand, requires reading closely, deciding what is important to remember, and selecting pertinent details. When students take notes they use several skills: reading, writing, and thinking. To teach students how to take notes, you can begin by explaining to the class that notes are to be in their own words to avoid plagiarism, that notes are never complete sentences, and that individuals may use different notes depending on their prior knowledge and their intent in taking the notes.

Peter Gray explains a method developed by Marcia Heiman to help students learn more effectively. Heiman taught students to engage in a mental dialogue with authors and lecturers (Gray 70). Students ask questions, then seek answers from the readings and lectures to create the dialogue. Heiman tells her students that unless they know the questions the reading and lectures are attempting to answer, they will not understand the material. She has her students use the following guide:

1. Skim the reading by section, read all the captions, and infer the section's main questions.
2. Write out the questions.
3. Read carefully to discover the answers to the questions.
4. If necessary, change the questions to more closely fit the information. (71)

As a modeling strategy, you can prepare a paragraph from a textbook on a transparency, one selected for appropriate information that would require notes if the material is to be remembered. Ask for a volunteer to read it aloud or do so yourself. The students can follow along as it is being read. Instruct the students to begin writing their notes, but turn off the overhead as they begin. The students usually protest, claiming they cannot write notes without looking at the material, but the point of the exercise is to encourage them to write notes in their own words. After they write their notes, you turn the overhead on and in small groups students compare what they wrote. Then in whole-class discussion, each group shares its experience.

To help students understand the importance of taking brief yet comprehensive notes, show them a paragraph on an overhead. Then display a copy of notes that essentially copies most of the material. Discuss with students how the notes could be cut down yet retain adequate information. Next show an example of sketchy notes taken on the same paragraph. Again, students discuss what needs to be added, what is the most important point in the paragraph, and what are the relationships between the thoughts in the paragraph. By modeling the note-taking, students understand more clearly how to be good note-takers.

Repeat this activity or some variation until students are comfortable with using their own words and realize everyone will not write the same notes. As much as possible use material based on current studies and gradually choose longer selections. Eventually students should use fairly long pieces, and they can have the piece in front of them. As they work, circulate around the room checking on their proficiency.

༄ຕ໑ *Reflection* ༄ຕ໑

In a group share your techniques for taking notes. What might you share with your future students?

Regie Routman suggests that the teacher collect the notes that students have taken from written material. Two or three days later the teacher can hand them back, asking students to write a paragraph or two based solely on the notes. This exercise is helpful because students can check their own skill at note-taking (284).

When students bring their reading notes to a class discussion, they participate more. Because they have the notes in front of them, even shy students are more apt to join in. In addition, their answers and contributions are more thoughtful and generate additional discussion. A way to encourage students to take notes is to allow them to use the notes when taking a test. This is especially helpful when they are answering essay questions.

We want students to take notes so that they can remember and understand the material, but teachers should refrain from grading the notes. This becomes busywork for us and can result in some students copying notes from friends just to qualify for a grade. We want students to take notes to help themselves, not to please the teacher.

A biology teacher, William Olien, devised a method that teaches students how to integrate notes from lectures and reading into a study digest. His method works particularly well when the student textbook is the basis for the class. Although this rarely is the case in English class, there are times when teachers require students to read for information, and for these times Olien's method is valuable, especially for the upper levels of high school. His syllabus in Figure 8.2 explains the system to students.

This method works very well because, as Judith Langer and Arthur N. Applebee have explained, the more content is manipulated the more likely students will remember and understand the information.

Figure 8.2   Integrating notes from lectures and reading

Class Notebook and Study Digest

You are required to keep three sets of notes: (1) Reading Notes, (2) Lecture Notes, and (3) a Study Digest. The procedure and purposes of these three sets of notes are

1. Reading Notes

   Read and take notes on the assigned readings before the lecture on the material.

2. Lecture Notes

   Take notes during the lecture. Review these notes later the same day to fill in, clarify, and revise.

3. Study Digest

   This is the third set of notes. The purpose of the study digest is to summarize and integrate your notes from lecture and reading. It is an essential stage in learning and will make a difference in your level of achievement in the course. The digest will be your best study guide for exams. Bring your study digest up to date within 24 hours of every class period. Review your study digest notes of material to be covered on the next exam at least twice a week. Review your study digest notes for the entire unit at least once a week.

 ## SUMMARIZING

An important skill for students to learn is the ability to summarize. When students write reports, research papers, or any paper that requires outside references, good summaries are essential. Summaries are brief, much shorter than the original piece, but still capture the essence of the material. To "make a long story short" is an apt guideline.

If students learn how to summarize well, they are not as likely to plagiarize. At the secondary level, most plagiarism is the result of students' inability to put someone else's ideas into their own words, especially from written sources. However, they need to be taught that using summaries in writing requires that we document where the material came from. Often students have the erroneous idea that if they put the material in their own words they do not have to cite the author information. This leads to serious plagiarizing. As with other skills, students need direct teaching to learn how to write summaries.

You can begin by modeling the following procedure: Provide copies of a short story or article. After reading it as a class, ask students to summarize without using the author's exact words. Direct them to look for the major points, but not all the supporting detail. In small groups, students compare what they wrote and discuss how adequate the summaries are. Explain that they won't all write the same points, but everyone needs to take care not to misrepresent the author's viewpoint. They must not change the meaning of the piece. Repeat this practice several times using different types of reading material. You will find that teaching how to write summaries takes time and patience. Do not evaluate students' practice but do provide feedback with a lot of comments. When students summarize for a written report or essay, they need to begin each summary with the title, author, and publication information to include in the works cited page.

 ## PARAPHRASING

Paraphrasing is different from summarizing and not used as frequently. Yet secondary students, especially juniors and seniors, will find the skill useful when the material they want to include in an essay or report is too long for a quote but they do not want to shorten the material. This is fairly sophisticated and should be used only in the upper levels of high school. When paraphrasing, writers do not shorten the piece, but re-phrase the author's words into their own. A good way to begin teaching this skill is to give students a copy of "The Gettysburg Address" and have them paraphrase Lincoln's words. As a whole class, go over what they wrote line by line and discuss what possibilities they have. Remind them that their paraphrasing will not be the same as an-other's, but they all have to be true to Lincoln's meaning.

One student example of paraphrasing Lincoln's speech is given in Figure 8.3.

Figure 8.3 Paraphrasing

Original passage of approximately the first ten lines

Four score and seven years ago our fathers brought forth, upon this continent, a new nation, conceived in Liberty, and dedicated to the proposition that all men are created equal.

Now we are engaged in a great civil war, testing whether that nation, or any nation, so conceived, and so dedicated, can long endure. We are met here on a great battle-field of that war. We have come to dedicate a portion of it, as a final resting place for those who here gave their lives that that nation might live. It is altogether fitting and proper that we should do this.

But, in a larger sense, we can not dedicate—we can not consecrate—we can not hallow—this ground. The brave men, living and dead, who struggled here, have consecrated it, far above our poor power to add or detract.

A paraphrase of the passage

The founders of the United States created a union based on liberty and the belief that all people are equal. Now a civil war is testing the idea that a nation based on that premise can last. We are meeting on a battlefield of this civil war to dedicate an area for the men who died so that the ideals may live on. It is right that we do this; however, it isn't we but the men who gave their lives who have made this land holy.

From *Writing Our Lives* Maxwell 28–32.

Exploration

Using Study Skills

As a practice exercise for teaching your future students, read the following article, "How to Bite Back," and take notes. Second, summarize the material, and lastly, paraphrase the second paragraph of the article. After you have completed all three, meet in groups and compare your work. What have you learned from this exercise that will help you teach the skills to students?

How to Bite Back

A rainy spring this year produced a bumper crop of mosquitoes, making for a very buggy summer. The good news: whether you are concerned about the West Nile virus or just want to enjoy the outdoors bite-free, there is a fresh crop of products out this year that promise to fight mosquitoes. There are candles, sandalwood sticks, zappers, and traps that emit carbon dioxide (part of what attracts mosquitoes to humans). A Korean cell-phone maker is selling a ring tone that it claims will repel bloodthirsty bugs. The bad news is that the effectiveness of some of these new offerings is questionable.

The only products that have been proven to help people avoid mosquito bites are insect-repellent sprays or creams containing 35% DEET (10% for kids). But a new report from the University of Manitoba in Canada warns of dangers associated with using DEET and sunscreen at same time. Applying them together may increase the skin's absorption of DEET, leading to side effects ranging from skin rashes to changes in blood pressure. For the safest use, apply either sunscreen or DEET first, then wait half an hour before applying the other. Folks who want to avoid DEET should look for soybean oil-based products, which according to a study in the *New England Journal of Medicine* are effective but for shorter periods of time.

To protect the whole yard from mosquitoes there are two promising options. Sandalwood Mosquito Sticks from New Mountain can repel the bugs from a patio-size area. Like giant incense sticks, the all-natural repellents smolder for three to four hours.

Carbon dioxide traps like the Mosquito Magnet work by emitting a plume of carbon dioxide, heat, moisture, and octenol. They do a great job of capturing mosquitoes, but there's a chance they could work too well and attract more mosquitoes than usual to your yard, some of which might bite you on their way to being trapped.

Reprinted by permission from Lisa McLaughlin, "How to Bite Back." *Time*, August 11, 2003: 65.

Graphic Organizers

Graphic organizers are useful for providing structure for students taking notes from both oral and written information. They are especially useful for students who need visual guides to follow. Although students at any level may find graphic organizers

---

Figure 8.4 Examples of graphic organizers

Note taking showing a cause–effect relationship

CAUSE   EFFECTS

_____   _____

                                         _____

                                         _____

Or depending on the material, reverse the order

EFFECT   CAUSES

_____   _____

                                         _____

                                         _____

                                         _____

From *Writing Across the Curriculum* Maxwell 68–69.

helpful, those who have special needs will find them particularly useful. Cathy Sakta, a university instructor, explains that graphic organizers help students to listen more effectively and to include essential information. The structure teaches students how to focus on main ideas and supporting details (482). Figure 8.4 shows an example of a graphic organizer.

Teachers can gradually reduce the amount of information provided on the organizers until students no longer need them at all. Sakta suggests the following plan (484):

1. First, have students use the complete organizer, including topics, main ideas, and essential details arranged in the order that students hear them in lectures or read them from texts.
2. Next, supply only the topics and the main ideas, leaving numbered spaces for supporting details.
3. Give the topic and main idea, but omit the number and placement of the details.
4. Only the topic is provided, and spaces are left for the remaining information.

You can first model the use of the graphic organizers and then provide the graphic for students to use on their own. Special-needs students will need additional teacher modeling, but by keeping the graphics simple in design, they will be able to work on their own.

Christen and Murphy, in a handbook written for secondary students, suggest a drawing of a graphic organizer that helps students find the topic, main ideas, sup-

---

Figure 8.5   Reading guide

Use this outline to guide students when they are reading an article.

TOPIC   _____

MAIN IDEAS   _____

SUPPORTING DETAILS   _____

                   _____

                   _____

                   _____

SUMMARY   _____

                   _____

---

porting ideas, details, and summary. Writing the summary helps students to understand the readings (60). Figure 8.5 provides an outline for students to follow.

Graphic organizers can differ in structure, but all focus on main idea, major points, and supporting details. The purpose of graphic organizers is to guide students into taking adequate notes, not to insist that they fill out teacher-prepared forms (Maxwell 68). The guides should not be evaluated at all. A quick read will tell a teacher if students are on the right track. We want students to become independent in their learning and studying; the notes they take are for their own use, not an assignment to satisfy a teacher.

 ## WRITING IN OUR EVERYDAY LIVES

We use writing in our everyday life in order to remember and learn. List making is an obvious technique we use to remember. Even if we misplace the list later, we will remember what we wrote. For instance, if we make a shopping list for the grocery store and leave it at home, the chances are high that we will buy everything we wanted. The act of writing helps us remember.

We can teach our students to use this property of writing to remember and learn. If students write what they want to remember from their reading, the information is remembered much longer. The same is true when studying for exams, remembering characters in a long novel, or writing points they want to include in a story or essay.

In addition, we use writing to communicate, mostly by e-mail, but letters and notes, too. If we are planning on buying a used car, the most successful way to keep track of the information we find is to use a chart, writing down facts about each one. Writing has many practical aspects, and when we teach writing to students, it is important to help them realize this.

TEACHING PERSUASION

We use persuasion often in our daily lives, and for that reason we need to teach the skill of writing persuasion to our secondary students. Requests are persuasive: Asking parents for money or a boss for a day off, applying for a scholarship or a job are all persuasive techniques. The more we show our students the practical side of persuasion, the more willing they are to learn how to be successful.

Convincing someone of our point of view is another use of persuasion. When we give students an assignment to write about their favorite place, they need to persuade a reader they had good reasons for choosing this favorite place. The more students use sensory details, the more likely readers will agree with their premise.

Readers respond to both logical and emotional appeals and writers often include both, although students may emphasize one approach more than the other depending on the topic and audience. For example, if a student was trying to persuade his or her parents to help buy a car, the emotional or personal approach might work the best; however, adding figures about how he or she will pay for insurance and gas or the money saved on bus fare could be convincing. An additional example to use with students is if they were writing to oppose road construction through a previously protected area, they might gather all the facts and arguments against the roadway, and also include an emotional appeal to save a species of butterflies. For some readers logical facts on money and time would be convincing. For others, the fate of the butterflies would be the deciding factor. We can teach students to use both styles to their advantage.

Rogerian Arguments

Carl Rogers, a psychologist, developed a pattern of persuasion that seeks to find a common ground between opposing viewpoints. Often secondary students have difficulty understanding a point of view different from their own, especially on topics they feel strongly about. By teaching students the Rogerian way of presenting their side, they learn to better understand opposing views. The advantage of this approach is that to convince people one must understand other's viewpoints and respond to them. Using the Rogerian approach, students first explain the issue and follow with their position. Then they state the opposing views and describe the points they agree with. They follow up with facts reinforcing their view (Maxwell, "Writing Our Lives," 178–179).

The following persuasive letter using the Rogerian approach was written by Pang Xiong, a student.

Dear Mom and Dad,

Ever since the beginning of this year, I have told the both of you about wanting to take a trip to California during winter break. I've been working extra hard and think I should be able to go. Although I understand your concerns, I want to be able to spend more time with my boyfriend to see if he is actually worth being with or not because I'm at the age where I'm starting to make decisions on who I'm going to be with in the future. Going to California is also a good opportunity for me to go see the atmosphere of California.

The both of you are great parents, but there is one thing that you have to overlook now that we are now in the American society. I know that in our culture it's bad for the girl to go visit her boyfriend, but now a days it shouldn't really matter if the guy's parents are okay with it. For instance, my boyfriend's parents have overlooked that certain issue so I believe that you should as well. I wish you could understand this and accept the way our society is. This is a great opportunity for me to go visit his family and him to see if they would be a good future family for me. It is around that where I'm thinking about my future life. You've always stated that you wanted me to end up with a good husband and the way I can do that is actually spend some time with him to see if he is the one. You both met him already and said you have trust in him. If so then you don't have to worry about me visiting him.

I have never had the chance to travel by myself. The only other places that I have been are Minnesota and Kansas City, both family trips. Gary has been telling me that weather over there is perfect. I think I've had enough of this ugly weather. Year after year I'm stuck here during the winter. Isn't it time that I get to go off and enjoy some beautiful weather during winter? I think so.

I've also been working my butt off to save for this trip. You didn't think that I could afford it so I started saving since the beginning of this year and so far have saved up to $1,200.00. I have money for the plane ticket, hotel, and even some left over for souvenirs and anything else that I find that I like. Don't you think that I've shown my responsibility by being able to save as much as I have? We all know that I have a hard time saving up money so I am very proud of myself and you both should be too.

I have shown both of you that I am responsible enough and deserve to be able to take this trip at the end of the year. Since I have saved enough money for this trip, I might as well take this money and actually use it for its purpose. California is a good place to visit and enjoy beautiful weather and also a good chance for me to spend some time with my boyfriend and his family.

Love,
Pang

༅ Reflection ༅

Where has Pang stressed the common ground? Where has she used facts and then, emotional appeals? How would you teach this approach to your students?

TEACHING CLASSIFYING

Knowing how to classify information is an important skill we use throughout our lives. When we are making a major purchase or looking for an apartment, or facing any decision where we compare a number of things, classifying the information we find is the best way to make the right choice. Classifying also gives us the opportunity to look at knowledge in a new way, perhaps to look at situations with added clarity.

A good place to begin when teaching high school students about classification is to show them how it can be used to solve problems. For example, if a police department is plagued with a number of robberies, it might look at classifying the characteristics of each one. The groups could be these: time of the robbery, number of people involved, type of place robbed, and what things were taken. By classifying the information in this way the officers could easily find patterns that would help them inform citizens and perhaps find the robber. Situations can be examined in several ways depending on the information needed.

A class assignment we have used successfully gives students a fictitious list of crimes over a period of time. Working in groups, they assume the roles of police writing a report to be published in the newspaper. The community is extremely worried about how to protect itself and the report is intended to provide information on what precautions to take. Following this activity, we discuss classifying for various reasons and we use many examples, including newspapers, magazines, and daily life.

The class then reads the essay, "Friends, Good Friends—and Such Good Friends," by Judith Viorst, followed by a discussion. The writing assignment asks students to write a classification essay on any subject. We remind them that the categories they select must fit the purpose of the paper. The following essay is an example of how one student, Brad Bucki, classified his friends (Maxwell, *Writing Our Lives* 84–86).

FRIENDS

By Brad Bucki

I have no clue how or why it turned out this way. Eight years ago I would rather have been dead than have this happen. Even today I wonder how I let that snot-nosed brat from fourth grade do the things he did to me; name-calling and daily pummelings were normal for me. After five years of this constant abuse, I had to retaliate. I was now bigger and stronger than he was; this was going to be the sweetest revenge of my life. That fateful night it happened; I won my first fight and made a new best friend all with one swing.

No one truly knows why or how people pick the friends they do. The simple fact is that it is unavoidable. At some time or another each person on this earth will have a friend. Of course, most people will have many friends throughout their lives. Be it a best friend, a classmate from second grade or the kid next door, friends have their own special place in a person's life. When I was young I considered every friend I had to be my best friend. I just knew it would stay that way for our entire life, no matter what. I was certain they thought the same. As the years go sweeping by, the reality sets in that this is an extremely narrow-minded view of the world. Best friends become ordinary everyday acquaintances and mortal enemies become invaluable friends. I now realize, as much as I do not want to admit it, friends can be labeled and grouped into several categories based on intensity and duration of the relationship.

The School Buddies

These are the people I sat next to in Mr. Alberti's history, study hall, lunch or shared a locker with in freshman gym class. After pure repetition, I began to learn their names and faces. I give them the name "buddies" because as the name implies these friends never get too close to my feelings nor do I get too close to theirs. At lunch, conversations covered a variety of subjects: sports, cars, parties or the always-popular girls. Rarely did subject matter sway toward more serious subjects. Even if it did, it was quickly dropped in order to preserve the all-important reputation. The main purpose of the school buddy is to make the day go by quicker; once the bell sounded we all went our separate ways until the next morning. Scott, the kid from history class, summed up the school buddy relationship eloquently when he poured his heart out to me and confessed, "Thank God, you're my friend or there wouldn't be no one around here to wake me up after class."

The Sports Friends

Much like the school buddies these friends are great for the social part of life. For the most part, this group of friends consisted of guys I met from playing sports since fifth grade. I am positive that somewhere there is a golden rule chiseled in stone that states it is a serious crime to show emotion in the presence of this group. They possess the unparalleled ability to turn one's emotions or misfortune into information that will be held over one's head for as long as possible. I have determined that the single most important function of this group is to pick on one another. It is impossible for two members of this group to be within twenty feet of each other for more than five minutes without teasing, picking on or harassing each other. This may seem terribly cruel for friends to do, but in fact the opposite holds true. This teasing has definitely taught me how to handle myself in adversity, how to think quickly for an answer and when to walk away. Most importantly, although it is hard to admit, these friends are always right. Be it the shirt I am wearing, the classes I am taking, or the girl I am dating, this group never has a problem telling me their opinions on any subject. They show absolutely no remorse in telling the harsh truth no matter how much it's going to hurt me.

Stand the Test of Time Friends

Even though time and distance will separate Shane and me, there will always be a special bond between us. The bond may be stretched and twisted, but it will never be severed. Good times and bad, we have been through it all, side by side. Who could ever forget the times we shared? Our innocent schoolboy crushes on Kim and Alison. The overnight camping expeditions into the mysterious woods behind my house. The two-hour rafting trip that took nine due to miscalculations in flotation capacity and poor navigation. All those sleepless nights before motorcycle races spent eating peanuts, drinking grapefruit juice and discussing the female gender. Those are all high points in our friendship, but friendships are defined by the low spots. Aesop once stated that genuine friends are proved through adversity. This was never more obvious than on May 7, 1989. That was the day Shane's dad was fatally shot by a worker he had laid off from the family business. In the following month, we spent many nights on Old Man Johnson's hill staring at the stars. I had absolutely no idea what to say. All I could do was listen, offer advice, and most importantly, provide a shoulder to cry on. We have since gone our separate ways, but we both know an irreplaceable part of our lives is still on Old Man Johnson's hill staring at the stars.

We're Just Friends

This group of friends is comprised completely of members of the opposite sex. These friendships can be just as intense and meaningful as same-sex friendships. However they do undeniably contain a small amount of attraction between the two individuals involved. Both parties also realize that it is in the best interest of both to not act on this attraction and keep the relationship purely a friendship. My good friend Sara once described it as, "The you can look, you can't touch friendship." The most outstanding trait of these friends is they can look past status, money, shortcomings, and forgive the unforgivable. They are always willing to lend an ear or give advice, never passing judgment. They accept with open arms the true me along with all my faults.

Why Am I Friends With You?

This perfectly describes my relationship between my best friend, Greg, and me. For five seemingly endless years we were mortal enemies. I hated everything he stood for. He was loud and obnoxious; I was quiet and reserved. He partied; I studied. I was in sports; he was on drugs. Never once did I consider him for a future friend. That all changed the day after he and I had our battle royal. The next day he appeared at my front door to apologize for everything he had done to me in the past. After he finished, I told him exactly what I thought of him, making sure not to leave out any adjectives describing his character. In the next two weeks, we talked a lot and discovered we had much more in common than we ever thought possible. We both were scared of the future. We had similar relationships with our parents and brothers. We both enjoyed hunting, fishing, snowmobiling, and especially girls. Eventually I realized he was not the rich spoiled bully he came across as. He realized that I was not the stuck-up preppy he viewed me as. We both realized we were two similar people trying to get through life the best we knew how. I admire Greg; not only has he put his own life back in order, but he has taught me a lot about my own life. He has shown me how to let loose and have a good time and how to approach life with a relaxed attitude. Greg has opened my eyes to the vast world around me and forced me to look at life in a new and interesting way. I now know that there is life outside of school and sports. People I deemed undesirable two years ago are now some of my closest friends. I consider Greg my one true friend in this world. He stands for everything I value in a friendship. He accepts me for who I am. He is always willing to listen to my problems no matter how trivial or insignificant they may seem. He respects my opinions and feelings even if he disagrees with them. I know that no matter what happens to us in the future, there will always be a special spot in my heart for that snot-nosed kid from fourth grade.

EXPLORATION

Lesson Plan for Classification

What topics might you use to design a lesson plan on classification for your future students? What other examples could you give to your class? Brainstorm as a class to come up with additional ideas. Design a lesson plan based on your ideas.

LIFELONG SKILLS

It is definitely our duty job as English Language Arts teachers to teach these lifelong skills. Taking notes, summarizing, classifying, and persuasion are ways for students become more efficient learners. We can provide activities to help students acquire these skills and adapt our own teaching styles to assist in the students' success. As students realize how writing is an aid to learning, they become more understanding of how reasonable and practical the skills are and become more willing to use them. These aids to learning are definitely lifelong and useful skills.

RELATED WEB SITES

http://www.readwritethink.org/lessons
http://search.thegateway.org/query
http: //www.iss.stthomas.edu/studyguides
http://ucc.vt.edu/stdysk/cornell.html

REFERENCES

Christen, William, & Thomas Murphy. *Smart Learning: A Study Skill for Teens.* Bloomington: Grayson Bernar, 1992.

Dana, Carol, and Margaret Rodriquez. "TOAST: A System to Study Vocabulary." *Reading Research and Instruction* 31.4 (1992): 78–84.

Gere, Anne Ruggles, ed. *Roots in the Sawdust.* Urbana: National Council of Teachers of English, 1985.

Gettinger, Maribeth, and Jill K. Seibert. "Contributions of Study Skills to Academic Competence." *School Psychology Review* 31.3 (2002): 350–65.

Gray, Peter. "Engaging Students' Intellects: The Immersion Approach to Critical Thinking in Psychology." *Teaching of Psychology* 20.2 (April 1993): 68–74.

King, Alison. "Comparison of Self-Questioning, Summarizing, and Note-taking—Review as Strategies for Learning from Lectures." *American Educational Research Journal* 29.2 (Summer 1992): 303–23.

Langer, Judith A., and Arthur Applebee. *How Writing Shapes Thinking.* Urbana: NCTE, 1987.

Maxwell, Rhoda J. *Writing Across the Curriculum in Middle and High Schools.* Boston: Allyn & Bacon, 1996.

_____ . *Writing Our Lives.* Boston: Allyn & Bacon, 1999.

Mc Laughlin, Lisa. "How to Bite Back." *Time* 11 Aug. 2003: 65.

Olien, William. "Biology syllabus." Unpublished, Winchester, VA: Shenandoah University.

Potts, Bonnie. "Improving the Quality of Student Notes." *ERIC/AE Digest.* U.S. Department of Education, October 1993.

Rafoth, Mary Ann, et al. *Strategies for Learning and Remembering: Study Skills Across the Curriculum.* Washington, DC: National Education Association, 1993.

Routman, Regie. *Invitations.* Portsmouth: Heinemann, 1991.

Sakta, Cathy G. "The Graphic Organizer: A Blueprint for Taking Lecture Notes." *Journal of Reading* 35.6 (March 1992): 482–84.

Washington, Valerie M. "Report Writing: A Practical Application of Semantic Mapping." *Teacher Education* 24:1 (Summer 1988): 24–30.

Writing Research Papers

9

> Inspiration is wonderful when it happens, but the writer must develop an approach for the rest of the time.
>
> *Leonard Bernstein*

Teaching students how to write research papers is a complex task. We must break such an assignment into segments and steps or we lose the students' interest and move beyond their capabilities. Reports and research papers are part of many subjects in addition to English language arts. However, teachers of other subjects often expect and want English teachers to teach the basics of these assignments. We can do this if we teach a process of writing research as our foundation.

Many problems occur in research paper assignments. Because research papers require a high level of cognitive ability, usually only students in eleventh and twelfth grades are able to successfully complete a traditional research paper. Too often, younger students are assigned research projects far beyond their developmental level and consequently are frustrated. We need to be mindful of the cognitive level of the task and the assignment.

Larry Johannessen, Northern Illinois University, stresses that we need "to design writing instruction to help students develop the tools they need to solve complex, unfamiliar problems, think for themselves and with others . . . " (38). To accomplish this, teachers must present a puzzling event, question, or problem so that the students

- formulate hypotheses to explain an event or solve a problem
- collect data to test the hypotheses
- draw conclusions
- reflect on the original problem and thinking processes needed to solve it (38)

What Johannessen is describing are important research skills to teach high school students; however, at middle school and sometimes at high school, too, what we are assigning students is more of a report than a research paper. Writing a report is not the same as writing a research paper, although some teachers tend to treat the two as if they were. Report writing requires students to gather information from sources and report what they find. This is the most common expository writing done in secondary schools. Research writing requires writers to consider the information gathered from many sources, and then come to a conclusion of their own based on what they've found. For example, if a student's topic is violence on children's television programs, a report would require that students read articles on the issue, and, in essence, discover what others have said about the topic. A research paper would require the same process, but include research on the topic as well; for example, a study by the student who watches specific programs and records acts of violence by categories. A higher degree of insight and commentary is required for research. The research would include the writer's opinion based on the data collected as well as the findings gained through other studies. High school students should know the difference between reports and research, but this probably is not necessary in middle school. Based on their students' levels, teachers can decide when the differences need to be explained. Throughout this chapter the guidelines and activities refer to both reports and research because the method is similar and appropriate for longer papers.

Reflection

What do you remember of the longer papers you wrote prior to college? Some of you may remember doing reports in elementary school that you enjoyed doing. What was there about these early reports that you enjoyed? What were the topics? How about high school papers? Were some enjoyable to do?

 ## RESEARCH WRITING IN THE CONTEXT OF COMPOSITION

Too often, teachers treat expository writing as if it were completely different from creative and personal writing. The lines of distinction between expository writing and so-called creative writing are not that distinct. Certain elements are unique to a particular type, but many occur in all writing. For example, descriptions occur in science writing, reports, letters (friendly and formal), and essays, as well as in fiction.

As writers we want readers to see and understand what we do. We can achieve this goal by describing in detail the physical appearances of a lake, a chemical reaction, a character, frog body parts, a graph, or a battlefield. Using figurative language in these descriptions helps, too, in providing a mind's-eye view for readers. Similes and metaphors work in any type of writing. A letter to the editor or a board member is more effective with personal examples, and political speeches are full of such examples.

As we teach specific ways to write reports, we also need to teach how and when to use descriptive language and personal experiences.

Although expository writing is required throughout the grades beginning at about the fourth, teachers are often dissatisfied with the students' papers. A major problem is that students are not taught steps to achieve good results, particularly at the beginning of the project. Beginning with their choice of the topic, students must have an active role in the project.

Writing reports and research papers provide students with opportunities to work in the library and on the Internet to look for information, take notes on what they find, and organize the notes into a first draft. When students self-select the topic, they enjoy the writing because it gives them a chance to pursue an interest; however, problems often occur when they are locating the information and organizing notes. Writing a report or research paper can overwhelm some students, but a structured method helps them keep track of what they are doing.

 A METHOD OF TEACHING STUDENTS HOW TO WRITE LONGER PAPERS

I developed this method because many of my special-needs students could not write and organize a report, no matter how much I hovered over them or gave suggestions. The first time I used the method that follows, students who usually did not complete the longer assignments not only handed in reports on time, but also their reports were better organized than other students'. From then on, everyone used the same method involving these specific steps.

- Self-select a topic.
- Develop questions.
- Organize note-taking.
- Write drafts.
- Revise, revise, revise.

Preliminary Work

Before students actually begin to compile reference information or begin their research, three elements must be in place: They must select a topic, they write what they already know about the topic (prior knowledge), and only then they develop the research questions they will address in their papers.

Selecting Topics

When teachers begin the process of helping students find an interesting subject, they generally begin with a fairly broad topic, usually one that comes from literature study or a unit. For example, if your students have read *The Great Gatsby* by F. Scott

Fitzgerald, you may want them to write a paper based on the novel. Or you may be doing a unit on issues facing teenagers. You need to begin with examples, perhaps topics from former students or ideas that have come up during discussion. But help them only to the extent that they understand enough to take over the exploration for their topic.

First as a whole class, students think of topics they find interesting. Often hearing others talk about topics gives students ideas. Encourage them to choose more than one, especially if they are having trouble thinking of appropriate choices.

The next step is to have students meet in small groups and share their choices. The purpose of the group is to help each other focus on a subject. You guide the group activity by having the students ask questions about what interests them about the subject, share views, discuss background, and ask what they want to find out. Each student in turn can add ideas about their choice, or sometimes they choose different topics depending on what others in the group say.

We often ask students to narrow their topic, but with the exception of advanced students, the request is of little use because students do not understand what that means. In fact, with special-needs students, quite the opposite is needed. Their choices are often very narrow and need to be broader. Students should select a topic they are interested in and have some idea of what they want to find out through research. As a teacher, you need to look at each student's choice and give suggestions if the topic is too general or too specific.

Prior Knowledge

Students always know something about a chosen topic if they selected it themselves. And what they know should be the beginning of their paper. Recognizing that what they already know is important and "counts" in school is highly motivating, especially for special-needs students. Educators are well past the notion that students are empty vessels waiting to be filled with teacher-generated knowledge, but nonetheless, what students do know is too often ignored. We need to build not only on students' interests but on their prior knowledge as well.

Have your students write or type the title of their topic at the top of a page. Next, without worrying about spelling or complete sentences, they write all they know about the topic. They should not use any sources, but rather try to recall everything they have read, heard, and seen about the topic. If they are not sure about some things, they can note that with a question mark. To do justice to the task, they need time to think through all they remember. When finished, they meet in small groups and share what they have written by reading their notes to the others. Members of the group respond with questions or comments. Although members help each other out by suggesting how to broaden or narrow the topic or by telling what they know about the topic, too, the biggest benefit of this exercise is in explaining the topic to other people. When we explain something to someone else, we realize what we are unclear about, what more we know, and what we want to find out. The oral sharing helps clarify the topic for the writer.

⌒⌒ *Reflection* ⌒⌒

Why is student prior knowledge important to you as a teacher? How will it help students become more effective writers?

_____

After students finish writing their prior knowledge, you then have students read over, on their own, what they wrote. Next they organize the material in outline form. As they organize, have them ask themselves the following questions:

- What additional information do I need?
- What am I not sure about?
- What do I need to support this idea?
- What areas do I know little about?

Adapt the questions to fit the age and experience level of your students. Students use this list as a guideline for developing their questions.

Developing Questions

In recent years, we have improved our own questioning abilities. We now ask questions that require higher-order thinking rather than simply using recall questions. Also, we use longer wait time when asking questions, thus encouraging students to think. But what about students developing their own questions? As with other strategies discussed in this chapter, the more students are involved in their own learning, the more they learn and the longer the knowledge is retained (Maxwell, *Writing Across the Curriculum* 70).

Without the questions, students go into the library or onto the Internet with only a vague idea of what they are looking for. Finding answers (information) is difficult if one doesn't know the question—somewhat like going into a room to get something and then forgetting what one was looking for. Finding an unknown is almost impossible.

By requiring students to develop their own questions, we are helping them become more active learners. When students receive a list of questions from the teacher, few regard it as a learning opportunity; rather they look at it as busywork. They write answers to receive grades, not to learn. Asking questions they themselves want to find answers to involve students in their own learning; however, students do need guidance in determining what type of questions to ask themselves.

Good questions are essential when reading for meaning and information. Without questions to guide the search and the reading, gathering information is very difficult. Students who begin their search either in the library or on the Internet with only a topic in mind spend their time unproductively. They become frustrated, especially those who struggle with writing. When students develop questions that need to be answered, they know better where to find the resources and can recognize an answer when they find it (Maxwell, *Writing Across the Curriculum* 72).

An important point is that the research questions must be developed by the students themselves. Toby Fulwiler believes that for research to be successful, what he refers to as "authentic," students must explore topics that interest them and then hunt for answers to questions that puzzle them.

EXPLORATION

Developing Research Questions

Choose a topic that you have an interest in and would like to explore more. Write everything you already know about the topic, then organize the information. Now write what questions you would like to answer if you were doing a research paper on your topic.

THE I-SEARCH PAPER

One type of research paper, the I-search paper, encourages students to search for a wide range of information well beyond the traditional sources. Students search for information, compare facts from various sources, and then draw conclusions. The original concept comes from Ken Macrorie and stresses genuine inquiry that the student writer is interested in, as opposed to locating information that has already been collected and summarized. To begin, then, the topic must be self-selected by the student.

After students select individual topics, they meet in groups to discuss how to locate resources and to generate possible questions to answer. A summary of Macrorie's advice to students includes thinking about the best way to interview people: what to ask, how to approach them, and what information to know before the interview. He suggests that the statements experts make need to be tested against what other experts say (Kearns 48). When writing the paper, a good method of organization is for a writer to explain the method of research in the order in which it was done (Kearns 48).

Because writers are searching for information they want and need to know, the I-search method develops lifelong skills in gathering information by listening, interviewing, reading, quoting, reporting, and writing (Macrorie 71).

Many teachers unnecessarily structure the research assignment by limiting the sources or specifying the number of sources to be used, rather than encouraging students to gather information. Robert Perrin, from Indiana State University, explains that students should be encouraged to look everywhere and explore every potential source of information. Why shouldn't students use personal and telephone interviews? Why shouldn't they conduct surveys when the results would be enlightening? Why shouldn't students use personal experience when it is appropriate? Why shouldn't students use films, pamphlets, lecture notes, records, or television programs when they supply helpful ideas, insights, and information (51)?

Tim Hirsch, a college educator, developed a research assignment for personal decision-making that uses many of the resources Perrin suggests. Hirsch believes research should center on a question students care about, one that has personal implications for them. High school students face important questions: Should they go to a postsecondary school? Should they work after school? Should they attempt to get on an athletic team? Hirsch explains:

> The first step, then, for student researchers is to begin with questions of critical importance to them. The answer to these questions should lead them to action. They should be questions that lead to choices rather than to simple accumulation of information and opinions about a topic. After the question is established, the student researchers need to define the "givens," and establish the criteria they are going to use to answer their questions. (11)

For example, if the topic is buying a used car, the "givens" might include how much money they can spend, the cost of insurance, and where they could park the car.

At first, students may think they can't find answers to questions like these, but they can. Hirsch notes that students are more apt to locate library and Internet resources when they have a "compelling need for information" (12). Other sources of information are important as well. We all discover information by talking to informed people, watching news broadcasts, or making direct personal observations. Evidence can come from a variety of sources, as long as it is verifiable. Students need to do their own calculations, comparisons, and evaluation (13). When students learn this type of research process, they can apply it to questions in other areas of their lives and become lifelong researchers.

Exploration

Locating Sources

List the possible resources a student might use in writing a long paper on cigarette smoking or any topic you choose. What kind of information would they find from the various sources?

Locating Sources

Carla Burmeister, a library media specialist, has devised a way of helping students choose appropriate sources from books, articles, and the Internet. She provides the guide shown in Figure 9.1 for eighth and ninth graders.

Burmeister discusses the sources with the students and explains where they can be found in the library. Students must make a list of possible sources before they begin gathering information. We need to model this with a class activity when we discuss with students possible sources for specific topics. We need to follow up the whole-class

---

Figure 9.1   Suggested sources

What type of source is the most appropriate for a given topic?
1. Magazine articles and newspapers—recent events
2. Online resources—ground-breaking discoveries
3. Primary sources—firsthand accounts
4. Reference/encyclopedias—basic background information
5. Almanacs—quick statistics
6. Monographs (nonfiction books)—in-depth analysis

Used by permission.

Figure 9.2   Determining the usefulness of a resource

How do you determine if this resource will be useful?
1. Look at the book's table of contents and index.
2. Read a chapter's or article's introduction and subheadings.
3. Examine a CD-ROM's main screen.
4. Look at the specific content of a source and ask these questions:
   a. What is the publication date?
   b. What is the author's background and perspective?
   c. Is the information fact or opinion?
   d. How does the author justify his or her opinion?
   e. What is the depth/detail of the information?

Used by permission.

practice by having the students do the activity in small groups on different topics. This is a good place to introduce them to the variety of resources available to them. When students know what sources are available and where they can find them, Burmeister provides the second guide in Figure 9.2.

Working with the classroom teacher, Burmeister teaches the types of resources, including why Internet sources need to be evaluated, and how to evaluate them. To give the students practice, she has them find one magazine article on their topic. After they have selected the research questions, she helps students work on sample keyword searches using terms that fit their topics. As they demonstrate readiness, students go to the Library Media Center and begin their research. To help students evaluate the resources, she gives them the handout shown in Figure 9.3.

Although the Internet is a marvelous source of information, it can also be an unreliable source. In "Teaching Healthy Skepticism About Information on the Internet," Reid Goldsborough explains:

Figure 9.3 Five C's for evaluating sources

1. Content
   What is the intent of the content? Who is the intended audience? Is the content popular, scholarly, satiric, or serious?

2. Continuity
   What is the copyright date of the article or document? Is it the most up-to-date information you can find on your topic? Is this important?

3. Credibility
   Is the author identified? How do you know this material is reliable?

4. Comparability
   Is the information verifiable? Do statistics match those found in other sources?

   How does this information fit the overall context of your research? What key idea or ideas does this article support?

5. Choice
   Will you choose this material as a source of information for your research? Why or why not?

Used by permission.

> The Internet is chockful of rumors, gossip, hoaxes, exaggerations, falsehoods, ruses, and scams. Though the Net can reveal factual, substantive information that students can learn from and use in homework assignments and term papers, it can also appear to be a gigantic electronic tabloid. (32)

Students need to be aware of the pitfalls of accepting what they read on the Net without applying critical thinking—critical thinking that will help them now and throughout their lives. Goldsborough provides a six-step approach to help students learn how to evaluate the information on the Internet (32).

1. *Don't be fooled by appearance.* Looks can deceive and a flashy site can be a marketing front for advertising or political propaganda.
2. *Locate guides you can trust.* There are authorities to help you find valuable educational sites. For example, the "T&L ultimate hotlist" (www.techlearning.com) has a number of resource collections with a good reputation. Argus Clearinghouse (www.clearinghou.net/chhome.html) rates topical guides in a variety of subject areas.
3. *Find out who's behind the information.* Check to see if the author is identified. Are there links to a page listing professional credentials? If no author is listed, users need to be skeptical.
4. *Look for the reason the information was posted.* Each web site has its own agenda and students should keep that in mind when evaluating the information.

5. *Look for the date the information was created or last modified.* To evaluate the information, either on the Internet or any published material, the reader must know how up-to-date the information is. In books and journals we look for copyright dates; have students check dates on the Net, too.

6. *Try to verify the same information elsewhere.* This is especially important if the information is different from other sources. Students should try to confirm the information from at least two other sources.

Goldsborough also lists sources for web site evaluation:

Evaluating Internet Information

www.medlib.med.utah.edu/navigator/discovery/eval.html

a medical library site

Evaluating Quality on the Net

www.tiac.net/users/hope/findqual/html

in-depth look at evaluation criteria

Internet Source Validation Project

www.stemnet.nf.ca/Curriculum/Validate/validate.html

offers guidelines for students using the Internet for research purposes and tips for teachers who want to teach their students to be critical users of the media. (35)

For middle school students, Burmeister uses the form in Figure 9.4 to help students evaluate the Internet sources.

The Internet as a Reference Source

The Internet is a major source of information and available in most U.S. schools. Even though students are familiar with the Internet, guidelines for reliable use as a reference are necessary. The information Burmeister provides goes a long way toward help-

---

Figure 9.4   Internet evaluation form

Authority: Who is the author/sponsor? What are the author's credentials and qualifications? Who sponsored this site? Is there a link on the page to the sponsoring organization? Is there any other form of contact to the author or sponsor?

Accuracy: Is the information consistent with that found in other sources? Is the factual information verifiable?

Audience: Who is the information intended to benefit? What is the purpose of this site?

Currency: When was this site first published? When was it last modified?

Used by permission.

ing students evaluate the Internet sources. Students must write the Internet address, the name of the organization, and the source of the information on their references list. Several sites are available to help students find reliable sources. Although sites can change, some long-time sites include the following:

- Search Engine Watch
- Internet Journalism Resources
- Internet Research Pointer
- Research It
- Gazetteer

Points to remind students of when they use the Internet for research:

- Students should print the articles they find, and then take notes as they would with any print material.
- Just because the information is on the Internet, they must not assume it's true.
- The information needs to be recorded under the appropriate questions that guide their research.

In an article, "Effective Internet Research," Janine Lim stresses the importance of guiding students as they do research on the Internet. We need to find appropriate sites in advance to make good use of classroom time. She suggests the web site <http://www. remc11.k12.mi.us/bcisd/classres/for good sites for teachers and students> (35).

Lim suggests an advanced treasure hunt to help students learn how to gather information. She recommends WebQuest, an inquiry-oriented activity available at <http://edweb.sdsu.edu/webquest/webquest.html> (36).

Also, Lim recommends a research planner for students to use as they search the Internet for information. A printable one is available at htpp://www.remc11.k12. mi.us/bcisd/classres/handouts/resplan.pdf> (36).

We must make students aware of the importance of giving credit to Internet sources just as they do for articles and quotations gathered elsewhere. Information on using the Modern Language Association style for citing Internet sources can be found at <http://owl.english.purdue.edu/handouts/research/rmla.html> (36).

Taking Notes on References

Before starting their information search, students write one question each on a sheet of paper. If they have four questions, they will have four sheets of paper. Then they take a final piece of paper and title it "References."

Now they are ready to begin searching for answers. As they locate a reference, they begin finding answers to their questions. First, they record the reference, including all of the necessary bibliographic information on the reference sheet, numbering it 1. Then they jot down notes under the appropriate question and place a 1 by the notes to signify where the material came from. The first reference might provide notes for two or three questions. The advantage of following this procedure over using note cards is that they are organizing the information at the same time they are writing it down. With the next reference they read, they go through the same procedure, numbering it 2. The question sheets soon will look like the following:

Fkdieand djs ejlewnj jpt ein eidjfks?	Rdfndx ygjokdv tde shumbale faxgew uro ds u ghe ty ste?	T de shumble faxge ?	Tredls ig wshge ak ?	References
1. Tle gwoun ora s hsaib rai nstzd				**1.** Hasde nstzd ds gaotbe fhotbe asif
2. Gaotbe awr o ghrpoe inhaib fhotbe asif yay	**2.** Tle gwoun ora s hsaib rai nstzd ds yay gaotbe awr o ghrpoe inhaib fhotbe	**1.** Ple grep ora s jasde rai nstzd ds gaotbe awr o ghrpoe inhaib fhotbe asif yay	**2.** Gasde rai nstzd ds gaotbe o ghrpoe inhaib fhotbe asif yay	**2.** Usahue Ives oru ptinvgeb sxoud avbgt
4. Rupths Ives oru ptinvgeb sxoud avbgt	**4.** Ptinvgeb rupths Ives oru sxoud avbgt	**3.** Usahue Ives oru nvgeb sxoud avbgt	**4.** Usahue Ives oru ptinvgeb sxoud avbgt	**3.** Lrugivg uwe wfibe pxingnte aspte uyv **4.** Fdgedge yfadbe sd o bitbat wcurt

When a direct quote is written down, the page number it was taken from should be added to the information sheet. If students have access to Alphasmarts, they will find them helpful for this method of note-taking. Each question and subsequent answer can be in a different file, with the documentation page in a separate file also.

If students need help in finding information, they can be specific about what questions they are trying to find answers to, making it much easier for someone to help them. When the pages fill up with notes, they staple on additional ones. When the questions are answered, it is time to write the report. Before using this method, students, especially ones who had trouble writing reports, never knew whether they had enough information to start writing. With this method they can see when they've answered each question. If they cannot find information to answer one of the questions, they may substitute another question if they clear it with the teacher. In addition, if they find interesting information they did not have a question for, they can write a question that fits.

With notes in hand, they begin writing the report. Because all of the notes about one subtopic are written right under the question, organizing is no problem. For many students, completing a report is a new experience. This method works for fourth through twelfth grade. More experienced writers may not need help with developing questions, although writing questions before looking for references is helpful for all writers. All of the students reported that keeping track of notes, seeing where more information is needed, and organizing the writing is much easier when they use this method, and the method works for all research papers and reports.

Guidelines for the Research Process

1. Students develop and choose their own questions for a topic they define and narrow.
2. As students do research (find answers), they may want to change their research questions.
3. Students write their notes (answers) under individual questions.
4. Organization of the report is determined by the questions and answers.
5. Conclusions explain the author's new knowledge and interest.

Developing Plans for Including Longer Papers

Research papers and reports are most successful if they are incorporated within a unit and not taught simply because the curriculum includes teaching research papers. The plan that follows illustrates how three teachers incorporated the research paper into other facets of their curriculum, creating an interesting and integrated activity that follows a process approach. The three teachers are Carla Burmeister, media specialist; Betsy Damon, eighth-grade teacher; and Wendy Mosley, ninth-grade teacher. The three worked together to develop a unit incorporating research skills, a Level 3 research report, and debates. They explain:

> As part of our language arts curriculum, we are required to teach research, writing, and speaking skills. The research work and writing act as a stepping stone to the junior year when students write longer and more in-depth research. The speaking part of the project provides students with basic speaking skills and prepares them for the sophomore year in which they spend a full quarter working on speech techniques. All aspects of the project, speaking, writing, and researching, develop the art of presentation.
>
> The eighth-grade debate unit is an approximately six-week project that focuses on thinking critically, researching current issues, and developing library skills, writing skills, and enhancing public speaking techniques. The unit culminates with students performing formal debates in teams of four.
>
> The ninth-grade research writing follows up on the eighth-grade experience by reviewing skills taught at that level and adding new skills, such as documentation. The debate portion adds presentation techniques, such as posture, body movement, facial expression, gesture, and voice. Here the students work in teams of two.

INSTRUCTIONAL UNIT

RESEARCH SKILLS/DEBATE

Narrative Outline

The eighth-grade research unit actually starts in the social studies classroom with a discussion about the importance of hearing all sides of an issue before making a decision. Students then brainstorm a list of current topics that have two opposing viewpoints. Once the students have a variety of topics, the teacher puts them into groups. After a 15–20 minute discussion, the groups share with each other what they know and don't know about these topics. Now the students are ready to move into teams of four. Each team decides on a current issue to use as a topic. The students in each team decide who will argue the affirmative side of an issue and who argues the negative side. At this point the media specialist comes into the classroom to begin the library skills section of the unit.

DEBATE REQUIREMENTS
(Handout for students)

1. You will complete a keyword search and turn it in for credit.
2. While you are working in the media center, you are required to show Mrs. Damon your research notes at the end of each class period.
3. Evaluate your sources. Be ready at any time to explain why you are using a source. How does it fit the evaluation criteria? (See Mrs. Burmeister's criteria)
4. Prepare a list of your references. Make sure you use the correct format. (Teacher handout shows correct form)
5. You may choose your outline format. Your outline is worth 10 points.
6. Your first draft is worth 25 points.
7. You must use two visual aids in your debate. Posters, overheads, videotapes are acceptable. Make sure the aids are visible to the audience.

Eighth-Grade Debates

A debate is a formal spoken argument for and against a particular topic. Two speakers will provide information, opinions, and facts to support opposing viewpoints on the chosen topic. The purpose of the debates is to provide students with information so that they can make informed decisions on important issues that affect their lives. The debates are not designed to advocate one position over another, but rather to allow students to make their own decisions.

INSTRUCTIONAL UNIT

RESEARCH PAPER/DEBATE

Narrative Outline

This unit begins with an introduction to the general theme of the research project for English 9: teen issues. Much of the content discovery occurs here before the research paper and debate guidelines. The research guidelines are passed out and discussed on day two. Also, the students are provided with a general description of the debate activity so that they understand the extent to which they will be working with their topic. The need for a genuine interest in the topic is stressed before the next activity, which is to choose partners and then together, a pro/con or two-sided teen issue. For the remainder of the next five weeks, students follow a step-by-step process from research to note-taking to drafting and revision to producing a Level 3 final mini-research paper. Once the paper is complete, students use the content to prepare debates. Students concentrate on preparing note cards and practicing the initial speech along with anticipating the rebuttal arguments. Students also develop presentation techniques such as gesture, facial expression, body movement, and voice volume and inflection. A variety of modeling and opportunities for practice are provided during the unit that extends over about seven weeks.

Although not included here, Wendy Mosley prepared a detailed timeline for her students, which included the writing levels for every assignment. The debate assignment was outlined with all the requirements. Also, she gave students a handout of strategies for speaking and debating.

She prepared the following outline for the research assignment:

MINI-RESEARCH PAPER
(Handout for students)

Guidelines: 2–3 pages; minimum 5 sources
Steps in writing the paper:

1. With your partner choose a two-sided teen issue.
2. Prepare your list of questions (4–6).
3. Evaluate your topic.
   Is there enough information available on the subject?
   Is the subject narrow enough to cover in 2–3 pages?
   Is the subject interesting to your audience?
4. Consider your purpose. In this case it is to persuade.
5. Write your thesis statement by stating your purpose in one sentence.
6. Gather information.

We will review IMC sources and spend a week in the library. Possible sources include books, magazines, interviews, pamphlets, videos, television, the Internet, and other electronic sources.

7. Prepare your bibliography.
8. Take notes using the one-question-per-sheet format.

As you locate sources, check each one against your questions on the top of each page. If a source is useable, add documentation information on the reference sheet. Turn to the appropriate question(s) in the note packet. Take notes by using quotations, summaries, and paraphrases. Write the number of the source beside the items every time you take notes. Include page numbers. This will ensure proper documentation when you begin writing your paper.

(continued)

> Remember not to plagiarize!
>
>   9. Prepare an outline.
> 10. Write a draft.
> 11. Revise in writer's group.
> 12. Prepare works cited page.
> 13. Edit in writer's group.
> 14. Print, assemble with title page, outline, text, reference page.

Once the research paper was completed, the students used their research for the debate assignment using the following guidelines.

Debate guidelines

- Each initial speech is 2 minutes.
- Debates are prepared from research papers.
- Two rebuttal opportunities.
- One notecard with notes only is allowed; a blank card is allowed for rebuttal notes.
- Each speaker stands behind a podium.
- All debates are videotaped.
- Audience members write comments for each speaker.
- Pair voted "most memorable debaters" wins a prize.

Burmeister, Damon, and Mosley created a research assignment that provides purpose and experience for their students. The learning and practice is interwoven in the assignments so that the work always has meaning for the students. The requirements are clearly explained every step of the way; students know what they need to do and how they will be evaluated.

A Research Assignment for a Paper on Careers

A research assignment I designed for my students has the familiar title of investigating a possible future career. However, it has a twist in that the students also had to discover how their personalities, preferences, and talents fit with their selected career. I gave students the following handout after explaining at length the parameters of the assignment. Additionally, we had already done much of the work by writing papers on birth order and influences of family and friends, and a reflective description of their lives.

RESEARCH PAPER ON A POSSIBLE CAREER

Assignment

Investigate a career you are interested in and explain how you are suited to it by examining your personality, talents, values, future plans, and hopes. The paper has three main parts and a conclusion that pulls it all together. To create a cohesive paper, pay special attention to the transitions between sections.

Section 1

How do your past experiences inform your future? What are the connections between your younger life and the kind of person you are now? The papers you wrote previously for this class, as well as your family, friends, teachers, school records, and experiences, are all sources of information.

Section 2

In this section, write about your present values, your personality, what is important to you, and your dreams for the future.

Section 3

Research a career. Begin by enumerating the questions you are exploring and explain why you chose these questions. You must include several references citing a variety of sources, including an interview. Use current information or it won't be of use to you.

Conclusion

Tie all the sections together. How does the information from Section 1 relate to Section 2? How do both sections relate to Section 3? What have you learned that will be of help to you? What additional information would you like to find?

You need to begin the paper with an introduction and include a "Works Cited" page using MLA documentation.

The students frequently met in peer groups while they were working on the paper. When the paper was finished, they used the following response guide in their peer-editing group:

Response Guide for Research Paper
1. What content does the writer want you to focus on?
2. In the section on careers, what questions still need to be answered?
3. Where can information be condensed or expanded?
4. In the first section, the background, how does the information tie into the careers section? What else could the writer add?
5. In all sections, what examples help explain the main ideas?
6. What does the writer want you to focus on in terms of writing skills?
7. Where can sentences be expanded? Combined? Check carefully for run-on sentences.

8. Read the introduction and then the conclusion. How can they better reflect the major points of the paper?
9. Check for introductions to references. Where could they be improved?
10. What is the strongest part of the paper?
11. What could you suggest as the area that needs the most work?
12. Where are strong examples used?
    (Maxwell, *Writing Our Lives* 294–295, 302)

 A PROCESS TO TEACHING THE IMPORTANCE OF SOURCES

Laura Apfelbeck describes her process for teaching the research paper.

> To begin we brainstorm ideas. I give them some ideas from previous student papers, current events, and career issues. I ask them to think about possible topics several weeks before they will begin to work on the research paper. To begin, students hand in a research paper proposal so I know they have thought about the topic, what the main question is, and where they might find information. Students who have poorly worded questions will have a difficult time. I warn them against topics that have been overused or ones that they have such strong views on that they would not be able to see other sides to the question. Students fill out the proposal in Figure 9.5. When their research proposal is okayed they begin locating sources. In fact, students prepare a working Annotated Works Cited page first because I have found that they need at least 10–15 sources available on their subject. If they cannot find that many, they need to choose another topic.
>
> We spend several days in the computer lab and/or library accessing various research tools such as the periodical and newspaper indexes available through our library (WilsonWeb, EbscoHost, ProQuest), interlibrary loan, Bagerlink, and so on. Our library is small so students have to depend on the University of Wisconsin system's lending library and online sources. Students are required to include an interview as one of their sources and we discuss how best to conduct interviews.
>
> After reading the sources, highlighting what they find useful, taking notes, and answering the main question they set out to answer, they create the MLA Annotated Works Cited Page.
>
> Next I have them make a preliminary outline using keywords and listing sources to accompany the main ideas. This lets me know if they have an understanding of how to answer their research question in an organized way. Once this is okay, they create a sentence outline because it helps them organize their thoughts. If they do this well the actual drafting flows quite easily.

Apfelbeck provides the handout in Figure 9.6 before students meet in peer-editing groups. By giving them steps to follow, they better prepare their papers for the peer edit.

After the students finish their research and edit their own papers, they meet in peer-editing groups. Apfelbeck uses Figure 9.6 for their group work.

Figure 9.5 Research topic proposal for _____

1. What is the topic?

2. What questions will you be answering?

3. How is this topic controversial?

4. Why are you interested in this topic?

5. What types of research will you need to do? Examples include interviews, articles, library, internet, periodicals, TV, newspapers, and government sources.

Used by permission.

Figure 9.6 Student handout: Editing your research paper

There are many steps to take in editing a lengthy paper. You will want to ask several people you trust to read it. What follows is a list of common mistakes I see in drafts. You can use it as a guide for your own work.

1. Avoid back-to-back ideas, whether they are quotations, paraphrases, or summaries. Instead add your own comments, analysis, transitional sentences, explanations, or comparative analysis between the borrowed material.
2. Be sure each section begins with a sentence related to your thesis and each section ends with a concluding sentence about that topic. Check to see if body paragraphs begin and end with your own writing, not borrowed material.
3. When showing that experts agree, you may summarize ideas of several sources. Be sure to include all the sources you use.
4. If you use two articles by the same author, make sure you distinguish between them in the citation.
5. Check your punctuation carefully. Read your paper aloud or ask someone else to read it aloud and listen carefully to check for correct punctuation.
6. Read the paper looking only for tags introducing borrowed material. Be sure you introduced borrowed material each time and the first time should establish the credibility of the source.

Used by permission.

Figure 9.7 Revising guide for research papers

Introduction:

How could the introduction be more interesting?

What "hook" did the writer use to interest the readers?

Body:

What are the major points?

What details are used to explain the major points?

How could the organization be improved?

Where could more information be added?

What questions do you have about the information and the points the writer is making?

Borrowed material:

Are the introductions to the material sufficient? Where might more be added?

Where could the writer discuss the borrowed material more?

Conclusion:

How could the writer sum up the major points more effectively?

Could the introduction and conclusion be more compatible?

In what ways could the conclusion be stronger?

Used by permission.

One of Apfelbeck's students wrote the following paper. As you read it, respond to Figure 9.7 as a guide and write comments.

EFFECTS OF FETAL ALCOHOL SYNDROME
Research paper by Andrea Monka

Even though Fetal Alcohol Syndrome (FAS) was "discovered" in the early 1970s, very few people today realize the devastation FAS has on a life. The sad part of this disease is that it can be prevented. The definition from Amy Nevitt states, "FAS is a birth defect caused by a woman's drinking of alcohol when she is pregnant" (13). This is a definition that is agreed upon by most experts. In the United States, FAS is the reason for most cases of mental retardation (Nevitt 1). FAS is a devastating disease that affects people throughout their lives, places a great burden on society, and the need for intervention is immediate.

FAS is more prevalent today than ever. The women with the highest rate of babies with FAS are from ages sixteen to twenty-three. On her website, On Any Given Day in the United States, Teresa Kellerman states that according to the US Census Bureau, every day in the United States there are about ten thousand babies born; studies have shown for every thousand live births, approximately three newborns are afflicted with FAS. Kellerman also notes that the book, Substance Abuse and the America Woman, states, "The latest estimate for the U.S. is a rate of nineteen point five per ten thousand live births, although estimates run as high as thirty per ten thousand—about twelve thousand babies a year" (1). This adds up to approximately eleven thousand children a year. There are many children afflicted every year for a disease that is preventable. Due to the woman's drinking, these unfortunate infants will never have an average life. These newborns face a life of hardship and uncertainty.

Many devastating physical and mental birth defects accompany FAS. One of these is facial characteristics that most people affected with FAS carry. Anastasia Neberezny and Alma Saddam published an article in the Ohio State University Extension Fact Sheet, titled "Human Nutrition and Food Management" describing these characteristics as "Narrow eyes, low nasal bridges, short upturned noses, and a thin upper lip" (1). A person who does not know what FAS looks like might not see these signs and they will not realize that a person has FAS. This can lead to many problems for the affected person: teachers may not understand why a child is having trouble in school, potential employers may think that the FAS person is unintelligent, and peers may tease them.

The devastating problems FAS poses for a baby are astronomical. Jodee Fulp is an author on FAS, a lobbyist for FAS, and a teacher of children with FAS. On her website in an article titled, "Prenatal Exposure," a description of newborns states babies born with FAS are usually underweight and small in stature (1). These children are at a disadvantage right from the start. The article continues to state that some of these babies are "failure to thrive" babies because they are not able to suck, due to facial deformities, so they lose weight after they are born (2). If babies have trouble eating, this may cause them to become fussy, and they may have trouble sleeping because they will need to eat more often and expend more energy trying to eat than a "normal" baby. This is just the beginning of life with FAS. This stage is hard, imagine what it would be like with a toddler in the "terrible twos."

Toddlers born with FAS are slow to learn. According to Amy Nevitt, these mental defects include having a hard time learning to put words together due to brain damage, difficulty walking due to balance problems, and problems being toilet trained because they cannot comprehend the feeling when they have to use the bathroom (21). Trying to potty train children that do not understand what they need to do can be a very difficult task. Nevitt also tells us why this is such a difficult task; it is hard enough trying to teach a toddler how and when to use the bathroom, adding FAS to the mix usually means they are not potty trained until they are four or five years old (21). As a parent, just answering all the questions posed by a two-year-old is trying enough; if that child has trouble communicating, it would be frustrating for both parent and child. Even at two years old, kids can be cruel. My two-year-old already gives his cousin, who is three, a hard time because he wears diapers, "Just like a baby." Children that are preschool age are starting to notice that they are different from other children. Most of these differences will be subtle, however, wearing diapers and not being able to communicate well, will stand out to other children. These physical and intellectual problems can lead to social problems as the children grow.

The devastating problems for school-age children with FAS grow with the child. According to the book, Fantastic Antone Succeeds!, a person afflicted with FAS has an average IQ of 65; a normal person has an IQ of 100 (Kleinfeld and Westcott 8). Children with FAS have a hard time learning. These devastating learning disabilities become clearer when a child starts school. Learning disabilities include trouble reasoning, trouble with short-term memory, trouble with words and numbers (25). Numbers and language are the hardest subjects for children with FAS. As a child progresses through school, the math and English classes may become too difficult for them and they are placed in special education classes. Instead of algebra in school, they may be in a special math class that teaches how to count money and make change.

Many children with FAS get hurt because they are not afraid of anything; they have no fear. FAS children are overly friendly even with strangers. They do not harbor the same fear of strangers that most children do. Many children with FAS will do anything that they know other children are afraid of doing to gain their acceptance like jumping from a dangerous height. Children with FAS also do not realize the consequences of their actions; they do not realize when they are doing something "bad." For example, spilling their milk accidentally, and then when others laugh do it on purpose for the attention. Continuing getting in trouble and being frustrated with school gets these children labeled as difficult. Many children with FAS also suffer from attention deficit disorder (ADD). ADD children have a hard time sitting still, paying attention in class and tend to act out their frustration. Once the label of "difficult" is made, it usually follows them throughout their school years. Being teased and being different are enough to handle, but add in the learning disabilities and this becomes devastating.

The teasing and school problems can lead to low self-esteem for FAS teenagers. There is a need for activities that restore self-esteem, otherwise these teen could have some serious problems. In a personal interview with Roxanne Brandenburg a foster mother, with two adopted children with FAS, she informed me about some of the problems her fifteen-year-old faces. Because he has trouble with language and numbers, he fell farther behind than his peers, and because he is smaller in size, his peers tease him. To help with his self-esteem, she enrolled him in karate class when he was about seven. The self-esteem that karate restored is a lifesaver. He knows it doesn't matter that he is small; he can take care of himself. Roxanne hopes he will be able to carry this into adulthood. Teenagers with FAS may not have the physical developments that other teens have and this may lead to more teasing. The naivete of these teens may lead them to become sexually active since they may believe that sex means they are loved. With low self-esteem that may be present and the additional teasing a teen with FAS may get depress and turn to drugs and alcohol. This can lead to trouble with law enforcement that follows them into adulthood.

Problems for adults are no less severe. Amy Nevitt states that some adults have trouble with money and numbers. This makes it difficult for an adult with FAS to hold a job, go shopping, and pay bills because the concept of money is difficult. Nevitt explains that because they "have difficulty with the concept of time, so scheduling and planning can be challenging" (40). Without the ability to hold a job, many of these adults live in group homes where supervision is available 24 hours a day, 7 days a week. Every day is a routine and they learn what is expected of them.

According to Sandy Imhoff at the Manitowoc County Social Services, the danger with some adults with FAS is that they have trouble distinguishing reality from fantasy. They cannot tell that what they see on Television is only a movie, and they may think of it as real. This poses a danger not only to themselves, but also to the public in general. Many adults with FAS end up getting in trouble with the law because, they do not realize, for example that shoplifting is a crime. Sometimes the crimes go further than shoplifting and that person ends up in prison. This is only a part of the cost of fetal alcohol syndrome.

The cost to society is an astronomical five million dollars throughout the lifetime for one baby born with FAS; 30 babies a day, approximately 10,000 babies a year; all this for a disease that is preventable. This is an enormous cost to society overall. In an article, "Whose Baby is This?" by Teresa Kellerman. The cost breakdown for one person with FAS is as follows:

Medical costs	$1,496,000
Psychiatric care	530,000
Foster care costs	354,000
Orthodontia	12,000
Respite care	6,000
Special education	240,000
Supported employment	624,000
SSI	360,000
Residential placement	1,376,000
TOTAL	$4,998,000

That is approximately $5,000,000 per person with FAS; remember there are about 30 babies with FAS born every day. Even if an FAS baby is adopted, the adoptive parents receive a medical card for the child, and taxpayers pay for their medications, doctor visits, and therapy. The costs do not stop there. Social Services are involved in a high percentage of cases, especially if the child lives with the biological mother and she is an alcoholic. Based on an interview with Kim Jacquart, a social worker with Manitowoc County, most children with FAS are put up for adoption; only about one fourth of the children live with their biological mothers. There is a tremendous cost to society because social workers must be involved, medications are needed, doctor appointments, and therapy; we pay for all of this with our tax dollars.

Fred Boland of the Correctional Service of Canada states that many people with FAS become involved with law enforcement at an early age and usually end up incarcerated. Many often resort to committing the same crime over again because they do not realize they did anything wrong. Since these adults are vulnerable, there is a need for special placement within the prison system. So, not only is the taxpayer paying for the incarceration, but the added burden of special incarceration. This is an added cost of $5,000,000.

With such a tremendous cost for a disease that is preventable, we need to do something now. Dr. Julie Newcomer, an OB/GYN at Froedert Medical Hospital, informed me in an interview that there is no safe amount of alcohol for a pregnant woman to drink. However, Dr. Rodney Halvorsen, an OB/GYN at Woodland Clinic, told me that a glass of wine with dinner occasionally is acceptable; however, binge drinking is the most dangerous form of intoxication for a fetus. According to both doctors, pregnant women rarely inform their doctors that they are drinking. If the woman is married, usually the husband or mother-in-law informs the doctor that the woman is drinking. If expectant mothers are confronted with this problem, it is more than likely that they will deny it. There is more than one way to intervene and all are tried before informing the authorities. Both doctors agree that if the woman is married, the husband is asked to take part in the intervention and try to talk his wife into some sort of treatment. If the woman is not married, a family member, usually her mother, is asked by the obstetrician to intervene. If there are no family members, a friend would be the next step. After all of these steps have been followed and the woman still refused to obtain treatment, both doctors said they would call Social Services. Once Social Services become involved, these women may not have the chance to voluntarily seek the help they need.

Once Social Services gets involved most women are informed that, in Wisconsin, there is a law called the "Cocaine Baby Law" that can be applied to them by Social Services. This law allows the state to place the woman into treatment against her will, or to arrest her and put her in jail until the baby is born. Usually the threat of becoming involved with law enforcement is enough to make the woman go into a treatment program. According to Sandy Imhoff, this law has been put to use in Wisconsin six times; it has only been successful twice. Imhoff explains why it so hard to invoke this law. She says, "the law lacks teeth," meaning that it is difficult to prove what the state requires to force a woman into treatment. The state has to prove that the woman is pregnant, drinking to excess, and knows and understands that this can be harmful to the fetus. However, the legislature is looking at the facts; FAS is a growing disease and the cost of this disease are not declining. There has been recent discussions on changing the law slightly so it is easier for law enforcement to intervene. In 12 states there are laws that remove the newborn from the mother immediately when they test positive for alcohol or drugs. These states are Florida, Illinois, Indiana, Maryland, Minnesota, Nevada, Rhode Island, South Carolina, South Dakota, Texas, Virginia, and Wisconsin. While Minnesota has the most stringent laws out of these 12, Wisconsin is not far behind. However, once the baby is born, the damage has already been done (Laws Pertaining to Pregnant Women Who Use Drugs).

Life is not easy for any of us, but for a person with FAS life is more complicated. From the struggling babies to the adult living in a structured environment, the devastation that FAS places on people afflicted with this disease is evident and lasts a lifetime. There is no cure for FAS. The costs for this disease are not going to diminish. The need for immediate intervention when a pregnant woman is drinking is evident. By involving a husband, mother, or friend in the intervention may help curb the need for the authorities to step in. However, involving the authorities early could force the woman into a treatment program that could change her life forever for the better. Alcoholics are no fun to have as parents; ask anyone who grew up with an alcoholic mother or father. The intervention taken early in a pregnancy could affect the way a child is raised. FAS is a horrific disease; the most disturbing fact about the disease is that it is one hundred percent preventable.

WORKS CITED

Boland, Fred J. "Fetal Alcohol Syndrome: Implication for Correctional Service." 1998. *Correctional Service of Canada.* 19 Apr. 2002 <http://www.csc-scc.gc.ca/text/rsrch/reports/r71/r71e.shtml>.

Brandenburg, Roxanne. Personal interview. 1 Apr. 2002.

Halvorsen, Rodney. Personal interview. 20 Apr. 2002.

Imhoff, Sandy. Personal interview. 19 Apr. 2002.

Jacquart, Kim. Personal interview. 18 Apr. 2002.

Kellerman, Teresa. "Whose Baby Is This?" 1999. FAS Community Resource Center. 1 May 2002 <http://www.come-over.to/FAS/WhoseBabyisThis.htm>.

_____. *On Any Given Day in the United States.* 1999–2002. FAS Community Resource Center. 6 May 2002 <http://www.come-over.to/FAS/USbirths.htm>.

Kleinfeld, Judith, and Siobhan Wescott, eds. *Fantastic Antone Succeeds!* U of AK P, 1993.

Kulp, Jodee. "Prenatal Exposure." *Better Endings, New Beginnings.* 7 Feb. 2002 <http://www.betterendings.org/FosterCare/MFIFAE.htm>.

_____. "Breaking Down Brick Walls for FAS." *Better Endings, New Beginnings.* 3 Apr. 2002. <http://www.betterendings.org/FASE/facts/FASdama.htm>.

"Laws Pertaining to Pregnant Women Who Use Drugs." *State Responses to Substance Abuse Among Pregnant Women.* 6 May 2002 <http://www.agi-usa.org/tables/gr030603t.html>.

Neberzny, Anastasia, and Alma M. Saddam, "Human Nutrition and Food Management." HYG-5534–93. *Ohio State University Extension Fact Sheet.* Ohio State U, Columbus, Ohio. 1 May 2002 <http://ohioline.osu.edu/hyg-fact/5000/5534.html>.

Nevitt, Amy. *Fetal Alcohol Syndrome.* New York: Rosen, 1996.

Newcomer, Julie. Personal interview. 18 Mar. 2002.

EXPLORATION

Creating a Research Assignment

Design a research paper or report assignment you could use for your future classroom within the context of a larger unit. Describe what the teaching unit would be based on. You might choose a topic or a theme—something you are interested in yourself. Designate the grade level the unit is for.

1. How would you spark interest in the topic for your students?
2. Describe a few discovery activities you could use to help students become involved and begin thinking about what they want to explore.
3. What main topic would you choose for their research or report or how would you help students choose their own topic?

To help yourself understand the research/information process discussed in this chapter, go through the process yourself. Pick a topic that you might assign to students. Then do a free-write listing what you already know about this topic.

After reading over and organizing your prior knowledge, write several questions that would direct further inquiry. Share this with class members and revise.

List several resources that would help you locate answers to your questions. Make the list as varied as possible.

List keywords that would help you perform an Internet search, and follow up with an actual search, noting the appropriate sites.

At the conclusion of this activity, you will have the foundation for a project that you can use in student teaching or as a first-year teacher.

REFERENCES

Fulwiler, Toby. *Teaching with Writing*. Upper Montclair: Boynton/Cook, 1987.

Goldsborough, Reid. "Teaching Healthy Skepticism About Information on the Internet." *Technology & Learning* (Jan. 1998): 32–35.

Hirsch, Timothy J. "Student Research for Personal Decision Making." *Wisconsin English Journal* 30.2 (1988): 9–14.

Johannessen, Larry R. "Teaching Thinking and Writing for a New Century." *English Journal* (July 2001): 38–45.

Kearns, Nancy J. "I-Search, I-Find, I-Know: A Summary of Macrorie's Alternative to the Traditional Research Paper." *Indiana English* (Winter 1995): 47–50.

Lim, Janine. "Effective Internet Research." *The Clearing House* (Sept./Oct. 2001): 35–36.

Macrorie, Ken. *The I-Search Paper*. Portsmouth: Boynton/Cook, 1988.

Maxwell, Rhoda J. *Writing Across the Curriculum in Middle and High Schools*. Boston: Allyn & Bacon, 1996.

_____. *Writing Our Lives*. Boston: Allyn & Bacon, 1999.

Mosley, Wendy, Betsy Damon, & Carla Burmeister "Research Project: Paper/Debate." Unpublished paper from *Research and Writing*, Cray Institute, July 1999.

Perrin, Robert. "Myths About Research." *English Journal* (Nov. 1987): 50–53.

Washington, Valerie M. "Report Writing: A Practical Application of Semantic Mapping." *Teacher Educator* 24.1 (Summer 1988): 24–30.

Selecting Literature

Every time we select a piece of literature to read, we are exposing
ourselves to a vision: a vision of people and places and things;
a vision of relationships and feelings and strivings.

G. Robert Carlsen (201)

 ## OBJECTIVES FOR TEACHING LITERATURE

Deciding what literature we should teach seems relatively easy at first glance. School
districts may have decided who reads what when, state and national standards also
guide literature choices, and new teachers have their literature notes from college.
However, a closer look at why we teach literature and what we want to achieve in
teaching reveals that literature choices can be difficult.

In general, we want students to read, to think about what they read, and to enjoy
the experience. More specifically, a list of objectives could include the following:

1. Develop an enjoyment of reading so that lifelong reading is realistic.
2. Understand the past by becoming more knowledgeable about not only
   what people did, but also how they felt.
3. Understand one's own experiences and how they may or may not fit with
   those of others.
4. Know and appreciate a wider view of life, both different cultures and
   different circumstances.
5. Learn how to make critical judgments about literature and to understand
   literary devices.

Only by using a variety of literature can we achieve these goals. One of our purposes in teaching literature is to help students read well and to enjoy reading; because students have different personalities, experiences, and abilities, we must provide as wide a range of literature as possible.

Many new teachers teach the literature they recently studied in college classes because they are most comfortable with it and know the most about it. Some of these selections may be suitable for high school seniors, but the way the literature was taught is never appropriate. The gap in linguistic and cognitive maturity between high school seniors and upper division college students prohibits use of the same teaching material and approaches. The wealth of literature from which to choose leaves no excuse for us not choosing selections appropriate for high school and middle school students.

The literature we select for students to read has both social and political implications and far-reaching consequences. We may think it is not difficult to decide what to ask our students to read, but a serious problem is what we do *not* ask them to read. For years multicultural literature has been ignored in the schools, and only recently have women authors been included in anthologies. In collections of American poetry, it is not uncommon for Emily Dickinson to be the only woman represented. By omission, teachers create the impression that great works are written only by white males. Northrop Frye calls literature an organization of human experience. The question is, whose experience? Because we can't teach everything, we make selections, and those selections determine if we are providing opportunities for students to become truly literate.

Being literate means having the ability to use knowledge to better understand the world and ourselves; it is not decoding words. Frank Smith, who has written many books and articles on language and learning, in "Overselling Literacy" describes what literacy is and is not and examines how our understanding of literacy affects how we teach literature. His main point is that the press makes too much of illiteracy and assumes too much for literacy. He writes that literacy "doesn't generate finer feelings or higher values. It doesn't even make anyone smarter." He further explains, "people who can't read and write think just as well out of school as people who can read and write, especially if they are members of a culture in which strong oral language traditions have prevailed" (354). The important point here for teaching is that literacy is not just a set of skills but an "attitude toward the world." "Individuals become literate not from formal instruction they receive, but from what they read and write about and who they read and write with" (355).

When students see their teachers read with pleasure, this goes far to convince students that they, too, can enjoy reading. Trying to talk students into believing that they will enjoy a piece of literature is usually not successful. Smith suggests the following:

> They [teachers] can promote interest by demonstrating their own interests. Nothing attracts young people more than activities, abilities, or secrets that absorb adults; they want to know the things that we find worthwhile. Demonstrating the imaginative possibilities of literacy and collaborating with students should be a classroom delight for teachers and students alike. (358)

Smith's statement emphasizes the responsibility teachers have to select literature that interests the diverse group of students we find in our classrooms. Being literate does not mean that students have read a particular list of titles, but rather that interest and understanding were generated when students read literature they could relate to.

 *Reflection*

What literature did you study in middle and high school? What were your favorites? What books did you read on your own? What literature selections in today's middle and high school are students reading? Visit a local school and check out the paperbacks the students are reading. If you have the opportunity, ask them what they like to read. Discuss your findings in class.

On what basis do we select literature? A strong influence is the society we live in. Northrop Frye writes that every society produces a social mythology or ideology, and he describes the two aspects of this mythology. One is a body of beliefs deeply held by a society. For Americans, these beliefs include self-reliance, independence, democratic process, and tolerance. All are important values for creating the kind of society we want to live in. The second is an adjustment mythology by which our ideology is learned by the society's citizens. One function of education is to teach this adjustment mythology, and we do so, Frye explains, by keeping alive a nostalgic version of the American past, relying heavily on Washington's honesty, Lincoln's concern, and stories about pioneers, hunters, and cowboys (16). Such a design is not intrinsically wrong; we value certain ideals and we want future generations to value them as well.

When the adjustment myth becomes perverted, however, some groups of people in society become subordinated. For example, in Victorian times women were thought to be exceedingly delicate—a perverted myth. Protecting women was taught as a social value. As a result, women were actually deprived of equal participation in society (Frye 22). For a variety of reasons, some more vicious than others, minority groups have remained outside the mainstream of the adjustment myth education. When bravery is studied in the classroom, for example, the literature chosen is still, too often, a story of whites fighting Native Americans or men defending helpless women. There are exceptions, of course, but the multitude of literature selections available leaves no excuse for promoting such stereotypes. Becoming aware of this situation and realizing that the literature we choose can help students develop an imaginative social vision make our society a better place to live—for everyone.

 ## CANONICAL LITERATURE

In the late 1980s a movement called cultural literacy gained popularity when Secretary of Education William Bennett argued that students need to read particular authors and works that represent great Western literature. The movement affected the public's opinion about what students should know. Cultural literacy gained momentum when E. D. Hirsch Jr. wrote *Cultural Literacy*, in which he listed the titles of texts he thought all students should read. A major difficulty with Hirsch's list is that he sponsors only the cultural literacy of rich and educated white Anglo-Saxon Protestants of the 19th and 20th centuries. At a time when our country's population is nearly 40 percent minorities, Hirsch's cultural literacy is too narrow in scope and limited in perspective to adequately meet the needs of teachers and students.

A second difficulty with Hirsch's concept of cultural literacy is its simplistic view of learning. Peter Elbow in *What Is English?* describes Hirsch's list as ideal for learning chunks of information that have right or wrong answers, but leaves no room for interpretative imagination or the ability to create meaning from reading texts (163). Hirsch has a specific plan to encourage the teaching of his list—a test of general knowledge for twelfth grade. He is planning to write tests for third, sixth, and ninth grades. For Hirsch, then, knowledge is a set of memorizable facts.

However, as Chris Anson explains in an article in *English Journal,* knowing about something is not the same as integrating content into prior knowledge, perceptions, and beliefs, or even more important, knowing how to know (17). We want to provide learning situations that encourage students to explore many varieties of discourse. This is a very different kind of learning from what Hirsch proposes. The best argument against an approach such as Hirsch's is a well-thought-out philosophy of one's own. We teachers need to take literature selection into our own hands by first establishing goals and then choosing literature that facilitates those goals. If we don't, we run the risk of someone else deciding for us.

EXPLORATION

Choosing Literature for Your Future Students

Individually make a list of what you believe is important in literature study for middle school and high school students. What selections do you think are important for them to read? What do you want them to learn? Remember, your future students will have different interests and abilities than you do. In small groups, discuss what you wrote. Develop your own philosophy for teaching literature.

Balancing Literature Selections

Current literature anthologies include more selections by women and minorities than they did 10 years ago, but many still contain writings by a disproportionate number of white, male, and middle-class authors. For example, in a twelfth-grade British literature text published recently, only 15 women authors are featured among a total of 102. Our literature curriculum should reflect the multicultural nature of our society. We need a variety of forms and perspectives. If the anthology does not provide such a spectrum, then we must supplement it with paperback books and copies of stories and poems that give students reading experiences that reflect the lives of all of us.

Making Choices

Because we come to know the abilities and interests of our students, as well as the units of study in which particular themes are appropriate, we should control the literature program for our schools. We want to choose "good" books for our students to read, but what criteria do we use? In *Experiencing Children's Literature,* Alan Purves and Dianne Monson suggest that teachers use three questions to judge the quality of a book:

1. Did the book arouse my emotions? (Are the emotions trite or realistic? Is the story interesting?)
2. Is the book well written? (Are characters believable and is the language appropriate to the theme?)
3. Is the book meaningful? (Is the audience respected? Is the theme treated seriously?)

In addition, the book should appeal to both students and the teacher. As teachers we are responsible for suggesting and selecting good and divergent literature for our students, literature that reflects their interests and reading levels.

ORGANIZING LITERATURE STUDY

We do not believe that particular types of literature should be taught at specific grade levels. Rather, we should select literature based on what we believe are important considerations for a unit or theme designed specifically for our classes. In many curricula, tall tales are designated for only one grade level, and fables for another. Instead of attaching a grade level to a kind of literature, we need to consider the developmental level of our students and what literature best meets our purpose. For instance, we find that it is appropriate to use Dr. Seuss books and Shel Silverstein's poetry at the senior high level when discussing how authors can integrate morals into literature or to understand the creativity of language play. Tall tales, myths, and legends can be used at any grade level because readers bring different levels of sophistication to their responses.

Literature study is often organized by genre. Our university, for example, offers courses in the short story, drama, novels, and poetry. Or the literature is organized by historical periods and geographical locations, such as British literature before the 18th century or American literature after World War II. We strongly believe that if we want to interest secondary students in literature we should not use these divisions. Students have little interest in literary periods, and this approach relies heavily on "teacher" knowledge. Literature tied to a unit in social studies or history is certainly appropriate; however, historical facts become more "real" to students when they understand them through the feelings and thoughts of people who lived at that time. But teaching John Dryden because he wrote before Oliver Goldsmith and after John Donne does not turn students on to reading. Providing literature by genre is just as troublesome. Rarely in the real world do we read only poetry for several weeks. The same is true for any genre. We mix forms, styles, and periods, and we believe the same should be true in our classrooms.

Jodi Resch, an English education student, illustrates the richness possible when a unit includes several genres. She wrote a unit on Mexican culture intended for twelfth-grade students.

INSTRUCTIONAL UNIT

MEXICAN CULTURE

Week One

The unit begins with a short story, "Un Drama de Familia" by Heriberto Frias. The theme is that although the family has no money, they still have each other—the most important thing in the world to them. The students write responses as they read (Level 1 writing) and also jot down any vocabulary words they have difficulty with. Students meet in small discussion groups to exchange views on the story, then write an in-class essay on the choice Antonia made and her reasons behind it. During the week students read two poems: "The Men of Dawn" by Efrain Hueta and "Humbly" by Ramon Lopez Velarde. Both poems are about labor on a ranch. Students write their own poem on a cultural aspect of Mexico (Level 2 writing).

Week Two

Resch shows the students slides and crafts from her travels to Mexico. They discuss the environment, people, and activities shown on the slides. Students follow up with a one-page paper of a description of a Mexican setting (Level 2 writing). Next students read a poem by Jaime Sabines, "la Casa del Dia." Students write a response to the poem (Level 1). She assigns the story "Rosamunda" by Carmen Laforet, followed by nonfiction material from Mexico: *Civilizaciones y Culturas* by Luis Leal. After discussion of the readings, students write a short paper comparing an aspect of Mexican culture with an aspect of U.S. culture (Level 2).

Week Three

Students read two poems: "Don't Talk to Him about Love" by Amado Nervo and "The Southern Cross" by Jose Juan Tablada. They compare these poems with "Rosamunda." Resch shows a video she made in Mexico that is a collection of interviews she conducted with people from many classes and lifestyles.

Week Four

Students write a Level 3 research-type paper on a cultural aspect or issue in modern-day Mexico.

By including short stories, poetry, nonfiction, slides, a video, and firsthand experience, Resch provides her students with an interesting and compelling view of Mexico.

ORGANIZING AROUND A THEME

Organizing around a theme has many advantages. First, several types of literature can be included, providing for a variety of reading levels and interests. Second, the choice of themes can include current issues, developmental stages, and selections from an anthology. In choosing a theme, we can keep our students' interests and ages in mind and also rely on our own enthusiasm for a topic, as Resch did. Your special interest in travel or sports can be the foundation for a successful unit.

The first unit you as a new teacher design is time-consuming and may be somewhat overwhelming, but once unit planning is under way, it becomes easier. A large file for each unit enables you to add material as you find it. For instance, when teaching a unit on heroes to middle school students, you might want to convey the idea that many ordinary people are heroes, and therefore collect newspaper articles that describe heroic deeds over a period of several weeks before teaching the unit. Then, during the unit, you may add several current nonfiction selections. After the unit is finished, you can continue to add new material and suggestions, so that the development of units is continual.

Thematic units work well in classrooms for both middle and high school for several reasons:

1. *They promote student interest.* Students are more likely to be interested in learning about "what is a hero" or "high adventure" than reading a single book title, even though that title may be included in the unit. Reading one book after another with no connection among them makes it difficult to compare books or develop serious discussions on, for example, relationships with parents. By using a variety of sources, students better understand the complexities of issues. Because units contain a variety of material, students are more likely to bring in suggestions and reading material for the class; in other words, they become more involved in their own learning.

2. *Thematic units integrate genre.* Choosing a variety of poems, stories, novels, plays, and nonfiction related by themes introduces forms of literature to students in a natural way. Students are not required to read a poem because it is the week to study poetry, but because the poem provides insights or other ways of looking at the theme. For example, in designing a unit titled "Who Am I?" eighth-grade teacher Liz Rehrauer included the following literature: a novel, *The Light in the Forest* by Conrad Richter; the short stories "The Moustache" and "Guess What? I Almost Kissed My Father," both by Robert Cormier, and "Raymond's Run" by Toni Cade Bambera; and several poems—"Me, Myself, and I" by Eve Merriam, "The Ballad of Johnny" by May Sarton, "Sometimes" by Eve Merriam, "Speak to Me" by Calvin O'John, "Celebration" by Alonzo Lopez, "The Question" by Karla Kuskin, "Self-Pity" by D. H. Lawrence, and "Will I Remember?" by Richard J. Margolis.

Including many forms of reading materials broadens students' concept of "school learning." For example, a comic book may provide an excellent model of one type of hero to begin a discussion on the attributes of heroism. This could be the basis for comparing heroic character traits in other forms of literature. Students then can develop their own definition of heroism.

3. *They provide for different reading levels.* Some thematic units are more appropriate for one level than another. The "Who Am I?" unit mentioned above is an excellent choice for middle school, whereas a unit on war might be more appropriate for high school. Many themes can be used at any level, but the literature selections should always reflect the level of the students. The following list provides a few suggestions for topics that might be used in grades 6 through 12:

- What is it like to grow old?
- Fantasy
- Choices
- The American West
- Friendship
- Values
- Love

Because students read a variety of literature in thematic units, the whole class does not have to read the same material, or they may read the same material but not at the same time. If the unit includes three or four novels, you may devote a class period to introducing all the novels by explaining a little about each. All the novels are related by theme, but the reading levels are different. For example, a unit on family relations might include *Home Before Dark* by Sue Ellen Bridgers, *Ordinary People* by Judith Guess, and *Tell Me a Riddle* by Tillie Olsen, listed in order of difficulty. Students are free to read all three novels and many do, especially the better readers, but they are required to read only the one assigned to them. You need to tell students during the time the books are introduced that they can read as many as they want but don't mention reading level. It is very important to avoid any stigma attached to who reads which book first.

General class discussions based on issues related to the theme involve all students. Students also meet in small groups to discuss their assigned book. Group projects might be based on just one of the novels, or two, or all three. Group members will not have to read all the novels because each one can make contributions based on one book. In this way, students of varying abilities can work together.

EXPLORATION

Beginning to Plan a Unit

Make a list of topics you are especially interested in that could be the basis for a unit, perhaps countries and cultures similar to Resch's unit or a hobby or interest you can share with your future students. Share your list in small groups and brainstorm literature selections appropriate to various themes.

READING LEVELS

The literature we select for students depends on many factors. The most obvious, of course, is the grade we teach, but we must also consider our students' age, interests, and developmental stage, as well as our own interests.

Reading levels are rarely considered in secondary schools. Students are handed *Hamlet;* if they can't read the text, they watch the film. We believe this practice is grossly unfair to students who have trouble reading difficult material. If we do not give them material they can read, their reading ability does not improve. Secondary school teachers must be as concerned with reading levels as elementary school teachers.

Reading levels vary greatly across a grade level. A rule of thumb in determining the span of reading levels in an "average" class is to divide the grade number in half, subtract that number to establish the low end and add that number to predict the high level. For instance, in teaching sixth grade one can expect reading levels to range from third grade to ninth grade. The higher the grade, the greater the differences; twelfth-grade levels range from sixth grade to well beyond a college education. We often think of reading problems as a concern of elementary grade teachers only, but they are also a major cause of problems in school for older students. We also must be concerned, and make our classrooms a place where more students can succeed. One way to achieve this is to choose literature that is interesting but at a lower reading level. Young adult literature is a good choice.

 ## YOUNG ADULT LITERATURE

Young adult literature deserves a solid berth in the literature programs of secondary schools. A growing number of talented authors are writing for adolescents. Writers such as Maya Angelou, Chris Crutcher, M. E. Kerr, Sue Ellen Bridgers, Cynthia Voigt, Ursula Le Guin, Robert Lipsyte, Emily Cheney Neville, Katherine Paterson, Gary Paulsen, Sandra Scoppettone, Ouida Sebestyen, and Brenda Wilkinson, to name just a few, hold their own with respected authors of adult fiction. As with literature for adult audiences, some pieces are trite or poorly written, but others receive critical acclaim. Intricate plot structure, multifaceted characterizations, interesting and various settings, symbolic interpretations, and artistry of language can all be found in young adult literature. Writing for a teenage audience is a serious undertaking for many fine writers. The results are important contributions to the study of literature in the secondary schools.

Young adult literature didn't come into its own as a genre until the 1950s. Since that time, novels for adolescents have become increasingly realistic. Young adult books cover a variety of topics: murder, theft, child abuse, mental illness, fatal illness, abortion, pregnancy, self-esteem, relationships, and responsibility. The protagonists are always teenagers and the stories are told from their point of view. Although the themes are as varied and universal as those in adult fiction, the stories are about the adolescent experience; it is this characteristic that defines the genre rather than a particular plot.

The study of young adult literature enhances students' understanding and appreciation of more difficult works. By including young adult literature, we can assure greater success in meeting the goals of teaching literature: to gain an understanding of themselves and others, to learn of a wider worldview, and to become lifelong readers. Specifically, we believe teaching young adult literature will achieve the following outcomes:

1. *Students learn to make critical judgments about what they read.* It is difficult for students to critically analyze the more sophisticated works, yet the skill of analyzing literature—that is, critically thinking about what they read—is important. By using young adult literature, students can more easily understand the motivation behind characters' actions. Students not only can discuss how fictional teenagers react to a situation, but they also can sense the validity of the author's perception. These books speak to experiences they know something about. As students consider cause and effect—that is, the relation between plot and characterization—they gain understanding beyond the work itself. Once students gain skill in analyzing fiction, they are better able to look critically at more difficult works.

2. *Students learn to support and explain their critical judgments.* The simpler vocabulary and sentence structure in most young adult literature allows students to understand the text better. Students often have trouble making appropriate judgments about what they read and explaining their opinions. Using literature with easier vocabulary and style helps students get beyond surface elements. Archaic language often has a beauty of its own, but it can interfere with comprehension. Because young adult literature uses simpler vocabulary, it is an excellent tool for teaching the difficult skills of documenting judgments because the language does not interfere.

3. *Students will gain an understanding of themselves and others.* Adolescence is a time when young people critically examine their own beliefs and values. As they grow away from dependence on their family, they are often confused by anxieties and uncertainties. The teenage fictional characters in young adult literature mirror the readers' experiences and provide helpful insights. The characters are realistically portrayed so readers relate to their concerns of physical appearance, family relationships, and sexual experiences. Teenagers feel reassured to discover through young adult literature that others have the same concerns they do, and in the process of understanding the fictional characters, they gain a better understanding of themselves. Maturity is enhanced as they learn more about themselves and others.

4. *Students learn about a wider view of life.* Young adult literature covers every historical period and country in the world. Because the teenager's point of view is central to the novels, the reader is likely to respond personally and reach a better understanding of historical concepts and different cultures. The vicarious experiences broaden students' views. Young adult literature celebrates the uniqueness of individuals. The central character must often overcome obstacles and prejudices. Accepting one's own disability or relating to people with

disabilities is a popular theme. Because ignorance fosters prejudice, the more knowledgeable students become, the more they will accept and understand individual differences.

5. *Students' enjoyment of reading will increase.* Because the protagonist is a teenager and the plot involves problems teenagers encounter, young adult literature provides high-interest reading. Every literature curriculum contains the objective of helping students to enjoy reading. Motivation occurs naturally when teenagers can read about situations they are knowledgeable about and interested in. Young adult literature does much to establish the habit of reading for pleasure.

EXPLORATION

Selecting Young Adult Literature

Read a young adult novel published since 1990. What themes are present in the novel? What grade level would enjoy the book? Choose a theme, either one present in the book you read or one you have a particular interest in and find another young adult book with this theme.

WORLD LITERATURE

Awareness of other cultures becomes increasingly important as the world shrinks via television and the Internet. Yet most secondary students know very little about cultures other than their own. We need to become aware of literature that helps students develop a wider worldview. Prejudice and fear come from ignorance; literature can do much to increase awareness of other people—their hopes, their fears, their dreams. Studying world literature helps students see not only the differences among cultures, but also the similarities. And by learning about other people, we learn about ourselves and the part our culture plays in shaping an individual's life.

Including world literature in English language arts classes generally means selecting literature from Third World countries. Students and teachers often know little about this body of literature, which is why we should include it. Teachers and students learning together create a dynamic class. Contemporary Third World authors are concerned with the tension between traditional values and ways of life and the changes the new life brings to their country; their themes often involve struggles between the old and the new. Young adults understand such struggles and find they have more in common with Third World people than they may have thought. Also, much of the literature is reminiscent of early American concerns as these countries work to develop strong, independent governments.

In the introduction of *Guide to World Literature,* editors Warren Carrier and Kenneth Oliver make the case for including world literature in English language arts classes:

> As we move into multinational economic, ecological, and cultural enterprises and interdependencies, it becomes increasingly important for students to recognize national similarities and differences, but above all to recognize our common bond, our common lot. A study of world literature contributes much to an appreciation and understanding of the heritage we share. (3)

Teaching world literature brings a special set of concerns. We rely on the same practices as we do in teaching any literature: encouraging responses, valuing students' opinions, helping students to think beyond the obvious. But how do we select the literature and organize it for teaching?

Thematic Approach

Carrier and Oliver believe the thematic approach is the best way to teach world literature. The thematic approach works for all literature and is especially important when reading about other cultures. When studying one country's literature apart from other cultures, we might emphasize differences between them. Although great differences may exist, we want students to realize they have more in common than may be apparent. Carrier and Oliver suggest themes of love, injustice, conflict, separation, and war, among others (3). They give as an example the theme of time. In *The Great Gatsby* by F. Scott Fitzgerald, Gatsby tries to recapture time. In a Japanese novel, *The Sound of the Mountain* by Yasunari Kawabata, the hero is very aware of the passing of time. The transience of time is also a theme in *My Mother's House* by Colette (French), *The Tale of Genji* by Murasaki (Japanese), and *Lucy Gayheart* by Willa Cather (American) (4). Selections can come from a variety of countries and be grouped around a common theme.

Studying One Culture

You may want to focus a unit on one particular culture if the area of study is largely unknown to students. An intense study of the literature is an excellent way to acquaint them with that culture. Alan Olds, a high school teacher in Colorado, explains in a recent article that he taught Chinese literature to his students to help them understand China's rich heritage. To understand our own culture, we need to understand ideas and traditions from other voices (21).

> I constantly remind my students (and myself) that we are visitors, not tourists, when we read literature from other cultures. We try to prepare for our visit, so that we do not stumble about in an unfamiliar setting. We are not reading these writers to check them off our list of books, the way a tourist checks off destinations without really tarrying to see beyond the surface attractions and rushes on to see the next stop. Instead, we intend to arrive informed and sensitive to a new culture, open to its wonders. We want to stay long enough to see beyond the clichés. If we are lucky, our visit will broaden our sense of what it means to be human. (21)

Olds wants his students to be able to read Chinese literature with an Eastern view-point. The article contains a rich variety of sources and a description of how he teaches the unit.

In writing about teaching South African literature, Robert Mossman, a high school teacher in Arizona, warns of the danger of choosing only one representative novel from a culture.

> A study of South African literature in an American classroom, to be valid and legitimate, cannot consist of merely one work and be successful. By the very fact of the polarized nature of the apartheid system and the literary responses to it, students must encounter and examine works which represent viewpoints from different racial perspectives. Reading only one work may do a disservice because it inevitably provides only one perspective. The richness and complexity of South Africa's literature deserves better (41).

Mossman explains the problems occurring when *Cry, the Beloved Country* is the only South African literature taught in English classes. Students read and learn only one perspective, which, particularly in South Africa, creates a false impression. "If *Cry, the Beloved Country* must be taught in the curriculum, then it should be taught in conjunction with *Mine Boy* by Peter Abrahams" (42). Mossman suggests six other pairings of South African literature that offer different perspectives:

- Nadine Gordimer's *Burger's Daughter* with Andre Brink's *Dry White Season*. This pairing presents two perspectives—one female, one male—of what it means to be white in South Africa.
- Richard Rive's *Buckingham Palace, District Six* with Andre Brink's *Rumors of Rain*. This pairing contrasts two communities through vivid and detailed portraits.
- Nadine Gordimer's *July's People* with J. M. Coetzee's *Life and Times of Michael K*. The pairing deals with what life might be like after a black revolution.
- Sipho Sepamla's *Ride on the Whirlwind* and Mongne Serote's *Every Birth its Blood*. These novels deal with the intense accounts of the uprising of the late '70s.

Resources for World Literature

An excellent resource for selecting African literature is *Teaching African Literature* by Elizabeth Gunner. Her handbook contains teaching suggestions, information about the novels and authors, and an extensive annotated bibliography of books, films, and recorded sound. In the introduction, Gunner emphasizes the importance of including African literature in the curriculum. "Texts by African writers often provide an alternative view of history, or illuminate an aspect of history and individual experience previously not available to a particular pupil or group of pupils" (v). In addition to the teaching ideas for individual novels, Gunner describes thematic units that include novels, poetry, and films. For those not well acquainted with African literature for secondary students, this book is invaluable.

Another book in the same series is *A Handbook for Teaching Caribbean Literature* by David Dabydeen. The format is similar to Gunner's and provides information about the authors and literature as well as teaching ideas. Dabydeen describes 12 units, each dealing with a particular novel or a set of poems. He includes related readings and audiovisual resources.

 ## LITERATURE BY WOMEN

Gender imbalance in literature choices for student reading continues in spite of numerous articles, reports, and editorials arguing for a change. One reason for the lack of change is that we often do not challenge the lists of required reading and do not reexamine literature choices, but teach what has always been taught. A second reason is that the literature canon is perpetuated by agencies that carry a voice of authority. Patricia Lake, a high school teacher, reports that the Advanced Placement Course Description published by the Educational Testing Service includes few women authors. Lake found that, "According to the guide book, only fourteen women (versus eighty men) have written prose of sufficient merit to warrant its study" (36). ETS is a powerful influence on literature selections for advanced placement English classes. Lake asks,

> Why then is there continued propagation of such severe gender imbalance in the reading lists provided by ETS? High-school literature courses should be broadening students' perspectives, not directing them into predetermined stereotypical channels that, by their exclusionary nature, actually prevent students from reading about life in other than traditional contexts. (36)

Often lists of books taught in secondary schools are interpreted as a list of what should be taught. We need to critically examine such lists because important authors are ignored and the lists give an erroneous message to young people. Lake explains,

> If we do not work for a greater gender balance in teaching literature, we present a distorted picture of our literary heritage and the society which spawned it. We do a wonderful job of showing that indeed men did—and do—receive most of the recognition, but we also suggest that there were no women doing anything of scholarly or literary merit. (37)

Another danger for the young women in our classes is that, when they read male authors almost exclusively, they develop a male perspective of understanding the women characters. They have no choice when both the authors and the critics are male. The readings need to be balanced to give young women a better sense of the value of their own experiences. Literature by women is as rich and varied as literature by men. We owe it to our students (and ourselves) to provide a gender-balanced literature curriculum.

Reflection

Male authors in any culture are published and recognized before female authors. Why is this the case? During your middle and high school years, what works by women authors did you read? Which ones would you teach?

The National Council of Teachers of English publishes a pamphlet, "Guidelines for a Gender-Balanced Curriculum in English, Grades 7–12." It suggests how a teacher can create a gender-balanced curriculum and includes a list of literature selections. The pamphlet is free and may be copied without permission. Ask for #19654 from NCTE, Order Dept., 1111 Kenyon Road, Urbana, IL 61801.

 ## MULTICULTURAL LITERATURE

The population of the United States is shifting from a predominately white culture to one with an increasing number of people of color. Nearly one out of every three Americans is from a non-English-speaking home. The Hispanic population is the fastest growing, about 17 percent of the total population. African Americans constitute 16 percent. America remains a land of immigrants, and Mary Sasse, a high school English teacher, stresses the importance of teachers gaining an understanding of the term *ethnic*.

> With those understandings comes an acceptance of the universality of human experience, which teachers can use as a bridge between themselves and other ethnic peoples and as a recognition of the richness and diversity of American ethnic literature. (171)

She provides three criteria for selecting minority literature:

1. Selections should be by minority authors, not just about minority people; otherwise, stereotyping can be a problem.
2. Selections must represent the total dynamic nature of an ethnic group. Historical accounts should be balanced with contemporary ones. Both urban and rural experiences need to be represented.
3. Selections should represent a broad spectrum of experiences to avoid romanticizing or stereotyping. (170–171)

Teaching minority literature is vital if we are serious about reaching all of our students. Roseann Duenas Gonzalez, a teacher at the University of Arizona, explains that classrooms changed dramatically in ten years. Our students come from widely diverse backgrounds, both culturally and linguistically, and minorities "are fast becoming a significant proportion of the school-age population" (16). We are not meeting the needs of these children. If these culturally and linguistically different children do not stay in school and receive an adequate education, "our society incrementally loses the productive capability of an entire generation" (16). Gonzalez discusses the problems teachers have in teaching minority literature and presents recommendations. Minority literature should not be taught as "special," but should be discussed in terms of the same criteria as any other literature: style, honesty, and language. To fail to do so sends a message to students that this literature is inferior and will not stand up to critical analysis (19).

It is difficult to select literature with which we are unfamiliar. The following resources provide annotated bibliographies for selecting appropriate literature:

- *Booklist*, an American Library Association publication
- *Bulletin of the Center for Children's Books*
- *English Journal*, a National Council of Teachers of English publication for secondary school teachers
- *The Horn Book Magazine*
- *Interracial Books for Children Bulletin*
- *Journal of Reading*
- *Media and Methods*
- *School Library Journal*
- *Wilson Library Journal*

Searching for appropriate books does take time, but the time is well spent and the books are interesting. Not taking the time ensures that we will continue to use the same books that have been used for the last 25 years with no changes. Arthur N. Applebee, Director of the Center for the Learning and Teaching of Literature, conducted a study to determine what book-length works were most commonly taught at secondary schools. The ten most commonly taught books included few by women and minority authors, and classics dominated the lists. While we should continue to teach classics, we need to make room in the curriculum for literature that all students can identify with and appreciate.

Native American Literature

A study of Native Americans is an essential part of our American past and does much to enrich our curriculum. Because of the Native Americans' oral traditions, students learn a great deal about the nature of language; the songs and chants provide beauty and meaning, helping students to understand the importance of lyrical quality. The themes carried through Native American literature are of special interest and importance to adolescents: developing self-identity, establishing values, understanding a relationship with nature, making decisions that are often at odds with the majority.

Not long ago, Native Americans were portrayed in negative or outdated stereotypes, which may persist in many students' minds. To discover what knowledge students have of Native Americans, a teacher can ask them to write everything that comes to mind when they think of Native Americans. The results are usually shocking, from comments that are ludicrous to cruelly misinformed. The contrast between such misinformation and actual Native American beliefs and behavior is startling. Students have much to learn from Native Americans: the spiritual nature of the universe, respect for the land, importance of ritual and ceremony, oneness with nature. Using literature by Native Americans, we can dispel erroneous impressions and replace them with understanding, knowledge, and empathy.

Excellent literature written by Native Americans is not difficult to find. Particularly appropriate books for middle and high school students include *The Education of Little Tree* (nonfiction) by Forrest Carver, *Tracks* by Louise Erdrich, *The Indian Lawyer* by James Welch, all of Tony Hillerman's books, and *Night Flying Woman: An Ojibway Narrative* by Ignatia Broker. A book published in 1999, *Passage to Little Bighorn* by Terry Kretzer-Malvehy, is recommended by *Booklist*. The story goes back in time and explores Lakota beliefs.

Hispanic Literature

Hispanic literature is poorly represented in anthologies, more so than other minority literature. For example, an anthology of American literature published by a major company contained more than 1,000 entries but had no literature about the Hispanic experience in the United States. What message does this give to our Hispanic students? If a particular literature is not included in a new anthology, it must not be important. Two teachers, Patricia Ann Romero and Don Zancanella, explain why they include Hispanic literature in their program:

> We believe that outside the traditional American canon lie works by less familiar names—classics of the future, we would argue—demonstrating to our students that the American story becomes much richer when we hear it told in all its voices. For example, alongside the traditional American anthology pieces, we place the works of contemporary Hispanic writers. (25)

Suggestions for Hispanic selections include novels and poetry by Gary Soto, Sandra Cisneros's *The House on Mango Street,* and poetry by Pat Mora, Carlos Cortez, and Lorna Dee Corvantes. A book by Rudoefo Anaya, *My Land Sings: Stories from the Rio Grande,* is especially appropriate for middle school readers.

Romero and Zancanella believe it is important for students "to read literature that validates their own experience and know that authors and artists of substance and value have come from their culture" (29). If you are fortunate enough to have cultures outside the mainstream represented in your classrooms, you can enrich the learning of not only these students but also all the students by including authors from various cultures.

African American Literature

Many high school graduates are familiar with African American male writers, such as Richard Wright, Ralph Ellison, and Langston Hughes. In recent years, African American women writers have been included in college literature classes but are not likely to appear at the high school level. There are, however, many wonderful selections to choose from, such as *Their Eyes Were Watching God* by Zora Neale Hurston, which are appropriate for upper levels or AP English. The story centers on a young woman who, in spite of immense difficulties, develops a strong sense of self, an ideal topic for adolescents. In addition to a good story, the book has an incredible lyrical quality, and

Hurston's use of figurative language stays with a reader long after the book is finished. Other outstanding African American authors include Maya Angelou, Virginia Hamilton, Alice Walker, Mildred Taylor, Terry McMillan, J. California Cooper, Nikki Giovanni, and Toni Morrison. We need to include both male and female African American writers from different literary genres and sources.

Asian American Literature

The term *Asian Americans* includes Chinese, Japanese, Filipino, and Korean Americans, as well as immigrants from Laos, Cambodia, Vietnam, and Thailand. Ogle Duff and Helen Tongchinsub describe the thematic concerns of modern Asian American writers as love, personal liberty, injustice, and inner struggles. However, when Asian Americans were first published, their writing tended to be nonthreatening, nonassertive, and self-negating because otherwise their work would not have been accepted. An example of this type of writing is Jade Snow Wong's *Fifth Chinese Daughter,* published in 1950. Although the story denigrates certain Asian values, it was often included in secondary literature anthologies. Some contemporary Asian American literary critics are critical of the story, others like it (222). In choosing literature, teachers need to look for accurate portrayals of other cultures. A balanced representation of positive and negative characters struggling with contemporary issues is important in literature selection to assure an honest view and to avoid stereotyping (238).

When selecting Asian American literature, teachers have many choices. Ellen Greenblatt in *Many Voices* suggests combining the reading of *The Joy Luck Club* by Amy Tan with the more difficult *The Woman Warrior* by Maxine Hong Kingston. *The House of the Spirits* by Isabel Allende, a Chilean writer, could also be a companion reading with *Joy Luck Club*. Another suitable book by Tan is *The Kitchen God's Wife*. *The Sound of the Waves* by Yukio Mishima, a book about forbidden love, could be paired with *Romeo and Juliet*. Greenblatt highly recommends *A Boat to Nowhere* by Maureen Crane Wartski, a novel of the boat people's desperate flight from Vietnam (7).

Readers and Literature

We are not suggesting the exclusion of traditional literature from the white, male, Protestant perspective. But to accurately present the American experience, the literary canon needs to be redefined and expanded to include American minority authors. At one time, the difficulty of finding literature by minorities, women, and Third World authors created a serious problem for us. Now, however, many readily available bibliographies and articles provide annotations of titles.

Should we teach literature from the cultures represented in our classrooms? Regardless of the cultural makeup of our class, should we teach literature from other cultures? The answer to both questions is yes. We live in a pluralistic society, and our literature selections need to help our students better understand and appreciate the multiple cultures in the United States and the world. Students may have difficulty understanding references and idioms from cultures other than their own. Even though the same can be said for Chaucer, teachers believe that the value of helping students understand *The Canterbury Tales* far outweighs any difficulties students have with its language. That belief should transfer to teaching a wider spectrum of literature than the canon.

Sharon McElmeel, a library media specialist, agrees: "*All* children should be exposed to a diversity of cultures and heritages—that is how they grow, become tolerant of differences, and learn to respect others and their ideas" (50). McElmeel argues that teachers and librarians must provide up-to-date multicultural books for students. Otherwise the images students remember from their reading too often depict Native Americans as wearing feathers and face paint, African Americans as making their mark only by playing sports, and all Hispanics as migrant workers. We must not limit our cultural awareness by using only folktales and ignoring modern-day, realistic images. We need to "show the faces of the real America" (50).

When we think of teaching multicultural literature, we must realize that "individuals do not belong to single, clearly identifiable cultures" (Fishman 75). Each of us represents several cultures, and at different times we represent different cultures. For example, a student might be identified at one time by her age and background, another time by her race, or another time by her occupation or political beliefs—all different cultures overlapping and combining (75). No one person can represent a single cultural group, and no one literature selection "effectively represents any single cultural group" (79).

 ## RECOMMENDED BOOKS BY OR ABOUT PEOPLE OF COLOR

What follows are personal choices or those recommended by other English teachers. (Special thanks to the Cooperative Children's Book Center, University of Wisconsin–Madison.) The list is in no way comprehensive but is a starting point.

Native American Literature
Anpao: An American Odyssey by Jamake Highwater
Brothers of the Heart: A Story of the Old Northwest, 1837–1838 by Joan W. Blos
Ceremony by Leslie Silko
House Made of Dawn by N. Scott Momaday
I Heard the Owl Call My Name by Margaret Craven
The Man to Send Rain Clouds: Contemporary Stories by American Indians edited by Kenneth Rosen
When the Legends Die by Hal Borland

African American Literature
Blue Tights by Rita Williams-Garcia
Cotton Candy on a Rainy Day (poems) by Nikki Giovanni
Grand Fathers (1999) and *Grand Mothers* (1994) edited by Nikki Giovanni
I Know Why the Caged Bird Sings by Maya Angelou

In Search of Our Mothers' Gardens by Alice Walker

Let the Circle Be Unbroken by Mildred D. Taylor

Marked by Fire by Joyce Carol Thomas

Out From This Place by Joyce Hansen

Rainbow Jordan by Alice Childress

Scorpions by Walter Dean Myers

Sweet Whispers, Brother Rush by Virginia Hamilton

Trouble's Child by Mildred Pitts Walter

The Women of Brewster Place by Gloria Naylor

Chicano Literature

Across the Great River by Irene Beltran Hernandez

Black Hair (poetry) by Gary Soto

Bless Me, Ultima by Rudolfo Anaya

Chicano Voices edited by Carlota Cardenas De Dwyer

Kodachromes in Rhyme by Ernest Galarza

Nuyorican Poetry: An Anthology of Puerto Rican Words and Feelings edited by Miguel Algarin and Miguel Pinero

Schoolland by Max Martinez

The Crossing by Gary Paulsen

The Day the Cisco Kid Shot John Wayne by Nash Candelaria

The House on Mango Street by Sandra Cisneros

The Iguana Killer: Twelve Stories of the Heart by Alberto Alvaro Rios

The Last of the Menu Girls by Denise Chavez

The Road to Tamazunchale by Ron Arias

Asian American Literature

Duff and Tongchinsub recommend many of these selections.

Aiieeee! an anthology of Asian American writers edited by Frank Chin, et al.

Asian American Authors, an anthology edited by Kai-Yu Hsu and Helen Palubinskas

Child of the Owl and *Dragonwings* by Laurence Yep

Citizen 13660 by Mine Okubo

Homebase by Shawn Hsu Wong

The Joy Luck Club by Amy Tan

Nisei Daughter by Monica Sone

Tule Lake by Edward Miyakawa

Woman from Hiroshima by Toshio Mori

Woman Warrior: Memoirs of a Girlhood Among Ghosts by Maxine Hong Kingston

Other Selections

Breaking Ice: An Anthology of Contemporary African-American Fiction edited
    by Terry McMillan

Bronx Primate: Portraits in a Childhood by Kate Simon (Jewish)

Call It Sleep by Henry Roth (Jewish)

The Honorable Prison by Lyll Becerra de Jenkins (South American)

Invented Lives: Narratives of Black Women edited by Mary Helen Washington

Jews Without Money by Michael Gold

Rebels of the Heavenly Kingdom by Katherine Paterson (19th century China)

The Return by Sonia Levitin (Ethiopian)

So Far From the Bamboo Grove by Yoko Kawashima Watkins (Japanese)

Somehow Tenderness Survives: Stories of Southern Africa, selected by Hazel
    Rochman

A Thief in the Village, and Other Stories by James Berry (Jamaican)

The Third Women edited by Dexter Fisher includes selections of Native America,
    Chicano, and Asian American literature

Waiting for the Rain: A Novel of South Africa by Sheila Gordon

Arlette Willis, in *Teaching and Using Multicultural Literature in Grades 9–12: Moving Beyond the Canon*, states, "It should be understood that minority cultural identities are not fixed or monolithic, but multivocal and even contradictory" (2). She suggests using thematic teaching to include more voices and attitudes. When we are selecting books to include in our teaching, Willis provides the following criteria: They should be

    a. historically relevant
    b. representative of specific time period
    c. illustrative of a range of life circumstances and experiences
    d. representative of unique cultural or linguistic use
    e. appropriate for and used in grades 9–12 (37)

In addition to the Asian American titles given earlier, Willis suggests the following Asian/Pacific American literature:

A Bridge Between Us by Julie Shigekuni "follows four generations of Japanese
    American women and explores the ties that bind them together" (126).

Go by Holly Uyemoto describes a 21-year-old woman searching for truth and
    reality. Her "writing is deftly woven with humor, the absurd, and a lucidity
    that makes every page enjoyable" (126).

Typical American by Gish Jen. Willis writes that it is a joy to read; it is lucid and
    lyrical with a well-constructed plot (125).

This is small sampling of the books Willis discusses in the chapter, "Asian/Pacific American Literature: The Battle Over Authenticity."

Exploration

Choosing Literature that Represent Various Cultures

Select several books that were published in the last two or three years representing a variety of cultures. Decide what grade levels they are appropriate for. Share your findings with the class.

Putting It All Together

Literature selections are appropriate in several different thematic units depending on what aspect or theme you want to emphasize. For instance, *Summer of My German Soldier* could be used in a unit on family relationships, war, or on the need for acceptance. The groupings of literature that follow are examples of how some teachers combine their selections.

Mary Beth Koehler, an English teacher, created a unit on self-expression using Native American resources. Her rationale for the unit is based on her knowledge that the United States is a country of diversity. In any class in her school district, a teacher might have students representing three types of Asian cultures; African Americans from inner cities and blacks from other countries, such as Nigeria; and Native American students from as many as five tribes as well as Caucasian students. Teaching to single Anglo-American background made no sense. Koehler designed her unit using culturally specific literature and resources. She explains that using this approach helps students understand the experience and concerns of a culture different from their own and they learn how to express their own individuality through the use of what's called "minority or ethnic" literature (2). Koehler's categories are music, dance, poetry, storytelling, and novels in the unit.

The groupings include novels at different reading levels, novels by multicultural authors, and a balance of male and female writers. Many selections are included to highlight the variety of literature available. Chapter 13 in this text describes detailed units with lesson plans and specific teaching ideas relating listening, speaking, writing, reading, and creative dramatics for a comprehensive view of how the units work.

Selections for a Unit on Family Relationships

Novels

But in the Fall I'm Leaving by Ann Rinaldi

Cold Sassy Tree by Olive Ann Burns

The Disappearance by Rosa Guy

Everywhere by Bruce Brooks

Family Reunion by Caroline Cooney

A Fine Time to Leave Me by Terry Pringle
Home Before Dark by Sue Ellen Bridgers
IOU'S by Ouida Sebestyen
Ordinary People by Judith Guest
Sarah, Plain and Tall by Patricia MacLachlan
Summer of My German Soldier by Bette Greene
Thief of Dreams by John Yount
Unlived Affections by George Shannon

Poetry
"Blaming Sons" by T'ao Ch'ien
"Fifty-Fifty" by Carl Sandburg
"My Papa's Waltz" by Theodore Roethke
"Those Winter Sundays" by Robert Hayden

Selections for Coming of Age or Developing a Sense of Self

Stories
"Thank You, Ma'am" by Langston Hughes
"Train Whistle Guitar" by Albert Murray
"The Tree in the Meadow" by Philippa Pearce

Novels
Anywhere Else but Here by Bruce Clement
The Birds of Summer by Zilpha Keatley Snyder
The Catcher in the Rye by J. D. Salinger
Come Sing, Jimmy Jo by Katherine Paterson
The Crossing by Gary Paulsen
Far From Shore by Kevin Major
A Day No Pigs Would Die by Robert Newton Peck
I Will Call It Georgie's Blues by Suzanne Newton
In Summer Light by Zibby Oneal
Lily and the Lost Boy by Paula Fox
Long Time Between Kisses by Sandra Scoppettone
Member of the Wedding by Harper Lee
The Moonlight Man by Paula Fox
The Moves Make the Man by Bruce Brooks
My Antonia by Willa Cather
Notes for Another Life by Sue Ellen Bridgers
Permanent Connections by Sue Ellen Bridgers

A Place to Come Back To by Nancy Bond
A Portrait of the Artist as a Young Man by James Joyce
A Solitary Blue by Cynthia Voigt
Spanish Hoof by Robert Newton Peck
To Myself by Galila Ron-Fender

Poetry
"Curiosity" by Alastair Reid
"Dreams" by Langston Hughes
"Well Water" by Randall Jarrell

Selections for a Theme of Courage

Novels
The Autobiography of Miss Jane Pittman by Ernest Gaines
Chernowitz! by Fran Arrick
Christopher Reeve by Megan Howard
Eyes of Darkness by Jamake Highwater
Ganesh by Malcolm J. Bosse
If Beale Street Could Talk by James Baldwin
M. C. Higgins, The Great by Virginia Hamilton

Poetry
"Icarus" by Edward Field
"They Tell Me" by Yevgeny Yevtushenko
"Wild Horses" by Elder Olson

Selections for a Unit Focusing on Women and Women Writers

These selections are provided by Dennis Crowe, a high school teacher.

Anne Bradstreet, selected poetry
Gwendolyn Brooks, selected poetry
Emily Dickinson, selected poems and letters
Amy Lowell, selected poetry
Marianne Moore, selected poetry
Animal Dreams by Barbara Kingsolver
Babe Didrikson by Russell Freedman
The Belle of Amherst by William Luce
The Chinchilla Farm by Judith Freeman

Crown of Columbus by Louise Erdrich and Michael Dorris
Extraordinary Women of the American West by Judy Alter
I Know Why the Caged Bird Sings by Maya Angelou
In Country by Bobbi Ann Mason
Pilgrim at Tinker Creek by Annie Dillard
A Room of One's Own by Virginia Woolf
The Scarlet Letter by Nathaniel Hawthorne
"Silences in Literature" by Tillie Olsen
The Splendid Outcast or *West with the Night* by Beryl Markham
Their Eyes Were Watching God by Zora Neale Hurston

MEDIA IN THE ENGLISH CLASSROOM

Movies

Young adults like to go to the movies; not surprisingly, movie studios make more money from teenagers than from any other segment of the population. Harold Foster, a high school English teacher, believes that ignoring movies in the English classroom prevents us from helping students become aware of how movies influence them (86). Objectives for teaching about movies are similar to those involving advertising. We want students to become more objective and to understand how they are influenced. Not all advertising is bad, or all movies poor, but we must help students learn to tell which are and which are not. Foster suggests the following goals:

1. Transform students into discriminating viewers who can distinguish good from bad, exploitation from communication.
2. Sensitize students so they perceive how these films are designed to influence and manipulate them.
3. Educate students to understand films visually and thematically, so they can analyze and critique films they see.
4. Develop critical awareness so students will occasionally pass up the worst of these films and stay home and read a book. (86)

To achieve these goals, we need to discuss current films in the classroom and use videos in the literature units. Visual literature can be powerful; we and our students benefit from this added dimension.

Television

Television is a major influence in our lives, yet rarely are television shows discussed in English class unless we tape and show something like *The Nature of English*. Many of the same goals for movies apply to TV. We want students to become more objective observers and to make critical judgments. Television is a showcase of American life and an excellent vehicle for making students aware of stereotypes. Teachers can move them away from passive viewing and into critical analysis.

To accomplish these goals, students choose an area to focus on and then write questions to guide their viewing. For instance, you can begin a class discussion of favorite or not-so-favorite TV shows. Ask why students like or dislike a show. Conversation will be lively, with strong opinions, and students will interrupt each other frequently. Students then choose a series, type of show, or commercials shown during particular shows. Individually they write three or four questions that will guide their viewing: Are there consistent stereotypes? Are stereotypes more apt to be of minorities or women? What image is portrayed of children, parents, and their relationships? What audience is the show or commercial geared to? Do the commercials and shows complement each other? Are sport announcers biased, and if so, in what way? In small groups, students share questions and help each other refine the questions and generate new ones.

To be effective critics, students must keep track of what they view. Taking notes while watching is almost impossible, but students can write notes at every commercial break. And when they get used to keeping a pen and paper handy, they become better at recording dialogue and action. Students see things they never saw before and become much more objective.

We owe it to our students to help them become more critical viewers, which leads to their becoming better critical thinkers. Discussing whether violence is essential for a particular show, whether humor is appropriate, and whether people are portrayed honestly also helps students grow confident that they have something important to say. Sometimes the confidence transfers to discussing similar elements in literature, but even if that doesn't happen, they have gained knowledge and objectivity.

Videos and DVDs

Because they are so easily obtainable and their visual aspect appeals to students, videos are an important addition to the study of literature. Videos make some literature selections accessible in ways that a book cannot. A common way to use a video is to have students read a novel or play and then see the video; however, teachers use videos in class in other ways as well.

1. Instead of showing the video of the book students have read, you may select a different title, but one on the same theme. Harold Foster, suggests that *Sixteen Candles* is a good choice for a thematic unit on coming of age. Also, *The Alfred G. Graebner Memorial High School Handbook of Rules and Regulations* fits in very well, describing with humor what life is like for a high school freshman (87). Many videos on the popular theme of growing up can be ordered from the school's catalogue. You do need to plan ahead because it takes several weeks for the films to arrive, and popular ones are booked early. We found it best to order the films for the following year in the spring.

2. You can show a video different from the novels read, but select one based on a novel that is too difficult for all or most of the students. Seeing the film first does not detract from their enjoyment of reading the novel later. In fact, often students report they liked and understood the novel better

because they saw the film first. Our students do not always need to read the book. We can greatly broaden their literary experience by showing the film only and discussing it in class.

3. The visual interpretation of literature is always different from the printed form, and helping students learn how to analyze these differences deepens their understanding of interpretations. *The Revolt of Mother,* based on a short story of the same title by Mary E. Wilkins, is an appropriate choice for secondary students. Observing expression and actions brings a different dimension. You might pose these questions:

   - Where do the two versions differ?
   - Is the film true to what students believe the author presented?
   - Why are changes made?
   - If you made a film based on this or another story, how would you film it?
   - How do music, shadows, and light affect the meaning?
   - In what ways does camera angle make a difference?

   An offshoot of this activity is to have students choose well-known television or movie actors for the characters in a literature selection and explain why they made their choices. Characterizations often become clearer when they think about matching a fictional character with an actor.

4. Classic films like *Stagecoach, The African Queen, The Wizard of Oz,* and *Gone with the Wind* are excellent for analyzing the use of prototypes, directing techniques, and story line. A unit on a film or films is appropriate in an English class. Incidentally, comparing the novel *The Wizard of Oz* with the film version is interesting because the two are quite different; yet the intended audience for both is children.

 ## CENSORSHIP

We cannot think about literature selections without considering censorship. It is a controversial and complex issue. The basic premise in censorship cases is that reading certain material results in a change of values, beliefs, and/or behavior. For years, researchers have been trying to prove or disprove the connection between books (or television) and behavior. If children see or read violent actions, will they then be more apt to perform violent acts? No clear conclusions either way emerged from the studies. Nonetheless, parents sometimes object to a reading selection a teacher has made and they want the book banned from the school.

The issue affects us as teachers and when we look at the ten most challenged books of 2002 published by the American Library Association (ALA) we can see why (2003). The books in order of the most frequently challenged are

Harry Potter series by J. K. Rowling, for its focus on wizardry and magic.

Alice series by Phyllis Reynolds Naylor, for being sexually explicit, using offensive language and being unsuited to age group.

The Chocolate War by Robert Cormier, for using offensive language and being unsuited to age group.

I Know Why the Caged Bird Sings by Maya Angelou, for sexual content, racism, offensive language, violence, and being unsuited to age group.

Taming the Star Runner by S. E. Hinton, for offensive language.

Captain Underpants by Dav Pilkey, for insensitivity and being unsuitable to age group, as well as encouraging children to disobey authority.

The Adventures of Huckleberry Finn by Mark Twain, for racism, insensitivity, and offensive language.

Bridge to Terabithia by Katherine Paterson, for offensive language, sexual content, and occult/Satanism.

Roll of Thunder, Hear My Cry by Mildred D. Taylor, for insensitivity, racism, and offensive language.

Julie of the Wolves by Julie Craighead George, for sexual content, offensive language, violence, and being unsuited to age group.

Lee Burress, an expert on censorship, compiled a list of reasons people object to books. Sex and obscene language were the most common complaints, but people also objected to references to God, comments they perceived as being un-American or Communist propaganda, references to homosexuality, and depressing story lines. It is important to note that 40 percent of the books most often attacked are written by women and minorities.

The American Library Association (ALA) points out that banning books just makes teenagers want to read them. When a book is challenged, the number of students reading it goes up because, as one teenager explained, they are at the age when they want to be independent and do not want adults telling them what they can't read. The ALA publishes a list of books banned or challenged each year and the reasons cited. You can access the list every year and receive material related to Book Banning Week by either calling the ALA at 1–800–545–2433 or on its web site: <http://www. ala.org>.

We can see that many different viewpoints are reflected in the reasons cited. Some of the books clearly reflect the common prejudices of the time in which they were written, and students need to understand that, but banning the book prevents any discussions that would correct misconceptions.

Our best defense against censorship is to know why we are teaching a particular book. Sometimes teachers think they can avoid trouble for themselves by not teaching a book someone might object to. But self-censoring is wrong because it is driven by fear and emotional response. Our reasons for teaching a book must come from our knowledge of literature, our desire to teach students about the diversity of America's culture through a multitude of voices, our ability to help our students learn about other ways of life, and a wider, more informed view of the world. Of course, we make choices based on personal preferences as well; we can't teach everything. However, choices should not be based on fear but on meeting our objectives for teaching literature.

Alleen Pace Nilsen and Kenneth L. Donelson, in *Literature for Today's Young Adults*, explain that we need to be considerate and kind when listening to parents' complaints and concerns about books. The underlying reasons for parents' concerns are not always easy to detect; they may be more of a fear of our economy, sexual diseases, or the eroding of family values (393). Parents may initially question a literature choice but often after hearing the reasons you are teaching it, understand and do not object. You can always select an alternative book for a student as long as it is on the same theme. Teaching thematic units with two or three selections makes this an easier solution. An important point in the censorship issue is that parents do have a right to influence what their children read; however, they do not have the right to decide what other children read. You must be prepared to provide options.

Elizabeth Noll, a former English teacher, is concerned with the ripple effect of censorship cases that compel teachers to self-censor the choices they make when selecting literature for their students (59). School censorship is on the rise and is not limited to a geographic region or a particular grade level or instructional area; therefore, every teacher is affected by censorship. Some teachers avoid the problem by offering students a choice of reading material. When the curriculum is based on units of study, the choices, although broad in scope, can still be on the same theme. Noll reports that one teacher tells her students that if they or their parents object to any of the material, she will substitute something else that fits into the unit (62). Many teachers have a lengthy list of related materials and allow students to freely select what they want to read. The National Coalition Against Censorship published a book edited by Judy Blume, *Places I Never Meant to Be*. The book is a collection of original stories by censored writers and is for seventh- to twelfth-grade readers.

Although censorship usually comes from outside the school, Dorothea Hunter and Winifred Madsen, both librarians, experienced censorship pressure from within their school when a library supervisor ordered eight titles to be removed from the school library. The district had established procedures for examining books that were called into question, but this 20-year-old policy was ignored. Hunter lost her job, and the entire book selection committee was dismissed. After two years of effort, the books were finally reinstated. Hunter and Madsen received help from People for the American Way and the American Civil Liberties Union. "Both organizations fight for intellectual freedom and can give you crucial outside support, including legal assistance" (140).

Because censorship problems occur all over the United States in every school district, we all are affected. We do not have to fight censorship problems alone, however. State departments of education, universities, the National Council of Teachers of English, the International Reading Association, and the Office for Intellectual Freedom of the American Library Association will provide assistance.

Schools need to have a written policy about censorship that explains how teachers handle parent objections to their reading selections. As new teachers, you must ask about the policy and understand it. Further, in department meetings, ask about former problems and how the school handled them. Knowing ahead of time what procedures are in place will make it much easier for you to answer parents' questions.

Additionally, Jane Agee, who studied 18 high school teachers in five different schools to find out how censorship influenced teachers, has this advice for new teachers: Regular conversations with administrators and teachers will help you learn more about the issues and how experienced teachers have developed effective strategies.

John Kean, a member of the NCTE Committee Against Censorship and the Commission on Intellectual Freedom, stresses the importance of teachers being prepared to explain their choices of literature and methods to critics. "The teacher needs to know what the district's goals are and what the expectations are for the English curriculum" (136). Schools need to have a policy in place, and teachers need to be well informed about the policy. Kean offers this advice:

> If you anticipate that some aspect of your program or material has the potential for controversy, discuss it with other teachers and administrators to ensure that they understand what you are doing or using and why you are using it. Although it is possible to invite trouble by such consultation, it forces you to think through your own curriculum carefully and is likely to lead to a more supportive environment in which to work. (141)

Kean's advice is especially important for new teachers as they work at balancing literature selections with the community's concerns.

Exploration

Dealing with Censorship

Role-play a situation where a parent has requested a teacher to stop using a particular book and wants it removed from the school. Your group chooses one of the books from the ALA list or another one you know has been called into question. The members of the group take one of the following roles: parent(s), teacher(s), librarian, and community members including ministers, student(s), and an administrator. Each one expresses his or her opinion about keeping or banning the book in question, giving specific reasons and quoting from the book. A classroom discussion should follow the role-playing activity.

Instructional Unit

Stereotypes: The Root of Aggressive Behavior

Anne Elliott, an English education student, developed a thematic unit on "Stereotypes: The Root of Aggressive Behavior." She planned the four-week unit for tenth- or eleventh-grade students. As with other instructional units we are using, Elliott's explanations, objectives, and rationale are omitted here. Why might Elliott have selected this theme? Before reading the unit, what literature and other resources can you think of that would fit this theme?

Week One

Introduction. Students are in groups of four with one person designated as a recorder. Every few seconds I will write a term on the board; for example, *drug addict, athlete, police officer, honor student,* or *nurse.* As each word is added to the board, students in the groups tell the recorder every image that comes to mind in association with the word. When the activity is over, students answer these questions:

1. Has your group made any stereotypes?
2. What effect do these labels have on people?

Before discussing their responses, I will provide students with the dictionary definition of stereotyping and give them time to rethink their responses to the questions. We will discuss what the differences are among stereotyping, prejudice, and racism. Students read Chapter 5 in *I Know Why the Caged Bird Sings* by Maya Angelou. They respond to the chapter in their journals. Later journal responses are shared in class, guided by the following questions:

1. How do you think people feel when they are labeled?
2. How have you reacted when you've been labeled?
3. How does Momma resist insulting behavior?
4. What are some strategies for dealing with insulting behavior?

Throughout the unit we consider strategies for coping with stereotype labels.

We will read the poem "Indian Blood" by Mary Tallmountain. Students respond in their journals to the following questions:

1. In the poem, the girl uses the words *stumbled, crouch,* and *trembled* to describe her actions. How do you suppose she felt that day on the stage?
2. Why do you think she waits until "late in the night" to draw her "Indian blood"? Do you think she is celebrating or resenting her heritage?

EXPLORATION

TYING OBJECTIVES AND GOALS TOGETHER

What do you think are Elliott's objectives for this unit? How might she prepare her students for the literature circles? Although Elliott assigns some literature, she has built into the unit the students' responsibility for choosing literature. What are the benefits of this? Are there any potential difficulties?

Week Two

Students meet in their groups and define stereotyping, giving specific examples. Also, they discuss if they think stereotyping will ever be eliminated and why they think it exists.

They read the short story "Learning the Language" by Haruhiko Yoshimeki. Students may choose one of the following questions to write a one-page response (Level 2).

1. Find two or three examples of people of one race making comments about other races. Decide if you consider them racist. How do you define *racist*?
2. Yoshimeki describes his experience of coming to terms with a culture different from his own. Think of all the ways we encounter cultural differences and compare to Yoshimeki's experience. Reach a conclusion about how racial attitudes are culturally determined.

I will introduce the selection of novels they will read: *Pickle and Price* by Pieter Van Raven, *Night* by Elie Wiesel, and *The Bluest Eye* by Toni Morrison. The books represent different levels of difficulty. Students choose which one they want to read and may change their selection if they wish. As a prereading activity, I will hand out a page of quotations from all three books, and the students guess which book each one comes from.

EXPLORATION

INTRODUCING LITERATURE TO STUDENTS

What are Elliott's objectives for the activities in week two? How might a teacher introduce the books and help students decide what they want to read? What additional literature selections could you add?

Week Three

As students are reading their books, other activities and discussions are ongoing. I do not plan to give tests or quizzes to make sure students are keeping up with their reading. The class will work on a definition of culture. As an assignment, students will make a family tree to discover the many cultures that exist within their own family. Students will read "Nikki-Rosa" by Nikki Giovanni. Students will respond to one or more of the following quotations from the poem: "Black love is Black wealth," "biographers never understand," and "all the while I was happy." Also, they will read "Thank You, Ma'am" by Langston Hughes. Students respond in their journals.

To help students realize how easy it is to make generalizations I will use the following artwork and ask the accompanying questions:

1. "Mother Courage" by Charles White. Why did White title this work "Mother Courage"?
2. "Sunny Side of the Street" by Philip Evergood. What associations do you make from this work? What kind of emotional response do you have?

The final activity for the week is role-playing. Each small group has a counselor role, and the others have been confronted with hostility, insulting behavior, labeling, or stereotyping. They discuss what has happened with the counselor who explains a process for dealing with the dilemma. Students take turns playing different roles.

EXPLORATION

TEACHING READING

How might Elliott monitor the students' reading progress?
What are the students learning? What are Elliott's goals?

Week Four

The final discussion is on how people respond to stereotyping. The students' discussion should be based on all the activities they have done during the unit.

The final project is to develop a conflict-resolution program for our own school. Some possibilities could include increasing awareness by creating announcements, posters, handouts; organizing a culture club to discuss diversity issues; or developing a peer mediation group to intervene in disputing parties. Students may create any project; they can work in a group, with a partner, or individually. This project will not end when the unit does. For this reason students set their own completion dates. They must turn in a written plan and purpose of their program. Also, they need to turn in a written weekly update.

EXPLORATION

PLANNING WITH UNITS

Elliott plans to integrate this theme into subsequent units. How might she do this? How would the theme fit into units you are thinking of creating?

Elliott states at the conclusion of her unit, "Aggression in American schools manifests itself in attacks on teachers and students as well as in vandalism and property damage. The trend has serious implications for our children as well as for our schools. A unit on stereotypes seems not only appropriate but necessary."

RELATED WEB SITES

http://english.byu.edu/alan/
http://edfu.lis.uiuc.edu/puboff/bccb/
http://www.indiana.edu/~eric-rec

REFERENCES

Agee, Jane. "How Censorship Affects High School English Teachers." 29 Sept. 2003 <http://cela.albany.edu/newslet/fall/censorship.htm>.

Anson, Chris M. "Book Lists, Cultural Literacy, and the Stagnation of Discourse." *English Journal* (Feb. 1988): 14–18.

Applebee, Arthur N. *A Study of Book-Length Works Taught in High School English Courses.* Albany: National Research Center on Literature Teaching & Learning, 1989.

"Book Bans for Teens Backfire, Group Says." Associated Press. *Leader-Telegram.* 14 Sept. 1995: 3A.

Burress, Lee, "Battle of the Books." Metuchen: The Scarecrow Press, 1989.

Carlsen, G. Robert. "What Beginning English Teachers Need to Know about Adolescent Literature." *English Education* 10 (1979): 195–202.

Carrier, Warren, ed., and Kenneth Oliver, associate ed. *Guide to World Literature.* Urbana: National Council of Teachers of English, 1980.

Crowe, Dennis. "Women and Women Writers." English 703, Teaching AP English. University of Wisconsin–Eau Claire, 1993.

Dabydeen, David. *A Handbook for Teaching Caribbean Literature.* London: Heinemann, 1988.

Duenas Gonzalez, Roseann. "When Minority Becomes Majority: The Changing Face of English Classrooms." *English Journal* (Jan. 1990): 16–23.

Duff, Ogle B. and Helen J. Tongchinsub. "Expanding the Secondary Literature Curriculum: Annotated Bibliographies of American Indian, Asian American, and Hispanic American Literature." *English Education* 22 (1990): 220–40.

Elbow, Peter. *What Is English?* New York: Modern Language Association of America, 1990.

Elliott, Anne. "Stereotypes: The Root of Aggressive Behavior." English 404, Teaching AP English. University of Wisconsin–Eau Claire, 1993.

Fishman, Andrea. "Finding Ways In: Redefining Multicultural Literature." *English Journal* (Oct. 1995): 73–79.

Foster, Harold M. "Film in the Classroom: Coping with Teenpics." *English Journal* (March 1987): 86–88.

Frye, Northrop. *On Teaching Literature.* New York: Harcourt Brace Jovanovich, 1972.

Greenblatt, Ellen. *Many Voices: A Multicultural Bibliography for Secondary School.* Berkeley: Bay Area Writing Project, 1991.

Gunner, Elizabeth. *A Handbook for Teaching African Literature.* 2nd ed. London: Heinemann, 1987.

Hunter, Dorothea, and Winifred Madsen. "The Enemy Within." *School Library Journal* 39.3 (March 1993): 140.

Kean, John M. "The Secondary English Teacher and Censorship." *Preserving Intellectual Freedom.* Ed. Jean Brown. Urbana: NCTE, 1994: 133–42.

Koehler, Mary Beth. "Native American Resources as a Catalyst for Self-Expression in the Language Arts." Unpub. paper, 1994.

Lake, Patricia. "Sexual Stereotyping and the English Curriculum." *English Journal* (Oct. 1988): 35–38.

McElmeel, Sharon L. "Toward a Real Multiculturalism." *School Library Journal* (Nov. 1993): 50.

Mossman, Robert. "South African Literature: A Global Lesson in One Country." *English Journal* (Dec. 1990): 41–46.

Nilsen, Alleen Pace, and Kenneth L. Donelson. *Literature for Today's Young Adults.* 6th ed. New York: Addison-Wesley Longman Inc., 2001.

Noll, Elizabeth. "The Ripple Effect of Censorship: Silencing in the Classroom." *English Journal* (Dec. 1994): 59–64.

Olds, Alan. "Thinking Eastern: Preparing Students to Read Chinese Literature." *English Journal* (Dec. 1990): 20–34.

Purves, Alan C., and Dianne L. Monson. *Experiencing Children's Literature.* Glenview: Scott, Foresman and Co., 1984.

Rehrauer, Liz. "Who Am I?" English 702, Literature for Teachers. University of Wisconsin–Eau Claire, 1994.

Resch, Jodi. "Mexican Culture Unit." English 404, Literature for Teachers. University of Wisconsin–Eau Claire, 1995.

Romero, Patricia Ann, and Don Zancanella. "Expanding the Circle: Hispanic Voices in American Literature." *English Journal* (Jan. 1990): 24–29.

Sasse, Mary Hawley. "Literature in a Multiethnic Culture." *Literature in the Classroom: Readers, Texts, and Contexts.* Ed. Ben F. Nelms. Urbana: NCTE, 1988: 167–78.

Smith, Frank. "Overselling Literacy." *Phi Delta Kappan* (Jan. 1989): 353–59.

Willis, Arlette, ed. *Teaching and Using Multicultural Literature in Grades 9–12: Moving Beyond the Canon.* Norwood Christopher-Gordon Pub., 1998.

Teaching Literature 11

I urge us to see our task in schools as helping students read literature
to understand the culture, to speculate on the ideas and the imaginative vision,
and to speculate on the nature and use of the language that is the medium
of the artistic expression.

Alan C. Purves (360)

 ## READING LITERATURE

The teaching of literature in secondary schools has undergone a dramatic change in the past two decades. Emphasis has shifted from the text to interactions between text and reader; that is, what the reader brings to the reading is as important as the words in the text. Texts provide many possibilities for interpretations. Bruce Miller describes reading as a subjective experience because readers bring their own experiences and knowledge to their understanding of a text (19–20). The research behind the reader response approach, which is based on the interaction between reader and text, has been going on for years, but not until recently has this research affected the secondary schools. Although the literature we choose to have students read is of concern, teachers acknowledge that even the most carefully selected literature will not benefit students if they do not read it. Students also benefit little if they read the selections with no interest or understanding. For students to become lifelong readers—a goal in every curriculum we've seen—they must see reading as an enjoyable activity. As we think of how to help students become lifelong readers, we have two major concerns as educators: how to teach literature and what literature to teach. In Chapter 10, we dealt with the selection of literature, and in this chapter we will examine the methods of teaching literature.

BACKGROUND OF LITERATURE STUDY

A brief review of literary analyses can help provide a perspective for teaching literature in secondary schools. *Historical criticism*—that is, studying literature in the context of the period in which it was written—is a method of learning about literature that has been used since the 1900s. The works were studied in relation to others written in the same time period and were also compared with those written during other periods. By the 1930s, *social criticism*, or literature studied through its reflection of society, became an important way of gaining insights into the works. The work of both Sigmund Freud and Carl Jung also had a strong effect on the way we examine literature. In these traditional approaches, the work is of secondary importance.

By the 1950s, *new criticism*, which began after World War II, had become the dominant method of analyzing literature and remains an important influence. New criticism is concerned only with the work itself and not with the author, period, or social influence. *Structuralism* and *deconstruction* are based on the same premise—that the meaning and understanding are found in the text itself and that information about the author or social and historical influences have no bearing on the study of literature. It is not within the scope of this text to discuss the various literary critical approaches. Such studies are more appropriate for college literature classes. However, future English teachers do need to consider how these critical approaches influence and inform the teaching of literature to secondary students.

Focus of Literary Study

Literary study in middle and high schools has two major focuses. The first is to continue to help students develop an appreciation and enjoyment of literature. In elementary school, students become familiar with a variety of literature and have many opportunities to appreciate different styles, story lines, and genres. Generally speaking, the emphasis is on a subjective analysis. In the higher grades, students are introduced to the use of formal analysis, and literature becomes the *study* of literature. Too often, students receive the impression that what they think and feel about literature no longer counts. In *A Handbook of Critical Approaches to Literature,* the authors explain that they do not see a dilemma between teaching literatures by subjective or formal analysis. Rather, they believe the "intelligent application of several interpretive techniques can enhance the study of literature" (Guerin, Labor, Morgan, and Willingham 7). However, formal analysis often takes precedence over subjective approaches, creating a rift between the student and the text. In addition, formal analysis can become mired in detail when inappropriately taught to secondary students.

Too often, studying literature meant finding hidden meanings in the text. Students assumed that there was "one meaning" and through careful reading and studying all readers should arrive at the same understanding of the text, regardless of their experiences and knowledge. Most of us have had the experience of thinking that we understood a text only to be told we were mistaken. What the story or poem really meant—the right meaning—was what an authority claimed. A reader's perception, experience, and personality had little to do with the meaning. Such theory established a hierarchy of readers with the renowned critic at the top and the inexperienced student at the bottom. Pedagogy based on this view divides readers into two groups—those who know the right answers and those who don't. For those in the latter group, and there are many, reading is not an enjoyable activity, and, consequently, they avoid reading. This approach allows no room for a variety of interpretations even when readers can back up their interpretations with examples from the text. The experiences and knowledge students bring with them when they read don't count in this kind of literature study; what does count is learning one particular interpretation. If students listen carefully in class, they can even "ace" the exam without reading the text! When there is no personal connection between the text and the reader, students don't have to understand or apply what they read. Reading in this way is a passive activity. With such an arrangement, how can we convince students that reading is pleasurable and to be enjoyed for the rest of their lives? And how can we help students learn formal analysis if they do not first see connections between themselves and the literature?

reading is not enjoyable for readers who think they can't find the right meaning

⚘ *Reflection* ⚘

Thinking back to your junior and senior high school years, what literature do you remember? What books did you talk about with friends? In small groups, compile a list of favorite books. Which ones were school assignments? Which ones would you consider teaching?

READER RESPONSE THEORY

The reader response theory is an approach to literature study that stresses the relationship between text and reader. Briefly, students respond to the text after careful reading and develop an understanding of the literature from their own and others' responses. Several scholars and researchers help us understand why the response theory makes sense in the English language arts classroom.

Wolfgang Iser has written extensively about the role of the reader in interpretation. He describes a literary work as having two poles: artistic and aesthetic. The artistic comes from the author in creating a work of art, and the aesthetic from the reader in responding to the art. The meaning of the text is the result of the interaction of the two poles. According to Iser, a meaning is not an absolute value, but a dynamic happening (21). If the meaning is dynamic, then it can change from reader to reader or even with multiple readings by the same person. A reader might have a somewhat different interpretation when reading a text for a second time or after learning what the text means to other readers. Iser dismisses attempts to discover a single hidden meaning in a text as a phase of interpretation that belongs to the past. He believes we have moved beyond the new criticism, which focused entirely on the text itself, to a belief that each reader brings to a text a uniqueness that shapes the interpretation. Iser quotes Susan Sontag, "to understand is to interpret," and the understanding comes from the reader, not from an outside source except the text itself (6).

Louise Rosenblatt is most responsible for advancing the theory of reader response. More than 60 years ago, Rosenblatt studied how her students responded to literature, and from her research she developed the transactional approach to teaching literature. Her philosophy parallels Iser's; she believes, "The reader counts for at least as much as the book or poem itself" (vi). The interaction between the reader and the text creates meaning. The reading becomes a "transaction": The text provides words and ideas; the reader provides the personal response to the words and ideas; and the relationship between the two creates meaning. Teachers of English language arts teach specific human beings with individual hearts and minds "to seek in literature a great variety of satisfactions" (35). The teacher's job is to help create a relationship between the individual book or play and the individual student (33).

Rosenblatt believes the human experience that literature presents is the primary reason for reading (7). We read through the lens of our own understandings. Rosenblatt explains that the reader "brings to the work personality traits, memories of past events, present needs and preoccupations, a particular mood of the moment . . . " (30–31).

Robert E. Probst, an educator whose work focuses on implementing response theory in the classroom, explains that readers sometimes discover the need to rethink initial conceptions and revise their notions about the text (31). Students must first feel free to deal with their own reactions to the text. Then the teacher has students share their reactions by asking questions and comparing their reactions with each other in small groups. Creating an atmosphere of security where students are comfortable with each other is essential (33). Through sharing, students examine their responses and come to a deeper understanding of the text. Rosenblatt believes firmly that readers do not stop with the initial responses, but that those responses lead them to reflection and analysis (75). She does not encourage the "uncritical acceptance of texts" (Probst 35). Teachers must help students assume responsibility for their own understandings of what they read.

EXPLORATION

Responding to Literature

Write responses to a book you are currently reading. Or choose a poem, article, or play to respond to. Share with others in a small group.

Implementing the Response Theory

Using Factual Information

If connections between reader and text are the most important things to stress in teaching literature, and we believe they are, what do we do with the literary facts and interpretations we learned in college and high school? Do you remember, for example, learning all about Shakespeare and the Globe Theatre before reading one of his plays? Rosenblatt describes such facts about the author, literary traditions, history of the age, and so forth as "merely secondary and peripheral," and stresses that such facts are "even distracting or worthless unless it is very clearly seen that they are secondary" (33). Knowing the background information is useful when teaching literature, not as lecture material but as supplemental material that comes up naturally in a discussion or in response to a student's question. Admittedly, keeping those wonderful bits of knowledge to yourself is difficult, but telling students too much puts you in the role of holder of the truth and the students as those who know little or nothing. Such an arrangement encourages passive learning. We all remember information better if we either discover it ourselves or acquire it when we actively wonder about it. No matter how wonderful our lecture, it is wasted effort if students are not interested. Our task, then, is to generate interest and convince students that what they know and feel counts in the English language arts classroom.

Writing Responses

Students using a reader response method respond in writing as they read. They can write what the story makes them think about, a particular word or phrase, or a feeling evoked by the piece. In short, they can write about anything the text makes them think of, although they may at first not understand what it is they are "supposed" to write. Students who are not accustomed to responding to literature initially need quite a bit of guidance. Many find it hard to believe that what they think counts, and they try to discover what the teacher wants them to put down. Getting students to trust themselves takes patience. The best way for us to counteract students' lack of faith in their own ideas is to comment positively on what they do write and encourage them to write more by asking questions that draw them out. Little by little, they learn to believe they do have something significant to say.

A list of questions can help guide middle school students to respond with some depth. Farnam and Kelly suggest guiding questions that help students think about connections with their own experiences. Also, asking them to respond to the most interesting or important part of a reading requires them to think more carefully about the text (47–49).

As an example, questions such as the following might provide the structure students need to get started:

1. What characters remind you of someone you know? In what ways do they make you think of the person or people you know?

2. What experiences in the text make you think of ones you have had?
3. What objects or places make you think of things you have had or places you know about?
4. Perhaps movies or television shows come to mind as you read. Describe the connections, such as similar action, characters, or setting.
5. If you were one of the characters, in what ways would you have reacted similarly or differently?
6. Describe how you feel at the end of the story (or chapter). In what ways does the story seem plausible? If you were the author, what might you write differently?

It is important to avoid yes or no questions as much as possible. We want the students to think about what they are reading, to make connections with the text. Yes or no answers are too simplistic, and students either don't see or ignore the "explain your answer" instruction.

Keep the list of questions short and ask students to respond to all of them if possible. Too many questions overwhelm them, whether they are senior high students or middle schoolers. On the other hand, asking them to write whatever comes to mind might be equally difficult. They need some guidance, especially when responding is new to them. As they become more comfortable with this approach, they write more. Some readers go off on tangents, following a thought or feeling evoked by the text; they might write pages without referring directly to the text. Others will follow the text in detail, commenting on a phrase or idea. Both responses are acceptable, as are all the responses that fall between these two.

What is not acceptable is a lack of a response or something so trite it is a nonresponse; for example, "This story is stupid." Talking to the student individually is most helpful. Go over the reading together, asking questions: "Is this a part you didn't care for? What did you think about this? Or how about when the character did this?" Often, students worry that their response is what will be "stupid" and cover up their feeling of inadequacy by giving flip comments. When people are told repeatedly their answers are wrong, they need courage to put themselves on the line again. We have to rebuild trust so students are willing to commit themselves to expressing an opinion.

Responding to literature does not suggest a quick reading. Smagorinsky and Gevinson explain that personal response objectives help students "to respond empathically to literary characters and their experiences" (73). This relating text to their own experiences helps students understand themes, patterns, and archetypes in the literature (73). Rather than reading for specific answers, they read to gain an understanding of the work.

However, often in literature class there is no room for students' interpretations. Judith Langer encourages teachers to help students explore "a horizon of possibilities" (204). We often rethink our first interpretations as our understandings become more complex. Literature is often taught "as if there is a predetermined interpretation" (205), thus leaving no room for students' own explorations. To promote deeper understandings, we need to "link their ideas with what they have already discussed, read, or experienced" (207).

EXPLORATION

Developing Response Questions

Choose a poem or short story and write suggestions that will help students write thoughtful responses. Remember, your ideas are not questions students must answer but should be ways of helping them think more deeply about the text and connect the literature with their own experiences.

Using Responses

Students' written responses are an integral part of literature study and may be incorporated into class activities in several ways. Using a variety of approaches will help you keep students interested and achieve different results.

1. *Use responses to improve or spark discussions.* Even if students do nothing other than write a response, their discussion skills will improve. When students write about literature, they must think more deeply about it. One substitute teacher's experience illustrates this point. The students had been assigned to read "Neighbor Rosicky" by Willa Cather. Although the regular teacher did not use reader response, the substitute teacher asked them to write about the main character for 10 minutes before they discussed the story. To help students understand what was expected, she suggested they describe the kind of person Rosicky was and whom he reminded them of. After 10 minutes, she asked them to share what they had written. They started out slowly, but soon they had a lively discussion going and talked to each other as much as to the teacher. More than one said, "Well, I didn't write this down, but what she (or he) just said made me think of. . . ." Granted, "Neighbor Rosicky" is an easy story to respond to, but, on the other hand, the students and the teacher didn't know each other, which always make discussion difficult. What got the class involved was the act of writing responses. It allowed students, reluctant to participate, to think through their responses before taking the risk of sharing publicly.

2. *Use responses as a written dialogue among students.* Students write their responses, form groups of four or five, and then each one reads what he or she has written. The teacher tells the students that they can add to their responses after hearing what the others have to say. They do not have to come to a consensus; each individual's responses are respected. Students will challenge each other, however, and ask why someone responded in a particular way. When students explain their responses, they have to start with the text that made them think of the event or feeling they recounted. For example, a student might say, "When he walks away from his father and doesn't look back, it made me think of. . . ." Or "It made me feel like. . . ." They don't defend their responses, but they do explain what part of the reading prompted it.

This way of sharing responses accomplishes three things: (a) Students must read with attention, (b) they learn how others think and read, and (c) they find out what others in the class are writing. Knowing what their classmates think gives students confidence in their own work. Those who are unsure of themselves discover their responses are as valid and interesting as anyone else's. Response writing does not depend on academic ability, provided the students are assigned readings they can handle.

Having students write and share responses is an excellent way to keep the students on task for reading. When they meet in groups to share and someone adds nothing, other students complain. Even students who have not read the assignment will often join in the conversation. Although it is obvious they are not prepared, listening to the others talk and adding comments of their own helps them understand the literature at least partially. Sharing responses in groups is far superior to giving a pop quiz to see if students have done the reading. The quiz method, although widely used, only affirms those who did the reading and lowers the self-esteem of those who did not. Exceptions occur, but most of the time the same students read or do not read the assignments. There is nothing motivating about failing yet another test. Students do not read to avoid the embarrassment of failing; that's not how it works for students who have trouble succeeding in school. They either act out, disrupting the class, or withdraw. Every person should be given opportunities to succeed in school, and setting it up so the same kids fail repeatedly is truly unfair.

3. *Use reader responses to create a dialogue between individual students and the teacher.* The responses are handed in, and you may write comments about the responses. These comments are not evaluations, but rather thoughts that occurred when reading what the student wrote. Your role is similar to that of students in a peer group, not a voice of authority that declares the student is right or wrong. Your support as a teacher is valuable to students, giving them the sense that their writing is interesting and important. On the other hand, negative evaluations or comments damage the relationship between you and the student. No one participates easily or works best in a threatening environment.

Students' written responses also give you a sense of how well the students understand and enjoy the literature selections. A student's question, "How come we never get to read a happy ending?" made one teacher realize the need to read something more lighthearted for a change. Even if they don't comment directly, it is not difficult to tell if they are interested in what they read. In addition, the dialogue allows you to encourage students to respond more fully to the text. Questions can help students expand on their written responses. For example:

- "I would like to hear more about when you. . . ."
- "Your comment about Maya made me think of how I felt when. . . ."
- "What happened after (whatever is appropriate)?"
- "I can really understand how you felt. Have your feelings changed at all now?"

Any comment that supports and encourages is appropriate. You and your students get to know each other better as you share thoughts and feelings with each other.

4. *Use responses as a source of discussion questions for the whole class.* As you read students' responses, keep notes on issues that are raised and disagreements students have on motivations of characters, the plot movement, and so forth. It is amazing how different students' reactions can be, and these differences are springboards for discussion. You act as a moderator, keeping the discussion focused on the text, perhaps playing devil's advocate if students seem too willing to accept an idea. The teacher is not the last word on who is right and who is wrong. Encouraging a variety of interpretations helps students think for themselves.

5. *Encourage students to use responses when they write papers based on the literature.* As students look through their responses, they can find patterns or themes that suggest writing topics. Going back to the text for a second reading adds detail and substance to the points they want to make. Because the focus for their paper comes from their own responses, their interest is high and they have a personal stake in writing a convincing paper. The bonus for you is that these papers are much more interesting to read than those where the topic is not student-selected.

You can use any combination of these responses. In fact, it is a good idea to vary activities based on responses. We all become tired of the same routine after a while, and the benefits decrease. The point of reader response is that students' thoughts and feelings about what they read are validated in their study of literature.

COMPREHENSION

Recent studies have focused on how to implement reader response in middle school classrooms. The most difficult part for teachers in changing over to this approach is to give up their study guides. Teachers fear they won't know whether students comprehend the material if they are not required to answer specific teacher-made questions.

In *Comprehension and Learning*, Frank Smith describes comprehension as "making sense of information" (10). Students comprehend what teachers want them to know when the new information meshes with what they already know. If the knowledge is completely foreign to their previous experience, they will have difficulty comprehending it. The better we can integrate new information with prior knowledge, the easier it is to not only learn in the first place but to remember (71). When teachers ask, "Don't you see what the author is trying to say?" they are probably asking the students, "Why can't you locate the same kind of information that I do?" (107). Actually both questions are based on the assumption of predetermined meanings that students are supposed to discover, without taking into account their individual responses. When teachers, through reader response, help students connect the text with their own experiences, comprehension is an easier goal to attain. The new information students discover is, right from the beginning, related to their prior knowledge.

The concern about discarding study sheets is a legitimate one for teachers. We want students to know certain information about the text. There is, however, a much better way to arrive at the same goal—better because it is not just busy work for a student, but comes from discussing the work with others in the class. First, teachers are surprised at the amount of information that comes up without teacher intervention in discussions based on students' responses. The students' wide-ranging interests and knowledge touch on most of the points found in a teacher-prepared study guide. A teacher who takes notes on students' discussions knows what is covered and what is not. For example, if the text is *No Promises in the Wind* by Irene Hunt and the setting of the Depression never comes up, a teacher might ask during the discussion, "Does it make a difference when the novel took place?" There is no right or wrong answer to this; the father's behavior might be the same today if he were out of work. The story focuses more on father-son relationships than on the Depression, but some students and teachers believe the novel is basically a way to learn about the 1930s. Who determines what is the correct reading? Through discussion, it becomes clear that the setting is the Depression era, and students remember this fact much longer when the information comes from people arguing whether the setting makes a difference to the reading of the novel than they do from filling in a blank on a worksheet answering, "What is the setting of the novel?" Teacher-posed questions should rarely have one factual answer, but rather, should be couched in "What do you think?" terms. Knowledge gained through discussion fits Smith's definition of comprehension.

Teaching *The Giver*

The following discussion questions for *The Giver*, by Lois Lowry, demonstrate this approach. We begin the teaching of this novel to seventh graders by asking them to answer questions in their reading journals before their reading, but after the books were handed out.

What do you think the book is about?

What is your guess about where and when it takes place?

What does the title suggest to you?

before they read them — setting mentally prepared

We handed out discussion questions for the assigned chapters. The students were to answer them as homework and bring them to class for the discussion. By having the questions and answers in front of them during the discussion period, more students joined in, even those who generally did not discuss literature. In addition to the questions, we gave them vocabulary words within the context of the story. For example,

Page 5 *defiant*

What did Lily do to show she was defiant?

Why was she defiant?

Good approach to vocab — u like it!

The vocabulary is not included here because of length restrictions; however, all of the discussion questions are provided.

Chapter 1
1. Why does Jonas feel apprehensive?
2. Do you think that all family units do the same ritual in the story? Can you imagine your family enjoying such a ritual? Why or why not?
3. What do you think it means when someone is "released"?

Chapter 2
1. How do the children get their names?
2. How did you get your name?
3. What do you think the Receiver does?
4. From what you know now about the community, what do you think is good or not so good about it?

Chapter 3
1. What do you think is the significance of the newborn's eyes being light like Jonas's?
2. Why did Lily speak petulantly? When might you speak this way?
3. What do you think the apple might stand for? Why an apple and not something else?

Chapter 4
1. What do you think is the purpose of the rule that they can't talk about accomplishments?
2. Where do you think people go when they are released?

Chapter 5
1. What do you think is the significance of the Stirrings and the pill?
2. How do the pills affect the community?
3. What is your opinion about the pills?

Chapter 6
1. Lily's front-buttoned jacket signified what?
2. When in your life have objects been significant? What were they?

Chapter 7
1. Jonas knows that "soon age would no longer matter." What does that mean to you? How would you compare someone who is 16 with someone who is 30?
2. Do you think Asher's punishments described on page 55 were fair? Explain your answer.
3. What do you think of the phrase "thank you for your childhood"?

Chapter 8
1. Describe what qualities you think a Receiver should have.
2. What kind of pain do you think the Chief Elder is talking about?

Chapter 9
1. What do you think of his instructions? Especially the last one about lying?

Chapter 10
1. What is the significance of the Attendant standing when Jonas enters the annex?
2. Why would Jonas know of so few books?
3. What memories is Jonas expected to receive?
4. What do you think is the significance of the Receiver's eyes?

Chapter 11
1. Why doesn't Jonas know about snow?

Chapter 12
1. Why can't people see colors?
2. Why did they relinquish sunshine?

Chapter 13
1. Why does Jonas think not seeing color is unfair? How is this new feeling important?
2. What do you think about protecting people from making wrong choices?
3. What does the Giver mean when he says that the instructors know nothing?
4. Why are memories important to knowledge?

Chapter 14
1. Why might protecting ourselves from certain kinds of pain not always be a good thing?
2. Why does it now seem ominous to Jonas that rules can't be changed?
3. Why did the idea that he could give a memory away frighten Jonas?

Chapter 15
1. Why is memory important?
2. What historical memories do we have that are important to keep alive even though they may be painful?
3. What is the purpose of having someone hold all the memories?

Chapter 16
1. Why is Jonas's memory of being treated as an individual a happy memory?
2. What good memories do you have?

3. What is good about the way older people are treated in the community? What isn't so good?
4. Why does Jonas lie to his parents?
5. Why does Jonas stop taking the pill?

Chapter 17
1. What is Jonas losing because of his new memories?
2. What do you think of Lily's story on page 137?

Chapter 18
1. What was the former Receiver's name and what is the meaning of that?
2. Why did she want to leave?

Chapter 19
1. Why do you think the Giver wants Jonas to see the release?
2. Do you think it is a good idea?

Chapter 20
1. What does the Giver mean when he says, "They can't help it."?
2. What does the Giver think is the worst part of holding memories?
3. What do you think of what the Giver tells Jonas at the end of this chapter?

Chapter 21
1. Do you think Jonas's plan to escape will work?
2. How did he escape and avoid detection?

Chapter 22
1. What was Jonas's new fear?
2. What does Jonas mean when he says he would have starved if he had stayed in the community?

Chapter 23
1. What is happening as they get closer to Elsewhere?
2. What begins to make Jonas feel happy?
3. What do you think happens at the end of the book?

After the conclusion of the book, we asked students to respond to the following questions, first in writing, then in small-group discussion:

What do you think are some of the main ideas the author wants readers to think about while reading her book?
What would you add or change in the book to make it better?
If you were to write a story similar to this one, what would it be about? *after reading— for summary*

FORMAL ANALYSES

We have emphasized reader response theory because we strongly believe that this approach achieves the desired results with secondary students. Furthermore, without the connections between reader and text, further analysis has limited effect. This is not to say, however, that no other critical analysis is appropriate. Teachers can use a variety of approaches depending on the developmental stages of the students, as well as the literature being read. A combination of critical analyses works best. Reader response requires close reading of a text as students search for meaning. Close reading is the mainstay of the new criticism. A reader's responses should lead to interpretation of the text.

Recognizing and understanding images is an important skill in literature. However, teachers often have a predetermined list of the images and what they signify, leaving no opportunities for students' own interpretations. By encouraging students to look for images that relate to their own experiences, they make connections that are often quite different from the usual interpretations, but are insightful and appropriate.

Teachers, however, must not emphasize information about the text more than they emphasize the text itself. Often the best approach is a matter of degree. We mentioned earlier that extensive information about Shakespeare's time is not appropriate for study before reading the play itself, but ignoring the historical implications of a plot during the reading process is not appropriate either.

Some historical or biographical information about the author's life and times or about a major fictional character helps readers understand what is happening. For example, students reading Dickens's *A Tale of Two Cities* need background information, but the information must be kept in perspective. We wouldn't read the book to learn only about the French Revolution. The social implications of an author's intentions help students understand Steinbeck's *The Grapes of Wrath* or Stowe's *Uncle Tom's Cabin*. If we use outside information only to help students understand the works, then students are not overwhelmed by the study of literature. The bottom line is that we are teaching students, not books.

 ## PREREADING ACTIVITIES

Generating interest may involve discussing some of the themes in a story or novel before the students read it. Contrary to what many students believe, there are many themes in a literary work, especially in the longer pieces. For example, *To Kill a Mockingbird* has several strong themes: a father's relationship with his children, growing up, prejudice against blacks, and fear of people different from ourselves. The themes a teacher chooses depend on the age and literary experience of the students. Whatever theme we choose to study, several resources can provide ideas for generating interest as a prereading activity. *Literature—News That Stays News,* edited by Candy

Carter, is an example of such a resource. The examples that follow are student suggestions from this text.

1. *Lord of the Flies*. Students do an impromptu writing on "What I would do if I were the leader of a group stranded on an island." The following day students share and discuss what they came up with. The teacher encourages students to compare what they wrote with the novel they are about to read (Beem 3–6).

2. "Young Goodman Brown." Students close their eyes and imagine they are in the world's most peaceful setting. They write down as many details as possible, using all of their senses. Then they imagine the most terrifying place and describe it in writing. The responses are grouped on a chart and discussed. The discussion helps students see the similarities in their images, and this helps them to understand the images in Hawthorne's story (Farbman 38–41).

3. *Romeo and Juliet*. The work is introduced with a brainstorming session in which the teacher asks students questions like, "What makes people fall in love?" and "What makes people fight?" Responses are encouraged, and the session ends with questions that lead into the actual reading. For example, "Do people ever decide whom they are going to love or how much they are going to fall in love?" Students keep their notes and refer to them as they read (Christ 66–69).

4. The following activity is from *Structuring Reading Activities for English Classes* (Graves, Palmer, and Furniss). "The Great All-American Cross Country Motorcycle Run" is designed for the "Prologue" to *Canterbury Tales* (11). Before students begin reading the "Prologue," the teacher describes an imaginary contemporary trek on motorcycles and then hands out pictures of interesting people who want to participate in the trek. Pictures from *National Geographic* work well. Tape them on brightly colored cardboard and give one picture to each group. Group members write an application letter for their participant. Each letter is read to the class, and students discuss what kinds of problems the travelers might have on the trip, how they could entertain themselves, and which travelers would get along with others and which would not.

   The scenario might be something like this: They are going to Colorado to see, for one last time, a beautiful river that will soon be destroyed by a dam project. One student group (Kimberly Paap, Jennifer Ulesick, and Colleen Ahern) wrote:

   > *Momma Mia! When I heard about the trip I knew this is what my late wife, Marie, would have wanted me to do. Being the owner of Anthony's Fish Market, I am aware of the importance of the wildlife of the river and would truly appreciate one last look at this environment.*

[handwritten margin note: prereading activities to gain stud's interest]

I would definitely enjoy spending time with a group of people. I have a large group of friends in the old neighborhood and am known as "the entertainer." I acquired this nickname from my talent as an accordion player and group comedian.

I still have my motorcycle from the old country; the one Maria and I rode around the country on when we were first married. This would be like a second honeymoon for me and my late Maria— although a little less romantic.

Sincerely,

Anthony "Tony" Rossel

5. When teaching *All Together Now* by Sue Ellen Bridgers, a book used in middle school, the teacher may ask students before they begin reading, "What are the characteristics of a good friend?" The responses are listed on the board as the class brainstorms what friendship means. Then students write about the most unusual friendship they have had. Students share these and discuss the responsibilities of friendship. This theme is only one of several in the novel. The prereading activity becomes a springboard for later discussions.

6. A teacher, Jan Sutton, planned a unit on diverse voices and designed the following activity to help students realize that stereotypes still plague our society.

Stereotypes—Small-Group Discussion

Write as many impressions/words as you can think of when you read the following words. Discuss your responses with the other group members.

- Football player
- Teacher
- Student with acid-green hair
- Women's libber
- Student with 4.0 average
- Police officer
- Fast-food worker
- Welfare recipient
- Banker
- Child molester

In general, prereading activities should generate interest in reading the text rather than provide factual information as "background." Some activities may be related to background, particularly a historical period. However, the discussions are always student-centered and not lectures. The teacher phrases questions in ways that increase student participation and refers to earlier discussions to strengthen the connections between readers and their responses.

Exploration

Developing Prereading Strategies

1. Choose a literature selection that is appropriate for high school but could be initially uninteresting to or difficult for students. One suggestion is *Great Expectations*, but choose any one you want. Write prereading activities that will increase students' interest and provide any necessary prereading knowledge.

2. Choose a literature selection that is appropriate for middle school but could be confusing at first for students of this age. You might use *The Giver* by Lois Lowry or *The Monkey Island* by Paula Fox, but any choice appropriate for middle school is fine. Write prereading activities that will increase students' interest and provide any information that they might need to begin reading the book.

Reading Activities

Assignments related to the text and given throughout the time students are engaged in reading add interest and understanding. Some activities come from students' written responses, whereas others are not directly related to responses. However, the responses always help students to complete assignments because they have developed clearer understandings of the text's characters, motivations, and outcomes. Activities that link the text with the readers' understanding help to heighten interest.

Activities from *All Together Now* by Sue Ellen Bridges, a book appropriate for middle school, provide an example of connections between text and experience. The main character is 12-year-old Casey, who is spending the summer with her grandparents. Her father is fighting in the Korean War, and her mother is working at two jobs, leaving little time to spend with her daughter. The story focuses on Casey's relationships throughout the summer.

1. After reading the description of Hazard in Chapter 2, describe in your response journal your impression of him. Whom does he remind you of?
2. Casey allows Dwayne to assume she is a boy. What is her motivation? Assume you were caught in a lie. Write a persuasive letter explaining your reasons for telling the lie and why you should be excused from blame.
3. In Chapter 8, Dwayne gives Casey a gift that means a lot to her. Why is it so significant?
4. Pansy and Hazard's honeymoon was not a happy experience. What values and expectations did each have that got in the way of their happiness?
5. In Chapter 11 Marge blows up at Dwayne. What words and images are used to describe Dwayne's feelings?

6. Describe your impression of Gwen when you first meet her in Chapter 6. Trace the development of her character throughout the novel, taking notes as you read. Reread your notes and describe how your impression of her changed, using passages from the text to explain.

7. Casey is angry because Dwayne has to spend the night in jail, and she feels the adults have let her down. How could the situation have turned out differently?

8. Point of view strongly influences our opinions of others. Write a description of someone you know very well; then write how another person might view that person.

9. By the end of the novel, Casey has learned much about responsibility and love. Describe the changes she has gone through and the results of those changes using passages that illustrate significant learning experiences for Casey (Maxwell 7–8).

We can create many different activities for our students. The following illustrate the possible variety and scope:

Creative, dramatic interpretations of lit.

1. Kurt Lothe, a high school student, wrote an article describing the activity his English teacher, Mr. Mead, had the class do for *Crime and Punishment*. He suggested they turn the story into a musical rather than write the usual paper. The students organized committees, and over the next few days worked on dialogue, created scenes, and wrote lyrics. They rewrote some of the scenes to add humor to the story. Showtime was in two weeks. Kurt explains, "What began as an alternative to another paper turned into one of the most memorable things I have done in my high school career. Not only does a musical like this provide an escape from the daily routine of the classroom, but it allows one to explore a character's feelings and emotions that reading alone cannot accomplish" (76–77).

writing predictions of plot

2. Vicki L. Olson describes several activities for *The Cay* by Theodore Taylor, a book used at middle school. As students began reading, she had them write predictions to help get them involved in the book. Then students listed three or four things that could happen to Philip and his family now that the Germans had attacked Aruba and brought war to the Caribbean. Students wrote predictions on the chances of Philip and his mother making it to Miami. Then students met in groups to share their predictions and the reasons behind them, later sharing orally with the large group. Writing predictions can be used at any grade level and for just about any reading to encourage readers to connect with the text. There is not a right or wrong answer, but students have to defend their ideas by explaining the evidence on which they built the prediction.

3. Assignments can build toward an activity that students complete after the literature is read. Karin Cooke, an English teacher, devised assignments for "Neighbor Rosicky" by Willa Cather that created the background for such an activity.

- Before assigning "Neighbor Rosicky," read the poem "Choices" by Nikki Giovanni. Have students write a response to the poem in their journals. They can explain what the poem meant to them or what it made them think of while they were listening.
- In their journal, students write a poem about either their best friend or someone they value highly. They are encouraged to share their poems with the rest of the class or in small groups.
- In their journals students write what they think the word *neighbor* means. They discuss their responses in small groups.
- After reading "Neighbor Rosicky," students write a short paper about why they think Cather titles the story "Neighbor Rosicky" instead of "Mr. Rosicky." Why was he considered a neighbor? (This is not to be evaluated as a formal paper.)
- Backed up with examples from the story, students write what they think was most valuable to Rosicky.
- The teacher divides the class into groups. The groups are the directors and producers for a film based on "Neighbor Rosicky." They use film and TV stars to cast their roles. Then they write a brief description of each character and give the reasons for their casting selections.
- The final assignment is writing a biography of Rosicky using facts and inferences gleaned from the reading.

 ## TEACHING SHAKESPEARE

Romeo and Juliet

Barbara Dressler, a high school English teacher, wrote the following three-week unit for teaching *Romeo and Juliet:* Students read the play aloud during class time. Frequent stops are made to clarify questions that arise from the language and vocabulary differences. Then students listen to audiotapes of certain acts to become familiar with the Shakespearean language style. After reading each act, a videotape of parts of that entire act will be shown. Following the videotape viewing, students work in small groups to outline the act. Writing activities follow this group work.

Small-Group Work

Students are divided into groups according to their choice of a minor character in the play (Paris, Tybalt, Mercutio, Lord and Lady Capulet, Friar Laurence, the Nurse, and so on). The groups discuss the traits of the character and how he or she influences the course of the play. Groups then report to the entire class.

Writing Assignments Given to Students

Act One
1. As Juliet, write a letter to a friend telling how you met and fell in love with Romeo.
2. As Romeo, write a letter to a friend telling about your new love and explaining why you've forgotten Rosaline.
3. As Benvolio, write an explanation of how and why you want to help your love-sick friend, Romeo.
4. As an attendant of the Prince, write a description of the street fight.

Act Two
1. Write a description of Friar Laurence. Tell why Romeo turns to him for help.
2. Write Tybalt's letter to Romeo.
3. Write a description of Scene 4 through the eyes of Peter.

Act Three
1. Imagine Juliet has asked you for advice. Write her a letter telling what you think she should do at this time.
2. As the Prince, dictate a letter to your secretary explaining why you are banishing Romeo.
3. Write a speech for Lord Capulet to give at Juliet's wedding.

Act Four
1. Write what Lady Capulet would say if she discovered that Juliet was planning to take the potion.
2. Write what Lord Capulet would say if he discovered that Juliet was planning to take the potion.
3. Write a letter from Friar Laurence to Romeo.

Act Five
1. As the page, tell what happened between Paris and Romeo.
2. Write a persuasive speech Friar Laurence could use to try to convince Juliet to leave the tomb with him.
3. As Friar Laurence, explain your involvement in this affair to your superior.

After reading and discussing the entire play, students select from the following assignments:

1. Using the play's prologue as a model, write an original epilogue for *Romeo and Juliet*.
2. As Romeo or Juliet, write a diary entry for each of the five days of the play.
3. As Juliet, write two letters to an advice columnist. As the columnist, write a letter in reply to each of them.

4. Rewrite the ending of the play, as it would have been if Friar John had not been quarantined but was able to deliver the message to Romeo.
5. Write a front-page news article that could appear in the newspaper the day after Romeo and Juliet were found dead.

There are many assignments a teacher can use for any work of literature. What is important is that the assignments occur throughout the reading, especially in longer works. The activities should be designed for individual work, small groups, and the entire class. Discussion is vital to provide students with opportunities to interact and discover what others are thinking and writing.

Romeo and Juliet is the most widely taught work of literature at the secondary level. Using activities that involve students as the ones Dressler described helps students who may have difficulty reading this selection. One teacher, Pamela E. Adams, suggests a preview as a way to help students see connections between their lives and the play. Adams explains that students "need to spend much effort understanding the antiquated English and often get bogged down at a literal level and fail to appreciate the humor, puns, and story line" (425). To alleviate this problem, she suggests a text preview that builds information with questions for discussion, synopsis of the story, and vocabulary introduction. The preview's purpose is to help students understand and enjoy the play, not to test them on what they learned.

ACTIVITY FOR *HAMLET*

Teacher Pat Stellick designed the following assignment for her high school students:
   Hamlet Journals

Directions to Students: *Choose a character from the list below.*

Hamlet
Gertrude
Claudius
Polonius
Horatio
Ophelia
Laertes
The Ghost

1. Following your reading of each act, write a journal entry. The journal entries should
   a. reveal the innermost thoughts and feeling of your character
   b. make specific references to the details and events in the story
   c. use your imagination to creatively explain your character's state of mind
2. If your character dies or is already dead have the character explain how he/she views the ensuing events of the drama.

An example of the assignment by Miranda, one of Stellick's students, is shown here.

OPHELIA'S JOURNAL
Act I

Since the death of his father, my dear Lord Hamlet has been so depressed. I am very worried about him. I can see the pain in his eyes.

Somehow it seems as though he is so overpowered by his grief that he doesn't love me anymore. But then I catch him glancing at me, and I see his feelings—for just a moment. It's encouraging. I know that the situation between the queen and Hamlet's uncle, the new King, is confusing him very much.

He continues to wear the mourning colors—somehow I do not blame him. I would be very distraught if something were to happen to my father. Oh, dear Hamlet. I miss us.

I hope things get better for him!

Act II

I am so confused that Hamlet is acting stranger than ever, and I am afraid his feeling for me is not what had once been.

Was father right?

I thought I knew Hamlet so well, but now I am not so sure. Dad thinks that Hamlet is lovesick for me since he has forbidden me to see him—but I know that isn't it.

Whatever is going through his mind is much deeper than that—much more detrimental.

Oh, it is so unnerving. I want everyone to stop acting so crazy. No one trusts anyone anymore. Father sent someone to spy on Laertes. Why won't he just let him be?

Laertes should be able to live his own life. It isn't fair for father to invade his personal life.

None of what is going on in our lives is anyone's business but our own.

Father needs to be concerned with his own issues.

Act III

Hamlet arranged for a group of players to perform. Before the performance, he was very rude to me. He treated me very cruelly. He is still upset with me about something. It's driving me nuts! I fear that he won't love me again!

In front of so many people he embarrassed me. I'm becoming afraid of him! I used to trust him completely. I can't anymore.

It's so hard for me to think of what we had once shared. It's all over.

Why? I need him—I thought he needed me. I was such a fool!

Act IV

Flowers oh. I love all the pretty flowers! Everyone needs a pretty flower. Everyone is a pretty flower! I am a pretty flower!

Flowers need water. I am a very pretty flower who needs water.

> *Here I go!*
>
> *Weeeeeeeeeeeee!*
>
> *Splash-woosh!*
>
> *Glug glug flower*
>
> > *Flowerrrrrrs. . . . .*
> >
> > *Fllloowerrrsss. . .*
> >
> > *Fll. . . ow. . . ers. . .*
> >
> > *Fll. . .*
>
> *Oh, damn.*
>
> *I died.*

EXPLORATION

Teaching Shakespeare

Choose a Shakespearean play other than *Romeo and Juliet*—perhaps one of the comedies—and design activities to help secondary students enjoy and understand the play.

TEACHING SHORT STORIES

Teaching short stories is not appreciably different from teaching novels. However, short stories are often overlooked when designing thematic units. Too often, short stories are taught, one after another, with little or no connection among them. The beauty of short stories is quite simply the length. For some students, a novel is overwhelming and they avoid even beginning one. As with other literature, teachers can find in short stories a wealth of subject matter, variety of settings, complex characters, and intricate plots. Stories themselves are an important part of our lives. All families share stories, and telling stories have a long, rich tradition. Using response activities with stories we assign students can help them connect school texts with their family stories.

Reflection

Recall as many of your family stories as possible. Which ones were repeated over a period of time? Why these and not others? Jot down some of your stories and share them with your future students.

Short Story Activities

The following student assignments were written by Anne Elliott, an English education major, to accompany "The Secret Life of Walter Mitty" by James Thurber.

1. Write a synopsis of the story as if you were describing it to a friend. Try to condense the story into a few sentences.
2. Pretend this story is going to be a TV series. Write a television announcement to advertise it. Include who will play the leading roles as well as what the series will be about.
3. Think about other books you have read, television shows you've watched, or stories that express a great deal of imagination. How do they compare with "The Secret Life of Walter Mitty"?
4. Many of Mitty's fantasies are interrupted. Choose one and finish it for him.
5. Before reading the story, students form groups of four or five. The teacher begins each group by reading one line from the story, and students create their own story by each contributing one sentence at a time. After reading the story, students compare their versions with Mitty's version. Discuss the power of the imagination.
6. Recall one event from your life and then write an exaggeration of it to create a tall tale. Then write the event as it actually happened.
7. Write a character description of Walter, including how he looks, acts, and sounds. Pantomime your description for the class or draw an illustration.
8. In a small group act out one of Mitty's fantasies, changing the ending as you wish.

A second group of activities is written by Renee McCarthy, an English education student, and is based on a collection of short stories, *Baseball in April*, written by Gary Soto. This book is an excellent choice for middle and high school students. The stories reveal day-to-day life of Mexican American youth in Fresno. The issues in the book include love, friendship, family, youth and age, success, failure, and self-esteem. Students write in a journal following every story or reading.

1. The first activity is for prereading. Answer the following questions in your journals:

   What does it mean to be attractive? Does it mean physically beautiful or can it mean something else? Explain what you mean.

   What does it mean to be popular? How does one get to be popular and whose decision is it? Do you think popularity is important? Explain your answer.

2. The second activity is done throughout the book, starting with Chapter 1. After each chapter write in your notebook the main points from the story you just read. What experiences in your life does it remind you of?

3. This activity deals only with the chapter on the Barbie doll. The issue in the story is self-esteem and self-perception, important concepts at this age. Write an essay about Veronica's treatment of her two Barbie dolls. How does she treat them differently? What does this say about the way people treat one another?

4. The final activity: Imagine you are asked to write an essay to a governor who does not support learning foreign languages in middle school. Explain why you think it is helpful to learn about another culture and its language. Use at least three examples from the book.

Short stories should be included in the literature program, not as a separate unit, but integrated throughout the curriculum. As with other literature selections, you need to offer choices to students and to have resources of interesting short stories available for them. Many of the following selections are written by authors popular with young adult readers.

- *8 Plus 1* by Robert Cormier
- *Angels and Other Strangers* by Katherine Paterson
- *Athletic Shorts* by Chris Crutcher
- *Baseball in April and Other Stories* by Gary Soto
- *Coming of Age* edited by Bruce Emra
- *Dear Bill, Remember Me?* by Norma Fox Mazer
- *The Illustrated Man* by Ray Bradbury

TEACHING POETRY

Activities for poetry are much the same as those described for short stories and novels. Too often, students' reactions to reading poetry are, "I don't get it," as if there is a hidden meaning. Student responses are as valid here as for other types of literature, and the same general guidelines are appropriate. Poetry is meant to be heard. When we share a poem with students, it is important to read the poem aloud as students follow along with a printed copy. You may want to ask them to allow their minds to react to the words, letting thoughts flow freely, and not to think about what the poem "means." Students then write responses without talking to anyone else. You may want to provide suggestions if students have difficulty responding.

- What images do I see as I hear the poem?
- What do the words remind me of?
- What feelings have I had that are similar to the ones expressed in the poem?

Students compare their responses and discuss the similarities and differences. Poetry, more than prose, elicits widely different comments. For example, when students read Theodore Roethke's "Papa's Waltz," some students believe the poem represents a joyful romp of a father with his son, whereas others see it as the father's abusive behavior, probably caused by alcohol. The differences arise out of different experiences of the students. Also, many of the young women believe the father is dancing with a daughter, and images of themselves as small children come back strongly. Both views are "correct," and students can point to specific examples in the poem to back up their interpretations.

In a study of student responses by Robert Blake and Anna Lunn, students read a poem and responded with no restrictions. In fact, the responses were done outside of a school setting to further remove any sense of a threatening or structured expectation. The findings of the study have important implications for classroom teachers (72–73).

1. Reading a poem is not a simple or linear process. Readers need time to read over particular lines and to think about the poem, to not be rushed through the process. A poem "needs to grow on us—adults and adolescents alike" (72).
2. When students say they do not like a poem or poetry in general, they often mean they are afraid they cannot understand the meaning. Further, they believe the teacher does know the "meaning."
3. Adolescents read and respond differently "from English majors and experienced teachers in many immensely important ways" (72). This does not mean that adolescents do not read poetry successfully, but they bring to the reading different backgrounds and experiences; few have acquired the critical techniques that took us years to develop.
4. Within the limits of meanings held by class members and the larger community, there are as many responses to complex poems as there are students in the class. It takes time for students to learn how to read and respond to poetry. Students need many opportunities to develop confidence so that they can respond in meaningful ways to complex poetry.

One of the problems with teaching poetry is that students often have had little experience with poetry since elementary grades. Moreover, it is usually taught in a separate unit pulled out of the regular context of literature. If students become more familiar with a variety of poetry, responding to it becomes easier. Poetry is best taught throughout all thematic units. Regardless of the day's activity, you need to try to read a poem to the students, not to "study" it, but to enjoy it.

EXPLORATION

Preparing for Poetry Teaching

Immerse yourself in poetry for a week. Read children's poetry, which is often in a picture-book format. Read funny poetry like those found in Shel Silverstein's books, poems in current magazines written by novice writers, award-winning poetry, poems written by elementary schoolchildren, and poems by minorities. Think about them; roll the words around in your mind. Bring your favorites to class to share.

Richard Beach and James Marshall, English professors, suggest the following guidelines for successfully teaching poetry:

- Never teach a poem you do not like.
- Teach poems you are not certain you understand.
- Teach poems that are new to you.
- Read poems daily in your life outside of school.
- Give students the freedom to dislike "great poetry." (384)

Activities for Teaching Poetry

images in poetry ←

1. Teacher John T. Kell Jr. devised a lesson that helped his tenth-grade students understand how description is used in poems to create images. He wrote a short descriptive poem based on a picture of Alaska. Without showing students the picture, he gave them copies of the poem. As they listened to the poem and read it to themselves, they drew a picture of what they thought the poem described. After completing their drawings, they circled words and phrases from the poem that helped create the images they drew (66). In discussion, help students see that the circled words created the images so that in future readings they can recognize imagery and understand the deeper meaning in their individual readings.

images in poetry ←

2. A similar assignment for developing student abilities to see images in poems comes from Linda Wall, a middle school teacher. One way to help students see images in poems is to help them realize that imagery is language that appeals to our five senses. "Students can understand poetry through the pictures we see, hear, touch, taste, and smell" (9).

Wall begins by handing out peppermint candy. Students write words or experiences that come to mind as they eat the candy, identifying what sensory impression they are reminded of. Students could later apply this technique when reading a poem.

Another approach Wall uses is to have students draw pictures or images they recognize from a poem. After hearing and reading the poem, they draw as many images as they can. The activity can be reversed by having students first draw pictures based on a sensory image, then write a poem based on the picture.

3. To help students recognize tone in poetry and, consequently, to come to a deeper understanding of the poem, Renee McCarthy, an English education student, developed a list of questions to guide students when they read "Hermana" by Gary Soto.

- What type of tone does this poem have? In other words, how does it make you feel? Is it uplifting, inspiring, melancholy, or depressing? Give examples from the poem that make you feel this way. Quote a line that made you feel the way you did.
- Who is the voice in the poem? Is she or he young or old? How do we know? Is this individual feeling pain? Why? Who else is affected by the father/brother-in-law's behavior? What types of problems are these people experiencing and how might they be helped? How would you act if you were a member of this group? Explain the living environment for the children and explain how justice could be found.

4. English education students brainstormed questions and activities they could use in a secondary English class after assigning the poem "The Belly Dancer" by Diane Wakoski.

To begin, place the poem on an overhead, cover the title and read it together, line by line. Have students write reactions to each line as it is read. They write a summary of reactions after completing the reading. How did their reactions change after they read the title?

- Write a list of words from the poem that appeal to our senses.
- Discuss attitudes toward the body as exhibited in the poem.
- What does the poem say to you about relationships between men and women?
- How does the poem use sounds to create meanings?
- How does the snake image function within the poem? Why a snake and not a different animal?
- What do you think is the tone of the poem? Specifically what words or thoughts provide the tone?
- Discuss the women's fear. Why are they uncomfortable in the presence of the belly dancer?
- What do you picture as the setting of the poem? If it were changed, would your reaction change?
- Think of another type of dance and write a list of words to describe it. Compose a poem based on these words.
- Explain with examples from the poem whether you feel the belly dancer presents a positive or negative image.

Although a teacher would not use all of these ideas or suggestions in guiding students to a deeper understanding of a poem, the list illustrates the many possibilities teachers have when we want to encourage students to read more closely and to explore a variety of meanings.

5. An activity that includes a poem and a short story helps students recognize common elements in different genres and may make poetry more accessible to them. Ella Shaw, a high school teacher, asked her students to read the story "Two Kinds," an excerpt from *The Joy Luck Club* by Amy Tan, and the poem "Thanking My Mother for Piano Lessons" by Diane Wakoski. Both works focus on the relationship between a mother and daughter and piano playing as a major force.

Shaw suggests the following: Have students list characteristics that describe first Wakoski's mother, then Tan's mother. After generating the lists, students discuss in what ways the two mothers are similar and in what ways different. Next they compare and contrast the tones of each piece and find examples in the texts. Their findings are turned in as group writing products. The following are questions for individual students to consider:

- What attitudes do Wakoski and Tan seem to have toward their mothers?
- How are their feelings about the piano as adults different from their feelings as children?

Students write a short essay discussing these questions and other points they want to include when comparing the two texts.

EXPLORATION

Poetry in the Curriculum

Select a poem you like and write as many ideas as possible that you could use if you taught the poem in class. How could the poem relate to other literature you are having students study?

Poetry Resources

We all have our favorite poems and may want to teach them in our classes. We should enjoy the poetry we teach; however, beginning teachers need to be careful about using poetry that they studied in college literature classes for two reasons:

1. Many of the selections are too difficult for young adult readers. The difficulties may come from vocabulary, allusions, content, word choice, and syntax.
2. Because you studied them in a college class, you may have learned only one way of understanding the poem, thus making it difficult for you to accept the various meanings your future students will find.

Rather than resorting to teaching the same poems you were taught, try to explore the wealth of resources available to us. Bushman and Bushman suggest the following texts for secondary students:

- *Class Dismissed!* and *Class Dismissed II* by Mel Glen
- *A Fire in My Hands* by Gary Soto
- *Now Sheba Sings the Song* by Maya Angelou (45–46)
- *Postcard Poems: A Collection of Poems for Sharing* by Paul Janeczko
- *Rainbow Writing* by Eve Merriam
- *Reflections on a Gift of Watermelon Pickle and Other Modern Verse* edited by Steve Dunning, Edward Lueders, and Hugh L. Smith

Beach and Marshall list several poetry collections, of which a small sampling is included here:

- *Bring Me All Your Dreams* by Nancy Larrick
- *Celebrations: The Poetry of Black America* by Arnold Adoff
- *I Am Phoenix: Poems for Two Voices* by Paul Fleishman
- *I Like You, If You Like Me: Poems of Friendship* by Myra Cohn Livingston (403–405)
- *To Look at Anything* by Lee Bennett Hopkins

TEACHING LANGUAGE IN LITERATURE STUDY

The study of tone, diction, imagery, and style is appropriate for older students—juniors and seniors—who are capable readers and are enrolled in college-bound or advanced placement English. If teachers stress these language elements for younger students, however, literature becomes a study of facts at the expense of reading, enjoying, and learning about others and ourselves. Even with the advanced students, teachers must present the study of language elements in an interesting and appropriate way; not the way college students are taught. Two experienced teachers share lesson plans to illustrate how they accomplish this goal.

A Closer Look at Tone (Jean Moelter)
1. To begin, we have a class discussion to define what is meant by tone. How do you decide what type of clothes to buy? Style? Color? Size? What does your style say about you? What does it mean when someone says, "Tone down your color"? What can tone of voice convey? Compare two versions of the same song by different artists. Discuss the differences between tone and style even though it is the same song.

2. Read "We Real Cool" by Gwendolyn Brooks and "The First Confession" by X. J. Kennedy. What is the message each writer is trying to convey? How do you know? How does tone create meaning? How does the tone in the poem support the meaning?

3. Students look at how a stereotyped group is portrayed from the movie *Grease* or a similar one. How did the director create tone to get the meaning across? After discussion, students model either Brooks's or Kennedy's style to write a poem or narrative that has a strong tone conveying meaning.

Metaphor Focus *(Andrea Kramer)*

Before Reading Hamlet

1. Students listen and respond to "I Am a Rock" by Simon and Garfunkel. Why does this voice identify himself as a rock and an island? Have you ever felt this way? When? Are a rock and an island good things to be when a person has had a struggle with a loved one or a friend? Why? What other choices would also work to describe a person in this mental state?

2. Students bring in lyrics of a song containing a metaphor. Together we analyze whether the metaphors "work." Is the comparison appropriate? Are enough connections drawn? What other words could they choose instead to create that metaphor?

3. Students listen and respond to "An Old Pair of Shoes" by Randy Travis. How is this comparison similar to and different from "I Am a Rock"?

4. Discuss the use of imagery and puns to create metaphors; use "An Old Pair of Shoes" to begin the example. Other examples from literature are also used.

5. Students write a personal metaphor or lyric form with the option of performing their metaphor in some fashion for the class.

During the Reading of Hamlet

6. Demonstrate the concept of extended metaphors with "Whose List to Hunt" (and other sonnets) and the disease imagery in *Hamlet*.

7. Students keep a list of words associated with imagery that continue the unweeded garden and disease metaphors.

8. Students brainstorm a list of words appropriate for creating a personal metaphor for *Hamlet*. Use that list to create a diamante poem for *Hamlet*; then choose one to further develop in essay form.

These two lessons involve students in their own learning rather than being told in a lecture format what style, tone, and metaphor are.

EXPLORATION

Planning Lessons on Literary Devices

Select another literary language device such as diction, irony, connotation, mood, or any other. Develop a lesson plan that is creative and interesting. Use any literature you like, but the lesson must connect to specific literature examples.

VOCABULARY STUDY IN READING

Purposes

Vocabulary study has several purposes, and how we teach vocabulary depends on the specific purpose. Teaching reading vocabulary does not require pronunciation or spelling because spelling has nothing to do with speaking or listening, and little to do with reading. Pronunciation is important only when speaking, and further, we know the meanings of many words that we neither speak nor write.

Vocabulary in reading has two purposes: to learn the meanings so the present text can be understood and second, to increase reading vocabulary so that meanings in future texts will be understood. It is important to realize that none of us needs to know the meaning of every word to comprehend what we read. Without thinking about it, we skip over many words when we read, inferring the meaning from the context. To stop and look up each word slows readers down so much that they lose interest. Occasionally, readers might write down words they don't know, but they often keep right on reading and look them up later. The only reason for doing this is a love of words, not a need to understand the story better.

Words in Context

Words are never to be taken out of context, either for learning or for testing. We know how important context is in figuring out meanings, and it goes against all common sense to give students a list of words to learn, ask them to look up the words in a dictionary, and use each in a sentence. To illustrate, I once assigned a list of words from a short story by Poe. A very competent student looked up the word *dank*. Learning that it meant moist, she wrote, "My, these brownies are dank." When I explained the connotation to her, she thought it so funny she shared it with the rest of the class. After that, every time we ate brownies someone would say, "Mmmmmm, good—so dank." Although that turned out to be a shared joke, I learned students must have context to understand connotations and never gave them words in isolation again.

Another experience involved a student who struggled with reading. While taking a vocabulary test, he commented that the teacher forgot to include the meaning of a particular word. The test was one where students were to match words to appropriate meanings. As she looked at the paper, the teacher could see the meaning he was supposed to choose; of course, she wrote the test and knew all the answers. She asked him what he thought the word meant, and in his own words he gave a reasonable definition. The teacher told him she had forgotten to include that meaning and wrote it on his paper. Many students could generalize the meaning supplied for the test and come up with the "right" answer, but she was penalizing those who could not. Yet, these students did know what the word meant. The tests were more "guess what meaning the teacher has in mind" than tests of vocabulary knowledge.

Because words must remain in context, one way to identify the ones you choose for study is to give the line and page number of each word. Another method is to reprint the sentence or part of a sentence on a handout. For example: "He usually agreed with her in earlier years, sometimes grudgingly, but without *rancor*" (from *No Promises in the Wind*). The directions to students are to write what *rancor* means in the context. To help them use context, they first write what they think the word means, and if unsure or just want to check, they look it up in a dictionary. The students meet in groups to go over the meanings and use dictionaries to solve arguments.

Testing Vocabulary

If you want to test students on reading vocabulary, use the same sentences in the test as were on the handout, perhaps in different order. In their own words, students write the definition of the word as used in that sentence. Spelling should not be evaluated, nor do students need to write complete sentences because that is not what is being tested. Rather, teachers look for accurate meanings of the words in the context in which they appeared in the text. Grading time is minimal, guessing doesn't help students, and the test is true to the principle that context provides clues for word meanings.

Words in the text are often esoteric or specialized, such as foreign phrases or words that are not commonly used, and students need not remember them beyond the passage they are reading. For these words, you simply tell students the meaning. For vocabulary instruction you may find the following web site useful: <http://www.indiana.edu/~eric_rec/eio/bibs/vocabsec.html>.

 ## SHARING BOOKS

This section might be called "Book Reports," except we are strongly opposed to them as they are generally used. Having students fill out a book report form or follow a particular format wastes the teachers' and students' time. When asked why they require the reports, teachers usually respond, "So I will know if the students are reading." Ironically, book reports do not provide that information. It is too easy to write a report without actually reading the book, which makes it difficult to know who reads and who does not. And book reports are boring. We try to make them more interesting by providing options to the standard report, but generally the options, although more fun, can also be done without reading. Teachers cannot be sure students actually read the books unless they ask, and students are surprisingly honest.

Sharing books, though, is a vital part of a literature class. Most of us like to read; after all, teaching English is our chosen field. When we read something we especially enjoy, we try to think of someone who would also like it. Friends and family pass books around, usually with the comment, "You have to read this! You'll love it." We can replicate that enthusiasm in the classroom if we provide the opportunities.

Book Talks

Students pay attention to what other students read, which can be frustrating when you take time to suggest books to a student who then ignores the advice and chooses a book a classmate casually recommends. The solution is to structure time so that students can share, and this can be done in various ways.

The most informal, and often most successful, way is setting aside part of a period to talk about books. Students know ahead of time when this will be, but they do not have to prepare anything. Not everyone has to talk about a book, although everyone is encouraged to do so. Some share information about a magazine article they read, which is fine. The requirement is that it must be reading material as opposed to a TV show. You, too, can share reading that would be of interest to the students. The discussions are casual, and students stay seated when sharing. Students show high interest in the discussions; questions and conversations are common.

One time in a book-sharing session, one student walked out of the room. A few minutes later he reappeared with a book under his arm. When I asked where he had gone, he explained he had left to check out the book one of his classmates was talking about. He said, "If I waited until class was over, I was afraid someone else would get it before I did." Such eagerness to read is precisely the objective of book sharing.

Interest Grouping

A more structured way to create book-sharing time is for students to form groups based on the type of book they read. After students select the book they want to read, they jot down the genre (e.g., biography, mystery, adventure), and then you form the groups, so that the mystery buffs talk about mysteries together, the biography readers talk together, and so on. The reason for doing this is that readers with a strong liking for one kind of book enjoy talking to others who share their reading tastes. This is especially true of science fiction fans, but everyone likes to share a common interest. The students meet in groups after they read the books. This grouping is appropriate only once in a while because, of course, we want to increase the variety of books students read, but interest groups are popular with students, and they increase reading enjoyment.

As a spin-off on the interest grouping, each group can create a skit involving characters from the books each student reads. Students perform the skits for the class, and it is a good idea to videotape them and have them available on Parents' Night. We've had talk shows with characters across historical times and from different fields; in one,

Joan of Arc and Einstein held a discussion about taking responsibility for making the world a better place. Another time, students dressed in gym clothes, dribbled and passed a basketball around while discussing feats of the various sport figures they had read about. Admittedly, students could do these without reading the whole book, but the activities provide opportunities for informal dramatics and are based on literature and are therefore well worth the class time.

Student Critiques

Another way to share books is to keep a card file in the room with student-written summaries and information about the books they have read. They include their name so others can ask more about the book if they care to. Many of the students use this source instead of browsing in the library when looking for a book to read. This also provides a way for shy students, who may be reluctant to speak in class, to share their reading.

At the end of the year, have all students write a paragraph about a book they would highly recommend for others to read over the summer. Every student goes home for the summer with a copy of all the book descriptions.

A middle school student (D. Stevens) wrote:

LORD OF THE FLIES BY WILLIAM GOLDING

When they land the boys are overjoyed to have no grownups. But soon work has to be done: the fire kept burning, the huts built, the hunting done. There is Piggy. He is fat and very grownup. He knows how to do things but the crowd rejects him. He gets killed by a rolling rock that cracks his skull open. Ralph is the "leader" because he blew the conch first. On the other hand, Jack, though he doesn't know at first, is bloodthirsty!

Reading in Class

Many teachers believe that reading in class is a waste of time, but Larry Johannessen believes that if students begin a reading assignment in class, this "significantly increased the likelihood that they will continue and finish the reading outside of class" (69). In addition, giving students class time to read promotes the idea of reading being an integral part of English class. That sounds obvious, but some students brag about their ability to never read a book and yet pass English courses.

To increase reading enjoyment and come closer to the goal of helping students become lifelong readers, reading and talking about books must become an integral part of the class. The groups work well because they focus the activity, but talking about books needs to be a common, almost daily, activity. We can set the stage for this to happen by talking about books we ourselves read. At first, students may seem surprised that we know about, let alone read, romance novels, Stephen King, or any contemporary popular authors. The same is true for magazine articles. When we first share articles from *Road Rider* or *Rolling Stone*, we may be met with looks of disbelief, but students do then begin to talk more freely about what they read. Book sharing increases enjoyment in reading and makes the goal of helping students become lifelong readers more attainable.

INSTRUCTIONAL UNIT

THE HOUSE ON MANGO STREET

An English education student, Melissa Rossing, prepared a teaching unit for *The House on Mango Street* by Sandra Cisneros. Because of space limitations we are able to include only a small portion of her entire unit. However, by using her resources you would be able to construct your own unit.

Rossing wrote the unit for eighth graders for a period of 20 days. The outcomes she planned for her students were

1. Identify issues in *The House on Mango Street* that have a personal meaning for them.
2. Understand the concept of character and aspects associated with creating a descriptive character.
3. Have a greater appreciation of cultural differences.
4. Relate their original personal meanings from the novel to societal issues, therefore demonstrating how literature can provide a personal connection to society as a whole.

Rossing's activities included writing journal prompts. The students had to have only one journal write a day and a total of 15 were required at the conclusion of the unit. She provided a list of prompts from which they could choose.

Journal Prompts

Day 1:	Describe some physical aspect of your family.
	Describe how you view "boy and girl" worlds.
	What do you think your name means? How did you get it?
Day 2:	How do you choose your friends?
	Recall a story about one of your friends.
	Describe a good day for you.
	Are you like any of your family? Describe how you are or aren't.
Day 3:	"Gil's Furniture Bought & Sold"—How would the vignette appear if it were in Gil's voice? Rewrite it in Gil's voice.
	Write about one of your neighbors, describing them in detail. Try writing a poem about them.
Day 4:	Have you ever been aware of a prejudice based on something unknown and feared?
	Write about the biggest family you know.
	How do you think the role of mothers has changed? Has it changed in all households?

Day 5:   Try to write a poem from "And Some More."
                How would you describe your feet?
                What is it like to get something new?
Day 6:   What are special occasions like in your family?
                Why do you think young people don't like their bodies?
                What do you want your first job to be when you "grow up"?
Day 7:   Esperanza experiences the death of her grandfather. What do
                you think she and her father are going through?
                Does birth order affect your personality?
                Would you ever go to a palm reader? Why or why not?
Day 8:   Write about a stranger you've met.
                Write about someone you know who is old but acts young.
                Create a mysterious character with an extraordinary life.
Day 9:   Write about a dream you've had that seemed so real you had
                trouble knowing if it happened or not.
                Write about what it would be like being in a foreign country and
                not knowing the language.
Day 10:   "Minerva Writes Poems" is a violent vignette. How do you feel
                towards her husband or her for staying with him?
                "What Sally Said" is another sad story. Write your response to
                it. How did you feel about her father and her for defending him?
Day 11:   What do you think the Sisters meant when they told Esperanza
                that she must come back for the others?
                Why do you think that Esperanza doesn't want to claim her
                house as her home?
Day 12:   What do think the significance of the assigned poems is?
Days 13–17: Reflect on any thoughts or questions you have about the book
                or the film.

The film Rossing is referring to is *Breaking Away*, directed by Peter Yates. It is about the first year after high school of four boys who are struggling to decide what to do with the rest of their lives. It is rated PG and has won many awards. A related web site for the film is <http://www.teachwithmovies/breaking-away.html>.

A selection of poems Rossing includes in her unit is

"Choices" by Nikki Giovanni
"The House in the Woods" by Randall Jarrell
"The House on the Hill" by Edwin Arlington Robinson
"The House on Moscow Street" by Marilyn Nelson
"Nikki-Rosa" by Nikki Giovanni
"The Road Not Taken" by Robert Frost

This is only a small sampling of the wealth of resources activities in Rossing's unit. Another source to help you plan your own unit is *Sandra Cisneros in the Classroom: Do Not Forget to Reach* by Carol Jago, NCTE, 2002. An additional resource, and one that Rossing used for book selections, is <http://scholar.lib.vt.edu/ejournals/ALAN/fall95/Ericson.html>.

INSTRUCTIONAL UNIT

THE AMERICAN DREAM

Stan Nesbit, a high school English teacher, developed a unit on the American dream for the tenth grade. He has chosen a theme commonly taught at the secondary level, but his presentation of the material is strikingly different from a traditional approach. He incorporates introductory activities to develop student interest and to broaden the concept of an American dream by including texts that represent the voices of American women, men, and children. His planned activities include not only reading, but writing, listening, and speaking. What follows is an abbreviated version of Stan's unit listing only the activities.

Activity 1. As students enter the first day of the unit, I will play the song "Born in the U.S.A." by Bruce Springsteen. To introduce the unit I will ask students to respond in their journals to the question "What is the American dream?" I will ask students for examples of this dream. Students share their individual responses in small groups, and then each group writes a Level 2 paper on the discussion. I will collect their individual responses and keep them on file for a comparison/contrast activity at the end of the unit.

Activity 2. I will ask students to do some research at home. They have one week to ask parents, grandparents, and friends about their family's immigration to the United States. Students then choose one of the stories they hear and write a paper in first person. These papers will be shared orally in pairs for a peer response activity and handed in as a Level 2 paper.

Reading a selection from the autobiography *Stelmark* by Harry Petrakis, a Greek immigrant, follows this assignment. Students write a response in their journal about the relationship between the main character and the old Greek man, the work ethic portrayed, and the relation to the theme of the American dream.

 *Reflection*

From these assignments what can you deduce about Stan's goals? What in particular is he accomplishing?

What was his point in having students write the stories they heard in first person?

Activity 3. Next we watch segments of a video recording of speeches by presidential candidates, all of whom claim to deliver the American dream to everyone. Students respond in their journal, stating first why the candidates all refer to our theme and then explaining which person they believe gave the most believable speech and why it was effective.

Activity 4. While the students do research for activity 2, we will read several early works of American literature to observe the establishment of the American dream and the effect of this ideal on our history.

    The first text we read is the "Description of New England" by Captain John Smith. Students respond in their journals to the following questions: Who is Smith's audience? What do you think Smith's audience is looking for in a new world? How does Smith sell America in this selection? How does this relate to the American dream?

    After the journal entry, we review advertising techniques (bandwagon, testimonial, name-calling, transfer, and so on). Students form groups, and each group is assigned a technique to use in writing an ad to sell the New World to the English back home. Each group presents the ad to the class, and the whole class tries to determine which technique was used.

Activity 5. As a prereading assignment to the next activity, we read two letters from Abigail to John Adams. In these letters, Abigail encourages her husband to "remember the ladies" when he helps establish the laws of the new nation. Students write a journal entry guessing what Abigail's response will be to John's letter. Students share their entries with the whole class.

◦∾ *Reflection* ∾◦

Stan has the activities flow from individual to small group to whole class. What is his purpose in organizing the time this way? How does this affect the learners?

Activity 6. As students enter the classroom, I will play the song "Pink Houses" by John Mellencamp. Together as a class, we will read aloud and discuss Jefferson's "Declaration of Independence." Then each student reads Elizabeth Stanton's "Declaration of Women's Rights." We will compare and contrast these two documents. Following the reading and referring back to the persuasive techniques we learned in activity 4, students write their own "Declaration of Independence" from adults, parents, teachers, administrators, or whomever they choose. We will have peer response groups for this Level 2 assignment. Students must consider the whole audience, as did the framers of the U.S. Declaration, and make this a persuasive document.

Activity 7. As students enter the classroom, I will play the song "My Hometown" by Bruce Springsteen. To introduce selections from Ben Franklin's *Autobiography* and *Poor Richard's Almanac,* we will define the term *aphorism* and brainstorm a list, followed by a class discussion. Then using *Poor Richard's*

Almanac, students choose two aphorisms that mean the most to them, paraphrase each one, and write a personal experience that illustrates the concept (Level 2).

ᴄᴍᴩ *Reflection* ᴄᴍᴩ

What is Stan's purpose in playing the music at the beginning of class periods? Do you think it is effective? What other selections might fit into the theme?

Activity 8. Activities 8 and 9 are transitions to the "dark side" of the American dream. I introduce the idea that nothing comes free; that every step we call progress carries with it a price. Students write a journal entry on the costs of the American dream. Next we watch a videotape of Dr. Seuss' *The Lorax*; students also have a hard copy. In discussion, they relate the poem to loggers and the proposed mines in northern Wisconsin. We will discuss the name "Once-ler," the chain of events in the story and other points the students contribute.

Activity 9. As an introduction to "Under the Lion's Paw" by Hamlin Garland, we will discuss economic hardships and question the myth that we can achieve our dreams if we work hard enough. Students write in their journal guided by the following prompts:

1. Is Bulter an evil man or is he simply a shrewd businessman trying to achieve his own dreams?
2. Why doesn't Haskins kill Bulter? What does this show about his goals for his children?
3. Does this story present a realistic or romantic view of life? Support your answer with evidence from the story. Journals are shared in large group.

Activity 10. I will ask students to brainstorm a list of Americans to whom the American dream is difficult or impossible to attain. Also, what Americans may reject the dream entirely? Students read several poems showing the variety of attitudes toward the quest for a satisfying life in America. The poems include these: "America" by Claude McKay, "From the Dark Tower" by Countee Cullen, "Weekend Glory" by Maya Angelou, and "The Bean Eaters" by Gwendolyn Brooks.

Students relate the poems to earlier definitions of the American dream and write a Level 2 paper on their response. Students listen to songs by Tracy Chapman, especially "Fast Car."

EXPLORATION

ADDING POETRY TO UNITS

What other poems can you find that would fit in this activity?

Activity 11. Students read "The Man Who Saw the Flood" by Richard Wright. Then they write responses to the following statements:

1. The African Americans portrayed are fundamentally still slaves.
2. Some Americans today have no more opportunity to realize the American dream than Tom and his family did. Compare Burgess in this story with Bulter in "Under the Lion's Paw." Students should support their responses with reason and evidence.

Activity 12. We view Martin Luther King Jr.'s "I Have a Dream" speech. I will encourage students to pay attention to the rhetorical devices King uses to persuade his audience. Students then write their own "Dream for the Nation" using King's rhetorical devices as a model. I will remind students that their dream must be for the good of the nation.

Reflection

We have not included all of the transitions Stan uses to introduce each activity and to create interest. For the last two activities, what might a teacher do to create good discussions and involve students in the issues?

———————————

Activity 13. We will read two poems by Langston Hughes, "Freedom" and "Dream Deferred," and discuss a person's responsibility for achieving one's own dreams. In a response journal, students respond to Hughes' question: What happens to a dream deferred?

Reflection

Stan usually gives students prompts to answer for journal entries. Discuss whether you agree with this technique. What else might you do?

———————————

Activity 14. Students view the video *A Raisin in the Sun* by Lorraine Hansberry. Following the video, they write a journal response using these questions as a guide:

1. Identify the dreams of the main characters in the play. Then consider these characters in light of the Hughes poem "Dream Deferred."
2. Compare the dreams of a character in the play with those described in King's speech.
3. Write a dialogue between Joseph Asagai and George Murchison that shows their different dreams, lifestyles, and perceptions of America.

4. In what way has Walter come into his manhood at the end of the play? In what ways will the change be favorable and unfavorable?

The writing assignment will be Level 2 and revised in peer groups.

Activity 15. I will play "Signs" by Tesla as the students enter the room. Students read "Stupid America" by Abelardo Delgado, a Chicano who expresses the clash between the American idea of progress and the Chicano way of life. Students respond in their journals to the following questions:

1. What is the source of misunderstanding between the man and "America"?
2. What is the source of frustration for the man?
3. What role does art play in the Chicano's life?
4. What was your emotional reaction to the title? To the poem itself?

After large-group discussion, we read the poems of the Chinese Americans of the "Town of Iron," the Angel Island Detention Center where, from 1910 to 1940, Chinese immigrants were imprisoned and interrogated. For a Level 2 assignment, students are assigned a flag, either China's or Mexico's, to designate their native country (these are assigned because we do not choose our birthplace). Students write a letter to a friend or family member back home telling about their life in the New World. The letter should end with a recommendation of whether the person should come to America.

Activity 16. Class begins with a discussion of the history of immigrants who have come to America and have been victims of prejudice, such as the Irish, Swedish, and Italians. Students watch *The Blue Hotel* by Stephen Crane and respond in their journals to who and what are responsible for the death of the Swede. In groups, students discuss their responses and write a Level 2 group paper.

Activity 17. Students read "The Sculptor's Funeral" by Willa Cather and then write a short Level 2 assignment comparing the values of the town with those of the sculptor and his friends.

Activity 18. I will read aloud a selection of Native American myths to help students understand that with their diverse beliefs and environments many Native Americans live satisfying lives without the idea of personal or national progress. Students then read selections from *Bury My Heart at Wounded Knee* by Dee Brown. They write responses in their journals.

Reflection

What suggestions can you add to Stan's unit to help students respond with depth and understanding?

Activity 19. Students will read *The Great Gatsby* by F. Scott Fitzgerald. I will play selections of jazz classics and give students some background about the Jazz Age. Students select from a list of possible topics to write a Level 2 assignment:

1. Write two biographies with time lines: one for Jay Gatsby and one for James Gatz.
2. Supply the dialogue between Gatsby and Daisy, the one Fitzgerald discreetly omitted from Chapter 5.
3. What is Gatsby's dream? What did he do to achieve it?
4. Contrast Gatsby's dream relationship with the real one that developed. How do you account for the differences?
5. Ben Franklin and Gatsby each had detailed plans for becoming successful. Write your own plans in detail. Students also complete a Level 3 assignment by writing a comparison paper for any two characters or people we have read about during this unit.

Activity 20. As a closure activity, students examine what it means to be an American. First they read "What Is an American" by Jean Crèvecoeur and then the preface to *The Pursuit of Loneliness* by Philip Slater. Students write their definition of an American, taking into account all of their readings. Then I hand back their definitions from the first day of the unit, and we discuss the differences in large group.

EXPLORATION

Examining the American Dream Unit

1. What do you think Stan's students learned from the unit? In what areas might some students have difficulty with the material? How could you provide for these students?
2. The unit is designed for the tenth grade. What parts of it might be appropriate for other grade levels?
3. Stan noted that he had trouble finding works by female writers whatever the culture. What additions can you suggest?
4. He wondered if the American dream is more of a male pursuit than a female one. What do you think? In groups, plan a unit on a more female pursuit.
5. What would you add or delete in Stan's unit?

How we teach literature is vitally important for our students. Your future classrooms will not be filled with students who feel the same way you do about literature. Our job as teachers is to make literature accessible and enjoyable for all our students. Arthur N. Applebee believes that "when books are taught well they will invite exactly the kinds of thoughtful discussion, reflection, and debate that we most need to foster" to help our students become responsible citizens (46).

RELATED WEB SITES

http://www.readwritethink.org/lessons/index.asp
http://www.cascd.org/recipteach.shtml
http://www.ops.org/reading/secondary stratl.htm

REFERENCES

Adams, Pamela E. "Teaching *Romeo and Juliet* in the Nontracked English Classroom." *Journal of Reading* 38.6 (March 1995): 424–32.

Applebee, Arthur N. "Literature and the Ethical Tradition." *Vital Signs* 1. Ed. James L. Collins. Portsmouth: Boynton/Cook, 1990: 39–47.

Beach, Richard, and James Marshall. *Teaching Literature in the Secondary School*. San Diego: Harcourt Brace Jovanovich, 1991.

Beem, Jane A. "Golding as a Key to Conrad." *Literature—News That Stays News*. Ed. Candy Carter. Urbana: NCTE, 1984: 3–6.

Blake, Robert W., and Anna Lunn. "Responding to Poetry: High School Students Read Poetry." *English Journal* (Feb. 1986): 68–73.

Bushman, John H., and Kay Parks Bushman. *Using Young Adult Literature in the English Classroom*. Upper Saddle River: Merrill/Prentice Hall, 1993.

Carter, Candy, ed. *Literature—News That Stays News: Fresh Approach to the Classics*. Urbana: NCTE, 1985.

Christ, Jim. "Exploring Emotion through Romeo and Juliet." *Literature—News That Stays News*. Ed. Candy Carter. Urbana: NCTE, 1984: 66–69.

Dressler, Barbara. "Families in Literature." Unpublished paper. UWEC, 1996.

Elliott, Anne. "Stereotypes: The Root of Aggressive Behavior." Unpublished paper. English 404, 1995.

Farbman, Evelyn. "One Writer to Another: An Approach to Young Goodman Brown." *Literature—News That Stays News*. Ed. Candy Carter. Urbana: NCTE, 1984: 38–41.

Farnam, Nancy, and Patricia K. Kelly. "Response-Based Instruction at the Middle Level: When Student Engagement is the Goal." *Middle School Journal* (Sept. 1993): 46–49.

Graves, M. F., R. J. Palmer, and D. W. Furniss. *Structuring Reading Activities for English Classes*. Urbana: NCTE ERIC, 1976.

Guerin, W. L., E. G. Labor, L. Morgan, and J. R. Willingham. *A Handbook of Critical approaches to Literature*. New York: Harper & Row, 1979.

Iser, Wolfgang. *The Act of Reading*. Baltimore: Johns Hopkins University Press, 1978.

Johannessen, Larry R. "Enhancing Response to Literature: A Matter of Changing Old Habits." *English Journal* (Nov. 1994): 66–70.

Kell, J. T. Jr. "Illustrating Imagery." *English Journal* (April 1995): 66–67.

Kramer, Andrea. "Metaphor Focus." Unpublished paper, 1996.

Langer, Judith A. "A Response-Based Approach to Reading Literature." *Language Arts* 71 (March 1994): 203–11.

Lothe, Kurt. "Crime & Punishment, The Musical." *Wisconsin English Journal* (Fall 1990): 76–77.

Maxwell, Rhoda J. "Exploring Characters in *All Together Now*." *Notes Plus*. Urbana: NCTE, Jan. 1989: 7–8.

McCarthy, Renee. "Teaching Activities for *Baseball in April* and 'Hermana.'" Unpublished paper, 1995.

Miller, Bruce E. *Teaching The Art of Literature*. Urbana: NCTE, 1980.

Moelter, Jean. "A Closer Look at Tone." Unpublished paper, 1996.

Nesbit, Stan. "The American Dream." Unpublished paper, July 1992.

Olson, Vicki L. "Connecting With Literature: Activities for *The Cay* and *The Bedspread*." *Literature—News That Stays News: Fresh Approaches to the Classics*. Ed. & Chair of the Committee on Classroom Practices, Candy Carter. Urbana: NCTE, 1985: 19–25.

Probst, Robert E. *Response Analysis: Teaching Literature in Junior and Senior High School.* Upper Montclair: Boynton/Cook, 1988.

Purves, A. C. "Toward a Reevaluation of Reader Response and School Literature." *Language Arts* 70 (Sept. 1993): 348–61.

Rosenblatt, Louise M. *Literature as Exploration.* 3rd ed. New York: Barnes & Noble, 1976. Original work published 1938.

_____ . *The Reader, the Text, and the Poem.* Carbondale: Southern Illinois UP, 1977.

Rossing, Melissa. "The House on Mango Street," Instructional unit. Unpublished. UWEC, 2003.

Shaw, Ella. "Activities for *Two Kinds* and *The Joy Luck Club.*" Unpublished paper, 1994.

Smagorinsky, Peter, and Steven Gevinson. *Fostering the Reader's Response.* Palo Alto: Dale Seymour, 1989.

Smith, Frank. *Comprehension and Learning.* New York: Holt, Rinehart & Winston, 1975.

Stellick, Pat. Syllabus for English. Unpublished, 2000.

Sutton, Jan. "Diverse Voices." Unpublished paper. University of Wisconsin–Eau Clair, 1998.

Wall, Linda. "Seeing Is Believing: A Method for Teaching Imagery in Poetry." *Notes Plus.* Urbana: NCTE, March 1994: 9–10.

Evaluating English Language Arts 12

> Practitioners must educate the public that strong correlations exist between qualitative measurements—student artifacts, exhibits, projects, portfolios, experiments, and other creative products—and workplace demands for self-directed, collaborative workers.
>
> *Jim Abbott (11)*

Evaluating students' work can be a teacher's most difficult task. Should we pay more attention to content or mechanics? How do we give credit for creativity? How does the evaluation of a research paper differ from an evaluation of a short story? The answers lie in the teacher's purpose for assigning the particular activity. Or put another way, what did the teacher want the student to learn? Evaluation means deciding if something worthwhile happened, not just measuring a skill. Consequently, teachers must be clear and specific about what they expect to happen when they give students a particular assignment.

 ## AUTHENTIC ASSESSMENT

Many teachers are changing what they teach and how they teach in response to John Goodlad's description of the curriculum in most schools as being dull and lifeless, filled with teacher talk and uninterested students. Classrooms have become more student-centered as students are allowed and encouraged to self-select topics for writing and texts for reading. Small groups provide more opportunities for interaction among students. As teacher talk declines and student input increases, interest and enthusiasm heighten student learning. However, even with the changes in teaching approaches, too often the students are evaluated with the same old tired tests and quizzes. Jim Abbott explains that "quantitative measurements, such as multiple choice, norm-referenced tests, reveal only a small portion of a child's knowledge" (11). How teachers evaluate their students' progress deserves a closer look.

Authentic assessment is a fair assessment of what students know. The problem with standardized tests and other tests that require one correct answer is that students may know the information called for, but the question may be worded in a way that does not make sense to them. This is especially true for ESL students or students of limited language proficiency. Testing becomes a frustrating experience. Often, to get a correct answer, students must guess what the author of the test was thinking rather than show that they actually know the information. For this reason, vocabulary, comprehension, and short-answer tests should allow students to answer in their own words rather than include formats such as matching columns or selecting multiple-choice or true/false answers. Students then can explain in their own way what they know.

Larry Johannessen explains that teachers continue to use the same tests because of habit; they have given the tests for years and feel comfortable with them (66). "The trouble is that most of us give quizzes without thinking about why we are giving them; and most important, we don't think about what the effect of giving them will be, especially over a long period of time" (67). Teachers must consider their purpose for each quiz and whether it really tells them what they want to know. For example, teachers give pop quizzes because they want to make sure students do the required reading. The problem is that pop quizzes do not serve this purpose. The threat of a pop quiz does not encourage students who have difficulty with reading nor those not interested in the required selections; consequently, they receive yet another F. They become discouraged and lose even more interest. Students who excel at reading often finish the literature far ahead of the others and when given a pop quiz have difficulty remembering the literal information required for these tests. Quizzes do not tell teachers how well students interpret literature or learn an interpretive skill or strategy (Johannessen 68). All students view them as unfair, even those who do well, because they have no input into the content or timing.

Students need to have a voice in the assessment process so they know what its purpose is, what it tells them about their learning, and what the teacher will use it for. "Assessment should teach students something, not just take time away from teaching" (Murphy 151). Both students and teachers need to learn something from evaluations other than a meaningless number or percentile. The criteria for evaluation needs to be "explicit to students, so that they can begin learning how to do it for themselves" (151). Assessment does not have to be something teachers "do" to students, but rather a process in which teachers can improve their teaching for individual students and in which students discover what they need to focus on in their learning.

༄ Reflection ༄

Do you remember a time when an assessment helped you learn? In what way? When have you experienced unfair assessment? What could you do in your future classrooms to make sure the assessments you make will truly help your students learn?

PURPOSES OF EVALUATION

Evaluation is not the same as measurement. We evaluate to see if something worthwhile was accomplished. We might evaluate our teaching methods or our students' learning. In *The Evaluation of Composition Instruction*, Davis, Scriven, and Thomas describe two purposes for evaluation: formative and summative. Formative evaluation is used to discover how writing can be improved; that is, what specific areas students need to work on to become better writers. Summative evaluation is used to report the overall quality of the writing (3–4). Both forms are useful when used appropriately. When teachers want to know if their teaching methods are improving student learning, summative evaluation provides that information. When teachers and students want to identify particular strengths and weaknesses, formative evaluation gives them that information. Holistic evaluation is an example of summative evaluation and is commonly used to assess the success of a curriculum. For example, a school district may collect student writing samples in several grades and evaluate the writing holistically to determine the effectiveness of the writing curriculum. This type of summative evaluation does not give information on individuals, only on the program as a whole. For individual assessment, analytical grading scales are examples of formative evaluation that furnish information on weaknesses and strengths of students' writing. Analytical grading is when the writing is judged by particular skills. For example, the scale may look like this for a comparison paper.

Thesis and introduction: 2 points
  Takes a stand
  Clear what paper is about
Major points: 8 points
  Consistent
  Easy to follow
Supporting details: 12 points
  For every major point
  Examples
  Quotes or paraphrases
Organization: 5 points
  For whole essay
  Paragraph level
  Conclusion
Punctuation, spelling, word usage 3 points
Comments:

(Maxwell 139)

Because of the amount of time needed for formative evaluation, it is used more often in individual classes than in large-scale assessment and is the type usually used in our classrooms.

ASSESSMENT

Most school districts have some method of assessing how well students do in reading, math, and writing, usually through state mandated tests. Assessment of writing can be either direct, as in a writing sample, or indirect, as in an objective test. Objective tests are editing tests in which students read test items to identify errors in punctuation, subject-verb agreement, pronoun-noun agreement, and other conventions of language depending on the grade level tested. However, the direct assessment of a writing sample more closely reflects what is taught in the classroom and provides a clearer idea of what needs to be improved. Because our goal is to help students become better writers, and objective tests are not a good measure of that, we should always assess the students' own writing. A student may be able to pick out writing errors, but not be capable of thoughtful, interesting writing, and the reverse may be true as well. Unless large-scale assessment and classroom grading reflect the teacher's purpose in teaching writing, the evaluations provide no useful information, and, in fact, can be harmful to teachers and students because the information is misleading.

 EXPLORATION

Purposes of Evaluation

What are the similarities and differences among assessment, evaluation, and testing? As a teacher, when and how would you use each one? What would be the goals of using each?

 EVALUATING LITERATURE

What matters to students is not the details of knowledge they pick up when studying literature, but the "internalized concepts that help them to cope with the problems they encounter in the world outside of school and throughout their lives" (Schuman 55). Because of this emphasis, educators are less interested in objective testing and are looking for ways to assess interpretive skills. When literature is presented through a whole language approach, the scope of reading sources widens greatly. Many teachers are uncomfortable with whole language because their students are reading books they themselves have not read (55). However, if teachers limit students to reading selections the teachers have read, they are narrowing the scope of reading experiences. Teachers do not have to read every selection their students read. When teachers use the whole language approach, the works themselves are not as important as the way students analyze the works.

Using reader response for literature study invalidates the true/false, multiple-choice, and even the short-answer tests. This doesn't mean that we can't evaluate students' knowledge and understanding of literature, but it does mean that we must truly test students' knowledge and not force them to guess what the teacher is thinking.

In *Testing Literature: The Current State of Affairs,* Alan C. Purves summarizes a longer report of a study funded by the U.S. Department of Education. He explains that tests published for secondary school students are, for the most part, multiple-choice questions that focus on comprehension at a relatively low level of understanding. The questions are based on the meaning of specific parts or the main idea of a passage and test literature as if it were the same as encyclopedia articles or research papers. Little attention is paid to the artistic characteristics of literature, such as language, structure, and point of view. Purves's report recommends not using purchased tests and encourages teachers to create their own methods of evaluation.

We can create our own evaluation methods in several ways. First, it is important to realize that not all assignments should be graded. For instance, response writing would be checked only for the effort the student made in reading and responding. The same is true for any journal writing, even when we give fairly specific assignments for journals. Length is not an accurate measure of the effort, but we can evaluate the extent of the reader's involvement with the text.

Another important area of literature study is discussion, but it should not be evaluated. Keeping track of who answers questions in class is a tricky and an unreliable way to assess interest and involvement. Some teachers believe that noting when students respond to a question motivates discussion, and occasionally that may indeed be the case. The danger, though, is that only high-achieving students will care about the discussion grade. Also, shy students may find it very difficult to talk in class, and it would be wrong to penalize them. Response and discussion are crucial to active class participation, but they are informal activities and, as such, do not need to be evaluated with a grade. To ensure active discussion you can have students write answers to discussion questions prior to the class discussion. However, they do not hand them in to the teachers before class discussion. With their notes in front of them, students are more comfortable answering in front of a group. Encourage students to add on to their answers from information they hear during discussion. Following the group discussion, they then hand their answers in for a Level 2 grade. This system encourages students to discuss more openly and to listen to other students more intently. An example of discussion questions based on literature is in Chapter 11, "Teaching Literature."

EXPLORATION

Establishing Teaching Goals

What goals might you have for assigning a short story to seventh graders? How would the goals change for a comparable story for eleventh graders? What goals would you have for assigning poetry?

Guiding Questions for Literature

Over the span of time that students are reading a text, you may use questions to guide their understanding. Students often answer questions as homework assignments, discuss their answers, and hand them in the following day. Specific questions, of course, depend on the literature selection, but as a guide, you might use questions like these:

What factors influenced the actions of the characters?

How did relationships among people influence actions?

Why do you approve or disapprove of a character's action?

Why do they behave the way they do?

In what ways are their actions realistic or unrealistic?

I like the idea of point scoring + it's objective + easier for stud's to understand

Students' answers will vary, but as with responses, you can tell if a student has read the material. Because the questions are more formal than reader responses, they are graded more formally. A point system works well, such as five points for each question; the total score rather than a letter grade goes on the paper. When you use points, they more clearly specify acceptable and unacceptable answers for each question, much more helpful than assigning a grade for the work as a whole.

Many assigned activities can be graded on a more formal basis, but you should clearly state the purpose of the assignment and grade accordingly. For instance, if the activity is to write down characteristics that will help readers understand characters' motives, then the evaluation must reflect that purpose. That is, did the student describe the characteristics? Too often, all activities are graded alike, even though the purposes are quite different. For example, we might count spelling, punctuation, and grammar even though the assignment was to discuss viewpoint in a fairly informal way. The levels of writing described in Chapter 6, "Teaching Composition," clarify the connection between purpose and evaluation.

EXPLORATION

Teaching a Short Story

Choose a short story you could teach at ninth grade and write ten discussion questions that you could use with students. What do you want students to understand about the story? What would you like them to remember? Share your questions in a group.

CONSTRUCTING TESTS

In a student-centered classroom, evaluation covers both academic and personal competence because we want students to learn not only material and strategies but also how to continue learning without a teacher's guidance (Everly 193). Testing for aca-

> **Figure 12.1** Adapted version of Everly's test
>
> Your assignment is to write a short story using what you have learned about the writing process and literary forms and techniques. Your story will be published in a class literary anthology and distributed at the end of school. You may choose the subject and format of your story, but you must include the following:
>
> 1. At least two well-rounded characters
>
> 2. A conflict
>
> 3. Direct and indirect characterizations
>
> 4. A believable setting
>
> 5. A developed plot
>
> 6. At least two techniques for building suspense

demic competence gives students opportunities to show they have subject area knowledge and understand structures for learning in an area. Testing personal competence includes showing that they can manage their time to reach goals and take responsibility for their work (193). A test that covers these areas must clearly define the required task, provide guidelines, and allow students to manage their work time on their own. Everly designed a test that resembles a unit, one that is a "complex, authentic task that requires one to two weeks of constant class time work to complete" (194). Peer tutoring and review are encouraged, but the teacher does not help except for procedural questions. Figure 12.1 shows an adapted version of Everly's test.

Editing guides, response sheets, and the grading criteria for this assignment are available for students. Everly publishes the stories so students have a clear sense of audience as they compose. Exams of this type evaluate subject knowledge, ability to use time wisely, and knowledge of how to organize a task—important skills for a lifelong learner.

Evaluation can take many forms besides an exam. We may require papers as a final project instead of an exam, oral presentations, or slide shows. Group projects are also valid ways of evaluating if students understand the literature. We believe it is wise to use a variety of evaluation methods to accommodate different learning styles and to encourage interest in class activities. We need to be as creative when evaluating as we are when providing choices of writing assignments, topics, and projects.

 ## WRITING TEST QUESTIONS

Test questions are based on the discussion questions used in class and not from passages in the book. We must ask ourselves what do we want students to remember and to think about, perhaps months after they finish the reading. Questions about specific details are not what we want our students to remember. If we forget the name of a character in a book we read some time ago, but recall how and why that character changed, what was important to the character and how other people reacted and why, then the literature becomes part of our lives. Our discussions and test questions need to reflect that goal.

A more formal evaluation is the essay exam. As new teachers you may be tempted to use a test written by either another teacher or a publishing company. But students don't always understand the questions even if they did understand the novel. Because the exams do not necessarily test what was covered in class, a teacher who wants to be fair to the students should teach the test material, whether it seems appropriate or not. Ready-made tests cannot reflect the dynamics of the classroom discussions and learning. Short-answer, true/false, and matching questions all test lower-level comprehension, and that is not what we want to test students on. Instead, we want to see if they grasp connections between ideas, make inferences about motivations and outcomes, analyze points of view, and judge a work's effectiveness; in other words, we want to test higher-order thinking. Only test questions that allow students to express their thoughts in their own words will assess higher-order thinking.

Teachers often express two objections to essay exams. First, some believe that the evaluation of essay answers is not objective. On a multiple-choice or true/false question, the answer is either right or wrong, and the teacher needs only to count up the number of correct answers and convert that number to a grade: 80 percent right is a B, 90 percent an A. The numbers make us believe we are being objective, and therefore fair. However, the test itself is subjective and unfair, even though we can count correct responses. It is difficult, if not impossible, to write multiple-choice, true/false, and matching questions that are not misleading. Fill-in-the-blank questions test recall, the lowest stage of critical thinking. When teachers or unknown test makers create a test, they decide what is important for students to remember and learn. That's where the subjectivity comes in. By giving students more latitude in explaining what they know and understand, we give them a more objective test; that is, one that is not as tied to our way of stating information. A true test of our understanding comes from our ability to explain in our own words. *true*

The second objection is that essay exams take longer to grade than op-scan sheets or short-answer tests. Yes, they do. However, it is not an impossible amount of time. As we read the answers, we must have a clear idea of what to look for, even though it may be expressed in a variety of ways. To help us achieve this, we need to write the essay answers ourselves in a list format. What points do we want the students to make? How many would they have to include to receive full credit? Also, we need to read and evaluate one question at a time on all the students' exams. By reading the same question on all the papers, we get a good idea of how the responses compare in the development of ideas and the use of details and examples. Then, the papers are shuffled before reading the second question. This method ensures that we are not influenced as much by the paper we read previously. Several studies have shown that the order in which essays are read does affect our evaluation. If we read a strong essay followed by a weaker one, the second one suffers by comparison. Also, the twentieth essay will probably seem less wonderful than the second one did, even though they are similar. It does take time to read essay exams, but they promote learning and give students opportunities to express ideas in their own words, and that makes them well worth the time.

It is also important to remember that students write the exams in class where time and test anxiety are factors, and students may not use correct punctuation or spelling. Therefore, it is inappropriate to consider these skills when evaluating. We are looking for understanding of the literature, and that is all we need to pay attention to. When students are concentrating on thinking, the most common word can be misspelled. Of course, mechanics are important, but not in a testing situation. *good point!*

EXPLORATION

Creating a Test

Using the discussion questions you wrote for the short story in the last exploration, write four essay test questions. Jot down what points you would like your students to include.

EVALUATING WRITING

Teaching writing through a process approach means that the purposes of activities vary. For example, the purpose of a discovery activity in which students practice how to develop a character is different from a library activity that acquaints students with Newsbank. The purpose of an assignment to practice dialogue is different from that of an assignment to write a story including dialogue. The differences in purposes of assignments shape evaluations. What we want students to learn determines how we evaluate.

Creating the assignment and deciding how to evaluate it should happen at the same time. If this connection is not clear in the teacher's mind, and therefore not clear to the students, evaluation can be troublesome. Students have the right to know how their work will be evaluated before they hand it in. Shelly Smede, a junior high school teacher, agrees: "Part of assessing student work fairly is to let them know exactly what you expect before they begin" (93). If teachers evaluate using levels, students know the teacher's expectations and never have to ask if spelling or neatness counts.

EVALUATION BY LEVELS

Using the levels of writing for evaluation helps us to focus our grading and helps our students to know how their writing is going to be evaluated. Parents, too, need to know how the students' papers are evaluated. With the process approach to writing, students have papers that contain mechanical errors, yet receive comments of praise and, perhaps, a high grade. When parents understand the three levels used to evaluate their children's writing, they are much less likely to criticize because they understand *concerns w/ parents grading*

the evaluation procedures. To create the home/school connection, you need to write letters to parents at the beginning of the school year explaining the levels of writing and emphasizing your expectations for each level. Also, at the beginning of the year, students write the level of the assignment on the paper. Then, when parents do read their child's work, they are more likely to understand the purpose of the assignment and the evaluation.

Level 1

brainstorm journal notes no distractions no correctness

For Level 1 assignments, your purpose is to provide a wealth of activities for ideas and practice. We want our students to engage in a wide range of thinking, such as brainstorming; making connections between thoughts, as in mapping; or practicing a variety of writing forms. If we add the layer of correctness to such activities, the purpose is lost. First drafts and journal writing are also Level 1. Here students concentrate on getting ideas down; if they stop to look up a word or even to consider how a word is spelled, their train of thought is interrupted. In Level 1 writing, the writer should be free from distractions as much as possible. The purpose is to get thoughts on paper and to try new forms of expression. Note-taking is also Level 1; writers jot down notes to help them remember, and that is the only purpose.

discovery activities

The audience for Level 1 is, first and foremost, the writer. The writer may be the only one who hears or reads the writing. However, peers may also be the audience when the writing is shared in groups. An example of using peer groups for Level 1 could be when students are thinking of questions to use for a report or when they share ideas for a collaborative story.

To evaluate, you may read the writing and make a comment or a checkmark to show that you read their work. Often, though, you do not read this level because there is no need to. Students may keep it in a notebook or folder, but no evaluation is necessary. Level 1 writing is the foundation for all other writing and is therefore assigned the most frequently, even daily. In Level 1 writing, students practice writing, try out ideas, take notes, write in journals, and respond to reading or listening. The major focus is on content; the main audience is themselves.

Level 2

HW essay tests drafts

Level 2 assignments are somewhat more formal. The purpose of these assignments is to explain, inform, or further develop a discovery writing activity. We assign Level 2 writing to see if students understand ideas and concepts. Examples of this level are homework assignments, essay tests, and multiple drafts students are working on. The audience is the writer, the teacher, and peers. The audiences are always known, and the writing is often read by others, not only shared orally. Because people other than the writer read the writing, a certain amount of formality is required. Writing conventions need to be adhered to so others can understand the work. On the other hand, Level 2 is not intended as a final draft and is not evaluated as such. When we evaluate a Level 2 assignment, we expect correct spelling of common words and the correct use of most punctuation marks. However, if a student uses an uncommon word and spells it incorrectly, the error is not noted. When teachers overemphasize spelling, students do not expand their vocabulary. Instead, they use a word they know how to spell rather than one that captures the connotation they want. In an essay test, a teacher may circle a misspelled word, but spelling errors should not be included in the evaluation. The teacher's purpose is to see if students understand the material, not to check their spelling ability. Level 2 assignments should reflect knowledge of common conventions of punctuation. The appropriate conventions depend on the abilities and grade levels of the students.

Organization is another area we do not want highly evaluated at Level 2. Thinking is not a highly organized activity, and students often think of other ideas and points too late to make coherent organization. For example, in an essay exam, students may write in the margins or crowd words in between lines because they are thinking hard about the subject and remember additional information.

In homework assignments, the intensity seen during essay tests is not present, but if students make an effort to organize their thoughts, that is sufficient. Again, teachers want students to add new ideas even if the paper looks messy because of the additions. Level 2 assignments are rarely recopied. The emphasis is on content with a common level of correctness. Level 2 writings are assigned two or three times a week.

Level 3

Level 3 assignments are the most formal. The purposes of these assignments are to give students an opportunity to write for audiences outside the classroom, to organize thoughts into a coherent form for readers outside the writers' circle of friends, and to learn the value of creating error-free writing when the occasion calls for it. Level 3 writings are polished drafts that students carry through all of the stages of the writing process. Examples of assignments include research papers, reports, stories, letters, plays, poetry, and essays. Length is not a factor in determining levels. Level 1 might be the longest, such as journal writing; Level 3 might fill one page or less when writing a poem.

The intended audience is oneself, the teacher, peers, and unknown readers. Level 3 writing might be for a class or school anthology, the school or city newspaper, or a gift for family or friends. It is used any time writing needs to be the best possible. Our purpose is to help students learn how to carry a piece of writing through revising, editing, and proofreading to create an error-free paper that is well organized and interesting to read.

Evaluating a Level 3 writing is similar to traditional grading of writing. Because the paper has been taken through all the writing process stages, you can expect it to be the writer's best work. However, the mechanical aspect of writing never outweighs the value of the content.

Students are more likely to value creating a polished piece of writing when the purpose is clear; if teachers require "perfect" papers every time a student writes, students lose interest in that objective. Common sense tells us that no one writes perfect papers all of the time because no one needs to. Writing done in the world outside of the classroom is largely at Levels 1 and 2, except for occasional reports. List making, notes to oneself, telephone messages, journal writing, and class notes are all Level 1. Letters we write to people we know are Level 2. College students write more Level 3 papers than anyone else, far more than they will after graduation. Secondary students learn how to produce a polished draft if we assign a Level 3 no more than once every four to six

	Level 1	Level 2	Level 3
Style	Informal	Semi-formal	Formal
Audience	Writer, teacher, and classmates.	Writer, teacher, classmates, and parents.	Writer, teacher, classmates, and parents. May have an audience outside the classroom.
Function	Thinking, organizing, generating ideas, fluency, and study skills.	Organizing, developing ideas, explaining, and informing.	Recognizing the value of error-free products, editing, and proofreading for a wider audience.
Form	Note-taking, journals, responses, lists, and mapping.	Exams, homework, drafts, reports, and summaries.	Letters, reports, poetry, books, and final drafts.
Evaluation	Content only. Often not evaluated.	Content and appropriate conventions.	Content, form, skills, word choice, neatness, and typed format.

Figure 12.2 The three levels of writing

weeks. Going through the entire writing process takes a great deal of class time. That in itself is not a negative aspect, but running out of time to include a variety of writing forms and activities is. We teachers never seem to have enough time to carry out all our ideas, and the work required to complete a Level 3 writing assignment more than once a month can crowd out creative dramatics, independent reading, discussions, and other activities. Figure 12.2 summarizes the three levels of writing.

Reflection

Discuss the importance of writing levels in improving student writing. Describe how the purposes would be different for an assignment to write a short story at Level 2 compared with one written at Level 3.

_____

EXPLORATION

Letter to Parents

Assume you have your first teaching job and you want to explain to parents how you will use the levels of writing as a basis for grading their children's writing. Write a letter to the parents or guardians of your students explaining how you will do this.

METHODS OF EVALUATION

Depending on the purpose of the writing assignment, evaluation varies from formal to informal. Evaluation does not necessarily mean a grade is assigned. We evaluate to see if students are learning what we want them to learn. A variety of methods can supply that information. In fact, teaching writing by the process approach requires many different evaluation techniques, depending on the stage or level of the writing.

Impression Grading

For discovery activities, we always use impression grading; that is, you read the writing quickly to see if the student put effort into the writing. You may write comments on the students' papers but not formally evaluate them. When reading journals, we respond in writing as an adult friend, someone who listens and nurtures. Other discovery activities may require only a short comment: "Good start, creative, interesting." Or the comment can encourage students to expand their thinking and writing: "Tell me more about. . . ." "How did _____ happen?" or "What did you think of the part where. . . ?" If you ask specific questions, students have an easier time expanding on what they wrote. In some cases, a simple checkmark at the top is sufficient to let students know you read their work and approved. Sometimes students ask if these discovery activities "count." Because discovery activities are essential to good writing, we want to make sure students value their work at this level, but we do not want to evaluate on a more formal basis. Informal grading and following up if a student does not turn in an assignment help students realize the teacher values their work, so that they, too, will come to value it.

Holistic Grading

Holistic grading gives an overall evaluation without identifying the particular weaknesses or strengths of the writing. Papers are evaluated on the overall success of the writing, not on specific elements. Papers are read as a "whole" piece, and the evaluator decides if the writing is competent or not. Because this type of evaluation is quite reliable and quickly done, it is useful for large-scale assessment, such as evaluating writing in an entire school district. In the classroom, holistic grading may also be used as an assessment tool when you want to know, in general, how well the students write or if your teaching methods are effective. At the beginning of the year, you may assign a writing task and evaluate the writing holistically. Then, later in the year, you give them a similar writing assignment and evaluate it in the same manner. By comparing the two pieces of writing, you can monitor students' progress.

good idea

Writing used for holistic evaluation is usually done during one class period, or it can go through the stages of the writing process. In either case, when assignments are holistically evaluated, the final draft is not returned to the student because the teacher makes no comments and the grade is only a number. Such evaluation, although useful to the teacher, means nothing to students. Receiving a holistic grade does not help students improve their writing because they do not know what specifically they did right or wrong.

When evaluating holistically, evaluators spend about two minutes on each paper and use scoring guides to decide the category of competency for each paper. Using an even number of categories works best because the top two describe acceptable writing and the lower two, unacceptable. For instance:

If an odd number of categories is used, the middle area becomes confusing: 5, 4, 3, 2, 1. Would papers that fall into the middle be considered competent or not? Evaluators tend to score near the center of the scale. Providing a middle number increases the chances of that. Holistic grading requires that decisions on the quality of writing be made quickly and decisively.

Scoring guides describe what is expected in each category. Criteria include the amount of detail; the extent the writing reflects the writer's own experience, organization of ideas, and control of the conventions of writing. Holistic evaluation determines overall fluency. Grammar, punctuation, spelling, organization, and expression of ideas together form a sense of fluency. Even the best papers contain errors; in fact, good writers tend to write longer papers and, therefore, may have more errors. Also, if the students had to produce the writing in a certain length of time, which is usually the case when collecting writing samples from a large number of students, the writing will contain more errors. The quality of writing is lower than if students wrote in a less stressful situation. Students may have time to read over what they wrote, but the writing looks more like Level 2 writing than Level 3. The scoring guide needs to reflect the limitations of timed writing.

Analytic Scales

Analytic scales evaluate the parts of a written piece. Because this method is slower than holistic evaluation, it is seldom used in large-scale evaluation but is a valuable tool in the classroom. Paul Diederich and associates at the Educational Testing Service (1974) developed a grading scale used for scoring SAT essays (see Figure 12.3). The scale emphasizes ideas and organization. The first four factors in the scale are on "general merit" and the last four on "mechanics" (54). Analytic scales are useful evaluation tools. You can adapt the scale to fit your assignment, the grade level, and the recent focus of your teaching. Using such a grading scale ensures a fair weighting of all the elements that create the final grade for a paper.

Rubrics

When an analytic scale is explained with descriptive terms, the form is referred to as *rubrics*. For example, in Diederich's scale, "Clear information" could be explained as including major points with specific examples, sufficient details, and organization easy to follow. What the rubric includes depends on the level of the students, the purpose of the assignment (the level), and the type of writing. The content of a paper should

Figure 12.3 Diederich rating scale

Quality and development of ideas	1	2	3	4	5
Organization, relevance, movement	1	2	3	4	5

_____ × 5 = _____

Style, flavor, individuality	1	2	3	4	5
Wording and phrasing	1	2	3	4	5

_____ × 3 = _____

Grammar, sentence structure	1	2	3	4	5
Punctuation	1	2	3	4	5
Spelling	1	2	3	4	5
Manuscript form, legibility	1	2	3	4	5

_____ × 1 = _____

Source: Diederich (1974, 54)

Figure 12.4 Sample analytical scale for evaluating a resume

Correct form (5)   _____

Sense of audience (2)   _____

Clear information (3)   _____

Mechanics (5)   _____

Total points (15)   _____

always be at least 50 percent of the total grade. If a student makes several errors in spelling, and spelling errors are designated as 10 percent of the grade, then regardless of how many words are misspelled, only 10 percent of the grade is affected.

The scale represents a contract between a student and the teacher. Before students write their final draft, they have a copy of the scale and know exactly how the paper will be evaluated. The scale is also used during peer response groups, particularly at the editing stage. The criteria on the grading sheet are the focus for the student editors.

We assign point values to each criterion rather than using the multiplication technique in Diederich's scale. The criteria and point values differ greatly from one assignment to another. The criteria reflect what the teacher wants students to achieve in each assignment. For example, form might be important in one assignment and not in another. When the assignment is for seniors to practice writing a resume, the points might be divided up as shown in Figure 12.4. The number in the parentheses represents the possible points for each criterion. The number of points actually received by the student is noted on the blank line. Students know exactly why they receive the grade they do.

For longer Level 3 assignments, the analytic scale is more detailed to reflect the amount of time available for students to work on the writing and the effort they put into it. Figure 12.5 is an example of a scale for a research project intended for juniors and seniors.

The first five items relate to the content of the paper and are 50 percent of the total grade. The reason the conventions count for so much in this assignment is that a main purpose is for students to learn how to use documentation. Several smaller assignments at Levels 1 and 2 gave students opportunities to learn these skills. The final draft went through a response group, an editing group, and a proofreading session.

Using scoring guides with rubrics helps teachers to more accurately evaluate. We all have biases about certain errors. Someone may be really bothered by incomplete sentences, another by subject-pronoun errors. Mistakes should be noted for a paper that went through all of the revision steps, but every error should be counted in fair proportion to the rest of the paper. A scoring guide makes it easier for a teacher to grade in an unbiased way. The scoring guide in Figure 12.5 was used with students who were familiar with analytical scales.

Figure 12.5 Sample scoring guide for a research project

Name _____

Thesis clearly stated	(5) _____
Organization of subject clear	(10) _____
Major points clear	(10) _____
Supporting details and examples well developed	(15) _____
Introduction and conclusion clear and concise	(10) _____
Correct word choice	(10) _____
Transitions clear	(5) _____
Punctuation acceptable	(10) _____
Spelling accurate	(10) _____
Introduced borrowed material	(5) _____
Correct documentation	(5) _____
Accurate work cited page	(5) _____

Total Points   (100) _____

Comments:

When students are not familiar with this type of grading, descriptions of the items are helpful. For example, students would not necessarily know what "Organization of subject clear" means. A description of organization might include the following:

Transitional words connect paragraphs. Paragraphs are in a logical order. Ideas in each paragraph are related. The paper as a whole has logical sequencing. Major points are supported by examples and support.

When scoring guides are used, we do not mark on the students' papers. A check-mark in the margin calls attention to a particular place, but the comments go on the guide. When papers are unmarred by our comments, the students can make revisions and hand the paper in for further evaluation. If we make all the needed corrections, students lose ownership of the paper. They just go through the motions when they revise, not thinking about how and why to make changes. However, we may use a teacher-edit after the student paper has been self-edited and gone through one or more response group sessions. For a teacher-edit, the teacher asks questions or offers suggestions, but does not correct. For example, a teacher may circle a word and write in the margin, "Better word choice?" Or the teacher could suggest that a writer "tell specifically what you did." Positive comments are also appropriate to encourage strong writing.

[handwritten margin note: Vis are useless]

EXPLORATION

Writing Rubrics

As a teacher you assign an eleventh-grade class a Level 2 short paper describing an event. They are to use descriptive phrases and all five senses. Write rubrics for this assignment using the format in Figure 12.5.

Some Final Points to Remember

- Scoring guides are a type of formative evaluation designed to help young writers improve their writing.
- The guides differ from one assignment to another and reflect the developmental age of the students.
- Students are familiar with the scoring guide before they turn in final drafts to the teacher.

Examples of Scoring Guides

Laura Apfelbeck devised the following criteria for a four-paragraph essay, seventh grade, literature assignment.

Introductory Paragraph

> The intro begins with a sentence that grabs the readers' attention.
>
> Background information includes author's name, story line, brief summary of the story, character name, and three to five physical traits.
>
> Intro ends with a thesis that tells the name of the character and two main personality traits.

Body Paragraph #1

> Begins with a topic sentence stating the character's name and one main personality trait.
>
> Supporting sentences prove the character has this trait by providing two to three examples from the story.
>
> The writer clearly explains how the examples from the story prove the character is evil, brave, and so on.
>
> The paragraph ends with a concluding sentence summarizing what was proven.

Body Paragraph #2

> Begins with a topic sentence stating the character's name and another personality trait.
>
> Supporting sentences prove the character has this trait by providing two to three examples from the story.
>
> The writer clearly explains how the examples from the story prove the character is evil, brave, and so on.
>
> The paragraph ends with a concluding sentence summarizing what was proven.

Concluding Paragraph

> The conclusion restates the thesis, naming the character and two traits.
>
> Concluding comments include opinion of the story and of the character.
>
> Ends with a memorable line, something catchy, clever, interesting.

This scoring guide was used for peer evaluation and teacher evaluation. In addition, Apfelbeck used the following form for the required steps in the writing assignment as part of her evaluation:

1. Student wrote an essay outline based on the handout.
2. Student completed a rough draft of the four paragraphs.
3. Student used the yellow criteria sheet with a parent or partner to evaluate rough draft.
4. Student completed a final draft in ink and on loose-leaf paper or typed.
5. Student was ready on time to evaluate the final draft in class using the peach criteria sheet.

A second evaluation example (see Figure 12.6) is by Wendy Mosley, a ninth-grade English teacher, for an English research paper.

Figure 12.6   Sample evaluation for English research paper

I. Content   1 2 3 4 5 ×2
   A. Introduction
      1. clear thesis statment   _____
      2. main points clearly stated   _____
      3. attention getter   _____
                          Total for introduction _____ (30)

   B. Body
      1. clear topic sentences   _____
      2. sufficiently developed paragraphs   _____
      3. clear transitions between paragraphs   _____
      4. used supporting information   _____
      5. citations in correct form   _____
      6. adequate number of references   _____
      7. minimum 5 sources on bibliography   _____
      8. paraphrased accurately   _____
      9. adequately revised draft   _____
                     Total for body _____ (90)

   C. Conclusion
      1. summary of points in body   _____
      2. persuasive clincher   _____
                   Total for conclusion _____ (20)

II. Process and Format
   A. Title page   1 2 3 4 5
   B. Outline   1 2 3 4 5 ×2
   C. Bibliography   1 2 3 4 5 ×2
   D. Neatness/form   1 2 3 4 5 ×2
   E. Mechanics   1 2 3 4 5 ×4
                     Total for process _____ (60)

III. Deductions: No revised draft: −30, not turned in on time: −10
                     Grand total _____ (200)

Comments:

Figure 12.7 Sample checkpoint scale

	Needs improving				Very good
Strong major points	1	2	3	4	5
Supporting vivid details	1	2	3	4	5
Lively specific language	1	2	3	4	5
Clear organization, easy to follow	1	2	3	4	5
Transitions that provide unity	1	2	3	4	5
Mechanics and grammar	1	2	3	4	5
Overall impression of the piece	1	2	3	4	5

EXPLORATION

Scoring Guides

Write a scoring guide for a report written by seventh graders. The report is worth 100 points and is a Level 3 assignment. What changes would you make in the scoring guide if it were a twelfth-grade assignment?

Checkpoint Scales

Checkpoint scales include specific criteria and an overall impression of the paper. You need to develop your own guides and vary them depending on grade level and assignment. The advantage of checkpoint scales is that they can be used quickly. Besides providing an in-progress evaluation, the guides suggest ways to improve the writing without actually doing the revision for the students. An example of a checkpoint scale is illustrated in Figure 12.7. Using a checkpoint scale is a quick way to help students gain a sense of "how they are doing"—something young writers often need for assurance.

SELF-EVALUATION

First and foremost, writing must please the writer. No matter who finally evaluates, if the writer is not pleased with the piece, the writing will lack spirit and flair. The more involved students are with the whole process, the more they personally care about what they wrote. Too often, however, evaluation comes from a source outside the process.

With help, students learn to be good judges of their own writing. Criteria for judging writing are developed by the whole class. Students tend to be critical when they discuss writing in the abstract. They often describe criteria far too difficult to achieve. Through discussion, teachers can help them understand what is important at each stage of the process and at each writing level. The list of agreed-on criteria then guides the self-evaluation.

The list should not be a checklist or a series of "yes" or "no" questions. Checks do not engage one's mind because it is too easy to just check "yes" for each item without really thinking about it. Student textbooks commonly include checklists to help students with their own editing, but such lists do not require a thoughtful response. Students do a better job if teachers give them opportunities to slow down their reading and think about the writing. Items on a checklist can be turned into directions that help students locate errors or into questions that require answers other than yes or no. For instance, "Did I spell all the words correctly?" can be changed to a more helpful suggestion: "Read your paper slowly, looking only for misspellings. Circle any word you are not sure of, and after reading through the paper, look up the words you questioned." Or on the subject of description, "Where is your best descriptive phrase? Where else might you add descriptive details?"

Assignments selected for self-evaluation should not then be evaluated by the teacher. Self-evaluation means assigning a summation comment or grade to one's own paper. This is different from reading over one's own work before receiving help from a response group or turning a paper in for a grade. Self-evaluation is a way of helping students understand what it means to evaluate, and the experience improves their own writing. Self-evaluated papers may go into a writing folder, or their portfolio.

 ## EVALUATION OF ORAL LANGUAGE

Teachers are sometimes puzzled about how to evaluate oral language activities. However, when we consider the similarities between oral and written expression, we see the potential for evaluation of oral work. Just as in written work, it is important to realize that not all oral activities are evaluated. Evaluation is based on the formality and purpose of the activity; in other words, according to the intended level. Practice is vital for increasing students' self-confidence and ability, and as in writing, practice is never formally evaluated.

Analytical grading scales are important, as they are in writing, to help students. Without the specific information students learn from the scale, it is difficult to improve—especially in speaking, where there is so much to attend to. Items on an oral activity grading scale include vocal and physical delivery, organization, and presentation of the material. What is emphasized depends on the type of activity: informational, storytelling, dramatic, explanatory, persuasive, or humorous.

Wendy Mosely, a ninth-grade teacher, devised the scoresheet in Figure 12.8 for her students' debate assignment.

In a classroom, the setting for oral language is often small groups. Discussion group responsibilities can be described and used as evaluation techniques for teachers and students. Les Parsons, in his book *Response Journals*, organizes the skills needed for effective group discussions into five areas:

1. Sharing with others (speaking up, listening to others, giving facts and reasons)
2. Replying to others (asking clarifying questions, replying to others, sharing equally in the talking)

Figure 12.8   Scoresheet for debate assignment

English 9

Debate Scoresheet

Topic _____

Each item is worth 10 points; 120 total points possible

Content

    Introduction

        Attention getter   _____

        Thesis statement   _____

        Main points   _____

    Body

        Main points restated with transitions   _____

        Examples and/or statistics   _____

        Direct quote   _____

    Conclusion

        Summary   _____

        Clincher *hela* " "   _____

Presentation

    Eye contact   _____

    Gestures & movement   _____

    Volume   _____

    Rate   _____

Rebuttal #1—bonus points   _____

Rebuttal #2—bonus points   _____

                         Total   _____

Comments:

---

3. Leading others (suggesting ideas, problem solving, keeping on topic)
4. Supporting others (helping others have a turn, acting interested in what others say, giving others credit)
5. Evaluating in a group (indicating if you agree, considering how to make the group work better, adjusting own ideas after listening to others)

Parsons suggests focusing on only one or two of these areas during a discussion. After the small-group discussions, students record in their journals whether they used a particular skill, how well they succeeded, and what they can do to increase their competence (58–59). Teachers can use the same criteria to evaluate an individual's group participation.

EVALUATION OF UNITS

Evaluation cannot be left until the end of a unit or any long-term assignment such as a research paper, but needs to occur as students progress through the unit. We evaluate journal writings as a Level 1 task and put a checkmark in a recordkeeping book to indicate a student completed the work. The same method is used for much of the group work. Collecting the work and responding to it is important. Students need to know the work "counts," and when you write a response or comment on their work, it gives them the sense that it was important. Level 2 writing, such as homework and some group work, deserves a grade or numerical evaluation. Level 3 writing, the final project for the unit, requires evaluation based on a grading scale described earlier. If the final project is not a writing assignment, then a different type of evaluation is required, one in which students help develop the criteria and know about well in advance before they perform or hand in the project.

Middle school students, in particular, need frequent evaluations as they progress through a long-term project. Individual conferences with students help keep them on track and aware of how they are doing. Students, for the most part, do not manage their time well, and we can't assume they are completing their work when the units extend over time. However, with help and encouragement, students can be taught to assume more responsibility for their own learning. Frequent checkpoints and group work, where students are responsible to each other, help students stay on task and complete their work. A project journal described in Chapter 8, "Writing for Learning," is part of the evaluation process that we can check as the students progress through the unit.

Peer critiquing is important to include, much as peer groups work in revising writing. Response forms that reflect the evaluation scales help direct students in making worthwhile comments and suggestions, as well as keeping them on task. Speaking and listening are linked activities, and learning to listen in order to make judgments about another's speech helps both the speaker and the listener.

Portfolio Evaluation

Portfolio evaluation is not a new way to evaluate student work. Artists have used portfolios for years to show employers the depth and breadth of their work. Only recently, however, have schools begun to use portfolios to evaluate student writing. The major advantage to portfolios is that we can look at students' work over a period of time. Too often we are judged on a one-time evaluation: SAT scores, unit test, musical performance, writing sample, and term paper. The thinking, planning, and effort that went into creating the final product are ignored in the evaluation, as is the possibility of not feeling well physically or emotionally the day of the test. The restricted time allowed for writing greatly affects the product. As Sandra Murphy notes, portfolios show what students do in a variety of situations, giving teachers a "broader and more accurate picture of student performance" (143). Because portfolios include writing intended for different audiences and purposes that draw on different strategies and skills, portfolio assessment is more fair to students (144). The overall evaluation of portfolios gives a much clearer picture of students' fluency and progress in writing.

Peter Elbow, a university educator, supports portfolio evaluation because of improvement in students' effort and interest. Students are more willing to revise their work because they receive credit for their effort. They are more likely to "try for what is exciting, not just what's acceptable" (*What Is English?* 167). Portfolios give students the chance to show their best work and to say, "Look how hard I worked," providing a more complete picture of student abilities than one piece of writing (Maxwell 143).

In *Portfolio News*, Martha Johnson, director of a cooperative writing program, lists several positive attitudes and behaviors that portfolios encourage in students:

- To take more responsibility for their work
- To see themselves as apprentices
- To value daily work as a meaningful part of learning
- To see mistakes as opportunities for learning
- To see revision as an opportunity to succeed
- To spend more time thinking about their teacher's response
- To spend more time conferring with classmates
- To spend more time reconsidering and improving their work
- To be more creative, to feel more confident, to be more productive
- To take pride in their work, to perform or display what they know (2)

Johnson's claims for portfolios might sound somewhat ideal, but involving students in evaluation does improve their attitudes toward writing.

Writing folders and portfolios serve different purposes. The difference lies in what each contains. Students keep all their writing in a folder, but they select only the best pieces of writing for placement in their portfolio. Depending on the grade level, you may want to keep the writing folders in the classroom. Older students keep track of their own. We can encourage or actually require that students keep everything they work on. In addition to portfolio selection, students may want to revise a paper they did several weeks ago or use one of their papers for a reference in a later assignment. The folder does not involve any self-selection on the part of the student, but the selection process is essential for portfolios.

The physical appearance of portfolios can vary considerably. Some teachers require neatly organized notebooks; others have bulky folders or expandable files. Some portfolios are covered with student artwork or handmade covers. Whatever their appearance, they share the common philosophy that teachers value what students are doing: their efforts, results, products, process, diversity, and standards (Tierney, Carter, and Desal 49).

Contents of Portfolios

Portfolios contain (a) a table of contents, (b) the selections of writings, (c) a rationale for the selections, and (d) future goals, all written and selected by students. Student involvement in their own evaluation is the most important reason for using portfolios. Evaluations should matter first to the students and secondarily to parents and teachers. To achieve this, students must be involved in creating the portfolios right from the start.

    a. *Table of contents.* A list of the contents gives the teacher an overview of what the portfolio contains and provides the context for the selections. Selections are listed in order by date so progress is more apparent.

    b. *Selections.* To begin, students choose what goes into the portfolios by going through their writing folders and other work they have accumulated and selecting what they believe best represents their effort, progress, and achievement. The selections vary depending on the teacher and level of the class, but basically they are a collection of work assigned by the teacher. However, students may want to include writing done on their own. Students are also encouraged to add assignments from other classes (e.g., a paper written for history or science). In addition to student-selected work, some teachers designate assignments they want included in the portfolio. Teachers can specify a minimum number of pieces that students select and then add one or two teacher-selected pieces, such as an assignment everyone has in common (e.g., a short story, a poem, or a report). Teachers may have general input in this choice by requiring a certain number of Level 2 writings, assignments based on particular readings, and types of activities; however, each student selects the actual piece to include. For example, one teacher requested that the following writings be included in her students' portfolios (Maxwell 146):

       1. A Level 3 writing, including all of the discovery activities, drafts, revisions, and response sheets

       2. An example of what you worked the hardest on

       3. An example of what you learned the most from

       4. The assignment you enjoyed the most

       5. Anything of your choosing (explain why you are including it)

    The selections do not have to be final copies; students may add a discovery activity they particularly like. We need to encourage students to look at writing done at each stage of the writing process for two reasons: (1) In evaluating improvement, early drafts may give more information on fluency and thinking than those that go through all of the steps of revising; and (2) when early drafts are part of the material to be evaluated, students learn to value all of the writing they do.

    Some teachers have students meet in groups to help each other decide what pieces to select. Whether students receive help from peers or select papers on their own, they write a rationale or explanation for the selections. Through this process of selecting and explaining their choices, students develop a sense of ownership in every step of the writing process.

    c. *Rationales.* This is the reflective part of the portfolio. Students write a letter to their teacher explaining why they chose the pieces they did and what they believe the choices show.

A student, Christa Przytarski, chose one piece because "it was a creative idea," another from her midterm because she "enjoyed the poetry," another because she "really had fun writing this story," and another because "it was a fun project to do, and I was very pleased with the way it turned out."

Thinking about their writing makes students begin to consider themselves as writers, and not just as students enrolled in a particular course. They could reflect about their learning, a novel experience for most secondary students; they are not often given that opportunity (Ballard 48).

Students in Mary Meiser's freshman composition class reflected on the writing they did over a four-month period. Excerpts from their comments include the following:

> *Just making a paper flow all together seems to be coming much easier. It is becoming more of a routine to check my sentences to see if they make sense and how they flow. (Krista Mickelson)*

> *It still is troublesome for me to get to the point I can say what I want to say in as few words as possible. I think the source of the problem is that I need more experience writing. (Angie Piper)*

> *At first I didn't write/include as many examples as I should have. My latest paper was on stereotyping. In this essay I did show concrete examples and let some of my feeling show, which resulted in a better paper. (Jessica Smith)*

d. *Reflecting.* Students look at all their accumulated work and write a reflection on their progress over a period of time. Based on this reflection, they write a number of goals for themselves; goals they plan on reaching during the next marking period. Alan Purves, Joseph Quattrini, and Christine Sullivan suggest that students ask themselves three things:

   1. What do I want to know about?
   2. What do I want to be able to do?
   3. What habits and practices do I want to develop? (11)

A student, Laura, wrote the following goals (Maxwell 147):

> *First I would like to increase my vocabulary so that I am not always searching for words to use. I think my writing would be more effective if I had a broader range of vocabulary to choose from. And second, I would like to expand my creativity. I am much better at writing accounts of something that has already happened. I lack in the area of coming up with my own story.*

Purves et al. urge students to take charge of their own writing. Directing their remarks to student writers, they write that students need to "focus on three facets of you as a writer: what you know, what you can do if you are really put to the test, and what you can do on your own" (10).

They suggest looking at portfolios as a self-portrait, showing the world the variety of things you know.

Each time students work on their portfolios, they read the goals from the last one. Part of their reflection, then, is to think about how well they met those goals. If teachers realize the student's goals are unrealistic, the teacher and student need to have a conference. Occasionally students write lofty goals that are impossible to achieve, and their expectations for themselves need to be more sensible. On the other hand, some students need to be encouraged to stretch themselves to achieve more difficult goals. When teachers evaluate the portfolios, they can specifically check to see if goals and student abilities are a good match.

Evaluating Portfolios

Because portfolios are designed to show progress, teachers, as a rule, do not include ungraded work. Every piece needs to include the date it was written and, if appropriate, the dates of revision. The writing level of each piece is included as well. If students place the papers in the portfolio in order by date, the teacher can evaluate progress more easily. A variation of an analytical scale helps the teacher during evaluation and helps the student to understand the evaluation. Figure 12.9 shows an example of a portfolio scale.

Figure 12.9   An analytical scale used for portfolio evaluation

1. The goals are specific enough to be helpful.
   Comments:

2. The goals are a realistic reflection of your past work.
   Comments:

3. The goals are realistic considering the period of time you have to achieve them.
   Comments:

4. Your reflection is a thoughtful response to your work.
   Comments:

5. The reasons for your selections are clear and thoughtful.
   Comments:

6. I think your effort and progress is:
   Comments:

7. Suggestions I want to make:
   Comments:

Your total points for the portfolio are _____ .

Teachers often assign a certain number of points as a grade for the portfolio; others record a pass/fail grade. The benefits come not from a specific grade, but from what both students and teachers learn in the process. An analytical response lets students know if a teacher's goals fit with what they see as their personal goals. Selecting and evaluating portfolios takes time, but it is the most successful way of involving students in evaluation.

TEACHERS' EXPERIENCES

Margie Krest, a high school teacher, has used portfolios for several years to document her students' growth and risk-taking (29). Her students keep all of their writing, "including drafts, revisions, prewriting material, and final papers" (29). Students date the papers so they can keep track of their own progress. Because not every piece of writing is graded, students are more willing to experiment and take more risks. Krest devised a method for evaluating that rewards multiple drafting, revising, and practice, all elements of the writing process. In addition to the graded work the students select for their portfolio, she includes an ungraded final draft. She gives two grades on the portfolio: one for all of the writing and one for a paper grade on one final product. She weights the two grades according to what she wants to emphasize. For instance, if fluency is more important than creating an error-free paper, then the portfolio grade might be 75 percent and the paper grade 25 percent. The reverse situation might be appropriate for seniors. By adjusting the percentages, Krest finds portfolios adaptable to different grade levels and student abilities (31).

High school teacher Roberta J. Herter used portfolio evaluation because she wanted a "fuller picture of a writer's growth over time" (90). She found portfolios helped students assume responsibility for their writing.

Portfolios involve students in assessing the development of their writing skills by inviting self-reflection and encouraging students to assume control over their writing. Accumulating a body of work to return to, to reject, revise, or simply revisit calls on students to become responsible for the content and quality of their portfolio, and ultimately to confront their personal writing inventories and investments in activities of the class (90).

Other teachers who have used portfolios echo this belief. One teacher reports, "The first thing that struck me was their insight into their own strengths and weaknesses and their willingness to be honest about their efforts" (Ballard 46). Students also realize the benefits of revision-substantive revision, not just editing changes (47).

Parents and Evaluation

Parents can also become involved in evaluation through portfolios. Teacher Ruth Mitchell has her students take the portfolios home and includes a questionnaire for parents asking them what they think of their child's work. Mitchell reports that parents, for the most part, have a positive response. They know what is happening at school and feel more involved in the school–home relationship (110–114).

Portfolios also help with the parent connection at parent–teacher conferences. They provide a concrete illustration of each child's work, which is more helpful than discussing evaluation in abstract terms. Parents can more easily see evidence of growth and progress (or lack of it), something a test grade does not tell them.

INSTRUCTIONAL UNIT

BIOGRAPHIES: EVALUATING A STUDENT PAPER

Teacher Pat Stellick shares an assignment she gives to her tenth graders. The assignment is part of a unit on biographies. The following is her explanation to the students:

> In "Open Letter to a Young Negro," "Hitler's Games Tarnished Gold," and *The Jesse Owens Story* video, we were given a variety of views of Jesse Owens. By referring to specific examples from our biographical selections (try to use all three sources), explain in a well-developed essay what you think are the most outstanding characteristics of Jesse Owens.

EXPLORATION

USING AN ANALYTICAL SCALE

Assume the role of a teacher and develop an analytical scale to use for evaluating the student paper that follows. The paper is worth 50 points, is a Level 3, and the class is tenth grade. Once you develop the scale, evaluate student Elizabeth Ehlert's paper using your scale.

JESSE OWENS

Jesse Owens was an incredible, well-rounded person who influenced the entire world, using his life to benefit others. I think one of Jesse Owens most outstanding characteristics was his selflessness. He respected everyone and was never too busy to take the time to help someone. In *The Jesse Owens Story* video, he went out in the middle of the night to get a young negro out of jail and talk to him. He also volunteered his time to help young black athletes succeed. During the 1936 Olympics, Jesse helped a broad jumper from Mexico to improve his jumping, even though this person was one of his competitors. In the article "Hitlers' Games Tarnished Gold," Jesse showed his unselfishness. When the Jewish runners were taken out of the relay race, Jesse was put in their place. He stood up for them saying they deserved to run, as he had already won three gold medals and was exhausted. These things took a lot of courage.

Another outstanding characteristic of Jesse Owens was his positive attitude and outlook throughout life. This was evident in the video. While his life was being picked apart by the investigator, Jesse was positive and very honest. He kept a glimmer of hope and responded positively towards the investigator. In "Open Letter to a Young Negro" he tells people that we can get along without violence. He tries to impress upon us that people are people. It doesn't matter what color their skin is, what their religion or beliefs are, or anything else. Jesse Owens used his life and well-known name to help others. He was very honest and was often treated unfairly, but he fought through those tough times. Jesse Owens made a great contribution to the world, and I feel we should all learn from him.

After you have evaluated Elizabeth's paper, meet in small groups and consider the following points:

Reflection

1. What did each of you write in your comments that would help Elizabeth with her next writing assignment?
2. What specific positive comments did you make?
3. Where you disagreed on scores or evaluations, what were the reasons for the discrepancies?
4. What mini-lessons, if any, could you use with this tenth-grade class to better prepare them for writing their essays?
5. What follow-up writing assignment could you ask students to do to build on the skills they learned from the activity?

THE FUTURE OF ASSESSMENT

Arthur Applebee makes a strong case that we need to make assessment decisions based on curricular grounds. He lists five principles that language arts assessment should reflect:

1. Assessment should be based on a wide range of situations where students read and write—the same situations we create in our classrooms.
2. The contexts of assessment must involve students in "higher literacy" activities that are "thought-provoking and that give students time and space to develop their own interpretations and defend their own points of view.
3. Assessment must include time for "reflection and revision" to allow students to use their abilities and return to a task over time.
4. Assessment must "provide room to discuss and make explicit the basis of judgments about quality." Reports on student performance at district, state, or national levels must include sufficient samples of student work.
5. Assessment must be classroom-based and in the context of a rich and varied curriculum. (45–46)

For assessment to be authentic, it must reflect an ongoing process of learning where varieties of activities provide the most favorable opportunities for a diverse group of students to learn.

REFERENCES

Abbott, Jim. "Changing the Perception of Assessment." *Center X Quarterly* (Spring 1995): 11.

Apfelbeck, Laura. "Literature assignment." English lesson plan, unpublished, 2000.

Applebee, Arthur N. "English Language Arts Assessment: Lessons from the Past." *English Journal* (Apr. 1994): 40–46.

Ballard, Leslie. "Portfolios and Self-Assessment." *English Journal* (Feb. 1992): 46–48.

Davis, Barbara Gross, Michael Scriven, and Susan Thomas. *The Evaluation of Composition Instruction.* New York: Teachers College Press, 1987.

Diederich, Paul B. *Measuring Growth in English.* Urbana: NCTE, 1974.

Elbow, Peter. *Embracing Contraries.* New York: Oxford UP, 1986.

_____ . *What Is English?* New York: Modern Language Association, 1990.

Everly, Pamela. *Teaching Teenagers and Living to Tell about It.* Englewood: Teachers Ideas Press, 1992.

Goodlad, John I. *A Place Called School: Promise for the Future.* Columbus: McGraw-Hill, 1984.

Herter, Roberta J. "Writing Portfolios: Alternatives to Testing." *English Journal* (Jan. 1991): 90–92.

Johannessen, Larry R. "Enhancing Response to Literature: A Matter of Changing Old Habits." *English Journal* (Nov. 1994): 66–70.

Johnson, Martha. *Portfolio News* (Spring 1991): 2.

Krest, Margie. "Adapting the Portfolio to Meet Student Needs." *English Journal* (Feb. 1990): 29–34.

Maxwell, Rhoda J. *Writing Across the Curriculum in Middle and High Schools.* Needham Heights: Allyn & Bacon, 1996.

Mitchell, Ruth. *Testing for Learning.* New York: Free Press, 1992.

Mosley, Wendy, Carla Burmeister & Betsy Damon. Research Project: Paper/Debate. Research and Writing Workshop Cray Academy, 1999.

Murphy, Sandra. "Writing Portfolios in K–12 Schools: Implications for Linguistically Diverse Students." *New Directions in Portfolio Assessment.* Eds. Laurel Black, et al. Portsmouth: Boynton/Cook, 1994: 140–56.

Parsons, Les. *Response Journals.* Portsmouth: Pembroke Publishers, 1989.

Purves, Alan C. *Testing Literature: The Current State of Affairs.* Bloomington: ERIC Clearinghouse, 1990.

Purves, Alan C., Joseph A. Quattrini, and Christine I. Sullivan. "Using Portfolios to Take Charge of Your Writing: Advice to Students." *Portfolio News* (Fall 1994): 10–12.

Schuman, Baird R. "Assessing Student Achievement in the Study of Literature." *English Journal* (Dec. 1994): 55–58.

Smede, Shelly D. "Flyfishing, Portfolios, and Authentic Writing." *English Journal* (Feb. 1995): 92–94.

Stellick, Pat. "Unit on Biographies." English lesson plan, unpublished, 1996.

Tierney, Robert, Mark A. Carter, and Laura E. Desal. *Portfolio Assessment in the Reading–Writing Classroom.* Norwood: Christopher-Gordon, 1991.

Developing Units

The use of thematic units permits a broadening of pedagogical concerns in English studies beyond those of genres, periods, and particular authors and works. The thematic approach reflects a concern with the personal growth of the reader/writer versus an emphasis on specific literary works as objects worthy of study for their own sake.

Robert C. Goldbort (72)

 ## INTERACTIVE TEACHING

Throughout this text, the different aspects of teaching English are presented in individual chapters, but only as a way of discussing each one. Language, composition, literature, speaking, and listening are all part of English instruction. The interaction among the parts is the foundation for planning the curriculum. For instance, a unit on listening is a poor way to teach the skills of listening. However, when listening is incorporated throughout the curriculum, teachers have a better chance of achieving their goal of improving students' listening habits.

The same is true for speaking. The most effective way to provide opportunities for both listening and speaking is the use of small groups, which shifts the class from being teacher-centered to being student-centered. Students listen to each other and contribute to the discussion. When groups become part of an instructional plan, the balance among reading, writing, listening, and speaking more closely approximates our use of these skills in the world outside the classroom. In real life, we speak and listen far more than we read and write. Creative dramatics also provides opportunities for interactions among the four components. One way to include a variety of activities that promote an ongoing interaction among all the components is through thematic units. The theme serves as an umbrella for a whole host of activities involving all strands of the language arts.

 ## ORGANIZING AROUND A THEME

Thematic units are designed with many focuses: art, music, history, literature, and language—although literature is the most common focus. One reason, of course, is that literature is a major part of an English class; more importantly, using a thematic approach is a more effective way to teach literature than using a single author or chronological organization.

In *Novels of Initiation*, David Peck agrees that the best way to teach literature is by theme. "Somehow our secondary literature curriculum has gotten locked into historical and genre approaches that have lost much of whatever usefulness they once had" (xxi). He explains that when students read thematically related works they are able to connect the ideas and characters to their own lives and to other works as well. As an example he writes, "Why is tolerance such an important idea in Harper Lee's *To Kill a Mockingbird*? How different is its treatment in Mildred D. Taylor's *Roll of Thunder, Hear My Cry*? What relevance does it have to our own lives? And what relationship does it have to the idea of self-respect that we find in both novels?" (xxi). To read with a focus, as in Peck's example of the theme of tolerance, helps students clarify their own ideas and values about things that matter in their lives. Such units allow students to pursue topics that concern and interest them while learning the course content mandated by the curriculum (Maxwell 152).

When literature is taught chronologically, the teacher must play the major role of one who knows the answers. George Hillocks explains, "Since the knowledge gained about one writer is unlikely to be applicable to the next, students are almost necessarily forced into the role of passive recipient of knowledge about individual writers and works" (149). Chronological organization doesn't help students make connections from one text to another or to connect the literature with their own life experiences.

A high school teacher, David T. Anderson, uses thematic units because a "problem with chronological sequencing is that it goes against a basic principle of education: Begin with simple experiences on which to base learning and move to complex understandings" (62). He explained to his students that the next novel they would be reading was easier than the one they just finished. "Upon saying this, one of my students raised her hand and asked, 'Then why didn't we read it first?' Even a junior in high school realized when this basic rule was compromised" (62). When novels for young adults are included in the units, students can read these easier works first and then be better able to understand the more difficult selections. Because the concepts are the same, the easier texts help students comprehend the ideas in the more difficult reading.

BEGINNING TO PLAN

Developing a unit that encompasses many components might seem overwhelming to a new teacher. One way to begin is to choose literature selections on a common theme. Every student in each class must be capable of reading at least one of the selections, and each unit must have at least three reading levels. Many other titles should also be available for students who want to read several books or for those who find the original choices too difficult or not interesting. Every poem, short story, drama, essay, or article included in the unit must be on the common theme. Themes can be a historical period or how a particular period in history affected art, education, and societal values. Themes might also focus on human emotions such as fear, love, envy, hate; or people's traits of bravery, pride, perseverance, generosity, or any other theme that would be interesting to the age group you are teaching.

examples of themes

large variety of reading, but not necessarily all genres

Not every unit will have every genre of literature represented, but as much as possible, a variety of readings should be included. One type of text enhances another. For instance, Faulkner's "A Rose for Emily," *To Kill a Mockingbird* by Harper Lee, poems by Dickinson, and current newspaper and magazine articles all contribute to students' wider understanding of the theme of societal values.

A high school teacher, Nina Hackett, describes a program in which she and three other teachers integrate the themes of adolescence and identity; family relationships and values; influence of the media, cinema, and TV; political administrations and court decisions with the ethnic groups of African Americans, Latinos, Asians, and Native Americans. They use literature, art, music, media, history, and sociology to explore contemporary America through the eyes of minorities. The themes provide the means for minority students to see their cultural contributions to society as a part of the classroom (8).

Organizing a unit around a theme provides opportunities to include poetry, nonfiction, short stories, drama, and novels. A unit ties all the literature together in a unified approach to teaching. The literature itself can be the basis for understanding a historical period, not just an add-on because the setting coincides with a time period. Carolyn Lott and Stephanie Wasta developed a unit using the theme of the American Civil War. Working in groups, students present material they discovered through research, their knowledge of the American Civil War coming from various sources of literature. Each group investigated through literature the roles of youth or women or military leaders and then presented their findings to the class. They needed to make connections between the literature and explain how each character or voice added to their background information of the American Civil War.

Teaching and Learning in Groups

Once a teacher selects a variety of literature, the next step is to devise ways to discuss and write about the literature. The listening and speaking strands of English are most naturally incorporated through small- and large-group discussion, although projects can also be designed to include oral presentations. Traditionally, teachers talked and students listened. But for students to improve their skills in listening and speaking, the focus must shift from the teacher to the students. Teachers do need to give information and explanation through a lecture format, but students need ample opportunities to talk among themselves. James Moffett describes discussion as "a process of amending, appending, diverging, converging, elaborating, summarizing, and many things" (46). He is referring to small-group discussion, not a whole-class discussion in which the teacher dominates the talk and only a few students join in. In a whole-class group, a teacher is often looking for specific answers to questions, but even if the questions are intended to draw out students' opinions, they succeed with only a few.

For an interchange of ideas, feelings, and opinions, four to six in a group works best, particularly if students are discussing literature or responding to each other's writing. Teachers must give directions to the groups that are clearly understood by students and have a well-defined purpose. To keep students on task, teachers may limit the length of time for the group work to be accomplished and then have each group present the results of their discussion orally to the whole class. Middle school students may need further structure, and a teacher can require written notes to be handed in following the discussion. Some type of activity as closure to the group work is vital to create purpose for the activity. Also, if a teacher walks around the room listening to one group and then another, students are more likely to stay on task. Group work should be part of every unit and should be a planned activity, not left to chance or used as a fill-in for extra time.

Including Writing Activities

A unit includes many opportunities for writing. All three levels of writing described in Chapter 6, "Teaching Composition," are appropriate throughout a unit. A Level 3 writing is usually the final project, whereas Level 1 activities occur almost daily, and Level 2 activities occur two or three times a week. However, every unit does not have to have a Level 3 writing. Also, a unit provides many opportunities for different types and purposes of writing: poetry, factual, autobiographical, analytical, summaries, responses, and informational.

Developing a thematic unit that includes all of the elements mentioned takes a great deal of time, but a beginning teacher can start slowly by designing writing activities for one literature selection and later adding other literature and activities to the unit. Teaching units may never be "finished." Even if the unit is repeated for several years, it should be revised each year, especially if the teacher regularly uses current news stories. Once teachers decide on the units and begin to develop them, material is not difficult to find. Files of poems, articles, clippings, notes, and suggestions are continually added to. Longer units often grow into two files, providing many choices, so that a unit isn't the same from one year to the next. All this takes a great deal of time, but if new teachers enter the classroom with one well-thought-out thematic unit, they will have a head start in their planning and be well prepared for the beginning of the year.

COMPONENTS OF A UNIT

Perhaps the easiest way to begin planning a unit is to choose a literature selection. The curriculum may specify that *Romeo and Juliet* be taught at ninth grade or *Great Expectations* at tenth grade. That is the place to start. Because many high school students are going to have difficulty with either of these selections, the first task is to choose additional literature on the same theme that is easier to read. Literature as complex as *Romeo and Juliet* or *Great Expectations* has several themes, and teachers decide what seems the most appropriate for their students. Young adult literature can be added fairly easily because many reference books are available with annotated bibliographies that are grouped thematically. Short stories are more difficult to find; however, anthologies available in the schools are a good source of short stories. In addition, authors of young adult literature have several books of short stories. Choosing poetry for a particular theme is even more difficult and requires reading poetry from a variety of sources. Literature chosen for units must represent a variety of authors and include both minorities and women. Once teachers make a few literature selections, they can add writing activities, group activities, language play, and creative dramatics.

The sequence described above varies. For example, sometimes a teacher selects a theme before deciding on any literature. However, in general, planning a unit might follow these steps:

step by step

- Select a theme.
- Choose literature for two or three reading levels.
- Decide on writing activities at Levels 1 and 2.
- Add short stories, poetry, drama, and nonfiction selections appropriate to the theme.
- Look at the connections among the literature selections, and between the literature and the students' lives. Include group activities that strengthen the connections and allow listening and speaking to be major activities.
- Add creative activities such as drama, drawing, and music.
- Looking at the unit as a whole, create several choices for a Level 3 writing assignment or some other type of final project or presentation, keeping in mind the students' varied interests and ways of learning.

Important Points to Remember

?'s to ask when planning unit

As you plan a unit of your own, you will need to consider your classroom. What interests do your students have? What is the variety of learning preferences for your students? How can you provide for gifted students and those with special needs? How can you include diversity? How much time will you have for teaching the unit? How can you make it interesting for your students? What standards are covered in the unit?

Planning a unit is hard work; however, you will enhance your teaching and the students' learning by considering these questions.

We describe many units in the following pages. Few are explained in full because of space limitations; however, our hope is that you will find many ideas that you can adapt into your own planning.

UNITS DEVELOPED AROUND ONE MAJOR LITERATURE SELECTION

An example of writing activities based on one work of literature comes from a former English education student, Cassie Scharber, who chose a young adult novel, *Finding My Voice* by Marie G. Lee.

INSTRUCTIONAL UNIT

FINDING MY VOICE

Summary of the Novel

It is Ellen Sung's last year of high school. She is a typical teenager preoccupied with good grades, fun, varsity letters, college, and boyfriends; however, one thing makes her different from her classmates is that she is Asian American. This leads to big problems for Ellen: name-calling, fistfights, and so on. This novel is about Ellen's year of decisions and discrimination, the year in which she finally "finds her voice" and stands up for what she believes in.

Writing Activities

1. (Level 2) This activity introduces the novel. Because Lee's book deals extensively with the issues of prejudice and discrimination, students need to understand the words before they begin reading. The teacher asks students to write in their learning logs their own definition for being prejudiced. The definition should include information about what prejudice is, whom it affects, why it occurs, and some examples of prejudice. Writing the definition is a homework assignment so that students can really think about the word and what it means. *[handwritten: I might do this in class, so they don't use dictionaries]*

   The next day the class is divided into groups of four or five students. Each group member reads his or her definition of prejudice to the group. The group discusses the definitions and develops one that the whole group agrees on. Each group then reports to the whole class, and the class develops a common definition of prejudice. The teacher discusses the difference between prejudice and discrimination (a belief or feeling and acting out of these beliefs).

2. (Level 1) Now that the class understands what prejudice and discrimination are, Scharber has the students observe behavior in the

school and communities to understand how common and widespread prejudice is—prejudice against age, sex, intelligence, religion, opinions, appearance, wealth, athletic skills, and so on. Students keep a journal for one week and record every act of discrimination they see, hear, or experience. They respond to their feelings and those of others. She hopes by keeping the journal the students come to realize how common and how unnecessary discrimination is. The activity helps students to identify with the character, Ellen.

3. (Level 1) After the week of journal writing, students write about a time when they were discriminated against, focusing on their feelings and reactions. Through discussion, the students compare their reactions to Ellen's.
   - In what ways were their reactions similar to Ellen's?
   - Why did Ellen react the way she did to the taunts and jeers of her classmates?
   - How do you think she felt?
   - How did you feel when you read about it?

4. (Level 3) Discussion continues throughout the reading of the book. When students have completed the reading, the final writing activity centers on the title *Finding My Voice*. Examples of discussion questions include the following:
   - What does the title mean?
   - When does Ellen "find" her voice?
   - How did she use it?
   - Does she use her "voice" when Marsha breaks the bottle over her head?
   - How does silence have a "voice"?

The final assignment for students is to write a paper about a time when they found their voice; the paper may be an essay or story. The following questions help guide their writing:

What if they haven't found their voice?

- When did you discover your "voice"?
- Who or what helped you discover your "voice"?
- How did you feel before you used your "voice"?
- What were the advantages and disadvantages of using your "voice"?

Students follow the writing process to produce a high-quality Level 3 paper.

The discussion and writing questions described for *Finding My Voice* are only the beginning of a unit. The next step is to find other novels, poetry, drama, and nonfiction on the same theme.

Exploration

Planning for Literature Study

Choose a novel for either middle school or high school that you have enjoyed. Write a list of Level 1 and Level 2 assignments you could use for your future students.

Teaching *To Kill a Mockingbird*

To Kill a Mockingbird by Harper Lee has been a perennial favorite for many years and is still frequently taught in secondary schools. For that reason, we are including a compilation of several approaches by English education students for teaching *To Kill a Mockingbird*.

In this first unit, Maureen McManus uses writing activities to connect the literature to students' lives. By making these connections, she helps students understand the characters in the novel and gain a deeper knowledge of the literature. She assigned the journal and in-class writing daily, and they were used for class or group discussions. The activities labeled "writings" are all Level 2 and are not daily activities; however, they too are the basis for class or group discussions. Although McManus wrote writing activities and discussion questions for every chapter, only a few are included here as examples of how a teacher could begin planning for a literature unit.

INSTRUCTIONAL UNIT

TO KILL A MOCKINGBIRD

Chapter 1

Journal Options

1. Describe a person, place, event, or TV show that frightened you when you were young, but now that you are older you realize you let your imagination get the best of you.
2. Discuss your family traditions or community customs. In what ways are they important to you?
3. Write a character sketch of Boo Radley. Describe his appearance, mannerisms, how he talks, and what he does.

Chapters 2 and 3

Journal Options

1. Reflect on how you felt about your experiences in kindergarten or first grade. How did you feel about school? Offer some examples.
2. What are some of Scout's innocent mistakes? How are ideas of good and bad, right versus wrong, manners, and politeness expressed so far in the story?

3. Write about a time when you didn't mean to be bad, but did something because you didn't know better and people were angry with you.

Chapter 11

Journal Options
1. How are Scout and Jem changing their attitudes about Atticus? What are some reasons for this new outlook?
2. What are the various evidences of prejudice, not only racial, but ways in which Scout notices a great difference between other characters and herself? When and where have you noticed some of these prejudices today?
3. Prepare a dialogue between Boo and Mrs. Dubose concerning Jem and Scout.

Chapters 13 and 14

Journal Options
1. What are the differences between the town's acceptance of Aunt Alexandra and those of Jem and Scout?
2. What are some evidences of Jem's growing maturity? How does this change his friendship with Dill? How does it affect the relationship between Scout and Dill?
3. Write a character sketch of Dill including his personality and physical attributes. Describe his family life and how it has affected him.

Chapter 16

Journal Options
1. In what ways are Aunt Alexandra's views even narrower than those of the children?
2. How are Scout and Jem finally beginning to realize the differences and similarities between blacks and whites? What are some questions they discuss about this?
3. Describe the atmosphere of the courthouse lawn and the moods of the various groups scattered about.

Chapters 18 and 19

Journal Options
1. Throughout the story what are the various ways Scout describes blacks? Name both physical and personality attributes. How is her particular association with the person a factor in her opinion?
2. Atticus once told Scout that she could never really understand a person unless she "wears his shoes." How is Scout's understanding of this statement becoming more apparent throughout the novel?
3. Write an account of the trial as it might appear in the Maycomb newspaper from Mr. Underwood's point of view.

Chapters 22 and 23

Journal Options

1. Jem gives serious thought to the trial and its outcome. What are various aspects of the trial that he questions? What people help Jem draw his conclusions?
2. What were the various reactions of different people when Bob Ewell spit in Atticus's face? How does this reflect their characters?
3. Show how Scout's thought process changes, especially about prejudice, after the trial. Compare her with other characters in how they changed or failed to change. In what ways has Scout learned to question what others say rather than simply accept it? Who does she question now and in what ways? Create dialogue or cite actual passages in the book.

Chapters 29 and 30

Journal Options

1. In what ways are both Boo and Tom Robinson like mockingbirds? How is the way they are treated like killing a mockingbird?
2. How are the lives of Tom Robinson and Boo similar or different? How do Scout and Jem change their attitudes about both Boo and Tom as the story progresses? What brings about this change?
3. Scout tells this story in retrospect. Describe her as she writes this book. How old is she? What is her occupation and education? Where does she live? What are her contributions to society?

Level 3 Writing Options [to be completed after students finish reading the novel]. Students select one from the list or may choose another option by conferencing with the teacher.

1. Choose one character from the book and describe one wish the character would choose and explain why. Who else is affected by the wish? What does this say about the character? How would the wish change certain aspects of the story?
2. If Atticus were the guest speaker at a high school graduation, what messages, warnings, and encouragements might he offer the graduates? How would he prepare them for the real world? Write his speech or take the standpoint of a graduate listening to him.
3. Write a series of letters between Scout and Dill. What would they share in a letter?
4. Choose a character from the book who keeps a journal or is a closet poet. Make a series of journal entries or prepare a collection of poetry by this character.
5. Write a collection of Letters to the Editor or journal entries from several different characters showing their various opinions of the trial.
6. Compile a list of guidelines for raising children. How could parents and teachers promote open-mindedness or instill values/morals in children?

⌇∿⌇ *Reflection* ⌇∿⌇

Why is *To Kill a Mockingbird* appropriate for teaching in secondary schools? What student outcomes would you like for your students?

In a second example of activities for teaching *To Kill a Mockingbird,* Nicole Marty, Joseph Mlinar, and Kristine Stein chose the theme of values.

INSTRUCTIONAL UNIT

TO KILL A MOCKINGBIRD

[handwritten margin note: Would use the definition of values approach used for p. 401]

The teacher begins by introducing the concept of values. What is a value? How are behaviors and values related? Students respond in their journals to the following prompts: What values do you think have been instilled in you by your parents? What values have you received from friends, your community, and your culture? After further class discussion, the teacher has the students meet in six groups. Three of the groups work on the poem "If" by Rudyard Kipling and the other three on "Mother to Son" by Langston Hughes. Each group makes a list of the values expressed in the poem. The class meets as a whole and each group share the lists with the class. Then the teacher leads a discussion on what values are important to the students. The values are listed on the board and students discuss how they relate to their lives. Students write the agreed-upon list in their journal to be used as they read the novel.

The teacher creates a wall chart with the values listed along the left-hand side. Columns across the top list the chapters in groups of three. In their journals, students write responses to their reading and list the behaviors of the characters that illustrate a particular value. The students share their journal writing in their reading groups. This is continued throughout the reading of the novel.

For the final project, students create a portfolio on a value they choose. The directions to the students are as follows:

1. Choose a value that we have discussed in class. Define it in your own terms.
2. Find two instances in the novel where you see the value illustrated. Write about how the value relates to the character and the novel in general. Use specific details and support your answers.
3. Find an instance in your own life where you see evidence of this value. Write about how this value connects with your life story.
4. Find a current event where you see evidence of your value. Explain how your value relates to the current event. Copy the current event and include it in your portfolio.
5. Find a text of your choice that relates to your value. It could be a song, short story, novel, article, poem, or artwork. Explain how the text relates to your value.

The portfolios will be shared in class where students can exchange ideas on values they have discussed during the unit.

∽ *Reflection* ∽

What other themes could you develop from *To Kill a Mockingbird?* What themes are you interested in that you could possibly develop into a unit? Discuss suggestions in a small group.

INSTRUCTIONAL UNIT

TO KILL A MOCKINGBIRD

A third example of activities for *To Kill a Mockingbird* was designed by Nicole Kind and Sarah Nyberg. Their goals in teaching this unit were to connect the text and all of its themes to their students' lives. They planned on achieving this through daily journal writing. They include prompts on personal likes and dislikes, peer pressure, music, and conformity. Diversity is included by using a wide variety of texts throughout the unit: the novel, political cartoons, poems, songs, videos, newspapers, and children's literature. To assure a variety of learning styles being addressed, they use lessons that appeal to audio, visual, musical, kinesthetic, artistic, logical, interpersonal, intrapersonal, and verbal learners.

Three major assignments are included:

Journal Writing   Students write in the journals daily to record their thoughts, spark ideas, and encourage deeper exploration. Teachers read and evaluate the journals with a ✓ −, ✓, ✓ + method.

Collaborative Research Project   In groups students research a historical topic associated with the setting of *To Kill a Mockingbird.* They present their finding to the class and lead a discussion that explores connections between their topic and the text.

Scrapbook   This project is an analysis of one of the characters in the novel. In creating the scrapbook, students must not only consider what their character is like but also what he or she might carry in a pocket, a favorite ice cream, what type of grades, or what a prized possession may be, anything that would enhance an understanding of the character.

To begin the unit, the students are divided into groups by counting off. First, the teacher engages them in a discussion of dress codes and point of view. Students have a discussion prompted by the following questions: What purposes do dress codes serve? What kind of threat can clothing pose? What can clothes say about a person? What interest do groups have in a dress code? What could a dress code add or subtract from the students' experience? Now the teacher directs students to make connections from the group's opinions to underlying values. An example might be an administrator's concern with safety.

They close the discussion by determining factors that influence point of view (belief systems, financial status, social status, mood, group affiliation, age, experience, and background). Each group now fills out the handout "The Dress Code Controversy," shown in Figure 13.1.

After each group has an opportunity to share its point of view with the class, the teacher makes the connections between this exercise and *To Kill a Mockingbird*. Throughout the reading of the novel, students keep a character analysis chart. The chart has three columns at the top: Character, Distinguishing Characteristics, and Textual Evidence. Along the left-hand side is a list of the characters. The characters, characteristics, and textual evidence are frequently discussed in class.

Historical Project Assignment

Because the novel takes place in the 1930s, to better understand the events and characters, each group will chose a topic to study and present to the class. An example of topics could include

The causes of the Great Depression
The plight of the farmers
President Roosevelt's New Deal
The Stock Market Crash
The failure of the banks
What the South was like during this period
Southern politics of the time

The teacher and students can brainstorm for additional topics.

Figure 13.1   The dress code controversy

A student at Method's High recently was suspended for her refusal to follow the school's dress code. A town meeting is being held tonight to discuss the issue of instituting school uniforms. Representatives from interested groups are going to have an opportunity to voice their opinions.

Your group will represent one of the groups. Consider the following questions when deciding on your point of view:

Which group do you represent?

Are you for or against school uniforms? Explain why.

What statements do clothes make? How do they do this?

What type of clothes should not be allowed in schools? Explain your answer.

What factors determine what students should wear?

What are the benefits to your clothing policy?

What problems might some people have with your policy?

Requirements for the Students
> Answers to the 5 Ws
> Include two interesting facts (can be trivia, anecdote, statistic, etc.)
> Include some form of multimedia and explain its connection to history
> Connect your presentation to the novel
> Lead a class discussion with two open-ended questions
> Hand in a written report

Other Material Included in the Unit
My Great Grandpa by Martin Waddell and Dom Mansell. This is a children's literature selection, used for a discussion on how elderly people are treated in our society and roles the elderly have in a student's life. Students related the discussion to Miss Maudie and Mrs. Dubose.

We are including sections of a fourth unit on *To Kill a Mockingbird* to illustrate an organization plan and a beginning activity introducing the setting to students. Elizabeth Fehr, Karla Geissler, and Lucas Harris designed the unit for 15 days. They handed out a Unit Outline to the students and discussed it with them for an overview of the activities. This enabled the students to know when assignments were due and helped to keep them on track.

Unit Outline

Day one
Introduction to the novel
Picture project

Day two
Character identification in the novel

Day three
Characters' attitudes

Day four
Multigenre connection to the novel
(short story/poetry)

Day five
Historical connection online research

Day six
Group presentations of research
Watch *Eyes on the Prize* video

Day seven
Introduction to final class project

Day eight
Character development
Discussion on "Loss of Innocence" theme

Day nine
Point of view

Day ten
Contemporary relevance of novel
Connect novel to song, "Worlds Apart"

Day eleven
Student reactions to the novel
Start writing final project
Collect journals

Day twelve
In-class writing workshop

Day thirteen
Rough drafts due
Small-group peer review

Day fourteen
In-class writing workshop
Working on class portfolio

Day fifteen
Finish revising/editing work
Final class portfolio due

INSTRUCTIONAL UNIT

TO KILL A MOCKINGBIRD

Keep in mind that this unit outline is only a suggestion for the organization of the unit projects. In the classroom, chances are that it will take more than 15 days depending on your students, always your first consideration.

Before students began reading the novel, they were assigned an Internet search on American Memory. They followed an outline shown in Figure 13.2.

Reading Guide

The students received three or four fairly general questions to answer based on their reading. For example, the questions for the first 32 pages are on the following handout:

Guide to Reading

Think about each question or comment and respond. Each question or response is worth one point unless otherwise specified.

1. What do you think about Atticus's family?

2. What do you know about Jem and Scout?

3. (2 points) What do you think about Calpurnia's relationship with the Finches? Scout? Jem? Atticus?

4. ". . . until you climb into his skin and walk around in it."

The answers were discussed in class following the reading. Even if students fell behind in reading, they at least knew some of the novel through the discussions.

A few of the related sites that students used in the *Mockingbird* units:

<http://www.slc.k12.ut/webweavers/jillc/mbird.html>
<http://library.thinkquest.org>
<http://memory.loc.gov>

Figure 13.2 Student handout

Internet Search
American Memory

Let's get to know the setting of the novel, *To Kill a Mockingbird,* before we begin reading. We are going to do some online searches for information, and then look at photographs to help us understand the historical period. Be ready to share what you have found.

1. Take some time to do a general search on the Internet using key words like the Great Depression or Racial Discrimination.

2. What do you come up with? Tell me what you found and if you think the sources are reliable (5 points).

3. Go to <http://www.kic.give.rr.orbut.085/085-dis.html> and <http://memory.loc.gove/ammem/sowhome.html>, to look for pictures that were taken from the Great Depression to the beginning of World War II. When you locate a picture you find interesting, write a paragraph explaining what is in the picture and what it may tell us about the time period (10 points).

4. As an overall summary, explain why you think the picture is important and interesting (5 points).

EXPLORATION

Locating Sites for Literature Study

Browse the Internet for additional sites related to *To Kill a Mockingbird.* Try NCTE sites as well as others.

Teaching *The Scarlet Letter*

We include a teaching unit on *The Scarlet Letter* by Nathaniel Hawthorne because it frequently is a required text. Melissa Rossing, an English education student, developed a comprehensive unit for a month-long study of *The Scarlet Letter.* Because of space limitations we are unable to include the entire unit; however, the overview will help you develop your own teaching plan.

INSTRUCTIONAL UNIT

THE SCARLET LETTER

Rossing's student outcomes are the following:

Students will

1. Identify issues in *The Scarlet Letter* that remain relevant today.
2. Understand the concept of symbolism in literature.
3. Have a greater appreciation for the colonial time period along with an understanding of the Puritan beliefs during that time.
4. Relate their original personal meanings from the novel to societal issues demonstrating how literature can provide a connection to society as a whole.

Before reading the novel, students use the Internet to find interesting facts about Puritan life. They can look at the dress and customs, religion and beliefs, historical events, or any related information. The students then share what they found with the class to help each other understand the Puritan culture.

Journal Writings

The students are to keep a reading journal. To assist them with this, Rossing provides the following handout:

The Scarlet Letter *Journal Prompts*

Remember that these are just to give you some ideas as to what to write in your journals. You can use these prompts or write something else if the readings inspire you to do so.

1. Keep a list of interesting, impressive, and/or amusing words, phrases, or passages used by the novel's narrator or characters. Two examples of such passages occur when the townspeople call Hester a "brazen hussy" and when the children say:

   > Behold, verily, there is the woman of the Scarlet Letter, and, of a truth moreover, there is the likeness of the Scarlet Letter running along by her side! Come, therefore, come and let us fling mud at them.

   You may want to include words such as "ignominy," "labyrinth," "propensity," and "precipice."
2. Develop profiles of Hester Prynne, Arthur Dimmesdale, Roger Chillingworth, and Pearl.
3. Respond to the actions, thoughts, and beliefs of one or more of the characters.
4. Try to figure out who is Pearl's father before Hawthorne actually tells you. Keep a record of your guesses with your reasons.

5. Keep a journal as if you were one of the main characters. Record your activities, thoughts, and feelings.

Symbolism Writing Activity

Directions to the students. Although the "A" is the most prominent symbol in *The Scarlet Letter,* Hawthorne uses many other symbols throughout the novel. Select one or more of the following symbols and explain its meaning within the context of the story:

Black (pp. 116, 129, 132, 168)
The forest (pp. 175, 189)
The brook (p. 178)
Roses (pp. 56, 112)
Indians (p. 66)
Hester's clothing, particularly her formal cap (p. 192)
Pearl's clothing (pp. 102–103)
Pearl's name (p. 91)
Meteor (p. 149)
Golden embroidery on the "A" (p. 60)

(Note: page numbers will vary depending on what text is used)

For the students who desire or require additional readings, they may choose from the following list of authors:

Author List
Fiction Authors

Lydia Child
Nathaniel Hawthorne
Herman Melville
Elizabeth Cady Stanton
Sojourner Truth

Frederick Douglass
Harriet Jacobs
Edgar Allan Poe
Harriet Beecher Stowe
Harriet Wilson

Essayists and Poets

Emily Dickinson
Margaret Fuller
Henry Wadsworth Longfellow
Henry David Thoreau
John Greenleaf Whittier

Ralph Waldo Emerson
Oliver Wendell Holmes
James Russell Lowell
Walt Whitman

Students who choose to read more than one text can share their literature in a group book talk. Guiding questions could include how the literature relates to *The Scarlet Letter,* what was interesting about it, and what they thought of the readings.

At the conclusion of the novel, students choose an essay prompt and write a one- to two-page out-of-class essay.

Essay Prompts

1. Did Hester and Dimmesdale really love each other? How do you know?
2. Was Roger Chillingworth evil or just strange? Use passages in the book to illustrate your opinions.
3. Were the townspeople of Boston fair to Hester? What did they do that was right? What did they do that was wrong?
4. Discuss the character of Pearl, how is she likable or not? Is she a believable character?
5. What are the effects of the symbols in the novel? Discuss how the symbols influence your views of the plot and characters.
6. The narrator remarks that there are sins worse than adultery and punishments more terrible than the scarlet letter. What do you consider the worse sins and punishments evident in *The Scarlet Letter?*

Related web sites for *The Scarlet Letter*

<http://www.sparknotes.com/lit/scarlet/study.html>
<http://school.discovery.com/lessonsplans/programs/greatbooks->
<http://www.awesomelibrary.org>

DEVELOPING WRITING ACTIVITIES FOR MORE THAN ONE NOVEL

A four-week unit written by teacher Gail Servoss for the ninth grade illustrates how a teacher begins planning activities for a unit using more than one novel.

INSTRUCTIONAL UNIT

FOUR-WEEK LITERATURE UNIT

Four novels are used in this unit. Students are required to read two of them; however, they can read all four if they wish. The novels are paired so that students have a choice during the first two weeks of reading *A Day No Pigs Would Die* by Robert Newton Peck or *The Bloodroot Flower* by Kathy Callaway. For the next two weeks, they choose from *Where the Red Fern Grows* by Wilson Rawls or *A Killing Season* by Barbara Brenner.

Student Guide

Week One
Read the first two chapters in the novel you chose. Write reading responses in your journal (Level 1). Meet in groups to discuss your responses and to compile a list of adjectives that describe the main character in the novel you are reading (Level 1).

Read the next two chapters and write responses (Level 1). The first four chapters in both novels give us information about the parents. In class, begin to write a short paper on what you think Peck's father and Carrie's father are like. What does the story say about each of them? Give examples from the story that support your own view. For example, look at their personalities: Are they strict, lenient, happy, sullen, friendly, mean, or understanding? The paper is due the next day. Before handing them in, meet in groups to read aloud and discuss (Level 2).

Read the next three chapters and write responses (Level 1).

Week Two

Share responses in groups from the last chapters read. Hand in the response journals for the teacher's comments. Working in small groups, discuss the characters' values. Find phrases or paragraphs that represent the values.

Continue reading and responding. In small groups discuss the feeling the text evokes through word choice and details about the weather, actions, and character behavior. Choose one scene and write descriptive words about it. Write a poem using the descriptive words (Level 2). Work on the poems in class, sharing in small groups. Continue reading.

Week Three

Read the first two chapters in a novel you chose and write responses in your journal (Level 1). In small groups discuss what effect the setting has on the characters. Collaboratively, write a description of what would change in the book if the setting were urban (Level 1). Continue reading and writing responses.

Choose one of the characters from a novel and write a dialogue this person might have with someone else in any situation. Be sure to keep the character true to his or her personality. Do not tell anyone which character you chose. Other students will try to guess your character by listening to the dialogue you write. Be prepared to tell each other why you chose the words you did for the character. Base your reasons on examples in the novel (Level 1).

The following day share your dialogues in small groups. Discuss the influences of dialogue on developing characterization and in moving plot along. Each group then reports to the whole class. Working in pairs, draw a map on a large sheet of paper showing all the places described in the novel. Trace the action with short descriptions from the book and use X's to denote important areas (Level 2).

Week Four

Continue writing responses. When you are through reading the novel, review the responses in your journal. In groups of four or five students who read the same book, discuss your feelings and thoughts about the book. Answer the following questions in writing:

- How did this book make me feel?
- How was the book believable?
- What do I think about the characters?
- What other places or situations does the book make me think of?
- What are the major differences or similarities between the main character and me?

Figure 13.3 Scoring guide for the Level 3 paper

	Possible points 30	Your points
Introduction explaining what paper is about	3	_____
Main points clear and related to each other	4	_____
Examples to support your ideas	7	_____
Conclusion states what you discovered	2	_____
Word choice: descriptive, appropriate, correct forms	4	_____
Mechanics: correct spelling, punctuation, capitalization	5	_____
Original, creative, interesting	5	_____
Comments:	Total points	_____

Discuss all the answers in the small group.

The final activity is to write a Level 3 paper using one of the novels. Possible topic choices include:

1. The connection between nature and setting in the plot.
2. The relationship between a character and an animal.
3. The trials some people have to go through in their life and how these trials change them.
4. What a character might be like in 10 years from the conclusion of the story.

You are free to choose any topic you wish. You will meet in groups to talk over possible choices. With any topic you develop, be sure to include examples from the book you read to back up what you write. In addition, you may use personal examples to help develop your ideas.

A suggestion for a Level 3 scoring guide is shown in Figure 13.3.

 ## A LITERATURE UNIT WITH MULTIGENRES OF LITERATURE

Literature units need to include a variety of genres, as well as literature with different reading levels. This example of a literature unit is based on the theme "Families in Literature" written for ninth graders by Barbara Dressler, a high school teacher. Dressler's unit begins with a rationale explaining why she chose this theme.

Instructional Unit

Families in Literature

This literature unit for ninth graders centers on families in different eras and different cultures. The unit is designed for approximately four weeks. Selections were chosen to show the wide variety of combinations of people held together by a bond that we call family. Male and female characters and authors from minority groups—including African Americans, Asian Americans, Shakers, and Native Americans—are included. Special emphasis is given to relationships between teenagers and other family members because these relationships trouble most teens. I hope reading and thinking about characters in situations similar to their own will help students discover that they can achieve their individual identities and still appreciate and enjoy their families.

The problems encountered by today's teenagers in understanding and communicating with other members of their families are certainly not new. Through the years, young adults in literature experienced difficulty in getting along with adults, especially parents. The rejection of "old ways and ideas," and even alienation from the rest of the family, is a common conflict. A goal of this unit is to allow students to experience vicariously the problems and resolutions that characters find. They will realize that they are not unique in having problems in their families and may find ideas for solving or living with the problems through reading the literature.

Introduction

The introductory activity for the unit starts with a short brainstorming period for students to write words and ideas they associate with the word *family*. After sharing the lists, commenting and questioning, students write a paragraph defining family (Level 1).

Part 1

- "Blues Ain't No Mockin' Bird," a short story by Toni Cade Bambara
- "Brother Carlyle," a short story by William Melville Kelley
- "To My Father," a poem by Wing Tek Lum
- "The Funeral," a poem by Gordon Parks
- "Believing It Will Rain Soon," a poem by Simon J. Ortiz

The first reading assignment is "Brother Carlyle," a short story that centers on the behavior of one of two black brothers and the disagreement between their parents about whether the boy's treatment of his younger brother is appropriate. Students write a response to the story when they finish reading. They share their responses in a group and discuss them with the large group. The issue of parents giving different treatment to children based on birth order will probably be part of the discussion. I chose this short story to begin the unit because students often feel that their parents treat them differently from their siblings. Students enjoy talking about the advantages and disadvantages of being the first born, a middle child, or the youngest.

The second reading is "Blues Ain't No Mockin' Bird." I chose this story because it shows a loosely structured, nontraditional family with grandparents and distant cousins living together. The theme concerns the need for pride and dignity regardless of family income. After the reading, students respond in writing and then choose specific details used for the development of one of the characters. With emphasis on significant details, students write a character description of someone they know well (Level 2).

Part 2

The poems are read aloud during class. The first, "The Funeral," tells of the great admiration and respect a young man feels for his father. Many things in the poet's childhood seemed enormous to him, but as an adult, only his father remains larger than life. Students select lines that show how the poet's perspective changed as he matured. Many examples of hyperbole are used. As a group activity, students write their own descriptive sentences using hyperbole (Level 1).

"To My Father" tells of the rebellion of the Chinese against the emperor. The speaker, whose grandfather was involved in the rebellion, knows his way of life changed because of the revolt. In a group, students discuss ways their lives are affected by actions of their grandparents or other ancestors.

"Believing It Will Rain Soon" expresses a faith that is passed from one generation to another as shown through the description of the promise of rain over the mountains. Students discuss how they learn their beliefs and values, including prejudices, through the family. Students write a letter to a future son or daughter expressing an important belief about the world (Level 2).

Part 3: Individual Novel Reading

Students choose one novel from a list that contains books at different reading levels. All feature different types of families.

- *To Kill a Mockingbird* by Harper Lee
- *Growing Season* by Alden R. Carter
- *Permanent Connections* by Sue Ellen Bridgers
- *A Day No Pigs Would Die* by Robert Newton Peck
- *What About Grandma?* by Hadley Irwin
- *A Figure of Speech* by Norma Fox Mazer
- *Kim, Kimi* by Hadley Irwin

Students keep a response journal while reading the novel. After writing responses, students meet in small groups based on the book they read. They choose a character from the book that they would like to interview and answer interview questions as they believe their character would. Possible interview questions include the following:

1. In what ways did the author describe you accurately? What would you like to change in the description?
2. How did you feel about your family early in the story?
3. How did your feelings change before the end?
4. What was the happiest time for you in the book?
5. What would you like to say to a member of your family that you didn't get a chance to in the book?
6. If you could change anything in the story, what would it be? (Level 1)

When the time for the novel reading is about half over, students write a want ad in search of a good mother, father, teenage son, or teenage daughter. Ads are shared in groups (Level 1).

After reading and discussing the novels, students choose from the following Level 3 writing assignments:

1. Write an obituary for the family member who dies during the course of the book.
2. As a friend of the main character, write a letter of condolence after the death of the family member.
3. Imagine you are a good friend of the main character. How would you have tried to help at any point in the story?
4. As one character, write a letter to another explaining your actions during the book.
5. Write a campaign speech that the main character could use to run for student council president at your school.
6. Write a summary of the story's events from the point of view of the main character after 10 years have passed.
7. Write your description of a good parent. Include your evaluations of the parents in the book.

Selecting Books

By including novels for different reading levels, Dressler allowed students to find the one they were comfortable with without embarrassing them. Some students choose books that are too difficult and later ask to switch to another book or they may find they don't care for the book they started. Students need the flexibility to change their minds about a self-selected book. We may check out four books from the library but read only two because the others didn't hold our interest. We must make sure we apply the same common-sense rules to our students that we use in our own lives.

Students who read well may decide to read all four books. Having a selection of books avoids the problem of what to do when students come to the teacher two days after the unit begins and say they have finished the assigned book. The readings provided for these students are on the same general theme as the current unit. What they read then is part of what is going on in class, and they can share their reading with others.

Because of the policy of mainstreaming, students with special learning problems are now included in the regular classroom rather than taught in a separate class. For these students to feel a part of the class, their work, however adapted for their needs, must be a part of the same thematic unit or topic that the rest of the class is involved in. That's why including texts on a variety of reading levels is critical.

The same is true for gifted students. Too often, these students are sent to the library to work on their own. Perhaps even more than the average student, the gifted ones need to interact with peers and feel part of a group. Social skills are vitally important and need to be part of the learning environment. Every student in a class is responsible for getting along with others and respecting their rights. Participating in groups that are all working on the same theme enhances a sense of community effort.

EXPLORATION

Selecting Literature for a Particular Theme

Select a theme or topic you would like to teach. Locate, with the help of your librarian and the Internet, at least three books at different reading levels on the same theme.

Selecting a variety of reading texts is the first step in providing for all the students in a class. In addition, optional activities create a wide range of activities. One way to incorporate the activities into the current thematic unit is to tape the suggestions on the inside of file folders. The folders can then be placed in an open box available to students when they want additional projects. To accommodate all students in a class, the ideas need to vary greatly in difficulty: puzzles, reports, interviews, word searches, articles, essays, and poems. Also, they should cover a wide range of interests, such as reading nonfiction, writing movie reviews, writing based on art or music, drawing, creating music, and reading and performing drama. Each unit has an accompanying box of activities, such as one on courage, growing up, choosing careers, or environmental issues. Finding additional materials is difficult for inexperienced teachers, but one starts with only a few ideas and gradually adds to the number and variety of the activities.

All the activities include a way to bring the work back to the class as a whole. Artwork is displayed on the walls, reports are available for others to read or are orally presented to the class, skits are acted out, videos shown, music played, and puzzles distributed. Students may work in the library on their own or do the work outside of school, but the result is enriching the learning for everyone in the class.

COMPREHENSIVE THEMATIC UNITS

Units need to include a list of other readings on the same theme. Cathy Steffen, teacher, wrote a unit on heroes intended for middle school. An abbreviated version of Steffen's unit shows how she includes listening, speaking, reading, and writing.

Instructional Unit

Heroes

My primary objective in teaching a unit on heroes is to introduce students to alternatives to the traditional hero and to offer new perspectives on the idea of heroes. The activities in this unit include music, all levels of composition, language study, listening, and speaking. Both fiction and nonfiction are included.

Part 1: Introduction to the Unit

Propose the following questions to the class and write responses on the board. First, explain that the term "heroes" refers to both genders.

1. What are some examples of heroes?
2. What qualities are found in heroes?
3. What does someone have to do to be considered a hero?
4. Which of these people do you consider heroes? (Suggest people whom students know through the media.)
5. Do you know any "quiet heroes"? Read a recent newspaper or magazine article to the students about a quiet hero.
6. Who do you know who fits the description of a quiet hero?

Students search for articles on people (or animals) who acted heroically. They write a short paragraph describing some action they consider heroic (Level 1).

Part 2: Reading

Students read *A Hero Ain't Nothing but a Sandwich* by Alice Childress, *Roll of Thunder, Hear My Cry* by Mildred Taylor, or *The Chocolate War* by Robert Cormier. Students must read one of the novels, but may read all three if they wish. Students keep response notebooks as they read (Level 1).

In class students write a description of one of the main characters based on these questions: What is she or he like? What do you like or dislike the most about the character? Students meet in small groups to share what they wrote. The group members then discuss how the character would react to the following situation:

> Your character is in charge of a public place where students and adults can come to read books and listen to music. He or she tries hard to give quality materials to the people who come in, but some have started to complain that the books and music are trashy. Your character is told to get rid of the books and records or else lose the job. What will your character do?

Then in one large group, the smaller groups report, and discussion follows of the possible consequences of the characters' actions.

Part 3: Language

Give the class examples of different ways that a sentence can be spoken. Point out that an author can establish the emotional tone of the speaker by using certain words. Such clues help readers understand how a character feels.

Students work in pairs for this activity. Give each pair a slip of paper with an expressive word written on it. Explain that all the words come from the novels they are reading. If necessary, students look up the meaning of the word in a dictionary and then discuss when the word might be used. Each pair writes the word on the board, pronounces it for the class, and gives an example of a sentence containing the word. A few examples of the words used are *consolingly, taunting, tentatively, abstractedly,* and *resignedly.*

Part 4: Music

Be sure the classroom has available several headphones, tape players, and tapes. All of the songs should suggest something about heroes. The following songs might be appropriate:

- "Wild West Hero" by ELO
- "Along the Road" and "Face the Fire" by Dan Fogelberg
- "Roy Roger" and "The Ballad of Danny Bailey" by Elton John
- "Holding Out for a Hero" by Bonnie Tyler
- "Never" by Moving Pictures

After listening to several songs, students discuss the themes and descriptions of the heroes. Each student writes a paragraph about one of the songs, exploring the concept of hero.

Part 5: A Final Writing Assignment (Level 3)

Students write a two- or three-page paper on some aspect of a hero. Suggestions could include the following:

- Describe a hero from your own family history.
- Compare any two of the heroes we talked about in class—from music, the newspaper, novels, or any other genre used.
- Create a fictional story about a hero.
- Write a poem about a hero—real or fictional.

Also, students are free to select any topic, as long as it deals with heroes.

The concept of hero can be the basis for many thematic units. Teachers design units representing their own interests and try to capture their students' interests and imaginations through literature choices and selected activities. This next unit written for high school students by Connie Flug, an English teacher, is also on heroes and illustrates the wealth of materials available. Only a small part of the total unit is presented here. Flug begins with her rationale for choosing the theme of heroism.

INSTRUCTIONAL UNIT

HEROISM

The theme of heroism has been present in all times and places. Mom and Dad are probably the earliest heroes in most youngsters' lives; however, other figures—both real and fictional—through media and literature soon become an integral part of a child's life and development.

This unit is intended for students in ninth or tenth grades and examines heroes in literature, art, film, music, and, most important, through the students' own lives. The unit is planned for seven to eight weeks because of the amount of material available. Tall tales, Western folklore, and many other stories and poems have much to offer but are not included in the unit. Two novels for young adults (taught simultaneously), ancient and modern poetry, a 30-year-old film, and a modern version of *Cyrano de Bergerac* are the "meat" of this unit. Bridges from past to present are important; teachers will want to emphasize the idea that heroism was "then" and is "now."

Flug begins the unit by sharing a quote with students.

> Heroes have within themselves the resonance that comes from imagination supplanting despair. These heroes can recognize the possibilities inherent in living a human life to win and lose, perhaps, but also to discover and use our own voices yet in a common tongue; to use and be used by our passion and intellect; to deal with complexity and ambivalence; to be proud, to err, to be humbled, to grieve, and to grow. To live in such a manner is noble and heroic. (Engle 32–33)

The materials selected for the unit include the following:

Literature
- *Close Enough to Touch* by Richard Peck
- *Chartbreaker* by Gillian Cross
- *The Miracle Worker* by William Gibson
- *Class Dismissed* by Mel Glenn
- *Collected Poems* by Robert Hayden
- *Strings: A Gathering of Family Poems* by Janeczko
- "Negro Hero" by Gwendolyn Brooks
- "Ex-Basketball Player" by John Updike
- "To an Athlete Dying Young" by A. E. Housman
- "The Lady Pitcher" by Cynthia MacDonald
- "That Stranger on the Lawn" by Ray Bradbury
- "Fist Fight" by Doug Cockrell
- "Ulysses" by Alfred, Lord Tennyson
- "Flowers for Algernon" by Daniel Keyes

Films

- *Helen Keller*
- *Man as Hero: Tragic and Comic*
- *The Miracle Worker*
- *Roxanne*

Music

- *West Side Story*
- "Free to Be"
- "Great American Hero"
- "You Won't Believe in If Anymore"
- "Wind Beneath My Wings"
- "Big Bad John"
- "Oh, Mine Papa"

Although the entire unit is not included here, the beginning of the unit is explained because introducing units is an important part of creating student interest and sets the tone for the next several days.

Day 1

The bulletin board contains many pictures, poems, lyrics, and paintings with room for student additions during the next several weeks. The day begins with student responses to an opinionnaire on heroes (Figure 13.4).

Figure 13.4   Opinionnaire on heroes

Directions: Write *agree* or *disagree* beside each statement.

1. A hero does better than just about anyone else.   _____
2. Heroes are forever.   _____
3. The values of heroes are old-fashioned.   _____
4. If you say something often enough, it becomes true.   _____
5. If you hear something often enough, you come to believe it. _____
6. Heroes never have to say, "I'm sorry."   _____
7. To become a hero, one must be lucky.   _____
8. TV has helped destroy today's heroes.   _____
9. A real-life hero fills a need for all of us.   _____
10. Anyone can be a hero.   _____

Students agree or disagree with the items, and discussion follows. Students brainstorm on the meaning of heroism. Responses are listed on the board. The following questions might be used to lead into the session:

1. What do you think a heroic quality is?
2. What are some qualities in real-life heroes?
3. What makes a hero? Is it more deeds or personality?
4. Consider heroes of different ages, nationalities, centuries, and interests. Do they bring to mind any other characteristics?

The next day's assignment is to bring in examples of today's heroes using newspapers, magazines, TV, record jackets, and comics as resources. Every Monday for the rest of the unit, students are asked to bring in information on heroes of the week.

Day 2

Students share their examples of today's heroes. Discussion in small groups gives students an opportunity to explore aspects of heroes. Then, students watch the slide/tape presentation, *Man as Hero: Tragic and Comic*. Discussion follows. Students write in their journals and choose from the following suggestions:

1. I was a hero once . . .
2. My hero at school is . . .
3. A local hero from this town is . . .
4. If I were a hero I think I would feel like . . .

Day 3

Students share their journal responses in small groups. The teacher writes a mystery formula poem on the board. For example:

Dedicated, brave,
Climbs, investigates, rescues,
Saves peoples' lives
Hero

The students try to guess the name that goes on the first line, which in this case is *Firefighter*. The class as a whole writes a similar poem using one of the heroes from the bulletin board. The formula for the poem is to write the person's name on the first line. Then:

- Write two adjectives that describe the person.
- Write three verbs that tell what the person does.
- Write a thought or four words about the person.
- Write another noun for the person or repeat the same name.

The assignment for the following day is for students to write their own poem, leaving off the name in line one.

Day 4

Students share their poems and others try to guess who they are about.

Two other sections of Flug's unit are included here. One is her list of suggested end-of-the-unit activities for the students. The other is a list of additional readings.

Suggestions for End-of-the-Unit Activities
1. Write your own song about heroes.
2. Create a comic strip featuring a hero.
3. Write a folktale about a hero.
4. Interview a local hero and write a news article.
5. Review the comic section of the Sunday paper and evaluate the images of heroes. Write a report of your findings.
6. Write a modern fairy tale.
7. Make a class scrapbook of all the heroes in the news over the duration of this unit.
8. Put together a slide presentation on heroes.
9. Write a poem about a personal hero.
10. Invite a local hero to class for a presentation. Write a follow-up report.

What follows is a list of readings students choose from as the unit progresses. The list demonstrates the wealth of readings available to teachers as they design units. Because Connie wrote annotations, the list is helpful to those looking at resources for units on heroes, survival, and self-esteem.

Reading List
- Aldrich, Bess Streeter. *A Lantern in Her Hand:* Abbie MacKenzie, a talented singer and aspiring artist, is 19 when she marries Will Deal in 1865. Homesteading in Nebraska, Abbie and Will face droughts, dust storms, blizzards, and locust infestations. Abbie's courage and her love for her husband and children lead her to sacrifice her dreams for theirs.
- Barrett, William E. *The Lilies of the Field:* Homer Smith, a young black man recently discharged from the army, comes upon a group of immigrant nuns who are trying to build a chapel in the desert. This is a delightful story about Smith's role in this undertaking.
- Brancato, Robin. *Uneasy Money:* Mike Bronti loses track of values after winning money in a lottery. Spending the money quickly, he finds himself losing family and friends.
- Chester, William L. *Kioga of the Wilderness:* This is the tale of Kioga, or Snow Hawk, who rises to the position of war chieftain in the wild region north of Siberia.
- Ching, Lucy. *One of the Lucky Ones:* An autobiography of a blind Chinese girl's fight for education and a future. Her nanny helps Lucy find a productive life that results in her helping other blind Chinese.

- Collier, James L., and Christopher Collier. *The Winter Hero:* After the Revolutionary War, Justin is caught up in the Shay's Rebellion. Through his experiences, he learns the truth about heroism, cowardice, and war.
- Crutcher, Chris. *Running Loose:* For Louie Banks, living by what is right is more important than being popular. When instructed to "play dirty," Louie walks off the playing field. This turns out to be the most important decision of his life.
- Easwaran, Eknath. *Gandhi the Man:* Gandhi's own words and an array of photos accompany this biography. A string of failures leads the young Gandhi to a job in South Africa where he begins his life of service to others.
- Froehlich, Margaret. *Reasons to Stay:* Babe's determination to piece together her past leads to hard discoveries, but she becomes a strong memorable hero.
- George, Jean Craighead. *The Talking Earth:* Billie Wind, a young Seminole, survives on her own in the Florida Everglades. Her courage finds a link between an ancient and modern culture.
- Haskins, James. *Sugar Ray Leonard:* This biography follows Sugar Ray from the beginning of his boxing career at age 14 to his turning pro.
- Hughes, Monica. *Hunter in the Dark:* Mike Rankin, star basketball player, is dying of leukemia. He goes to the Canadian wilderness to escape overprotective parents. Through his experiences he comes to understand that death is not always the enemy.
- Magill, Kathleen. *Megan:* An independent woman struggles for freedom and a sense of self. She runs away to a boomtown where she discovers the truth about herself.
- Mazer, Harry. *The Island Keeper:* Cleo runs away from her family pressures and the death of her sister. She proves herself as she struggles to survive on a deserted island.
- McKinley, Robin. *The Hero and the Crown:* Aerin, with the help of a wizard and the blue sword, battles the Black Dragon. She wins her birthright as the daughter of the Damarian king and alters the history of Damar.
- Myers, Walter Dean. *Hoops:* Lonnie is at a key point in his life. If his team does well in a citywide tournament, he may have a professional career. Integrity becomes as important as talent.
- Portis, Charles. *True Grit:* Mattie Ross and Rooster Cogburn, an old federal lawman, set out on an incredible journey to avenge her father's death.
- Rosa, Joseph G. *They Called Him Wild Bill: The Life and Adventures of James Butler Hickok:* Hickok led an eventful life, working as a U.S. marshal, an army scout, and a Wild West performer. This biography describes the man beyond the legend.
- Roth, Arthur. *The Castaway:* This novel is based on a true story of a young man who is the lone survivor after a shipwreck. He survives alone for five years on a rocky reef.

- Savage, Deborah. *A Rumour of Otters:* This wilderness survival story takes place in New Zealand where 14-year-old Alexa sets off on her own to prove she is as heroic as her brother.
- Townsend, Peter. *The Girl in the White Ship:* Tran Hue, a 13-year-old, and her family must flee Vietnam in 1978. She battles to survive and escape.
- Valens, E. G. *The Other Side of the Mountain:* This is the true story of Jill Kinmont, who became paralyzed while training for the Olympic ski team. Jill's determination to lead a meaningful life is inspiring.
- Voigt, Cynthia. *The Runner:* A dedicated runner distances himself from other people. His experience in coaching his teammates helps him to change.
- Wheeler, Robert W. *Jim Thorpe: World's Greatest Athlete:* Thorpe is probably best known for winning both the decathlon and pentathlon in the 1923 Olympics, only to be disqualified later. His early life on the reservation, Indian school, football triumphs, and Olympic feats are recounted.

INTERDISCIPLINARY UNITS

The units previously described are not interdisciplinary ones, although they encompass a wide range of topics and interests. English language arts teachers designed them, and then taught the units during their classes. However, when teachers of other subjects join together to plan units that include topics and activities related to several disciplines, they create interdisciplinary units. Interest in planning curriculum around such units is increasing because of the recognition that teaching across subject lines more closely resembles "real life." Consequently, student motivation increases because the subject matter appeals to a wider range of learning styles, abilities, and interests. Students have questions about their world and wonder about the environment, human rights, race issues, and justice. Heidi Hayes Jacobs, an authority on designing interdisciplinary curriculum, writes that the "idea is to bring together discipline perspectives and focus them on the investigation of a target, theme, issue, or problem" (54). Units that are organized around a range of topics and approaches help learners understand the variety of perspectives and the complexity of issues involved.

An example of a unit that connects the "real" world with school learning is one on an environmental issue designed for middle school by Jackie Williams and Terry Deal Reynolds. In the area of science, activities centered on wastewater discharge and water pollution. The social studies activities were based on the political, economic, and social implications. English language arts focused on current readings, interviews, vocabulary, note-taking, and oral presentations. Students learned there are many sides to an issue; in this case, jobs and livelihoods had to be balanced with concerns for the environment and natural resources (14). Students learn that there are no simple solutions.

A unit on an environmental issue might include some literature, but the major focus is current media information and community involvement. A unit on aging would include community work, trips to nursing homes, and interviews, as well as literature. Language provides the focus for many different units, such as politics, advertising, history, and cultures. In the following unit on advertising, developed for middle school, the theme is the power of language to persuade and its effect on middle schoolers who are becoming critical consumers of goods.

INSTRUCTIONAL UNIT

ADVERTISING

The first purpose for teaching the unit is to help middle school students become better informed as consumers and more aware of the role of advertising in their lives. Because of the age of the students, literature isn't included, although many essays and articles are appropriate for older students. The second purpose for teaching the unit is to give students opportunities to draw, sing, compose music, and act—in general, to be creative. This is a long unit—four to six weeks—and because of the amount of independent and unstructured work, it is best to include it in the curriculum later in the year. The teacher needs to know students well enough to know who can work on their own and who needs supervision. The unit is divided into sections, not weeks, because the amount of time needed for each part depends on the students' interests and could be quite different from one year to the next.

Section 1: Analyzing Advertisements

The first activity is to ask students what their favorite advertisements are. They talk about TV ads exclusively. Actually, they do more than talk; they sing the songs, repeat dialogue, act out the scenes, and interrupt and correct each other. After a time, you ask what their least favorite ads are. Although less enthusiastic, they report several, with some saying one's most disliked was their favorite. Then the conversation shifts to why they liked or disliked certain ads, which leads to a discussion of audience. Most of the ads they dislike are not meant for teenagers. From this point we move to the purposes of ads and discuss how advertising companies conduct market research. Next, we look more closely at the ads, examining the particular approach used to entice consumers. Together we put the responses into categories. The responses are not the same from one year to the next, but they fall roughly into the same categories: popularity with the opposite sex, you owe it to yourself, everyone has one, having fun, being healthy, staying young and beautiful, loving one's family, and owning the best. The assignment that follows is to collect printed ads that represent each of the categories, put them in booklet form, and label each one. Although students considered the activity fun, they were improving a critical skill of classifying.

Section 2: Designing a Product

Next, students design a new and unknown product that later is advertised for sale. The design is on paper only and they do not actually construct it. The following questions help get them started: What new product would make your life easier? Can you think of a product that might become a new fad? What item might be improved if you made major changes in the design? The assignment was to describe the product and draw it if they desired. They have to keep their product a secret since they do not own a patent on the design. Descriptive language is vital for an activity later in the unit, so we spent time on choosing specific words and using comparisons. Because of the secret nature of the project, they cannot ask other students if the descriptions are clear, so the teacher acts as the editor. Students turned in the designs for the teacher's safekeeping. Students think of a variety of products: a watch-radio-telephone, edible dishes, a walkie-talkie AM-FM radio pen, computerized pencil, convertible shoes, a shoe phone, and instant moat mix (in case you have a dry moat—it comes with creatures and muck).

Section 3: Advertising Media

This is a short section where the class members explore all the places ads might appear. People who work in ad agencies are invited to speak to the class. Also, people who design ads for newspapers or billboards talk to the class. The students write interview questions before the visitors speak to the class. Students need to prepare for a class visitor by planning ahead. Asking appropriate questions is not easy, and they meet in groups to brainstorm questions. Following the visits, students—again working in small groups—write letters thanking the presenters.

Section 4: Media Groups

Students become part of a media group. The types of groups are newspapers, magazines, billboards, radio, and television. Students write their top two choices on a card and hand it in to the teacher, who then forms the groups. Each media group first selects a name for itself, then researches the cost of advertisements placed in their media. Next they design an ad for advertising space, trying to make their company the most attractive for people who want to advertise, but the rates have to be realistic. Each group makes one poster to try to entice customers.

At this point, each student receives five copies of the product description he or she wrote earlier. Individually they decide on where to place ads for the products. They all have a set amount of money to use on advertising so it is impossible for anyone to buy the top advertising five times. If they decide on a back-page ad and a one-minute TV commercial, they will be out of money. However, if they use the money sparingly, they can afford five ads in a variety of media. To maintain secrecy, the teacher is the only one who knows who designed each product and serves as the broker. When students decide on the type of ad, they write the specific information on the back of each card, such as, "1/2 page on an inside sheet of Wonder Magazine." The teacher then delivers the card to the Wonder Magazine group. This procedure is repeated until all the students have selected the advertising they want for their product, and each group has received all the advertising jobs.

Before the ad production goes into full swing, we review techniques we discussed before: use of statistics, well-known personalities, humor, music, color, drawings, logos, animals, and children.

Section 5: Production

Each media group designs the ads it received orders for. Except for the billboard group, the ads are placed in a larger context. The newspaper group produces a newspaper with local news, pictures, human-interest stories, announcements, and sports. The television group produces a show: a situation comedy, soap opera, mystery, or talk show. The radio group usually uses music as the content. If the billboard company has extra time, the members draw a public service ad.

At the conclusion of the unit the students display their work for other students, teachers, and parents. The last assignment is to write a one- to two-page paper explaining what they learned.

Units planned across disciplines are advantageous for a number of reasons. They provide a model for students who erroneously believe writing and reading fiction belong only in the English language arts classrooms. Also, breaking down the walls among disciplines creates more true-to-life experiences for students and, consequently, often heightens interest. Teachers of a variety of subjects can plan the objectives and activities together. Depending on the school's organization, teachers may team-teach the units, but even if the classes have to remain separate, the students and teachers benefit from the shared planning. A word of caution is in order here. By working with other teachers, we do not mean that the English teachers only grade a social studies paper for mechanical errors, but rather that planning and carrying out the ideas are a joint effort.

Exploration

Beginning to Plan an Interdisciplinary Unit

In a group, brainstorm topics that could be used for interdisciplinary units. Choose one or two and suggest reading material and activities that could be used. Later you may want to develop one into a full-size unit.

A unit designed by Becky Olien, a teacher, demonstrates how English, social studies, art, and music are woven together to create a rich tapestry of experiences for young people. Olien is particularly fortunate because her classroom is multicultural. The unit can be used for a variety of age levels.

Instructional Unit

Tracing One's Roots

Olien begins the unit with a discussion about students' ancestors. She might ask what it means to say one has ancestors or an ethnic background. After students have an opportunity to talk about ancestors, ask questions, and listen to others, she gives them a survey on ethnic background to be filled out in class. The survey includes questions about where their ancestors came from, how long ago they came to America, whether they were married, whether they had jobs, and whether they came with friends or traveled alone. By filling out the survey, students become aware of what they know and don't know about their family history. They take the survey home and ask parents and grandparents to help complete the information.

Once the surveys are completed as much as possible—and this may take a while—the discussion continues and students share their information with each other. Students then choose a person who is knowledgeable about their family to interview. Usually this is a relative, but not always. A Native American, for example, may interview a tribal leader; another student may talk to a family friend who knows a great deal about a particular immigrant group. Before the interview takes place, students develop the questions, meeting in groups for ideas and feedback. Once the interviews are completed—and again this may take a few days—the students write a report based on the information from the survey, interview, and additional sources as needed. Because many students are a mixture of ethnic backgrounds, they choose which one they want to work on.

While the students are working on these activities, they also are reading historical fiction. The literature is discussed in class, and they consider what makes historical fiction interesting. When the reports are finished and the novels and short stories are read, the next activity is to write a fiction story based on their reports. Most of the stories are patterned after historical fiction, but students may wish to make the work more contemporary. (This is especially true of the Hmong and Native American students in Olien's class.)

The culminating activity is a cultural week in which students work in groups to present their culture to the class. Students select the cultural group they want to work in; usually it is the one they wrote the report on. They may focus on any aspect they wish, but music, crafts, dance, and food are usually part of the presentations. Students bring maps, flags, or any artifact that helps explain the family background. Many teach the other students a few words of the language their ancestors spoke. Some dress in native costumes (particularly the Hmong girls). Everyone learns from listening, talking, and sharing.

Instructional Unit

Historical Homes

The focus of this unit designed by teachers Sue Klapatauskas and Becky Milliren, and librarian Diana Coffey was to teach students about the historical homes in their small town (population 1,500). The unit was called "History Through the Homes of Thorp" and planned for middle school.

The activities for the unit included photographing the homes, interviewing, writing information about each house creating a quilt, writing a class booklet, and learning how to use Power Point.

They began the unit with a discussion of the older homes. What did students know about them? Where were they located? Did any of them live in a home at least 100 years old? Students then talked to parents and, if possible, older members of the community, asking about the older buildings in town. As they collected the information, they made a list and then students chose a home they would research.

The teachers led a discussion about what information would be interesting to others. The students decided on key questions that everyone should ask during the interview of the people who presently lived in each house. These were the age of the house, how long they had lived there, and who were the former owners. In addition, students could ask questions based on the particular house. They might include who built the house, what remodeling had been done, was it originally a farmhouse, and had it been moved from one location to another. A newspaper reporter came to the class and taught students how to conduct an interview. Then students practiced interviewing in school.

Each student had a disposable camera to use for taking the photographs. A local photographer came to teach students how to take effective pictures. After students gained permission for the interviews, they conducted them at the various homes and took their pictures.

The pictures were scanned onto squares of fabric for the quilt. A woman from the community sewed the quilt squares together and constructed the quilt. The students tied the quilt with yarn. The quilt was displayed at the library.

Because the information on the historical homes was going to be shared with the public, the students used the entire writing process with several drafts, revisions, and editing sessions to write the booklets. The booklets were presented to the homeowners and displayed in the library.

Using Power Point, the students created a slideshow presentation for the historical society, school board, and several district-wide locations. The students learned a great deal from the project: using technology, conducting interviews, taking effective pictures, creating a slide show, writing a booklet for the public, and how to work cooperatively with other class members.

Units are a way to organize reading, writing, speaking, and listening to ensure continuity among the activities. They give purpose to classroom activities and actually are a much easier way to teach than using disjointed lesson plans because their flow carries students along. Often students themselves will think of activities to do and, therefore, can play a major role in planning curriculum. Once a theme or topic is decided on, students can suggest stories, poems, music, films, and activities that complement the unit. The more students are involved, the more ownership and responsibility they accept, and that is the beginning of a learning/teaching partnership between student and teacher.

We include one last unit here to help you as a beginning teacher to see how comprehensive thematic units can be. The unit is written by Don Heil for high school.

INSTRUCTIONAL UNIT

LITERATURE OF CONFLICT: SOCIETAL AND PERSONAL

Rationale for Selecting This Theme for This Age Group. We are all exposed, directly or indirectly, to various forms of conflict. There is possibly no greater time of turmoil and conflict in a person's life than adolescence into young adulthood. At this time in our lives, we find out that the world is bigger than the limited scope of our experiences. We discover that the conflicts in which we have been embroiled as adolescents are just a part of the bigger conflicts that go on in the world every day. As tenth graders, these kids have begun to understand the greater implications of many kinds of conflicts and are at a crossroads in their lives. They are no longer children, but they are not yet adults. They are no longer as naive about the world as they once were, but they have not yet made the connection between themselves and the wider world. Because of this, I feel that presenting a unit on conflict in literature at this point in their lives provides an insight into what they have experienced already and what is yet to come. By further dividing the topic into two parts, societal and personal conflicts, they are exposed to types of conflict that affect them immediately and directly, as well as conflict of a farther reaching and longer lasting quality. It is my hope that by seeing conflict on both a personal and societal level they will be able to make the connection between the two levels of conflict and that they understand that there is more in the world than their own problems—that they are part of something much bigger than themselves.

Unit Objectives

I want my students to gain or further develop:

- An awareness of the various forms of conflict around them on a personal and societal level.
- An understanding of how literature portrays conflict and how it is a means of recording, discussing, and resolving conflict.
- An understanding of how conflicts are best resolved and, if irresolvable, how they are best dealt with.
- The ability to read literature critically to extract its meaning and value.

- The ability to express their own thoughts and talents through writing and other means of expression.
- An awareness of the wider world outside of their personal lives and their connection to that world.
- A love of literature and, more generally, a love of reading.

Overview

The first part of the unit covers conflict on a societal level, touching on sub-themes of race, religion, economics, politics, and war. The second part is conflict on a personal level and includes family, peer, and internal conflict. The third part is reading a novel students choose from a selection of three, which represent three levels of difficulty in reading. The shorter readings and writings are in the first two parts to provide background information and make the novel and final writing more meaningful.

Introduction to the Students

Students first do free writing in their journals on the topic of conflict, responding to these questions:

- What is conflict?
- What do you think of when you hear the word *conflict?*

Students write for 10 to 15 minutes and then share their ideas. The teacher lists their responses on the board, demonstrating the possible perceptions and variety of conflict. The students and teacher then group the conflicts under the headings of societal and personal conflicts. The following class period the teacher provides students with a copy of the list that students keep in their writing folders. Students also create bulletin boards to further define the theme of the unit.

Part 1

Activity 1. To begin, the teacher shows clips from the PBS television series *The 60s: A Decade of Conflict* to show various kinds of societal conflict and how they were manifested in the turmoil of that time. Also, the clips give a historical perspective on much of the literature the students will read for the unit. After viewing the clips, students write in their journals describing what they think societal conflict is.

Activity 2. The students then read and discuss Chapter 27 from *I Know Why the Caged Bird Sings.* They respond in their journals; they may respond to the following guide questions:

- What main themes do you see in this passage? What is going on?
- What has happened to the Japanese in San Francisco? Why are they disappearing and being replaced?
- What reasons did the woman on the streetcar give for refusing to sit with the black man? Are these valid reasons?

Activity 3. The class reads and discusses "Ruby's Drawings," "Self-Portrait," and "The Sign," all from the Robert Coles anthology, *A Festering Sweetness*. These poems emphasize conflict caused by racial differences. Students also read a selection of poems focusing on conflict caused by war from *Class Dismissed* by Mel Glenn.

Activity 4. The students read and discuss the short story "The Other Foot" by Ray Bradbury. The story focuses on conflict caused by both racial differences and warfare.

Activity 5. Students watch an episode from the television series *M*A*S*H,* which focuses on the effects of war on various people at a fictitious field hospital. The students are asked to bring in newspapers, magazine clippings, songs, and examples from TV shows as further examples of war-related conflict and its effect on individuals.

Part 2: Personal Conflict

Activity 1. Students write in their journals about various conflicts they may have experienced at home, school, or other places. They compare their list to the one the whole class generated at the beginning of the unit to reflect on their own experiences.

Activity 2. Students view the film *The Three Warriors,* which deals with contemporary Native American culture and their efforts to survive in the modern world. Students write a paper from the perspective of one of the film's characters.

Activity 3. The students read and discuss "Everyday Use" by Alice Walker.

Activity 4. The teacher plays songs expressing a conflict from his or her adolescence. The class then listens to a short selection of songs with historical significance. The students are encouraged to bring in songs they believe are examples of conflict. Discussion and journal writing follow.

Activity 5. The students form groups and each group is given a scenario that includes a conflict. They finish the story by resolving the conflict or at least getting the parties involved in a process of resolution. Each group acts out the scene for the class.

Part 3: Individual Novels

Activity 1. The three literature selections chosen for this unit are *The Chocolate War* by Robert Cormier, *All Quiet on the Western Front* by Erich Maria Remarque, and *Romeo and Juliet* by William Shakespeare. Each student must complete one selection but are encouraged to read more if appropriate. After students choose which one they will read, they write a journal entry about why they made their choice, what they think it is about, and what kinds of conflicts they think are presented in the book.

Activity 2. The activities for this part of the unit are of two types: whole-class and novel-specific. The whole-class activities include activities and questions that pertain to all three of the readings because they are of a general nature on the theme of conflict. The novel-specific activities are done in conjunction with part 4 of the unit. When one group meets to discuss one selection, others may work on their final projects. Some students prefer more reading and discussions, whereas others will want more time for the individual work. Students are free to move in and out of the activities that appeal to them and best meet their needs. The students are required to write a response journal entry every day after completing the reading. Discussion groups are held throughout the time the students are reading.

Part 4

In this part of the unit students complete a major project related to a thematic literature unit. The following are choices for the project:

- Write a research paper with the theme of conflict as your focus.
- Write at least two poems with the theme of conflict as your focus.
- Write a song on the theme of conflict or collect at least five such songs on a tape. You must include a short description of how each song includes conflict.
- Write a short story on the theme of personal conflict.
- Write a one-act play on the theme of conflict.
- Suggest your own final project. This must be approved by the teacher and submitted in writing.

All of these options are Level 3 writing projects and involve the entire writing process.

In summary, units are as varied as the teachers who teach them. The major advantage of units is that the teacher has great flexibility in planning and choosing activities that meet a wider range of student abilities and interests. Units are rich sources of material so all students can find literature selections, activities, and topics that appeal to them. Students who wish to explore a topic in depth can do so. Others who prefer a wide spectrum of readings and activities can use this approach. No students are left out or made to feel that they do not fit in. Although units may be more work for teachers initially, they are much more interesting to teach than the "one book at a time with no continuity" approach.

EXPLORATION

Developing Your Own Instructional Unit

Throughout this chapter, we have shown several examples of how teachers plan for thematic units. Now, work through a unit of your own following these suggested guidelines.

1. In small groups, brainstorm ideas for unit themes. Decide on one that the group can work on. Now brainstorm ideas for readings that fit the theme. Share with the rest of the class.
2. Individually choose a theme you are interested in. Decide what grade level you would like to develop it for. Choose one or two pieces of literature that would be appropriate for this grade level. In small groups, share your ideas and help each other think of additional literature. Write a rationale for teaching the theme you have chosen and explain why it is appropriate for the grade level you selected. What do you want the students to learn from the unit?
3. Choose literature for young adults on the same theme to include in your unit.
4. Select poems that are appropriate.
5. Add film and music selections. Remember to add a variety of readings (for example, nonfiction, drama, journals, articles, and so on). Selections may be found in local newspapers, television, magazines, and a wide variety of anthologies. Don't limit yourself to what you were taught in school.
6. Plan activities that include listening and speaking (for example, creative dramatics and small-group activities).
7. Plan writing activities throughout the entire unit and specify what levels they are. Remember to have many Level 1 activities, several Level 2, and only one Level 3. Develop a grading scale for your Level 3 assignment.

How will you encourage students' interest in the unit? How will you focus on the theme? How will you accommodate the different ability levels and interests you will have in your classroom?

Developing this unit will help you in two ways: You have a teachable unit all set to go when you enter the classroom, and it is a wonderful example of your abilities to add to your portfolio when you are interviewed for a teaching position.

REFERENCES

Anderson, David T. "An Apology for Teaching American Literature Thematically." *Wisconsin English Journal* (Fall 1989): 58–66.

Dressler, Barbara. "Unit on Families in Literature." English 705. University of Wisconsin–Eau Claire, 1989.

Engle, Sandra A. "Of Jocks and Heroes" *English Journal* (Dec. 1984): 32–33.

Fehr, Elizabeth, Karla Geissler, and Lucas Harris. "Unit on *To Kill a Mockingbird* Unpublished University of Wisconsin–Eau Claire, 2003.

Flug, Connie. "Heroism." English 406/606. University of Wisconsin–Eau Claire, 1992.

Goldbort, Robert C. "Science in Literature Materials for a Thematic Teaching Approach." *English Journal* (Mar. 1991): 69–73.

Hackett, Nina. "Humanities." *CAIP Quarterly* (Winter 1992): 8.

Hawthorne, Nathaniel. *The Scarlet Letter*. Reissue. Bantam Books, 1981.

Heil, Don. "Literature of Conflict—Societal and Personal." Unpublished paper, 1995.

Hillocks, George, Jr. "Literary Texts in Classrooms." *Socrates to Software: The Teacher as Text and the Text as Teacher*. Eds. Philip W. Jackson and Sophie Haroutunian-Gordan. Chicago UP, 1989. 135–58.

Jacobs, Heidi Hayes, ed. *Interdisciplinary Curriculum Design & Implementation*. Alexandria: Association for Supervision & Curriculum Development, 1989.

Kahn, Elizabeth A., Carolyn Calhoun, and Larry R. Johannessen. *Writing About Literature*. Urbana: NCTE, 1984.

Kind, Nicole, and Sarah Nyberg. "Unit on *To Kill a Mockingbird*." Unpublished, University of Wisconsin–Eau Claire, 1993.

Klapatauskas, Sue, Becky Milliren and Diana Coffey. "History Through the Homes of Thorp." Unpublished, Wisconsin Department of Education grant, 1999.

Lott, Carolyn and Stephanie Wasta. "A Civil War Unit." *Clearing House* (July 1999): 56–61.

Marty, Nicole, Joseph Mlinar, and Kristine Stein. "Unit on *To Kill a Mockingbird*." Unpublished University of Wisconsin–Eau Claire, 2003.

Maxwell, Rhoda J. *Writing Across the Curriculum in Middle and High Schools*. Boston: Allyn & Bacon, 1996.

McManus, Maureen. "Writing Activities for *To Kill a Mockingbird*." English 404. University of Wisconsin–Eau Claire, 1993.

Moffett, James. *A Student-Centered Language Arts Curriculum*. Boston: Houghton Mifflin, 1973.

Olien, Rebecca. "Tracing One's Roots." Unpublished paper, 1994.

Peck, David. *Novels of Initiation: A Guidebook for Teaching Literature to Adolescents*. Teachers College, Columbia University, 1989.

Rossing, Melissa. "Teaching *The Scarlet Letter*." Unpublished, University of Wisconsin–Eau Claire, 2002.

Scharber, Cassie. "Writing Activities for *Finding My Voice*." English 404. University of Wisconsin–Eau Claire, 1995.

Servoss, Gail. "Four-Week Literature Unit." English 402. University of Wisconsin–Eau Claire, 1988.

Steffen, Cathy. "Unit on Heroes." English 404. University of Wisconsin–Eau Claire, 1994.

Williams, Jackie, and Terry Deal Reynolds. "Courting Controversy: How to Build Interdisciplinary Units." *Educational Leadership* (Apr. 1993): 13–15.

Your Starting Role: Student Teacher

14

In Chapter 1, "Becoming a Teacher," we asked you to explore your motivation and goals for becoming an English language arts teacher. Here we are asking you to explore a more immediate professional role, that of student teacher. Why? Because not only is student teaching a required part of your program and state certification, it is also your first sustained teaching experience. Moreover, student teaching differs rather significantly from your first year as a newly hired teacher. As a student teacher, you are not completely independent. That is, you are not always able to construct curriculum and implement instruction as you desire, nor are you able to claim the students as your own for an entire academic year. Nonetheless, as a student teacher you are indeed learning to negotiate the world of secondary teaching, and you are a final step away from a classroom with your name on the door. It's an important time for learning more about teaching and, especially, more about yourself.

But what actually happens in those 18 weeks of student teaching? What questions and issues confront student teachers? What surprises them? What gives them immense satisfaction? What lets them know that teaching English is the right profession—or not—for them? Through weekly e-mail dialogues and monthly seminars, many of our student teachers have asked good questions and worked out some answers that we think are applicable to most student teachers. Thus, we are going to take you through their experiences, asking you questions along the way. In doing so, we will also be reviewing student traits, curricular and instructional issues, classroom management, grading, parent conferences, and many other aspects of being a teacher. Again, we would like you to keep a journal, completing your reading of this text as you began it: reflecting on becoming a teacher.

THE COMMUNITY, THE SCHOOL DISTRICT, THE SCHOOL

Although you may be quite well acquainted with the community in which your student teaching assignment will lie, there may also be a few surprises when you become part of the teaching staff for a semester, mainly because you have not yet had to take the perspective of a professional working in the community.

Reflection

List some schools where students in your program are assigned to student teach. What do you know about the community? About the district's schools? About the profile of the district's students? Where did you get your information? Is it reliable? What do you think you should know about the community and school district in which you will teach?

The community is the context for the district's schools; that is, things that are important to the community are often reflected in its schools (e.g., emphasis on sports or music). If the community has a diverse cultural base, the schools will be enriched by it, but also have some challenges to meet varying needs and expectations. If the community is scrambling for fiscal support for its schools, the number of teachers, class size, and availability of new materials may be affected. In brief, there are variables in every community that touch on the lives of its schools, its teachers, and, ultimately, its students. As you make the transition from student to student teacher, knowing the pulse of the community is an important aspect of becoming a professional within it. Similarly, knowing the resources of the community will serve you well as you develop lessons.

Learning about your school district is another important pre-student teaching task. What is the typical number of classes per semester and number of students per class? Does the district have in-house support for special needs students? How does the district support its teachers through professional development? Through social events? If you are in a large district, how many students comprise a single middle school or senior high school? Does the district use a team or pod concept in its larger secondary schools? If you are in a small district, how does everyone knowing everyone else make your job easier or more difficult? What are the advantages of a large district? A small one? And do you come into your student teaching thinking that you prefer one over the other?

When you receive your student teaching assignment, you need to "physically" learn your school: classrooms, media center and library, computer lab, lunch area, study hall area, teachers' lounge, teachers' work room, counseling office, and main office. You also need to get your personal e-mail address and voice mail box. Large schools will have floor plans for you, but it's a good idea to walk the school corridors yourself in advance of your start date. Things will look very different when halls are filled with students and everything is in full tilt. In addition to knowing the physical layout of the school, you need to know student rules and regulations set down by the district and the specific school. Usually, these are laid out in a student handbook, governing everything from classroom behavior to parking a car. And although often unwritten, there are teacher "rules" (procedures, really) you need to learn about as well. Whom do you contact if something is not working in your classroom (e.g., heat, windows, media equipment, computer)? Where do you get materials copied? Who will show you how to run the copy machine and other equipment? What are your responsibilities with school keys and entrances into the building? Do you wear an ID badge at all times? Where do you park? What are the appropriate or expected procedures for contacting parents/guardians? For posting homework assignments on the school web site? And within the English language arts department, you should explore with your cooperating teacher the nature and amount of homework assigned, grading practices, and other "this is how we do it here" topics.

Reflection

Out of all the "need to know" topics just listed, which to you are most important? Why? Which do you think you might learn gradually and which do you believe are most pressing when you first contact your cooperating teacher?

 ## YOU AND YOUR COOPERATING TEACHER: THE CT

Typically, your cooperating teacher (the CT) is a veteran, usually someone who has not only accepted the task of mentoring a student teacher but who also may have done additional university training in preparation for this role. There is no extra pay for this work, and there is no "time off" in this work, as your cooperating teacher remains ultimately responsible for the students—and for you.

Reflection

What traits do you expect a cooperating teacher to have?
What traits do you bring to your cooperating teacher?
Are you afraid that you may not be "good enough" for your CT?
Are you afraid that you will be embarrassed if something goes wrong?
Are you afraid that you and your CT will have very different approaches to teaching?
Are you afraid that your CT, who may not have taken a grad course in years, will be less than open to new approaches in learning or in English language arts?
Are you afraid that your CT may be threatened by your energy and enthusiasm? Or skeptical of your idealism?

Most often, rapport between the cooperating teacher and the student teacher is very good, and the mentoring process is strong and effective. However, personality and teaching style differences may turn up—and that's okay. You just need to be prepared and practical about any differences; you can work them out.

⚬ᴡ᷾᷃᷑ᴡ᷾ *Reflection* ᴡ᷾᷃᷑ᴡ᷾ ⚬

1. Here's what Jennifer, one of our student teachers, had to say:

   One of the things I have discovered about my cooperating teacher and myself is that we have very different expectations about classroom conduct. She tends to be more lenient most of the time but very touchy at others. I want to work toward consistency.

   My CT told me that I had to be more tolerant of the group shouting out answers as opposed to raising their hands. I have a hard time with students talking when other students are answering a question or when I am talking. I suppose this is one of the problems with student teaching—students are used to behaving in a certain way in certain environments, and it's hard to expect them to act differently when a student teacher comes in.

   What are Jennifer's options? If she were in your student teaching seminar, what advice would you give her and why? As a novice teacher, what is understandably on her mind?

2. Because you may have more than one placement, you may find, as Mel did, that there will be differences between one CT and another. However, Mel made some progress in figuring out her feelings as she changed CTs and curricular levels:

   I am still having a hard time finding my own style in the high school classroom. In the middle school classroom, it was so natural and instinctive. Here I feel like I can't be my own teacher. My CT and I have very different teaching styles; I like him very much, but it [his style] isn't how I am comfortable teaching. He has told me to feel free to do things differently, but I find that nearly impossible. I feel like the students (and him) need some sort of consistency. I feel obligated to teach the way he does. It is frustrating.

   How is Mel going to resolve this "pickle"? There are nine weeks to go in this placement, and students who need to be taught. What questions would you have for Mel? What advice would you give her?

3. Sara found herself in quite a different situation. A previous supervisor noted she was an exemplary, even gifted, student teacher—one of those naturals who can "knock the socks off" students almost immediately. But her current cooperating teacher found her lacking, and thus evaluated her with a somewhat mediocre "acceptable" rating. What might account for the difference? What could Sara do to reassure herself, to remain a confident student teacher?

4. We have noted some problematic situations with cooperating teachers, but we want to emphasize once more that the vast majority of relationships are not only good but also extremely supportive, through thick and thin. Note what Rachel had to say:

   The whole classroom was chaos, and the students were out of control. By the end of the period I was so frustrated with them; I think they were doing everything in the book that frustrates a teacher—not paying attention, talking over one another and me. After all this, and the kids were gone, Mrs. B. asked how I was doing—and I broke down into tears.

And in the midst of my tears, a few other English teachers came into the room. It was really embarrassing, but they all offered suggestions and ideas to improve the situation. What Rachel experienced, losing class control, is not uncommon for a student teacher, and her cooperating teacher, as well as other colleagues, no doubt recall their own novice teaching days quite vividly. Thus, the CT knows that mentoring a novice requires such understanding, along with some good, practical advice on how to handle an unruly group.

What would you say to Rachel if she were in your seminar? Should you anticipate some class management problems and ask your CT about ways to handle them? Or should you wait until the need arises?

There are as many different personalities and styles in CTs as there are in student teachers. And that's good. But as the student teacher, you need to be flexible and open-minded, and perhaps set aside a bit of what you have been taught as best practice. Why do we say that, especially when you have been working hard to be a good practitioner? Because you have to get through student teaching before you can be a solo practitioner. You have to be pragmatic, as well as respectful of your CT, even when you know for sure that a steady stream of worksheets doesn't really work or that kids really benefit from structured group work.

We have seen some of our student teachers make good decisions when they realized that they can have it both ways: follow the requirements and preferences of the CT but also bring in new strategies and materials as they take over the classes. We should note here that many CTs want student teachers because student teachers bring new strategies and materials, or as one CT told us, "I don't have to take additional coursework all the time; my student teachers bring the best of English language arts to me."

 ## YOU AND YOUR UNIVERSITY SUPERVISOR

Colleges and universities set up their supervision differently, but in most cases, someone from the departments of English or education, or both, will observe your teaching. Some colleges also make good use of recent retirees from area school districts, hiring these veteran teachers as supervisors in specific fields. Your supervisor will talk with you about what happened in those 45 minutes of classroom observation—and probably, far more often than that. In our experience, supervisors have been extremely helpful and wonderfully supportive of our student teachers. They don't sugarcoat areas where improvement is needed (and they provide specific strategies to help), nor do they fail to mention areas of strength. Both are essential to your growth. And keep in mind that your university supervisors have seen just about everything happen: the good, the bad, and the ugly. Here are some things our students told us about things going awry.

Rebecca noted in her weekly e-mail:

Monday, Dr. L. observed my communications class (tenth grade), and it was awful. They are usually a pretty rowdy bunch, but Monday was especially bad.

Amanda noted in hers:

Mr. K. was here this week, and everything went wrong. I got lost in my lesson, the kids didn't pay attention—not that I could blame them—and I felt so stupid, especially with him observing me.

Ellie also had her lesson fall apart—due to the antics of a ninth grader who didn't like *The Odyssey* in particular and being in school in general. Ellie finally ejected the student from the class, but she was upset that it came to that—and in front of her university supervisor (who, incidentally, told Ellie that what she did was exactly right).

Sometimes, everything that could go wrong, does. That happens to veteran teachers too, and it has no doubt happened to your supervisors. So even though you may be apprehensive at first, keep in mind that your supervisors are not there to be hypercritical or undermine your confidence. They are there to see what you cannot see from the front of the classroom, to help you tackle the curriculum and strengthen your teaching methods. We have had student teachers ask us to notice things, to see if their perceptions were on target. For example, one student teacher had the sense that she was paying more attention to one side of the classroom, responding to them more, asking them more. And she was. This situation could have led to trouble, but it was headed off because the student teacher was up-front, using her supervision well.

Brad noted something unexpected during one of his university supervisor observations.

I am so angry. She [U. supervisor] sat there, grading papers or something, but not paying any attention to my teaching. She then gave me high marks on the evaluation, but how could she do that? She didn't even watch me or listen to me.

This, we hasten to point out, is a rare exception in the world of classroom supervision. The supervisors we know are attentive, detailed in their observations, and very good at talking with and listening to our student teachers. But Brad's comment reminds us of something important: As a student teacher, you need feedback; you will want feedback. Your university supervisor, as well as your CT, is there to provide it.

ᴑᴍᴑ *Reflection* ᴑᴍᴑ

At the very beginning of the semester, before your university supervisor visits your classroom, what conversation do you need to have with him or her? In what ways do you envision your university supervisor(s) and your cooperating teacher consulting about your teaching? How might you prepare yourself for constructive criticism? What might you do if you feel criticism is neither fair nor constructive? What questions should you ask about formal evaluation; that is, who has responsibility for your semester grade? Will he or she write a professional recommendation for your job search?

THE SCHOOL UNIVERSE

Your Colleagues

Being a good colleague is important, and you begin that journey during student teaching. Getting along with fellow teachers is important not just in daily interactions or shared projects and committees, but also in forming authentic working relationships and friendships. Many teachers we know formed these early in their careers, and 30 years later, the friendships are still operating, even into retirement. As a student teacher, you will be in and out of faculty lounges and lunch areas, and many things, both positive and negative, are heard in these sites. Here's what Jon discovered:

Sometimes I am really shocked at the topics of conversation. I realize we need an outlet during the day and some of these kids are a real handful, but when the comments are about physical appearance, it upsets me, especially when I have the 'topics of conversation' in class the next hour.

Jon is right: Teachers do need an outlet, just as their students do. And lunch break is often the time for both groups to let loose. Unfortunately, lunchroom talk can be or appear to be insensitive, cruel even. Michele noted in her e-log that her "biggest challenges were not in the classroom. Rather they were in developing social relationships with other teachers. I found it hard to find my comfort level with them." She goes on to explain that although kids do and say stupid things, she expected more from teachers: "I find it challenging to sit in the lunchroom with those few bad adults that I have met, knowing that I came into the profession because I love kids, and wondering if they are in it for the dental plan." Harsh words indeed but Michele's idealism was taking its first hit, and she was wise to talk about it in her e-log. Veteran teachers may be of two minds on this issue. Some view the insensitive talk as dark humor, but not malicious, and that it's normal and necessary to let off steam among colleagues who know the cast of characters. Some veteran teachers are apathetic, for a variety of reasons, and they use school gathering places to sound off. Colleagues may simply ignore it. At the same time, some dislike the unprofessional, on-the-edge talk as much as Jon and Michele did, but understand straining collegial relations over lunch-time comments isn't worth it.

 *Reflection*

It's easy to be around colleagues whom you like and respect, less easy with others who rub you wrong—or you them—for whatever reason. How would you handle situations where you don't like the conversation or you think other teachers are somewhat unprofessional or uncaring?

Addressing Apathy

Unfortunately, student teachers running into schoolhouse insensitivity and apathy is common enough that NCTE's *English Journal* recently addressed the issue. In one article, Amanda Richey relates her fieldwork experience at an urban high school: "I expected to learn and see something positive in the classroom. Instead, what I saw in the teachers and their attitudes toward education and their students was heartbreaking." What precipitated Amanda's view: Teachers who were burned out, had given up on their students, did nothing to engage them in learning, or even teach. "I couldn't believe what I saw there. It took me completely off guard and soon I found my enthusiasm going down the tubes right along with the teachers'." Amanda's fear lay in what was ahead for her: "What will I do about teachers around me who are [apathetic]?"

In response to Amanda, Dante Petretti, a teacher at John F. Kennedy High School in Paterson, New Jersey, provided some needed perspective (20–23). Although Petretti agreed that the behavior of some teachers is disturbing and unprofessional, he pointed out that "many, many teachers are dedicated, hardworking, and positive." Further, he reminded us that in some districts, teachers work under extremely difficult conditions—large classes, too few supplies and books, underfunded in every way. These teachers may also be isolated from one another and from the community at large, thereby lacking support. Petretti does not excuse the behavior that Amanda (and some of our own students) have witnessed, but he does ask that students doing field work "acknowledge the contextual circumstances that contribute to teacher apathy." This is an important point of view, and one that should be heeded, not just when you are student teaching but also when you enter the job market. The apathy factor, or morale, is a critical consideration when checking out school districts to work for.

Petretti offered suggestions. If the teachers' room is a breeding ground for negative and apathetic attitudes, avoid it and recognize that the vocal minority is just that— a minority. Seek out engaged, positive teachers, who will be avoiding the teachers' room as well. Take charge of your professional development, joining organizations, attending workshops, and so forth, where you will be surrounded with others who share your zest for teaching. Included in his advice are some wise words about trying to change other teachers: First, you will find you have enough to do just learning your way as a new teacher; moreover, teachers, especially urban teachers, are wary of people who come into their school with a mission. Set yourself as an example—do your own thing and do it well. We would add: be the professional that you set out to be. Don't bad-mouth colleagues to your CT or other teachers in the building. It's best not to make comments in the school community, either. If the situation is thus that you feel you *have* to say something, then say it to that teacher only. Also, recognize the efforts of colleagues. When you hear a good idea, tell that teacher, or when you know a teacher has special expertise, ask for some help (Petretti 20–23).

 ## CHANGES, PLANNED AND OTHERWISE

Temporary Chaos: Schedules

We've mentioned before the need for teachers to be flexible—to adjust to changing school situations. Here are a few of those that our student teachers reported.

The prom:

Irritating. The juniors were all in a dither over prom and were also excused from class quite a bit [to decorate for it].

Class pictures day:

Instead of just shortening hours and calling all the kids to the gym, or doing it before or after school, they [administration] kept interrupting class.

Homecoming week:

The kids seem to think that this is a five day weekend, like we don't have to do anything but get ready for the game and dance.

State basketball tournament:

Okay, it's great that the team is going to state, but the administration doesn't seem to know what it wants to do—it can't shut down the school, but everybody who can leave, is leaving. Am I supposed to teach anything to those still here?

Standardized testing:

I couldn't believe it. The kids were all herded into gym, of all places, to take a state test. That was bad enough, but my CT was pretty upset at both the setting and her schedule being shredded for the week. She made comments to the kids, which only made some of them more anxious. The whole gym thing made some pretty apathetic too. I know we are supposed to plan for testing days, but I didn't see any adjustments in the teaching plan—only resentment at the interruption.

Just Chaos

Kate provided us with this situation, about which she was, forgive the pun, powerless.

We had the power go out on Friday around 2:00, so we had English in the dark. It was very difficult to make the kids take a spelling test when they could barely see the paper. The rest of the period they just read their books in the hallway, near the window, cafeteria—anywhere we could find some light.

Chris had to problem-solve this one:

Last week I was playing a video when I went into the hall for a minute to check on a student. When I came back, my class was complaining and covering their noses. I figured some trouble-making student had set up a stink bomb. My CT wasn't around, so I had to figure it out on my own and search the options. I didn't want to punish those students who hadn't been involved, and I didn't want to give the culprit the satisfaction of knowing he/she had caused a huge class disruption. I stopped the video, told them we would take a break to get some fresh air. When we returned the odor was still unbearable, so I found an empty classroom with a VCR and moved the class.

 *Reflection*

How do you respond when your own schedules (school or personal) are disrupted or changed? If you tend to get upset, how will you prepare yourself for the inevitable disruptions in middle or senior high schedules?

TEACHERS' WORKLOADS

As Chad pointed out,

It [student teaching] has really opened my eyes to the fact that a teacher's work never really stops and it definitely is not limited to the classroom.

As a student teacher, you will be logging many hours to prepare and "clean up" class work, student work, assessment and grading, and look ahead to another week. Many of our student teachers tell us that they expected to be busy, but not *that* busy— nor so tired. The energy that goes into learning a school, a class, a new lesson or unit is immense; it's no wonder that student teachers are tired. Most student teachers observe their CT's classes for a couple of weeks, and then gradually take over the teaching—one class at a time, until they are teaching three or four classes daily. Although the CT may have laid out the material to be covered, he or she most often will expect you to develop lessons, bring in new materials, and implement teaching strategies that work for your plans and style. Your work in methods classes will have prepared you for this moment, but the brain power and emotions that go into "for real" will be more intense.

One of our very capable student teachers remarked at mid-term:

I made myself relax [on a long weekend] and didn't spend a single second working on anything for school. I baked cookies, and Friday night, I actually rented a movie and took time to sit down and watch the whole thing. I really think I needed that break to re-energize myself.

Heidi's right—she did need to shut down the schoolwork and do things for her-self and just for fun. She, like every student teacher we have known, needed renewal. You can't sustain as a student teacher without some time for yourself—whether it is baking, playing basketball, hanging out in a coffee shop with the morning newspaper, jogging, reading something unrelated to school, watching a favorite television show, working out, or having a 45-minute phone conversation with a friend. You will need that time, some alone and some with others, without any feelings of guilt for having taken it. If you don't take such time, you will likely end up run down, both emotion-ally and physically, and susceptible to every illness making its rounds in the school. Thus, taking care of yourself—carving out time for yourself, getting enough sleep, eat-ing well—is integral to your teaching success.

 ## Reflection

Make a list of your typical responses to schoolwork pressure (e.g., when you have had a major project or presentation to prepare). Now make a list of the things you do to relax, to take a break. Do you give yourself enough time to re-energize? How will you build in time during student teaching? What activity is so important to your well-being that you know it simply cannot be "dumped," regardless of school tasks? What is your daily eating and sleeping schedule right now? How might you have to adjust that once you are teaching? Do you eat "healthy" foods that sustain energy for hours? Since there won't be any snacking between meals, what adjustments might be needed in your diet?

Another student teacher (and she was not the only one) discussed her dilemma with time, pressure, and her friends and family. She noted:

They just don't understand. They don't know what it's like to continually prepare, to be responsible for what happens to 25 kids, to deal with the daily emotions of so many kids. And in English, to be reading and evaluating student work. So they don't get it when I say I can't go out, or I don't have time for visiting right now. And some of them get angry with me.

 Reflection

How can you avoid this student teacher's dilemma? If your family and friends have little or no experience with the profession, what can you say—without sounding whiney or angry? What if they are right, that you tend to be overly zealous in preparation or are somewhat disorganized—both of which leave you with less personal time?

DAILY CHALLENGES

The Kids

One of the earliest, and perhaps most vexing, problems that student teachers face is that of student apathy or defiance regarding assignments or class participation. The reasons for such responses vary, everything from a student who is disappointed not to have Ms. Jones, the teacher she had been waiting to have, to one who can't believe an AP English class will be taught by a student teacher. Other reasons, of course, stem from real learning problems or a long history of non-participation in classes. We will offer some suggestions about "what to do," but first, we would like you to consider the following situations and your own first response.

In his weekly e-log, Jake wrote:

This student is one of the brightest kids in the class (IQ over 140) and has a lot of interesting insight to offer a group of students—the problem is he is just so unmotivated. He is literally failing these classes because he does not do the work—not at all. Not alternative reading—nothing.

EXPLORATION

Gifted but Failing

Brainstorm some reasons why a gifted middle school student might refuse to take part in class or complete any assignments. Then, with a partner, problem-solve: What action might a student teacher take?

Karen wrote about her situation with a high school student who refused to work:

One of my students has stopped participating in class. He has been tested on several occasions, and although he has some short-term memory problems, he has not been specifically labeled [as disabled]. He stopped working, suddenly, after a weekend, and he refused all offers of me helping him. I am really uncertain how to handle this. We [CT and Karen] have decided he will be receiving zeros for the work he has not handed in. He was told exactly how it would hurt his grades, and it did not seem to have any effect on him last week. What do you do with an 18-year-old who has decided he doesn't want to do homework for whatever reason? At what point do you leave it up to him?

Reflection

What would you say to Karen if she were in your seminar? At what point *do* we leave it up to the student to pass or to fail? Or are we then failing as teachers? What possible reasons are there for her student's refusal to work?

———————————————————

Michael noted two different situations in his ninth-grade classes:

One area of concern that I have right now is my two young men in fourth hour who refuse to turn in any homework. I did talk with them about their failing grades—and that they will be taking English over.

I have a student who refused to cooperate. When it was writing time, he did not take out his paper . . . when I asked, he refused, and when I asked again more firmly, he said: "No, I don't think I am going to write today." I talked with him privately—and he said, "I don't have to." I called his mother. The next day the kid had paper and wrote.

Reflection

Michael has two different problems in two different classes: a refusal to do homework and a refusal to work in class. You have his immediate response to both. What else do you think Michael did or might have done? What might be happening with the rest of the class during this verbal exchange? What do you think kids have to know about you as the teacher?

———————————————————

Emily brought us quite a different situation: A ninth-grade girl had "issues" with a couple of boys in her class. If the boys even looked at her, she was set off, verbal and volatile in varying degrees of intensity. Needless to say, nothing else could happen in class while the gender fireworks were displayed.

EXPLORATION

Based on your knowledge of teens, what would you do? Make a list of potential strategies for defusing the situation.

wow... do I know that feeling...

Since our students presented these issues in their weekly e-logs, here are some of our immediate responses.

Jake's student was gifted but silent. Gifted students, especially in middle school, who refuse to do anything may be afraid of failure and thus do nothing rather than risk it. A student who has been #1 all through grade school faces more competition and more difficult work in middle school—along with high expectations from family. Consequently, some kids feel that the only control they have is to fail. If they don't try, they have a built-in reason for the failure—lack of effort rather than lack of being "smart enough." This is an extreme situation, and one that you may never face; nonetheless, it happens. Other more obvious reasons for failure may lie in legitimate boredom with everything at grade level, some natural "testing" of teacher, or reinforcement from peers (it's not cool to be smart). Ruling out experimentation with drugs should also be considered. You should first talk with the student—not around him. There will be plenty of "around him" with guidance counselors, specialists, and teams of teachers who will become part of his "situation." But oddly and sadly, sometimes no one talks directly to the student as a first approach to "what's going on?"

Karen's student presented a different situation. Marginal students, especially in senior high school and of legal age, who suddenly refuse to work may be responding to serious questions of worth—the school's, that is. We have to wonder if telling a marginal student that he is going to get zeroes, and to no effect whatsoever, is the best approach. After all, he already knows he's barely making it, so zeroes simply give a failing student more of the same. The sudden "I quit" that Karen noted also makes us wonder what happened over that weekend: an argument with family or friends, humiliation of some sort, a family problem or urgency, or just tired of playing what seems to be a school game? Again, directly asking the student why (even if he won't respond) seems an appropriate first step.

Michael's students provide yet another view of "I won't." The first instance of the two who refuse to do homework conjures up once more the question of why. The old mantra of " what are the kids doing, what is it good for, and how do you know" comes into play, as does the "already failing, so what?" syndrome. If Michael has talked with the kids, been clear in his expectations, and provided support—even if the boys didn't take it—he has done his part. If he talked with their parents/guardians, he has once again done his part. However, he also needs to take a hard, honest look at his lessons and assignments. When kids' interests and involvement are not even a consideration in teacher planning and implementation, it's not surprising that some kids won't do anything. As a teacher, you have an obligation to work out a good curriculum and diverse instructional strategies—and invite the kids in. But you can't save every student, no matter how much you care and how hard you try. Try you must, but learning to live with that reality is part of being a teacher. Similarly, you must be prepared for another reality: Some kids don't actually refuse to do the work, but they do refuse to get it in on time. As a student teacher, you need to be ready for this situation; have a written policy for late work—and then stick to it.

The other student refusal Michael faced is perhaps simpler: The boy wanted to know who's in charge. This was a teenager, and most teenagers test adults. What's more, sometimes, like us, kids just have a bad day. What's important in this situation is Michael's attitude to not take things too personally and to keep a perspective of "this is a 15-year-old." Further, it *never* works to confront or humiliate a student in front of his peers, nor does a threat. So talking with the student privately is one avenue; contacting a parent if needed is another. Michael did both, and he got back his student.

To Emily's firecracker, the most immediate response, and an easy one, is moving the student out of the guys' sight. If the girl sits in a front, center seat, and the boys are separated and in back seats, Emily will know who's lighting the fuse: the girl or the guys. Emily might also attempt to find out the story behind these three kids, which may take some investigation with other teachers or just quiet concentration on classroom gossip. In any case, talking with the students individually and privately is in order.

Classroom Management

If there is one area that student teachers write and talk about often, it is classroom management. The fear of losing control is real and understandable. As a result, our student teachers tell us that they know they are being inflexible and rigid, handing down too many rules—and not at all how they want to be or how they envisioned themselves as teachers. Thus, we asked some veterans for advice.

- If a student should be removed from class, know school procedures and follow them.
- Remember you are not their friend, and not their peer.

We would add that class management is closely related to curriculum and instruction. The stronger and more stimulating your selection of materials, the more diverse and appropriate your instructional methods, the fewer problems in class control. The more often and deeply kids are involved in their own learning, making real choices and decisions, the less often they are fooling around. And finally, setting the tone of your classroom on Day One leads to a community of learners where kids can feel respected and safe. Use initial class periods for "ice-breakers" and integrating activities, survey the kids to learn their interests, share your own interests, and engage them in "small talk" at the start or close of class. For decades, novice teachers were told "don't smile until Christmas." That was bad advice. You should smile, and you should have humor in your classroom. At the same time, set the parameters for appropriate behavior; that's your job.

Curriculum and Instruction

helpful tips

- Have your daily plan carefully structured, so there is no "down time," no time when kids don't know what's coming next or what they are to do.
- Help kids with organization (middle schoolers are notoriously disheveled) by having files and crates for their work, a class log or calendar for assignments, and a class plan that is somewhat predictable in structure.
- Put time limits on various activities (e.g., 10 minutes to write a response or work with a partner); don't expect kids to stay totally engaged on one task for an extended time.
- Use structured but engaging oral activities; give kids space to talk or move about.
- Use challenging, stimulating questions or materials and keep kids on their toes.
- Give kids some choices, authentic decision-making, in assignments and projects.
- Develop classroom rules or expected behavior with the kids; implement fairly and consistently; do not give empty threats or put off consequences.
- Act on the knowledge that kids need predictability, structure, stability—even if they complain about it.
- If a student is a problem, handle it privately and calmly.

Student teachers can find themselves in situations where their very recent knowledge of curriculum and instruction is at odds with the district's or with their CT's. In a middle school classroom, one of our student teachers was caught between methods of teaching grammar: directly, as his CT did, or indirectly, as he had learned in his methods courses. When his university supervisor visited the class, Steve was quick to say that the lessons that were about to unfold were not his idea, even though he was teaching them. The university supervisor was struck by the complete absence of books (other than workbooks and dictionaries), as well as by the only décor in the room being lists of punctuation rules. In the conversation that followed his lesson, Steve explained that "all the young adult lit books are used in the reading class; this is composition and grammar class."

⟨⟩ *Reflection* ⟨⟩

Steve knew, of course, that the curriculum and methodology in this classroom did not fit with state standards, nor did they generate authentic student writing. But was there anything he could do in this situation, where the middle school itself had determined "no reading" in composition class? Is it the student teacher's role to encourage or bring about curricular change? Do you think Steve should have found ways to use literature, for example, to teach about grammar and language? Or is it a matter of survival?

In a rural senior high school class, Amy faced a different curricular issue:

And they all [class of seniors] informed me that no one should know this junk about someone that's been dead that long.

The someone was Shakespeare. Shakespeare is perhaps the one requirement in the senior high school literature curriculum, and in some states he is required reading at every high school level, 9 through 12. Thus, even if Amy wanted to take Shakespeare out of her plans, she couldn't have.

Reflection

How would you respond to this class? (Being shocked and dismayed isn't the answer.) Think about the 21st-century high school student; think about the issues in Shakespeare's plays, especially *Macbeth* or *Romeo and Juliet,* the most commonly taught. How do they connect with these very modern kids? What might Amy have told this class?

_____

In that same rural high school, Amy faced another Shakespeare issue, but this time, with a small, senior British literature class—all female. She noted in her weekly e-mail:

I'm really excited to teach this [Macbeth] because several of the women are into witchcraft and the like. I do worry about how to approach what can be a highly controversial subject, however . . . I've already told them several times that they cannot cast spells in school.

Reflection

Amy was not joking. Although her situation may appear as an extreme example, underneath it lies a curricular reality—controversial issues or topics associated with required literature. How do you prepare for controversy, possible misinterpretation of what you are doing or using in class? What discussion do you need to have with your CT, other teachers, the school librarians?

_____

Assigning Work

As student teachers plan their first assignments, they often aren't thinking of student reaction, at least not what Holly met up with one week:

Tuesday was pretty, um, interesting. I assigned their first formal piece of writing. You'd think I had asked them [seniors] to donate organs rather than turn out a 2–3 page paper. . . . Apparently, there was a discussion at lunch on Tuesday about what would happen if they simply refused to do their papers. They arrived at the conclusion that I would either cry, or laugh at them and give them all zeros. The latter would have been more correct.

As part of her discussion about student revolt, Holly noted something else:

It is a constant tug of war with the seniors as a lot of their teachers have given in to their demands for more time, extended deadlines, pared down assignments, etc.

⟲⟲⟲ *Reflection* ⟲⟲⟲

Holly was student teaching in a small community and school, where she knew all of the teachers, and thus, she also knew a lot about what went on. Do you think Holly's senior situation is typical—that is, do you think seniors, especially during spring semester, are going to challenge almost everything assigned? Should Holly be working with her CT on this? Or, what if she already knows her CT is one of those teachers who "give in"? What should a student teacher know about school "tradition" and expectations? What if you don't agree with them? What, for a student teacher, is realistic?

Planning for Absentees

Among the most dreaded words a teacher hears are these: "What did we do yesterday? Did I miss anything?" Although you will be tempted to say something to the effect that "Oh, we didn't do a thing, not with you absent!"—you instead need to have a system in place that saves you from saying anything at all. Here are two systems that we believe are practical.

The first, from Lani Eklund:

Establish a student-kept class log with the date, details of assignments, and the events of that day's class period. Students rotate keeping the log, signing it for the day kept. On the cover, put the class/period and a class roster for keeping track of who's been a recorder. The log is not only a place where absentees can find information, but also serves as a useful reference to what was covered in different class periods. You can ask the recorder to make a final note of where class ended its discussion or activity.

And the second, which we have seen our student teachers do successfully, from Marylou Guentert:

Give the students a calendar for four or six weeks, a duplicated sheet with squares for each day of that time period. Write the day's assignment on board or on transparency; have the kids copy onto their calendar. Keep a large laminated sheet of poster board, with 30 squares on it. With a water soluble pen, copy that day's work into the appropriate square of big calendar. On table next to calendar, keep a wire rack with folders which are numbered in sequence. Every "paper" the kids do is then numbered sequentially. Students who were absent go directly to big calendar, copy the missed assignments on their calendar, and get whatever is needed from the appropriate folder. The only papers not in folders are tests. If a student misses test, it is his/her responsibility to arrange a time to take it.

Reflection

What adjustments, if any, might you make for different age groups—that is, would the same system work for seventh or eleventh graders? How would you ensure that students have the "lion's share" of responsibility for making up work?

THE EXTRA-CURRICULARS

We encourage student teachers to become involved in the extra-curricular activities of their schools, to become part of the fabric making up a large part of their students' lives. Because of your background in English language arts, people will associate you with drama, the newspaper, the yearbook, and other language arts-based clubs. However, turning up at athletic events, chaperoning a dance, or visiting the science fair will bring you some valuable insights into the kids—and much more.

Kristy was not a sports fan, but she decided to attend a basketball game at her small, rural high school:

I really didn't have time to go, but I'm glad I did. Nearly all of the teachers and most of the kids commented on my presence at the game—especially the table of male faculty who discuss the game at great length during lunch. I guess I was struck with what an effect my going to one game had on people's perception of me. I had not realized the degree to which people had ascribed my Coop's [cooperating teacher] personality to mine. Interesting.

Kristy's cooperating teacher was heavily into drama, and very successful with productions both at school and in the community; however, he did not pay much attention to any other aspect of extra-curricular life. By association, Kristy was labeled. Although she did indeed prefer drama club and productions, Kristy also found out the value of showing up at non-drama events. The kids noticed, the kids cared—as did teachers who coach. A few of our student teachers, male and female, became athletic coaching volunteers or workers at athletic events, using their interest in these sports and the kids' participation to good advantage.

EXPLORATION

But I Only Like . . .

Rank your extra-curricular school activities from "favorite" to "tolerate." Which of these would you want to help with as a student teacher? Which of these do you think might make a difference when you apply for teaching positions? Which of your least favorite activities would be important to a majority of kids? Will the size of the school and community make any difference in your decision to turn up at school-sponsored events?

While student teaching at a middle school, Mark went to a science fair:

When I got there that night, I saw those sixth graders who participated in such a different light. They were excited about education and what they learned from their project outside of the classroom. I saw them acting silly with their friends, and as someone's child when they talked to their parents; they weren't just my students. I walked around and talked to all of them individually and learned a lot about their personalities—things you don't always see in the classroom. They also saw me in a different light. I remember growing up and thinking that my teachers didn't have a life outside of school. When I saw them shopping at a store or driving in their car, I remember thinking, "What are they doing here? They're supposed to be in school!"

 *Reflection*

Mark gives strong evidence of the importance of extra-curricular events—and student teachers attending. Why do you think some student teachers don't ? Do you think attending or participating in extra-curriculars or school-sponsored events should be required as part of student teaching?

You can help your students, as well as yourself, by knowing their talents and interests. One of our student teachers did just that. Kevin was an avid hunter and fisherman, but he really didn't care for pro football; however, his mostly male ninth graders did. So Kevin found out what he needed to know about the Green Bay Packers and the Minnesota Vikings, the two teams his students loved or loved to hate. Monday mornings brought lively discussions of Sunday's games—and even a story or two of the deer or fish that escaped Kevin's weekend attempts. A couple of weeks into the fall football scene, Kevin realized he could use information from the games as illustrations in lessons about writing. In honoring his kids' outside interests, Kevin found his teaching was enhanced. But even had he not woven pro football into his lessons, the time spent talking about the teams was time well spent. Building a community of learners depends on knowing the outside interests and activities—of both kids and teacher.

EXPLORATION

These—Always in My Life

List your favorite, sustained interests and hobbies; list your real passions. Which of these might mesh well with middle school kids? With senior high kids? What is the potential relationship between what you love to do outside of school and what you are developing in your lessons and units?

Lexi found out something unexpected when she took on an extra-curricular that she loved—directing the school play at a middle school. She stressed that the experience helped her learn many things about herself as a teacher, and that "extra-curricular activities are more than worth the time, effort and money each person puts into them . . . knowing the students on a different level, interacting with them differently than in class." But, here is the unexpected:

[This experience] made me realize that I would never take on an extra-curricular event in my first year of teaching. I wasn't one hundred percent my best in any capacity: teacher, director, student, friend, girlfriend, person. Each part of me was compromised by the way I was spreading myself.

Lexi's CT told her that it was a healthy decision, but that Lexi had to be realistic. Some school districts who won't hire teachers unwilling to take an extra-curricular activity; they will hire the teacher, regardless of qualifications, who is willing to take it on. Lexi's immediate response was one of "I don't want to teach in a district where a teacher's knowledge of her own well-being isn't important."

Do you think Lexi will change her mind when faced with "if you want this position, you will be responsible for drama club and the school play"? Or do you think Lexi is wise to listen to her experience as a student teacher? Should you seek out extra-curricular roles to find out how you balance your responsibilities?

WORKING WITH PARENTS

As a student teacher, you will either be a listener or a full participant in parent-teacher conferences, usually held twice a semester. Depending upon the amount of work that you have been responsible for, and the amount of grading that you have done, your CT will determine your role at the conferences. In our experience, student teachers have played a very active role in school-wide conferences, as well as in contacting parents or guardians informally as warranted.

One of our students at an urban high school had this initial reaction to her first formal parent conferences: "I was very, very nervous!" Many of her classmates also used that adjective when they wrote about conferences. We'll share some ideas for conferences a bit later, but first, we would like you to think about this important topic on your own.

EXPLORATION

Preconference Butterflies

Why was Cindy "nervous"? Make a list of the reasons or scenarios that would cause a student teacher to have a few butterflies. What do you expect to happen at conferences? What do you expect parents/guardians to say or to ask? How do you prepare?

Learning from your CT can be invaluable experience for your solo conferences to follow.

Becky wrote about her first parent conferences:

Some parents were mad at the administration for sending out failing notices so late. By the time they knew what was going on with their kids, it was too late. Some seniors aren't turning in work, and even those kids who were good students earlier are letting their grades drop. One kid got in with a bad crowd and the parents are beside themselves. I felt bad for some of the parents who don't know what to do with their kids. Some of them have seniors, and they are desperate for answers because their kids are in danger of failing and not graduating. My CT simply listened, let them talk, giving advice only in the educational arena.

EXPLORATION

Anticipating and Responding to Parental Concern

What should you say when parents complain about administrators? Or other teachers? Why did Becky's CT stick strictly to educational advice? Regardless of what the school does with progress reports, what should you do about students not faring well? Make a list of specific actions or strategies.

Some conferences occur because either the parent or teacher believes a problem needs solving immediately. A case in point came from Lori, who was student teaching in a large middle school. A sixth grader, gifted by all accounts, refused to do any work at all; moreover, he was so rude to his classmates that the CT didn't want him in group work. Lori noted that this student really didn't communicate much, giving only one- or two-word answers to her or the CT. So, his mother was asked to come for a conference. Lori was completely (and understandably) unprepared when the mother's response to the litany of problems came: "He hasn't been raised how I wanted him to be."

Reflection

Even though Lori was a student teacher, she had been responsible for large segments of the class; thus, she was an integral participant in this conference. How do you think she prepared for talking with this mother? How do you think she responded to the mother's response? What should be the outcome of conferences? Are conferences always helpful? Should they be scheduled regardless of doubtful outcomes?

Preparing for Conferences

Your CT will guide you through school procedures and expectations for conferences, but sometimes you have to handle conferences on your own, even as a student teacher.

This is good experience, and if you prepare well, the first-time butterflies will settle down. Listen to what some veteran teachers suggest.

Mary C. Rose tells novice teachers that:

> It's unavoidable. Amidst all your parent conferences that are enjoyable and flow with ease, once in a while a really tough one comes along that tests your preparedness, your professionalism, and at times even your patience.

The items to be discussed—disruptive behavior, poor study habits, low test scores—are difficult for parents to hear, even if they already know of the problems. Some will deny them, some will be angry with you, and others will be apathetic, thus Rose's "test your patience."

Rose has some ideas of what you can do:

- Document the student's progress or lack thereof. Keep a log of behavior, keep track of missing assignments.
- Let parents know early on if there are problems. But don't shock them with things they might not be prepared for. Ongoing communication is important and will help to eliminate "shockers."
- Keep records of all your contact with parents.
- When parents arrive, put them at ease. Have some "small talk" first, and try to share something positive you noticed about their child. Keep in mind your remarks can be easily interpreted as criticism of parents or cultural practices. Allow for anger, allow them to vent—don't lose your composure.
- Seek suggestions and ideas from the parents as to how to solve the problem.
- Have responses ready, some solutions in mind (e.g., tutoring, change in your classroom practice, testing); try to offer concrete suggestions for parents to use at home—in writing if possible. Schedule a follow-up conference—keep communicating.
- Try to find the student's greatest strength and build on it.

Linda Shalway, another veteran teacher, had other useful suggestions for conferences.

- "Plan questions to ask, points to make, suggestions to offer."
- Collect samples of student work. Have them ready for the conference, and be ready to explain the assignment.
- Prepare to explain your goals and teaching strategies in plain language, not teacher talk.
- If there is a problem, focus your comments only on things that can be changed.
- Limit the number of suggestions or improvements expected; don't overwhelm parents.
- Avoid jargon, speak plainly. Be tactful but not so tactful that you don't really communicate the problem.

- Ask for and listen to parents' reactions, questions, and suggestions.
- After a conference, jot down the gist of what was said. Unless there are specific questions parents want answered, don't take notes during conference time.
- For your own protection in this age of litigation, keep records of all personal contact—phone call, e-mail, on-site conversations. Include the commitment you or the parent made to assist the student. Follow up and stay in touch.
- Evaluate the conference—honestly and fully.

We especially like Shalway's final point: Evaluate yourself. Were you well prepared? Did you begin on a positive note? Did you allow the parents to give their point of view? Did you remain professional, regardless of criticism directed at you?

Talking with Parents and Guardians

Our student teachers reported diverse situations and personal responses to interaction with parents. Dan noted some frustration:

This week I had some interesting dealings with parents. Two parents of failing students e-mailed to find out what assignments were missing and what kids needed to do to pass the class. I spent a lot of time preparing letters to the parents. I replied to their e-mails, sent packets of material through regular mail and left messages at their homes. I feel like a lot of my week was spent making sure all the students' grades were updated. I was really disappointed when, after several hours of work for one of the students, I found out she dropped my class and all the work I had done was unnecessary.

⊙⊙⊙ *Reflection* ⊙⊙⊙

Was Dan's work unnecessary? Should he have considered it as wasted time? What practical lessons do you take away from Dan's experience?

In secondary schools, letting parents know what is going on right from the start of a unit or major project is worth your time. In fact, it takes less time to prepare a brief handout on the goals and assignments of a unit or project than it does to explain them after the fact, when parents may be upset. Also, keep in mind that parents who are interested, calling or e-mailing, regardless of the extra work and nervousness you experience, are a plus—compared to those who don't or won't respond. One caution, however: Don't let e-mail communication get out of control, or you will be spending all your prep time answering parent e-mails. Always keep good records, updated and accurate, and be prepared to talk to a parent or guardian at any time—not just at major grade reporting times. If you have students with special needs or individual curricular plans, you will have to be prepared to talk with special education personnel and parents at regular intervals, not just at school-designated conferences.

[handwritten in margin:] send letters to parents early about units

Another of our student teachers, Carrie, noted that she had sent e-mails to several parents and planned letters to all the parents of failing students. In her opinion,

Some parents give their kids all the responsibility while others are very involved and they want to know everything their kids are doing. Students who are passing are clearly showing that they are responsible while those who have neglected to turn in their assignment are irresponsible so their parents should be involved.

We would caution here that most kids goof up and goof off some of the time. And unless teachers have fair and high expectations, and hold kids to them, kids—being kids—won't do much. They are not automatically "irresponsible," as Carrie mistakenly labeled them.

Jamie noted,

My week started on a pretty negative note because of two parental phone calls I received. The first came from a mother who felt that I gave her son an unfair grade on his autobiography project (he earned a "C"). The second call was from a mother who was concerned about her son's "F" in my class. As I listened to the messages on my voice mail, in preparation to return the calls, my CT informed me that both mothers are known for causing problems and feeling that their children are perfect and can do no wrong. This knowledge made me even more nervous to speak to them.

 *Reflection*

What is your first response to Jamie receiving this warning from the CT?

_____

I called the first mother back right away. Initially, she was very pleasant, saying that Steven had worked very hard on the project and they both felt he deserved a higher grade.

I asked her if she had looked at a copy of the assignment, and she hadn't. I explained to her that the class had been given examples and plenty of time to fulfill requirements, in-class work in which to get help. In addition Steven turned it in late. She complained that he was up two hours past his bedtime to complete the project—and I explained that he had over two weeks to do this work. She was very persistent that his grade be changed and I said no, but invited her to the classroom to see the other students' projects and understand why Steven has a "C". She finally backed down and thanked me for my time.

 *Reflection*

What has Jamie learned?

_____

Jamie then noted the second parent call, which turned into a 5 P.M. conference. She asked that the student attend with the parents and in the course of the conference,

Jamie noted that Robbie was very smart, and he was getting an F because he doesn't hand in any work. What transpired next was a revelation:

Robbie had been lying to his parents. He had told them he had only two days to complete the autobiography project, so the parents thought this was very unfair—which it would have been if true. I showed them my lesson plans, so they could see the dates, and they saw that he had many chances to work in class. We brainstormed some solutions, and Robbie will bring a red folder to class where we will keep an extra copy [of any handouts/assignments] to go home to Mom and Dad. I called Robbie's mom the next day because he had done so well on The Outsiders. She started to cry and thanked me, told me they felt foolish when they got home and knew that Robbie's low grade was his own fault.

I learned two things from this experience. First, I was terrified to call the parents. Fellow teachers had told me the parents were impossible to work with. However, I had the opposite experience. I attribute this to my careful preparation for both contacts. I had the due dates, assignment description, notes about behavior all at my fingertips. I was also confident and firm. Second, I learned that I need to call parents early, when their child starts to slip. Robbie's parents had no idea he was failing until progress reports went home.

⁓ *Reflection* ⁓

When you sense or are told that certain parents are considered a "nuisance," how will you deal with potential bias toward those parents, and possibly, their child?

SHARING WITH STUDENTS

Student teachers may be caught between two worlds, that of adult—the person in charge of this class, the person responsible, poised and restrained—and that of the person subject to all the same emotions as the students in those desks. Caitlin learned that there may be times when a teacher has to let down her guard and trust those kids.

I called home last night and learned that our family kitten had died, and I could hear my sisters sobbing in the background. Losing a pet is devastating, even if she is only your fur niece. My 3rd-hour class noticed—and one student said, "You seem a lot less happy today, Miss C." So I told them. One girl cried but so did I. I hesitated to share something so personal but I felt it was only fair because it was affecting my personality and therefore my teaching. They [students] handled it with much more maturity and sensitivity that I could have imagined. I felt so much better having it out there because then the kids did not attribute my mood to something they had done. great point!

⁓ *Reflection* ⁓

Caitlin's final comment, "then the kids did not attribute my mood to something they had done" is critical insight. But there is a fine line between appropriate sharing of personal information and indulging oneself or inadvertently manipulating kids' feelings. What are some personal situations that you believe could or should be shared with students? For example, those that may enhance positive student values or good decision-making skills? What are some that you believe should remain yours alone? What should you do if you are facing personal issues serious enough that your students might be affected?

———————————

 ## MAKING THE MOST OF STUDENT TEACHING

Reflection is an essential component in student teaching; being positive, realistic, and pro-active are similarly important.

Sam took notice of his own state of mind about a month into the semester:

I have come to the realization that I have been incredibly negative lately. Grading projects and quizzes tends to put me in a bad mood. As I prepared mid-quarter progress reports on failing students, I was disappointed that so many are failing simply because they don't turn in their work or fail to follow directions. I find myself complaining about them and about my day on a regular basis. I am going to make an effort to change my attitude: First, I am sure my roommates, girlfriend, and family are sick of hearing my complaining. Second, I don't really have anything to complain about; only a few are failing; third, pessimism, like optimism, is contagious. If I have a negative attitude as a teacher, I can't expect my students to be positive. No one wants to work for a grouchy teacher.

We pointed out to Sam that it's normal to feel down now and then, and that grading is an activity that can produce myriad emotions. We tend to worry a lot about those kids failing (and may see it as our failure); consequently, we also forget to celebrate the many students who are productive and doing well. We also noted to Sam that he was right to get the grouch out of his life, or he will precipitate a downward spiral. He also has to remember that learning occurs at different times, in different ways, and at different rates. Those kids' names in the grade book represent "different," and even when Sam thinks he's not getting through, he probably is. One of the things we have to accept about teaching is that the rewards are not always immediate, nor even in the foreseeable future at times. What is immediate is our ability to take charge of the situation, fix what needs fixing, and thus eliminate any excessive griping to friends, family—and self.

 *Reflection*

What kind of things might send you into a funk while student teaching? How do you already know these things? Are there prior experiences that suggest you may get discouraged too easily? Do you have personality traits that push you into perfectionist or worry-wart behaviors? Or to procrastinate when non-fun chores are at hand? Make a list. Then, make a counter-list of how you will combat tendencies that can undermine your student teaching.

———————————

Those who mentor student teachers have written rather extensively about concrete, positive things student teachers can do during their field work. We have adapted some that we hope you will consider as you make the transition from student to teacher.

- *Seek opportunities to observe other teachers.* Ask them questions about: their teaching styles and materials, assessment, working with different ability levels, and classroom management strategies.
- *Be yourself.* Learn from other teachers but don't attempt to copy them.
- *Set realistic goals for yourself.* Don't compare yourself to veteran teachers with a wealth of accumulated experience, but keep an eye on them, learn from that experience.
- *Recognize that you are well-trained and well-educated, but that you are a learner, a novice teacher.* Don't be a perfectionist! No one expects you to have all the answers or know how to do everything well. Be truthful when you don't know something, especially with students, and tell them you can check it out together.
- *Realize that you need to unpack your own school experiences.* Dan Lortie, an eminent researcher of teachers, writes of the "apprenticeship of observation" that student teachers have had in 16 or more years of being students themselves, thus influencing their conception of the role of teachers. Be aware that you have to overcome a mental stereotype of "teacher." Unpack your preconceptions.
- *Overcome perceptions of failure if or when students don't respond or do poorly on assignment or exam.* Kids are, as with every generation before you and no doubt after, self-absorbed. Their main interest is themselves. And that means some of them, some of the time, and some of them all of the time, may not respond, no matter how good the lesson or unit and your implementation of it.
- *Make a commitment to your cooperating teacher, and understand that he or she is making a commitment to you, to your professional growth.* Be ready to accept some risks in this partnership, take some leadership, and maintain a strong work ethic. (Adapted from McWilliam 39–42)

We realize that some of these are far easier in the abstract than in the classroom. However, you have reached this point in your professional goal through the kind of hard-minded thinking delineated above. You have had to sort through commitment, self-evaluation, and goal-setting many times. We know you can do it again—this time, from the other side of the desk.

THOUGHTS, ADVICE, AND SUPPORT FROM A VET

Recognizing the issues critical to novice teachers, the *English Journal* turned its full attention on the newest members of the teaching profession: students like you and first-year teachers. In her editorial, Leila Christenbury writes:

Those of us in the school want the universities to send us perfectly polished teachers; those of us in the universities want the schools to finish what we haven't already done. While there are notable exceptions, many in the schools often want beginning teachers to fit neatly into the system; many in the universities often expect beginning teachers to revolutionize that system. What, it appears, all of us veterans expect is, perhaps, the most impossible of all: We not only want the best from our new teachers, we want them, in essence, to be better, from the very beginning, than we ever were. (13)

Although Christenbury confronts us with a dilemma, her recognition that veteran teachers want you to be better than they were, right from the beginning, is also a positive force: We believe in you. Right from the start. But we also want you to recognize, as Eileen Simmons points, out, that you will always be in transition. Simmons, a veteran teacher from Tulsa, Oklahoma, notes that she is still becoming a teacher: "Twenty-five years of experience have taught me that teaching and teachers are always 'in process,' never completed" (73). Simmons adds an important step in this process: Trust your students and yourself to explore the subject area together. Simmons explains:

No teacher's guide taught me the connection between Shakespeare's play *The Tempest* and Ray Bradbury's novel *Fahrenheit 451*. But a high school sophomore saw that Prospero and Beatty were both into "mind control." A junior English literature student spotted the similarity between King Arthur's Court and modern society: Gang members are controlled by a code as rigid as that of any medieval knight. (73)

Simmons is right: Students are wonderful teachers, smart and insightful, if only we give them the sense of a shared journey and the importance of their responses. And they are ever so much more fun than a teacher's guide.

One piece of advice we hadn't thought of is a very useful one: Enroll yourself in a class in an area where you're not proficient. Simmons relates that she became a "back row aerobics student" who takes two weeks to master a new routine and when faced with a new step is puzzled again. What Simmons gains (in addition to stress relief through intense physical activity) is an invaluable reminder:

My instructor is patient. She never singles me out; she lets me learn at my own rate; she encourages any kind of progress—the very model of what a writing teacher should be with students for whom writing is as challenging as aerobics is for me. I know how my students feel. . . . (74)

Simmons also encourages you to keep a journal: "Set aside some time during the school day to write and reflect on your teaching and your students." For her, it is the quiet time when school is out, when she can reflect on that day, the frustrations, the bright spots, think about lesson plans, "and generally bring order to the chaos of a normal teaching day." The journal is a place where perspective can be gained. As Simmons put it: "Mastery teaching is reflective teaching—a journal is essential for reflection" (74).

We know that for many teachers, keeping a daily journal simply doesn't happen, even though they believe in the idea. For this reason, we urge you to begin a teaching journal when you student teach. It can become, as Simmons put it, a place where you "bring order to the normal teaching day." It can become a habit. If you don't maintain a journal, then at the very least, be sure to make margin notes on your lesson plans and your handouts. You need to know where you are and where you are headed: what worked; what didn't; what needs review; what needs changing; and what ideas popped into your head as the day wore on. Without a written record, you will forget, you won't reflect in the same way. And mastery, as well as great personal satisfaction, does come from reflection, from thinking deeply about what you do and why you do it— and then figuring out how to do it even better.

Simmons reveals a good ending to that lifelong process of becoming a teacher— expect great rewards:

> From the perspective of twenty-five years, I can tell you that the rewards will be greater than you ever expect. They may not be immediate, nor will they be readily apparent, but when one of your former students says—five or ten or twenty years later—"You know, you taught me so much. You're a great teacher"—you'll be ready to do it again for another five, or ten, or twenty years. (74)

Like Eileen Simmons, we've been teaching for a long time, and we too know the rewards. You are about to discover them.

 ## FINAL THOUGHTS

We began our journey by asking you to explore your motivation and goals in choosing this profession; we asked you to look at your personal traits and think about being a teacher of English language arts. Then, we asked you to consider each of the English language arts in turn, to learn how to make them interesting and useful as you work with adolescent learners. Now, we have ended the journey by asking you to reflect on what will be, for most of you, the final semester of your professional preparation, student teaching. The many voices of our student teachers have provided you with authentic glimpses of what awaits and with, we hope, the certain knowledge that you can problem-solve; you can be the teacher that you want to be. We end, then, with one more student voice:

Since I began my journey as an English education major, I secretly feared student teaching. I remembered as a child how my classmates had treated student teachers. They tormented these poor individuals, being greatly aware of the student teacher's inexperience, enjoying taking advantage. Thus over this summer I tossed and turned every night, imagining what my future students would do come fall. However, from the moment I stepped into the classroom, I realized I had worried over nothing. My students were not monsters, and in fact, have surprised me with their good behavior and obvious desire to learn. Yes, there are a few students who enjoy testing my strengths and weaknesses but they are far and few between. And it is important to note, without these students, I would not be as aware of the areas where I need improvement. The semester I secretly feared for four years has begun on a high note. Further, the students appear to be far greater tools of learning than I could have imagined, teaching me what it takes to be an effective educator.

Like Robin, you may have wondered and worried as you think about your new role. However, we believe that you will step into it and find that you are in the right place—being a learner, now and always.

REFERENCES

Christenbury, Leila. "From the Editor." *English Journal* (Feb. 1995): 13.

Eklund, Lani. "No Aggravation: What Did We Do Yesterday?" 29 May 2003 <http://www.ncte.org/notesplus/solutions/log.shtml>.

Guentert, Marylou. "No Aggravation: What Did We Do Yesterday?" 29 May 2003 <http://www.ncte.org/notesplus/solutions/yesterday/shtml>.

McWilliam, Jean A. "Is It Finding or Following a Path? A Guide for Student Teachers and Their Mentors." *English Journal* (Feb. 1995): 39–42.

Petretti, Dante. "Response to Amanda Richey." *English Journal* (Nov. 2002): 20–22.

Richey, Amanda. "View from the Field." *English Journal* (Nov. 2002): 19–20.

Rose, Mary C. "Handle With Care." 3 June 2003 <http://teacher.scholastic.com/professional/parentconf/handlewithcare.htm>.

Shalway, Linda. "Planning for Parent Conferences." 3 June 2003 <http://teacher.scholartic.com/prof . . . rentconf/planning parent confe.htm>.

Simmons, Eileen. "A Quarter of a Century and Not Finished Yet." *English Journal* (Feb. 1995): 73–74.

Student Teachers. "E-Logs from English 408, Seminar in Teaching." University of Wisconsin–Eau Claire. Spring Semester 2001 and Fall Semester 2002.

Index